Don Doherty
Michelle M. Manning

SAMS
Teach Yourself
JBuilder™ 2
in 21 Days

SAMS

A Division of Macmillan Computer Publishing
201 West 103rd St., Indianapolis, Indiana, 46290 USA

Sams Teach Yourself JBuilder 2™ in 21 Days
Copyright © 1998 by Sams Publishing

International Standard Book Number: 0-672-31318-9

Library of Congress Catalog Card Number: 98-84521

Printed in the United States of America

First Printing: July 1998

00 99 98   4   3   2   1

Trademarks

All terms mentioned in this book that are known to be trademarks or service marks have been appropriately capitalized. Sams Publishing cannot attest to the accuracy of this information. Use of a term in this book should not be regarded as affecting the validity of any trademark or service mark. JBuilder is a trademark of the Inprise Corporation.

Warning and Disclaimer

Every effort has been made to make this book as complete and as accuate as possible, but no warranty of fitness is implied. The information provided is on an "as is" basis. The authors and the publisher shall have neither liablility nor responsiblilty to any person or entity with respect to any loss or damages arising from the information contained in this book.

EXECUTIVE EDITOR
Brian Gill

ACQUISITIONS EDITOR
Ron Gallagher

DEVELOPMENT EDITOR
Scott Warner

MANAGING EDITOR
Jodi Jensen

PROJECT EDITOR
Susan Ross Moore

COPY EDITORS
Geneil Breeze
Sarah Burkhart
Cheri Clark

INDEXER
Christine Nelsen

TECHNICAL EDITOR
Andrew Bennett

PRODUCTION
Marcia Deboy
Michael Dietsch
Jennifer Earhart
Cynthia Fields
Susan Geiselman

Contents at a Glance

Contents

Acknowledgments

I thank Brian Gill for being fun to work with and, especially, for making sure that I'm not bored and with too little work to do. Thanks go out to Scott Warner's excellent job at editing. Special thanks go out to the JBuilder team at Inprise Corporation, especially to Nan Borreson and Andrew Bennett. Andrew Bennett's thorough and conscientious technical editing job warrants special mention.

About the Authors

Dr. Donald Doherty is a neuroscientist and a computer expert. He received his Ph.D. from the Department of Psychobiology at University of California, Irvine. Don's computer experience includes programming large-scale computer models of brain systems. He's written on a wide range of computer topics. His books include *Sams Teach Yourself JavaBeans in 21 Days*. Don is a research associate in the Department of Neurobiology at the University of Pittsburgh School of Medicine. Visit his Web site at `http://ourworld.compuserve.com/homepages/brainstage/`.

Michelle Manning, the principal of Triple-M Consulting, specializes in software quality assurance and documenation. Michelle's computer industry experience spans 25 years as a developer, QA engineer, and technical writer. She is also the author of *Borland's Official No-Nonsense Guide to Delphi 2*.

Tell Us What You Think!

As the reader of this book, *you* are our most important critic and commentator. We value your opinion and want to know what we're doing right, what we could do better, what areas you'd like to see us publish in, and any other words of wisdom you're willing to pass our way.

As the Executive Editor for the Programming group at Macmillan Computer Publishing, I welcome your comments. You can fax, email, or write me directly to let me know what you did or didn't like about this book—as well as what we can do to make our books stronger.

Please note that I cannot help you with technical problems related to the topic of this book, and that due to the high volume of mail I receive, I might not be able to reply to every message.

When you write, please be sure to include this book's title and author as well as your name and phone or fax number. I will carefully review your comments and share them with the authors and editors who worked on the book.

Fax: 317-817-7070
Email: prog@mcp.com
Mail: Executive Editor
          Programming
          Macmillan Computer Publishing
          201 West 103rd Street
          Indianapolis, IN 46290 USA

Introduction

Learn the Java language and how to use JBuilder to create exciting and useful applets, applications, and software components with *Teach Yourself JBuilder 2 in 21 Days*. Java is now the language of choice for creating applications, applets, and software components for computers and the entire computing enterprise. JBuilder is a powerful integrated development environment that brings every level of Java software development within easy reach, including visual programming or RAD (Rapid Application Development). With Java and JBuilder there is no limit placed on your imagination and creativity. The Internet, the World Wide Web, in fact, the entire computing enterprise, are yours to create the Java programs for today and the future. *Teach Yourself JBuilder 2 in 21 Days* will teach you all you need to know to start you on your path.

How This Book Is Structured

Teach Yourself JBuilder 2 in 21 Days is intended to be read and absorbed over the course of three weeks. Nevertheless, the pace you keep is up to you. During each week you'll read seven chapters that present concepts related to Java and JBuilder and the creation of Java software. Each week covers a different general area of Java software development. The following is an outline of what to expect.

Week 1

During Week 1, you're introduced to the Java language and the JBuilder integrated development environment. You create Java applications and applets using JBuilder and use JBuilder's rapid application development (RAD) capabilities including visual programming.

Day 1

Day 1, "Introduction to JBuilder," explains what Java is, how it relates to JBuilder, and how to install JBuilder properly.

Day 2

Day 2, "Java Basics," shows you the building blocks of your Java programs, such as variables, types, expressions, operators, arrays, strings, conditionals, and loops.

Day 3

Day 3, "Java Intermediate," discusses classes and objects and how they relate to each other. You also explore behaviors and attributes.

Day 4

Day 4, "Java Advanced," discusses protection for class variables and methods, constant variables, classes that can't be subclassed, and methods that can't be overridden.

Day 5

Day 5, "JBuilder IDE," examines JBuilder's extensive menu system and shows you how to customize the JBuilder integrated development environment.

Day 6

Day 6, "User Interface Design," shows you the UI Designer, the Component Palette, and the Java Abstract Windowing Toolkit (AWT).

Day 7

Day 7, "JavaBeans Component Library," concludes Week 1 with an exploration of the Component Palette, which presents tabbed pages containing a wide range of JavaBeans software components that you can use in your JBuilder visual programming, or RAD, projects.

Week 2

During Week 2 you dig into building solid Java software, whether it be applets, applications, or software components. All of the elements you learned about Java and JBuilder in Week 1 come together in Week 2, enabling you to create Java programs.

Day 8

Day 8, "Applets, Applications, and Wizards," begins Week 2 by showing you how to create Java applications, including how to pass arguments to a Java program from a command line.

Day 9

Day 9, "Graphics, Fonts, and Multimedia," discusses how the graphics system works in Java. You explore the Graphics class and Java coordinate system used to draw to the screen. You also see how applets paint and repaint to a window.

Day 10

Day 10, "Streams and I/O," explains how you create, use, and detect the end of input streams. You learn how to use and nest filtered input streams. And you learn how to create, use, and close output streams.

Day 11

Day 11, "Compiling and Debugging," explores using the Make and Rebuild commands to compile your Java programs in the JBuilder integrated development environment. You also learn how to get context-sensitive help to correct errors in your code.

Day 12

Day 12, "Handling Events," shows you how your Java application responds to messages sent to it by the system. You learn how to handle event messages in your Java applications.

Day 13

Day 13, "Exception Handling," shows you how to allow your program to cope with exceptions easily and to occasionally execute alternative code rather than simply shutting down.

Day 14

Day 14, "JBuilder Database Architecture," teaches you JDBC and how it affects applet and application development.

Week 3

During Week 3 you learn about advanced Java and JBuilder topics including how to create JavaBeans software components, building database applications, and creating network-aware Java applications.

Day 15

Day 15, "Building Database Applications," shows you how to set up Local InterBase, along with data sources. Create, update, and delete database tables. Design database application user interfaces.

Day 16

Day 16, "Multithreading," explains what threads are and how they can make your programs work better.

Day 17

Day 17, "Persistence," explores serializable and externalizable objects and teaches you about persistence security issues.

Day 18

Day 18, "Building JavaBeans," shows you the JavaBeans software component model and how to create these reusable software components known as beans. You also learn how to distribute the functionality of your code without distributing the source code itself.

Day 19

Day 19, "Deploying Java Programs," teaches you how to prepare and place program files making sure that the program works properly in its intended environment.

Day 20

Day 20, "Java Network Communications," teaches you how to create networking links in applets using the `URLConnection`, `Socket`, and `SocketServer` classes and handle network-related exceptions.

Day 21

Day 21, "Inside Java," explores the inner workings of the Java system, including the Java Virtual Machine, bytecodes, garbage collection, and security.

Conventions Used in This Book

Text that you type and text that you see on-screen appears in `monospace` type:

`It will look like this.`

to mimic the way text looks on your screen.

Variables and placeholders (words that stand for what you will actually type) appear in `italic monospace`.

Each chapter ends with questions pertaining to that day's subject matter, with answers from the author. Most chapters also include an exercise section and a quiz designed to reinforce that day's concept. (The answers appear in Appendix A.)

Note	A Note presents interesting information related to the discussion.

Tip	A Tip offers advice or shows you an easier way of doing something.

> **Caution**
>
> A Caution alerts you to a possible problem and gives you advice on how to avoid it.

NEW TERM   New terms are introduced using the New Term icon.

TYPE   The Type icon identifies code that you can type in yourself. It usually appears next to a listing.

OUTPUT   The Output icon highlights the output produced by running the Java application or applet.

ANALYSIS   The Analysis icon designates the author's line-by-line analysis.

When a line of code is too long to fit on one line of this book, it is broken at a convenient place and continued to the next line. The continuation is preceded by a special code continuation character (➡).

Web Sites for Further Information

Two Web sites are particularly useful to the Java programmer who uses JBuilder. The offical Java Web site is provided by JavaSoft, a subsidiary of Sun Microsystems Inc., at `http://www.javasoft.com`. The official JBuilder Web site is provided by Inprise Corporation at `http://www.inprise.com/jbuilder/`.

WEEK 1

At a Glance

1

2

3

4

5

6

7

DAY 1

Introduction to JBuilder

Welcome to *Teach Yourself JBuilder in 21 Days*. During the next few weeks, you'll learn all about Borland's JBuilder visual development environment and the underlying language—Java. You'll discover how to program standalone Java applications and how to create Java applets that will run over the Internet and the World Wide Web.

NEW TERM An *applet* is an interactive program that runs inside a Web page when that page is displayed by a Java-capable browser, such as Netscape's Navigator, Microsoft's Internet Explorer, or Sun's HotJava browser.

You'll also learn how to debug, test, and deploy your applications and applets. This will be critical, due to the nature of Java programming and the fact that Java programs can be run on any number of platforms.

Those are the overall goals for this book. Today, you'll begin your journey by learning about the following:

- What Java is and how it relates to JBuilder
- How to install JBuilder properly
- Where to look for help in the disk files and documentation

- Where to look online for additional resources
- How to create your first applet and application program

What Is Java?

Java is an object-oriented programming language developed by Sun Microsystems, a company best known for its high-end UNIX workstations. Originally modeled after C++, the Java language was designed to be small, portable, robust, and object-oriented. These features make it the "language of choice" for the World Wide Web, which can be accessed from many different platforms and operating systems.

Java applets are dynamic and interactive, so they expand the types of transactions that users can accomplish on the Web. After you've created and compiled a Java applet, you embed it in an HTML (Hypertext Markup Language) Web page and then publish the Web page on a Web site. If the user is accessing the Web site with a Java-enabled browser, the browser will download the embedded applet's binary code to the user's computer system and execute it.

Technically, you won't need to have a browser available on your system to test your applets because JBuilder has its own integrated debugger (Day 11, "Compiling and Debugging") and also includes Sun's appletviewer. However, it is recommended that you do your final testing under commercially available browsers.

Not all browsers are created equal, so you will want to have several of them handy to test your applets. Currently, the most popular browsers are Netscape Navigator and Microsoft Internet Explorer, which you can download from the Netscape or Microsoft Web sites at http://www.netscape.com or http://www.microsoft.com, respectively. Sun's HotJava browser is also available for downloading from the HotJava Web page at http://java.sun.com/products/hotjava.

In addition to creating applets that can be run from browsers, you can create full-fledged application programs to solve the same programming problems as you can in other programming languages, such as C, C++, Pascal, or Visual Basic. In fact, Sun's HotJava browser is itself written in Java, as is much of JBuilder.

Java's Past and Present

The Java language was originally created to solve the problems surrounding personal digital assistants (PDAs) and consumer electronic products, such as microwaves and toaster ovens. The language had to be robust, small, and portable. None of the programming languages available at the time (circa 1990) would fill the bill. Some were too complex to write really robust code, and none of them was portable. Code had to be

1

recompiled for each target chip, and consumer electronics chips were proprietary and frequently updated.

The language that met all those requirements didn't exist, so the folks at Sun decided to create a new language that would. PDAs fizzled (although they are threatening to make a comeback), and the consumer electronics market never really made use of the new language. However, the Java team discovered that Java's design made it ideal for another purpose: programming on the Internet. In 1993, the World Wide Web was just becoming popular, with its myriad platforms and operating systems, and it desperately needed a platform-independent language—so Java found a new home.

Java Is Platform-Independent

The Java language was designed specifically to be platform-independent. This means that programs written in Java can be compiled once and run on any machine that supports Java. So, what exactly does platform-independence mean, and how does it differ from what was available before Java?

NEW TERM *Platform-independence* refers to a program's capability to run on various computer systems without the necessity of being recompiled. A *platform* means a particular processor, like the Intel 80x86, the Intel Pentium, the Motorola 68*xxx*, or the PowerPC.

Traditional compiled programming languages are compiled to machine-level binary code that is, of course, specific to the machine or platform on which it is compiled. The advantage is that the compiled binary runs quickly because it is running in the machine's native language. The disadvantage is that a program written in a traditional language has to be recompiled to binary code for each different hardware platform before it can be run on that machine. On the other hand, whereas traditional interpreted programming languages are machine-neutral and can be run without recompilation on various platforms, they generally run much slower than compiled applications.

Java has incorporated the best of both worlds. The Java team created a platform-specific layer, called the Java Virtual Machine (Java VM), which interfaces between the hardware and the Java program. When you install a Java-capable browser on your computer, for example, a copy of the Java interpreter is also installed, which is what enables your browser to execute Java applets and your system to run standalone Java programs.

Note A virtual machine is a software implementation of the heart of a computing machine, the central processing unit, along with an operating system. The Java VM provides an operating system with threading, input, output, and display capabilities.

NEW TERM *Java interpreter* and *Java runtime* are alternative terms for the Java Virtual Machine (VM).

The Java VM presents the same interface to any applets that attempt to run on the system, so to applets, all machines look the same. The applet itself is compiled into a form of interpretable code called Java bytecodes. This special form of code can be run on any platform that has the Java VM installed.

NEW TERM *Bytecodes* are a set of instructions that are similar to machine code but are not processor-specific. They are interpreted by the Java VM.

Sun's trademark phrase "write once, run anywhere" is the promise that is fulfilled by Java. This, above all other features of the language, is what makes it so essential for interactive Web programming.

Java Is Object-Oriented

Java is a real object-oriented language, which enables you to create flexible, modular programs. It includes a set of class libraries that provide basic data types, system input and output capabilities, and other utility functions. It also provides networking, common Internet protocol, image handling, and user-interface toolkit functions. Java's object classes provide a rich set of functionality, and they can be extended and modified to create new classes specific to your programming needs.

Java Is Easy to Learn

Among the original design goals of the Java team members was to create a language that was small and robust. Because they started from scratch, they were able to avoid some of the pitfalls of other more complex languages. By eliminating things such as pointers, pointer arithmetic, and the need to manage memory explicitly, the Java development team made Java one of the easier languages to learn. However, you still can do anything in Java that you can do in traditional languages. If you have previously used a high-level object-oriented programming language, such as C++, much of Java will look familiar to you.

What Is JBuilder?

JBuilder is Borland's visual development environment for Java. It includes a project browser, a code editor, a visual designer, a Component palette, a property inspector, an integrated debugger, and a compiler. Each of these elements will be introduced on Day 5, "JBuilder IDE." JBuilder also includes Sun's latest Java Development Kit (JDK), and together they form a complete programming environment that enables you to be instantly productive with Java.

1

JBuilder Makes Java Even Easier

JBuilder has incorporated Borland's "Two-Way Tools" (originally introduced by Borland in the Delphi product), which keep your visual design and the source code synchronized. Any changes you make to the visual design are added automatically to the source code for you. Any changes made to the source code that affect the visual interface are also reflected in the visual design. This synchronization enables you to build your program in whichever mode is the most appropriate for the program element on which you're working, making development faster and easier.

JBuilder Extends Functionality

JBuilder encapsulates and extends much of Java's functionality in components that are also known as *JavaBeans*.

NEW TERM   *JavaBeans* is a specification for reusable software components containing properties (attributes), methods (behaviors), and events (messages). One of these components, known as a Java bean, can be as simple as a text label or as complex as a real-time Internet communications program.

JavaBeans gives you a way to visually design your Java programs with drag-and-drop components. JavaBeans components extend Sun's Java classes to enhance the visual and nonvisual design elements of your programs. The programs you design using JBuilder's components follow Sun's standards.

JBuilder's Component palette contains a rich set of ready-made JavaBeans for you to use in your Java applets and applications. Based on the JavaBeans Component Library (JBCL), these components are covered in more detail on Day 7, "JavaBeans Component Library."

Installing JBuilder

JBuilder's install program takes care of most of the details of installation, but there are still a few things you should do to make sure things go smoothly. Preparation is the key. This section discusses how to install JBuilder 2.0 for Windows from the CD, what to back up after installation, and how to uninstall.

Before you install JBuilder, you should read a few things:

- The CD-ROM sleeve
- The SETUP\JBUILDER\INSTALL.TXT file
- The SETUP\JBUILDER\README.TXT file

It's very important that you read these before invoking the install program so that you can be prepared in case anything goes wrong. You might also want to print INSTALL.TXT so that you'll have the troubleshooting information handy—just in case.

Tip

When installing large software packages, it's best to take the time to do a full system backup before proceeding. Also, it's typically a good idea to disable any virus-detection software running on your computer during the install process.

JBuilder is distributed in three editions: Standard, Professional (Pro), and Client/Server (C/S). Most of the installation instructions apply to all three versions, and any differences are appropriately noted.

Requirements

JBuilder's install program (InstallShield) requires at least 15MB of available disk space in your Windows TEMP directory to hold its temporary files during installation, no matter what drive you choose for your JBuilder installation. JBuilder itself requires approximately 100MB of disk space for a compact install.

Installation

JBuilder 2.0 for Windows is distributed on CD. Before beginning, be sure to save your work and close all other applications. You can invoke the InstallShield installation program in several ways. The following is a very common method of starting the installation:

1. Load the CD-ROM into your CD-ROM drive.
2. From the Start menu, select Programs | Windows Explorer.
3. Locate your CD-ROM drive in the left pane, and double-click to expand the node.
4. In the right pane, double-click on INSTALL.EXE to launch the install program.

After the install program starts, it launches the setup programs associated with each application you want to install. The InstallShield setup program starts, and you are given an opportunity to read the INSTALL.TXT file. If you haven't read it yet, be sure to do so now, and then click the Next button. The install program is initialized, and in the next dialog you are asked to choose which type of installation you want to perform: Typical, Compact, or Custom. Fill out the requested information in each dialog box, and click the Next button to proceed. If you need assistance with any of the options, click the Help button.

1

After you've answered all its questions, InstallShield begins uncompressing and writing files to your hard disk. On a 200MHz Pentium MMX, the Typical install takes less than five minutes. At the end of the installation, you are given the opportunity to view the README.TXT file. If you didn't read it prior to installation, you should read it now. It contains important information that will save you time and trouble later.

Tip

> If you have a modem, take advantage of the online registration offered by the JBuilder installation program. If not, be sure to fill out the registration card to qualify for *Installation Hotline* technical support and notification of upgrades and new product offers.

After Installing

During the installation, changes are made to the Windows Registry. Nevertheless, JBuilder doesn't automatically set the environmental variables that the Java command-line tools depend on. A batch file is provided in the JBuilder package to set the environmental variables used when running JDK and Borland command-line tools from your console window or DOS prompt.

Caution

> Don't unzip files such as classes.zip. These are *not* regular zip archives. These are special compressed Java archives that Java and JBuilder require in order to work properly. If you've already unzipped them, you'll need to reinstall to recover those files.

Setting Windows Environmental Variables

The best way to ensure that the environmental variables necessary to run command-line Java tools in Windows are set every time you spawn a DOS session is to insert the following line in your AUTOEXEC.BAT file:

```
c:\jbuilder2\bin\setvars.bat c:\jbuilder2
```

To do this, select Shut Down from the Start menu, click the Restart the computer in MS-DOS mode? radio button, and then click the Yes button. When at the DOS prompt, edit your AUTOEXEC.BAT file, save it to disk, and then type exit and press Enter to return to Windows. Now, you'll be able to use any of the Java command-line tools from a DOS session window.

Setting Windows NT Environmental Variables

Under Windows NT, use the `setvars.bat` file to set environmental variables for a particular console window session. Type the following at the command prompt, and you're ready to use the Java command-line tools:

```
c:\jbuilder2\bin\setvars.bat c:\jbuilder2
```

Your console windows can be ready to run command-line Java tools anytime they're opened if you set the environmental settings manually. First, be sure that you are logged in using an Administrator account. Contact your computer administrator if you don't have administrative permissions. Point to the My Computer icon on your desktop and click your right mouse button. A shortcut menu appears. Select the Properties command from the menu, and the System Properties dialog box appears. Click on the Environment tab to switch to the dialog box's Environment page, shown in Figure 1.1.

FIGURE 1.1.

Change environment variable settings on the System Properties dialog box Environment page.

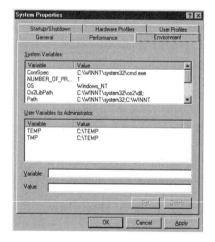

You need to do two things: modify the `Path` variable in the System Variables list and add a `CLASSPATH` variable in the User Variables for Administrator list.

Select the `Path` variable from the System Variables list. The variable name and value appear in text boxes at the bottom of the dialog box page. At the end of the existing values, add a semicolon followed by the path to the Java Development Kit programs, typically `C:\jbuilder2\java\bin\`. Your System Properties dialog box Environment page should look as shown in Figure 1.2. Click the Set button when you're done.

FIGURE 1.2.

Your Path *variable values should look similar to these.*

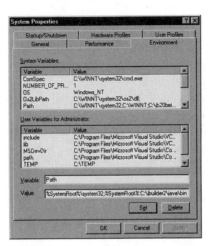

Next, type CLASSPATH into the Variable text box at the bottom of the dialog box page, deleting any variable name that was previously there. In the Value text box, type the path to the Java Development Kit classes, typically C:\jbuilder2\java\lib\classes.zip, followed by a semicolon and the path to the root of your personal class library, typically C:\jbuilder2\myclasses\. Your System Properties dialog box Environment page should look as shown Figure 1.3. Click the Set button when you're done.

FIGURE 1.3.

Your CLASSPATH *variable values should look similar to these.*

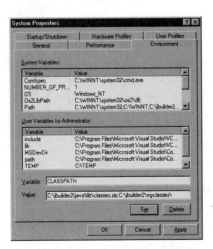

Close the System Properties dialog box by clicking the OK button. You should now be able to run command-line Java tools.

Uninstalling

The UnInstallShield utility is copied to your Windows directory during installation. In addition, an InstallShield Uninstall (ISU) file containing information about your JBuilder installation is created:

```
C:\JBuilder\DelsL1.ISU
```

The ISU file contains information that the uninstall utility needs in order to complete its work, so be sure not to inadvertently delete this file.

 Note | You should always use Add/Remove Programs in the Windows Control Panel when you uninstall programs from your computer.

If the Local InterBase Server was installed (Pro and C/S Editions), you must shut it down to prepare for uninstallation. In the Windows taskbar, right-click on the Local InterBase Server glyph (the CPU with the green globe), and select Shutdown from the pop-up menu.

To uninstall, follow these steps:

1. From the Start menu, select Settings | Control Panel.
2. Double-click the Add/Remove Programs icon.
3. In the Add/Remove Programs Properties dialog's Install/Uninstall page, select Borland JBuilder in the list box, and then click the Add/Remove button. Add/Remove Programs calls the UnInstallShield utility provided by JBuilder (UNINST.EXE), which removes the numerous Registry entries made by JBuilder's installation program, along with all the JBuilder files.
4. In the Confirm File Deletion dialog, click the Yes button. You will be asked to confirm deletions of any shared files that the uninstall program determines are no longer used by any other programs (per Registry entries).
5. When the uninstallation is complete, in the Add/Remove Programs Properties dialog's Install/Uninstall page, click the OK button.

There might be files that are created during use of JBuilder that the uninstall program is unaware of. In particular, any project files that you've created and left in the JBuilder directory tree will not be deleted, so you might want to check for such files after uninstalling and before deleting the directory tree.

1

Where to Get Help

JBuilder is very intuitive and easy to use. However, at times you will need suggestions on how to complete a task or aid in understanding how to use the product. JBuilder's Help menu gives you access to online HTML help files with full search capabilities. There are also several electronic documents, such as README.TXT, that contain last-minute revisions and updates to the product. In addition, extensive documentation in the form of paper manuals (*User's Guide*, *Component Writer's Guide*, and so on) are provided in the Pro and C/S Editions of JBuilder.

Help Files and E-Docs

Select Help | Help Topics to see how JBuilder's help files are organized. JBuilder presents its HTML help files in a browser-style window with a contents tree in the left pane and the relevant help text in the right pane.

You can also open these files independently of JBuilder by loading the HTML file into your Internet browser. Opening help files this way can be particularly useful when you want to examine multiple help files simultaneously. This procedure also makes it possible to Alt+Tab between the help file and the IDE.

Tip

> Instructions on how to use the online help in a browser can be found in the Online help under the topic "Using a Web browser to view JBuilder documentation" in the "Welcome to JBuilder" book under the section titled "Using the Help Viewer."

Paper Documentation

JBuilder's printed documentation consists of the following:

- *User's Guide* (Pro and C/S): Covers fundamental skills, programming topics, and sample applications. The demo files discussed in this manual are in the JBuilder\samples\borland subdirectories.

- *Programmer's Guide* (Pro and C/S): Is made up of the "Component Writer's Guide" and the "Database Application Developer's Guide." The "Component Writer's Guide" covers the JavaBeans component model and the tasks associated with creating JavaBeans components from scratch. The "Database Application Developer's Guide" covers the DataBroker architecture and database functionality for developing database applications.

• *Component Library Reference*: (C/S only) Covers the definitions for the JavaBean Class Library's objects, components, variables, constants, types, properties, methods, and events.

Online Resources

In addition to the documentation provided with the product, Borland provides JBuilder support on the Web at `http://www.borland.com/jbuilder/`. There is also a set of forum newsgroups that you can reach by setting your newsreader to access `forums.borland.com`. These official Borland forum newsgroups are supported by TeamB volunteers, who are developers chosen for their expertise and desire to help. And don't forget the premier Java resource at `http://www.javasoft.com`, Sun's Java Web site.

JBuilder's Integrated Development Environment

Borland pioneered the idea of an Integrated Development Environment (IDE), where the developer could create, compile, debug, and run a program all from the same interface. When Borland first introduced the IDE in its DOS compilers, the concept was revolutionary. Today, we take this type of interconnected functionality for granted, but Borland has continued to improve and refine its IDE. Certainly, the JBuilder IDE is another step forward in programming environments.

Although you won't be formally introduced to the JBuilder environment until later this week (Day 5, "JBuilder IDE"), here's a quick overview that will help you when you begin entering code later today in the "Applets and Applications" section. Launch JBuilder, and when it has finished loading, click on the node `WelcomeApp.java` in the upper-left pane of the project window so that it looks as shown in Figure 1.4.

The main window contains the main menu bar, tool bar, Component palette, and status bar. The main menu bar, of course, presents the JBuilder command set in text form. The toolbar displays a subset of those commands in iconic form and is configurable, so you can display your most commonly used commands for easier access. The Component palette comprises drag-and-drop JavaBeans components for building programs using rapid application development (RAD) techniques. The status bar is used for displaying various status messages (such as file-saving information and compiler status) in the IDE.

The AppBrowser has three panes: the Navigation pane (upper left), the Structure pane (lower left), and the Content pane (on the right). The Navigation pane shows the various files that compose the current project. For example, in Figure 1.4, you can easily see that `Welcome.jpr` contains an `.html` file and two `.java` files. With the `WelcomeApp.java` node selected in the Navigation pane, the Structure pane displays a hierarchy of the members that compose that file, both internal (such as methods) and external (such as imports). In the Content pane, the file itself is displayed. When an editable file is displayed, the Content pane becomes the Editor. The AppBrowser status bar is used to display the Line:Column, Modified, and Insert/Overwrite indicators for the Editor and various other AppBrowser-specific status messages.

FIGURE 1.4.

JBuilder's Integrated Development Environment.

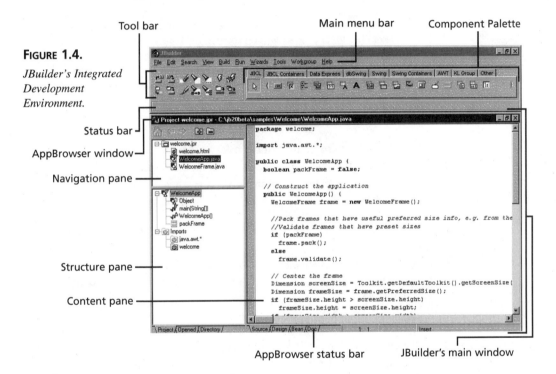

There are other windows and panes in the IDE, but these basic elements will get you through your first few projects. Next, you'll use the main menu bar and the AppBrowser to create your first Java programs.

Applets and Applications

There are two types of Java programs: applets and applications. To finish up the day, you'll create one of each type. What if you want your program to run as a standalone application and also be able to run as an applet across the Web? Java enables you to combine these into a single program that can be run either way. In this book, you concentrate on creating separate applets and applications.

Applets are Java programs that are usually embedded in an HTML Web page and down-loaded from the Web to be run by a browser on the user's computer system. The browser must be Java-capable for the user to get the full effect of applets that contain animation and other advanced Java features. Applets can also be viewed using Sun's appletviewer utility.

 Tip

You can turn any Web browser into a Java-capable Web browser by using the Java Plug-in. The Java Plug-in provides 100% Java compatibility, it's free, and you can download it from the JavaSoft Web site at http://java.sun.com/products/plugin/. Some Java-capable browsers such as the Microsoft Internet Explorer are not 100% Java compliant. Use the Java Plug-in to make the browser 100% Java compliant.

Applications are full-fledged programs written in Java. They don't require a Web browser to run, but they do require the Java VM to be installed on the target platform. The best-known example of a Java application program is Sun's HotJava browser, which is written entirely in Java. Run Java applications by invoking the Java interpreter.

 Caution

Java is case-sensitive, so be careful that you type uppercase and lowercase where necessary when entering code. This applies to filenames too. For many novice Java programmers, this proves to be the most common stumbling block.

Go ahead and try the steps in the following sections in the IDE. If you get stuck, select File | Close All from the JBuilder menu bar and a Save Modified Files dialog box will appear, as shown in Figure 1.5.

FIGURE 1.5.

The Save Modified Files dialog box appears if the file you're closing contains unsaved changes.

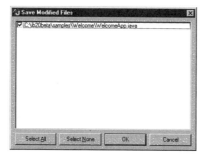

1

Click the Select None button so that none of the modified files is selected to be saved, and then click the OK button to close the file. Now you're ready to begin again. (If you have already saved files and want to delete them before starting over, you can find your source-code files in JBuilder's myprojects subdirectory and your compiled class files in the myclasses subdirectory.)

Before you begin, if the Welcome.jpr project is being displayed in JBuilder (or any other project, for that matter), select File | Close All so that you can start fresh.

Creating an Application

In JBuilder, select File | New Project from the main menu bar. The Project Wizard: Step 1 of 1 dialog box appears, as shown in Figure 1.6.

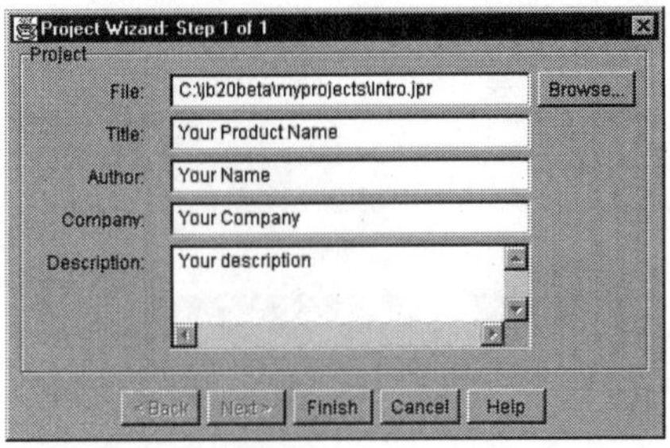

FIGURE 1.6.

Enter your project's name and information into the Project Wizard: Step 1 of 1 dialog box.

In the File: field, change the project filename to c:\JBuilder\myprojects\Intro.jpr and click the Finish button. An AppBrowser window appears, as shown in Figure 1.7.

Click the Add to Project icon (plus symbol on the folder) in the Navigation pane to display the File Open / Create dialog box, shown in Figure 1.8.

On the File page of the File Open / Create dialog box, type HelloWorld.java in the File name: field, and then click the Open button. The HelloWorld.java file should be added to and currently selected in the Intro project's Navigation pane list.

In the Content pane, enter the Java program shown in Listing 1.1. Type this program exactly as shown (except for line numbers), being careful that all parentheses, braces, and quotation marks are entered properly. When typing the code from the listings that follow, do not type the line number and colon at the beginning of each line. They are there only as reference points for the ensuing discussion of the code itself. As you type each line, watch what happens in the Structure pane.

FIGURE 1.7.

A new AppBrowser window opens for your Intro project.

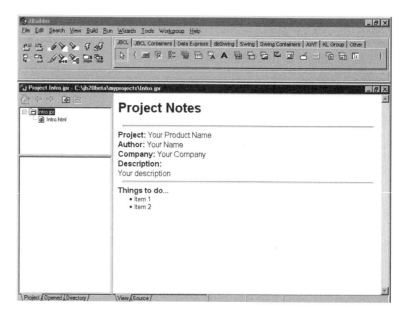

FIGURE 1.8.

Create a new Java source file in the File Open / Create dialog box.

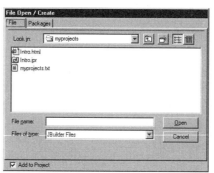

TYPE   **LISTING 1.1.** HelloWorld.java.

```
1:   class HelloWorld {
2:     public static void main (String args[]) {
3:       System.out.println("Hello World!");
4:     }
5:   }
```

After you're finished typing the program, select File | Save All to preserve your work. You should see a confirmation message in the main window's status bar. Now your Intro project should look as shown in Figure 1.9.

FIGURE 1.9.

The Intro project now includes a Java source file named HelloWorld.java.

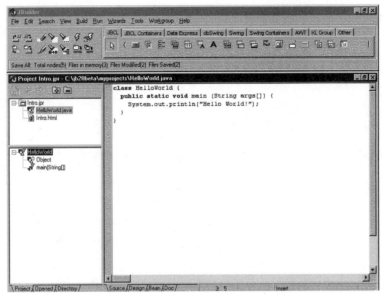

This program has three parts:

- A `class` definition that encloses the program—in this case, it's named `HelloWorld`. It begins on line 1 and ends on line 5. All classes in Java automatically descend from the top-level `Object` class, and you'll notice that there is an `Object` node in the Structure pane.

- The body of the program, the `main()` method—for this application, lines 2 through 4. The `main()` method is the subroutine that is executed when your application is run. There is also a node for this method in the Structure pane.

- The code that produces the actual output of the program—line 3. In this line of code, the application tells the system to print the words "Hello World!" to the screen. This line is part and parcel of the `main()` method, so there is no separate entry for it in the Structure pane.

Note that the name of the class and the filename are the same. In Java, source-code files must always be named the same as the class they define, with the `.java` extension added at the end. Your source files are stored in JBuilder's `myprojects` subdirectory tree by default.

Now that you have written your first Java application, you'll want to compile and run it. HelloWorld is a command-line Java application. That means that, like DOS applications, HelloWorld writes directly to the screen without using the Windows graphical user interface. JBuilder sends command-line program output to a Console window, another name for a DOS window, by default. The default isn't usually very handy, however, because the Console window typically opens and closes too quickly for you to read what the output actually was. JBuilder provides a useful alternative.

You can tell JBuilder to display command-line Java program output in a special window called the Execution Log. Select File | Project Properties from the JBuilder main menu bar to open the Intro.jpr Properties dialog box. Click on the Run/Debug tab to display the dialog box's Run/Debug page, shown in Figure 1.10.

FIGURE 1.10.

Open the Intro.jpr Properties dialog box to the Run/Debug page.

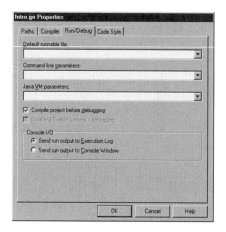

Find the Console I/O area toward the bottom of the Intro.jpr Properties dialog box. Select the Send run output to Execution Log radio button so that JBuilder automatically sends command-line Java program output to the Execution Log. Then click the OK button.

Now you're ready to compile and run the HelloWorld program. Make sure that the HelloWorld.java file is selected in the Navigation pane of the AppBrowser. Then compile and run your program in a single step by clicking on the Run icon in the toolbar—the one that looks like a lightning bolt.

Tip

When working with the toolbar, hold the mouse cursor over an icon for a moment to learn what it's used for. A ToolTip appears with the icon's command name.

The compiler should complete the compilation without error. If you get errors, they will be displayed in the lower portion of the Editor window in the Content pane. Make any necessary corrections so that the program appears exactly as it is in Listing 1.1 (including uppercase and lowercase), and try again.

When the program is successfully compiled, a new file named `HelloWorld.class` appears in JBuilder's `myclasses` subdirectory. This is the Java bytecode file that can now be run from any Java VM installation.

After you run the HelloWorld program, look at its output by opening the Execution Log window. Select View | Execution Log from the JBuilder main menu bar, and the Execution Log window appears with the program's output, as shown in Figure 1.11.

FIGURE 1.11.

Your first Java application says, "Hello World!"

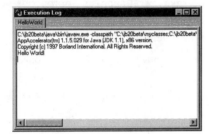

Creating an Applet

You will, of course, want to say hello to all your friends out there on the World Wide Web, so you'll need to create a HelloWorld applet as well. Because applets are displayed from an HTML Web page, they typically require more complex programming to do the same thing as an application. For example, you can't simply print "Hello World!" to the standard output because a Web page doesn't include that concept. You need to define coordinate space on the Web page within which your applet runs, and then use graphics functions to paint the message in that coordinate space.

Note

If you attempt to print to the standard output in an HTML Web page, the output appears in a special log file or window—depending on how your browser handles standard output messages. In Netscape Navigator, this is the Console window.

To create the applet, click the Add to Project icon to once again display the File Open / Create dialog. On its File page, type `HelloWorldApplet.java` in the File name: field, and then click the Open button.

In the Content pane, enter the Java program shown in Listing 1.2.

TYPE   **LISTING 1.2.** HelloWorldApplet.java.

```
1:   import java.awt.Graphics;
2:   public class HelloWorldApplet extends java.applet.Applet {
3:     public void paint(Graphics g) {
4:       g.drawString("Hello World!", 20, 50);
5:     }
6:   }
```

ANALYSIS   This program has four parts:

- The first line imports the java.awt.Graphics library code into your program, which enables you to use the drawString() method later. (The import statement is similar to the #include statement in C/C++.)

- The class definition is named HelloWorldApplet. It begins on line 2 and ends on line 6.

- The body of the applet is the paint() method—lines 3 through 5. There is no main() method because the applet is run as a subprogram by the browser.

- The code that produces the actual output of the applet is in line 4. In this line of code, the application tells the system to paint the words "Hello World!" beginning at the graphic coordinate (25,50) as the lower-left anchor for the text string within the applet's coordinate space.

Compiling this program creates a new file named HelloWorldApplet.class. This is the Java bytecode file, which you can then run by embedding it into a Web page, called an HTML (Hypertext Markup Language) page.

To create the HTML page, click the Add to Project icon. In the File Open / Create dialog's File page, type HelloWorldWideWeb.html in the File name: field, and then click the Open button.

Click on the Source tab just below the Content pane, click on the Content pane itself, and press Ctrl+Home. Enter the text shown in Listing 1.3. This text is just a simple HTML page that enables you to run your applet in a Java-enabled browser.

TYPE   **LISTING 1.3.** HelloWorldWideWeb.html.

```
1:   <HTML>
2:   <HEAD>
3:   <TITLE>Hello to the World Wide Web!</TITLE>
4:   </HEAD>
```

```
5:   <BODY>
6:   <APPLET CODE="HelloWorldApplet.class" WIDTH=150 HEIGHT=50></APPLET>
7:   </BODY>
8:   </HTML>
```

Be sure to save your work when you're finished.

ANALYSIS The part of this HTML file that is of interest here is line 6, where you reference your `HelloWorldApplet.class` file. This is done with the `<APPLET></APPLET>` tag pair. You'll learn more about this tag pair later, but for now, just remember these things:

- The `CODE` attribute is used to name your `.class` file. This is what causes the applet to be executed when the HTML Web page is viewed in the browser.
- The `WIDTH` and `HEIGHT` attributes reserve the graphical space within which the applet runs on the HTML Web page. In this example, a box that is 150 pixels wide and 50 pixels high is set aside for the applet's use.
- The `<APPLET>` tag must always be followed by the `</APPLET>` tag.

Although you might find it useful to name your `.html` file the same as your applet `.class` file, it's not a requirement. If you have a Java-enabled browser installed on your system, use it to open the `HelloWorldWideWeb.html` file. If you don't yet have a browser available, you can use Sun's appletviewer utility to view your applet. It is located in the `JBuilder\java\bin` subdirectory.

The appletviewer is used quite often in this book to illustrate applet behavior because it is the one viewer you are assured to have available. It can be run from within the IDE, but first you have to accept Sun's license.

To do this using the `HelloWorldWideWeb.html` file you've just created, right-click on that file's node in the Navigation pane, and select the Run menu item. This causes Sun's Copyright Notice window to appear; click the Accept button. Now, the appletviewer is displayed, as shown in Figure 1.12. (Typically, you'll need to resize the appletviewer window to see the applet displayed property.) From now on, you'll be able to launch the appletviewer anytime you run an HTML file from within the JBuilder IDE.

Note Using appletviewer, you won't be able to see the entire HTML Web page, but it does show you what the applet part of the page looks like.

FIGURE 1.12.

Java applets can be viewed in the appletviewer.

You've created your first Java application and Java applet and viewed the results. Be sure to save all your work and select File | Close All to close the `Intro` project.

Summary

Today, you've been introduced to the Java language and how it came into being. You've also learned a bit about JBuilder and how it makes developing your Java programs easier.

You've learned how to install JBuilder, what to do after installation, and how to uninstall JBuilder. You also know where to look for help in the disk files and paper documentation, and you're aware of some of the online resources that are available to you.

Most important, you've created your first applet and application programs in Java, using JBuilder's Integrated Development Environment (IDE). Tomorrow, you'll get your first look at the basics of the Java language itself.

Q&A

Q Do I need to buy an Internet browser to use JBuilder?

A Earlier today, you used the appletviewer utility to check out your first applet. Later, you'll also use JBuilder's integrated debugger to test your programs. So it isn't really necessary for you to have an Internet browser to build your programs. However, it is recommended that you have several different browsers available for testing your applets so that you can see what users of your applets will actually see when they run your programs in their local environments. These are the major ones to obtain:

- Sun HotJava (`http://java.sun.com/products/hotjava`)
- Netscape Communicator (`http://www.netscape.com/try/download`)
- Microsoft Internet Explorer (`http://www.microsoft.com/ie/download`)

1

Q **You said that applets have to be run from inside an HTML Web page. How do I learn more about HTML coding?**

A Although HTML coding is not part of the scope of this book, you'll be using it enough that you'll be able to run your applets. But, to answer your question, several good books on HTML coding are available, including *Teach Yourself Web Publishing with HTML in 14 Days, Premier Edition*, by Laura Lemay (Sams.net).

Q **According to today's lesson, Java applets are downloaded using a Java-enabled browser, such as Navigator, Internet Explorer, or HotJava. Isn't that a huge security hole? What stops someone from writing an applet that compromises the security of my system—or damages my system?**

A Sun's Java team thought a great deal about the security of applets within Java-enabled browsers and implemented the following restrictions:

- Java applets cannot read or write to the local system's hard disk.

- Java applets cannot execute any programs on the local system.

- Java applets cannot connect to any machines on the Web except for the server from which they originated. Except in two cases.

Some browsers allow the user to turn off restrictions as an advanced option. However, as an applet designer, you cannot expect any of these capabilities to be available. In addition, the Java compiler and interpreter check both the Java source code and bytecodes to make sure that the programmer has not tried any sneaky tricks (for example, overrunning buffers or stack frames). Obviously, these checks cannot stop every potential security hole (no system can promise that), but they significantly reduce the potential for hostile applets.

You can acquire a digital certificate and digitally sign an applet. The applet can perform the preceding tasks as long as the user accepts the signature.

Q **Why use Borland's JBuilder to create Java programs?**

A Day 5, "JBuilder's IDE," gives you an in-depth look at the many advantages JBuilder offers over using just command-line utilities. But as a quick summary, here are the highlights. Borland's IDE was the first integrated development environment, and JBuilder's IDE takes full advantage of Borland's experience in the field of creating premier development products. JBuilder inherits "Two-Way Tools" from Borland's award-winning Delphi. These tools enable you to design the parts of your program in the way that's most intuitive for you—to drag-and-drop when visual designing is best, to type code when that's the best approach—and then synchronize your code and visual design so that you get the best of both worlds. JBuilder's AppBrowser, integrated debugger, and online help files give you all the tools you need to develop your Java programs with less typing, less redundancy, and fewer errors. Also, JBuilder is the first visual development environment to support rapid application design (RAD) using JavaBeans components.

DAY 2

Java Basics

Yesterday, you wrote your first Java application and applet. Today, you'll begin to examine the language in some depth so that you'll understand each of its basic constructs and know how to use them when programming with Java.

> **Note**
>
> There are enough differences among Java, C, C++, and Pascal that it will be well worth reviewing today's information even if you've been programming for some time. For example, C or C++ programmers might be surprised to find that Java does not include typedef, whereas Pascal programmers will be shocked to discover that a semicolon is required before an else statement.

These constructs represent the basic building blocks of your Java programs, such as variables, types, expressions, operators, arrays, strings, conditionals, and loops. Today, you'll learn about these topics:

- Program statements and comments
- Variables, literals, and data types
- Expressions and operators

- Creating and accessing arrays and strings
- Declaring and using multidimensional arrays
- Manipulation techniques for instances of the `String` and `StringBuffer` classes
- `if-else` and `switch`, for conditional tests
- `for`, `while`, and `do-while` loops, for iteration or repeating a statement or block multiple times

Program Statements

A program statement is where all the action takes place. There are three categories of statements:

- Simple
- Compound
- Comments

Simple and compound statements are compiled and become part of your application's binary image; all compiled statements must end with a semicolon (`;`). Comments are not compiled and are visible only in the source code, but they can be invaluable several months later when you (or someone maintaining your code) is trying to determine the original purpose of that code.

Simple Statements

Simple statements can assign values, perform an action, or call a method.

 A *method* is the term used in Java to indicate any subprogram (subroutine, function, or procedure).

Here are some examples of simple statements:

```
currpoint = new Point(x,y);
if (i==8) j = 4;
g.drawString("Hello world!", 10, 30);
repaint();
```

Java supports various statement types, including assignment, block, conditional, declaration, looping, and method calls. All except method calls will be covered today; method calls will be covered tomorrow.

Block Statements

You generally can use a block anywhere that a single statement is valid, and the block creates a new local scope for the statements within it. This means that you can declare and use local variables within a block, and those variables will cease to exist after the block is finished executing.

NEW TERM   A *block statement* (or simply, a *block*) is a group of other program statements surrounded by braces ({}). This is the same way braces are used in C and C++ and is analogous to the begin..end pair in Pascal. It is also sometimes known as a *compound statement.*

Here's an example that highlights the differences in scope. In the following method definition, x is declared for the method as a whole, and y is declared within the block:

```
void testblock() {
  int x = 10;
  { // block begin
    int y = 50;
    System.out.println("inside the block:");
    System.out.println("x:" + x); // prints 10
    System.out.println("y:" + y); // prints 50
  } // block end
  System.out.println("outside the block:");
  System.out.println("x:" + x); // prints 10
  System.out.println("y:" + y); // error, outside the scope
}
```

Note   The preceding example code does not compile because the y variable is undeclared outside of the block where it is defined.

When the value assigned to x is printed from inside the block, a 10 is sent to the console window. Likewise, when the value assigned to the y variable is printed, there is no problem because the scope of the y variable is within the block. There's also no problem with printing the value assigned to the x variable outside the block and in the method as a whole, because its scope is throughout the method. However, the second attempt at printing the value associated with the y variable fails because the y variable is defined only within the block, not outside it.

Blocks usually are not used alone like this in a method definition. A very common use of block statements is in the control-flow constructs you'll learn about later today.

Comment Statements

Comments are noncompiled statements that can contain any textual information you want to add to the code for later reference. Java provides you with three kinds of comments: single-line, multiline, and documentation comments.

Comments are useful as internal documentation for your program. You might want to use comments to add information about how a particular part of the program was designed, why a particular data structure was chosen, or what dependencies are inherent in the code. If you have an external specifications document, comments are a good place to reference that document and tie the internal and external documentation together.

Single-Line Comments

A single-line comment can be placed on a line by itself. It is indicated by placing two slashes (//) at the beginning of the line:

```
// A single-line comment looks like this.
```

A single-line comment can also be placed at the end of a line of code after the semicolon. This is sometimes called an inline comment:

```
x = y;      // An inline comment goes here.
```

Multiline Comments

You can designate a multiline comment by typing a slash-asterisk (/*) at the beginning and an asterisk-slash (*/) at the end of the comment:

```
/* For purposes of this calculation, the number of
   days per cycle will be assumed to be 30. */
```

Here is an alternative way to style multiline comments:

```
/* The AvgDailyBal procedure calculates the Average
 * Daily Balance, which is the sum of each day's
 * unpaid balance of any Purchases itemized on
 * statements prior to the current month's statement
 * divided by the number of days in the current
 * billing cycle.
 */
```

Note that the asterisks at the beginning of the middle lines in this example are for visual effect only. You can use any style of multiline comments you desire, as long as they begin with /* and end with */. The compiler will simply disregard anything between these special character pairs.

 Caution Nested multiline comments are not allowed in Java. In other words, you cannot place one multiline comment within another multiline comment.

Documentation Comments

Documentation comments are specially designed to generate public class documentation in HTML format. In fact, the HTML pages that document the Java language were generated using this technique, by placing documentation comments in the Java language source code. Everything between the slash-asterisk-asterisk (/**) and asterisk-slash (*/) is regarded as part of this special kind of comment. The comments are extracted from the source code by a utility called javadoc, which also recognizes certain keyword variables within the comment that start with the "at" (@) symbol, such as @author and @version:

```
/** This public class is designed to extend
  * the functionality of the awt.Graphics
  * class to display corporate logos.
  * @author mmm
  * @version 3.51
  */
public class mySpecialClass extends java.awt.Graphics {
...
};
```

2

Documentation comments usually are placed directly before the class declaration, as in this example.

Variables, Literals, and Data Types

Variables are named placeholders where values are stored during program execution. Before you can use a variable, you need to decide what kind of value it needs to hold. The kind of value determines which data type you will use to declare the variable. After the variable is declared, it can be initialized by being assigned a value and can be used in expressions. The value assigned can be a literal value (a specific number, letter, or string) or the result of an expression evaluation.

There are three categories of variables in Java: class variables, instance variables, and local variables. All three are declared the same way; however, class and instance variables are accessed somewhat differently than local variables. Class and instance variables are covered tomorrow. Today, you'll learn about local variables, which are declared and used in methods.

 Note   Java does not support the concept of global variables, which would be available to all parts of your program. Rather, instance and class variables are used to communicate information among objects.

Data Types

By declaring a variable to be of a specific data type, you define the kinds of values that can be stored in that variable. For example, a variable declared to be of type byte can hold a numeric value from -128 to 127 inclusive. There are eight value data types and two reference data types.

The eight value types include integral, floating-point, Boolean, and character data types, as shown in Table 2.1. These are also sometimes called *primitive types*. All data types in Java have default values and consistent properties across all platforms.

TABLE 2.1. JAVA'S VALUE DATA TYPES.

Data Type	Size	Default	Values
byte	8 bits	0	-128 to +127
short	16 bits	0	-32768 to +32767
int	32 bits	0	-2,147,483,648 to +2,147,483,647
long	64 bits	0	-9,223,372,036,854,775,808 to +9,223,372,036,854,775,807
float	32 bits	0.0	±3.40282347E+38 (min) ±1.40239846E-45 (max)
double	64 bits	0.0	±1.79769313486231570E+308 (min) ±4.94065645841246544E-324 (max)
boolean	1 bit	false	false, true
char	16 bits	\u0000	\u0000 to \uFFFF

Integral types (byte, short, int, long) are all signed. Floating-point values (float, double) follow the IEEE 754 floating-point standard for single- and double-precision numbers. In addition to the normal numeric values, floating-point operations can return four special values, defined as constants: POSITIVE_INFINITY, NEGATIVE_INFINITY, NEGATIVE_ZERO, and NaN (not a number). The boolean values will not evaluate to integers, as they will in other languages; they can represent only the values true or false.

If the char character values look a bit odd, it's because Java supports the two-byte Unicode character standard. However, for purposes of this book, you'll be using only the ASCII or Latin-1 subset of Unicode characters.

 Note

The Unicode character set is 16 bits and includes 34,168 characters. The Unicode subset that represents ASCII characters is \u0020 to \u007E, and for Latin-1 the range is \u0020 to \u00FF. Because ASCII and Latin-1 are 8 bits, they are both simply subsets of Unicode. Unicode is quickly becoming the world standard because it can represent the symbols and characters from most natural languages. To learn more about Unicode, visit the Unicode Consortium site on the World Wide Web at http://www.unicode.org.

The two reference data types hold objects (discussed tomorrow) and arrays. The object reference type can hold a class instance and defaults to null. The array reference type can hold elements of either value or reference type, and it defaults to the elements' type default value. In other words, a byte array's elements default to 0, and an object array's elements default to null.

Note

In Java, there is no typedef statement, as there is in C and C++. To declare new types, you must first declare a new class, and then variables can be declared to be of that class's type.

2

Variable Naming

A variable identifier can begin with a letter, an underscore (_), or a dollar sign ($) and can be followed by a combination of letters and digits. Symbols are problematic because so many of them are used in Java operators. Also, it is recommended, although not mandatory, that you not use the underscore (_) or dollar sign ($) as the first character to avoid conflicts when linking in C/C++ libraries.

The de facto standard is to name variables with letters and numbers only, with the first word all lowercase, and with the second and subsequent words initially capitalized. For example, a variable that will hold retirement ages might be named retireAge, whereas one to represent an insurance value limit could be named insValueLimit.

Java keywords cannot be used as identifiers. There are two keywords listed in Table 2.2 that, although not in use, are still reserved by Java. They are designated by the dagger (†) symbol.

TABLE 2.2. JAVA KEYWORDS.

abstract	boolean	break	byte	case
catch	char	class	const†	continue
default	do	double	else	extends
final	finally	float	for	goto†
if	implements	import	instanceof	int
interface	long	native	new	package
private	protected	public	return	short
static	super	switch	synchronized	this
throw	throws	transient	try	void
volatile	while			

Don't forget that Java is case sensitive. In other words, variables named
watchOut, WatchOut, and WATCHOUT are not the same. So be careful to be consistent in typing identifiers when creating code.

Declaring Variables

Now that you know what type you want the variable to be and have chosen a name for it,
it's time to declare the variable. There are several ways to declare a variable in Java, and
the declaration can be placed anywhere in the method. A variable will have effect from
the block in which it's declared and throughout blocks nested inside that block.

NEW TERM The group of program statements during which a variable exists is called the
variable's *scope*. When a program is run, the variable is created during execution
of the variable's declaration statement. All statements following the variable declaration
can access and manipulate the variable until the right brace (}) at the level of the block
or method in which the variable was declared is encountered. At that point, the variable
ceases to exist in memory and is now *out of scope*.

The simplest form of variable declaration contains just the type and variable name. For
example, the following declaration statements create variables named retireAge and
birthYear of type short and a variable named insValueLimit of type float:

```
short retireAge;
short birthYear;
float insValueLimit;
```

When declaring variables of the same type, you can declare them together on the same
line by separating them with commas. All three variables in this declaration are of type
short:

```
short retireAge, birthYear, stdRetireAge;
```

Initializing

To assign an initial value when the variable is declared, you use the equal sign (=), which
is Java's assignment operator, followed by the desired value. The following declaration
statement initializes insValueLimit to 10000.00:

```
float insValueLimit = 10000.00;
```

You can initialize multiple variables by giving each a value and declaring them on separate lines. In this declaration, isInsured and isCurrent are both initialized to true:

```
boolean isInsured = true;
boolean isCurrent = true;
```

Alternatively, you can initialize several variables of the same type by putting them on the same line and separating them with commas. Either way is fine, and it is mainly a matter of personal preference and visual style. Here's an example:

```
boolean isInsured = true, isCurrent = true;
```

In the next example, `retireAge` and `birthYear` are not initialized, but the last variable `stdRetireAge` is assigned the value of `65`:

```
short retireAge, birthYear, stdRetireAge = 65;
```

Note Although variables take on the default values of their declared type, the Java compiler gives you a warning if you attempt to use a local variable without initializing it first.

Literals

Literals are used to indicate values in your Java programs. In the preceding section on assigning values to variables, the values assigned (`10000.00`, `true`, and `65`) were all literals.

 A *literal* is a value that can be assigned to a value data type variable, as when initializing a variable in a declaration. A literal can also be used directly by your program, such as the literal value `8` in the expression `i==8`.

There are Boolean, numeric, character, and string literals. Each kind has some special information that you will need in order to make decisions about how to represent these values.

Boolean Literals

The Boolean literals in Java cannot take on integral values. They will not evaluate to anything other than the values `true` or `false`, and they are of type `boolean`.

Numeric Literals

A numeric literal is any number that can be assigned to an integral or a floating-point type. You can specify a literal's type by using special type designators, which can be in either lowercase or uppercase.

By default, an integral literal such as `8` is assumed to be of type `int`. However, if an integral literal is too large to fit into an `int`, such as `3000000000` (3 billion), it automatically becomes a `long`. Also, you can specifically designate the literal to be a `long` by adding an `l` or `L` type designator to the end of the number: `8L` becomes a `long` literal. All integral types can be used as negative numbers by preceding the number with a minus sign: -78 is a negative int literal.

Integrals can also be expressed as octal or hexadecimal. Prefixing a number with 0 designates the number as an octal (base 8) literal: 0347. Prefixing a number with a 0x or 0X indicates that the number is a hexadecimal (base 16) literal: 0x2FA3. Although you can use the octal or hexadecimal number system to represent the literal, it is still stored in memory as one of the integral data types, according to the rules explained in the preceding paragraph.

Floating-point literals are always assumed to be of type double, no matter what their stated value: 5.67 is a double literal. You can make the literal a float by adding an f or F to the end of the number: 5.67f becomes a float literal. You can also use scientific notation to express floating-point literals by adding an e or E, followed by the exponent, to the end of the number: 5.964e-4 is the representation of 0.0005964 in scientific notation and is stored as a double.

 Note   To store a number expressed in scientific notation as a float, add an f or F to the end of the literal, such as 5.964e-4F.

Character Literals

Character literals in Java, represented by Unicode characters of the char data type, are surrounded by single-quote (') symbols: 'a', '*', and '8' are all character literals. Nonprinting characters, such as the Tab and the Backspace, can also be represented as character literals by using what are known as character escape codes.

 A *character escape code* is created by prefacing the nonprinting or special symbol with the backslash (\). This allows the nonprinting or special symbol to be used as a character literal.

In addition, because certain symbols are used by the Java language, such as single-quote symbols ('), they are also represented as character literals by using the backslash (\), as indicated in Table 2.3.

TABLE 2.3. CHARACTER ESCAPE CODES.

Escape Code	Nonprinting Character or Symbol
\b	Backspace
\f	Formfeed
\n	Newline

Escape Code	Nonprinting Character or Symbol
\r	Return
\t	Tab
\\	Backslash
\"	Double quote
\'	Single quote
\ddd	Octal (for example, \347)
\xdd	Hexadecimal (for example, \x2FA3)
\udddd	Unicode character (for example, \u0C00)

2

For octal codes, the d character represents an octal digit (0–7). For hexadecimal and Unicode character codes, the d character represents a hexadecimal digit (0–9, a–f, A–F).

String Literals

A string simply is a combination of character literals and is delimited by double-quote (") (double-quotes)> symbols: "Hello world!" is a string literal. To an empty string— that is, one without any characters—just type the double-quote (") symbol twice: "" is an empty string.

Following is a code snippet with statements that each contain a string literal:

```
System.out.println("This string prints\nmultiple lines.");
System.out.println("\"I want to be alone,\" she said.");
System.out.println("Most 4th-graders are \11 years old.");
```

In the first line, a \n literal indicates that a newline character should be printed after the word prints. In the second, double-quotes are printed by using the \" literal. The third line uses an octal literal, \11 to produce the number 9 in the output. Here's what the actual printed output looks like:

```
This string prints
multiple lines.
"I want to be alone," she said.
Most 4th-graders are 9 years old.
```

In Java, strings are instances of the class String and are true objects, not arrays as in other languages. When you use a string literal, you are implicitly creating an instance of the class String and initializing it with the value of the string literal. The other literals don't do this because they are all primitive value data types, not objects like strings. You'll learn more about strings later today.

Expressions and Operators

Expressions and operators combine to let you perform evaluations with data.

NEW TERM An *expression* is a statement or part of a statement with variable and literal terms that resolve to a specific value, such as i==8, which evaluates to either true or false.

NEW TERM An *operator* is a symbol used to control how the terms of an expression are to be evaluated or manipulated. In the example i==8, the operator == tells the compiler to compare the values of the variable i and the literal 8, which are called *operands*.

You can think of operators as minifunctions that take parameters (the operands) and return a result. The data type of the result depends on the operator used. For example, a logical operator can take int values as operands, but it returns a boolean result. The operator and its operands are the smallest form of an expression.

Each operator has a precedence that governs the order in which it and its operands are evaluated within the expression. You have several other aspects to consider when dealing with operators. There are three kinds: unary operators take one operand; binary operators take two operands; ternary operators take three operands. Unary operators can also be prefix or postfix, causing quite different results. Binary and ternary operators are all infix.

NEW TERM A *unary prefix operator* is placed before its operand:

    op b

NEW TERM A *unary postfix operator* is placed after its operand:

    a op

NEW TERM A *binary infix operator* is placed between its two operands:

    a op b

NEW TERM A *ternary infix operator* is actually a pair of operator symbols and it takes three operands. The first symbol of the pair is placed between operands one and two, and the second is placed between operands two and three:

    a op1 b op2 c

Java has a large set of assignment operators, which you'll learn about later today. For the moment, you need to know only that the assignment operator (=) assigns the value of the expression on the right side of the operator to the variable on the left side.

> **Note** In Java, the = assignment operator does the same operation as the Pascal := assignment operator.

In the following sections, you'll be exposed to all these aspects of evaluating expressions and using operators. Don't worry about memorizing them at this point. You just need to get a good idea of the principles involved.

Arithmetic Operations

Operations that deal with numeric operands and produce numeric results are called *arithmetic operations*. The unary operations include incrementing, decrementing, plus, and minus. The binary operations include addition, subtraction, multiplication, division, and modulus. There's even an arithmetic binary operation for strings called *concatenation*.

Incrementing and Decrementing

The increment (++) and decrement (- -) operators are both unary prefix and unary postfix. If the operator appears before the operand (prefix), the operation takes place before your program uses the resulting value. If the operator appears after the operand (postfix), your program uses the value and then completes the operation. Incrementing a value adds 1; decrementing subtracts 1 from the value. In other words, the expressions in the two statements

```
myAge = myAge + 1;
daysLeftUntilVacation = daysLeftUntilVacation - 1;
```

represent the same values as these two expressions:

```
myAge++;
daysLeftUntilVacation--;
```

The value can be either any integral or floating-point value or any expression that evaluates to one of these numeric types.

For example, consider the following program fragment:

```
int x, y, z = 7;
x = ++z;    // In this example, x is assigned the value 8.
y = z;      // The variable y is also assigned the value 8.
```

The variable z is first incremented. The result, 8, is then assigned to x. Because z is now 8, y is also assigned that value. Now consider this program fragment:

```
int x, y, z = 7;
x = z++;     // In this example, x is assigned the value 7.
y = z;       // The variable y is assigned the value 8.
```

The value in variable z (7) is assigned to x. Then z is incremented and now contains the value 8. Because z is 8, y is assigned that value.

Signs

To sign a numeric value or expression, simply prefix it with either the unary plus (+) for positive numbers or the unary minus (-) for negative numbers. Here is an example:

```
int x, y = +4, z = -7;
x = y;          // Here, x is assigned the value of 4.
x = -y;         // Here, x is assigned the value of -4.
x = -z;         // Here, x is assigned the value of 7.
x = z;          // Here, x is assigned the value of -7.
```

Basic Math

This group of binary infix operators accomplishes basic math operations, such as addition (+), subtraction (-), multiplication (*), division (/), and modulus (%). These operations are all demonstrated here:

```
int x, y = 28, z = 8;
x = y + z;     // Variable x is assigned the value 36.
x = y - z;     // Variable x is assigned the value 20.
x = y * z;     // Variable x is assigned the value 224.
x = y / z;     // Variable x is assigned the value 3.
w = y % z;     // Variable x is assigned the value 4.
```

The division (/) operator drops the remainder of the division and uses only the integral part for the result, and the modulus (%) operator uses only the remainder of the division for its result.

String Math

How do you add strings together? By using the concatenation (+) binary infix operator:

```
String helloWorld, hello = "Hello", space = " ", world = "World";
helloWorld = hello + space + world + "!";
```

This has the same effect as the following line:

```
String helloWorld = "Hello World!";
```

With the concatenation (+) operator, you can use any strings or character literals for operands.

Relational Operations

All relational operators return a boolean result. The expression formed by the operator and its operands is either true or false. These operators are also known as *comparison operators*. In addition to comparisons of arithmetic values, you can compare objects and types.

2

> **Note**
>
> In Java, the == is-equal-to operator does the same operation as the Pascal = is-equal-to operator for arithmetic comparisons.

The arithmetic relational operators are less than (<), less than or equal to (<=), greater than (>), greater than or equal to (>=), is equal to (==), and is not equal to (!=). Here are some examples of how they work:

```
int w = -8, x = -9, y = 28, z = 8;
boolean isThatSo;
isThatSo = y < z;        // isThatSo is assigned the value false.
isThatSo = x <= w;       // isThatSo is assigned the value true.
isThatSo = y > z;        // isThatSo is assigned the value true.
isThatSo = x >= w;       // isThatSo is assigned the value false.
isThatSo = y == z;       // isThatSo is assigned the value false.
isThatSo = w != z;       // isThatSo is assigned the value true.
```

Several relational operators are also available for object comparisons: type comparison (instanceof), refers-to-same-object (==), and refers-to-different-object (!=). These last two operators look the same as the is-equal-to (==) and is-not-equal-to (!=) operators shown previously, but they take objects as operands rather than arithmetic values.

The type comparison (instanceof) operator determines whether the object in the left operand is an instance of the type (or implements the interface) in the right operand. If it is, the result is true; if it isn't or if the object is null, the result is false.

The refers-to-same-object (==) operator evaluates whether the object in the left operand points to the same instance as the object in the right operand. If it does, the result is true; if it doesn't, the result is false.

The refers-to-different-object (!=) operator evaluates whether the object in the left operand points to a different instance than the object in the right operand. If it does, the result is true; if not, the result is false.

Logical Operations

Logical operators take `boolean` operands and return a `boolean` result. There is one unary prefix logical operator: logical NOT (!). Almost all the rest are binary infix operators: logical AND (&), logical OR (¦), logical XOR (^), conditional AND (&&), and conditional OR (¦¦). Last, but not least, is the ternary infix operator: conditional if-else (?:).

The logical NOT (!) operator simply toggles the `boolean` value it prefixes. If its operand is `true`, the result is `false`; if its operand is `false`, it returns `true`.

The logical AND (&) operator evaluates both operands, and if both are `true`, the result is `true`; if either operand is `false`, the result is `false`. The logical OR (¦) operator determines whether either operand is `true`, and if so, the result is `true`; if both are `false`, the result is `false`. The logical XOR (^) operator ascertains whether the operands are different (one must be `true`, and one must be `false`). If so, the result is `true`; if both are `true` or both are `false`, the result is `false`. Table 2.4 outlines these results.

TABLE 2.4. LOGICAL BOOLEAN OPERATIONS AND RESULTS.

Left Operand	Right Operand	AND (&) AND (&&)	OR (¦) OR (¦¦)	XOR (^)
true	true	true	true	false
true	false	false	true	true
false	true	false	true	true
false	false	false	false	false

The conditional AND (&&) operator and the conditional OR (¦¦) operator are short-circuit Booleans. The results are the same as the logical AND (&) and logical OR (¦) operators, but the evaluations of the expressions happen a bit differently.

The conditional AND (&&) operator first determines whether the left operand is `false`; if so, the result is `false`, and the evaluation stops right there. However, if it evaluates the left operand as `true`, it then evaluates the right operand. If the right operand is also `true`, the result is `true`; if it's `false`, the result is `false`.

The conditional OR (¦¦) operator first determines whether the left operand is `true`; if so, the result is `true`, and the evaluation stops at that point. But if it evaluates the left operand as `false`, it then evaluates the right operand. If the right operand is `true`, the result is `true`; if it's `false`, the result is `false`.

The ternary-infix conditional (?:) operator is a kind of shorthand for the familiar `if-else` statement. If the first operand is determined to be `true`, the second operand is evaluated/performed, or else the third operand is evaluated/performed:

```
isInsured ? payClaim() : doNothing();
```

In this example, if isInsured is true, the method payClaim() is called; if isInsured is false, the method doNothing() is called. You'll learn more about method calls tomorrow.

Bitwise Operations

Bitwise operations manipulate the bits in the variable's memory space. Bitwise operators take integral operands and return an integral result. There is one unary-prefix bitwise operator: bitwise NOT (~). The rest are binary infix operators: bitwise AND (&), bitwise OR (¦), bitwise XOR (^), bitwise left shift (<<), signed right shift (>>), and zero-fill right shift (>>>).

The bitwise NOT (~) operator simply toggles the bits of the integral value it prefixes. For example, if the integral value is 00101001, applying the bitwise NOT (~) operator would result in the integral value 11010110.

In an actual program statement, the two integral values would be to the left and the right of the bitwise operator. But for ease of comparison, it is best to show them in a columnar format. For the bitwise AND (&), bitwise OR (¦), and bitwise XOR (^), you will be comparing bits paired by their positions in the integral value. For example, consider the following two numbers:

```
00101001
11101110
```

The first pair is (0,1), the second pair is (0,1), and the third pair is (1,1). Remember to pair them vertically in columns so that you're using the same position for each pair. In this example, the number 00101001 represents the left operand, and the number 11101110 represents the right operand. Table 2.5 outlines the results of each possible bit pairing in bitwise operations.

TABLE 2.5. BITWISE OPERATIONS AND RESULTS.

Paired Bit in Left Operand	Paired Bit in Right Operand	AND (&)	OR (¦)	XOR (^)
1	1	1	1	0
1	0	0	1	1
0	1	0	1	1
0	0	0	0	0

The bitwise shift operators are bitwise left shift (<<), signed right shift (>>), and zero-fill right shift (>>>). These operators take an integral value as the left operand and a numeric literal as the right operand, which specifies how many positions to shift.

The bitwise left shift (<<) operator moves each digit in the integral value in its left operand to the left by as many places as the numeric literal in the right operand indicates. As the numbers shift left, the digits on the left "fall off," and zeros are added to the right to fill out the new number.

 Caution   When you're using the left shift operator (<<), the sign drops off as you shift left.

The signed right shift (>>) operator moves each digit in the integral value in its left operand to the right by as many places as the numeric literal in the right operand indicates. In this case, however, the sign is not lost. The leftmost digit remains unchanged, and the number is padded on the left with the value of the leftmost digit.

If you want to explicitly left-fill with zeros, use the zero-fill right shift (>>>) operator. Because this operation always fills with zeros, it does not preserve the sign of the number.

Assignments

Java has a rich collection of assignment operators. The basic assignment (=) operator is supplemented by a set of operators that enable you to do an operation and an assignment at the same time. They take the form *op=*, where *op* is an operator belonging to the following set:

    { *, /, %, +, -, <<, >>, >>>, &, ^, ¦ }

For example, rather than using the statements

```
totalCharges = totalCharges + newItemPrice;
isInsured = isInsured & hasRenewed;
```

you could use these statements to accomplish the same operations:

```
totalCharges += newItemPrice;
isInsured &= hasRenewed;
```

These assignment operators can be real time-savers when using long identifiers and can make your code more readable.

Operator Precedence

You've examined each of the Java operators, but one last consideration remains. The precedence of the operators determines in what order the expression's arguments are evaluated. In Table 2.6, each operator is listed in order of precedence with the type of operands it takes, the operation it performs, and the placement of the operator in the expression. For example, in the program fragment

```
int g, x = 6, y = 7, z = 8;
g = x + y * z;
```

the multiplication of y and z is done first, resulting in the value 56; then the result is added to x, giving a value of 62. Finally, that result is assigned to g. But what if you wanted to add x and y first and then multiply by z? You can accomplish this by using parentheses to change the order of evaluation:

```
int g, x = 6, y = 7, z = 8;
g = (x + y) * z;
```

In this case, x and y are first added together, resulting in 13, and that value is then multiplied by z, giving 104. Finally, 104 is assigned to g. Operators in the same precedence level are evaluated left to right, except nested unary and ternary operators, which are evaluated right to left.

TABLE 2.6. PRECEDENCE OF OPERATIONS.

Precedence	Operator	Operands	Operation	Placement
1	++	arithmetic	increment	unary prefix/postfix
	- -	arithmetic	decrement	unary prefix/postfix
	+	arithmetic	plus (positive)	unary prefix
	-	arithmetic	minus (negative)	unary prefix
	!	Boolean	logical NOT	unary prefix
	~	integral	bitwise NOT	unary prefix
2	*	arithmetic	multiply	binary infix
	/	arithmetic	divide	binary infix
	%	arithmetic	modulus	binary infix
3	+	string	concatenate	binary infix
	+	arithmetic	add	binary infix
	-	arithmetic	subtract	binary infix
4	<<	integral	bitwise left shift	binary infix
	>>	integral	signed right shift	binary infix
	>>>	integral	zero-fill right shift	binary infix
5	<	arithmetic	less than	binary infix
	<=	arithmetic	less than or equal to	binary infix
	>	arithmetic	greater than	binary infix
	>=	arithmetic	greater than or equal to	binary infix
	instanceof	object, type	type comparison	binary infix
6	==	arithmetic	is equal to	binary infix
	!=	arithmetic	is not equal to	binary infix
	==	object	refers to same object	binary infix
	!=	object	refers to different object	binary infix
7	&	integral	bitwise AND	binary infix
	&	Boolean	logical AND	binary infix
8	^	integral	bitwise XOR	binary infix
	^	Boolean	logical XOR	binary infix
9	¦	integral	bitwise OR	binary infix
	¦	Boolean	logical OR	binary infix
10	&&	Boolean	conditional AND	binary infix
11	¦¦	Boolean	conditional OR	binary infix
12	?:	Boolean, any, any	conditional if-else	ternary infix
13	=	variable, any	assignment	
	op=	variable, any	assignment with operation	

In addition to these operations, a package of mathematical constants and operations is defined in the `java.math.lang` class. Explanations of how these functions are used are beyond the scope of this book. However, if you should need them, they include constant values for e and pi, trig functions (sine, cosine, tangent, arc sine, arc cosine, arc tangent), exponential e, natural logarithm, square root, IEEE remainder, ceiling, floor, rectangular to polar coordinates, exponent, round, random, absolute, max, and min functions.

Arrays and Strings

Arrays are some of the most useful constructs in Java. They enable you to collect objects or primitive types into easy-to-manage structures. Strings are a special type of array, and so also are full-fledged objects in Java. In this section, you'll learn how to create and manipulate these objects.

In the following discussion, the term *constructors* is used. You'll learn more about constructors tomorrow (Day 3, "Java Intermediate"). But for now, just keep in mind that constructors are special methods that enable you to create an object in memory, optionally giving some value to the object at the same time.

Array Objects

In Java, arrays are implemented as full-fledged objects, so they can be compared and manipulated as objects. Because arrays are true objects, they have constructors, methods, and variables especially designed for use with arrays.

NEW TERM   An *array* is a way to store a list of items. Each slot in the array holds an individual item or element. You can place elements into slots or change the contents of those slots as needed.

Array elements can contain any type of value (primitives or objects), but you can't mix types in an array. That is, an array's elements must all be the same data type. For example, you can have an array of integers or an array of `String` objects, but you cannot have an array that contains both integer and `String` elements.

Creating an array in Java involves three steps:

1. Declare a variable to hold the array.
2. Create a new array object, and assign it to the array variable.
3. Store things in the array object by accessing its elements.

Declaring Array Variables

The first step in creating an array is to create a variable that will hold the array. Array variable declarations can take one of two equally valid formats. Both formats include the name of the array, indicate the type of object the array will hold, and have empty brackets ([]) to indicate that the new variable is an array. Here are some typical array variable declarations:

```
int[] theTenBestGameScores;
Date games[];
int averageRBI[];
```

The first declaration denotes that you are declaring an array of type `int` named `theTenBestGameScores`. The second declares an array of type `Date` named `games`. The third declares an `int` array named `averageRBI`.

As you can see, the brackets ([]) can be after the type or after the variable identifier. Either way is accepted by the Java compiler, and the two declaration styles can be mixed. By putting the brackets directly after the type, you can easily see that you are declaring an array of that type. However, the Java source code uses the format shown in the last two examples, so this book follows that standard and places the brackets directly after the variable identifier.

Creating Array Objects

The second step is to create an array object and assign it to that variable. You can do this in two ways:

- Use `new` to explicitly create the array and then initialize the elements separately.
- Directly initialize the contents to create the array implicitly.

When you create an array object using `new`, you must explicitly indicate how many slots or elements that array will hold:

```
int games[] = new int[10];
```

This creates a new array of integers with 10 elements. In this case, each of the 10 elements in the integer array is initialized with the value `0`. The initialized value depends on the type of array you have created, as shown in Table 2.7.

TABLE 2.7. DEFAULT VALUES FOR ARRAY INITIALIZATION.

Array Type	Default Initial Value
boolean	false
char	'\0'
byte, short, int, long float, double	0
Object, String	null

You can also create and initialize an array at the same time, just as you can for other variables. Instead of using new to create the array object, enclose the elements of the array inside braces, separated by commas, to denote the set of initial elements:

```
float rates[] = { 12.9, 14.5, 16.5, 18.95, 23.0 };
```

The elements inside the braces must be of the same type as the variable that holds the array. The array is created with the number of slots matching the number of elements you've specified. So in this example, an array of five float elements is created and named rates. The first element in the array contains the value 12.9, the second contains 14.5, and so on.

Attempting to store the wrong type of data in an array will cause a compiler error. For example, this line of code will cause the compiler to complain about type mismatch:

```
float rates[] = { 'M', 'i', 'a', 'm', 'i' };
```

An attempt to assign the wrong type at runtime will cause an ArrayStoreException object to be thrown.

NEW TERM   An *exception* is an error that occurs at runtime. The Java Exception class is divided into various categories so that when an exception is thrown, you will have some idea of what caused the error.

To properly declare the array for the preceding values, you would need to declare an array of type char:

```
char chArr[] = { 'M', 'i', 'a', 'm', 'i' };
```

Accessing and Changing Array Elements

After you have an initialized array, you can test and change the values in each slot of that array. To access a value stored within an array, use the array *subscript* expression:

```
arrayName[subscript];
```

The *arrayName* is the variable holding the array object. The *subscript* is an integer or an integer expression that specifies the slot to access within the array.

 Caution   Subscripts in Java always begin with zero (0).

Let's take another look at this example:

```
float rates[] = { 12.9, 14.5, 16.5, 18.95, 23.0 };
```

Here is a code snippet that illustrates how these elements might be assigned to other variables:

```
float platinumRate == rates[0];    // value is 12.9
float goldRate == rates[1];        // value is 14.5
float preferredRate == rates[2];   // value is 16.5
float regularRate == rates[3];     // value is 18.95
float probationRate == rates[4];   // value is 23.0
```

All array subscripts are checked to make sure that they are inside the boundaries of the array. That is, they must be greater than or equal to zero but less that the array's length. This check occurs when your Java program is compiled or when it is executed. It is impossible in Java to access or assign a value to an array slot outside the boundaries of the array. Examine the following two statements:

```
int myArr[] = new int[10];
myArr[10] = 73;
```

A program with these statements in it produces a compiler error at the second line when you try to compile it. The array stored in myArr has only 10 slots, numbered from 0 through 9. The element at subscript 10 would be in slot number 11, which doesn't exist, so the Java compiler complains about it.

If the array subscript is calculated at runtime (for example, as part of a loop) and ends up outside the boundaries of the array, the Java interpreter will produce an ArrayIndexOutOfBoundsException object. If at runtime you attempt to allocate an array with fewer than zero elements (for example, by using a subscript expression that resolves to a negative number), you will receive a NegativeArraySizeException object.

To avoid throwing an exception caused by exceeding the bounds of an array accidentally in your own programs, you can find out the number of elements in the array by checking its length instance variable. This variable is defined for all array objects, regardless of type:

```
int len = arr.length;  // returns 10
```

To modify the value of an array element, simply put an assignment statement after the array access expression. Here are two examples:

```
myArr[1] = 15;
sentence[0] = "The";
```

Arrays of primitive types such as int or float can copy values from one slot to another. However, an array of objects in Java is an array of references to those objects (similar in some ways to pointers). When you assign a value to a slot in an array, you're creating a reference to that object, just as you do for a plain object variable. When you assign one array object to another, as in the line

```
sentence[10] = sentence[0];
```

you just reassign the reference. You don't copy the value from one slot to another. After this line of code is executed, both `sentence[10]` and `sentence[0]` would point to the same memory allocation.

Arrays of references to objects, as opposed to arrays of the objects themselves, are particularly useful because they enable you to have multiple references to the same objects both inside and outside arrays. For example, you can assign an object contained in an array to a variable and refer to that same object by using either the variable or its array position.

▼ SYNTAX

There is also a method in `java.lang.System` called `arraycopy()`, which enables you to copy data from one array to another. The syntax of this method is

```
arraycopy(srcArr, srcOffset, dstArr, dstOffset, copyLength)
```

The arguments are defined as shown here:

srcArr	The identifier of the source array
srcOffset	The position where you want to begin copying
dstArr	The identifier of the destination array
dstOffset	The position where you want the copied data to be written
copyLength	The number of array elements to be copied.

▲ This method does not allocate any memory, so the destination array must already exist.

Multidimensional Arrays

Java supports multidimensional arrays. A very easy way to think of a multidimensional array is to picture it as an array of arrays. In Java, you declare and create an array of arrays (and those arrays can contain arrays, and so on) and access their elements by using subscripts for each dimension. Here's an example of a two-dimensional array of coordinates:

```
int coords[][] = new int[12][12];
coords[0][0] = 1;
coords[0][1] = 2;
```

Multidimensional arrays can have as many dimensions as you want—just keep adding brackets ([]) for each dimension. Here's an example of a six-dimensional array declaration:

```
int sixDimArr[][][][][][] = new int [2][4][8][3][][];
```

In this example, the first four dimensions are explicitly sized, whereas the last two are not. Memory is allocated for the first four dimensions; the last two dimensions are not allocated until they are later initialized. You can specify as many explicitly sized dimensions as you like, followed by as many unsized dimensions as you like, but they must be in that order. For example, the following is not allowed in Java:

```
int threeDimArr[][][] = new int [3][][3];  // invalid
```

Another thing to notice about multidimensional arrays is that it is not necessary for each subarray to be the same size. Consider this example:

```
byte threeDimByteArr[][][] = new byte [2][4][3];
```

This array contains eight subarrays, each containing three byte elements. The `threeDimByteArr` array contains 2 elements that are subarrays. Each of those two subarrays has four elements that are also subarrays. Each of those four subarrays has three byte elements. You can also declare nonrectangular multidimensional arrays by specifying literal values, such as the following:

```
String encryptStrArr[][] = new String {
  {"ab", "cd", "ef", "gh", "ij"},
  {"kl", "mn"},
  {"op", "qr", "st", "uv"},
  {"wx", "yz"}
};
```

This example creates a multidimensional `String` array allocating four subarrays with 5, 2, 4, and 2 `String` elements, respectively.

String and StringBuffer Objects

In this section, you'll take a look at how to declare and create strings, how to access string elements, and how to use methods to manipulate strings. In addition, you'll take a look at how to use the `StringBuffer` class.

The `String` class is used to represent strings that are constant. The `String` class does provide a few basic manipulation methods, but the result must always be assigned to a second `String` object. Any significant change in a string value requires an interim assignment to a `StringBuffer` object. The `StringBuffer` class enables you to manipulate strings directly inside the original `StringBuffer` object. This generally requires more memory to be allocated, however, so it is recommended that you use `String` objects whenever possible.

Declaring String and StringBuffer Objects

Declaring a variable of the `String` or `StringBuffer` data type is simple:

```
String myString;
StringBuffer myStringBuff;
```

However, declaring the variable only sets aside the identifier; it doesn't allocate any memory for the `StringBuffer` or `String` object. To do that, you must either initialize using a string literal or call a constructor.

Creating `String` Objects

Because strings are used so often, the `String` class in Java defines several shortcuts to create strings without explicitly calling a constructor. The most common way of allocating a `String` object is to assign a string literal to the declared variable:

```
myString = "I'll see you on Saturday.";
```

The resulting allocation is based on the number of characters contained in the literal. Another way to create a new string is to use one of the `valueOf()` methods to convert a value of another type, such as an integer, to its text equivalent:

```
myString = String.valueOf(17);
```

This creates a `String` containing two characters, 1 and 7. The `valueOf()` method can convert primitive types (`boolean`, `char`, `int`, `long`, `float`, `double`), the `Object` type, and `char` arrays. For `char` arrays, the `valueOf()` method provides two method signatures: one that takes the entire array as its parameter and another that takes a `char` array, an *offset*, and a *count* as parameters. Here's an example of the latter:

```
char chArr[] = { 's', 'p', 'o', 'r', 't', 's' };
String chString = String.valueOf(chArr, 1, 4);
```

This creates a `String` named `chString` containing the characters defined in `chArr`, starting at position 1 (the offset) for 4 characters (the count) and resulting in the value `port`.

Note that these techniques for creating `String` objects do not require the explicit use of a constructor. In addition, the `String` class defines several constructors from which to choose. Here are some of the more common examples.

The following constructor takes no parameters and is the default constructor:

```
String str1 = new String();
```

It creates a `String` object named `str1` with a `length` of `0`.

This constructor takes a `string` literal as its parameter:

```
String str2 = new String("Good Afternoon");
```

It creates a `String` object named `str2` containing the value `Good Afternoon` with a `length` of `14`.

This one takes a chArr as its parameter:

```
char chArr[] = { 'S', 'a', 'm', 's' };
String str3 = new String(chArr);
```

It creates a String object named str3 containing the value Sams with a length of 4. (This method is identical in result to the valueOf() method, which takes a char array as its parameter.)

And this one takes a char array, an offset, and a count as its parameters:

```
char chArr[] = { 'I', 'n', 't', 'e', 'r', 'n', 'e', 't' };
String str4 = new String(chArr, 5, 3);
```

It creates a String object named str4 containing the value net and a length of 3, which is obtained by starting at offset 5 in chArr and taking a count of 3 characters. (This method is identical in result to the valueOf() method, which takes a char array, an offset, and a count as its parameters.)

This last constructor takes a StringBuffer object as its parameter:

```
String str5 = new(myStringBuff);
```

It creates a String object named str5 containing the contents of the myStringBuff variable.

Accessing String Elements

The elements of a String object can be accessed the same way you access array elements, and you can use integer or integer expression subscripts to identify individual String array elements. If a String subscript ends up outside the boundaries of the array at runtime, the Java interpreter will produce a StringIndexOutOfBoundsException object.

Here's an example of a for loop that initializes all the values of a String object to the char A by accessing its individual array elements:

```
String aString[] = new String[3];
for (int i = 0; i < aString.length; i++)
  aString[i] = 'A';
```

In addition to accessing the characters as array elements, the String class defines numerous methods to facilitate access to values within strings. Create an application using the AccessString class in Listing 2.1, which illustrates some of these methods.

TYPE **LISTING 2.1.** AccessString.java.

```
1:  class AccessString {
2:    public static void main(String args[]) {
3:      String str = "Time is too slow for those who wait.";
4:      System.out.println();
5:
6:      System.out.println("The string is: " + str);
7:
8:      System.out.println("Length of string: "
9:                          + str.length());
10:
11:     System.out.println("Character at position 17: "
12:                         + str.charAt(17));
13:
14:     System.out.println("String begins with \"those\": "
15:                         + str.startsWith("those"));
16:
17:     System.out.println("String ends with \"wait.\": "
18:                         + str.endsWith("wait."));
19:
20:     System.out.println("Index of the first \"w\" character: "
21:                         + str.indexOf('w'));
22:
23:     System.out.println("Index of the last \"w\" character: "
24:                         + str.lastIndexOf('w'));
25:
26:     System.out.println("Substring from 0 to 2: "
27:                         + str.substring(0, 3));
28:
29:   }
30: }
```

2

After you compile and run the program, you should see this output in the Execution Log window, which you open by selecting the Execution Log command from the View menu:

OUTPUT
```
The string is: Time is too slow for those who wait.
Length of string: 36
Character at position 17: f
String begins with "those": false
String ends with "wait.": true
Index of the first "w" character: 15
Index of the last "w" character: 31
Substring from 0 to 2: Tim
```

ANALYSIS In this example, you create an instance of String and then print various values returned by methods defined in the String class:

- Line 3 creates an instance of `String` called `str` with the literal `Time is too slow for those who wait.` as its initial value.

- Line 6 prints the current value of the `str` variable.

- Line 9 calls the `length()` method and returns the value `36`. (Don't forget to count the period at the end of the sentence in the string.)

- Line 12 calls the `charAt()` method and returns the character at the given index position in the string. Note that string indexes start at `0`, so the character at position `17` is `f`.

- Line 15 calls the `startsWith()` method, which looks for the substring `those` at the beginning of `str`. This is a `boolean` method, and the result is `false`.

- Line 18 calls the `endsWith()` method, which looks for the substring `wait.` at the end of `str`. This is also a `boolean` method whose result is `true`.

- Line 21 calls the `indexOf()` method with a `char` argument, which returns the index position of the first observation of the given character. The first `w` in the string is at position `15` in the word `slow`.

- Line 24 calls the `lastIndexOf()` method with a `char` argument, which returns the index position of the last observation of the given character. The last `w` is at position `31` in the word `wait`.

- Line 27 calls the `substring()` method and begins at index position `0` (inclusive) and ends before index position `3` (exclusive) in the string. This results in the substring `Tim` (the 0th, 1st, and 2nd characters).

The `substring()` method warrants a bit more explanation. The character at the beginning index position is included in the substring, but the character at the ending index is not included in the substring. For this reason, the `substring()` method can take a second form that enables you to get the substring from a specified index position to the end of the `String`. For example, to get the last two characters of the `String` containing the value `Hello`, you could use this second form:

```
String str = "Hello";
String loStr = str.substring(3));   // using correct method
```

If you attempt to use the first form to accomplish this same task, you will get a runtime `StringIndexOutOfBounds` exception object:

```
String str = "Hello";
String loStr = str.substring(3, 5));   // throws an exception
```

To get those last two characters, you would have to specify a beginning inclusive index of `3` but an exclusive ending index of `5`. This causes the exception to be thrown because the valid indices for `str` are `0` through `4`.

Several other methods have more than one form (such as the indexOf() and lastIndexOf() methods), but for purposes of this example, only one form was shown for each method. For more details, be sure to refer to the online documentation for the String class in the online Java Reference help file.

Comparing and Manipulating Strings

The String class also provides methods for comparison and manipulation. When objects are compared, the comparison returns a boolean value telling you whether two object variables point to the very same object in memory. Also, don't forget that if you define two string literals with the same value, they will actually point to the same memory allocation.

Caution

> String literals are optimized in Java. This means that if you store a string value and then attempt to assign another string value by using the same literal, the Java compiler will realize that it has that literal already stored and will very helpfully return the existing object rather than creating a new object. Therefore, you must explicitly use new to create two distinct String object instances with the same string value.

So assuming you've used new to create two separate and distinct strings, how do you compare the two strings? The String class defines three comparison methods for this purpose. The first method, which is called equals()and is case sensitive, tests the corresponding characters in both strings and returns true if they have identical values. In addition, the String class defines a version that's not case sensitive called equalsIgnoreCase(), which, as you would expect, compares the corresponding characters without regard to whether they are uppercase or lowercase.

A third comparison method, compareTo(), compares two strings and returns an integer value representing the numeric difference between them:

```
String firstStr = new String("JBuilder");
String secondStr = new String("C++Builder");
System.out.println(firstStr.compareTo(secondStr));
```

The integer Unicode values of each pair of characters are compared until two are encountered that don't match (and the remaining characters are ignored). In this example, the first character pair, J and C, don't match, and because the method is called by firstStr, the compareTo() method subtracts the integer value for C (99) from J (106). The result is 7, a positive integer, which indicates that JBuilder is greater than C++Builder (at least from a String point of view). A negative integer result indicates that the calling string is less than the passed string; a zero result indicates that the two strings are the same.

Although StringBuffer objects are recommended to hold strings that you know in advance will need to be manipulated, the String class does define a few techniques for changing String object values. However, you cannot assign the result to the original String object; you must define another String object to receive the result of these methods. They include concat(), replace(), trim(), toLowerCase(), and toUpperCase().

Create a program using the ChangeString class in Listing 2.2, which shows the use of some of these methods.

TYPE   **LISTING 2.2.** ChangeString.java.

```
 1:   class ChangeString {
 2:     public static void main(String args[]) {
 3:       System.out.println();
 4:
 5:       String aStr = "   Geed ";
 6:       String bStr = "Merning!";
 7:       String cStr = aStr.concat(bStr);
 8:       System.out.println(cStr);
 9:
10:       String dStr = cStr.replace('e', 'o');
11:       System.out.println(dStr);
12:
13:       String eStr = dStr.toLowerCase();
14:       System.out.println(eStr);
15:
16:       String fStr = eStr.toUpperCase();
17:       System.out.println(fStr);
18:
19:       String gStr = fStr.trim();
20:       System.out.println(gStr);
21:
22:     }
23:   }
```

After you compile and run the program, you should see this output:

OUTPUT
```
    Geed Merning!
    Good Morning!
    good morning!
    GOOD MORNING!
GOOD MORNING!
```

ANALYSIS In this example, you use the various manipulation methods defined in the String class:

- Line 5 creates a `String` object with the literal
`<space><space><space>Geed<space>` as its initial value and assigns it to the `aStr` variable. Line 6 creates a `String` object with the literal `Merning!` as its initial value and assigns it to the `bStr` variable. Line 7 concatenates the objects assigned to the `aStr` and `bStr` variables and assigns the resulting `String` object to the `cStr` variable. Line 8 produces the first line of output:

OUTPUT   `Geed Merning!`

- Line 10 replaces every instance of the `e` character in the `String` object assigned to the `cStr` variable with an `o` character. A new `String` object is created, encapsulating the new array of characters, and is assigned to the `dStr` variable. Line 11 prints the resulting value encapsulated by the `String` object assigned to the `dStr` variable:

OUTPUT   `Good Morning!`

- Line 13 changes every character encapsulated by the `String` object assigned to the `dStr` variable to lowercase (if necessary). In this example, the `G` and `M` characters are changed to the lowercase `g` and `m` characters. The resulting new `String` object is assigned to the `eStr` variable. Line 14 prints the resulting value encapsulated by the `String` object assigned to the `eStr` variable:

OUTPUT   `good morning!`

- Line 16 changes every character encapsulated by the `String` object assigned to the `eStr` variable to uppercase (if necessary). In this example, the method changes every character in the `string` to uppercase. The resulting new `String` object is assigned to the `fStr` variable. Line 17 prints the resulting value encapsulated by the `String` object assigned to the `fStr` variable:

OUTPUT   `GOOD MORNING!`

- Line 19 removes any leading or trailing spaces in the array of characters encapsulated by the `String` object assigned to the `fStr` variable. In this example, the three leading spaces are trimmed. The resulting new `String` object is assigned to the `gStr` variable. Line 20 prints the resulting value encapsulated by the `String` object assigned to the `gStr` variable:

OUTPUT   `GOOD MORNING!`

Also, you'll want to remember that Java defines the concatenation operator (+) for concatenating strings.

As you can see, doing this much manipulation of a string value requires many allocations of memory, due to the fact that you cannot assign the result back to the calling String object. If you actually had to do this much manipulation of the string value, it would be much more efficient to use string buffers. In fact, you'll revisit this same listing in the section "Manipulating StringBuffers," later in this chapter.

There are still other methods defined in java.lang.String that are not illustrated in this section, including copyValueOf(), getBytes(), hashCode(), intern(), and regionMatches(). Once again, refer to the online Java Reference included in JBuilder for further information on these more advanced methods for dealing with String object values.

Creating StringBuffer Objects

For a StringBuffer object, in addition to the length, which tells how many characters are actually contained within, it also has a capacity method, which returns the number of characters that were allocated to the buffer. To create a StringBuffer object, you can use one of its three class constructors. For example,

```
StringBuffer myStrBuff = new StringBuffer(myString);
```

has just one parameter, myString, which takes a String object. It creates a StringBuffer object, which contains the contents of a String object passed to the myString parameter, and assigns it to the myStrBuff variable. The length of the string assigned to the myStrBuff variable is set equal to the length of the string passed to the myString parameter. The capacity is dynamically allocated. You can also pass a string literal to the myString parameter.

This constructor takes no parameters and is the default constructor:

```
StringBuffer myStringBuff = new StringBuffer();
```

It creates a StringBuffer object, with a length of zero, and assigns it to the myStringBuff parameter. Once again, the capacity is dynamically allocated.

This one takes an integer parameter, which represents both the length and the capacity of the StringBuffer object that is created:

```
StringBuffer aBuff = new StringBuffer(25);
```

This example creates a StringBuffer object, with an initial static allocation capacity of 25 filled with spaces and a length of 0, and assigns it to the aBuff variable.

Accessing StringBuffer Elements

Once again, accessing individual elements encapsulated in StringBuffer objects can be done by using subscripts, just as with any other array access. However, because string buffers are indeed objects, the `StringBuffer` class defines its own methods for determining the number of characters actually in the buffer, the number of characters that the buffer can contain, and the character at a particular position. Create a program using the `AccessBuffer` class shown in Listing 2.3, which displays these methods.

TYPE   **LISTING 2.3.** `AccessBuffer.java.`

```
 1:  class AccessBuffer {
 2:    public static void main(String args[]) {
 3:
 4:      System.out.println();
 5:      StringBuffer aBuff = new StringBuffer("Time flies!");
 6:      System.out.println("The contents of aBuff: " + aBuff);
 7:      System.out.println("Capacity: " + aBuff.capacity());
 8:      System.out.println("Length: " + aBuff.length());
 9:      System.out.println("Character at position 7: "
10:                          + aBuff.charAt(7));
11:
12:      System.out.println();
13:      StringBuffer bBuff = new StringBuffer();
14:      System.out.println("The contents of bBuff: " + bBuff);
15:      System.out.println("Capacity: " + bBuff.capacity());
16:      System.out.println("Length: " + bBuff.length());
17:
18:      System.out.println();
19:      StringBuffer cBuff = new StringBuffer(25);
20:      System.out.println("The contents of cBuff: " + cBuff);
21:      System.out.println("Capacity: " + cBuff.capacity());
22:      System.out.println("Length: " + cBuff.length());
23:    }
24:  }
```

When you compile and run the program, you should see this output:

OUTPUT
```
The contents of aBuff: Time flies!
Capacity: 27
Length: 11
Character at position 7: i
The contents of bBuff:
Capacity: 16
Length: 0
The contents of cBuff:
Capacity: 25
Length: 0
```

ANALYSIS   In this example, you create several instances of `StringBuffer` and then print the values returned by methods defined in the `StringBuffer` class:

- Line 5 creates an instance of the `StringBuffer` class, with the literal `Time flies!` as its initial value, and assigns the object to the `aBuff` variable. Line 6 prints the initial value of the object assigned to the `aBuff` variable.

- Line 7 prints the `capacity`, which was dynamically allocated for the object assigned to the `aBuff` variable, returning 27. Line 8 calls the `length()` method, which returns the value 11.

- Line 9 calls the `charAt()` method, which returns the character at the given index position in the buffer. The `StringBuffer` object indexes are array subscripts and start at 0, so the character at position 7 is `i`.

- Line 13 creates an instance of the `StringBuffer` class with no initial value specified and assigns the resulting object to the `bBuff` variable. Line 14 shows that the object assigned to `bBuff` is indeed empty.

- Line 15 prints the `capacity` dynamically allocated to the object assigned to `bBuff`, returning 16. Line 16 calls the `length()` method on the same object, which returns the value 0.

- Line 19 creates an instance of the `StringBuffer` class, specifying its `capacity`, and assigns the resulting object to the `cBuff` variable. Line 20 shows that the object assigned to `cBuff` is empty.

- Line 21 prints the `capacity` statically allocated to the object assigned to `cBuff`, returning 25. Line 22 calls `length()` on the same object, which returns the value 0.

You'll notice that when `capacity` is dynamically allocated, it is sometimes double the `length` of the actual contents assigned to the buffer. This is the extra overhead required for string buffers to be able to manipulate their contents and is why you should use `String` objects unless you really need a `StringBuffer`. Next, you'll learn how to use the `StringBuffer` manipulation methods.

Manipulating `StringBuffers`

The `StringBuffer` class provides various methods for manipulating the contents of buffers. They include `setLength()`, `setCharAt()`, `append()`, `insert()`, `reverse()`, and `toString()`. In contrast to `String` objects, in which the result of a `String` object manipulation must be assigned to a second `String` object, a `StringBuffer` object can assign the method result directly to the calling `StringBuffer` object. The `ChangeBuffer` class in Listing 2.4 illustrates these buffer manipulation methods defined in the `StringBuffer` class. Create a new program using Listing 2.4.

TYPE **LISTING 2.4.** ChangeBuffer.java.

```
 1:  class ChangeBuffer {
 2:    public static void main(String args[]) {
 3:      System.out.println();
 4:
 5:      StringBuffer aBuff = new StringBuffer("Time plies!");
 6:      System.out.println("aBuff contents: " + aBuff);
 7:      System.out.println("Capacity, length: "
 8:                          + aBuff.capacity() + ", "
 9:                          + aBuff.length());
10:      aBuff.setLength(10);
11:      System.out.println("aBuff contents: " + aBuff);
12:      System.out.println("Capacity, length: "
13:                          + aBuff.capacity() + ", "
14:                          + aBuff.length());
15:      aBuff.setCharAt(5, 'f');
16:      System.out.println("aBuff contents: " + aBuff);
17:      System.out.println("Capacity, length: "
18:                          + aBuff.capacity() + ", "
19:                          + aBuff.length());
20:      aBuff.append(" having fun!");
21:      System.out.println("aBuff contents: " + aBuff);
22:      System.out.println("Capacity, length: "
23:                          + aBuff.capacity() + ", "
24:                          + aBuff.length());
25:      aBuff.insert(11, "when you're ");
26:      System.out.println("aBuff contents: " + aBuff);
27:      System.out.println("Capacity, length: "
28:                          + aBuff.capacity() + ", "
29:                          + aBuff.length());
30:      String aStr = aBuff.toString();
31:      System.out.println("The string is: " + aStr);
32:      System.out.println("Length: " + aStr.length());
33:
34:      StringBuffer bBuff = new StringBuffer("Bob//");
35:      System.out.println("Original contents of bBuff: " + bBuff);
36:      bBuff.reverse();
37:      System.out.println("Reversed contents of bBuff: " + bBuff);
38:    }
39:  }
```

After you compile and run the program, you should see this output:

OUTPUT
```
aBuff contents: Time plies!
Capacity, length: 27, 11
aBuff contents: Time plies
Capacity, length: 27, 10
aBuff contents: Time flies
Capacity, length: 27, 10
aBuff contents: Time flies having fun!
```

```
Capacity, length: 27, 22
aBuff contents: Time flies when you're having fun!
Capacity, length: 56, 34
The string is: Time flies when you're having fun!
Length: 34
Original contents of bBuff: Bob//
Reversed contents of bBuff: //boB
```

ANALYSIS   In this example, you use some of the manipulation methods defined in the
StringBuffer class:

- Line 5 creates a StringBuffer object, with the Time plies! literal passed as its
  initial value, and assigns the object to the aBuff variable. Line 6 prints the encapsulated value.

- Lines 7 through 9 print the current values of capacity and length for the
  StringBuffer object assigned to the aBuff variable, which are 27 and 11, respectively.

- Line 10 uses the setLength() method to truncate the value encapsulated in the
  object assigned to aBuff to 10 characters. Line 11 prints Time plies, which is the
  new value.

- Lines 12 through 14 print the current values of capacity and length for the
  StringBuffer object assigned to aBuff, which are 27 and 10, respectively.

- Line 15 uses the setCharAt() method to change the character at offset 5 to f. Line
  16 prints Time flies, which is the new value.

- Lines 17 through 19 print the current values of capacity and length for the
  StringBuffer object assigned to the aBuff variable, which are again 27 and 10,
  respectively.

- Line 20 uses one of the append() methods to add the string literal <space>having
  fun! at the end of the string encapsulated in the object assigned to aBuff. Line 21
  prints Time flies having fun!, which is the new value.

- Lines 22 through 24 print the current values of capacity and length for the
  StringBuffer object assigned to aBuff, which are now 27 and 22, respectively.

- Line 25 uses one of the insert() methods to insert the string literal when
  you're<space> at offset 11 in the string encapsulated in the object assigned to the
  aBuff variable. Line 26 prints Time flies when you're having fun!, which is
  the new value.

- Lines 27 through 29 print the current values of capacity and length for the
  StringBuffer object assigned to aBuff, which are 56 and 34, respectively.

- Line 30 uses the StringBuffer class's toString() method to assign the current
  value encapsulated by the StringBuffer object assigned to aBuff to the aStr

variable. Line 31 prints `Time flies when you're having fun!`, which is now the value encapsulated by the `String` object assigned to `aStr`.

- Line 32 prints the current value of `length` for the `String` object assigned to the `aStr` variable, which is `34`.

- Line 34 creates a new `StringBuffer` object, using `Bob//` as its initial value, and assigns it to the `bBuff` variable. Line 35 prints this initial value.

- Line 36 calls the `StringBuffer` class's `reverse()` method to reverse the order of the character array encapsulated by the `StringBuffer` object assigned to `bBuff` to `//boB`, which is printed by line 37.

As hinted at in this analysis, both the `append()` and the `insert()` methods are overloaded. That is, each has numerous method signatures. The `append()` method can take primitive values (`boolean`, `char`, `double`, `float`, `int`, and `long`), object values (such as `Object` and `String`), and `char` array values. There are two `char` array signatures; the first takes the `char` array as its parameter, and the second takes a `char` array, an offset, and a count. The `insert()` method takes an integer offset as its first parameter, and for its second parameter it can take the same primitive or object values as the `append()` method.

Not every method defined in `java.lang.StringBuffer` was demonstrated here. Some not mentioned are `ensureCapacity()` and `getChars()`. For more details on these methods, refer to the online Java Reference included in JBuilder.

Conditionals and Loops

Although you could write Java programs using what you've learned so far, those programs would be pretty dull. Much of the good stuff in Java or in any programming language results when you have flow control constructs (loops and conditionals) to execute different bits of a program based on logical tests.

`if-else` Conditionals

The `if-else` conditional, which enables you to execute different lines of code based on a simple test in Java, is nearly identical to `if-else` statements in other languages.

▼ SYNTAX

Here is its syntax:

```
if condition
  statement(s);
else statement(s);
```

The keyword `if` is followed by the `condition`, which is a Boolean test. The `condition` is immediately followed by `statement(s)` (either a single statement or a block of statements) to execute if the `condition` returns `true`. An optional `else` keyword provides the

▼ `statement(s)` to execute if the `condition` is `false`:

```
if (x < y)
   System.out.println("x is smaller than y");
else System.out.println("x is larger than or equal to y");
```

> **Caution**
>
> There are three common syntax errors that novice Java programmers make when using if-else statements:
>
> 1. In Java, if-else conditionals *must* return a boolean value (that is, either true or false) unlike most other languages, in which if-else conditionals can return an integer value.
>
> 2. There is no then keyword in Java's if-else conditional statement as there is in other languages. You simply put the statement to be executed directly after the test.
>
> 3. Don't forget to put a semicolon (;) at the end of the if statement as well as before the else. In some other languages, a semicolon before an else would cause a compiler error; in Java it is *required*.

Here is an example of an if-else conditional using a block in the else part of the statement:

```
if (engineState == true)
   System.out.println("Engine is already on.");
else {
   System.out.println("Now attempting to start engine.");
   if (gasLevel >= 1)
      engineState = true;
   else System.out.println("Low on gas -- cannot start engine!");
}
```

This example uses the test (engineState == true) in the first if statement, which is actually redundant and causes an unnecessary comparison. Because engineState is a boolean variable, you can simply use the value of the variable itself rather than comparing its value to true:

```
if (engineState)
   System.out.println("Engine is on.");
else System.out.println("Engine is off.");
```

Sometimes, when nesting if-else statements, you need to distinguish which if the else belongs to. Here's an example:

```
if (condition1)
   if (condition2)
      statement;
else statement;
```

In this example, the indentation indicates to the reader that the else belongs with the first if statement and should execute when *condition1* is false. Unfortunately, the Java compiler isn't as astute. It will assume that the else goes with the if statement that immediately precedes it. Therefore, in the preceding example, it will assume that the else goes with the second if and will execute when *condition2* is false. Here's how to keep Java in line:

```
if (condition1) {
  if (condition2)
    statement;
}
else statement;
```

Even though the second if statement is not a block, you can use the curly braces ({}) to force the issue and indicate its scope as if it were a block. This will prevent the else from associating itself with the second if because scoping makes this new block invisible to any statements outside the block.

The Conditional ?: Operator

An alternative to using the if-else statement in a conditional statement is to use the conditional operator, which is a ternary operator.

The conditional operator is an expression, meaning that it returns a value (unlike the if-else statement, which simply controls execution). The conditional operator is most useful for very short or simple conditionals.

▼ SYNTAX ▲

The syntax for the conditional operator is as follows:

```
condition ? trueresult : falseresult;
```

The *condition* is a boolean expression that returns true or false, just like the *condition* in the if-else statement. If the *condition* is true, the conditional operator expression returns the value of *trueresult*; if the *condition* is false, the conditional operator expression returns the value of *falseresult*.

 Caution Both *trueresult* and *falseresult* must be expressions that resolve to a single value. In other words, you cannot use assignment or block statements for these operands.

Here is an example of a conditional that tests the values of x and y, returns the smaller of the two, and assigns that value to the variable smaller:

```
int smaller = x < y ? x : y;
```

The conditional operator has a very low precedence. The only operators lower in precedence are the assignment operators. So the conditional operator is generally evaluated only after all its subexpressions are evaluated. For more information on operator precedence, refer to Table 2.6.

In the preceding example, here is the order of evaluation:

1. The value of x is compared to the value of y.
2. If the comparison is true (that is, x is less than y), the value of x is returned; or else the comparison is false, and the value of y is returned.
3. The value returned is then assigned to the int variable smaller.

Here is the same comparison using the if-else statement:

```
int smaller;
if x < y
 smaller = x;
else smaller = y;
```

As you can see from these examples, you can accomplish a lot with just a single line of code by using the conditional operator.

Note

> You cannot use assignment or block statements as one of the operands with the ternary operator. If you want to use these more complex statements, you will need to use the if-else statement instead.

switch Conditionals

A common programming practice in all languages is to test a variable against each value in a set of values and then perform different actions based on which value the variable matches. Using only if-else statements, this can become unwieldy, depending on how it's formatted and how many different values are in the set of possible matches. For example, you might end up with a set of if-else statements like this:

```
if (oper == '+')
  addargs(arg1, arg2);
else if (oper == '-')
  subargs(arg1, arg2);
else if (oper == '*')
  multargs(arg1, arg2);
else if (oper == '/')
  divargs(arg1, arg2);
```

This form of if-else statement is called a *nested* if-else because each statement in turn contains yet another if-else, and so on. In this example, four possibilities are accounted for, so the code isn't too unreadable. But what if you had 20 possibilities to deal with? Because this situation is so common, there is a special conditional to handle it: the switch conditional, also sometimes called the "case" statement.

Here is the syntax for the switch conditional:

```
switch (expression) {
  case constant_1;
    statement(s);
    break;
  case constant_2;
    statement(s);
    break;
  ...
  default:
    statement(s);
}
```

The switch structure consists of a series of case values (constant_1, constant_2, and so on) and an optional default statement. The expression (which must result in a primitive type of byte, char, short, or int) is compared with each of the case values in turn. If a match is found, the statement(s) after the case value execute until a break statement or the end of the switch statement is reached. If after checking all the case values no match is found, the default statement is executed. The default is optional, so if it is not used and there is no match with any of the case values, the switch statement completes without doing anything.

▼ SYNTAX

▲

2

> Tip
>
> Because the default statement is optional when the switch conditional is used, it's easy to leave it out by mistake. If you really don't want to do anything in the event of no case-value matches, it is recommended that you put in a comment statement for the default, such as this:
>
> `default: /* do nothing */ ;`
>
> This way, when someone looks at your code several weeks (or months) later, it will be obvious that the no-op for the default was intentional.

Here's the nested if-else statement shown earlier, rewritten as a switch statement:

```
switch (oper)
  case '+';
    addargs(arg1, arg2);
    break;
  case '-';
```

```
      subargs(arg1, arg2);
      break;
   case '*';
      multargs(arg1, arg2);
      break;
   case '/';
      divargs(arg1, arg2);
      break;
   default: /* do nothing */ ;
}
```

> **Note**
>
> Within switch statements, it is not necessary to group statements as blocks by using brackets ({}). Any statements between a case statement and its break statement will automatically be treated as an implicit block, creating a local scope.

Note the break statement at the end of each case. Without the explicit break, when a match is found, the statements for that match and all the statements further down within the switch are executed until either a break or the end of the switch is found (whichever occurs first). Normally, this is not the behavior desired, so you'll want to be sure to include the break to delimit which statements should be executed upon finding a match.

On the other hand, this characteristic can be useful. Consider the instance in which you want a set of statements to be executed for more than one case value. Specifying the same statements for each case value would be redundant, so Java provides a way for multiple case values to execute the same statement(s). When you leave out the result statement for a case value, execution will "fall through" to the next case value, and the next, until a result statement is found. Here's an example of this kind of construct:

```
switch (x) {
   case 2:
   case 4:
   case 6:
   case 8:
      System.out.println("x is an even single-digit number");
      break;
   default:
      System.out.print("x is not an even single-digit number");
}
```

The significant limitation of the switch in Java is that the tests and values can be only simple primitive types (and then only those primitive types that are castable to int). You cannot use larger primitive types (long, float, double), strings, or other objects within a switch statement, nor can you test for any relationship other than equality. This limits the usefulness of switch to all but the simplest comparisons. However, nested if-else statements can be used for any kind of test on any type of value.

for Loops

The for loop tests a condition and, if the condition is true, executes a statement or block of statements repeatedly until the condition is false. This type of loop is frequently used for simple iteration in which you repeat a block of statements a certain number of times and then stop, but you can use for loops for just about any kind of loop.

Here is the syntax for the for loop:

```
for (initialization; test; increment) statement(s);
```

The start of the for loop has three parts:

- *initialization* is an expression that initializes the starting counter of the for loop. This expression is evaluated only once, when the for statement is first encountered. If you have a loop index, this expression might declare and initialize it; for example, int i = 0. Variables that you declare in this part of the for loop are local to the loop itself; they cease to exist after the loop has finished executing.

- *test* is the condition that must be met before each pass of the loop. The *test* must be a boolean expression or function that returns a boolean value; for example, i < 10. If the *test* returns true, the loop executes. As soon as the test returns false, the loop stops executing. If *test* returns false the first time it is tested, the loop won't be executed at all.

- *increment* is any expression or function call. Commonly, the *increment* is used to change the value of the loop index to bring the state of the loop closer to returning false and completing, such as i++.

The *statement(s)* part of the for loop represents the statement or block of statements that is executed each time the *test* returns true and the loop executes. Here's an example of a for loop that initializes all the values of a String array to null strings:

```
String strArray[] = new String[10];
for (int i = 0; i < strArray.length; i++)
  strArray[i] = "";
```

Any of the parts of the for loop can be empty statements. That is, you can simply include a semicolon without an expression or statement, and that part of the for loop will be ignored.

Note

> If you use an empty statement in your `for` loop, you might have to initialize or increment loop variables or loop indices yourself elsewhere.

You can also have an empty statement for the body of your `for` loop, if everything you want to do is accomplished in the start of the loop. For example, here's one that finds the first prime number higher than 4,000. Again, it is recommended that you put a comment statement anywhere you want to put an empty statement so that it is obvious that the empty statement was intentional:

```
for (i = 4001; notPrime(i); i += 2)
  /* do nothing */ ;
```

Be careful about placing a semicolon (;) after the first line in the `for` loop, however. Consider the following code snippet:

```
for (int i = 0; i < 10; i++);
  System.out.println("Loop!");
```

What was intended was for the string `"Loop!"` to be printed 10 times, but what actually would occur is that the loop would iterate 10 times doing nothing but testing and incrementing, and then print `"Loop!"` just once. Why? It's the misplaced semicolon (;) at the end of the `for` loop's first line.

while Loops

The `while` loop is used to repeat a statement or block of statements as long as a particular condition is `true`.

▼ SYNTAX

▲

Here is the syntax of the `while` loop:

```
while (condition) statement(s);
```

The *condition* is a `boolean` expression, which returns a `boolean` result. If it returns `true`, the `while` loop executes the *statement(s)* and then tests the condition again, repeating until the condition returns `false`. If the condition is `false` the first time the condition is tested, the `while` loop's *statement(s)* will not execute.

Here's an example of a `while` loop that copies the elements of an array of integers (in `arrInt`) to an array of `float`s (in `arrFloat`), casting each element to a `float` as it goes. To make things more interesting, there are two conditions that must return `true` for the loop to execute:

- The count must be less than the array's length.
- The current integer element must not be 0.

To accomplish this task, the loop features a compound test, which checks for more than one condition. When you use the && operator, both must be `true` for the condition to return `true`. This loop also uses the postfix increment operator (++) to increment the count each time the loop is executed:

```java
int count = 0;
while ( (count < arrInt.length) && (arrInt[count] != 0) ) {
  arrFloat[count] = (float) arrInt[count];
  count++;
}
```

Suppose that `arrInt` had a length of 20. If none of `arrInt`'s values was 0, this `while` loop would execute 20 times because the test would be `true` while the `count` variable iterated though the values 0 to 19. On the other hand, if any one of `arrInt`'s values was 0, the loop might execute anywhere from 0 to 19 times, depending on the position of the first 0 value in `arrInt`.

do-while Loops

In the discussion of the `while` loop, it was noted that it might not execute even once, if the *condition* returns `false` on the first try. If you want to execute the loop at least once, a do-while loop is what you need. It does essentially the same thing as a `while` loop, with the exception that it executes the *statement(s)* first, and then it performs the test on the *condition*.

Note	The do-while loop in Java corresponds to the `repeat-until` loop in Pascal.

▼ SYNTAX

Here is the syntax for the do-while loop:

```java
do statement(s) while condition;
```

Here, the *statement(s)* execute first, and then the *condition* is tested. If the *condition* returns `true`, the *statement(s)* execute again; if the *condition* returns `false`, the loop ends. Here's an example that prints 20 lines of output:

```java
int x = 1;
do {
  System.out.println("Looping, round " + x);
  x++;
} while (x <= 20);
```

▲

Remember, do-while loops always execute at least once and test at the end, whereas while loops test at the beginning and might not execute even once.

Breaking Out of Loops

In all the loops (`for`, `while`, `do-while`), the loop ends when the condition you're testing for returns `false`. What happens if something odd occurs within the body of the loop and you want to exit the loop early? For that, you can use the `break` and `continue` keywords.

You've already seen `break` as part of the `switch` statement; it stops execution of the `switch`, and the program continues with the next statement following the end of the `switch`. The `break` keyword, when used with a loop, does the same thing—it immediately halts execution of the current loop. If you have loops nested within loops, execution picks up in the next outer loop. Otherwise, the program merely continues executing the next statement after the loop.

 Tip

> Although using nested loops can help you handle complex data-flow management, using more than two or three levels can make your code very difficult to read and understand. So use nesting of loops sparingly.

For example, take that `while` loop that copies elements from an integer array into an array of `float`s until the end of the array or until a `0` is reached. You can test for the latter case inside the body of the `while` and then use a `break` to exit the loop. Here's the example rewritten to accomplish the job:

```
int count = 0;
while (count < arrInt.length) {
  if (arrInt[count] == 0)
    break;
  arrFloat[count] = (float) arrInt[count];
  count++;
}
```

The `break` statement causes the loop to cease as soon as the *condition* is met; in this case, the loop ceases as soon as one of the `arrInt` values is equal to `0`. In contrast, the `continue` keyword ceases to execute the current iteration of the loop but then continues with the next iteration of the loop. For `do-while` loops, this means that the loop begins execution at the top again; for `while` and `for` loops, the loop is executed again starting with the evaluation of the *condition*.

The `continue` keyword is useful when you want to restart the loop without finishing all its *statement(s)*. Consider the earlier example of copying one array to another. You can test whether the current integer element is `0`. If it is, you can restart the loop so that the resulting array of `float`s will never contain a zero value. Note that because you're skipping some elements in the first array, you will now have to track and increment two array counters:

```
int iCount = 0;
int fCount = 0;
while (iCount < arrInt.length) {
  if (arrInt[iCount] == 0) {
    iCount++;
    continue;
  }
  arrFloat[fCount++] = (float) arrInt[iCount++];
}
```

This example will now iterate through both arrays, copying the integer values from arrInt to arrFloat only if the element in arrInt is not equal to zero.

Labeled Loops

Both break and continue can have an optional label that tells Java which specific program statement it should continue with. Without a label, break continues execution with the next program statement following its enclosing loop, and continue restarts its enclosing loop. Using labeled break and continue statements enables you to continue a loop outside the current loop or to break completely out of several layers of nested loops at once.

To use a labeled loop, add the label before the initial part of the loop with a colon (:) rather than a semicolon (;) at the end of the label. Then, when you use a break or continue statement, add the name of the label after the keyword itself:

```
out:
  for (int i = 0; i < 10; i++) {
    while (x < 50) {
      if (i * x == 400)
        break out;
      ...
    } // end of while loop
    ...
  } // end of for loop
... // execution continues here after break out
```

In this code snippet, out: labels the outermost block. Then, inside both the for and the while loops, when a particular condition is met, the break statement causes the execution to break out of both loops and continue program execution with the line of code after the end of the for loop.

The Breakers program in Listing 2.5 is an example that contains nested for loops and a labeled break. Within the innermost loop, if the summed values of the two counters is greater than four, both for loops exit at once. Create a new program using the code in Listing 2.5.

TYPE   **LISTING 2.5.** Breakers.java.

```
 1: class Breakers {
 2:   public static void main(String args[]) {
 3:
 4:     ers:
 5:       for (int i = 1; i <= 5; i++) {
 6:         for (int k = 1; k <= 3; k++) {
 7:           System.out.println("i is " + i + ", k is " + k);
 8:           if ((i + k) > 4)
 9:             break ers;
10:         }
11:       }
12:     System.out.println("end of both loops");
13:   }
14: }
```

When you run the program, you should see the following output:

OUTPUT
```
i is 1, k is 1
i is 1, k is 2
i is 1, k is 3
i is 2, k is 1
i is 2, k is 2
i is 2, k is 3
end of both loops
```

ANALYSIS   In this example, the label is ers: (line 4). The loops execute (lines 5 through 11) and continue to iterate as long as i + k is not greater than 4 (line 8). When the sum of i and k is greater than 4, the break statement (line 9) causes both loops to exit back to the outer block, and the last line is printed (line 12).

Summary

Today, you learned about many aspects of JBuilder's underlying language, Java. You learned about program statements, including Java's special documentation comments. You also examined data types, variables, and literals. In addition, you reviewed the operators available in Java and how they are used in expressions, including precedence rules. You also were made aware of the availability of advanced mathematical functions in Java.

You also learned quite a lot about arrays, strings, and string buffers. You learned how to declare array, String, and StringBuffer variables and create their objects. You exercised most of the methods that access the data contained in these structures and now know where to look for additional information on some of the more obscure methods.

You can declare and use multidimensional arrays. You now know when to use `StringBuffer` objects rather than `String` objects.

Two topics also covered that you'll probably use quite often in your own Java programs were conditionals and loops. Conditionals include the `if-else` and `switch` statements, with which you can branch to different lines of code depending on the result of a `boolean` test. The loop statements include the `for`, `while`, and `do-while` loops, each of which enables you to execute certain statements repeatedly until a specified condition is met.

Now that you've learned these language constructs, the next thing to tackle is the larger issues of declaring classes and creating methods within which instances of those classes can communicate with each other by calling methods.

2

Q&A

Q I didn't notice any way to create local constants. Doesn't Java have constants?

A Yes; however, you can't create local constants in Java. You can create only instance constants and class constants. You'll learn how to do this tomorrow.

Q What happens if you assign a numeric value to a variable that is too high (or too low) for that variable to hold?

A You might think that the variable would just be converted to the next larger type, but that's not what happens. Instead, if the value is a positive number, the variable "overflows," which means that the number wraps around and becomes the lowest negative value for that type, and counts up from there. If the value is a negative number, the variable "underflows" by becoming the highest value for that type and counts down from there. This can cause wrong results, so make certain that you declare the right type for your numeric values. When in doubt, assign the next larger type.

Q If arrays are objects and you have to use `new` to create them, where is the `Array` class? I didn't see it in the Java class libraries.

A Arrays are implemented rather strangely in Java. The `Array` class is constructed automatically when your Java program runs and therefore cannot be subclassed. `Array` provides the basic framework for arrays, including the `length` instance variable. Additionally, each primitive type and object has an implicit subclass of `Array` that represents an array of that class or object. When you create a new array object, it might not have an actual class, but it behaves as if it does.

Q You say that you can use the `arraycopy()` method with arrays, but because instances of the `String` and `StringBuffer` classes are implemented as arrays, can I use the `arraycopy()` method with these too?

A Yes, with one exception. Because `String` values are not directly modifiable, you cannot use a `String` as the destination array. Other than that, as long as the destination array or `StringBuffer` is already allocated in memory, you can use `arraycopy()` to write data to it.

Q If an array can be any kind of primitive type or object, how do I figure out exactly how much memory an array will be allocated?

A To calculate the amount of memory that will be allocated for an array, multiply the number of elements by the number of bits for the elements' declared data type. Then add 32 bits for the `length` field (which is always an `int`). Divide by 8 to obtain the number of bytes that will be allocated for the array. For example, if you declared an array of 6 `double` elements, which are 64 bits each, the memory allocated would be

$$((6 * 64) + 32) / 8$$

for a total allocation of 52 bytes of memory.

Q I noticed that you didn't use any `import` statements in today's code listings. Why is that?

A All the methods pertaining to arrays, strings, and string buffers are part of the `java.lang` package, and the `String` and `StringBuffer` classes are defined in `java.lang.String` and `java.lang.StringBuffer`, respectively. Because the entire `java.lang` package is implicitly imported into all Java programs, it is not necessary to add an explicit `import` statement.

Q Does Java have the `goto` statement?

A The Java language defines the keyword `goto`, but it is "reserved" and currently not in use. Labeled breaks are as close as you'll get.

Q I declared a variable inside a block statement within an `if-else` statement. When the `if-else` was done, that variable vanished. What happened?

A Block statements inside braces form a local scope. This means that if you declare a variable inside a block, it's visible and usable only from within that block. After the block finishes executing, the variables you declared within the block are no longer accessible.

Q Why can't you use the `switch` statement with `String` values?

A Strings are objects, and `switch` in Java is defined only for the primitive types `byte`, `char`, `short`, and `int`. To compare other types, you have to use nested `if-else` statements, which enable more general expression tests, including `String` comparisons.

Workshop

The Workshop provides two ways for you to affirm what you've learned in this chapter. The Quiz section poses questions to help you solidify your understanding of the material covered. You can find answers to the quiz questions in Appendix A, "Answers to Quiz Questions." The Exercises section provides you with experience in using what you have learned. Try to work through all these before continuing to the next day.

Quiz

1. True or False?

    a. Boolean variables can be assigned numeric values.

    b. The add operator has precedence over the multiply operator.

    c. The elements of an array can contain different data types.

    d. An `if-else` conditional can return either an integer or a `boolean` value.

    e. As long as you can cast the resulting value to an `int`, you can use an expression as a `switch` statement's *condition*.

2. What symbols are used to enclose statements that are to be treated as a group?

3. With what integer value do subscripts in Java begin, 0 or 1?

4. What's wrong with the following snippet of code?

```
int scores[] = new int[10];
int a = 3;
int b = 5;
scores[a-b];
```

5. What is the value of wwwStrLength in the following code fragment?

```
char chArr[] = { 'I', 'n', 't', 'e', 'r', 'n', 'e', 't' };
String wwwStr = new String(chArr);
int wwwStrLength = wwwStr.length();
```

6. How many strings would the following code create?

```
String firstStr = "Here I am!"
String secondStr = "No, I'm over here!!"
String thirdStr = "Here I am!"
```

7. You've declared a variable inside a block of statements. After the block has finished executing, is the variable's value the same, the opposite, or undefined?

8. How many iterations will the following `for` loop go through, and what will the output look like?

```
for (i = 0; i <= 100; i += 15);
  System.out.println("Hidey, hidey, hidey, ho!");
```

9. You want to execute the body of a loop, and then re-execute the loop body as long as a specified condition is `true`. Which type of looping construct should you use?

Exercises

1. Write program statements for the following:

   - Declare a floating-point variable named `bodyTemp` with `98.6` as its initial value.

   - Assign the word `retired` to a variable named `status`.

   - Write a documentation comment that explains that the method following the comment initializes the billing records for the month.

2. Given the declared integer array and strings

   ```
   int nums[] = {2, 10};
   String aStr = "doesn't";
   String bStr = "will get you that chicken across the road.";
   String cStr = "make it"'
   String dStr = "I say,"
   String aSpace = " ";
   ```

   create a class called `Splat`; use array subscripts, the concatenation operator (+), and the `substring()` and `valueOf()` methods to create a `String` that, when printed to the screen, reads as follows:

   ```
   I say, two will get you ten that chicken doesn't make it across the
   road.
   ```

3. Using the program in Listing 2.5 as a base, make the following modifications:

   - In the inner `for` loop, modify the code so that if the sum of `i` and `k` is greater than 4, the loop will continue execution at the top of the inner `for` loop.

   - Remove the `break` statement and its label `ers:` from the program.

   - Move the `println` statement so that it occurs only when the sum of `i` and `k` is less than 4.

   - Change the `class` name to `ContinueOn` and save the modified file.

Run the program and verify that the sixth line of output from running
`Breakers.java` (Listing 2.5), which is

`i is 2, k is 3`

is replaced by the following output in the new program:

`i is 3, k is 1`

Verify that this is the only change in the output.

2

Java Intermediate

Object-oriented programming (OOP) is one of the biggest programming break-throughs in recent years. You might think that you must spend years learning all about OOP methodologies and how they can make your life easier than traditional programming techniques. But the concepts are really not that difficult to understand. It all comes down to organizing your programs in ways that echo how things are put together in the real world.

Today, you will get an overview of object-oriented programming concepts in Java and how they relate to structuring your Java programs. If you are already acquainted with object-oriented programming, much of today's lesson will be familiar to you. You will still want to skim over the material and create the Java examples, just as a review.

Because Java is an object-oriented language, you are obviously going to be working with a lot of objects. You'll create them, modify them, move them around, change their variables, call their methods, combine them with other objects, and, of course, develop classes and use your own objects as well. So, today you'll learn all about the care and feeding of a Java object and how and why to create classes of your own.

Today's topics include the following:

- What classes and objects are, and how they relate to each other
- The two major parts of a class: behaviors and attributes
- Class inheritance and the class packages in the Java Class Library
- The parts of a class definition
- Declaring and using class and instance variables
- Creating objects (instances of classes)
- Casting and converting objects and primitives
- Comparing objects and determining an object's class
- Calling methods in the objects you create
- Defining, using, overloading, and overriding methods
- Creating constructors and finalizer methods

Thinking in Objects

You can walk into a computer store and assemble an entire PC system from various components: a motherboard, a CPU chip, a video card, a hard disk, a keyboard, and so on. Ideally, when you finish assembling all the various self-contained units, you have a system in which all the units work together to create a larger system that enables you to solve the problems you bought the computer for in the first place.

Internally, each of those components might be complicated and engineered by different companies with different methods of design. But you don't need to know how each component works, what every chip on the board does, or how an "A" gets sent to your computer screen when you press the A key. Each component you use is a self-contained unit, and as the assembler of the system, you need only be interested in how the units interact. After you know what the interactions are among the components and can match them, putting together the overall system is easy.

Object-oriented programming (OOP) works in exactly this same way. When you use OOP, your overall program is made up of lots of different self-contained components (objects), each of which has a specific role in the program and all of which can communicate with each other in predefined ways.

Object-oriented programming is similar in many ways to creating programs using software components, introduced later this week. The main difference is that OOP provides objects for programmers to plug together into working applications, while users still deal with monolithic applications. (Imagine that when your motorcycle gets a flat tire you must send the whole motorcycle back to the manufacturer to get it repaired.) With component software, such as JavaBeans components, the end user has access to the software components as working entities and can link them together into larger custom applications without the help of a programmer. (You can change your own tire without sending the whole motorcycle back to the manufacturer.) OOP brought the object-oriented software revolution to programmers; software components bring the object-oriented software revolution to everyone.

Understanding Objects and Classes

OOP is modeled on how, in the real world, objects are made up of many kinds of smaller objects. This capability of combining objects, however, is only one very general aspect of object-oriented programming. OOP provides several other concepts and features that make creating and using objects easier and more flexible. The most important of these features is the class.

NEW TERM   A *class* is a template from which objects with similar aspects can be created. Classes embody all the features of a particular set of objects.

When you write a program in an object-oriented language, you don't define actual objects; you define classes. For example, you might have a `Tree` class that describes the features of all trees (has branches and roots, grows, and gives off oxygen). The `Tree` class serves as an abstract model for the concept of a tree. The `Tree` class is not a particular tree, but simply a model for creating tree objects. To interact with a tree, you have to create a concrete instance of that tree. Of course, after you have a `Tree` class, you can create lots of different instances of that tree (see Figure 3.1). Each tree instance can have different features (has leaves or needles, produces flowers, bears fruit) while still behaving and being immediately recognizable as a tree.

NEW TERM   A *class instance* is an actual object. The class is the generic representation of an object; an instance is the concrete thing created from the instructions provided by a class. Think of the class as the architectural plans and the class instance as the actual building.

So what, precisely, is the difference between a class instance and an object? There is no difference. Object is the more generic term, but instances and objects are both terms for the concrete representation of a class. In fact, the terms *instance* and *object* are used interchangeably in OOP terminology.

FIGURE 3.1.

A Tree *class and* Tree *instances.*

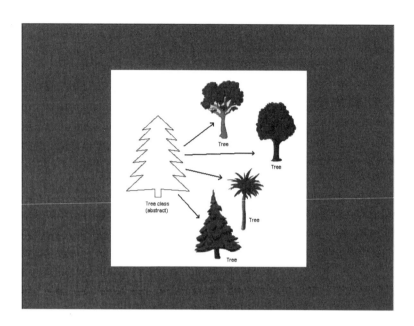

> **Tip**
>
> If you've programmed in C, you can think of a class as creating a new composite data type by using `struct` and `typedef`. Classes, however, can provide much more than just a collection of data, as you'll discover later today.

When you write a Java program, you design and construct a set of classes. Then, when your program runs, instances of those classes are created and discarded as needed. Your task, as a Java developer, is to create the right set of classes to accomplish what your program needs to accomplish.

NEW TERM A *class library* is a collection of classes. A class library can consist of any mixture of classes that define applets, JavaBeans components, or support classes that can't be instantiated on their own.

Fortunately, you don't have to start from scratch: the Java environment comes with a library of classes that implement a lot of the basic behavior you need—not only for basic programming tasks (basic math functions, arrays, strings, and so on), but also for graphics and networking behavior. In some cases, the Java Class Library and JBuilder Class Library classes might provide enough functionality so that all you have to do in your Java program is create a single class that uses the standard class library. For more complex Java programs, you might have to create a whole set of classes with defined interactions between them.

Every class you write in Java has two major parts: attributes and behaviors. In this section, you'll learn about each one as it applies to a hypothetical class called Motorcycle.

Using Attributes

Attributes are the individual aspects that differentiate one object from another and determine the appearance, state, or other qualities of that object. Let's create a hypothetical class called Motorcycle. The attributes of a motorcycle might include the following:

Color	red, green, silver, brown
Style	cruiser, sports bike, standard
Make	Honda, BMW, Harley

Attributes of an object also can include information about its state. For example, you could have features for engine condition (off or on) or current gear selected.

Attributes are defined by variables. Because each instance of a class can have different values for its variables, each variable is called an instance variable.

NEW TERM   An *instance variable* defines the attributes of an object. The class defines the type of the attribute, and each instance stores its own value for that attribute in the instance variable.

Each attribute, as the term is used here, has a single corresponding instance variable. Changing the value of a variable changes the attribute of that object. Instance variables can be set when an object is created and stay constant throughout the life of the object, or they can be changed at any time during program execution.

In addition to instance variables, there are also class variables. Class variables are analogous to global variables that apply to all instances of a class and to the class itself. Unlike instance variables, whose values are stored in the instance, class variables' values are stored in the class.

Understanding Behaviors

A class's behaviors determine what instances of that class do to change their internal state or how that instance responds to messages from other classes or objects. Behaviors define how a class or object can interact with the rest of the program. For example, some behaviors that the hypothetical Motorcycle class might have are start the engine, stop the engine, speed up, change gear, and stall.

To define an object's behavior, you create methods, which look and behave just like functions and procedures in other languages, but are defined inside the class. Java does not allow subprograms to exist outside classes as do some other languages.

NEW TERM   A *method* is a function (subroutine or procedure) defined inside a class that operates on instances of that class.

Methods don't always affect just a single object. Objects communicate with each other
using methods as well. A class or object can call methods in another class or object to
communicate changes in the environment or to request a state change in the object.

Just as there are instance variables and class variables, there are instance methods and
class methods. Instance methods (which are commonly just called methods) apply and
operate on an instance of a class. Class methods apply to and operate on the class itself.

Using Classes

Defining classes is pretty easy. You've seen how to do it numerous times in previous
lessons. To define a class, use the `class` keyword and the name of the class:

```
class MyClassName {
/* body of class */
}
```

NEW TERM   A *superclass* is the class from which the current class is derived. A superclass is
above the current class in the class hierarchy.

NEW TERM   A *subclass* is a class derived from the current class. A subclass of the current
class is lower in the class hierarchy.

If this class is a subclass of another class, use the `extends` keyword and the name of the
superclass:

```
class MyClassName extends mySuperClassName {
/* body of class */
}
```

If this class implements a specific interface, use the `implements` keyword and the name
of that interface:

```
class MyClassName implements Runnable {
/* body of class */
}
```

Both `extends` and `implements` are optional. The `implements` keyword pertains to interfaces, which you'll learn more about tomorrow. For today, let's dig into the details on all
the other things that comprise a class definition.

Creating a Class

Up to this point, today's lesson has been mostly theoretical. In this section, you'll create
a working example of the `Motorcycle` class so that you can see how instance variables

and methods are defined in a class. You also will design a Java application that creates a new instance of the Motorcycle class and shows its instance variables. You'll also build the Java source code that implements your design and then run the Motorcycle application.

 Note You won't learn the details here about the syntax of this example. Don't be too concerned if you're not really sure what's going on; it will become clear to you later. What's important about this example is that you understand the parts of the class definition.

Let's start with a basic class definition:

```
class Motorcycle {
}
```

Congratulations, you have just created your first Java class. Of course, it doesn't do much at the moment, but it's a Java class at its very simplest. To add functionality, you need to define instance variables (which define attributes) and methods (which define behaviors).

Using Instance Variables

To create some instance variables (attributes) for this class, immediately after the first line of the class definition, add the following three lines:

```
String make;
String color;
boolean engineState;
```

Here, you've created three instance variables: two of them, make and color, can contain String objects. (The String class is part of the standard class library mentioned earlier.) The third, engineState, is a boolean that can be set to reflect whether the engine is off or on.

Using Methods

Now you will add some behaviors (methods) to the class. There are all kinds of things a motorcycle can do, but to keep things manageable for this example, let's add just one method that starts the engine. Add the following lines after the instance variables in your class definition:

```
void startEngine() {
  if (engineState)
    System.out.println("The engine is already on.");
  else {
```

3

```
      engineState = true;
      System.out.println("The engine is now on.");
  }
}
```

The `startEngine` method tests to see whether the engine is running already (if `true` is assigned to the `engineState` variable) and, if it is, merely prints a message to that effect. If the engine isn't running already, it changes the state of the engine to `true` and then prints a message. At this point, you are constructing a class with specific behaviors and attributes.

Before you actually implement this class in JBuilder, you need to add one more method. The `showAtts` method prints the values of the instance variables in the current instance of your `Motorcycle` class:

```
void showAtts() {
  System.out.println("This motorcycle is a "
    + color + " " + make);
  if (engineState)
    System.out.println("The engine is on.");
  else System.out.println("The engine is off.");
}
```

The `showAtts` method prints two lines to the screen: the make and color of the motorcycle object, and the state of the engine—on or off.

Before continuing, let's review one of the major differences between Java applications and Java applets. A Java applet doesn't require a `main()` method because it is run as a subprogram of the Web browser from which it is viewed. However, in a Java application, the body of the program is contained in the `main()` method, and it is the first method to be run when the program is executed. You'll add the `main()` method to the `Motorcycle` class next.

Implementing Classes

Before you begin creating class files, let's create a project in which to keep them. Select File|New Project, and modify the File field so that it says `C:\JBuilder\myprojects\JIntermediate.jpr`, and then click the Finish button.

Now, to implement the `Motorcycle` class in JBuilder, first create the source code file. In the AppBrowser, click the Add to Project icon, type `Motorcycle.java` in the File name field, and then click Open. In the AppBrowser, click on the Content pane, and enter the code in Listing 3.1.

> **Note**
>
> Remember, don't type the line number or colon preceding each line of code. They are included here so that you can easily locate lines mentioned in the analysis, but they are not part of the code itself.

TYPE **LISTING 3.1.** Motorcycle.java.

```
1:  class Motorcycle {
2:
3:    String make;
4:    String color;
5:    boolean engineState;
6:
7:    void startEngine() {
8:      if (engineState)
9:        System.out.println("The engine is already on.");
10:     else {
11:       engineState = true;
12:       System.out.println("The engine is now on.");
13:     }
14:   }
15:
16:   void showAtts() {
17:     System.out.println("This motorcycle is a "
18:       + color + " " + make + ".");
19:     if (engineState)
20:       System.out.println("The engine is on.");
21:     else System.out.println("The engine is off.");
22:   }
23:
24:   public static void main (String args[]) {
25:     Motorcycle m = new Motorcycle();
26:     m.make = "Yamaha RZ350";
27:     m.color = "yellow";
28:     System.out.println("Calling showAtts...");
29:     m.showAtts();
30:     System.out.println("Starting engine...");
31:     m.startEngine();
32:     System.out.println("Calling showAtts...");
33:     m.showAtts();
34:     System.out.println("Starting engine...");
35:     m.startEngine();
36:   }
37: }
```

Select File | Save All to save both the project and the source code. Because you've written a program that prints to standard output, tell JBuilder to display command-line Java program output in the Execution Log window, as described on Day 1, "Introduction to JBuilder." Right-click on the Motorcycle.java node in the Navigation pane, and then select Run from the pop-up menu.

OUTPUT Select View | Execution Log from the JBuilder main menu to see the Motorcycle program's output:

```
Calling showAtts...
This motorcycle is a yellow Yamaha RZ350
The engine is off.
Starting engine...
The engine is now on.
Calling showAtts...
This motorcycle is a yellow Yamaha RZ350
The engine is on.
Starting engine...
The engine is already on.
```

Though most of the other code in this sample has already been described, some of the contents of the main() method in Listing 3.1 is going to be new to you. Let's go through it so that you have a basic idea of what it does.

ANALYSIS Line 24 declares the main() method. This should look familiar to you from the Java application you wrote on Day 1, "Introduction to JBuilder."

Line 25, Motorcycle m = new Motorcycle(); creates a new instance of the Motorcycle class and stores a reference to it in the variable m. In other words, a Motorcycle object is assigned to the m variable. Remember, you don't usually operate directly on classes in your Java programs. Instead, you create objects from those classes and then call methods in those objects.

Lines 26 and 27 set the instance variables for this motorcycle object: the make variable is assigned Yamaha RZ350 (a very pretty motorcycle from the mid-1980s) and the color variable is assigned yellow.

Line 29 prints the instance variables by invoking the showAtts() method, as defined in your Motorcycle object, producing the rest of the second and third lines of output.

Line 31 calls the startEngine() method to start the engine, producing the fifth line of output.

Line 33 prints the instance variables again, by invoking the showAtts() method, producing the sixth and seventh lines of output.

Line 35 calls the startEngine() method to attempt to start the engine again. Because it was on when the method was called, it produces the last line of output.

Using Inheritance

Now that you have a basic grasp of classes, objects, methods, and instance variables and how to use them in a Java program, it's time to explore inheritance. Inheritance is one of the features that makes object-oriented programming so powerful.

NEW TERM *Inheritance* is the mechanism that allows a new class to receive (inherit) the basis of its functionality from an existing class and build on that base by adding new functionality.

This means that when you write a class, you have to specify only how that class is different from some higher-level class, giving you automatic access to the information defined in that higher-level class.

With inheritance, all classes—those you write, those from other class libraries that you use, and those from the standard Java class library as well—are arranged in a strict hierarchy (see Figure 3.2).

FIGURE 3.2.

A class hierarchy.

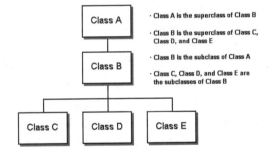

- Class A is the superclass of Class B
- Class B is the superclass of Class C, Class D, and Class E
- Class B is the subclass of Class A
- Class C, Class D, and Class E are the subclasses of Class B

Each class has a superclass (the class above it in the hierarchy), and each class can have one or more subclasses (classes below it in the hierarchy).

 Note In C++, a superclass is known as a base class, and a subclass is a derived class. In Object Pascal (Delphi), a superclass is known as an ancestor, and a subclass is a descendant.

A subclass inherits all the methods and variables from its superclass. By creating a subclass, you don't have to redefine attributes or behaviors or copy the code from the superclass. Your class automatically inherits that behavior from its superclass, which inherits behavior from its superclass, and so on all the way up the hierarchy. Your class becomes a combination of all the features of the classes above it in the class hierarchy through inheritance.

At the top of the Java class hierarchy is the `Object` class, the most general class in the hierarchy. The `Object` superclass defines behavior inherited by all other classes in the Java class hierarchy. Each subclass further down in the hierarchy adds more information and becomes more tailored to a specific purpose. You can think of a class hierarchy as defining very abstract concepts at the top with those concepts becoming more concrete as you travel further down the chain of superclasses.

Most of the time, when you write new Java classes, you'll want to create a class that has all the information some other class has, plus some extra information. For example, you might want a version of the `Button` class with its own built-in label.

Note   The `Button` class is part of the Java Class Library, which is included in all implementations of the Java language and Java VM. Specifically, you'll find the `Button` class in the `java.awt` package.

To get all the `Button` information, all you have to do is define your class to inherit from the `Button` class. Your class will automatically receive all the behavior and attributes defined in `Button` (and in `Button`'s superclasses), so all you have to define are the things that differentiate your class from the `Button` class itself. This technique for defining a new class as the difference between it and its superclass is called *subclassing*.

NEW TERM   *Subclassing* is creating a new class (the subclass) that inherits from some other class (its superclass) in the class hierarchy. By using subclassing, you need only to define the differences between the new subclass and its superclass, and the rest of its behaviors and attributes are available to the new class through inheritance.

What if your class defines entirely new behavior and isn't really a subclass of another class? Your class can inherit directly from the `Object` class, which still allows it to fit neatly into the Java class hierarchy. In fact, if you create a class definition that doesn't indicate its superclass in the declaration, Java automatically assigns `Object` as the default superclass. For example, the `Motorcycle` class you created earlier today inherited directly from `Object` as its superclass by default.

Creating a Class Hierarchy

If you're creating a large set of classes, it makes sense for your classes not only to inherit from the existing class hierarchy, but also to form a hierarchy themselves. This will take some planning beforehand when you're trying to figure out how to organize your Java code, but the advantages are significant after it's done.

- When you develop your classes in a hierarchy, you can factor out information common to multiple classes into superclasses. Then you can reuse that information over and over through inheritance.

- Modifying (or inserting) a class further up in the hierarchy automatically changes the behavior of the subclasses. There's no need to modify or recompile any of the subclasses because they get the new information through inheritance and not by copying code. However, you must be sure to supply any methods in the new or modified class that are expected by its subclasses.

- By following the object-oriented model that Java presents in its class library, your classes have the same advantages of reuse in other projects, as well as the current project.

For example, let's revisit that Motorcycle class and suppose you've created a Java program to implement all the features of a motorcycle. It's done, it works, and everything is fine. Now, you've been assigned a new task—to create a Java class called Car. Car and Motorcycle have many similar features. Both are vehicles powered by engines. Both have transmissions and headlamps and speedometers. So your first impulse might be to open up your Motorcycle class file and copy over a lot of the information into the new Car class.

A far better plan is to factor out the common information for Car and Motorcycle into a more general class hierarchy. This might look like a lot of work for just the classes Motorcycle and Car, but after you add bicycles, scooters, mopeds, trucks, and others, having common behavior in a reusable superclass significantly reduces the amount of work you must do overall.

Let's design a class hierarchy that might serve this purpose. Starting at the top is the class Object, which is the superclass of all Java classes. The most general class to which a motorcycle and a car both belong might be called Vehicle. A vehicle is generally defined as a thing that propels someone from one place to another. In the Vehicle class, you define only the behavior that enables someone to be propelled from point A to point B, and nothing more. These behaviors might include speed and directional control.

What should go below Vehicle? How about two classes: HumanPoweredVehicle and EnginePoweredVehicle? EnginePoweredVehicle has a mechanical engine, exhibits behaviors that might include stopping and starting the engine, and requires certain amounts of gasoline and oil. HumanPoweredVehicle has a human engine and exhibits behaviors that might include using pedals. Figure 3.3 shows what you have in the hierarchy so far.

3

FIGURE 3.3.

The basic vehicle hierarchy.

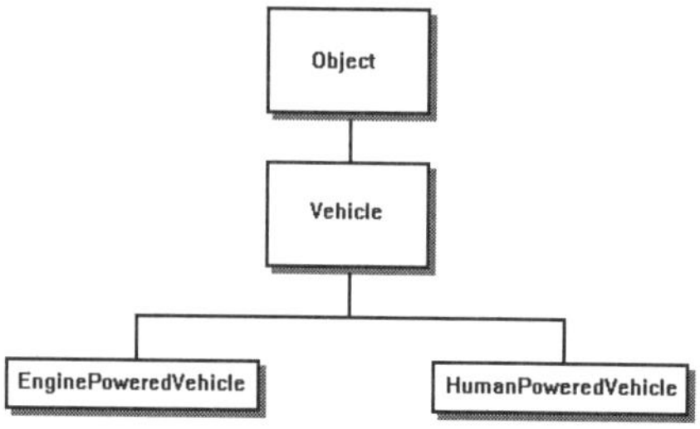

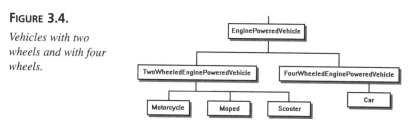

Now, let's get more specific. With `EnginePoweredVehicle`, you might have classes such as `Motorcycle`, `Car`, and so on. Or you can factor out still more behavior and have intermediate classes for two-wheeled and four-wheeled vehicles, with different behaviors for each (see Figure 3.4).

FIGURE 3.4.

Vehicles with two wheels and with four wheels.

Finally, with a subclass for `TwoWheeledEnginePoweredVehicle`, you can have a subclass for `Motorcycle`. You could also now define `Scooter` and `Moped`, both of which are two-wheeled engine-powered vehicles but which have different qualities from motorcycles. In addition, you can subclass `Car` under the `FourWheeledEnginePoweredVehicle` class.

Understanding How Inheritance Works

How does inheritance work? How is it that instances of one class can automatically have access to variables and methods from the classes further up in the hierarchy?

For instance variables, when you create a new instance of a class at runtime, memory is allocated for each variable defined in the current class and for each variable defined in all its superclasses. In this way, all the classes combine to form a template for the current object, and then each object fills in the information appropriate to its unique situation.

Methods operate similarly. New objects have access to all the methods named in its class and its superclasses, but method definitions are chosen dynamically when the method is called at runtime. That is, if you call a particular object's method, the Java interpreter first checks the object's class for the method definition. If it's not defined in the object's class, it looks in that object's superclass, and so on up the chain of the hierarchy until the method is found (see Figure 3.5).

FIGURE 3.5.

*How methods are
dynamically chosen.*

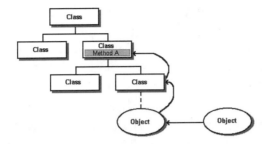

How does Java know when it has reached the correct method? When it locates a method whose signature matches the called method's signature.

> **NEW TERM** A method's *signature* is the way in which methods are identified. A signature comprises the method's name, the number of its arguments, and the type of each of the arguments.

But what happens when a subclass defines a method that has the same signature as a method defined in a superclass? In this case, the method definition that is found first (starting with the object's class and working upward in the hierarchy) is the one that actually gets executed. Because of this, you can intentionally define a method in a subclass that has the same signature as a method in a superclass, which overrides the superclass's method.

> **NEW TERM** *Overriding* a method is done by creating a method in a subclass with the same signature as a method in a superclass. That new method is then used in preference to the superclass's method by instances of the subclass at runtime.

You'll learn more about overriding methods later today.

Single and Multiple Inheritance

Java implements single inheritance, which means that a subclass can have only one superclass (although any superclass can, of course, have many subclasses). Java does not support multiple inheritance, as do some other object-oriented languages (such as C++).

> **NEW TERM** *Single inheritance* allows a subclass to inherit from one superclass only. *Multiple inheritance* allows a subclass to inherit from more than one superclass.

Multiple inheritance can provide enormous power, but it also can significantly complicate class definitions, reduce maintainability, and adversely affect performance. For these reasons, Java's developers declined to implement multiple inheritance. Instead, most of the same functionality is provided by interfaces, which are introduced tomorrow.

Using Java Class Library

The Java class library provides the set of classes that are guaranteed to be available in any commercial Java environment (for example, Netscape browsers). Those classes are in the `java` package and include all the classes you've seen so far, plus a lot more classes you'll learn about later in this book.

The Java Development Kit (JDK) comes with documentation for all of the Java class library, which includes descriptions of each class's instance variables, methods, interfaces, and so on. Exploring the Java class library and its variables and methods is a great way to figure out what Java can and cannot do.

Here are some of the class packages that are part of the Java class library:

`java.lang`	Classes that apply to the language itself, which includes the `Object`, `Math`, `String`, `System`, and `Thread` classes. Also contains the special classes for primitive types (`int`, `char`, `boolean`, and others).
`java.util`	Utility classes, such as `Date` and `Random`, as well as simple collection classes, such as `Vector` and `HashTable`.
`java.io`	Input and output classes for writing to and reading from streams (such as standard input and output) and for handling files.
`java.net`	Classes for networking support, including `Socket` and `URL` (a class to represent references to Web pages).
`java.awt`	Classes to implement a graphic user interface (GUI), including classes for `Window`, `Menu`, `Button`, `Font`, `CheckBox`, and image processing. Also known as the Abstract Window Toolkit (AWT).
`java.applet`	Classes to implement Java applets, including the `Applet` class itself, as well as the `AudioClip` interface. This package is subclassed from the `java.awt` package and so inherits that package's functionality as well.

In addition to the Java classes, your development environment might also include additional classes that provide other utilities or functionality. These classes might be useful, but because they are not part of the standard Java library, they won't be available to other people trying to run your Java program unless you provide them with a licensed copy. This is particularly important for applets because applets are expected to be able to run on any platform, using any Java-enabled browser. Only classes inside the java package are guaranteed to be available on all Web browsers and in all Java environments, so it's best to use only the standard library classes when creating applets.

Creating a Subclass

Now that you know all about inheritance, you can create a subclass and override some methods. Probably the most typical example of creating a subclass, at least when you first start programming in Java, is in writing an applet. All applets are subclasses of the class Applet which is part of the java.applet package. By creating a subclass of Applet, you automatically inherit all the functionality from the AWT and the layout classes that enable your applet to be drawn in the right place on the page and to interact with system operations, such as keypresses and mouse clicks.

Let's add to the JIntermediate.jpr project you created earlier today. To create an HTML page for testing your new applet, complete the following steps:

1. Click the Add to Project icon.

2. Type HelloAgain.html.

3. Click Open.

4. Click on the AppBrowser's Content pane, and then click on its Source tab.

5. Type the HTML code given in Listing 3.2.

TYPE   **LISTING 3.2.** HelloAgain.html.

```
1:  <HTML>
2:  <TITLE>Hello to Everyone!</TITLE>
3:  <BODY>
4:  <APPLET CODE=HelloAgainApplet WIDTH  = 250 HEIGHT = 100></APPLET>
5:  </BODY>
6:  </HTML>
```

This code is similar to the HTML code you wrote on Day 1, "Introduction to JBuilder." Now, to create the source code file for the applet, complete the following steps:

1. Click the Add to Project icon.

2. Type HelloAgainApplet.java

3. Click Open.

4. When the AppBrowser window appears, click on the Content pane, and enter the code shown in Listing 3.3.

TYPE **LISTING 3.3.** HelloAgainApplet.java.

```
 1:  import java.awt.Graphics;
 2:  import java.awt.Font;
 3:  import java.awt.Color;
 4:
 5:  public class HelloAgainApplet extends java.applet.Applet {
 6:
 7:    Font f = new Font("TimesRoman", Font.BOLD, 36);
 8:
 9:    public void paint(Graphics g) {
10:      g.setFont(f);
11:      g.setColor(Color.red);
12:      g.drawString("Hello again!", 5, 50);
13:    }
14:  }
```

As soon as you've finished typing the source code, select File I Save All to preserve your work.

ANALYSIS In lines 1 through 3, you are importing the classes that you need: Graphics, Font, and Color. All three of these are part of the java.awt package. Lines containing import statements go at the top of your program, before the actual class definition.

In line 5, you're creating a class called HelloAgainApplet. Note the part that says extends java.applet.Applet—this is what defines your applet class as a subclass of the Applet class. Remember, because the Applet class is contained in the java.applet package (and not the java.lang package), you don't have automatic access, and you have to refer to java.applet.Applet explicitly by package and class name.

Also in line 5 is the public keyword. This is an access modifier which means that your class will be available to the Java system at large after it is loaded. Most of the time you need to make a class public only if you want it to be visible to all the other classes in your Java programs. But applets, in particular, must be declared to be public. (You'll learn more about the public keyword tomorrow.)

In line 7, the f instance variable is assigned a new instance of the Font class, which is part of the java.awt package. This particular Font object is a Times Roman font, boldface, 36 points high (½ inch). In the previous HelloWorld applet, the font used for the text was the default font: Times Roman, 12 points. By using a Font object, you can change the font of the text you draw in your applet. By creating an instance variable to reference this Font object, you make it available to all the methods in your class. Now you can create a method that uses it.

When you write applets, there are several standard methods defined in the applet super-classes that you will commonly override in your applet class. These include methods to initialize the applet, to start it running, to handle operations such as mouse movements or mouse clicks, or to clean up when the applet stops running. One of these standard methods is the `paint()` method, which actually displays your applet on the Web page. The default definition of `paint()` doesn't do anything—it's an empty method. By overriding (redefining) the `paint()` method, you tell the applet just what to draw on the screen when it is run.

There are two things to remember about the `paint()` method. First, this method is declared `public`, just like the applet itself. However, the `paint()` method is `public` for a different reason—because it's overriding a `public` method. You'll see shortly why the superclass's method is `public`. In the meantime, just be aware that any time you override a `public` method, the new method declaration must also be `public` or you'll get a compiler error.

Second, the `paint()` method takes a single argument: an instance of the `Graphics` class. The `Graphics` class provides platform-independent behavior for rendering fonts, colors, and basic drawing operations. (You'll learn a lot more about the `Graphics` class in Week 2, when you create more complex applets.)

Inside your `paint()` method, you've done three things:

- In line 10, you've told the `Graphics` object assigned to the g variable to set its drawing font to the font specified in the Font object assigned to the instance variable f.

- In line 11, you've told the `Graphics` object assigned to g to set its default color to the instance of the `Color` class `red`.

- You've drawn `Hello Again!` onto the applet's work area on the Web page, at the screen `x,y` coordinates `5,25`. The string will be rendered in the new font and color.

The AppBrowser graphically displays the different parts of your new applet in the Structure pane, as shown in Figure 3.6.

One of the handiest features of the AppBrowser is that the imports are all shown in the Structure pane, and by double-clicking on one of the nodes indented below the Imports node, you can examine the JDK source code for that package. So if you want to see how Java implements the Font object, you can easily do so by double-clicking the `java.awt.Font` node.

3

FIGURE 3.6.

*The AppBrowser
Structure pane shows
the applet's parts.*

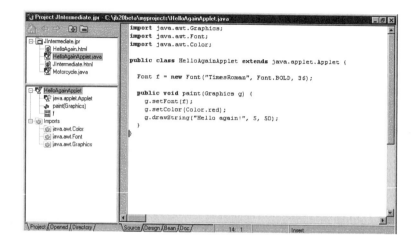

 Tip

While viewing other code, click the Home icon at the top of the Navigation
pane to return to your applet's source code.

Figure 3.7 shows the running applet displayed in appletviewer.

FIGURE 3.7.

*HelloAgainApplet in
appletviewer.*

Remember that to run an applet, you must first point to its associated HTML file in the
Navigation pane, right-click, and then select the Run command from the pop-up menu.

Creating Instance and Class Variables

Usually, when you create a class, you have something you want to add to make that class
different from its superclasses. Inside each class definition are declarations and definitions for variables, or methods, or both—for the class and for each instance of the class.
In this section, you'll learn all about instance and class variables. The section after this
one discusses methods.

Defining Instance Variables

Yesterday, you learned how to declare and initialize local variables—that is, variables
inside of method definitions. Instance variables, fortunately, are declared and defined in

almost exactly the same way as local variables. The main difference is their location in the class definition. Variables are considered instance variables if they are declared outside a method definition. Customarily, however, most instance variables are defined just after the first line of the class definition. For example, here's a simple class definition for the Bicycle class, which inherits from the PersonPoweredVehicle class:

```
class Bicycle extends PersonPoweredVehicle {
    String bikeType;
    int chainGear;
    int rearCogs;
    int currentGearFront;
    int currentGearRear;
}
```

This class definition contains five instance variables:

bikeType	The kind of bicycle this particular bicycle is (for example, Mountain or Street)
chainGear	The number of gears in the front
rearCogs	The number of minor gears on the rear axle
currentGearFront	The front gear the bike is currently in
currentGearRear	The rear gear the bike is currently in

Defining Class Variables

Class variables are global to a class and to all of that class's instances. You can think of class variables as being even more global than instance variables. Class variables are good for communicating between different objects with the same class or for keeping track of global states among a set of objects. Class variables are variables that are defined and stored in the class itself. This gives the class and all objects instantiated from that class access to the variable's value.

When using instance variables, each new instance of the class gets a fresh copy of the instance variables that the class defines. Each instance then can change the values of those instance variables independently, without affecting the values in other instances. However, with class variables, there is only one copy of the variable, and it can hold only one value. The class and each instance of the class has access to that same variable. Changing the value of a class variable changes it for all instances of that class at once.

You define class variables by including the static keyword before the variable declaration. For example, in the partial class definition

```
class FamilyMember {
  static String surname = "Matzenfrazzer";
  String name;
  int age;
  ...
}
```

each instance of the class `FamilyMember` has its own values for `name` and `age`, but the class variable `surname` has only one value for all objects created from the class. Change `surname`, and all the instances of `FamilyMember` are affected.

To access class variables, use the same dot notation as you do with instance variables. To examine or change the value of the class variable, you can use either the instance or the name of the class on the left side of the dot and the variable name on the right. Both lines of output in this example print the same information:

```
FamilyMember baby = new FamilyMember();
System.out.println("Family's surname is " + FamilyMember.surname);
System.out.println("Family's surname is " + baby.surname);
```

Because you can use an instance to change the value of a class variable, it's easy to become confused about class variables and where their values are coming from (remember, the value of a class variable affects all the instances). For this reason, it's best to use the name of the class when you refer to a class variable; `FamilyMember.surname` is preferred to `baby.surname` in the preceding example. This practice will make your code easier to debug and read later.

Defining Constants

Constants are useful for defining shared values for all the methods of an object and for giving meaningful names to object-wide values that will never change. In Java, you can create constants only for instance or class variables, not for local variables.

NEW TERM   A *constant* is a variable whose value never changes (which probably seems a tad strange given the meaning of the word "variable," but there you are).

To declare a constant, use the `final` keyword before the variable declaration, and include an initial value for that variable:

```
final float pi = 3.141592;
final boolean debug = false;
final int maxsize = 40000;
```

Tip

The only way to define constants in Java is by using the `final` keyword. Neither `#define` (a keyword in C and C++) nor `const` (a keyword in C, C++, and Pascal) is available for use in Java. The `const` keyword is reserved in Java, however, to help prevent its accidental use.

Constants can be useful for naming various states of an object and then testing for those states. For example, suppose you have a test label that can be aligned left, right, or center. You can define those values as constant integers:

```
final int LEFT = 0;
final int RIGHT = 1;
final int CENTER = 2;
```

The variable `alignment` also is declared as an `int`:

```
int alignment;
```

Then, later in the body of a method definition, you can either set the alignment, like

```
this.alignment = RIGHT;
```

or test for a given alignment:

```
switch (this.alignment) {
  case LEFT: // deal with left alignment
          ...
          break;
  case RIGHT: // deal with right alignment
          ...
          break;
}
```

Changing Values

To modify the value of a class or instance variable, just put an assignment operator on the right side of the expression:

```
myObject.myVar.state = true;
```

The `CheckPoint` class in Listing 3.4 is an example that checks and modifies the instance variables in a `Point` object. The `Point` class is part of the `java.awt` package and refers to a coordinate point with an x and a y value.

By now, you know how to add a new source code file to a project and to name, save, build, and run a Java program in JBuilder, so those instructions are omitted here. If you're unsure, just refer to the instructions for any of today's earlier listings.

3

TYPE   **LISTING 3.4.** CheckPoint.java.

```
 1:  import java.awt.Point;
 2:  class CheckPoint {
 3:    public static void main(String args[]) {
 4:      Point aPoint = new Point(100,100);
 5:
 6:      System.out.println("Original Coordinate:");
 7:      System.out.println("X,Y is " + aPoint.x + "," + aPoint.y);
 8:
 9:      aPoint.x = 50;
10:      aPoint.y = 150;
11:
12:      System.out.println("New Coordinate:");
13:      System.out.println("X,Y is " + aPoint.x + "," + aPoint.y);
14:    }
15:  }
```

When you run the program, you should see the following output:

OUTPUT
```
Original Coordinate:
X,Y is 100,100
New Coordinate:
X,Y is 50,150
```

ANALYSIS In this example, you create an instance of the Point class, with initial values of 100 for both x and y, and assign it to the aPoint variable (line 4). You then print the values encapsulated in the Point object using dot notation to refer to aPoint.x and aPoint.y (line 7). You change the variable values, again using dot notation (lines 9 and 10). Finally, you print out the changed values (line 13).

Using Objects

When you write a Java program, you define a set of classes. As you learned earlier today, classes are templates for objects. For the most part, use the class to create object instances and then work with those instances. In this section, therefore, you'll learn how to create and work with objects from any given class. Creating an object is also called instantiating an object.

Note   The words *object* and *instance* are interchangeable. An object is an instance of a class; an instance is an object.

Instantiating Objects

Yesterday, you learned that using a string literal—a series of characters enclosed in double quotes—creates a new instance of the class String with the value initialized to the string literal. The String class is unique in that respect. Although it's a class, there's an easy way to directly create instances of that class using a literal. The other classes don't have that shortcut. To create instances of those classes you have to do so explicitly, as you'll soon see.

 Note

> Number literals and character literals are primitive data types and are not implemented as objects for efficiency. However, you can use special class methods to treat them like objects if it should become necessary. (You'll learn how to do this later today, in the section named "Converting Between Primitives and Objects.")

Creating the Object

To create an object, you will use the new keyword, for example:

```
String str = new String();
```

This example shows how to explicitly create a String object. Notice that the class name, String, is used twice. The first time it is used to declare the variable str to be of type String (on the left of the equals sign). The second time, the String class name is followed by a pair of parentheses indicating that it is a method call that creates an object from the class. Don't forget the parentheses at the end; they are essential to indicate that you are calling a method.

When you use the new keyword, several things happen. First, an object of the specified class is created and memory is allocated for it. This instantiates the object (creates an instance). In addition, and more importantly, when the object is created, a special class method defined in the specified class is called. This method is known as a constructor.

NEW TERM A *constructor* is a class method used to create instances of the class. Calling a constructor initializes the object and its variables, creates any other objects that the object needs, and generally performs any other operations the object needs in order to initialize itself.

When you call the constructor, the parentheses can be empty, indicating that the object is created using the class's default values, or the parentheses can contain arguments that determine the initial values of instance variables or other initial aspects of the object.

The number and type of arguments you can use are defined by the class itself in the constructor's class method definition. You'll learn how to create constructors in your own classes later today.

 Caution

> Some classes might not allow you to create a new instance without any arguments. When in doubt, be sure to check the documentation or examine the class source code for the constructor(s) to find out what is required.

Classes might also have more than one constructor method for creating the same object, each with a different set of arguments. The constructor that gets called is determined by the method's signature (type and number of arguments). For example, Listing 3.5 shows the code for the `CreateDates` class, which illustrates two different ways to create a `Date` object using the `new` keyword with the two constructors that are available in the `java.util.Date` class. Click Add to Project, type `CreateDates.java` and click Open. In the AppBrowser, enter the code in Listing 3.5.

TYPE   **LISTING 3.5.** `CreateDates.java`.

```
 1:  import java.util.Date;
 2:  class CreateDates {
 3:    public static void main(String args[]) {
 4:      Date d1, d2;
 5:
 6:      d1 = new Date();
 7:      System.out.println("Date 1: " + d1);
 8:
 9:      d2 = new Date(26000);
10:      System.out.println("Date 2: " + d2);
11:    }
12:  }
```

Select File | Save to preserve your changes, then right-click on the `CreateDates.java` node in the Navigation pane and select Run from the pop-up menu.

Select View | Execution Log from the JBuilder main menu bar to display the Execution Log window. You should see output similar to this:

OUTPUT
```
Date 1: Tue Mar 17 00:09:54 EST 1998
Date 2: Wed Dec 31 19:00:26 EST 1969
```

> **Note**   Your output will look different depending on the date and time when you run the application and the time zone that your computer is set to

ANALYSIS   In this example, two different dates are created by using different arguments to construct each of the instances of the Date class. The first instance (line 6) uses no arguments, which creates a Date object that contains the current system date for the computer on which the program is run.

The second Date object you created in this example (line 9) has one long integer argument. The argument represents the number of milliseconds since January 1, 1970. I randomly picked 26,000 milliseconds, which happens to be 7:00 p.m. (and 26 seconds) on December 31, 1969, Eastern Standard Time.

To see what arguments the constructors for Date will accept, go to the Structure pane in the AppBrowser and double-click on the node labeled java.util.Date in the Imports section. This will display the source code for the class. Once again, in the Structure pane, find the second-level node labeled Date and click on the plus (+) symbol to expand the node. Now you can click on any of the Date constructors shown to see the source code for that constructor and learn more about it. Figure 3.8 displays one of the constructors you used in CreateDates.java (line 9).

> **Note**   You might see more than two class constructors listed for the Date class. Make sure that the constructor you're interested in isn't deprecated by checking the documentation or by keeping your eyes open for the compiler error message for deprecated elements. Deprecated constructors, methods, and classes have been removed from the official implementation of the Java language and temporarily remain for backward compatibility. Avoid using any deprecated language elements because they might not exist in the future.

When you learn more about creating your own classes later today, you will also learn that you can define as many constructors as you need to implement that class's behavior.

FIGURE 3.8.

AppBrowser displaying class constructors for the Date class.

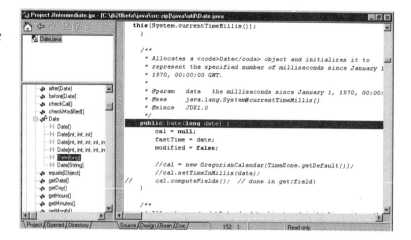

Managing Memory

If you've programmed in other languages, you might be wondering how memory management is handled in Java. For example, in the program you just created, you didn't need to explicitly allocate memory; the new keyword took care of it for you. In Java, memory management is dynamic and automatic. When you create an object using new, Java automatically allocates the right amount of memory for that object type on the heap.

NEW TERM A *heap* is an area of memory reserved for a program to store temporary information, and is allocated dynamically. In Java, the default initial heap size is 1MB and the default maximum heap size is 16MB (both values can be specified explicitly, as well, with a minimum of 1KB).

When your program is finished with the object, Java automatically deallocates the memory that the object uses. Java periodically looks for references to an object in other objects and in the method calling stack. If it no longer finds any references to the object, Java automatically deallocates the memory the object was using. This process of reclaiming memory is called garbage collection.

Making References to Objects

As you work with objects, one important thing going on behind the scenes is the use of references to those objects. When you assign objects to variables, or pass objects as arguments to methods, you are passing references to those objects, not copies of those objects or the objects themselves. Examine the ReferencesTest program in Listing 3.6 which declares two variables of type Point, and assigns a new Point object to pt1, then assigns the value of pt1 to pt2.

TYPE **LISTING 3.6.** ReferencesTest.java.

```
 1: import java.awt.Point;
 2: class ReferencesTest {
 3:   public static void main (String args[]) {
 4:     Point pt1, pt2;
 5:     pt1 = new Point(100, 100);
 6:     pt2 = pt1;
 7:
 8:     pt1.x = 200;
 9:     pt1.y = 200;
10:     System.out.println("Point1: " + pt1.x + ", " + pt1.y);
11:     System.out.println("Point2: " + pt2.x + ", " + pt2.y);
12:   }
13: }
```

Now, here's the tricky part. After changing pt1's x and y instance variables, what will pt2 look like?

Here's the program output:

OUTPUT
```
Point1: 200, 200
Point2: 200, 200
```

ANALYSIS This example shows that pt2 was also changed in lines 8 and 9. In line 6, when you assign pt1 to pt2, you actually create a new reference from pt2 to the same object to which pt1 refers.

Change the value of the object that pt1 refers to, and you also change the object that pt2 points to, because both are references to the same object instance. The fact that Java uses references becomes particularly important when you pass arguments to methods, so keep these references in mind.

> **Note**
>
> There are no explicit pointers or pointer arithmetic in Java. However, with references and with Java arrays, you have most of the capabilities that you have with pointers without the confusion and lurking bugs that explicit pointers can cause.

Casting and Converting

There will be times in your Java programs when you will have a value stored in one type, but you really need to use it as a different type. Maybe it's an instance of a class but you need to use it as an instance of some other class, or perhaps it's a floating-point value and what you really need is an integer value. To convert the value of one type to another, you use a mechanism called casting.

NEW TERM *Casting* is a way to convert the value of one object type to another object type, or of one primitive type into another primitive type. The result of a cast is a new reference or value. Casting does not affect the original object or value being cast.

Although the concept of casting is a simple one, the rules for what types in Java can be converted to what other types are complicated by the fact that Java has both primitive types and object types. As the preceding definition implies, you can't cast objects to primitives, nor primitives to objects. However, there is a way to convert from one to the other. There are three forms of explicit casts and conversions to talk about in this section:

- Casting between primitive types: `int`, `long`, `float`, and so on.
- Casting between object types: `String`, `Point`, `Window`, and so on.
- Converting primitives to objects, and objects to primitives.

In the following sections, the value to be converted is referred to as the source, and the type it's to be converted to is referred to as the destination.

Casting Primitives

Primitives can be converted either automatically or by explicit casting. In automatic type conversion, if the destination type is larger (has more precision) than the source, the conversion can take place by simply assigning the smaller to the larger. This is also known as promoting the value. Table 3.1 summarizes what types can be promoted to what other types.

TABLE 3.1. PROMOTIONS THAT DON'T RISK DATA LOSS.

Source Type	Destination Type
byte	char, short, int, long, float, double
char	int, long, float, double
short	int, long, float, double
int	long, float, double
long	float, double
float	double

However, assigning a value of a larger type to a smaller type will generally result in a loss of data. Of course, if the larger type's value just happens to be small enough (for example, the value of a long is 10 and you assign it to an int), the value will be preserved. However, to convert a larger value to a smaller type, you should use an explicit type cast to avoid the risk of data loss.

Casting between primitives enables you to convert the value of one primitive type to another primitive type—for example, to assign an floating-point value to an integer. Casting between primitive types most commonly involves the numeric types and chars; booleans cannot be cast to other primitive types. Explicit type casts look like this:

```
(destination-typename) source-value
```

In this form, *destination-typename* is the name of the type you're converting to (for example, short, int, float), and *source-value* is an expression whose result you want to convert. The following expression divides the value of x by the value of y and casts the float result to an int:

```
(int) (x / y)
```

Note Because the evaluation precedence of casting is higher than that of arithmetic, you have to use parentheses so that the result of the division is calculated first, and its floating-point result is what gets cast to an integer value.

Casting Objects

Some objects might not need to be cast explicitly. In particular, because subclasses contain all the information in the superclass at minimum, you can use an instance of a subclass anywhere the superclass is expected. Suppose you wanted to call a method that takes two arguments: one of type Object, and one of type Number. You don't have to pass instances of those particular classes to that method. For the Object argument, you can pass any subclass of Object (in other words, any object) and for the Number argument, you can pass an instance of any subclass of Number (Integer, Double, Float, and so on).

Casting an object to one of that object's superclasses loses the information pertaining specifically to the original subclass and requires an explicit cast. Instances of classes can be cast to instances of other classes, with one restriction: The class of the source object and the class of the destination object must be related by inheritance. That is, you can only cast an object to an instance of its class' subclass or superclass—not to any random class. To cast an object to another class, you use the same casting operation that you use for base types:

```
(destination-classname) source-object
```

In this form, *destination-classname* is the name of the class you're converting to, and *source-object* is a reference to the object you want to convert. Note that casting creates a new reference to the *source-object* of the type *destination-classname*; the original object continues to exist.

The following code fragment is an example of a cast of an instance of the class GreenApple to an instance of the class Apple (where GreenApple is a subclass of Apple):

```
Apple anApple;
GreenApple aGreenApple;
aGreenApple = new GreenApple();
anApple = (Apple) aGreenApple;
```

Note that the special attributes that made the GreenApple green are now lost in anApple. All the other behavior (methods) and attributes (variables) that GreenApple originally inherited from Apple, however, survive the conversion.

In addition to casting objects to classes, you can also cast objects to interfaces—but only if that object's class or one of its superclasses actually implements that interface (in other words, it belongs to the same inheritance tree). Casting an object to an interface then enables you to call one of that interface's methods even if that object's class does not directly implement that interface. You'll learn more about interfaces tomorrow.

Converting Between Primitives and Objects

Now that you know how to cast a primitive type to another primitive type and how to cast between classes, how can you cast one to the other? Well, as we mentioned at the outset of this section, you can't actually cast between primitives and objects in Java. However, Java does provide another way to do these kinds of conversions.

There are several special classes in the java.lang package that correspond to each primitive data type: Integer for int, Float for float, Boolean for boolean, and so on. Using class methods defined in these classes, you can create an object-equivalent for all the primitive types using the new keyword. The following line of code, for example, creates an instance of the Integer class with the value 35:

```
Integer intObject = new Integer(35);
```

After you have created this object, you can treat its value as an object. Then, when you want the primitive value back again, there are also methods to do that. In this example, the intValue() method extracts the int primitive value of 35 from the Integer object, and assigns it to theInt:

```
int theInt = intObject.intValue();
```

To read the specifics on how to use these methods, select Help|Java Reference and refer to the "package java.lang" topic in the JDK API Reference section.

Comparing Objects

Yesterday, you learned about operators for comparing values: is equal to (==), is not equal to (!=), less than (<), greater than (>), and so on. Most of these operators take arithmetic values as operands, and the Java compiler will display an error if you attempt to use any other type of value as operands.

The exceptions to this rule are the two operators for equality: is equal to (==), is not equal to (!=). When given objects as operands, these operators do not compare two separate objects; they test whether the two objects refer to exactly the same object. In this context, the operators become: refers to same object (==), refers to different object (!=). So how can you compare two different object instances for equality? You have to implement custom methods in your class, and you have to call those methods using their method names.

3

Note	Java does not support the concept of operator overloading—that is, the capability of redefining the behavior of built-in operators by defining methods in your own classes.

A good example of this is the String class. It is possible to have two independent String objects in memory with the same values. That is, you might have two strings with the same characters in the same order. However, the results of the == operator will be false, because although their contents are the same, the two strings are not the same object.

The String class, therefore, defines a method called equals() that tests each character in the string and returns true if the two strings have identical values. The EqualString.java class in Listing 3.7 illustrates this functionality.

TYPE   **LISTING 3.7.** EqualString.java.

```
1:  class EqualString {
2:    public static void main (String args[]) {
3:      String str1, str2;
4:      str1 = "Did you want me to repeat that?";
5:      str2 = str1;
6:
7:      System.out.println();
8:      System.out.println("String1: " + str1);
9:      System.out.println("String2: " + str2);
```

continues

LISTING 3.7. CONTINUED

```
10:        System.out.println("Same value?: " + str1.equals(str2));
11:        System.out.println("Same object? " + (str1 == str2));
12:
13:        str2 = new String(str1);
14:
15:        System.out.println();
16:        System.out.println("String1: " + str1);
17:        System.out.println("String2: " + str2);
18:        System.out.println("Same value? " + str1.equals(str2));
19:        System.out.println("Same object? " + (str1 == str2));
20:    }
21: }
```

When you compile and run this program, you will see this output:

OUTPUT
```
String1: Did you want me to repeat that?
String2: Did you want me to repeat that?
Same value? true
Same object? true
String1: Did you want me to repeat that?
String2: Did you want me to repeat that?
Same value? true
Same object? False
```

ANALYSIS In the first part of this program, line 3 declares two String variables, str1 and str2; line 4 assigns the literal value Did you want me to repeat that? to str1; and line 5 assigns str1 to str2. As you know from the earlier discussion of object references, both str1 and str2 now point to the same object, and the test at line 11 proves just that.

In the second part, line 13 creates a new String object with the value of str1. Line 18 shows that both str1 and str2 have the identical value; line 19 shows that they are two separate and distinct String objects.

 Caution
> Remember that string literals are optimized in Java. So you must explicitly use new to create two distinct String object instances with the same string value.

Determining an Object's Class

If you want to know an object's class, you can use the following line of code:

```
String myObjName = myObj.getClass().getName();
```

The getClass() method is defined in the Object class and so is available to all objects. The result of that method is a Class object (which is itself a class) that defines the getName() method. The getName() method returns a String object representing the name of the class and therefore tells you of which class the object is an instance. Lastly, this return value is assigned as myObjName's initial string value.

If you want to test whether an object is an instance of a particular class, you can use the instanceof operator. The instanceof operator takes two operands, an object on the left and the name of a class on the right. This boolean expression returns true or false based on whether the object is an instance of the named class or any of the named class's subclasses. For example:

```
"Meow!" instanceof String;  // returns true
Point pt = new Point(10,10);
pt instanceof String;  // returns false
```

The instanceof operator can also be used for interfaces. If an object implements an interface, the instanceof operator with that interface name as the operand on the right returns true. You'll learn more about interfaces tomorrow.

Using Methods

Methods are arguably the most important part of any object-oriented language. Whereas classes and objects provide the framework, and class and instance variables provide a way of holding that class's or object's attributes and state, it is the methods that actually provide an object's behavior and define how that object interacts with other objects in the system.

In this section, you'll also learn about some of the more advanced features of methods that make them really powerful and that make your objects and classes more efficient and easier to understand. These additional features include:

- **Overloading methods:** creating methods with multiple signatures and definitions but with the same name
- **Overriding methods:** creating a different definition for a method from what was defined in a superclass
- **Constructor methods:** methods that enable you to initialize objects to their initial state when the instance is created
- **Finalizer methods:** a way for an object to clean up after itself before it is removed from the system

Calling Methods

The format for calling a method in objects is similar to referring to its instance variables: Method calls also use dot notation. The object whose method you're calling is on the left side of the dot; the name of the method and its arguments are on the right side of the dot:

```
myObject.methodOne(arg1, arg2, arg3);
```

Note that a method must always have a pair of parentheses after it, even if the method takes no arguments:

```
myObject.methodNoArgs();
```

If the method you've called results in an object that itself has methods, you can nest methods as you would variables. In this example, the getClass method results in an object that contains the getName method:

```
myObject.getClass().getName();
```

You can nest variable references and method calls as well. In this example, the variable xVar refers to an object instantiated from a class that defines the methodTwo method:

```
myObject.xVar.methodTwo(arg1);
```

System.out.println(), the method you've been using so far, is a good example of nesting variables and methods. The System class (part of the java.lang package) describes system-specific behavior. System.out is a class variable that refers to an instance of the class PrintStream that points to the standard output of the system. PrintStream instances have a println() method that prints a string to that output stream.

This code fragment shows an example of calling a method defined in the String class, the length() method:

```
System.out.println("Length of string: " + str.length());
```

Strings include methods for string tests and modification, similar to what you would expect in a string library in other languages.

OUTPUT   The output produced for a string with 35 characters would be this:

```
Length of string: 35
```

Using Class Methods

Class methods apply to the class as a whole and not to its instances. Class methods commonly are used for general utility methods that might not operate directly on an instance of that class but fit with that class conceptually. For example, the String class defines a class method called `valueOf()`,which can take one of many different types of arguments (integers, Booleans, other objects, and so on). The `valueOf()` method then returns a new instance of `String` containing the string value of the argument it was given. This method doesn't operate directly on an existing instance of `String`, but getting a string from another object or data type is definitely a string-like operation, and it makes sense to define it in the `String` class.

Class methods can also be useful for gathering general methods together in one place (the class). For example, the `Math` class, defined in the `java.lang` package, contains a large set of mathematical operations as class methods—there are no instances of the class `Math`, but you can still use its methods with numeric or Boolean arguments.

To call a class method, use dot notation as you do with instance methods. As with class variables, you can use either an instance of the class or the class itself on the left side of the dot. However, for the same reasons noted in the discussion on class variables, using the name of the class for class methods makes your code easier to read. The last two lines in this code fragment produce the same results and highlight the reasons for prefer-ring the use of the class name on the left of the dot:

```
String s1, s2, s3;
s1 = "Mandy";
s2 = s1.valueOf(7);
s3 = String.valueOf(7);
```

The class method `valueOf()`, when given an integer, returns the string value associated with the integer. In the preceding example, both `s1.valueOf(7)` and `String.valueOf(7)` return the string value `seven`. However, the line of code containing the expression `s1.valueOf(7)` doesn't really involve the variable `s1`, but rather, simply uses it as a con-duit to call the class method. Using the instance name in this way will be misleading to the casual reader. The last line that uses the expression `String.valueOf(7)` is preferred because it is clearly referring to a class method.

Creating Methods

Methods, as you learned earlier today, define an object's behavior—what happens when that object is created and the various operations that the object can perform during its lifetime. In this section, you'll get a basic introduction to method definition and how methods work. Later today, you'll go into more detail about advanced things you can do with methods.

Defining Methods

Method definitions have four basic parts: name, return type, arguments, and body. The method's signature is a combination of the name of the method, the type of object or primitive type this method returns, and the list of its arguments.

To keep things simple today, two optional parts of the method definition have been left out: a modifier such as `public` or `private` and the `throws` keyword, which indicates the exceptions a method can throw. You'll learn about these tomorrow.

In other languages, the name of the method (or function, procedure, or subroutine) is enough to distinguish it from other methods in the program. In Java, you can have different methods that have the same name but a different argument list. This is called method overloading, which you'll explore in depth later today.

Here's what a basic method definition looks like:

```
returntype methodName(type1 arg1, type2 arg2, type3 arg3...) {
/* body of the method */
}
```

The `returntype` is the type of value this method returns. It can be one of the primitive types, a class, or `void` if the method does not return a value at all, such as the `main()` method.

Note

If a method returns an array object, the array brackets can go after either the `returntype` or the argument list. Because the former version is considerably easier to read, it is normally used, as in the following:

```
int[] makeRange(int lower, int upper) {...}
```

The method's argument list is a set of variable declarations, separated by commas, inside parentheses. These arguments become local variables in the body of the method, whose values are the objects or primitive values passed in when the method is called.

Inside the body of the method you can have statements, expressions, method calls to other objects, conditionals, loops, and so on—everything you've learned about yesterday. If your method has an actual return type (that is, it has not been declared to return `void`), somewhere inside the body of the method you need to return a value. To do this, use the `return` keyword.

Notice the `return` statements while you type Listing 3.8.

TYPE **LISTING 3.8.** RangeClass.java.

```
1:   public class RangeClass {
2:
3:     int[] makeRange(int lower, int upper) {
4:       int arr[] = new int[ (upper - lower) + 1 ];
```

```
 5:        for (int i = 0; i < arr.length; i++) {
 6:          arr[i] = lower++;
 7:        }
 8:        return arr;
 9:      }
10:
11:      static public void main(String[] args) {
12:        int theArray[];
13:        RangeClass theRange = new RangeClass();
14:        theArray = theRange.makeRange(1, 10);
15:        System.out.print("The array: [ ");
16:        for (int i = 0; i < theArray.length; i++) {
17:          System.out.print(theArray[i] + " ");
18:        }
19:        System.out.println("]");
20:      }
21:    }
```

OUTPUT After you compile and run the project, here is what the output looks like:

```
The array: [ 1 2 3 4 5 6 7 8 9 10 ]
```

ANALYSIS The main() method in this class tests the makeRange() method by creating a range (line 3) where the lower and upper bounds of the range are 1 and 10, respectively (line 14). It then uses a for loop to print the values of the new array (lines 16 to 18).

Using the this Keyword

In the body of a method definition, you might want to refer to the current object—the object the method was called by—to refer to that object's instance variables or to pass the current object as an argument to another method. To refer to the current object in these cases, you can use the this keyword. The this keyword refers to the current object, and you can use it anywhere that object might appear—in dot notation to refer to the object's instance variables, as an argument to a method, as the return value for the current method, and so on. Here are some examples:

```
t = this.x;  // the x instance variable for the current object
this.myMethod(this);  // calls the myMethod method, defined in
                      // the current object's class, and
                      // passes it the current object
return this;  // returns the current object
```

In many cases, however, you might be able to omit the this keyword. You can refer to both instance variables and method calls defined in the current class simply by name. The this keyword is implicit in those references and could have been left out.

Note
> Omitting the `this` keyword for instance variables depends on whether there are no variables of the same name declared in the local scope. See the next section, "Understanding Variable Scope and Method Definitions," for more details.

Keep in mind that because `this` is a reference to the current instance of a class, you should use it only inside the body of an instance method definition. Class methods—that is, methods declared with the `static` keyword—cannot use `this`. Class methods are not tied to a particular instance of the class; therefore, the `this` keyword is never relevant.

Understanding Variable Scope and Method Definitions

When you refer to a variable within your method definitions, Java checks for a definition of that variable first in the current scope (which might be a block) and then in the outer scopes up to the current method definition. If that variable is not a local variable, Java then checks for a definition of that variable as an instance or class variable in the current class. Finally, Java checks each superclass in turn.

Java makes it possible in certain situations for you to create a variable in an inner scope that hides a variable in an outer scope. When the definition of a variable in an inner scope is exactly the same as a variable in an outer scope, the value for the outer variable is hidden. This, of course, is not a recommended programming practice because it can introduce subtle and confusing bugs into your code. For example, consider this small Java program:

```
class ScopeTest {
  int test = 10;
  void printTest() {
    int test = 20;
    System.out.println("test = " + test);
  }
}
```

In this class, you have two variables with the same name and definition. The first, an instance variable, has the name `test` and is initialized to the value `10`. The second is a local variable also called `test` but with the value `20`. Because the local variable in the inner scope hides the instance variable in the outer scope, the `println()` method will print `test = 20`. However, you can circumvent the default scoping behavior by using `this.test` to refer to the instance variable and just `test` to refer to the local variable.

A more insidious example of the problem occurs when you redefine a variable in a subclass that already occurs in a superclass. Again, this can create bugs in your code. For example, you might call methods that are intended to change the value of a certain instance variable but instead end up changing an inner scope variable and cause the value of the outer one to be left unaltered. Another bug might occur when you cast an object from one class to another. The value of your instance variable might mysteriously change (because it is getting that value from the superclass instead of from your class). The best way to avoid this behavior is to make sure that, when you define variables in a subclass, you're aware of the variables in each of that class's superclasses and don't duplicate what is already defined in those superclasses.

Passing Arguments to Methods

When you call a method with object arguments, the variables you pass into the body of the method are passed by reference, which means that whatever you do to those objects inside the method affects the original objects as well. This includes arrays and all the objects that arrays contain. When you pass an array into a method and modify its contents, the original array is affected.

Note

Primitive types are passed to methods by value.

Here's an example to demonstrate how this works. First, you have a simple class definition, which includes a single method called oneToZero():

```
class PassByRef {
  int oneToZero(int arg[]) {
    int count = 0;
    for (int i = 0; i < arg.length; i++) {
      if (arg[i] == 1) {
        count++;
        arg[i] = 0;
      }
    }
    return count;
  }
}
```

The oneToZero() method does two things:

- It counts the number of ones in the array and returns that value.
- If it finds a one, it substitutes a zero in its place in the array.

In this code snippet, you create the main() method for the PassByRef class and pass an array of integers to the oneToZero() method:

```
public static void main (String arg[]) {
  int arr[] = { 1, 3, 4, 5, 1, 1, 7 };
  PassByRef test = new PassByRef();
  int numOnes;
  numOnes = test.oneToZero(arr);
}
```

The first three lines set up the initial variables. The first one is an array of integers. The second one is an instance of the class PassByRef, which is assigned to the test variable. The third is an integer to hold the number of ones found in the array. The fourth line calls the oneToZero() method, defined in the test object, and passes it the array stored in arr. This method returns the number of ones in the array, which you then assign to the numOnes variable. The oneToZero() method returns 3. Also, the old values in the {1,3,4,5,1,1,7} array are changed to {0,3,4,5,0,0,7} by the method call.

Using Class Methods

Just as you have class and instance variables, you also have class and instance methods, and the difference between the two types of methods is analogous. Class methods are available to any instance of the class itself and can be made available to other classes. Therefore, some class methods can be used anywhere regardless of whether an instance of the class exists or doesn't exist.

For example, the Java class libraries include a class called Math. The Math class defines a whole set of math operations that can be used in any program or with the various numeric types:

```
float root = Math.sqrt(453.0);
System.out.print("The larger of x and y is " + Math.max(x, y));
```

To define class methods, use the static keyword in front of the method definition, similar to the way you create a class variable. For example, here's the sqrt class method signature:

```
static float sqrt(float arg1) {...}
```

Java also supplies "wrapper" classes for each of the primitive types—for example, the Integer, Float, and Boolean classes. Using class methods defined in those classes, you can convert to and from objects and primitive types. For example, the parseInt() class method in the Integer class takes a string and a radix and returns the value of that string as an integer:

```
int count = Integer.parseInt("42", 10);   // returns the integer 42
```

Note Radix is the name for the base of a particular number system. The radix is 10 in decimal, 16 in hexadecimal, 8 in octal, and 2 in binary.

Most methods that operate on or affect a particular object should be defined as instance methods. Methods that provide some general utility but do not directly affect an instance of that class are better declared as class methods.

Overloading Methods

Earlier today, you learned how to create methods with a single name and single signature. Methods in Java can also be overloaded. That is, you can create methods that have the same name, but with different signatures and different definitions. Method overloading enables instances of your class to have a simpler interface to other objects and allow them to behave differently based on the input to the method.

When you call a method in an object, Java matches up the method name, the number of arguments, and the argument types to choose which method definition to execute. (You might want to review Figure 3.5 and the section "Understanding How Inheritance Works," where this concept was introduced.)

To create an overloaded method, all you need to do is create several different method definitions in your class, all with the same name but with different argument lists. The argument list might differ in the number of arguments, the data types of the arguments, or both. The variable names you choose for each method argument are irrelevant; all that matters is the number and the type.

Java allows method overloading as long as each method of the same name has a unique argument list. However, in Java, overloaded methods must have identical return types. That is, if you try to create two methods with the same name and same arguments but different return types, you will receive a compiler error for your efforts.

The following shows a simple class definition for a class called MyRect, which defines a rectangular shape. The MyRect class has four instance variables to define the upper-left and lower-right coordinate pairs for the rectangle's corners: x1, y1, x2, and y2. When a new instance of the MyRect class is created, all its instance variables are initialized to 0:

```java
class MyRect {
  int x1 = 0;
  int y1 = 0;
  int x2 = 0;
  int y2 = 0;
}
```

Tip

> Remember to avoid using names that are already defined in other classes or the Java class libraries. For example, there is a `Rectangle` class in the `java.awt` package, so you should name a new class something different than `Rectangle` to prevent problems later.

Let's define a `buildRect()` method that takes four integer arguments, sizes the rectangle to have the appropriate values for its corners, and returns the resulting rectangle object. (Note that because the arguments have the same identifier names as the instance variables, you have to use the `this` keyword to refer explicitly to the instance variables.) The method takes each of the arguments in the argument list (x1, y1, and so on) and assigns the value to the corresponding instance variable (`this.x1`, `this.y1`, and so on):

```
MyRect buildRect(int x1, int y1, int x2, int y2) {
  this.x1 = x1;
  this.y1 = y1;
  this.x2 = x2;
  this.y2 = y2;
  return this;
}
```

What if you want to allow the user to specify a rectangle's dimensions in a different way—for example, by using `Point` objects rather than individual coordinates? You can overload `buildRect()` so that its argument list takes two `Point` objects instead. (Note that you would need to import `java.awt.Point` to make this work.) This version of the method takes each `Point` object and assigns its x and y field values to the corresponding instance variables:

```
MyRect buildRect(Point topLeft, Point bottomRight) {
  x1 = topLeft.x;
  y1 = topLeft.y;
  x2 = bottomRight.x;
  y2 = bottomRight.y;
  return this;
}
```

Perhaps you want to define the rectangle using a top corner and a width and height. Just create another definition for the `buildRect()` method:

```
MyRect buildRect(Point topLeft, int w, int h) {
  x1 = topLeft.x;
  y1 = topLeft.y;
  x2 = (x1 + w);
  y2 = (y1 + h);
  return this;
}
```

Method overloading enables you to provide this type of flexibility to users of your class definition. Keep in mind that you can define as many versions of a method as you need to in your own classes to implement the behavior you need for that class. You cannot, however, define two separate methods that have the same name and the same arguments in the same class. If you attempt to do so, you will receive a "duplicate definition" compiler error.

Overriding Methods

When you call an object's method, Java looks for that method definition in the class of that object. If it doesn't find one, it passes the method call up the class hierarchy until a matching method signature is found. Method inheritance enables you to define and use methods repeatedly in subclasses without having to duplicate the code itself in each subclass.

However, there might be times when you want an object to respond differently to the method call than the behavior that is defined in the object's superclass. In this case, you can override the method. Overriding a method involves redefining a method in a subclass that has the same signature as a method in a superclass. Then, when that method is called, the method in the subclass is found and executed instead of the one in the superclass.

Creating Override Methods

To override a method, all you have to do is create a method in your subclass that has the same signature (name and argument list) as a method defined by one of your class's superclasses. Because Java executes the first method definition it finds that matches the signature, this effectively hides the original method definition from the current object's scope.

To demonstrate, click the Add to project icon, type `PrintClass.java`, and click Open. Click on the Content pane, and enter the code shown in Listing 3.9.

TYPE   **LISTING 3.9.** `PrintClass.java`.

```
 1: class PrintClass {
 2:    int x = 0;
 3:    int y = 1;
 4:
 5:    void printMe() {
 6:      System.out.println("X is " + x + ", Y is " + y);
 7:      System.out.println("I am an instance of the class "
 8:                         + this.getClass().getName());
 9:    }
10: }
```

Next, you want to create a subclass of `PrintClass` whose only difference is that the subclass has a z instance variable. This subclass will also contain the application's `main()` method. Click on the "Add to project" icon again to add `PrintSubClass.java`, and then enter the code shown in Listing 3.10.

TYPE **Listing 3.10**. `PrintSubClass.java`.

```
1:  class PrintSubClass extends PrintClass {
2:    int z = 3;
3:
4:    public static void main(String args[]) {
5:      PrintSubClass obj = new PrintSubClass();
6:      obj.printMe();
7:    }
8:  }
```

OUTPUT Here's the output when you compile and run `PrintSubClass.java`:

```
X is 0, Y is 1
I am an instance of the class PrintSubClass
```

In the `main()` method of `PrintSubClass`, you created a `PrintSubClass` object and called the `printMe()` method. Note that `PrintSubClass` doesn't define this method, so Java looks for it in each of `PrintSubClass`'s superclasses. In this case, it finds it in `PrintClass`. Unfortunately, because `printMe()` is defined in `PrintClass`, it doesn't know anything about the z instance variable and prints only x and y.

Now, add `PrintSubClass2.java` in Listing 3.11 to the project.

TYPE **Listing 3.11**. `PrintSubClass2.java`.

```
1:  class PrintSubClass2 extends PrintClass {
2:    int z = 3;
3:
4:    void printMe() {
5:      System.out.println("X is " + x + ", Y is " + y
6:                       + ", Z is " + z);
7:      System.out.println("I am an instance of the class "
8:                       + this.getClass().getName());
9:    }
10:
11:   public static void main(String args[]) {
12:     PrintSubClass2 obj = new PrintSubClass2();
13:     obj.printMe();
14:   }
15: }
```

When you run `PrintSubClass2.java`, it will instantiate the `PrintSubClass2` subclass and call the `printMe()` method defined in this subclass.

The output shows the new behavior obtained from overriding the `printMe()` method:

OUTPUT
```
X is 0, Y is 1, Z is 3
I am an instance of the class PrintSubClass2
```

Calling Original Methods

Usually, there are two reasons why you want to override a method that a superclass has already implemented:

- To replace the definition of that original method completely
- To augment the original method with additional behavior

You've already learned how to do the first task. By overriding a method and giving that method a new definition, you've replaced the original method definition as far as the subclass is concerned. But sometimes you might just want to add behavior to the original definition rather than hide it altogether. This is particularly useful when you end up duplicating behavior in both the original method and the method that overrides it, as you just did in the `PrintClass` example. By being able to call the original method in the body of the overriding method, you can add only the additional behavior.

To call the original method from inside a method redefinition, use the `super` keyword to pass the method call up the hierarchy:

```java
void myMethod (String a, String b) {
  // do some things here
  super.myMethod(a, b);
  // do more things here
}
```

Note

> The `super` keyword is a placeholder for this class's superclass. You can use it anywhere you can use the `this` keyword, but you use it to refer to the superclass rather than to the current class.

Rather than duplicating most of the behavior of the superclass's method in the subclass, you can define the superclass's method so that additional behavior can be added easily. Here's a revised version of the earlier example, showing how this can be done. Add `PrintRevClass.java` to the project, and enter the code shown in Listing 3.12.

TYPE   **Listing 3.12**. PrintRevClass.java.

```
 1:  class PrintRevClass {
 2:    int x = 0;
 3:    int y = 1;
 4:
 5:    void printMe() {
 6:      System.out.println("I am an instance of the class "
 7:                         + this.getClass().getName());
 8:      System.out.println("X is " + x);
 9:      System.out.println("Y is " + y);
10:    }
11:  }
```

Then, again click on the Add to project icon. Name this new class
PrintRevSubClass.java and click OK. Click on the Content pane and enter the code
shown in Listing 3.13.

TYPE   **Listing 3.13**. PrintRevSubClass.java.

```
 1:  class PrintRevSubClass extends PrintRevClass {
 2:    int z = 3;
 3:
 4:    void printMe() {
 5:      super.printMe();
 6:      System.out.println("Z is " + z);
 7:    }
 8:
 9:    public static void main(String args[]) {
10:      PrintRevSubClass obj = new PrintRevSubClass();
11:      obj.printMe();
12:    }
13:  }
```

Select File | Save All. When you run PrintRevSubClass.java, it will instantiate the
PrintRevSubClass subclass, call the printMe() method as defined in PrintRevClass
(the superclass), and then continue on to perform the additional behavior defined in the
method of this subclass.

Here's the output:

OUTPUT
```
I am an instance of the class PrintRevSubClass
X is 0
Y is 1
Z is 3
```

Understanding Constructor Methods

In addition to regular methods, you can also define constructor methods in your class definition.

NEW TERM A *constructor* is a special kind of method that determines how an object is initialized when it's instantiated.

Unlike regular methods, you can't call a constructor method by calling it directly by name. Instead, constructor methods are called by Java automatically. Here's how it works when you use the new keyword to create a new instance of a class; the Java language does three things:

1. Memory is allocated for the object.
2. The object's instance variables are initialized, either to the initial values specified in the class definition, or to the appropriate default value for their types.
3. The class's constructor method is called (which can be one of several methods).

If a class doesn't have any special constructor methods defined, you'll still get an object, but you might have to set its instance variables or call other methods that the object needs to initialize itself. Most of the classes you've created up to this point have done the latter, simply allocating memory for the object and not much more.

By defining constructor methods in your own classes, you can set initial values of instance variables, call methods based on those instance variables, call other objects' methods, or calculate initial properties for your object. You can also overload constructors, as you would regular methods, to create an object that has specific properties based on the arguments passed when instantiating an object with the new keyword.

Using Default Constructors

Constructors look a lot like regular methods with two basic differences:

- Constructors always have the same name as the class in which they are defined.
- Constructors don't have a return type.

For example, Listing 3.14 shows a simple class called Person which defines a constructor that initializes its instance variables based on the arguments passed with the new keyword. The class also includes a method for the object to "introduce" itself, and a main() method to see how it all works.

TYPE   **Listing 3.14**. `Person.java`.

```
 1:  class Person {
 2:    String name;
 3:    int age;
 4:
 5:    Person(String n, int a) {  // constructor
 6:      name = n;
 7:      age = a;
 8:    }
 9:
10:    void printPerson() {
11:      System.out.print("Hi, my name is " + name);
12:      System.out.println(". I am " + age + " years old.");
13:    }
14:
15:    public static void main(String args[]) {
16:
17:      Person p;
18:      System.out.println("----------");
19:      p = new Person("Michelle", 44);
20:      p.printPerson();
21:      System.out.println("----------");
22:      p = new Person("Phil", 49);
23:      p.printPerson();
24:      System.out.println("----------");
25:    }
26:  }
```

Be sure to save your work.

Here's the output from running this program:

OUTPUT
```
----------
Hi, my name is Michelle. I am 44 years old.
----------
Hi, my name is Phil. I am 49 years old.
----------
```

ANALYSIS   Lines 5 through 8 are the constructor (the name is the same as the class, and there is no return type). In line 17, you declare the variable p to be of the object type `Person`. However, the constructor doesn't get called until you reach the `main()` method, where it is called twice (lines 19 and 22).

Calling Another Constructor

Some constructors you write might be a superset of another constructor defined in your class. That is, they might have the same basic behavior as another constructor plus some additional behavior. Rather than duplicating identical behavior in multiple constructor methods in your class, it makes sense to be able to just call that first constructor from inside the body of the second constructor. Java provides a special syntax to do just that. To call a constructor defined on the current class, use this general form:

```
this(arg1, arg2, arg3...);
```

The arguments to `this` are the arguments to the constructor. Using the `this` keyword as a method call, calls the current class's constructor. After calling the `this()` method to invoke the original constructor, you can add whatever additional functionality your new constructor needs.

Overloading Constructors

Like regular methods, constructors can also take varying numbers and types of arguments, enabling you to create your object with exactly the properties you want it to have or with the capability to calculate properties from different kinds of input.

For example, the `buildRect()` methods you defined in the "Overloading Methods" section are good candidates for constructors because they're initializing an object's instance variables to the appropriate values. So instead of the `buildRect()` methods you defined, you can create constructors instead. Listing 3.15 shows a class named `MyRect.java` which shows the same functionality defined as several overloaded `MyRect()` constructors rather than the original overloaded `buildRect()` methods.

TYPE   **Listing 3.15**. `MyRect.java`.

```
1:  import java.awt.Point;
2:
3:  class MyRect {
4:      int x1 = 0;
5:      int y1 = 0;
6:      int x2 = 0;
7:      int y2 = 0;
8:
9:      MyRect(int x1, int y1, int x2, int y2) {
10:         this.x1 = x1;
11:         this.y1 = y1;
12:         this.x2 = x2;
13:         this.y2 = y2;
14:     }
15:
16:     MyRect(Point topLeft, Point bottomRight) {
17:         x1 = topLeft.x;
18:         y1 = topLeft.y;
19:         x2 = bottomRight.x;
20:         y2 = bottomRight.y;
```

continues

Listing 3.15. CONTINUED

```
21:    }
22:
23:    MyRect(Point topLeft, int w, int h) {
24:        x1 = topLeft.x;
25:        y1 = topLeft.y;
26:        x2 = (x1 + w);
27:        y2 = (y1 + h);
28:    }
29:
30:    void printRect() {
31:        System.out.print("MyRect: <" + x1 + "," + y1);
32:        System.out.println(" , " + x2 + "," + y2 + ">");
33:    }
34:
35:    public static void main(String args[]) {
36:        MyRect rect;
37:
38:        System.out.println("----------");
39:        System.out.println("Calling MyRect() with "
40:                            + "coordinates 25, 25, 50, 50:");
41:        rect = new MyRect(25, 25, 50, 50);
42:        rect.printRect();
43:        System.out.println("----------");
44:
45:        System.out.println("Calling MyRect() with "
46:                            + "points (10,10) and (20,20):");
47:        rect = new MyRect(new Point(10,10), new Point(20,20));
48:        rect.printRect();
49:        System.out.println("----------");
50:
51:        System.out.println("Calling myRect() with "
52:                            + "point (15,15), width 50 and "
53:                            + "height 60:");
54:        rect = new MyRect(new Point(15,15), 50, 60);
55:        rect.printRect();
56:        System.out.println("----------");
57:    }
58: }
```

There are several things to remember when converting methods to constructors:

- Remove the return type in the signature.

- Change the method name to match the class name.

- Remove the return method (for example, return this;).

OUTPUT When you compile and run this code, you get the following output:

```
- - - - - - - - - -
Calling MyRect() with coordinates 25, 25, 50, 50:
MyRect: <25,25 , 50,50>
- - - - - - - - - -
Calling MyRect() with points (10,10) and (20,20):
MyRect: <10,10 , 20,20>
- - - - - - - - - -
Calling MyRect() with point (15,15), width 50 and height 60:
MyRect: <15,15 , 65,75>
- - - - - - - - - -
```

Overriding Constructors

Technically, constructors cannot be overridden. Because they always have the same name as the current class, you have to create new constructors instead of inheriting constructors from a superclass. Much of the time, this is fine because when your class's constructor is called, any constructors with the same signature in your superclasses are also called to ensure that all inherited parts of the object are properly initialized.

However, when you're defining constructors for your own class, you might want to change how your object is initialized, not only to initialize new variables that your class adds, but also to change the contents of variables that are inherited. You do this by explicitly calling your superclass's constructors and then making the changes you require.

To call a regular method in a superclass, you use this form:

```
super.methodName(args)
```

But with constructors, you don't have a method name to call, so use this form instead:

```
super(arg1, arg2, ...);
```

Similar to using the this() method in a constructor, the super() method calls the constructor for the immediate superclass. For example, the following code shows a class called NamedPoint that extends the class java.awt.Point. The Point class has only one constructor, which takes an x and a y argument and returns a Point object. NamedPoint has an additional instance variable (a String to hold the point's name) and defines a constructor to initialize x, y, and name:

```java
import java.awt.Point;
class NamedPoint extends Point {
  String name;
  NamedPoint(int x, int y, String name) {  // constructor
    super(x, y);  // calling Point's constructor
```

```
        this.name = name;
    }
}
```

The constructor calls the `Point` class constructor, using the `super()` method, to initialize the `Point` class instance variables (x and y). Although you might just as easily initialize x and y yourself, you might not know what other things `Point` is doing to initialize itself, so it's always good form to pass constructors up the hierarchy to make sure that everything is set up correctly.

Understanding Finalizer Methods

Finalizer methods are the opposite of constructor methods. Whereas a constructor method is used to initialize an object, a finalizer method is called just before the object is garbage-collected and its memory reclaimed.

 Note   Finalizer methods are the equivalent of C++ destructors. Because Java uses garbage collection, however, class destruction is done automatically by the program. This results in Java being much easier to use because you do not have to keep track of the destruction of your classes. In addition, because it's done automatically, you do not have to worry about your classes inadvertently not being destroyed.

The Object class defines the default `finalize()` method, which does nothing. To create a finalizer method for your own classes, override the `finalize()` method using this signature:

```
protected void finalize() {...}
```

Inside the body of your `finalize()` method, include any cleanup you want to do for that object. You can also call `super.finalize()` to make use of finalizer method definitions in your class's superclasses, if necessary.

You can always call the `finalize()` method yourself at any time; it's just a plain method like any other. However, it is always implicitly called just before an object's memory allocations are freed during garbage collection. Also, you need to know that calling `finalize()` does not trigger an object to be garbage-collected; it simply causes the code in the method to be executed. Only removing all references to an object will cause it to be marked for deletion.

Finalizer methods are best used for optimizing the removal of an object—for example, by removing references to other objects, by releasing external resources that have been acquired, or for other behaviors that might make it easier for that object to be removed. In most cases, you will not need to use `finalize()` at all.

Summary

If this is your first encounter with object-oriented programming (OOP), a lot of the information today probably seemed really theoretical and somewhat overwhelming. Don't let that bother you—the further along in the book you go, and the more Java programs you create, the easier it will be to understand.

One of the biggest hurdles in OOP is not necessarily the concepts; it's the jargon. To summarize this material, here's a glossary of terms and concepts you learned today:

Class method   A function defined inside a class that operates on the class itself and can be called by the class or any of its instances.

Class variable   A variable that belongs to all the instances of a class simultaneously and whose value is stored in the class.

Class   A template for an object that contains variables and methods representing attributes and behaviors. Classes can inherit variables and methods from other classes.

Instance method   A subprogram defined inside a class that operates on instances of that class; commonly just called a *method.*

Instance variable   A variable that belongs to an individual instance and whose value is stored in the instance.

Instance   Same as an object; an instance is the concrete representation of a class.

Object   An actual instance of a class. Multiple objects that are instances of the same class have access to the same methods but often have different values for their instance variables.

Subclass   A class further down in the class hierarchy that is based on one superclass, due to single inheritance. Creating a new subclass is called *subclassing.*

Superclass   A class further up in the class hierarchy from which other classes can inherit. A superclass can have numerous subclasses.

Today, you learned a great deal about objects: how to create them, how to find out and change the values of their variables, and how to call their methods. You also learned how to convert objects into other objects or primitives, how to convert primitives into objects, and how to compare objects. With just about everything you do in your Java programs, you always end up working with objects.

You can now define methods, including the parts of a method's signature, how to return values from a method, how arguments are passed in and out of methods, and how to use the `this` keyword to refer to the current object. You learned all about the `main()` method and how it works.

Other method techniques were introduced, such as overloading, overriding, constructors, and finalizer methods. You also learned how to use the `super` keyword to reuse method functionality from a superclass, the `this()` method to call a constructor within the body of another method definition, and the `super()` method to call a superclass's constructor from within a subclass's method body.

You now have the fundamentals of how to deal with most aspects of the Java language. Tomorrow, learn about the Java language's more advanced features in putting together Java programs and working with the Java class libraries.

Q&A

Q I understand instance variables and methods, but not class variables and methods. Could you explain them in more detail?

A Almost everything you do in a Java program will be accomplished with objects. Some behaviors and attributes, however, make more sense if they are stored in the class itself rather than in the object. For example, to create a new instance of a class, you need a method that is defined for the class itself, not for the object (which doesn't yet exist). You need to call the method to create the object, but you don't have an object yet, so how can you call the method? This type of problem is solved by having class methods. Class variables, on the other hand, are often used when you have an attribute whose value you want to share with all instances of a class. Most of the time, though, you'll use instance variables and methods.

Q Is there any limit to the number of subclasses a class can have?

A Theoretically, no. However, practically speaking, there is a limit based on the computer's file system. Because the `.class` files are stored on the hard disk, you are limited to the number of files that can be stored on that hard disk. Also, the `.class` files belonging to a package are stored in a subdirectory with the same name as the package, and nested packages are stored in subdirectories of their parent packages, so you might be limited by the directory structure as well. This limitation will be covered in greater detail tomorrow.

Q What is the advantage of not having operator overloading in Java?

A The argument against operator overloading is that because the operator can be defined to mean anything, it is sometimes difficult to figure out exactly what it *does* mean in any particular context. This makes the code more prone to error and less maintainable. Java was designed to be simple and more robust than languages that have operator overloading, so this feature was not implemented.

Q I tried creating a constant variable inside a method, and I got a compiler error. What did I do wrong?

A The problem is that you cannot create a constant local variable; only class or instance variables can be created as constants using the `final` keyword.

Q I created two methods with the following signatures:

```
int total(int arg1, int arg2, int arg3) {...}
float total(int arg1, int arg2, int arg3) {...}
```

The Java compiler complains about "duplicate definition" when I try to compile the class, but their signatures are different. What have I done wrong?

A. For purposes of overloading, Java does not consider the return type as part of the method signature, so the compiler complains that the signatures are the same if that is the only difference (which in this case, it is). Overloading works only if the argument list is different (either in number, in type, or both). Because the return type would not be known until after Java decided which method to execute at runtime, it considers the return type irrelevant in determining whether the method is overloaded.

Q Can I overload overridden methods? That is, can I create methods that have the same name as an inherited method but a different parameter list?

A No reason why not! As long as the argument list varies, it doesn't matter whether the original definition of the method is in the same class or a superclass—you can overload an inherited method just the same as you can any other method.

Workshop

The Workshop provides two ways for you to affirm what you've learned in this chapter. The Quiz section poses questions to help you solidify your understanding of the material covered. You can find answers to the quiz questions in Appendix A, "Answers to Quiz Questions." The Exercises section provides you with experience in using what you have learned. Try to work through all these before continuing to the next day.

Quiz

1. Why should you avoid creating lots of custom classes to use with your applets?

2. If you don't specify a superclass, your class will inherit from what class by default?

3. True or False? Java supports multiple inheritance.

4. What do you think the following lines of code do?

```
boolean aBoolean = true;
Boolean boolObject = new Boolean(aBoolean);
```

5. When a class takes advantage of method overloading and contains several methods with the same name, what determines which one will be used when you call the method?

6. What keyword is used when declaring a class variable?

7. What do this and super refer to?

8. What is the purpose of these methods: this() and super()?

Exercises

1. Modify the program in Listing 3.6 so that when you change pt1, you don't change pt2. Name the new program RefTest2.java, and confirm that when it runs, it produces this output:

    OUTPUT
    ```
    Point1: 200, 200
    Point2: 100, 100
    ```

2. Figure out what's wrong with the following LunchTime constructor, and then see whether you can fix it so that it works properly.

```
void LunchTime(String n, String f, int a) {  // constructor
  name = n;
  food = f;
  age = a;
  return this;
}
```

DAY 4

Java Advanced

The larger your program becomes, and the more you reuse your classes for new projects, the more you'll want some sort of control over their visibility. One of the solutions to this problem that you can use within a class is modifiers.

Another large-scale solution is packages, which, along with interfaces, help you implement and design groups of classes and class behavior.

Today, you'll learn how to create and use the following things:

- Protection for class variables and methods, constant variables, classes that cannot be subclassed, and methods that cannot be overridden
- The abstract modifier for classes and methods
- How to organize methods and classes when designing Java programs
- How to implement your design using packages and interfaces

Using Modifiers

After you've been programming in Java for a while, you'll discover that making all your classes, methods, and variables public can become quite annoying.

Besides, one of the main goals of OOP is encapsulation, or information-hiding. However, `public` has various sibling keywords that can help you protect your classes and their members, called modifiers.

NEW TERM *Modifiers* are keywords that can be applied in various combinations to the methods and variables within a class and, in the case of some modifiers, to the class itself.

There is a long and varied list of modifiers. The order of modifiers is irrelevant to their meaning—your order can vary and is really a matter of taste. Pick a style and then be consistent with it throughout all your classes. Here is the recommended (canonical) order:

`<access> abstract static final <unusual> native synchronized interface`

Here, `<access>` can be `public`, `private`, or `protected`, and `<unusual>` can be `transient` or `volatile`.

All the modifiers are optional; no modifiers are required in a declaration. You'll want to add as many as are necessary to describe the intended use and restrictions on what you're declaring. In some special situations (inside an interface, for example), certain modifiers are implicitly defined for you, and you needn't type them in—they are assumed to be there. For example, if you don't type an `<access>` modifier, Java assumes that you want the default, which is access from within the same package that the element is a part of (package-level access) and for which there is no keyword.

A few of these modifiers are advanced topics: `transient`, `volatile`, `synchronized`, and `native`. However, for the sake of completeness, here is a brief description of each. The `transient` modifier is used to declare a variable to be outside the persistent part of an object. This makes persistent object storage systems easier to implement in Java. The `volatile` and `synchronized` modifiers have to do with multithreading. The `native` modifier specifies that a method is implemented in the native language of your computer (for example, compiled C, C++, or Pascal) rather than in Java. Again, you don't need to know these modifiers to follow the rest of today's lesson, so don't be concerned if their meaning is not totally clear to you.

The `interface` modifier, as you would expect, is used to indicate classes that are interfaces. You'll learn more about interfaces later today. In this section, you'll take a closer look at the `<access>` modifiers `public`, `private`, `protected`, `abstract`, `static`, and `final`.

Controlling Access to Methods and Variables

Access control is about controlling visibility. When a method or variable is visible to another class, its methods can reference (call or modify) that class member.

NEW TERM   A *class member* is a method or variable of the class.

To protect a class or class member from such references, you use the levels of visibility described in the next subsections. Each, in turn, is more restrictive and thus provides more protection than the one before it.

Learning how to use the protection modifiers comes down to understanding the fundamental relationships a method or variable within a class can have to other classes and subclasses in the system.

public

Because any class is an island unto itself, the first of these relationships builds on the distinction between the inside and the outside of a class. Any method or variable is visible to the class in which it is defined, but what if you want to make it visible to all the classes outside this class?

The answer is fairly obvious: simply declare the class member to have `public` access. Almost every class member defined this week will be declared, for simplicity's sake, to be `public`. When you use any of the examples provided in your own code, you'll probably decide to restrict this access somewhat. While you're learning though, it's not a bad idea to begin with the widest possible access you can use (package-level access or `public`) and then narrow it as you gain more experience. Soon, it will become second nature for you to know what access your class members should have when you declare them. Here are some examples of `public` declarations:

```
public class APublicClass {
  public int aPublicInt;
  public String aPublicString;
  public float aPublicMethod;() {
    ...
  }
}
```

A class or class member with `public` access has the widest possible visibility. Anyone can see it; anyone can use it.

Package-Level Access (Default)

In some languages, there is the notion of hiding a class or class member so that only the functions within a given source file can see it. In Java, this notion is replaced by the more explicit idea of packages, which can group classes; you'll learn about these in the "Using Packages" section of this chapter. For now, you need to know how to support the relationship of a class to its sibling classes that implement one piece of a system, library, or program. This defines the next level of increased protection and narrowed visibility.

Due to an idiosyncrasy of the Java language, this level of access has no keyword associated with it. Although Java does have a package keyword, it is not used in this context; rather, it is used to designate whether a class is a member of a package. The package level of access is indicated by the lack of any access modifier in a declaration and is therefore thought of as the default access level. Historically, it has been called "friendly" and "package." The latter term seems most appropriate and is the one used here, so it's known as package-level access.

Note

Why would anyone want to make more typing for themselves and desire to explicitly declare a method or variable with package-level access? It's mainly for consistency and clarity. If you have a pattern of declarations with varying access modifier prefixes, you might always want the modifier to be stated explicitly, both for the reader's benefit and because, in some contexts, you want the compiler to notice your intentions and warn you of any conflicts.

Tip

If you would prefer to explicitly label the package level of protection, consider using a comment at the beginning of the line of code. For example:

```
/* package-level */ float aPackageMethod() {...}
```

Most of the declarations you've seen so far have used this default level of protection. Here's an example of how this works:

```
public class ALessPublicClass {
  int aPackage Int = 2;
  String aPackageString = "a 1 and a ";
  float aPackageMethod() {  // no access modifier means package-level
                            // access
  ...
  }
}
public class AClassInTheSamePackage {
  public void testUse() {
    ALessPublicClass aLPC = new ALessPublicClass();
    System.out.println(aLPC.aPackageString + aLPC.aPackageInt);
    aLPC.aPackageMethod();  // all these references are okay
  }
}
```

If a class from any other package tried to access aLPC the way that AClassInTheSamePackage does in this example, it would generate compile-time errors.

Why was package made a default? When you're designing a large system and you partition your classes into workgroups to implement smaller pieces of that system, the classes often need to share a lot more with one another than with the outside world. The need for this level of sharing is common enough that it was made the default level of protection.

Another interesting feature of this level of protection is that any subclasses that are declared in other packages cannot access or inherit class members that have this level of protection in the superclass. Only subclasses in the same package as their superclass can access or inherit these class members.

protected

This level of protection can be applied only to class members, not classes. Other classes must be content with the public face that the protected class presents. To support the level of intimacy reserved for subclasses, modern programming languages have invented an intermediate level of access narrower than the previous two levels but more open than full privacy. This level gives more protection and less visibility to the rest of the world.

When a class member is declared to be protected, it is accessible to classes in the same package, accessible and inheritable by subclasses in the same package, and can be inherited by subclasses declared in other packages. However, the protected class's members cannot be accessed by anything in another package, even its own subclass.

What if you have some details of your implementation that you don't want to share even with sibling classes of the same package, but you still want your subclasses to be able to inherit? The answer to this question leads you to the next level of protection, private protected.

private protected

The relationship between a superclass and its present and future subclasses is even more restricted by this next level of access. Classes cannot be declared private protected; only class members can be given this level of protection. No other class can access a private protected class member, not even subclasses in the same package. The only visibility provided at this level is that subclasses are allowed to inherit these class members, regardless of whether the subclass is declared inside or outside the package. The following code presents three classes; two are created from scratch and one is extended from another class:

```
public class AProtectedClass {
  private protected int aProtectedInt = 4;
  private protected String aProtectedString = "and a 3 and a ";
```

4

```
  privte protected float aProtectedMethod() {
    ...
  }
}
public class AProtectedClassSubclass extends AProtectedClass {
  public void testUse() {
    AProtectedClassSubclass aPCS = new AProtectedClassSubclass();
    System.out.println(aPCS.aProtectedString + aPCS.aProtectedInt);
    aPCS.aProtectedMethod();  // all of these references are okay
  }
}
public class AnyClassInTheSamePackage {
  public void testUse() {
    AProtectedClassSubclass aPCS = new AProtectedClassSubclass();
    System.out.println(aPCS.aProtectedString + aPCS.aProtectedInt);
    aPCS.aProtectedMethod();  // these references are invalid
  }
}
```

Even though `AnyClassInTheSamePackage` is in the same package as `AProtectedClass`, it is not a subclass of it (by default, it's a subclass of `Object`). Remember, only subclasses are allowed to inherit `private protected` class members.

private

The most restrictive of these relationships is represented by the modifier `private`. This is the most narrowly visible, highest level of protection you can get—the diametric opposite of `public`. Class members that are declared to be `private` cannot be accessed by any other class or even inherited by a subclass; they can be used only by the class within which they are defined.

```
public class APrivate Class {
  private int aPrivateInt;
  private String aPrivateString;
  private float aPrivateMethod(); {
    ...
  }
}
```

This might seem extremely restrictive, but it is actually a commonly used level of protection. Any private data, internal state, or representations unique to your implementation—anything that shouldn't be directly shared with subclasses—should be `private`. Remember that an object's primary job is to encapsulate its data, to hide it from the world's sight and limit its manipulation. The best way to do that is to make as much data as private as possible. Your methods always can be less restrictive, as you'll see a bit later, but keeping a tight rein on your internal representation is important. This approach does the following:

- Separates design from implementation
- Minimizes the amount of information one class needs to know about another to get its job done
- Reduces the extent of code changes generated when your representation changes

Understanding Instance Variable Access Conventions

A good rule of thumb is that unless an instance variable is constant, it should almost certainly be `private`. If you don't do this, you have the following problem:

```java
public class AFoolishClass {
  public String aUsefulString;
  aUsefulString = "something really useful";
}
```

This class might have been intended to set up `aUsefulString` for the use of other classes, with the expectation that they would only read it. Because this class isn't `private`, however, the other classes can say this:

```java
AFoolishClass aFC = new AFoolishClass();
aFC.aUsefulString = "oops!";
```

Because there is no way to specify separately the level of protection for reading from and writing to instance variables, they should almost always be `private`.

Note

> The careful reader will notice that this rule is violated in many examples in this book. Most of these violations are for pedagogical reasons, to increase the clarity of the examples and to keep them short. (You'll soon see that it takes more space to do the right thing.)
>
> One use cannot be avoided: the `System.out.print()` and `System.out.println()` calls scattered throughout the book must use the `public out` variable directly. You cannot change this system class (which you might have written differently). You can imagine the disastrous results if anyone accidentally modified the contents of this global `public` variable!

If instance variables are private, how can you give the outside world access to them? The answer is to write accessor methods. Using methods to control access to an instance variable is one of the most frequently used idioms in object-oriented programs. Applying it liberally throughout all your classes repays you numerous times over with more robust and reusable programs. Here's a simple example that shows how this can be accomplished:

```java
public class ACorrectClass {
```

```
private String aUsefulString;

public String getAUsefulString() {
  return aUsefulString;
}

private protected void setAUsefulString(String aStr) {
  aUsefulString = aStr;
}
}
```

Notice how separating the reading and writing of the instance variable (using getAUsefulString() and setAUsefulString(), respectively) enables you to specify a public method to return its value (making it read-only to the outside world) and a private protected method to set it (making it read-write within the class). This is often a useful pattern of protections because everyone probably needs to be able to ask for the value, but only you (or your subclasses) should be able to change it. If it is a particularly secret piece of data, you could make its set method private and its get method protected or any other combination that suits the data's sensitivity to the light of the outside world.

Note The Java software component model, JavaBeans, defines properties as private data that must be accessed only through accessor methods—that is, through public set and get methods.

Whenever you want to append to your own instance variable, try writing this:

```
setAUsefulString(getAUsefulString() + " some appended text");
```

In this example, you're using accessor methods to change aUsefulString in the same way as if you were accessing it from outside the class. Why do this? You protected the variable in the first place so that changes to your representation would not affect the use of your class by others. You should take advantage of that same protection. That way, if you need to change the representation of aUsefulString, you will not need to individually update every use of that variable in your class (as you would if you didn't use the accessor methods); rather, the change affects only the implementations of the variable's accessor methods.

One of the powerful side effects of maintaining this level of indirection in accessing your own instance variables is that if, at some later date, some special code needs to be performed each time aUsefulString is accessed, you can put that code in one place, and all other methods in your class (and in other classes) will correctly call that special code.

Here's an example:

```
private protected void setAUsefulString(String aStr) {
  aUsefulString = aStr;
  performSomeImportantBookkeeping();
}
```

It might seem like more trouble to call the accessor method rather than using the instance variable directly in your code, but the minor inconvenience will reward you with future reusability and easier maintenance.

Protecting Class Variables and Methods

What if you want to create a shared variable that all your instances can see and use? If you use an instance variable, each instance has its own copy of the variable, defeating your whole purpose. If you place it in the class itself, however, only one copy exists, and all the instances of the class share it. This is called a *class variable*.

NEW TERM   A *class variable* is one that belongs to all the instances of a class simultaneously and whose value is stored in the class itself.

Here's an example:

```
public class Circle {
  public static float pi =   3.14159265359F
  public float area (float r) {
    return pi * r * r;
  }
}
```

4

Instances can refer to their own class variables as though they were instance variables, as in the preceding example. Because pi is declared public, methods in other classes can also refer to pi:

```
float circumference = 2 * Circle.pi * r;
```

Note

> Instances of a class can also use the form *instanceName.classVarName* to access a class variable. However, in most cases, the form *className.classVarName* is preferred because it clearly indicates that this is a class variable. It also helps the reader to know instantly that the variable referenced is global to all instances.

Class methods are defined analogously. They can be accessed in the same two ways by instances of their class, but other classes can access them only by their full class name (which is the preferred reference style). Here's a class that defines class methods to help it count its own instances:

```
public class InstanceCounter {
  private static int instanceCount = 0;    // a class variable

  private protected static int getInstanceCount() {
    return instanceCount;                        // a class method
  }

  private static void incrementCount() {  // a class method
    ++instanceCount;
  }

  InstanceCounter() {  // the class constructor
    InstanceCounter.incrementCount();
  }
}
```

In this example, an explicit use of the class name calls the method `incrementCount()`. Although this might seem verbose, in a larger program, it immediately tells the reader which object (the class, rather than the instance) is expected to handle the method. This is especially useful if the reader needs to find where that method is declared in a large class that places all its class methods at the top (the recommended practice, by the way).

Note the initialization of `instanceCount` to `0`. Just as an instance variable is initialized when its instance is created at runtime, a class variable is initialized when its class is created at compile-time. This class initialization happens before anything else can happen to that class, or its instances, so the class in the example will work as planned.

Finally, the conventions you learned for accessing an instance variable are applied in this example to access a class variable. The accessor methods are therefore class methods. (There is no set method here, only a get method and an increment method because no one is allowed to set `instanceCount` directly.) Note also that only subclasses are allowed to ask what the `instanceCount` is because it is considered a relatively intimate detail. Here's a test of `InstanceCounter` in action:

```
public class InstanceCounterTester extends InstanceCounter {
  public static void main(String args[]) {
    for (int i = 0; i < 10; ++1)
      new InstanceCounter();
    System.out.println("made" + InstanceCounter.getInstanceCount());
  }
}
```

Not surprisingly, this example prints the following output:

```
made 10
```

Using the `final` Modifier

Although it's not the last modifier to be discussed, the `final` modifier is very versatile and has several effects:

- When the `final` modifier is applied to a class, it means that the class cannot be subclassed.
- When applied to a variable, it means that the variable is a constant.
- When applied to a method, it means that the method cannot be overridden by sub-class methods.

Each of these possibilities is discussed in the following sections.

`final` Classes

Here's what a `final` class declaration looks like:

```
public final class AFinalClass {...}
```

You declare a class `final` for one of two reasons. The first reason is security. You expect to use its instances as unforgeable capabilities, and you don't want anyone else to be able to subclass and create new and different instances of the class. The second reason is efficiency. You want to count on instances of only that one class (and no subclasses) being present in the system so that you can optimize the class.

Note

> The Java class library uses final classes extensively. Some examples of the first reason (security) to use `final` are the classes `java.lang.System`, `java.net.InetAddress`, and `java.net.Socket`. A good example of the second reason (efficiency) is `java.lang.String`. Strings are so common in Java, and so central to it, that the runtime handles them specially.

You'll rarely need to create a `final` class yourself, although you'll have plenty of opportunity to be annoyed at certain system classes being final (thus making extending them rather difficult). Oh well, such is the price of security and efficiency.

`final` Variables

To declare constants in Java, use `final` variables:

```
public class AnotherFinalClass {
  public static final int aConstantInt = 123;
  public final String aConstantString = "Hello Java Enthusiasts!";
}
```

Note that the first constant is a public class constant (indicated by the `static` modifier), and the second is simply a public constant.

The `final` class and instance variables can be used in expressions just like normal class and instance variables, but they cannot be modified. Therefore, `final` variables must be given their (constant) value at the time of declaration, as in the preceding example. Classes can provide useful constants to other classes by using class variables, such as `aConstantInt` in the preceding example. Other classes reference them just as before: `AnotherFinalClass.aConstantInt`.

Local variables (those inside blocks of code surrounded by braces—for example, in `while` or `for` loops) can't be declared `final`. In fact, local variables can have no modifiers in front of them at all:

```
{
  int aLocalVariable;  // I'm so lonely without my modifiers...
  ...
}
```

`final` Methods

Here's an example of using the `final` methods:

```
public class MyPenultimateFinalClass {
  public static final void aClassMethodThatCannotBeOverridden() {
    ...
  }

  public final void aRegularMethodThatCannotBeOverridden() {
    ...
  }
}
```

These `final` methods cannot be overridden by subclasses. It is a rare thing that a method truly wants to be the last word on its own implementation, so why does this modifier apply to methods?

The answer is efficiency. If you declare a method `final`, the compiler can then "inline" it right in the middle of methods that call it because it knows that no one else can ever subclass and override the method to change its meaning. Although you might not use `final` right away when first writing a class, you might discover as you tune the system later that a few methods must be made `final` to make your class fast enough. Almost all your methods will be fine, however, just as they are.

The Java class library declares a lot of commonly used methods `final` so that you'll benefit from the speed increase, which is essential for this partly compiled, partly interpreted language. In the case of classes that are already `final`, this makes perfect sense.

The few `final` methods declared in non-`final` classes will no doubt annoy you—your subclasses cannot override them. When efficiency becomes less of an issue for the Java environment, many of these `final` methods might be made non-`final`, restoring flexibility to the system.

> **Note**
>
> Methods declared `private` are effectively `final` because they cannot be overridden in a subclass. So are all methods declared in a `final` class because such a class cannot be subclassed. Marking these methods `final` (as the Java library sometimes does) is legal, but redundant; the compiler already treats them as `final`.
>
> It's possible to use `final` methods for some of the same security reasons you would use `final` classes, but it's a much rarer event.

If you use accessor methods a lot (as recommended) and are worried about efficiency, take a look at this much faster rewrite of `ACorrectClass`:

```java
public class ACorrectFinalClass {
  private String aUsefulString;

  public final String getAUsefulString() {
    return aUsefulString;              // now faster to use
  }

  private protected final void setAUsefulString(String aStr) {
    aUsefulString = aStr;              // also faster now
  }
}
```

It might be that future implementations of Java will be smart enough to automatically inline simple methods, but for now, using the `final` keyword does the trick.

Using `abstract` Methods and Classes

Whenever you arrange classes into an inheritance hierarchy, the presumption is that higher-level classes are more abstract and general, whereas lower-level subclasses are more concrete and specific. Often, as you design a set of classes, you factor out common design and implementation into a shared superclass. If the primary reason that a superclass exists is to act as a common, shared repository, and if only its subclasses expect to be used directly, that superclass is called an `abstract` class.

Classes that are `abstract` cannot create instances, but they can contain anything a normal class can contain and, in addition, are allowed to prefix any of their methods with the `abstract` modifier. Non-`abstract` classes are not allowed to use this modifier for their class members; using it on even one of your methods would require you to declare the whole class abstract. Here's an example:

```
public abstract class MyFirstAbstractClass {
  int anInstanceVariable;

  public abstract int aMethodNonAbstractSubclassesMustImplement();

  public void doSomething() {
    ...    // a normal method
  }
}

public class AConcreteSubclass extends MyFirstAbstractClass {
  public int aMethodNonAbstractSubclassesMustImplement(); {
    ...
    /* this subclass *must* implement this method for
       it to be of any use to us in this subclass */
    ...
  }
}
```

Here are two attempted uses of these classes:

```
Object a = new MyFirstAbstractClass();  // illegal, abstract class

Object c = new AConcreteSubclass();     // legal, a concrete class
```

Notice that abstract methods need no implementation; it is required that non-abstract subclasses provide an implementation. The abstract class simply provides the template (by defining the method signature) for the methods that are implemented by other subclasses later. In fact, in the Java class library, several abstract classes have no documented subclasses in the system but simply provide a base from which you can subclass in your own programs. Interface classes are a good example of this.

Using an abstract class to embody a pure design—that is, nothing but abstract methods—is better accomplished in Java by using an interface. Whenever a design calls for an abstraction that includes instance variables or a partial implementation, however, an abstract class is your only choice. In previous object-oriented languages, abstract classes were just a convention. They proved so valuable that Java supports them not only in the form described here, but also in the purer, richer form of interfaces, as you'll see later today.

Using Packages

Packages are a way of relating certain classes and interfaces so that they can be referred to and imported as a group.

NEW TERM A *package* is a collection of related classes and interfaces.

Grouping classes and interfaces into packages also eliminates potential class name conflicts, and you can use package names to fully qualify a class name so that there is no doubt to which class you are referring. Packages can comprise multiple source code files as long as each contains the package's name. Packages also help govern access and protection, as you learned earlier today.

Packages can be nested within other packages, further organizing the classes within. For example, the fully qualified class name java.awt.Color indicates that the class named Color is contained within the awt (Abstract Windowing Toolkit) package, which itself is contained in the java package.

The classes in the JDK are contained in a package named java. This package is guaranteed to be available in any Java implementation, and its classes are the only ones guaranteed to be available across different implementations. Classes in other packages (such as sun or netscape) might be available only in specific implementations.

Your Java classes have default access only to the classes in java.lang (the basic Java language package). To have access to classes and interfaces in any other packages, you need to refer to them explicitly by package name or import them in your source code.

To give your program access to a JDK package, use the import keyword and the fully qualified class name. For example, to import the java.awt.Color class into your program, use the following syntax:

```
import java.awt.Color;
```

You can also import an entire package by substituting an asterisk (*) in place of a specific class name. For example, to import the entire java.awt package, use this syntax:

```
import java.awt.*;
```

Packages are Java's way of doing large-scale design and organization. They are used both to categorize and group classes. Let's explore why you might need to use packages in your own Java programs.

Designing Packages

When you begin to develop Java programs that use a large number of classes, you will quickly discover some limitations in the model presented thus far for designing and building them.

For one thing, as the number of classes you build increases, the likelihood of your wanting to reuse the short, simple name of some class increases. If you have classes that you've built in the past or that someone else has built for you (such as the classes in the Java library), you might not remember—or even know—that these class names are in conflict. Being able to "hide" a class inside a package becomes useful.

Here's a simple example of creating a package in a Java source file:

```
package myFirstPackage;
public class MyPublicClass extends ItsSuperclass {...}
```

Note

> If a `package` statement appears in a Java source file, it must be the first thing in that file (except for comments and whitespace, of course).

You first declare the name of the package by using a `package` statement, then you define a class, just as you would normally. That class, and any other classes also declared with this same package name, are grouped together. (These other classes usually are located in other separate source files, each with an identical `package` statement at the top.)

Packages can be organized further into a hierarchy somewhat analogous to the inheritance hierarchy, where each level usually represents a smaller, more specific grouping of classes. The Java class library itself is organized along these lines. The top level is called `java`; the next level includes names such as `io`, `net`, `util`, and `awt`. The last of these, `image`, is at an even lower level. The `ColorModel` class, located in the `java.awt.image` package, can be uniquely referred to anywhere in your Java code as `java.awt.image.ColorModel`.

Note

> By current convention, the first level of the hierarchy specifies the globally unique name of the company that developed the Java package or packages. For example, Sun Microsystems's classes, which are not part of the standard Java environment, all begin with the prefix `sun`, and Borland's classes begin with the prefix `borland`. The standard package, `java`, is an exception because it is so fundamental and because it might someday be implemented by multiple companies.
>
> Sun has proposed a more formal procedure for package naming to be followed in the future, reserving the top-level package name for the top-level domains of the Internet in all uppercase (`EDU`, `COM`, `GOV`, `ORG`, `FR`, `US`, `RU`, and so on). These are then to be followed by the Internet domain name. By this procedure, the Sun packages would be prefixed with `COM.sun` and the Borland packages with `COM.borland`. (Note, however, that neither Sun nor Borland is currently following this proposed procedure.)

> The idea is to keep adding segments to the package name as you go further down the company's internal organizational hierarchy, such as `EDU.harvard.cs.projects.ai.myPackage`. Because domain names already are guaranteed to be unique globally, this technique nicely solves a thorny problem, and as a bonus, the applets and packages from the potentially millions of Java programmers out there would be stored automatically into a growing hierarchy below your classes directory, giving you a way to find and categorize them all in a comprehensible manner.

Because each Java class usually is located in a separate source file, the grouping of classes provided by a hierarchy of packages is analogous to the grouping of files into a hierarchy of directories on your file system. The Java compiler reinforces this analogy by requiring you to create a directory hierarchy under your `jbuilder2\myclasses` directory that exactly matches the hierarchy of the packages you have created and to place a class into the directory with the same name and level as the package in which it's defined.

The directory hierarchy for the Java class library is made compact by compressing them all into a single zip file called `classes.zip`. For example, the class referenced as `java.awt.image.ColorModel` is found as the file named `ColorModel.class` in the `classes.zip` file in the `jbuilder2\java\lib` subdirectory. If you examine `classes.zip` using WinZip or another similar program, you will see that the path listed for `ColorModel.class` is `\java\awt\image` (see Figure 4.1), which mirrors its package name.

4

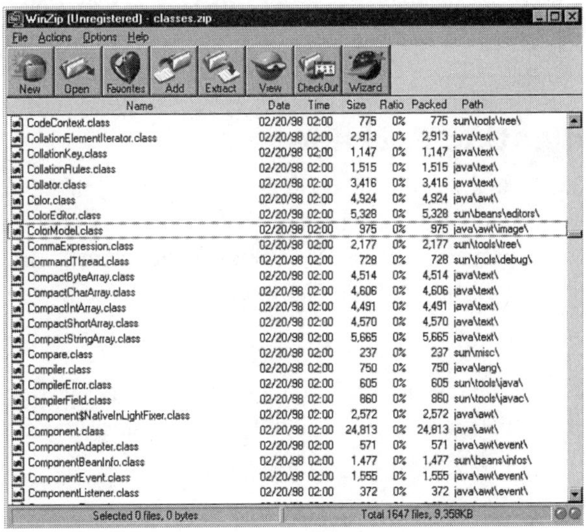

FIGURE 4.1.

The `classes.zip` *file contains compressed Java class files and the directory structures mirroring their package names.*

If you have created a package within `myFirstPackage` called `mySecondPackage`, by declaring a class like

```
package myFirstPackage.mySecondPackage;
public class AnotherPublicClass extends AnotherSuperclass {...}
```

the Java source file (called `AnotherPublicClass.java`) must be located in the JBuilder subdirectory named `myprojects\myFirstPackage\mySecondPackage`. When you compile the file, `AnotherPublicClass.class` is placed in JBuilder's `myclasses\myFirstPackage\mySecondPackage` subdirectory so that the Java Virtual Machine can find it.

Today's first example, `APublicClass.java` would have been placed in `myprojects\myFirstPackage`, and the `APublicClass.class` file would have been placed in the `myclasses\myFirstPackage` subdirectory. Both Java-based compilers and interpreters expect and enforce the hierarchy. But what happens when, as in earlier examples in the book, classes are defined without a `package` statement?

If there is no explicit package statement in the class source file, the compiler places them in a default, unnamed package, and their `.java` and `.class` files can be located at the top level of JBuilder's `myprojects` and `myclasses` subdirectories, respectively.

 Tip

> You can customize the source and output root directories for each JBuilder project. To do this, select File I Project Properties. When the `ProjectName.jpr` Properties dialog appears, display its Paths page by clicking on the Paths tab. Add the preferred path to your source files in the Source root directory text box, and add the preferred path to your output files in the Output root directory text box. Click the OK button, and your changes take effect.

Implementing Packages

When you refer to a class by name in your Java code, you are using a package. Most of the time, you aren't aware of it because many of the most commonly used classes in the system are in a package that the Java compiler automatically imports for you, the `java.lang` package. So, for example, whenever you saw

```
String aString;
```

something more interesting than you might have thought was occurring. What if you want to refer to the class you created at the start of this section, the one in the package `myFirstPackage`? If you try

```
MyPublicClass someName;
```

the compiler will complain. The class `MyPublicClass` is not defined in the package `java.lang`. To solve this problem, Java allows any class name to be prefixed by the name of the package in which it is defined to form a unique fully qualified reference to the class:

```
myFirstPackage.MyPublicClass someName;
```

Note

> By convention, package names begin with a lowercase letter to distinguish them easily from class names in fully qualified class references. For example, in the fully qualified name of the built-in `String` class, `java.lang.String`, it's easier to visually separate the package name from the class name because of this convention. Also, because of Java's case-sensitivity, this helps to reduce potential name conflicts between package names and class names.

Suppose you want to use a lot of classes from a package, a package with a long name, or both. You certainly wouldn't want to refer to your class as `that.really.long.package.name.ClassName` every time you use it. So Java allows you to import the names of those classes into your program for your convenience. These classes then act just as `java.lang` classes do, and you can refer to them without using their fully qualified names. For example, to use that really long class name more easily, you can do the following:

```
import that.really.long.package.name.ClassName;

ClassName anObject;   // that's much better!
```

Now you can use `ClassName` directly as many times as you like. All `import` statements must appear after any `package` statement but before any class definitions, so they will always near the top of your source code file.

What if you want to use several classes from that same package? Here's an attempt from a soon-to-be-tired-of-typing programmer:

```
that.really.long.package.name.ClassOne first;
that.really.long.package.name.ClassTwo second;
that.really.long.package.name.ClassThree andSoOn;
```

Here's one from a more savvy programmer who knows how to import a whole package of `public` classes:

```
import that.really.long.package.name.*;

ClassOne first;
ClassTwo second;
ClassThree andSoOn;
```

4

Note

> The asterisk (*) does not import all the subpackages of the specified package. For example, `import java.awt.*` imports all the `public` classes from the `java.awt` package, such as `java.awt.Font` and `java.awt.Graphics`. However, it does *not* import the `java.awt.image` or `java.awt.peer` subpackages (or their `public` classes, for that matter).
>
> To import all the `public` classes of a package and its subpackages, you must write a separate `import` statement for each package and subpackage at each level of the package's hierarchy.

If you plan to use a class or a package only a few times in your source file, it probably is not worth importing it. The question to ask yourself is, "Does the need for clarity outweigh the convenience of having fewer characters to type?" If it does, don't use `import`; use the fully qualified class name instead. Remember that the fully qualified class name includes the package name, which lets the programmer immediately know where to find more information about that class, rather than having to hunt down the `import` statement. Also, if there are a number of `import` statements, it will be unclear to which imported package the shortened class name belongs.

What if you have the following in `ClassA`'s source file?

```
package Motorcycle;
public class startEngine {...}
public class ClassA {...}
```

And in `ClassB`'s source file you have this:

```
package Car;
public class startEngine {...}
public class ClassB {...}
```

Then you write the following lines somewhere else:

```
import Motorcycle.*;
import Car.*;

startEngine YamahaObject;          // compiler error
startEngine CrownVictoriaObject;   // me too
```

You might be asking yourself, *Which* `startEngine` *did you mean?* as well you should. There are two possible interpretations for the class you intended; one in `Motorcycle` and one in `Car`. Because this is totally ambiguous, what is a poor compiler to do? It generates a compiler error, of course, and you have to be more explicit about which one you intended. Here's an example that resolves the problem:

```
import Motorcycle.*;
import Car.*;

Motorcycle.startEngine YamahaObject;    // corrected
Car.startEngine CrownVictoriaObject;    // corrected
```

Note

> You might be wondering about the numerous declarations that appear as examples in today's lesson. Declarations are good examples because they're the simplest possible way of referencing a class name. Any use of a class name—in your extends clause or in new startEngine(), for example—will obey these same rules.

Hiding Classes

The astute reader might have noticed that the discussion of importing with an asterisk (*) stated that it imported a whole package of public classes. Why would you want to import classes of any other kind? Take a look at this:

```
package collections;

public class LinkedList {
  private Node root;

  public void add(Object o) {
    root = new Node(o, root);
  }
  ...
}

class Node {
  private Object contents;
  private Node next;
  Node(Object o, Node n) {
    contents = o;
    next = n;
  }
  ...
}
```

If this were all in one file, you would be violating one of the compiler's conventions: only one class should be located in each Java source code file. (In fact, that is how it decides what to name the .class file.) Actually, the compiler cares only about every public class being in a separate file, although it's still good style to use separate files for each and every class.

The goal of the `LinkedList` class is to provide a set of useful `public` methods (such as the `add()` method) to any other classes that might want to use them. It is irrelevant to the other classes if `LinkedList` uses any other supporting classes to get its job done. In addition, `LinkedList` might feel that the `Node` class is local to its implementation and should not be seen by any other classes.

For methods and variables, this would be addressed by the protection modifiers discussed earlier today: `private`, `protected private`, `protected`, package (default), and `public`. You already have explored many `public` classes, and because both `private` and `protected` really make sense only when you're inside a class definition, you cannot put them outside of one as part of defining a new class. `LinkedList` might need to be visible only to its source file, but because each class is located in a separate source file by convention, this would be an overly narrow approach.

Instead, `LinkedList` declares no protection modifier, which gives it the same privileges as if it were declared as `package`. Now the class can be seen and used only by other classes in the same package in which it was defined. In this case, it's the `collections` package. You might use `LinkedList` as shown here:

```
import collections.*;  // only imports public classes

LinkedList aLinkedList;
/* Node n; */  // would generate a compile-time error

aLinkedList.add("THX-");
aLinkedList.add(new Integer(1138));
...
```

You can also import or declare an instance of `aLinkedList` using `collections.LinkedList`. Because the `public` class `LinkedList` refers to the `package` class `Node`, that class is automatically loaded and used, and the compiler verifies that `LinkedList` (as part of the `collections` package) has the right to create and use the `Node` class. However, you still would not have that right, as demonstrated in the preceding example.

One of the great powers of hidden classes is that even if you use them to introduce a great deal of complexity into the implementation of a `public` class, all the complexity is hidden when that class is imported or used. Thus, creating a good package consists of defining a small, clean set of `public` classes and methods for other classes to use and then implementing them by using any number of hidden (`package`) support classes.

You'll see another use for hidden classes later today in the "Implementing Interfaces" section. For now, let's leave them behind and look into interfaces.

Using Interfaces

Remember that Java classes have only a single superclass and that they inherit variables and methods from that superclass and all its superclasses. Although single inheritance makes the relationship between classes and the functionality that those classes implement easier to understand and to design, it can also be somewhat restricting. This is especially true when you have similar behavior that needs to be duplicated across different branches of the class hierarchy. Java solves this problem of shared behavior by introducing the concept of interfaces.

NEW TERM   An *interface* is a collection of method declarations without actual implementations.

Although a single Java class can have only one superclass due to single inheritance, that class can implement any number of interfaces. In implementing an interface, a class provides method implementations (definitions) for the method signatures declared in the interface. If two disparate classes implement the same interface, they both can respond to the same method calls as declared in that interface, although what each class actually does in response to those method calls might be very different.

Interfaces, like the abstract classes and methods you saw earlier today, provide templates of behavior that other classes are expected to implement, but interfaces are much more powerful than abstract classes. Let's see why you might need such power.

4

Designing Interfaces

When you first begin to design object-oriented programs, the class hierarchy seems almost miraculous. Within that single tree, you can express a hierarchy of numeric types (number, complex, float, rational, integer), many simple-to-moderately-complex relationships between objects and processes, and any number of points along the axis from abstract and general to concrete and specific. After some deeper thought, or more complex design experience, this wonderful tree begins to feel restrictive—at times, like a straitjacket. The very power and discipline you've achieved by carefully placing only one copy of each idea somewhere in the tree can come back to haunt you whenever you need to cross-fertilize disparate parts of that tree.

Some languages address these problems by introducing more flexible runtime power, such as the code block and the `perform:` method of Smalltalk; others choose to provide more complex inheritance hierarchies, such as multiple inheritance. With the latter complexity comes a host of confusing and error-prone ambiguities and misunderstandings, and with the former come a harder time implementing safety and security and a harder language to explain and teach. Java has chosen to take neither of these paths but has instead adopted a separate hierarchy altogether to gain the expressive power needed to loosen the straitjacket.

This new hierarchy is a hierarchy of interfaces. Interfaces are not limited to a single super-interface, so they allow a form of multiple inheritance. But they pass on only method descriptions to their children, not method implementations or instance variables, which helps to eliminate many of the problematic complexities of full multiple inheritance.

Interfaces, like classes, are declared in source files, one interface to a file. Like classes, they also are compiled into .class files. In fact, almost everywhere that this book has a class name in any of its examples or discussions, you can substitute an interface name. Java programmers often say "class" when they actually mean "class or interface." Interfaces complement and extend the power of classes, and the two can be treated almost exactly the same. One of the few differences between them is that an interface cannot be instantiated: new can create only an instance of a non-abstract class. Here's the declaration of an interface:

```
package myFirstPackage;

public interface MyFirstInterface extends Interface1, Interface2, ... {
    ...
    // all methods in here will be public and abstract
    // all variables will be public, static, and final
    ...
}
```

This example is a rewritten version of the first example in today's lesson. It now adds a public interface to the package myFirstPackage, rather than a public class. Note that multiple parents can be listed in an interface's extends clause.

Note   If no extends clause is given, interfaces do not default to inheriting from Object because Object is a class, and interfaces can extend only other interfaces. In fact, interfaces have no topmost interface from which they are all guaranteed to descend. Therefore, if there is no extends clause, the interface becomes a top-level interface (potentially, one of many).

Any variables or methods defined in a public interface are implicitly prefixed by the modifiers listed in the last example's comments (that is, public abstract for methods and public static final for variables). Exactly those modifiers can (optionally) appear, but no others:

```
public interface MySecondInterface {
  public static final int theAnswer = 42;                  // OK
  public abstract int lifeTheUniverseAndEverything();  // OK

  long theWordCounter = 0;  // OK, becomes public static final
  long ageOfTheUniverse();  // OK, becomes public abstract

  private protected int aConstant;  // not OK
  private int getAnInt();           // not OK
}
```

If an interface is not declared public (in other words, it is a package), no public modifiers are implicitly prefixed. If you say public inside such an interface, you're making a real statement of public-ness, not simply a redundant statement. It's not often, though, that an interface will be shared only by the classes inside a package, and not by the classes using that package as well.

Comparing Design Versus Implementation

One of the most powerful things interfaces add to Java is the capability of separating design inheritance from implementation inheritance. In the single-class inheritance tree, these two are inextricably bound. Sometimes, you want to be able to describe an interface to a class of objects abstractly, without having to implement a particular implementation of it yourself. You could create an abstract class, such as those described earlier today. For a new class to use this type of "interface," however, it has to become a subclass of the abstract class and accept its position in the tree. What if this new class also needs to be a subclass of some other class in the tree, for implementation reasons. What can be done without multiple inheritance? Watch this:

```
class FirstImplementor extends SomeClass implements MySecondInterface
{...}
```

```
class SecondImplementor implements MyFirstInterface, MySecondInterface
{...}
```

The first of these two classes is "stuck" in the single inheritance tree just below the class SomeClass but is free to implement an interface as well. The second class is stuck just below Object but has implemented two interfaces. (It could have implemented any number of them.) Implementing an interface means promising to implement all the methods specified in it.

Note

An abstract class is allowed to ignore this strict promise, and it can implement any subset of the interface's methods (or even none of them). But all its non-abstract subclasses must still obey this dictum.

Because interfaces are in a separate hierarchy, they can be mixed in with the classes in the single-inheritance tree, allowing the designer to sprinkle an interface anywhere it is needed throughout the tree. The single-inheritance tree can thus be viewed as containing only the implementation hierarchy. The design hierarchy (full of abstract methods, mostly) is contained in the interface tree.

Let's examine one simple example of this separation by creating a new class, Orange. Suppose you already have a good implementation of the class Fruit and an interface, Fruitlike, that represents what Fruit objects are expected to be able to do. You want an orange to be a fruit, but you also want it to be a spherical object that can be tossed, rotated, and so on. Here's how to express it all:

```
interface Fruitlike extends Foodlike {
  void decay();
  void squish();
  . . .
}
class Fruit extends Food implements Fruitlike {
  private Color myColor;
  private int daysTillRot;
  . . .
}
interface Spherelike {
  void toss();
  void rotate();
  . . .
}
class Orange extends Fruit implements Spherelike {
  . . . // toss()ing may squish() me (unique to me)
}
```

You'll use this example again in the next section. For now, notice that class Orange does not have to say implements Fruitlike because, by extending Fruit, it already has.

One of the nice things about this structure is that you can change your mind about what class Orange extends (if a really great Sphere class is suddenly implemented, for example), yet Orange will still understand these two interfaces:

```
class Sphere implements Spherelike {  // extends Object
  private float radius;
  . . .
}
class Orange extends Sphere implements Fruitlike {
  . . . // users of Orange need never know about the change!
}
```

The canonical use of the mix-in capability of interfaces is to allow several classes, scattered across the single-inheritance tree, to implement the same set of methods. Although these classes share a common superclass (at least, Object), it is likely that below this common parent are many subclasses that are not interested in this set of methods. Adding the methods to the parent class, or even creating a new abstract class to hold them and inserting it into the hierarchy above the parent, is not an ideal solution.

Instead, use an interface to specify the methods. It can be implemented by every class that shares the need and by none of the classes that would have been forced to inherit in the single-inheritance tree. Design is applied only where needed. Users of the interface can now specify variables and arguments to be of a new interface type that can refer to any of the classes that implement the interface (as you'll see below)—a powerful abstraction. Some examples are object persistence (via read() and write() methods), producing or consuming (the Java library does this for images), and providing generally useful constants. The last of these might look like this:

```java
public interface PresumablyUsefulConstants {
  public static final int oneOfThem = 1234;
  public static final float another = 1.234F;
  public static final String yetAnother = "1234";
  . . .
}
public class AnyClass implements PresumablyUsefulConstants {
  public static void main(String args[]) {
    double calculation = oneOfThem * another;
    System.out.println("hello " + yetAnother + calculation);
    . . .
  }
}
```

This outputs the thoroughly meaningless hello 12341522.756, but in the process it demonstrates that the class AnyClass can refer directly to all the variables defined in the interface PresumablyUsefulConstants. Normally, you refer to such variables and constants via the class, as for the constant Integer.MIN_VALUE, which is provided by the Integer class. If a set of constants is widely used or their class name is long, the shortcut of being able to refer to them directly (as oneOfThem rather than PresumablyUsefulConstants.oneOfThem) makes it worth placing them into an interface and implementing it widely.

Implementing Interfaces

How do you actually use these interfaces? Remember that almost everywhere you can use a class, you can use an interface instead. Let's try to make use of the interface MySecondInterface defined previously:

```
MySecondInterface anObject = getTheRightObjectSomehow();

long age = anObject.ageOfTheUniverse();
```

After you declare anObject to be of type MySecondInterface, you can use anObject as the receiver of any message that the interface defines (or inherits). So what does the previous declaration really mean?

When a variable is declared to be of an interface type, it simply means that any object the variable refers to is expected to have implemented that interface—that is, it is expected to understand all the methods that the interface specifies. It assumes that a promise made between the designer of the interface and its eventual implementers is a promise kept. Although this is a rather abstract notion, it allows, for example, the previous code to be written long before any classes that qualify are implemented (or even created). In traditional object-oriented programming, you are forced to create a class with stub implementations to get the same effect as you get with interfaces.

NEW TERM   A *stub* is a routine (method, class, and so on) that is used as a placeholder, usually containing comments describing what the routine will do when it is fully implemented. This technique enables programmers to come back and "fill in the blanks" later when it is more convenient, while allowing them to refer to the routine in other parts of the code without causing compiler errors.

Here's a more complex example of interfaces:

```
Orange     anOrange    = getAnOrange();
Fruit      aFruit      = (Fruit) getAnOrange();
Fruitlike  aFruitlike  = (Fruitlike) getAnOrange();
Spherelike aSpherelike = (Spherelike) getAnOrange();

aFruit.decay();        // fruits decay
aFruitlike.squish();   // fruits squish

aFruitlike.toss();     // not OK
aSpherelike.toss();    // OK

anOrange.decay();      // oranges can do it all
```

```
anOrange.squish();
anOrange.toss();
anOrange.rotate();
```

Declarations and cast interfaces are used in this example to restrict an orange to act more like a mere fruit or sphere, simply to demonstrate the flexibility of the structure built previously. If the second structure built (the one with the Sphere class) was being used instead, most of this code still would work. In the lines bearing Fruit, all instances of Fruit need to be replaced by Sphere. Almost everything else would remain the same.

> **Note** The direct use of implementation class names is for demonstration purposes only. Normally, you would use only interface names in declarations and casts so that none of the code would have to change to support a new structure.

Interfaces are implemented and used throughout the Java class library whenever a behavior is expected to be implemented by a number of disparate classes. For example, you'll find the interfaces java.lang.Runnable, java.util.Enumeration, and java.util.Observable, among others. Let's use one of these, the Enumeration interface, to revisit the LinkedList example—and tie together today's lesson—by demonstrating a good use of packages and interfaces together.

In JBuilder, select File | New Project, modify the File field to read C:\JBUILDER\ myprojects\JAdvanced.jpr, and click Finish. To add the first three files, you must create a subdirectory named collections for the package. Click the Add to Project icon in the AppBrowser, and when the File Open / Create dialog box appears, click the Create New Folder icon. Type collections, and then press Enter. Double-click the newly created folder to make it the current directory. Type LinkedList.java into the File name text box, and then click the Open button. Type the code in Listing 4.1 into the Content pane with the LinkedList.java file selected in the Navigation pane. Use the Add to Project icon in the AppBrowser to add each of two other files to the project (see Listings 4.2 and 4.3).

TYPE   **LISTING 4.1.** LinkedList.java.

```
1:  package collections;
2:
3:  import java.util.Enumeration;
4:
5:  public class LinkedList {
6:    private Node root;
7:
```

continues

LISTING 4.1. CONTINUED

```
 8:    public void add(Object o) {
 9:      root = new Node(o, root);
10:    }
11:
12:    public Enumeration enumerate() {
13:      return new LinkedListEnumerator(root);
14:    }
15:
16:  }
```

TYPE **LISTING 4.2.** Node.java.

```
 1:  package collections;
 2:
 3:  class Node {
 4:    private Object contents;
 5:    private Node next;
 6:
 7:    Node(Object o, Node n) {
 8:      contents = o;
 9:      next = n;
10:    }
11:
12:    public Object contents() {
13:      return contents;
14:    }
15:
16:    public Node next() {
17:      return next;
18:    }
19:
20:  }
```

TYPE **LISTING 4.3.** LinkedListEnumerator.java.

```
 1:  package collections;
 2:
 3:  import java.util.Enumeration;
 4:
 5:  class LinkedListEnumerator implements Enumeration {
```

```
 6:     private Node currentNode;
 7:
 8:     LinkedListEnumerator(Node root) {
 9:       currentNode = root;
10:     }
11:
12:     public boolean hasMoreElements() {
13:       return currentNode != null;
14:     }
15:
16:     public Object nextElement() {
17:       Object anObject = currentNode.contents();
18:
19:       currentNode = currentNode.next();
20:       return anObject;
21:     }
22:
23:   }
```

To add the next listing, click the Add to Project icon in the AppBrowser, and when the File Open / Create dialog box appears, click the Up One Level icon. Type LinkedListTester.java, and then press Enter to add Listing 4.4, which shows a typical use of the enumerator.

TYPE **LISTING 4.4.** LinkedListTester.java.

```
 1:   public class LinkedListTester {
 2:
 3:     public static void main(String argv[]) {
 4:
 5:       collections.LinkedList aLinkedList = new
collections.LinkedList();
 6:
 7:         aLinkedList.add(new Integer(1138));
 8:         aLinkedList.add("THX-");
 9:
10:         java.util.Enumeration e = aLinkedList.enumerate();
11:
12:         while (e.hasMoreElements()) {
13:           Object anObject = e.nextElement();
14:           // do something useful with anObject
15:           System.out.print(anObject);
16:         }
17:         System.out.print("\n");
18:     }
19:
20:   }
```

4

OUTPUT When you compile and run `LinkedListTester`, this is the output:

```
THX-1138
```

Notice that although you are using the `Enumeration` e as though you know what it is, you actually do not. In fact, it is an instance of a hidden class `LinkedListEnumerator` that you cannot see or use directly. By a combination of packages and interfaces, the `LinkedList` class has managed to provide a transparent public interface to some of its most important behavior (through the already-defined interface `java.util.Enumeration`) while still hiding its two classes that actually do the implementation.

Handing out an object like this is sometimes called *vending*. Often, the vendor gives out an object that a receiver can't create itself but that it knows how to use. By giving it back to the vendor, the receiver can prove it has a certain capability, authenticate itself, or do any number of useful tasks—all without knowing much about the vended object. This is a powerful metaphor that can be applied in a broad range of situations.

Summary

Today, you learned how variables and methods can control their visibility and access by other classes by using modifier keywords. Table 4.1 summarizes those keywords and their associated protection levels.

TABLE 4.1. LEVELS OF PROTECTION AND VISIBILITY IN JAVA.

	public	(default) package	protected	private protected	private
Package Class (modify access)	Yes	Yes	Yes	No	No
Package Subclass (modify access)	Yes	Yes	Yes	No	No
Package Subclass (inheritance)	Yes	Yes	Yes	Yes	No

	public	*(default)* *package*	protected	private protected	private
Outside Class (modify access)	Yes	No	No	No	No
Outside Subclass (modify access)	Yes	No	No	No	No
Outside Subclass (inheritance)	Yes	No	Yes	Yes	No

You also learned that although instance variables are most often declared private, declaring accessor methods enables you to control the reading and writing of them separately. Protection levels enable you, for example, to separate your public abstractions cleanly from their concrete representations.

You saw how to protect class variables and methods, which are associated with the class itself, and how to declare final variables, methods, and classes to represent constants, and fast and secure methods and classes that cannot be overridden or subclassed.

You discovered how to declare and use abstract classes, which cannot be instantiated, and abstract methods, which have no implementation and must be overridden in subclasses. Together, they provide a template for subclasses to fill in and act as a variant for interfaces.

Also covered was how packages can be used to collect and categorize classes into meaningful groups and in a hierarchy, which not only better organizes your programs, but allows you and all the other Java programmers out on the Internet to name and share uniquely named projects with one another. You also learned how to use packages—both your own and the many preexisting ones in the Java class library.

You then discovered how to declare and use interfaces, a powerful mechanism for extending the traditional single inheritance of Java's classes and for separating design inheritance from implementation inheritance in your programs. Interfaces often are used to call common (shared) methods when the exact class involved is not known.

4

Packages and interfaces can be combined to provide useful abstractions that appear simple yet actually are hiding almost all their complex implementation-based components from their users—a very powerful technique.

Q&A

Q Won't using accessor methods everywhere slow down my Java code?

A Not always. Soon, Java compilers will be smart enough to make them fast automatically, but if you're concerned about speed, you can always declare accessor methods to be `final`, and they'll be just as fast as direct instance variable accesses.

Q Are class (`static`) methods inherited just like instance methods?

A No, class (`static`) methods are currently `final` by default. How, then, can you ever declare a non-`final` class method? The answer is that you can't. Inheritance of class methods is not supported, breaking the symmetry with instance methods. Because this goes against the part of Java's philosophy about making everything as simple as possible, perhaps it will be reversed in a later release.

Q Based on what I've learned today, it seems as though `private abstract` methods and `final abstract` methods or classes don't make sense. Are they legal?

A No, they produce compile-time errors, as you've surmised. To be useful, `abstract` methods must be overridden, and `abstract` classes must be subclassed, but neither of those two operations would be allowed if they were also `private` or `final`.

Q What will happen to package/directory hierarchies when some sort of archiving is added to Java?

A Archiving has been added to Java, but the package/directory hierarchies are still relevant; and to prepare your packages for archiving, you would still need to arrange your files in that hierarchy. The archives are called JAR (Java ARchive) files. These compressed files dramatically decrease the amount of time necessary for downloading an applet's class files over the Internet. The JDK provides a command-line tool named `jar.exe` (located in your `JBuilder\java\bin` directory), with which you can examine the contents of JAR files, uncompress a JAR file, or JAR up your own files for distribution.

Q Is there any way that a hidden class can somehow be forced out of hiding?

A A bizarre case in which a hidden class can be forced into visibility occurs if it has a `public` superclass and someone casts an instance of it to the superclass. Any `public` variables or methods of that superclass can now be accessed or called through your hidden class instance, even if those variables or methods were not thought of by you as `public` in the hidden class. Usually these `public` methods/variables are ones you don't mind having your instances give access to, or you wouldn't have declared them to have that `public` superclass. This isn't always the case, though. Many of the system's built-in classes are `public`—you might not have a choice. Hopefully, this is a rare combination of events.

Q The `abstract` classes don't have to implement all the methods in an interface themselves. Do all their subclasses have to?

A Actually, no. The rule is that an implementation must be provided by some class for each method, but it doesn't necessarily have to be yours. That is, whatever the `abstract` class doesn't implement, the first non-`abstract` class below it must implement. Then, any further subclasses need do nothing.

Workshop

The Workshop provides two ways for you to affirm what you've learned in this chapter. The Quiz section poses questions to help you solidify your understanding of the material covered. You can find answers to the quiz questions in Appendix A, "Answers to Quiz Questions." The Exercises section provides you with experience in using what you have learned. Try to work through all these before continuing to the next day.

Quiz

1. True or False?

    a. If you want to declare a constant and make it global to all instances of the class, you must use both the `static` and `final` keywords.

    b. All classes that belong to a particular package must be declared in the same file.

    c. Interfaces that do not extend another interface automatically extend `Object`.

    d. A class is limited to implementing only one interface.

2. You want to declare a class method that your subclasses can override. What modifiers should you use?

3. What convention can you use to create a variable that is read-only?

4. What parts of an abstract method do you need to declare in the abstract class?

5. What program statement(s) would you have to add to your source code to import all the `java.util` classes and subclasses, including its subpackage `zip`?

6. Where in your source code file does a `package` statement belong? What about an `import` statement?

Exercises

1. Using this example from earlier today, modify the code to add access for classes and subclasses within the same package for the `getInstanceCount()` method:

```
public class InstanceCounter {
  private static int instanceCount = 0;    // a class variable

  private protected static int getInstanceCount() {
    return instanceCount;                  // a class method
  }

  private static void incrementCount() {  // a class method
    ++instanceCount;
  }

  InstanceCounter() {  // the class constructor
    InstanceCounter.incrementCount();
  }
}
```

2. Add a second interface named `PlymouthLaserConstants` with the following attributes: 38 miles per gallon, 19-gallon tank size, and model name "Plymouth Laser Turbo RS" to the following code. Then change the `RentalCars` class so that it implements both interfaces. Add the code necessary to calculate the Laser's range, and print information about the Plymouth Laser, similar to that printed for the Ford Taurus.

```
public interface FordTaurusConstants {
  public static final int mpgFTC = 25;
  public static final float tankSizeFTC = 13.5;
  public static final String modelNameFTC = "Ford Taurus GL";
```

```
    }

public class RentalCars implements FordTaurusConstants {
  public static void main(String args[]) {
    double totalMilesFTC = mpgFTC * tankSizeFTC;

    System.out.println("Total range for the "
                       + modelNamePLC + " is "
                       + totalMilesFTC + " miles.");
...
  }
}
```

OUTPUT The modified code, when run in a Java application, should provide the following output:

```
Total range for the Ford Taurus GL is 337.5 miles.
Total range for the Plymouth Laser Turbo RS is 722 miles.
```

4

DAY 5

JBuilder IDE

In the halcyon days of character-mode programming, Borland pioneered the concept of the Integrated Development Environment or IDE. The IDE was a breakthrough in development environments because it allowed the developer to have access to all the tools necessary to create a project from a single program interface, including an editor, a compiler, and a debugger. Now that most of us use graphical environments and can switch among many programs easily, this doesn't seem so revolutionary, but when it was first introduced, it was a time-saving concept that greatly increased productivity.

With JBuilder, Borland brings this same concept to Java programming, which formerly had been accomplished mainly with command-line tools. The JBuilder IDE comprises a menu system, browser, editor, designer, component palette, toolbar, property inspector, compiler and linker, and debugger—everything you need to create your Java programs easily and efficiently. Borland's *Two-Way Tools* technology enables you to work either graphically or textually so that you can use whichever medium best suits you while keeping everything synchronized.

Today, you'll be introduced to the features of JBuilder's IDE and get a feel for how each benefits your development efforts. The following topics will be covered:

- The IDE's main window and context-sensitive help
- JBuilder's extensive menu system, which exposes the majority of the IDE's feature set, including customizing the IDE
- A brief introduction to the Object Gallery and Component Palette
- AppBrowser's modes, editing and debugging views
- Visual Designer, Component Inspector's Properties and Events pages, and Menu Designer

Using Context-Sensitive Features

Before you get to know the rest of the IDE, it's nice to know that it has context-sensitive help hints that pop up on the screen to assist you in identifying various parts of the IDE. If you leave your mouse cursor over any of the buttons in JBuilder's main window for more than a half-second, a small ToolTip appears with some text in it (see Figure 5.1). JBuilder's ToolTips are there to help explain what those buttons are all about.

FIGURE 5.1.

A help hint displayed for the Debug toolbar button.

JBuilder also provides help specific to the context in which you're working. Pressing F1 almost anywhere in JBuilder's IDE causes the appropriate topic to be displayed in a Help window.

For example, if you want to find out what a particular menu item does, display the menu and use the arrow keys to highlight the menu item without selecting it. Press F1, and the help topic for that menu item is displayed. Of course, you can always access the Help files directly by selecting one of the items on the Help menu or by pressing the Help button in dialog boxes.

Context-sensitive pop-up menus appear when you right-click in almost any IDE window, pane, or view. Some of these commands might not be available from the main menu bar, and the command set changes according to what currently has focus. For example, place the mouse over any of the panes in the AppBrowser window and right-click. A pop-up menu containing the commands specific to that pane will appear. Pop-up menus give you quicker access to essential commands in the context where you need them.

Identifying Sections of the Main Window

When you first load JBuilder, its main window will be displayed. Figure 5.2 shows JBuilder's main window containing the main menu bar, the toolbar, the Component Palette, and the status bar.

FIGURE 5.2.

JBuilder's main window.

Main menu bar

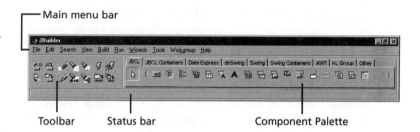

Toolbar   Status bar   Component Palette

The main menu bar gives you access to JBuilder's commands in hierarchical text form, whereas the toolbar contains the most commonly used commands in iconic form. The Component Palette displays a selection of the drag-and-drop JavaBeans components that you will use to create your program's graphical user interface (GUI). The status bar displays various messages including file saving and compiler status messages.

In addition to the visible parts of the main window, JBuilder has another way to access commands—local pop-up menus that are available in each of JBuilder's individual windows and views. These pop-up menus appear when you right-click in the IDE, and the commands are context-sensitive to each window. For example, in the main window, the Component Palette has a pop-up menu that enables you to display a dialog box where you can add and remove components from the palette.

Using the Main Menu Bar

JBuilder's extensive menu system gives you a large number of commands necessary to complete tasks in the IDE. The main menu bar is similar to that of other Windows applications. It contains menu items that are enabled and disabled in response to the current context. Figure 5.3 shows JBuilder's main menu bar.

FIGURE 5.3.

JBuilder's main menu bar.

5

Note

The actual menu items you see on each menu depend on which edition of JBuilder you purchased: Standard, Professional (Pro), or Client/Server (C/S). This information is noted in the description of the appropriate menus and menu items presented shortly.

For a definitive description of what features are available in each edition, refer to your JBuilder documentation.

Using File Menu Commands

The File menu contains the commands that pertain to project contents and source code files (in memory and on disk), project properties, print commands, and exiting the JBuilder IDE. Figure 5.4 shows the File menu.

FIGURE 5.4.

The File menu.

These menu items are enabled or disabled depending on which project file is selected, if any, and on the state of the currently active project.

New

The New command displays the New dialog box, shown in Figure 5.5.

Here, you can choose from a number of different file and object types to open in the AppBrowser window. The New dialog box includes several pages of widgets that compose the Object Gallery, which you'll be introduced to later today in the "Creating Files with the Object Gallery" section.

New Project

The New Project command displays the Project Wizard dialog box, shown in Figure 5.6.

FIGURE 5.5.

The New dialog box.

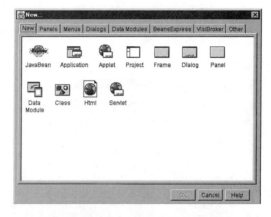

FIGURE 5.6.

The Project Wizard dialog box.

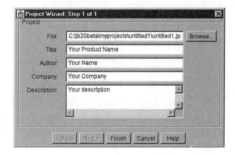

In this dialog box, you can name your project and package, product title, project author, company, and a description for internal documentation.

Open / Create

The Open / Create command displays the File Open / Create dialog box. Figure 5.7 shows the File Open / Create dialog box's File page.

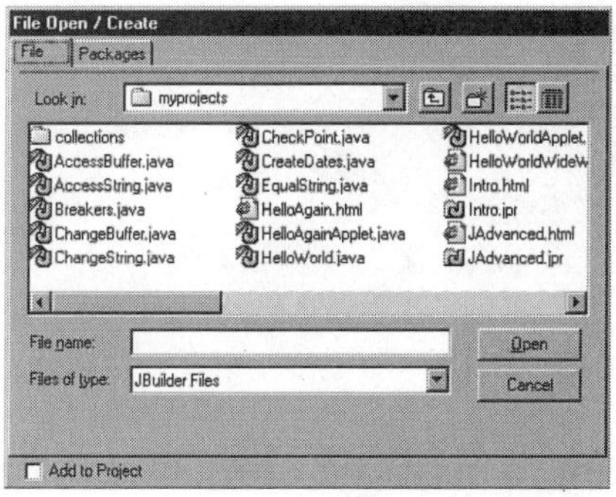

FIGURE 5.7.

The File Open / Create dialog box File page.

The File page gives you access to the local file system to open an existing file or create a new one in memory. Figure 5.8 shows the File Open / Create dialog box's Packages page.

FIGURE 5.8.

The File Open / Create dialog box Packages page.

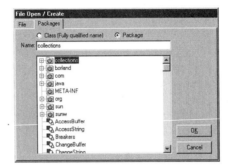

On the Packages page, you can either open one of the existing Java packages on disk or specify a new package of your own. When you create a new package, the corresponding directory is created on disk.

Both pages display the Add to Project check box which, when checked, adds the newly created or opened file to the currently active project.

Reopen

Selecting the Reopen menu item displays a submenu containing the JBuilder project and Java files that you have recently opened. Figure 5.9 shows what this submenu might look like after you've created the projects and files over the past four days in this book. Notice that the project files with the .jpr extension are listed at top. The bottom part of the list, under the menu separator, displays the .java files.

FIGURE 5.9.

A sample Reopen sub-menu.

Close

Selecting the Close command closes the current AppBrowser window. If any files in the current AppBrowser window have been modified, you are prompted to save those changes or discard them. All files are checked for modifications before the AppBrowser window is closed.

Close All

The Close All command closes all open AppBrowser windows, including all your open projects. If any files have been modified, you are prompted to save those changes or discard them.

Save

The Save command saves the currently selected file to disk. Files are saved to disk under their current name.

Save As

The Save As command displays the Save As dialog box, shown in Figure 5.10.

FIGURE 5.10.

The Save As dialog box.

In the Save As dialog box, you can save the file under a new name, a new location, or both.

Save Project

The Save Project command saves the currently active project's .jpr file to disk. Projects are saved to disk under their current name.

Save All

The Save All command automatically invokes the Save command for each modified file in a project and across multiple projects.

Remove from Project

The Remove from Project command enables you to disassociate the selected file from the project. It doesn't delete the file from the disk; it simply removes the file's entry from the project file.

5

Rename

The Rename command invokes the Save As dialog box (see Figure 5.10) so that you can rename the selected file. In this dialog box, you can save the file under a new name, a new location, or both.

Project Properties

The Project Properties command displays the *ProjectName*.jpr Properties dialog box. This dialog box's Paths page, shown in Figure 5.11, enables you to modify the JDK version used to create your project, the paths of the project's source and output root directories, and access to external Java libraries.

FIGURE 5.11.

The ProjectName.*jpr*
Properties dialog box
Paths page.

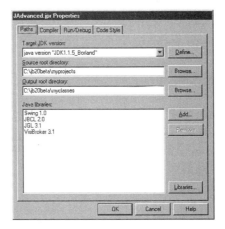

The *ProjectName*.jpr Properties dialog box's Compiler page, shown in Figure 5.12, enables you to set various compiler options.

FIGURE 5.12.

The ProjectName.*jpr*
Properties dialog box
Compiler page.

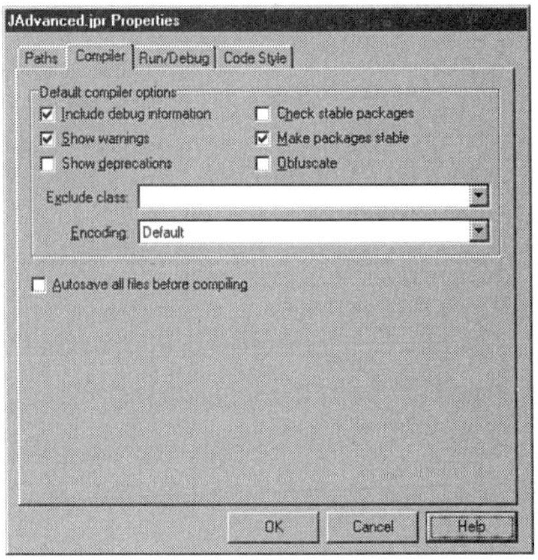

The *ProjectName*.jpr Properties dialog box's Run/Debug page, shown in Figure 5.13, enables you to set debug session options, such as command-line parameters and where to send the console (that is, command-line) output.

FIGURE 5.13.

The ProjectName.*jpr Properties dialog box Run/Debug page.*

Finally, the *ProjectName*.jpr Properties dialog box's Code Style page, shown in Figure 5.14, enables you to set the way your code is automatically formatted in the JBuilder editor.

FIGURE 5.14.

The ProjectName.*jpr Properties dialog box Code Style page.*

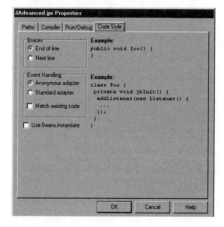

Printer Setup

The Printer Setup command invokes the Print Setup dialog box, shown in Figure 5.15, where you can specify which printer, paper, and orientation you prefer.

FIGURE 5.15.

The Print Setup dialog box.

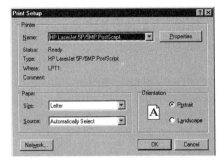

Print

The Print command reacts differently depending on which file you have selected and which Content pane tab is active. If you have a `.jpr` or `.html` file selected and the AppBrowser is in View mode (the View tab is selected), this command prints the graphical view being displayed in the Content pane.

If you have a file selected and the AppBrowser is in Editor mode (the Source tab is selected), this command invokes the Print Selection dialog box, where you can specify how you want the selected file to be printed. If you have a block of text selected, the check box labeled Print selected block will be enabled, as shown in Figure 5.16. You can also choose from other printing options, such as whether to use syntax print, color, line numbers, header/page numbers, and whether to wrap long lines (or truncate).

FIGURE 5.16.

The Print Selection dialog box.

This dialog box's Setup button invokes the Print Setup dialog box (see Figure 5.15).

Exit

The Exit command exits JBuilder entirely, closing all files and projects that are open in the IDE. If there are unsaved files, JBuilder will inquire whether you want to save them before closing, displaying the Save Modified Files dialog box as shown in Figure 5.17. In this dialog box, you can choose which files to save.

FIGURE 5.17.

The Save Modified Files dialog box.

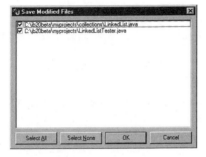

Using Edit Menu Commands

The Edit menu contains the commands that are used to manipulate text blocks in the AppBrowser Editor and components in the AppBrowser UI Designer. These commands include the usual cut, copy, paste, undo, redo, and selection commands. Figure 5.18 shows the Edit menu.

FIGURE 5.18.

The Edit menu.

Undo

Use the Undo command to reverse sets of keystrokes performed in the Editor, including cursor movements. You can use the Undo command an unlimited number of times; the number of undoable actions is limited only by the number set in the Environment Options dialog box Editor page. Open this dialog box by selecting the IDE Options command from the Tools menu. The default undo limit is 32,767 times.

Redo

Use the Redo command to reverse your Undo operations.

Cut

The Cut command removes the selected text blocks or components from the JBuilder IDE and places them on the Windows Clipboard.

Copy

The Copy command places the selected text blocks or components on the Windows Clipboard without deleting them from the JBuilder IDE.

5

Paste

The Paste command pastes text blocks or components to the JBuilder IDE from the Windows Clipboard.

Delete

The Delete command deletes the selected text blocks or components from the IDE without placing them on the Windows Clipboard.

Select All

The Select All command selects all the text in the Editor or selects all the components in the UI Designer.

Using Search Menu Commands

The Search menu contains the commands used to search and replace text, search text in multiple files across source paths, position the cursor at a specific line number, and browse code symbols. Figure 5.19 shows the Search menu.

FIGURE 5.19.

The Search menu.

Find

The Find command displays the Find Text dialog box, shown in Figure 5.20.

FIGURE 5.20.

The Find Text dialog box.

This dialog box enables you to specify a text string to locate. If text is selected in the Editor, it will appear in the Text to find field. You can also choose search options such as direction, scope, and origin, as well as case-sensitive, whole word, and regular expression searches.

Replace

The Replace command displays the Replace Text dialog box, shown in Figure 5.21.

FIGURE 5.21.

The Replace Text dialog box.

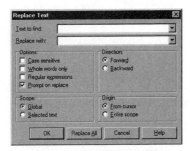

The Replace Text dialog box enables you to specify a text string to locate and a text string with which to replace the located string. If text is selected in the Editor, it will appear in the Text to find field. In addition to the options available in the Find Text dialog box, you can choose to be prompted for each replace by clicking the OK button, or you can replace all occurrences at once by clicking the Replace All button.

Search Again

The Search Again command repeats the last search, search and replace, or incremental search operation.

Incremental Search

The Incremental Search command moves the cursor directly to the matching text as you type each letter.

Search Source Path

The Search Source Path command searches for text across all the files specified in the project's Source Path (as specified in the *ProjectName*.jpr Properties dialog box). Figure 5.22 shows the Search Source Path dialog box.

FIGURE 5.22.

The Search Source Path dialog box.

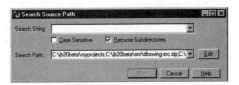

Go to Line Number

The Go to Line Number command displays the Go to Line Number dialog box, shown in Figure 5.23.

5

FIGURE 5.23.

The Go to Line Number dialog box.

This dialog box enables you to specify the text line number to which you want the cursor to be moved.

Browse Symbol

(Pro and C/S) The Browse Symbol command displays the Browse Goto dialog box, shown in Figure 5.24.

FIGURE 5.24.

The Browse Goto dialog box.

In this dialog box, you can specify a class, an interface, or a package to browse.

Using View Menu Commands

The View menu commands invoke or toggle the display of the JBuilder IDE views and windows, and also let you show or hide portions of the main window. Figure 5.25 shows the View menu.

FIGURE 5.25.

The View menu.

The following sections present descriptions of some of these windows to give you an idea of what they typically look like.

Loaded Classes

Selecting the Loaded Classes command during a debugging session opens the Loaded Classes window, which displays a list of all the classes associated with the program being debugged. Figure 5.26 shows the Loaded Classes window displayed while the LinkedListTester program developed during yesterday's lesson is being debugged.

FIGURE 5.26.

The Loaded Classes window.

Execution Log

Selecting the Execution Log command opens the Execution Log window, which displays all the command-line messages and errors that a program displays during execution or debugging. This includes standard output from command-line Java programs, when console I/O is set to output to Execution Log on the Run/Debug page of the projectName.jpr Properties dialog box. Figure 5.27 shows a typical Execution Log window.

FIGURE 5.27.

The Execution Log window.

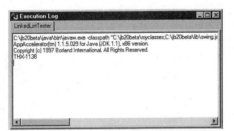

The Execution Log window creates a new tabbed page for each executable that it receives output from. If you run a program multiple times, you can scroll back to see the results of previous runs. You can remove pages by selecting the Remove Page command from the Execution Log window's pop-up menu.

Breakpoints

Select the Breakpoints command to open the Breakpoints window (see Figure 5.28), which shows a list of the breakpoints set in the current debugging session.

5

FIGURE 5.28.

The Breakpoints window.

Debugger Context Browser

The Debugger Context Browser command displays the Debugger Context Browser window, which shows various pieces of information about the current debugging session, including threads, call stack, and data. Figure 5.29 shows an example.

FIGURE 5.29.

The Debugger Context Browser window.

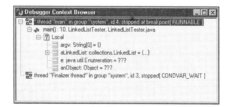

Multiple Debugger Context Browser windows can be open simultaneously.

New Browser

The New Browser command opens a new AppBrowser window with another copy of the same project. This enables you to have two or more views of the same set of files.

Next Error Message

The Next Error Message command shows the next error message in the Message view (automatically displayed at the bottom of the AppBrowser window's Content pane when a compiler error occurs) and positions the cursor in the Editor on the line where the error occurred.

Previous Error Message

The Previous Error Message command shows the previous error message in the Message view (automatically displayed at the bottom of the AppBrowser window's Content pane when a compiler error occurs) and positions the cursor in the Editor on the line where the error occurred.

Message View

Message View is a toggle command, alternately showing and hiding the Message view in the AppBrowser window's Content pane. This command shows a check mark to its left when the Message view is being displayed; it is not checked when the Message view is hidden.

Inspector

The Inspector command is active only when the AppBrowser window is in UI Designer mode. (You'll learn more about the UI Designer tomorrow.) When the Inspector pane in the AppBrowser window has been hidden, you can use this command to show it again. Figure 5.30 shows the Inspector pane.

FIGURE 5.30.

The Inspector pane in the AppBrowser window.

Toolbar

Toolbar is a toggle command, alternately showing and hiding the toolbar in the main window. If you don't use the toolbar often or you want more room in the main window to display the Component Palette, use this command. The Toolbar command shows a check mark to its left when the toolbar is being displayed; it is not checked when the toolbar is hidden.

Component Palette

Component Palette is a toggle command, alternately showing and hiding the Component Palette in the main window. This command shows a check mark to its left when the Component Palette is being displayed; it is not checked when the it is hidden.

Toggle Curtain

Toggle Curtain is a toggle command, alternately causing the Content pane of the AppBrowser to cover the entire AppBrowser window, and resetting the AppBrowser to its default state (showing multiple panes). This command shows a check mark to its left when multiple AppBrowser panes are being displayed; it is not checked when the Content pane is expanded.

5

Next Pane

The Next Pane command sets the focus to the next pane in the AppBrowser window. The order is as follows:

1. Navigation pane
2. Structure pane
3. Content pane
4. Message view

Using Build Menu Commands

The Build menu commands make and rebuild both individual files and entire projects. Figure 5.31 shows the Build menu.

FIGURE 5.31.

The Build menu.

The Make commands do conditional compilations, whereas the Rebuild commands do unconditional compilations. Rebuild is especially useful when you are getting ready to distribute your application and you want to rebuild the entire project without the debugging information you use to test and track bugs in your applications during development.

Make Project *ProjectName*.jpr

The Make Project command compiles any source files in the current project that either don't have a `.class` file or are newer than their `.class` files.

Rebuild Project *ProjectName*.jpr

The Rebuild Project command compiles all the source files in the current project, whether they have a current `.class` file or not. This command also causes all imported files and packages to be recursively compiled (except `java`, `jbcl`, and `jgl` standard packages).

Make *FileName*.java

The Make command compiles the currently selected source file if it either doesn't have a `.class` file, or is newer than its `.class` file.

Rebuild *FileName*.java

The Rebuild command compiles the currently selected source file in the project, whether it has a current `.class` file or not.

Using Run Menu Commands

The Run menu contains the commands used to run and debug your application from the
JBuilder IDE and to access the debugging views. Figure 5.32 shows the Run menu.

FIGURE 5.32.

The Run menu.

These menu items will be enabled or disabled depending on whether you are in a debug
session or not and at what stage in the debug session you are at any point in time.

Debug *Filename*

The Debug command starts a debugging session in the JBuilder IDE. Any modified project files are compiled before running.

Run *Filename*

The Run command runs your application from the JBuilder IDE. Any modified project
files are compiled before running.

Parameters

The Parameters command displays the Compiler page of the *ProjectName*.jpr Properties
dialog box (see Figure 5.12), which enables you to specify the compiler options that will
be used when JBuilder compiles your Java source files.

Step Over

The Step Over command executes a procedure call, its statements, and its return as a single step while debugging.

Trace Into

The Trace Into command executes a procedure call, its statements, and its return as separate steps while debugging.

Run to Cursor

The Run to Cursor command runs your application until it reaches the current cursor
position in the code while debugging.

5

Run to End of Method

The Run to End of Method command runs your application until it reaches the end of the current method in the code while debugging.

Show Execution Point

The Show Execution Point command positions the debugging cursor at the next line to be executed while debugging.

Program Pause

The Program Pause command pauses the execution of your application while it is running in the JBuilder IDE while debugging.

Program Reset

The Program Reset command unloads the application currently running in the JBuilder IDE while debugging.

Add Watch

The Add Watch command displays the Add Watch dialog box, shown in Figure 5.33.

FIGURE 5.33.

The Add Watch dialog box.

Specify an expression to watch in the Add Watch dialog box; all watches are displayed in the Watch page of the Debugging window.

Add Breakpoint

The Add Breakpoint command displays the Breakpoint Options dialog box, in which you can modify an existing breakpoint or add a new breakpoint for debugging. If the Breakpoint Type is Source Breakpoint, the Breakpoint Definition page shown in Figure 5.34 is displayed.

In this Breakpoint Definition page, you can specify options for the source breakpoint, including filename, line number, condition, pass count, and thread options. If the Breakpoint Type is Exception Breakpoint, an alternative Breakpoint Definition page is shown, as in Figure 5.35.

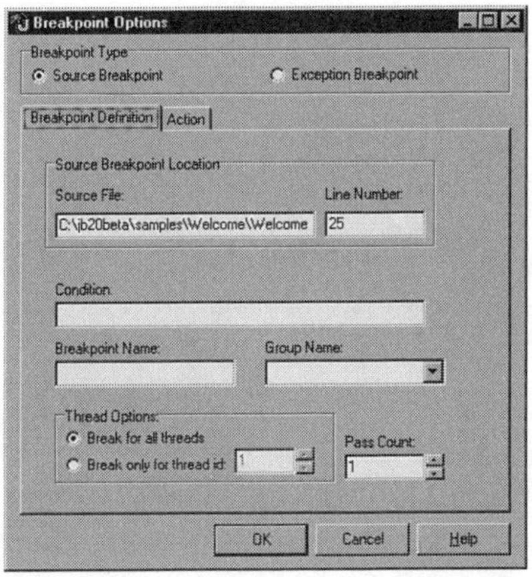

FIGURE 5.34.

*The Breakpoint
Options dialog box
Breakpoint Definition
page that is displayed
when Source
Breakpoint is selected.*

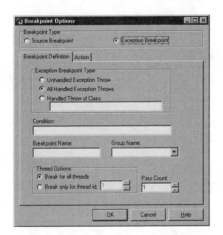

FIGURE 5.35.

*The Breakpoint
Options dialog box
Breakpoint Definition
page that is displayed
when Exception
Breakpoint is selected.*

5

In this Breakpoint Definition page, the filename and line number options are replaced by choices that tell the debugger for which type of exception you want the breakpoint to stop execution.

Both source and exception breakpoint types display the same Action page in the Breakpoint Options dialog box, as shown in Figure 5.36.

In the Action page, you can specify what action or combination of actions you want to occur when the breakpoint is reached.

Inspect

The Inspect command displays the Inspect dialog box, shown in Figure 5.37.

Figure 5.36.

The Breakpoint Options dialog box Action page.

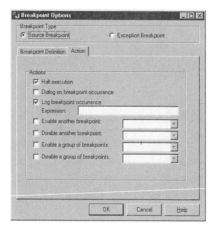

Figure 5.37.

The Inspect dialog box.

In the Inspect dialog box, you can specify an expression that you want to inspect. Both the expression and its current value are displayed and its value updated as you continue your debugging session.

Evaluate/Modify

The Evaluate/Modify command displays the Evaluate/Modify dialog box, shown in Figure 5.38.

Figure 5.38.

The Evaluate/Modify dialog box.

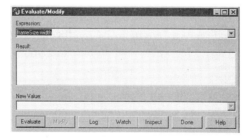

The Evaluate/Modify dialog box enables you to evaluate or temporarily change values or properties while debugging.

Using Wizards Menu Commands

(Pro and C/S) The Wizards menu items invoke various helper utilities that ask you a series of questions regarding a task and then present you with a new project that contains all the elements you've chosen. Figure 5.39 shows the Wizards menu.

FIGURE 5.39.

The Wizards menu.

The illustrations of the menu items in the following sections were created by selecting the WelcomeFrame.java file in the Welcome project and then invoking the wizard.

Use DataModule

Data modules enable you to separate the database logic in your applications from their visual containers. Use an existing data module in your project with the help of the Use DataModule Wizard. Select the Use DataModule command to start the Use DataModule Wizard. The Choose a DataModule dialog box appears, as shown in Figure 5.40.

FIGURE 5.40.

The Choose a DataModule dialog box.

5

Implement Interface

Use the Implement Interface Wizard to help you create an interface class. Select the Implement Interface command to start the Implement Interface Wizard. The Implement Interface dialog box appears, as shown in Figure 5.41.

Override Methods

Use the Override Methods Wizard to pick a superclass method that you want to override. From that method, the wizard then creates an empty method in your source code. You can then add your own code that overrides the original superclass method. Select the Override Methods command to start the Override Methods Wizard. The Override Inherited Methods dialog box appears, as shown in Figure 5.42.

FIGURE 5.41.

*The Implement
Interface dialog box.*

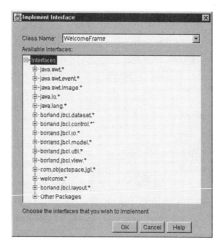

FIGURE 5.42.

*The Override Inherited
Methods dialog box.*

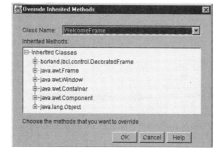

Resource Strings

Use the Resource Wizard for assistance with converting hard-coded strings in your program into identifiers, which it then puts into a resource file. Select the Resource Strings
command to start the Resource Wizard. The Resource Wizard dialog box appears, as
shown in Figure 5.43.

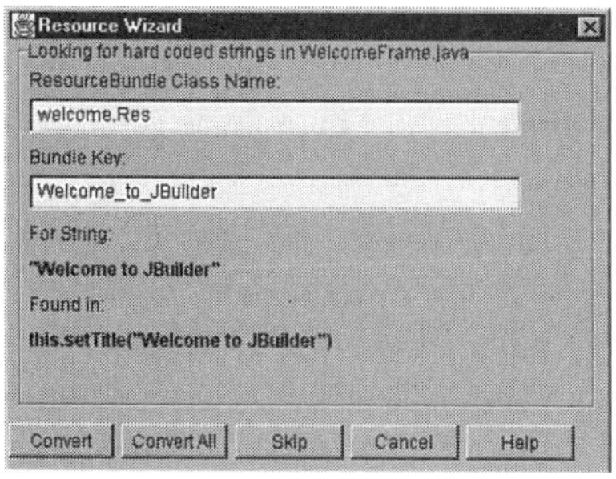

FIGURE 5.43.

*The Resource Wizard
dialog box.*

Deployment Wizard

Use the Deployment Wizard for assistance in gathering all files needed to distribute your application or applet, including creating compressed Java Archive (.jar) files. Select the Deployment Wizard command to start the Deployment Wizard. The first page of the Deployment Wizard dialog box appears, as shown in Figure 5.44.

FIGURE 5.44.

The first page of the Deployment Wizard dialog box.

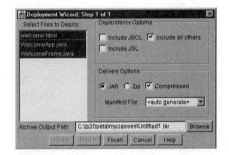

Data Migration Wizard

Use the Data Migration Wizard to move data between files and databases. Select the Data Migration Wizard command to start the Data Migration Wizard. The first page of the Data Migration Wizard dialog box appears, as shown in Figure 5.45.

FIGURE 5.45.

The first page of the Data Migration Wizard dialog box.

5

The Data Migration Wizard is provided with the JBuilder Client/Server edition.

Using Tools Menu Commands

The Tools menu contains the commands used to configure the Component Palette and the JBuilder IDE, and other miscellaneous utilities. Figure 5.46 shows the Tools menu.

FIGURE 5.46.

The Tools menu.

Configure Palette

Select the Configure Palette command to display the Palette Properties dialog box, shown in Figure 5.47. Use the Palette Properties dialog box to add, remove, and rearrange both pages and components in the palette. This dialog box is discussed in detail on Day 7, "JavaBeans Component Library."

FIGURE 5.47.

The Palette Properties dialog box.

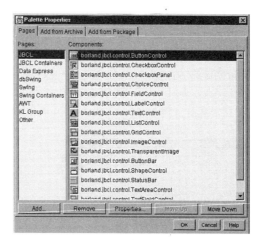

JDBC Monitor

Monitor and manipulate JDBC traffic using the JDBC monitor. Select the JDBC Monitor command to display the JDBCMonitor window, shown in Figure 5.48. Use the JDBCMonitor window to monitor and manipulate JDBC (Java Database Connectivity) traffic.

> **Note**
>
> The JDBC Monitor is provided with the JBuilder Client/Server edition.

FIGURE 5.48.

The JDBCMonitor window.

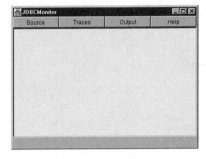

IDE Options

Select the IDE Options command to display the Environment Options dialog box, which comprises seven pages: Paths, Compiler, Editor, Display, Colors, AppBrowser, and Code Style. In these pages, you can configure your working environment to your personal tastes. By changing various JBuilder IDE options, you can customize your development environment. Certain options, such as syntax highlighting, can also help you spot errors. Other options control whether specific information is saved between project sessions. Still other options are used to set the appearance of JBuilder IDE windows, such as the AppBrowser options.

The Paths page shown in Figure 5.49 might look familiar. It's essentially identical to the Paths page in the *ProjectName*.jpr Properties dialog box, with one major exception. The paths and options are the default options for all new projects.

FIGURE 5.49.

The Environment Options dialog box Paths page.

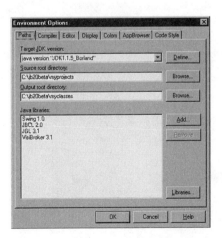

The Compiler page shown in Figure 5.50 is essentially identical to the Compiler page in the *ProjectName*.jpr Properties dialog box, except that the settings apply to all new projects. You set various compiler options on this page.

FIGURE 5.50.

*The Environment
Options dialog box
Compiler page.*

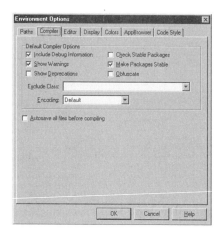

The Editor page is where you customize the editor's handling of text, including tabs, undo limit, block settings, and whether syntax highlighting is used for certain types of files. The Editor SpeedSetting option automatically sets certain individual editor options and also controls the default settings for two options on the Display page (BRIEF cursor shapes and Keystroke mapping). You can also set an individual option differently than the SpeedSetting choice. If you do so and later decide you want the SpeedSetting choices back, you can recover by selecting any other SpeedSetting and then reselecting the original SpeedSetting. Figure 5.51 shows the Editor page with the installed defaults.

FIGURE 5.51.

*The Environment
Options dialog box
Editor page.*

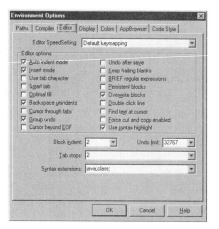

The Display page is where you set a number of miscellaneous Editor-related features. Some options deal with how the Editor pane itself is displayed, such as right margin, visible gutter, font, and cursor shapes. Other options determine whether backup files are created and keystroke mappings (controlling which set of keyboard shortcuts are in effect). This page is also where you can specify how the Editor maximizes: whether it takes up the whole screen or just the space available under JBuilder's main window. Figure 5.52 shows the Display page with the installed defaults.

FIGURE 5.52.

The Environment Options dialog box Display page.

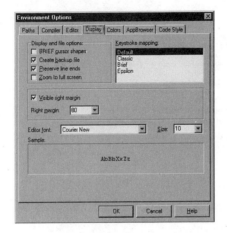

The Colors page of editor-related options is where you set how the color syntax highlighting will look, including font attributes for specific code elements. A separate style can be chosen for each code element, such as `Identifier` or `String`. Using syntax highlighting provides an effective way to help you spot coding mistakes and makes your code more readable. The appearance of your code printouts will also be affected by these choices, to the extent that your printer supports the attributes and colors.

The scrollable sample text window reflects the choices made in this page of the Environment Options dialog box, but it can also be used to select a code element. For example, click on the first line, which is a comment. As you do, note that the options are updated to reflect your choice. This provides an easy way for you to choose a code element to examine its settings without having to know what it is called. Figure 5.53 shows the Colors page with the installed defaults.

The AppBrowser page of the Environment Options dialog box enables you to configure the behavior of the AppBrowser itself. This page has options for specifying the sorting order by <access> modifier and by structure type. The Grouping options determine how data members and methods are displayed and whether items are grouped by accessibility. You can also control how the items are sorted, both by structure and by accessor. There is also an option that specifies whether to reload the project on which you were working last, when JBuilder opens its IDE. Figure 5.54 shows the AppBrowser page with the installed defaults.

5

FIGURE 5.53.

*The Environment
Options dialog box
Colors page.*

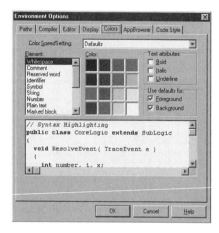

FIGURE 5.54.

*The Environment
Options dialog box
AppBrowser page.*

The Code Style page of the Environment Options dialog box enables you to set the way in which the Editor automatically formats your Java code. For instance, some people prefer to put the brace for a new block of code at the end of the statement preceding the new code block. Others prefer to put the brace on its own line. You can set your favorite method on the Code Style page of the Environment Options dialog box, shown in Figure 5.55 with the installed defaults.

Treat As Text

The Treat As Text command displays a Treat As Text dialog box, shown in Figure 5.56. This dialog box enables you to extend the types of files that JBuilder treats as text files.

FIGURE 5.55.

*The Environment
Options dialog box
Code Style page.*

FIGURE 5.56.

*The Treat As Text
dialog box.*

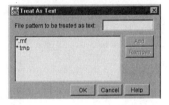

JBuilder Web Updates

The JBuilder Web Updates command displays a JBuilder Web Updates dialog box, shown in Figure 5.57, that enables you to check the Inprise Web site for JBuilder updates and patches. You can also schedule a monthly reminder to check the Web site.

FIGURE 5.57.

*The JBuilder Web
Updates dialog box.*

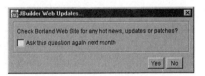

VisiBroker Smart Agent

VisiBroker Smart Agent is a toggle command that opens a VisiBroker Smart Agent window, as shown in Figure 5.58. A check mark is displayed next to the command when the VisiBroker Smart Agent window is open; the check mark is removed when the window is closed.

FIGURE 5.58.

The VisiBroker Smart Agent window.

VisiBroker is provided with the JBuilder Client/Server edition.

RMIRegistry

Applications using Remote Method Invocation register distributed objects in an RMI registry. Use the RMIRegistry toggle command to start the rmiregistry utility provided with the Java Development Kit. The rmiregistry utility starts remote object registries on specified ports.

The RMIRegistry command is provided with the JBuilder Client/Server edition.

Notepad

The Notepad command opens the Windows Notepad program. If you select a file in the Navigation pane before selecting the Notepad command, the contents of that file are opened with Notepad.

Calculator

The Calculator command opens the Windows Calculator program. This is handy, for instance, when you want to convert values between number systems, such as decimal and hexadecimal.

SQL Explorer

Select the SQL Explorer command when you want to display the SQL Explorer. The SQL Explorer is a hierarchical database browser with editing capabilities.

The SQL Explorer is provided with the JBuilder Client/Server edition.

Using Workgroup Menu Commands

The Workgroup menu contains commands to set up a project so that it can be worked on by more than one person—a workgroup. The menu contains commands for setting up a workgroup, including security, and for software version control. Figure 5.59 shows the Workgroup menu.

FIGURE 5.59.

The Workgroup menu.

The Workgroup menu is provided with the JBuilder Client/Server edition.

5

Browse PVCS Projects

The Browse PVCS Projects command displays the Version Control window shown in Figure 5.60. Use this window to create and manage archived versions of an application development project. You can go back and examine older versions of your project and track Java code revision histories.

FIGURE 5.60.

The Version Control window.

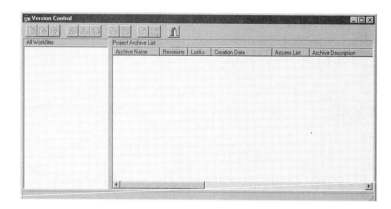

Manage Archive Directories

Manage the directories holding your project archives through the Archive Directories dialog box, which you can open by selecting the Manage Archive Directories command from the Workgroup menu.

Add *ProjectName* to Version Control

The Add *ProjectName* to Version Control command opens the Create Project for *ProjectName* dialog box, shown in Figure 5.61.

FIGURE 5.61.

The Create Project for welcome dialog box.

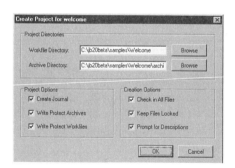

Use the Create Project for *ProjectName* dialog box to begin archiving and tracking your project.

Set Data Directories

The Set Data Directories command opens the Data Directories dialog box, shown in Figure 5.62.

FIGURE 5.62.

The Data Directories dialog box.

Using Help Menu Commands

The Help menu contains commands to access the JBuilder Help and documentation reference files. There are menu commands for directly accessing frequently used documentation on BeansExpress, the JDK, JBCL, and version control. You can also directly access Borland Online the Welcome Project (Sample) and display the About box. Figure 5.63 shows the Help menu.

FIGURE 5.63.

The Help menu.

Help Topics

The Help Topics command loads the JBuilder Help system with the JBuilder online documentation set: Distributed Application Developer's Guide, Component Writer's Guide, and many others.

Note When accessing help topics, JBuilder automatically loads the documentation appropriate for the version you have.

BeansExpress

The BeansExpress command loads the JBuilder Help system displaying the BeansExpress User's Guide, which explains how to use the JBuilder BeansExpress tools and examples found on the BeansExpress page of the Object Gallery.

Java Reference

The Java Reference command loads the JBuilder Help system displaying Sun's JDK (Java Development Kit) Documentation.

5

JBCL Reference

The JBCL Reference command loads the JBuilder Help system displaying the JBCL Reference documentation for the JavaBeans Component Library (JBCL).

Version Control Help

The Version Control Help command loads the JBuilder Help system displaying the PVCS Version Manager documentation.

> **Note**　The Version Control Help command is provided with the JBuilder Client/Server edition.

Borland Online

The Borland Online command opens your default Web browser with the Borland Web site URL, giving you direct access to Borland Online from the JBuilder IDE.

Welcome Project (Sample)

The Welcome Project (Sample) command opens the `Welcome` project in an AppBrowser window.

About

The About command displays the About JBuilder dialog box.

Creating Files with the Object Gallery

The items that compose the Object Gallery are displayed in the New dialog box, which you invoke by selecting File | New. This dialog box has eight pages: New, Panels, Menus, Dialogs, Data Modules, BeansExpress, VisiBroker, and Other.

To use the items in the Object Gallery, either click to select the item and click the OK button, or simply double-click the item and you're on your way. You can also add your own custom components, containers, and reusable code snippets by right-clicking on the appropriate page and selecting Add Snippet from the pop-up menu.

Using the New Page

The New page, shown in Figure 5.64, contains various file types, including JavaBean, Application, Applet, Project, Frame, Dialog, Panel, Data Module, Class, Html, and Servlet. By selecting one of these object or file types, you instruct the JBuilder IDE to prepare a skeleton source code file of that type and display it in an AppBrowser window.

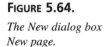

FIGURE 5.64.

The New dialog box New page.

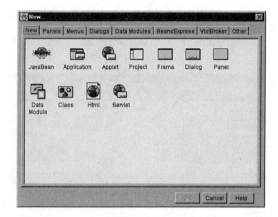

Selecting any of the object or file types when no project is open results in starting the Project Wizard to create a project for the object or file.

After a project is created, the JavaBean, Application, Applet, Project, and Servlet objects or files are created by invoking a wizard that asks you for information regarding the task at hand and generates the source code based on your answers. In contrast, the Frame, Dialog, Panel, Data Module, and Class files are created by invoking a secondary dialog box that asks you for the item's package, class name, and filename before generating the appropriate code. Here is a brief explanation of each of these file types:

Frame	Generates a new GUI frame in your UI design
Dialog	Aids in creating a new type of dialog box in your UI design
Panel	Helps you to create a new container panel for your UI
Data Module	Produces a file in which you can gather nonvisual data connection components together in your UI design
Class	Creates a skeleton class source code file with the appropriate package name and class declarations

The Html item creates a skeleton .html file and places the source code directly into the Content pane of the AppBrowser window.

Using the Panels Page

The Panels page, shown in Figure 5.65, gives you access to predesigned source code snippets that enable you to quickly and easily create standardized panels:

5

Tabbed pages   Creates a panel with tabbed pages and command buttons

Dual list box   Creates a panel with list boxes and command buttons

FIGURE 5.65.

The New dialog box Panels page.

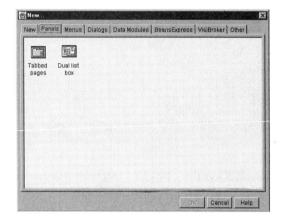

Using the Menus Page

The Menus page, shown in Figure 5.66, gives you access to a predesigned source code snippet that enables you to add a standardized menu to your project:

StandardMenu   Creates a main menu bar with generic File, Edit, and Help menus

FIGURE 5.66.

The New dialog box Menus page.

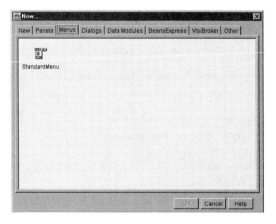

Using the Dialogs Page

The Dialogs page, shown in Figure 5.67, gives you access to predesigned code snippets that enable you to add standardized dialog boxes to your project:

About Box	Creates an about box dialog with product name, copyright, version labels, an image control, and a command button
Standard Dialog1	Creates an empty dialog box with horizontally aligned command buttons
Standard Dialog2	Creates an empty dialog box with vertically aligned command buttons
Password Dialog	Creates a dialog box with a password field and command buttons

FIGURE 5.67.

The New dialog box Dialogs page.

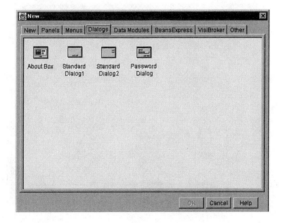

5

Using the Data Modules Page

The Data Modules page, shown in Figure 5.68, contains a predesigned code snippet that enables you to connect to the Dataset Tutorial database. You can use this snippet as a template for creating connections to other databases, as well.

Employee Data	Generates source code that provides database connection and query dataset examples

Using the BeansExpress Page

The BeansExpress page, shown in Figure 5.69, contains predesigned code snippets that provide you with examples of how to create your own custom JavaBeans components.

FIGURE 5.68.

*The New dialog box
Data Modules page.*

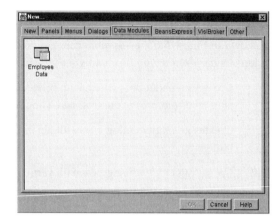

FIGURE 5.69.

*The New dialog box
BeansExpress page.*

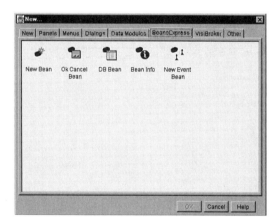

For all the details on these items, including a tutorial highlighting each one, select Help |
BeansExpress from the JBuilder IDE main menu bar. Here is a brief description of each
item:

New Bean	Creates a new generic component
Ok Cancel Bean	Creates a component containing command buttons
DB Bean	Creates a database-browsing component
Bean Info	Creates a BeanInfo class that exposes information about the corresponding component to its intended users (UI designers)
New Event Bean	Creates the pieces necessary for a new event set to go with your new JavaBeans component

Using the VisiBroker Page

The VisiBroker page, shown in Figure 5.70, contains a predesigned code snippet that creates an ORB server that serves an object.

CORBA Server   Generates source code that provides a connection to CORBA
                servers

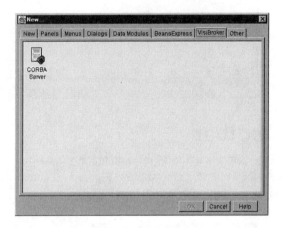

> **Note**   VisiBroker is provided with the JBuilder Client/Server edition.

5

Using the Other Page

The Other page, shown in Figure 5.71, can be used to gather up miscellaneous code snippets that you want to reuse. It starts you off with a predefined chunk of code that can be pasted into your file. Selecting the Example Snippet object from this page displays a secondary dialog box, where you can select all or part of the snippet to be pasted.

FIGURE 5.71.

*The New dialog box
Other page.*

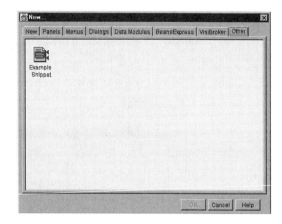

FIGURE 5.71.

*The New dialog box
Other page.*

Using the Toolbar

The toolbar gives you access to the 14 most commonly used commands as icons in one
convenient place—the JBuilder main window. Figure 5.72 shows the toolbar as it appears
in the JBuilder main window after installation.

FIGURE 5.72.

The toolbar.

> **Tip**
>
> Remember, to see which command a toolbar icon represents, move the
> mouse pointer over the icon, and a ToolTip displaying the command name
> appears momentarily.

You can adjust the size of the palette in the main window by placing your mouse over
the divider between the toolbar and Component Palette and then clicking and dragging
the divider until the toolbar is the desired size. If you hide the Component Palette, the
toolbar will expand to the entire width of the main window, leaving lots of blank space
for you to add new toolbar icons. You can also hide the toolbar by toggling the View |
Toolbar command.

Using the Component Palette

JBuilder contains JavaBeans components that can be accessed through the Component
Palette, which is located in the JBuilder main window. The palette is a collection of

tabbed pages filled with icons representing a selection of the components provided with JBuilder. You can add your own custom components, as well as components that you've purchased from third parties, to the Component Palette. You'll see examples of how each component on the Component Palette is used on Day 7, "JavaBeans Component Library."

Tip

> Positioning the mouse pointer briefly over a component displays a ToolTip containing the component's fully qualified class name. After you know its name, select the appropriate help command from the Help menu and drill down through the classes to the component's help page for more information.

You can adjust the size of the palette in the main window by placing your mouse over the divider between the Component Palette and the toolbar and then clicking and dragging the divider until the palette is the desired size. If you hide the toolbar, the Component Palette will expand to the entire width of the main window. You can also hide the Component Palette by toggling the View|Component Palette command.

If a palette page is not wide enough to display all its components, you can use the broad arrowheads at each end of the palette page to scroll through that page's components. If the area containing the palette is not wide enough to display all the palette page tabs, a pair of small arrowheads will appear in the upper-right corner of the palette, enabling you to scroll the page tabs.

Using the AppBrowser

The AppBrowser window is where you'll do most of your work in the JBuilder IDE: creating and adding files to projects, editing and debugging source code, and structuring your program. Figure 5.73 shows an AppBrowser window displaying the Welcome project in Debug mode.

You set the mode by selecting one of the tabs at the bottom left. The AppBrowser has seven modes:

- Project
- Opened Files
- Directory
- Debug

- Watch
- Class Hierarchy
- Search Results

FIGURE 5.73

An AppBrowser win-
dow in Debug mode.

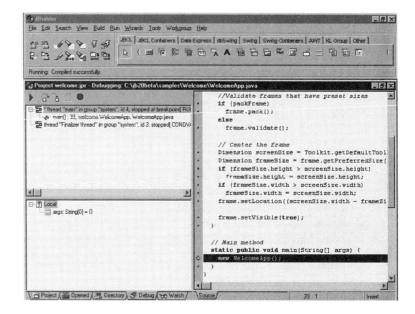

The last two modes don't show up as tabs in Figure 5.73. In the figure, both an icon and text are displayed in each mode tab. These tabs adjust their display depending on how much room they are given. If you want to see both the icon and the text, use the AppBrowser window's splitter to resize the panes by positioning your mouse over the divider between the left and right "halves" of the AppBrowser window, and then click and drag until the tabs are displayed as you desire. At a minimum, the tabs display the icon only.

In each mode, the panes on the left change to display information pertinent to that context and so are covered in the individual mode sections later in this section.

However, the Content pane on the right is always visible. It has its own set of tabs, which control how you want to view or edit the material in the Content pane. These tabs are Source, Design, Bean, Doc, View, Viewer, and Error pane. They appear in combination according to the context of the selected item in the AppBrowser.

If an item is selected for which there is a text representation, such as a .java or .html file, the Source tab appears. Selecting the Source tab displays the text in the Content pane, and it becomes the Editor.

If the selected item has an associated user interface design, the Design tab appears. This causes the AppBrowser window to become the UI Designer (see the "Using the UI Designer" section later today).

The Doc tab appears whenever the selected item can have an associated HTML documentation file, such as you would generate using the javadoc utility. (Remember that javadoc extracts documentation comments from your files and automatically creates an HTML file for you.) If the javadoc HTML file has been generated, it will be displayed in the Doc page of the Content pane; if not, a message stating this fact will be displayed instead.

If the selected item has a visual representation, such as a GIF, a JPEG, or an HTML file, the View tab appears. Selecting the View tab causes that graphic to be displayed in the Content pane.

One more feature of the Content pane is that you can toggle it so that it expands to cover the entire AppBrowser window by using either Alt+Z or the View|Toggle Curtain command. This can be very handy when working with large graphics or laying out your user interface design.

Using Project Browser Mode

When the AppBrowser window is in Project Browser mode, three sections appear: the Navigation pane, the Structure pane, and the Content pane. The Content pane might also display a secondary section, the Message view, when compiler errors occur. Figure 5.74 shows the Project Browser mode.

Navigation Pane

The upper-left pane of the Project Browser is the Navigation pane. This pane displays a tree representing the parts of the current project. As each node is selected in this pane, the other two panes are updated to reflect the new selection. Figure 5.74 shows the WelcomeFrame.java file selected in the Navigation pane.

Structure Pane

The lower-left pane is the Structure pane, and it displays the structure of the item currently selected in the Navigation pane. This tree structure shows all the classes, objects, methods, resources, and import files that compose the current project node. Selecting one of these structures will cause its content to be displayed in the Content pane. Figure 5.74 shows the structure of the WelcomeFrame.java file, with the jbInit() method selected.

FIGURE 5.74.

The AppBrowser window in Project Browser mode.

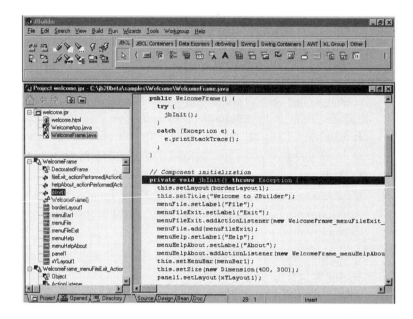

Content Pane

The pane on the right is the Content pane. What is displayed in this pane depends on what nodes are selected in the Navigation and Structure panes. If a .java file is selected in the Navigation pane, the Content pane will display the file and will be positioned according to the structure selected in the Structure pane. In Figure 5.74, because the WelcomeFrame.java file is selected in the Navigation pane, its Java source code is shown in the Content pane. And because the jbInit() method is selected in the Structure pane, that method is highlighted in the Content pane.

When a .java file is being displayed, the Content pane becomes the Editor. The page contains the source code for your program and its event handlers (methods) in text format. In addition to the code you add manually, code is also automatically generated and inserted into the source code in a number of ways. Changing the user interface (UI) design in the UI Designer invokes the *Two-Way Tools* feature and automatically inserts generated source code for the item you visually designed in the UI Designer.

The Editor provides Brief-style editing commands, syntax highlighting, search and replace functions, and the choice of four sets of key mappings to facilitate this task. When the Editor page is active, the bottom of the Content pane displays a panel containing status information: the Line:Column Indicator (*line:column*), the Modified Indicator (blank or Modified), and the Mode Indicator (Insert or Overwrite).

Using Opened Files Browser Mode

When the AppBrowser window is in Opened Files Browser mode, which is invoked by clicking the Opened tab, the Navigation Pane displays those files you have opened during that session. These files might or might not actually be part of the project, and you can add or remove files from the working set as desired without affecting the contents of the project. If you edit a file in the AppBrowser, it is automatically added to your Opened page. You can also add files to the Opened page by dragging and dropping files from other views onto the Opened tab.

When in Opened Files Browser mode, the Structure pane displays the structure of the file selected in the Navigation pane, and the Content pane displays the content of the file selected. If the file has a textual representation, the Source tab of the Content pane is an Editor.

Using Directory Browser Mode

Clicking on the Directory tab puts the AppBrowser window into Directory Browser mode and causes your computer's disk drive directory trees to be displayed in the Navigation pane. This gives you easy access to files you might want to add to your project or opened files. The Structure and Content panes have the same functionality in this mode as they do in Project Browser and Opened Files Browser modes.

Using Debug and Watch Modes

When you are ready to debug your program, JBuilder adds debugging views to your AppBrowser window for your convenience. You use the integrated debugger to execute your program by stepping over, tracing into, and pausing your code. While paused, you have access to several views that enable you to examine and change the values of variables and determine the state of objects.

In Debug mode (shown in Figure 5.73), the upper-left pane is the Threads and Stack pane, which lists the threads, methods, and parameters that were called to bring you to a certain point in program execution. The lower-left pane is the Data pane, which enables you to examine the state of an object's data. The Content pane displays the source, but now execution lines are indicated by a dot in the left gutter of the Editor, and an arrow is displayed to indicate the current execution line.

In Watch mode, the single left pane displays identifiers or expressions that you want to examine as they change while your application is running. These watches can be set with the Run | Add Watch command. The Content pane looks the same as it does in Debug mode.

5

The debugging views comprise the AppBrowser in Debug mode (Threads and Stack pane, Data pane, and Content pane), the AppBrowser in Watch mode (Watch pane and Content pane), the Breakpoint window, and the Inspector and Evaluate/Modify dialog boxes. These debugging views are covered in detail on Day 11, "Compiling and Debugging."

Using the UI Designer

To invoke the UI Designer, select a Frame node in the Navigation pane, and then click on the Content pane's Design tab. (You'll learn more about Frame components and how to add them to projects tomorrow.)

Selecting the Design tab invokes the UI Designer, converting the Content pane into the UI Designer, the Structure pane into the Component Tree, and displaying the Inspector window. These elements, shown in Figure 5.75, are used to design your program's user interface (UI).

FIGURE 5.75.

The UI Designer.

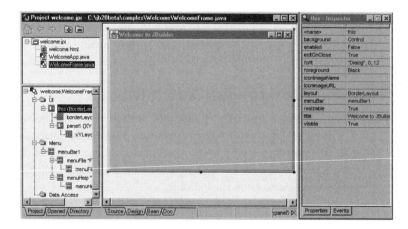

The Component Palette in the main window contains the drag-and-drop components you use to visually design your program. After you've placed menu components on the Frame in the UI Designer, the Menu Designer becomes available, which is used to lay out your program's menu system, both main menus and context menus. The AppBrowser window's Editor and the UI Designer views are synchronized so that any changes made to the Frame in the UI Designer are automatically reflected in your source code displayed in the Editor.

The UI Designer is the place where you design your application's user interface (UI). The Frame component acts as a container or parent of the components placed on it. The project can have multiple Frames to represent your application's windows, dialog boxes, and other interfaces with the application's underlying code.

In the JBuilder programming environment, the visual UI for your Java program is based on the contents of the Frame. The UI Designer gives you a graphical way to modify the Frame's properties, including placing and manipulating child components. The UI Designer's context menu conveniently provides many of the commands you need to arrange and manipulate the items in the Frame, such as alignment and spacing.

Controlling Projects Using the Component Tree

When the Content pane becomes the UI Designer, the Structure pane displays a structure hierarchy of the components in the current Frame in the UI Designer. This is the Component Tree, and it reflects all visual components that are added the to UI Designer. You can also add nonvisual components to the project by dropping them onto this pane.

 A *visual* component is one that can be viewed as a graphic in the UI Designer, such as a button or a label.

 A *nonvisual* component is one that has no graphical representation in the UI Designer, such as a dialog box or data access component.

When you select a node in the Component Tree, that item becomes selected in the UI Designer, and its properties and events are displayed in the Inspector.

Working with Components Using the Inspector

The Inspector is a separate window that is invoked when the Design tab is selected. In this window, event handlers and component properties are set at design time. When a component is selected in the Component Tree or UI Designer, its properties and event handlers are displayed in the Inspector. If the component is selected in the Inspector, it becomes the selected component in the UI Designer and Component Tree.

The Inspector window holds two multicolumn pages, the Properties page and the Events page. The component properties that are graphically represented in the UI Designer, such as size, color, and position, are listed and can be modified in the Properties page. The Events page is the point of origin for creating event handlers, which are methods that respond to messages.

Double-clicking on one of the entries in the Inspector window's Events page for the component inserts a skeleton method into the source code to hold your event-handling instructions.

After a skeleton method has been inserted, you need to add lines of code to instruct your program how to handle the event.

5

Note

Pressing F1 while your mouse cursor is pointing to a component in the Inspector or the component tree opens Help on that particular JavaBeans component.

Properties

On the Properties page, shown in Figure 5.76, the Property column on the left alphabetically lists the properties, and the Value column on the right lists the property values. Click on the property you want to change, or use the incremental search by typing the name of the desired property. In the Value column, click on the value you want to change. When multiple objects are selected, the changes you make to the Values column for a property are set for all the selected objects.

FIGURE 5.76.

The Inspector window
Properties page.

Events

On the Events page, shown in Figure 5.77, the Event column on the left alphabetically lists the events, and the Handler column on the right lists the event handlers. Click on the event you want to navigate to, or use the incremental search by typing the name of the desired event. In the Handler column, double-clicking a blank entry causes an event handler link to be formed and inserts skeleton procedure code into the source code in the Editor, positioning the cursor at the end of the first line of the newly created method.

After an event handler has been created, it can be associated with another event by clicking on the drop-down arrow to the right of the column and selecting it from the list of compatible handlers (those with matching parameter lists).

FIGURE 5.77.

The Inspector window Events page.

Menu Designer

The Menu Designer is invoked by double-clicking a Menu or PopupMenu in the Component Tree when the AppBrowser window is in Design mode. You can also right-click on a menu component and choose Activate designer from the pop-up menu. This object editor enables you to edit your menus graphically. As you add and delete menu items, the Menu Designer displays the menu just as it will look in your application.

NEW TERM   A *menu-bar item* refers to a menu item that, when invoked, displays a drop-down menu.

NEW TERM   A *menu-command item* refers to an menu item that, when invoked, executes a command or displays a dialog box.

The Menu Designer is shown in Figure 5.78. It shows the Help menu-bar item with an About menu-command item in `WelcomeFrame.java`. It also shows the Inspector displaying the Help menu-bar item's properties.

The Menu Designer enables you to immediately visualize how the menu you are creating will look at runtime. The ability to drag-and-drop menu items and whole submenus to rearrange the order of your menu makes creating menus one of the simplest tasks in creating your project.

5

FIGURE 5.78.

The AppBrowser window in Menu Designer mode.

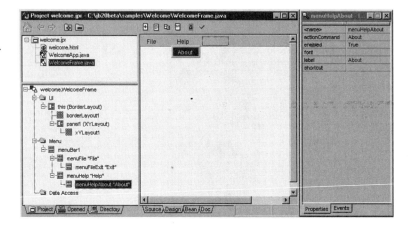

Summary

Today, you've taken a whirlwind tour of the JBuilder IDE and learned about its context-sensitive Help, the main window, and the AppBrowser window where you can navigate, edit, compile, and debug the elements of your projects. You've also explored the UI Designer comprising the UI Designer and Component Tree panes in the AppBrowser window and the Inspector, and you've explored the Menu Designer.

Q&A

Q Will Borland's JBuilder be available for platforms other than Windows?

A At the time of this writing, JBuilder is supported on Windows 95 and Windows NT. Although JBuilder might be supported on other platforms in the future, it is unknown at this time what platforms are currently under consideration. For the latest information, be sure to check out the JBuilder Web site at `http://www.inprise.com/jbuilder/`.

Q I prefer to use the Explorer for locating files, and I'd like to remove the Directory tab to make more room for the other tabs. How do I do this?

A To remove a mode tab from the AppBrowser, right-click on the tab and select the Drop *Tabname* tab command from the pop-up menu.

Workshop

The Workshop provides two ways for you to affirm what you've learned in this chapter. The Quiz section poses questions to help you solidify your understanding of the material covered. You can find answers to the quiz questions in Appendix A, "Answers to Quiz Questions." The Exercises section provide you with experience in using what you have learned. Try to work through all these before continuing to the next day.

Quiz

1. How can you get context-sensitive help in the JBuilder IDE?

2. When you select a .java file in the AppBrowser window's Navigation pane, what is displayed in the other two panes?

3. How do you invoke the UI Designer? The Menu Designer?

4. What command compiles the files in a project if the .class file is older than the .java source code file or if there is no .class file yet?

Exercises

1. Open and explore some of the Help files from the Help menu in the JBuilder IDE.

2. Try pressing F1 from various places in the JBuilder IDE and see what gets displayed!

3. Right-click in some of the JBuilder IDE panes, views, and windows, and explore what commands are available in each location.

3. See whether you can find the documentation for the <APPLET> tag in the Java Reference. (This will be very handy later.)

5

WEEK 1

DAY 6

User Interface Design

So far, you've been concentrating on Java programs that do very simple things. However, you probably want to start creating more complex programs that behave like real GUI (Graphical User Interface) applications, with buttons, menus, text fields, and other elements of user interface design. For the next two days, you'll be immersed in the components provided by Java class libraries. These components reside on the Component palette, and you can use them to design a wide array of user interfaces for your Java programs.

Today, you'll be introduced to the features of the Java Abstract Windowing Toolkit (AWT). Classes from the AWT can be used to create a complete user interface. In fact, the HotJava browser user interface was built using the AWT.

The AWT provides the following:

- A full set of UI widgets and other components, including windows, menus, buttons, check boxes, text fields, scrollbars, and scrolling lists

- Support for UI containers, which are components that can have other UI elements embedded in them

- Mechanisms for laying out components in a way that enables platform-independent UI design, called layout managers

You'll also learn how to use JBuilder IDE's UI Designer and Menu Designer to drag-and-drop your way through UI design, set properties, and provide initial values for your interface.

To create today's project, select File | New Project, modify the File field so it reads `C:\JBuilder\myprojects\UIDesign.jpr`, and then click the Finish button. You will add listings to the project later in this chapter by clicking the Add to Project icon above the Navigation pane, naming the file, and then typing the code.

Using the UI Designer

In the JBuilder IDE, several elements combine to provide you with a way to visually design your program's user interface. These elements—Component palette (main window), Navigation pane, Context Tree (Structure pane), UI Designer (Content pane), and Inspector—compose the UI Designer, which is invoked when you click on the Design tab in the Content pane of the AppBrowser window. After you've switched to the UI Designer, you can add components, set properties, and connect event handlers that will govern how your program interacts with the user.

For example, select File | New, select the Application icon, and then click OK. The first page of the Application Wizard dialog box appears. Delete the contents of the Package field, type `UITest` in the Class field, and then click the Next button. In the second page of the Application Wizard dialog box, type `MyFrame` in the Class field. Make sure none of the check boxes are checked, and click the Finish button. When the two `.java` files have been generated, click on the `MyFrame.java` node in the AppBrowser window Navigation pane, and then click the Design tab in the Content pane.

At this point, several things will happen. A message will appear in the Structure pane, `Opening designer...`, which will be replaced by a Context Tree of components. The Content pane becomes the UI Designer and displays your new user interface window, which includes the Inspector pane, with its Properties page on top. Figure 6.1 shows what the JBuilder IDE looks like in this configuration.

The Context Tree in the Structure pane shows you all the components that compose your UI design, and the levels show which components are contained by other components, called nesting. You can click on any item in the Context Tree, and it will become the selected component in the UI Designer pane, and its attributes will be displayed in the Inspector. The Context Tree view displays all the components (like the Frame, referred to as `this`) divided into top-level categories: UI, Menu, and Data Access.

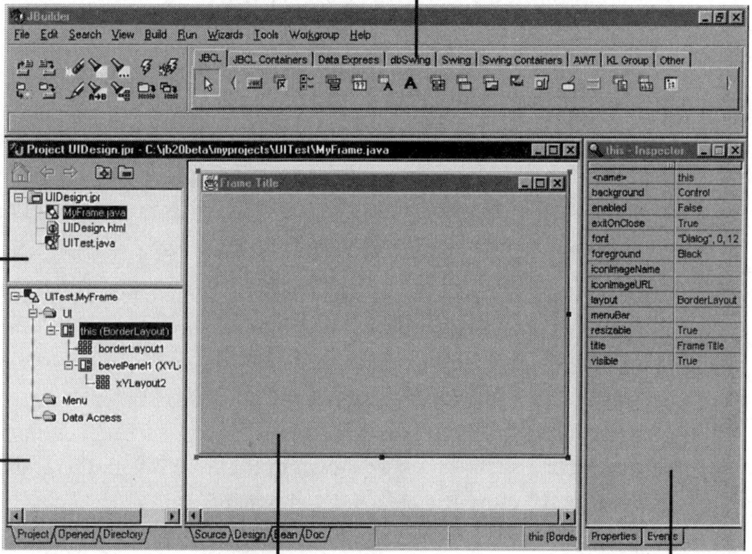

Component Palette (main window)

FIGURE 6.1.

The JBuilder IDE in UI Designer mode.

Navigation pane

Context Tree (Structure pane)

UI Designer (Content pane)   Component Inspector

Note

Some categories are displayed in the Context Tree view only when necessary. For example, a node named Other will appear if you add nonvisual components, such as dialogs, to your UI.

The Content pane, which now functions as the UI Designer, is waiting for you to add more components to your UI design, such as labels, text fields, and other graphical elements. When you select an item here, its node becomes selected in the Context Tree, and its attributes are displayed in the Inspector. In the UI Designer, you'll notice a number of small black boxes around the edges. These are grab handles that enable you to manipulate the component, and they indicate which component is selected.

The Inspector has two pages: Properties and Events. On the Properties page, the attributes associated with the selected component are listed, along with their current values. Here, you can set initial values for the attributes, and if the attribute has a visual representation, it will be reflected in the UI Designer pane. For example, if you change the font property for a label, you will see immediately the effect on the label itself. The Events page lists all the events to which the component is capable of responding and gives you access to existing event-handling methods that your component can use.

6

Although you'll create a few event-handling methods in today's examples, you'll mainly
be working with the Properties page. (Events and how to add event methods to your code
are discussed in detail on Day 12, "Handling Events.")

Modifying the GUI

Let's make a few modifications to this program, so you can see how to use the UI
Designer for adding components and setting properties and the Menu Designer for
adding and modifying menu items. For this program, you'll add a menu, an event
method, and a label field to display your message.

Click on the AWT page tab of the Component palette, click on the `java.awt.Label`
component (the one with the large capital A), and then click in the middle of the Frame
in the UI Designer. In the Inspector pane Properties page, click on the right column of
the `text` property, type `Anybody Home?`, and press Enter. Next, click on the `alignment`
property in the Inspector window, type `1`, and press Enter. When you're done, the UI
Designer pane should look as shown in Figure 6.2 with the grab handles indicating that
the label is the currently selected component.

FIGURE 6.2.

*The UI Designer pane
with a label.*

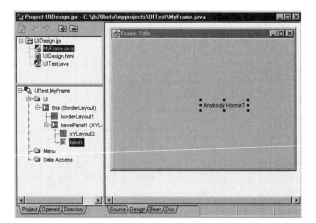

Now, click on the right column of the `<name>` property, type `lblAnybodyHome`, and press
Enter to give the identifier a more meaningful name than `label1`.

Note

The `<name>` property is not a standard Java property. JBuilder provides this
pseudo-property as a convenient way for you to change a component's identifier without having to do a search and replace throughout your code.
When you set this pseudo-property, the JBuilder IDE automatically finds
each occurrence of the old identifier name in JBuilder-generated code and
replaces it with the newly entered identifier name for you.

Notice that when you press Enter, the label's name is also updated in the Context Tree.

Next, in the Component palette's AWT page, click on the `java.awt.MenuBar` component, and then click in the UI Designer, somewhere near `lblAnybodyHome`. A component named `menuBar1` is added to the Context Tree. When you double-click the new `menuBar1` node, the Menu Designer is invoked, replacing the UI Designer in the Content pane (see Figure 6.3).

FIGURE 6.3.

Menu Designer in the AppBrowser window's Content pane.

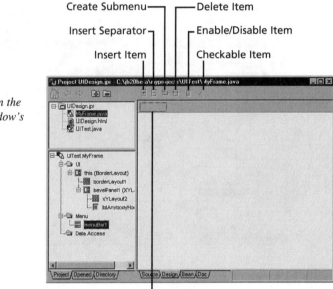

Create Submenu ─── ── Delete Item

Insert Separator ─ ┌── Enable/Disable Item

Insert Item ┌─ Checkable Item

Placeholder

Tip

If you've done something else in the meantime or closed the Menu Designer inadvertently, just double-click on the `menuBar1` component in the Context Tree to reopen the Menu Designer.

6

Before you add menu items, rename the menu component by clicking on the right column of the <name> property. Then, type `myMenuBar` and press Enter. To add your first menu-bar item to `myMenuBar`, click on the placeholder in the Menu Designer, type `File` as the first menu-bar item, and press Enter. As you do this, notice that two more placeholders are added: one below for the `File` menu's first menu-command item, and another to the right for the `myMenuBar`'s next menu-bar item. Also note that the Menu Designer has automatically named this new item `menu1`. Before adding any more items, rename this component `menuBarFile`.

To add the next item, click on the placeholder below the `File` menu-bar item, type `Say Hello`, and press Enter; rename it `menuItemFileSayHello`. Click on the placeholder below `Say Hello` in the Menu Designer, type `Exit`, and press Enter; rename it `menuItemFileExit`.

Let's add a second menu-bar item, to make this look more like a complete menu. Click on the placeholder to the right of the `File` menu-bar item, type `Help`, and press Enter; rename it `menuBarHelp`. When you're done, click on `File` in the Menu Designer. Figure 6.4 shows what the AppBrowser window looks like at this point.

FIGURE 6.4.

Menu Designer with the menu additions.

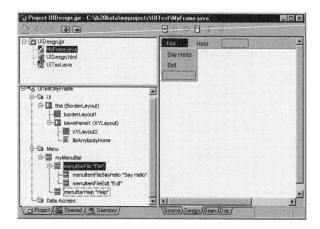

The Context Tree shows a complete outline of your menu's structure, whereas the Menu Designer shows its visual representation. As you select each item, either in the Context Tree or Menu Designer, its attributes will be displayed in the Inspector.

Tip

> Some of you who have created Windows menus are probably wondering why accelerators are not used here. The reason is that the & character used to indicate accelerators on Windows platforms is not recognized as being special on other platforms and shows up as a literal & character in your menu item label. Because this functionality is platform-specific, you should refrain from using menu accelerators in Java programs.

Next, you'll create simple event handlers for `menuItemFileSayHello` and `menuItemFileExit` so that they do something useful when invoked by the user.

 An *event-handler* is a method that responds to an event, such as a mouse click, mouse move, or keystroke.

In the Menu Designer, click on the `Say Hello` menu-command item, and then click the Events tab of the Inspector. For a menu-command item, there is only one event it can respond to, the `actionPerformed` event. Click the right column next to `actionPerformed`, and a new event-handling method name will be generated by combining the component's <name> property value with the event name. In this case, the method name becomes `menuItemFileSayHello_actionPerformed`, as shown in Figure 6.5.

FIGURE 6.5.

The Inspector pane displays the new event-handling method name.

Double-click in the right column next to `actionPerformed` after this method name is generated. This causes the AppBrowser window to return to Project Browser mode, closing the Inspector pane and setting the focus to the event-handling method name in the Structure pane. At the same time, JBuilder creates the method stub in the Source tab of the Content pane, ready for your event-handling code. Add this line of code to the method:

```
lblAnybodyHome.setText("Here I Am!");
```

The Content pane should now look as shown in Figure 6.6.

When the user selects the `Say Hello` menu item from the File menu, this code will change the label's text to `Here I Am!`

Because menu item nodes are listed in the Context Tree, you don't have to have the Menu Designer open to create an event handler for a menu-command item. However, you do have to have one of the designers open so that the Inspector pane is available. So click on the Design tab to switch back to UI Designer mode, and then click on the `menuItemFileExit` node in the Context Tree to display its attributes in the Inspector pane.

6

FIGURE 6.6.

The Content pane with new method code.

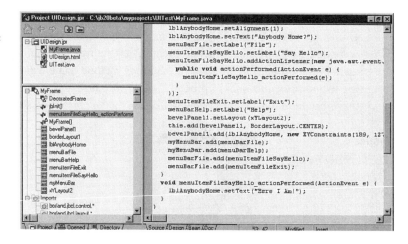

To create an event handler for the Exit menu-command item, click on the Events tab in the Inspector pane, and click on the right column to generate the new event-handling method name. Then double-click the method name to return to Project Browser mode, and add this line of code to the newly generated `menuItemFileExit_actionPerformed` method stub:

```
System.exit(0);
```

> **Tip**
>
> To switch between UI Designer mode and Project Browser mode, just click the Design and Source tabs, respectively. When you're in UI Designer mode, you can also switch easily between Menu Designer and UI Designer by double-clicking any node listed beneath the Menu and UI folder nodes, respectively.

Just to make the UI a bit more interesting, let's add another AWT control, using an alternate placement technique. Switch back to UI Designer mode by clicking on the Design tab of the Content pane. On the Component palette's AWT page, click on the `java.awt.Button`, and then click on the `bevelPanel1` in the Context Tree to add the button to the panel. Click on the Properties tab of the Inspector pane, then change the new `button1` component's `<name>` property to `btnWhereAreYou` and its `label` property to `Where Are You?` Remember to press Enter after changing each property to save your changes.

You want the `Where Are You?` button to update the label the same way that the `Say Hello` menu item does. So rather than create a new event handler, you're going to reuse the existing one. To do this, click on the Events tab, and then click on the right column next to the `actionPerformed` event. Because this component has an `actionPerformed` event, it is compatible with the one you've already created for the Say Hello menu item. To make the button use the existing event handler, just type `menuItemFileSayHello_actionPerformed` in the right column next to the `actionPerformed` event, and press Enter. (If you've already clicked and generated a method name, just highlight it and type over it.) When the user presses the Where Are You? button, the Anybody Home? label will change its text to say Here I Am!

Select File | Save All, and you're done. Notice that when the files are saved, that fact is reflected in the Status Bar in JBuilder's main window.

Viewing Generated Code

Now you can click on the `UITest.java` node in the Navigation pane, and click the Run button on the toolbar to try out your new GUI test application. Figure 6.7 shows what the application looks like after you click the Where Are You? Button.

FIGURE 6.7.

The running UITest *application.*

Listing 6.1 shows what is generated by the JBuilder IDE for the `UITest.java` file.

TYPE   **LISTING 6.1.** UITest.java.

```
1:    import com.sun.java.swing.UIManager;
2:
3:    public class UITest {
4:      boolean packFrame = false;
5:
6:      //Construct the application
7:
8:      public UITest() {
9:        MyFrame frame = new MyFrame();
10:       //Validate frames that have preset sizes
```

continues

6

LISTING 6.1. CONTINUED

```
11:        //Pack frames that have useful preferred size info,
              ➥e.g. from their layout
12:        if (packFrame)
13:          frame.pack();
14:        else
15:          frame.validate();
16:        frame.setVisible(true);
17:      }
18:      //Main method
19:
20:      public static void main(String[] args) {
21:        try  {
22:          UIManager.setLookAndFeel(new com.sun.java.swing.plaf.
              ➥windows.WindowsLookAndFeel());
23:          //UIManager.setLookAndFeel(new com.sun.java.swing.plaf.
              ➥motif.MotifLookAndFeel());
24:        }
25:        catch (Exception e) {
26:        }
27:        new UITest();
28:      }
29:  }
```

Listing 6.2 shows the entire MyFrame.java file, including your event-handling methods.

TYPE   **LISTING 6.2.** MyFrame.java.

```
1:   import java.awt.*;
2:   import java.awt.event.*;
3:   import borland.jbcl.control.*;
4:   import borland.jbcl.layout.*;
5:
6:   public class MyFrame extends DecoratedFrame {
7:
8:      //Construct the frame
9:      BorderLayout borderLayout1 = new BorderLayout();
10:     XYLayout xYLayout2 = new XYLayout();
11:     BevelPanel bevelPanel1 = new BevelPanel();
12:     Label lblAnybodyHome = new Label();
13:     MenuBar myMenuBar = new MenuBar();
14:     Menu menuBarFile = new Menu();
15:     MenuItem menuItemFileSayHello = new MenuItem();
16:     MenuItem menuItemFileExit = new MenuItem();
17:     Menu menuBarHelp = new Menu();
18:     Button btnWhereAreYou = new Button();
19:
20:     public MyFrame() {
```

```
21:      try {
22:        jbInit();
23:      }
24:      catch (Exception e) {
25:        e.printStackTrace();
26:      }
27:    }
28:    //Component initialization
29:
30:    private void jbInit() throws Exception{
31:      this.setLayout(borderLayout1);
32:      this.setSize(new Dimension(400, 300));
33:      this.setTitle("Frame Title");
34:      lblAnybodyHome.setAlignment(1);
35:      lblAnybodyHome.setText("Anybody Home?");
36:      menuBarFile.setLabel("File");
37:      menuItemFileSayHello.setLabel("Say Hello");
38:      menuItemFileSayHello.addActionListener(new
           ➥java.awt.event.ActionListener() {
39:        public void actionPerformed(ActionEvent e) {
40:          menuItemFileSayHello_actionPerformed(e);
41:        }
42:      });
43:      menuItemFileExit.setLabel("Exit");
44:      menuItemFileExit.addActionListener(new
           ➥java.awt.event.ActionListener() {
45:        public void actionPerformed(ActionEvent e) {
46:          menuItemFileExit_actionPerformed(e);
47:        }
48:      });
49:      menuBarHelp.setLabel("Help");
50:      btnWhereAreYou.setLabel("Where Are You?");
51:      btnWhereAreYou.addActionListener(new
           ➥java.awt.event.ActionListener() {
52:        public void actionPerformed(ActionEvent e) {
53:          menuItemFileSayHello_actionPerformed(e);
54:        }
55:      });
56:      bevelPanel1.setLayout(xYLayout2);
57:      this.add(bevelPanel1, BorderLayout.CENTER);
58:      bevelPanel1.add(lblAnybodyHome, new XYConstraints(197, 133, -1, -
1));;
59:      bevelPanel1.add(btnWhereAreYou, new XYConstraints(0, 0, -1, -1));
60:      myMenuBar.add(menuBarFile);
61:      myMenuBar.add(menuBarHelp);
62:      menuBarFile.add(menuItemFileSayHello);
63:      menuBarFile.add(menuItemFileExit);
64:    }
65:    void menuItemFileSayHello_actionPerformed(ActionEvent e) {
```

6

continues

LISTING 6.2. CONTINUED

```
66:        lblAnybodyHome.setText("Here I Am!");
67:     }
68:     void menuItemFileExit_actionPerformed(ActionEvent e) {
69:        System.exit(0);
70:     }
71: }
```

ANALYSIS In these two listings, all but two lines of code were generated either by the JBuilder IDE when the files were created or by your actions in the UI Designer windows. Lines 66 and 69 of Listing 6.2 are the lines for which you had to manually write code to instruct the event handlers what specific actions should be performed. The other lines of code were created for you through your visual design efforts.

In this example, you've exercised most of the features of the UI Designer: placing components, changing properties, creating event handlers, hooking up existing event handlers, and designing menus. In the following section, you'll examine each of the AWT controls, learning about their properties and the events to which they respond.

Understanding AWT

The AWT is Java's Abstract Windowing Toolkit, which comprises graphic control elements as defined in the java.awt package. This is the same package you've been importing all week to use the Graphics, Color, Font, and FontMetric classes. Java's AWT was designed to give Java programmers a way to create graphical user interfaces (GUIs) in the days before JavaBeans (components) were created. Before visual development environments, such as JBuilder, arrived on the scene, you had to instantiate AWT objects, set their properties, and create event handlers, all by manually writing source code.

 Note The AWT components have been modified to conform to the JavaBeans component standard since JDK version 1.1. All Java components are Java beans.

In JBuilder, these objects are presented as components on the Component palette so that, within the IDE, you can just drag-and-drop them onto the Frame. You don't have to know (or look up) what events a component responds to—the Inspector presents you with a list on its Events page. You don't have to remember (or look up) all the properties that a component has—the Inspector lists them on its Properties page. Much of the code that you would have written to instantiate AWT objects and connect events to event handlers is generated for you and placed into your source code automatically. Still, it's a smart idea to get a good grounding in the basics of how the AWT is put together because it forms the basis for the other components provided on the Component palette.

The basic idea of Java's Abstract Windowing Toolkit (AWT) is that a Java window is a set of nested components, starting from the outermost window all the way down to the smallest UI component. Components can include both visual components, which have a representation on the screen that you can see (such as windows, buttons, and panels), and nonvisual components, which don't appear until they're invoked (such as menus and dialogs). Some visual components are containers that can have other visual components nested within them.

The AWT components fall into two basic categories:

Containers	AWT components that can contain other components, including other containers. The most common form of container is the panel, which represents a container that can be displayed on-screen. An applet's drawing area is a form of panel, and in fact, the `Applet` class is a subclass of the `Panel` class.
UI Components	Buttons, lists, menus, check boxes, text fields, and other typical graphical user interface elements

The classes in the `java.awt` package are written and organized to mirror the abstract structure of containers and individual UI components.

The root of most of the AWT components is the class `Component`, which provides basic display and event-handling features. The `Container` class and many of the other UI components inherit from `Component`. Inheriting from the `Container` class are objects that can contain other AWT components—the `Panel` and `Window` classes, in particular. Note that the `java.applet.Applet` class, even though it resides in its own package, inherits from the `Panel` class, so your applets are an integral part of the hierarchy of components in the AWT system.

A graphical user interface-based application that you write by using the AWT can be as complex as you like, with dozens of nested containers and components inside each other. The AWT was designed so that each component can play its part in the overall AWT system without needing to duplicate or keep track of the behavior of other parts in the system.

6

In the JBuilder IDE, the AWT components are found on the AWT tab of the Component palette, as shown in Figure 6.8.

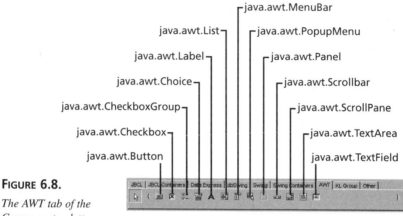

java.awt.MenuBar
java.awt.List
java.awt.PopupMenu
java.awt.Label
java.awt.Panel
java.awt.Choice
java.awt.Scrollbar
java.awt.CheckboxGroup
java.awt.ScrollPane
java.awt.Checkbox
java.awt.TextArea
java.awt.Button
java.awt.TextField

FIGURE 6.8.

The AWT tab of the Component palette.

In the next two sections, you'll explore the basic categories of AWT components: UI Components and Containers.

Using UI Components

The simplest form of AWT component is the basic UI component. You can create and add these to an applet without needing to know anything about containers—your applet is already an AWT container and is itself contained within another container, the browser window. Because an applet is a container, you can put other AWT components into it, nesting them as needed.

The basic procedure for adding the component to your user interface design is always the same. Simply click on the desired component in the Component palette, and then click in the UI Designer at the location where you want the component to appear. If you want to size the component at the same time you are placing it, click and hold down the left mouse button, drag until the outline is the desired size, and then release the mouse button. If you didn't get the component quite where you wanted it, click on it (anywhere but the grab handles), and drag it to the appropriate location. To resize the component after you've placed it, position the mouse over one of the grab handles until the cursor changes to the double-headed sizing cursor, and then click and drag the grab handle until the component is the size you desire.

> **Tip**
>
> Sometimes using the Inspector to set properties affecting size and locations makes it easier to create components of the same size.

In this section, you'll learn about these UI components, their key properties, the methods to get and set those property values, and their key events.

In the property descriptions that follow, the get*Xxxx*() method is used to obtain the property value and the set*Xxxx*(*datatype*) method is used to set the property value. These methods are generally used at runtime because you can easily set properties using the Inspector at design time. But you can also use these methods in event handlers at design time, such as when you used the label's setText() method in the Say Hello menu item's event handler earlier today.

Button

The java.awt.Button component is used to trigger some action in your interface when it is clicked. For example, a calculator applet might have buttons for each number and operator, or a dialog box might have OK and Cancel buttons. Button components have these key elements:

- label property—String value representing the visible text on the Button; getLabel(), setLabel(String)
- actionPerformed event—names the method called when the Button is pressed

Figure 6.9 shows a few buttons as they might appear in your user interface.

FIGURE 6.9.

Button *components.*

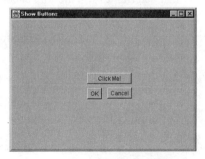

6

Checkbox

The java.awt.Checkbox component can be selected or unselected to provide options or indicate preferences. A check box can have two states: on or off (or checked and unchecked, selected and unselected, and so on). Unlike buttons, check boxes don't normally trigger direct or immediate actions in the interface, but rather are used to allow the user to select optional features that you want to occur for some future action in the interface.

Check boxes can be used in two ways:

- Non-mutually exclusive, which means that any Checkbox in a series of check boxes can be selected or not selected. This is the default.

- Mutually exclusive, which means that any Checkbox in the group that is selected automatically causes the rest of the check boxes in the group to be unselected. To make a Checkbox exclusive, you must set its checkboxGroup property; all check boxes with the checkboxGroup property value set are displayed as radio buttons.

Note   Radio buttons are commonly referred to as option buttons.

Checkbox components have these key elements:

- checkboxGroup property—CheckboxGroup component to which the Checkbox belongs, selected from a drop-down list of available CheckboxGroup components (if set, Checkbox becomes exclusive); getCheckboxGroup(), setCheckboxGroup(CheckboxGroup)

- label property—String value representing the visible text next to the Checkbox; getLabel(), setLabel(String)

- state property—boolean that determines whether the Checkbox is checked (true) or unchecked (false); getState(), setState(boolean)

- itemStateChanged event—names the method called when the state property of the Checkbox changes

Figure 6.10 shows two nonexclusive check boxes, one checked and the other unchecked.

FIGURE 6.10.

Nonexclusive Checkbox
components.

> Checkbox components in Java that belong to the same CheckboxGroup are the same as radio buttons in other languages. However, they are not automatically physically co-located, as a group. When creating check boxes that will belong to a group and will function as radio buttons, you might want first to place a container component, such as a Panel, to group them visually. Then place the check boxes within the container to visually cue the user that these components work together.

CheckboxGroup

The java.awt.CheckboxGroup component is a nonvisual component that serves to group exclusive check boxes together into radio button groups. Checkbox components with their checkboxGroup property value set to the same CheckboxGroup will become members of a radio button group, only one of which can be selected (state = true) at a time.

CheckboxGroup components have this key element:

- selectedCheckbox property—Checkbox in the group that is the currently selected radio button (automatically unselects the previously selected radio button); getSelectedCheckbox(), setSelectedCheckbox(Checkbox)

This component has no events. Figure 6.11 shows three exclusive check boxes (radio buttons) with the second one in the CheckboxGroup selected.

FIGURE 6.11.

Exclusive Checkbox *components in a* CheckboxGroup *component.*

6

> When placing Checkbox components into a CheckboxGroup component, the easiest procedure is as follows:

1. Place all the Checkbox components that you want to be in the group, and then add the CheckboxGroup component.

2. Use the multiple selection feature to select all the Checkbox components that will become members of the group by clicking the first one and then Shift-clicking the additional group member candidates.

3. When all the check boxes that belong in the group are selected, set the CheckboxGroup property for all of them at once by selecting the CheckboxGroup from the drop-down list on the Properties page.

When the check boxes are members of a group, setting the state property of any one to true will automatically set the state of all other check boxes in the group to false.

Label

The Label component displays nonselectable, non-editable text; however, it can be changed programmatically at runtime. Labels are usually used in conjunction with some other component, to identify the purpose of the other component. Labels can also be used to identify groups of components.

Label components have these key elements:

*   alignment property—int constant representing the horizontal alignment of the text string: 0 (Label.LEFT), 1 (Label.CENTER), 2 (Label.RIGHT); getAlignment(), setAlignment(int)

*   text property—String value representing the default text for the Label; getText(), setText(String)

For an example of Label components, refer to Figure 6.12 in the next section, "TextField."

TextField

The java.awt.TextField component is an editable field that enables the user to enter a single line of text and can also display a single line of text.

Tip

TextField components include only the editable field itself. You usually need to add a Label component next to the TextField to indicate what belongs in that editable field.

In addition, you can use the TextField component to create a text field that obscures the characters typed into it—for example, to implement password fields—by setting its echoChar property. Read-only fields are created by setting the editable property to false. TextField components have these key elements:

- columns property—int value representing the limit for the number of characters that can be typed or displayed in the field; getColumns(), setColumns(int)

- echoChar property—char value representing the character which is echoed to the screen for masking input; echoCharIsSet() returns a boolean, getEchoChar() returns a char, setEchoChar(char)

- editable property—boolean value representing the read-only attribute for the field: true is read-write and false is read-only; isEditable(), getEditable(), setEditable(boolean)

- text property—String value representing the default text for the field; getText(), setText(String)

- textValueChanged event—names the method called when the text property is modified or updated

Figure 6.12 shows two TextField components, each preceded by an identifying Label component, as they might appear in a login dialog.

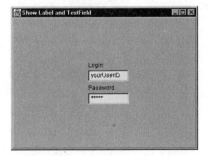

List

The List component displays a list of items from which one or more can be chosen. If the list is longer than the list box, a scrollbar is automatically provided. You can limit selection to a single item or allow multiple selections, by setting the multipleMode property.

List components have these key elements:

6

- `multipleMode` property—`boolean` value that determines whether to allow multiple selections (`true`) or limit to single selection (`false`); `setMultipleMode(boolean)`
- `items` property—`String` array representing the initial set of items to be displayed in the `List`; `getItem(int)` returns the `String` at the `int` index, `getItems()` returns a `String` array
- `selectedItem` property—`String` value representing the currently selected item; `getSelectedItem()` returns a `String`, `getSelectedItems()` returns a `String` array
- `itemStateChanged` event—names the method called when the `List` item selection changes

If the items are too long to fit, either horizontally or vertically, scrollbars will automatically be displayed. Figure 6.13 shows a `List` component with several items entered.

FIGURE 6.13.

`List` *component with several items and scrollbars.*

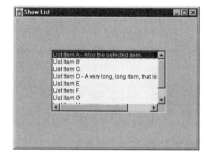

Choice

The `java.awt.Choice` component combines capabilities of a read-only `TextField` and `List` components. The `List` part of the `Choice` component is displayed when the user clicks the drop-down arrow to the right of the `TextField` part of the component. `Choice` components combine the key elements of `TextField` and `List` components.

Figure 6.14 shows how a `Choice` component looks in a running application when it first appears. Figure 6.15 shows how the same component looks with its list dropped down and the second item in the list ready to be selected.

MenuBar

The `java.awt.MenuBar` component enables you to display a hierarchical menu system, including submenus. Each new window in your user interface can have its own menu system. You can enable and disable menu items, have checkable menu items for toggling commands, add separator bars to group menu items, and add shortcuts to menu items (such as Ctrl+C for Copy). `MenuBar` components are composite components comprising

Menu components (menu-bar items) and MenuItem components (menu-command items), which have these key elements:

FIGURE 6.14.

Choice *component in a running application.*

FIGURE 6.15.

Choice *component with dropped list and second item highlighted.*

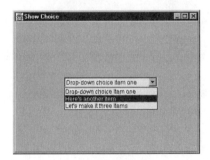

- label property—String value representing the text displayed for the menu item; getLabel(), setLabel(String)

- shortcut property—String value representing the text displayed to the right of the menu's label, which designates the keyboard shortcut for that item; getShortcut(), setShortcut(String)

- actionPerformed event—names the method called when a MenuItem is selected

For an example of what a MenuBar component with Menu and MenuItem components looks like, refer to Figure 6.4 in the "Using the UI Designer" section earlier today.

PopupMenu

The java.awt.PopupMenu component enables you to display a context menu in your user interface. The show() method controls how the PopupMenu is displayed in response to a call in an event-handling method of another component. For example, to show popupMenu1 in response to a user clicking on button1, you would insert the code line

```
popupMenu1.show(Frame1, 10, 30);
```

6

in button1's actionPerformed event handler, which would display popupMenu1 at coordinates 10,30 relative to the origin of Frame1 when button1 was clicked. Figure 6.16 shows what a sample PopupMenu looks like in the Menu Designer.

FIGURE 6.16.

PopupMenu *component in the Menu Designer.*

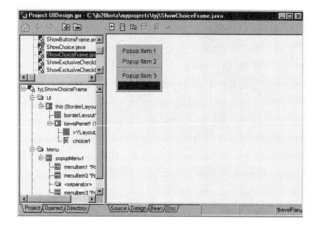

The Menu Designer's PopupMenuItem components inherit their functionality from the MenuBar component's MenuItem component.

Scrollbar

The Scrollbar component gives you a way to add scrollbars to manipulate a range of values. Scrollbars are used to select a value between a maximum and a minimum value. To change the current value of that Scrollbar, you can use three different parts of the component (see Figure 6.17, which shows a horizontal and a vertical scrollbar):

- An arrow on either end which, when clicked, increments or decrements the value by a small unit (1 by default).
- A shaft which, when clicked, increments or decrements the value by a larger amount (10 by default).
- A thumb (also sometimes called an elevator) whose position indicates the current value in the range. Dragging the thumb will scroll the value; releasing the thumb will set the value to the thumb's position.

Choosing any of these visual elements causes a change in the value; you don't have to update anything or handle any events. All you have to do is set the maximum and minimum properties, and Java will handle the rest. Scrollbar components have these key elements:

FIGURE 6.17.

Two Scrollbar *components, horizontal and vertical.*

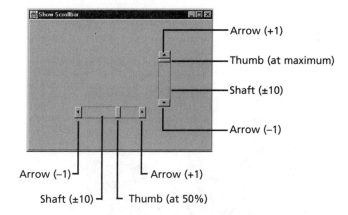

Arrow (+1)

Thumb (at maximum)

Shaft (±10)

Arrow (−1)

Arrow (−1)

Arrow (+1)

Shaft (±10)

Thumb (at 50%)

- maximum property—int value representing the upper bound for the range of values; getMaximum(), setMaximum(int)

- minimum property—int value representing the lower bound for the range of values; getMinimum(), setMinimum(int)

- orientation property—int constant: 0 (Scrollbar.HORIZONTAL) or 1 (Scrollbar.VERTICAL); getOrientation(), setOrientation(int)

- blockIncrement property—int value representing how many units the Scrollbar will increment or decrement when the shaft is clicked; getBlockIncrement(), setBlockIncrement(int)

- unitIncrement property—int value representing how many units the Scrollbar will increment or decrement when an arrow is clicked; getUnitIncrement(), setUnitIncrement(int)

- value property—int value representing the absolute value and therefore the position of the trailing edge of the thumb; getValue(), setValue(int)

- adjustmentValueChanged event—names the method called when the value property is modified

6

TextArea

The TextArea component is similar to a TextField, except that it allows multiple lines of text. Because TextArea components can be any given width and height and have scrollbars by default, you can deal with larger amounts of text more easily. TextArea components share the properties and methods of TextField and Scrollbar components, plus these additional key elements:

- rows property—int value representing the number of rows of text the text window can display; getRows(), setRows(int)

- textValueChanged event—names the method called when the text property value is modified

Figure 6.18 shows a TextArea control with a horizontal scrollbar.

FIGURE 6.18.

A TextArea *component with some text.*

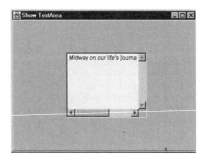

Using Containers

Containers are components in which you can place other components. The Panel and ScrollPane components on the AWT page are both containers, and they can be nested as many levels deep as you desire. You can use them to group and arrange other UI components and to add visual depth to your interface. The other really handy thing about containers is that when you have placed other components into them, you can move them as a group by moving the container component.

Panel

The java.awt.Panel component displays a rectangle, whose background color you can set, within which you can nest other components, including other container components. Panel components have this key element:

- layout property—sets the arrangement of the components nested within the Panel; setLayout(int, int), setLayout(Point). This property is discussed in the "Arranging Controls with Layout Managers" section later today.

Note

The JBuilder Application Wizard automatically adds a panel to all your applications. It adds the BevelPanel component, which is part of the borland.jbcl.control package.

Tip

Check the Use Only Core JDK and Swing Classes check box on the first page (Step 1) of the JBuilder Application Wizard dialog box if you don't want the `JBCL BevelPanel` component to be used.

ScrollPane

The `java.awt.ScrollPane` component displays a rectangle with horizontal and vertical scrollbars as needed. This is a special container component that provides a scrollable "view port" onto a single child component nested within. `ScrollPane` has these key elements:

- `scrollPosition` property—`Point` coordinates of the child component which will appear at the 0,0 coordinates in the `ScrollPane`; `getScrollPosition()`, `setScrollPosition(int, int)`, `setScrollPosition(Point)`.

- `layout` property—sets the arrangement of the components nested within the `ScrollPane`; `setLayout(int, int)`, `setLayout(Point)`. This property is discussed in the "Arranging Controls with Layout Managers" section later today.

Figure 6.19 shows how a `Frame` might look with a `TextField` component nested in a `ScrollPane` component.

FIGURE 6.19.

A ScrollPane *component containing a* TextField *component.*

Arranging Controls with Layout Managers

You know at this point that a `Panel` can contain UI components or other `Panel` components. The question now is how those components are actually arranged and displayed on the screen.

In other windowing systems, UI components are sometimes arranged using hard-coded pixel coordinates, the same way you used the graphics operations to paint squares and ovals on the applet's drawing area. In Java, the window can be displayed on many

6

different windowing systems on many different screens, with many different fonts using different font metrics. Therefore, you need a more flexible method of arranging components on the screen so that a layout that looks nice on one platform doesn't appear to be a jumbled mess on another platform. For this purpose, Java has layout managers, insets, and hints that each component can provide to assist with laying out the screen.

The actual appearance of components on the screen is determined by two things: the order in which they were added to the Panel that holds them, and the layout manager that Panel is currently using to lay out the screen. The layout manager determines how portions of the screen will be sectioned and how components within that Panel will be placed.

Note that each Panel component in your user interface can have its own layout manager by setting its layout property. By nesting panels within panels and using the appropriate layout manager for each one, you can often arrange your UI to group and arrange components in a way that is both functionally useful and also looks good on a variety of platforms and windowing systems.

The AWT provides eight layout managers, which are listed in the layout property's drop-down list:

BorderLayout	Arranges components designated as North (top), South (bottom), East (right), West (left), and Center (middle) within the Panel
CardLayout	Arranges components as cards that can be seen one at a time within the Panel
FlowLayout	Arranges components linearly left to right in rows, top to bottom, with each line of components horizontally centered in the Panel
GridLayout	Arranges components in specified rows and columns within the Panel
GridBagLayout	Arranges and resizes components according to specified constraints within the Panel
XYLayout	Arranges components according to their x,y origin coordinates within the Panel
PaneLayout	Arranges components as separate panes within the ScrollPane

| VerticalFlowLayout | Arranges components linearly top to bottom, with each line of components vertically centered in the Panel |

Once the layout is set, you can start adding components to the Panel. The order in which components are added is often significant, depending on which layout manager is currently set. In the UI Designer, you'll notice that below each Panel component, the first item listed is the layout for that Panel. That's because setting the layout property for the Panel actually creates a corresponding layout component, each with properties of its own.

In the following sections, the layout managers are presented in order of increasing complexity. You'll learn about each layout manager component, its properties and methods, and how it controls presentation of components within the Panel.

FlowLayout

The FlowLayout is the most basic of layouts. Using FlowLayout, components are added to the Panel one at a time, row by row. If a component doesn't fit onto the current row, it's wrapped onto the next row. FlowLayout also has an alignment, which determines the alignment of each row. By default, each row is center aligned.

After you have set the layout property of the Panel to FlowLayout, a new FlowLayout component is added to the Context Tree just below the Panel component. By selecting the new FlowLayout component in the Context Tree, you can examine its properties on the Properties page of the Inspector:

- alignment property—int constant representing alignment of FlowLayout rows: 0 (FlowLayout.LEFT), 1 (FlowLayout.CENTER), 2 (FlowLayout.RIGHT); getAlignment(), setAlignment(int)

- hgap property—int value representing the number of units between components in the rows (defaults to 5); getHgap(), setHgap(int)

- vgap property—int value representing the number of units between rows (defaults to 5); getVgap(), setVgap(int)

Figure 6.20 shows a FlowLayout and its effect on a row of five buttons.

GridLayout

The GridLayout offers more control over the placement of components inside a Panel. Using a GridLayout, you portion the area of the Panel into rows and columns. Each component you then add to the Panel is placed in a cell of the grid, starting from the top row and progressing through each row from left to right. Here's where the order of adding components becomes relevant. By using GridLayout and nested grids, you can often place UI components precisely where you want them.

FIGURE 6.20.

FlowLayout *and five buttons.*

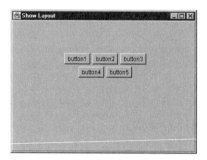

When you have set the layout property of the Panel to GridLayout, selecting the new GridLayout component in the Context Tree displays these properties:

- columns property—int value representing the number of columns in the grid (defaults to 0); getColumns(), setColumns(int)
- rows property—int value representing the number of rows in the grid (defaults to 1); getRows(), setRows(int)
- hgap property—int value representing the number of horizontal units between cells (defaults to 0); getHgap(), setHgap(int)
- vgap property—int value representing the number of vertical units between cells (defaults to 0); getVgap(), setVgap(int)

Figure 6.21 shows the same five buttons in a Panel with the layout changed to GridLayout, and the GridLayout component's rows property set to 2.

FIGURE 6.21.

GridLayout *of two rows of buttons.*

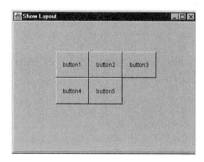

BorderLayout

The BorderLayout arranges components within the Panel by geographic location: Center, South, West, North, and East. After you have set the layout property of the Panel to BorderLayout, select the new BorderLayout component to see its properties:

- hgap property—int value representing the number of horizontal units between components (defaults to 0); getHgap(), setHgap(int)
- vgap property—int value representing the number of vertical units between components (defaults to 0); getVgap(), setVgap(int)

Figure 6.22 shows a BorderLayout of those same five buttons.

FIGURE 6.22.

BorderLayout *of five buttons.*

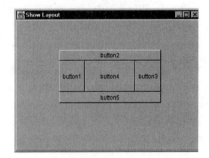

VerticalFlowLayout

The VerticalFlowLayout arranges components within the Panel vertically, from top to bottom. After you have set the layout property of the Panel to VerticalFlowLayout, select the new VerticalFlowLayout component to see its properties:

- alignment property—int value that sets the vertical alignment of the container's components: 0 aligns them to the top (default), 1 centers them vertically, and 2 aligns them to the bottom
- hgap property—int value representing the number of horizontal units between components (defaults to 0); getHgap(), setHgap(int)
- horizontalFill property—Boolean value
- verticalFill property—Boolean value
- vgap property—int value representing the number of vertical units between components (defaults to 0); getVgap(), setVgap(int)

Figure 6.23 shows a VerticalFlowLayout of buttons.

6

FIGURE 6.23.

VerticalFlowLayout
of buttons.

CardLayout

The CardLayout manager doesn't actually visually arrange components. Instead, it produces a slide show of components, which are shown one at a time within the Panel. If you've ever used the HyperCard program, you've seen how this works.

Generally, when you create a CardLayout, the components you add to it will be other container components—usually Panel components. You can then use different layouts for those individual "cards" so that each one has its own look. When you add each card to the Panel, you can give it a name. Then you can use methods defined in the CardLayout class to move back and forth between different cards in the layout.

After you have set the layout property of the Panel to CardLayout, select the new CardLayout component to see its properties:

- hgap property—int value representing the number of horizontal units between components (defaults to 0); getHgap(), setHgap(int)
- vgap property—int value representing the number of vertical units between components (defaults to 0); getVgap(), setVgap(int)

XYLayout

The XYLayout enables you to arrange components precisely according to their x,y origin coordinates within the Panel. This is a custom layout manager supplied by JBuilder so that you can place components exactly where you want them without having a layout manager interfere while you are prototyping.

Tip

> After you've decided on a layout using the XYLayout manager, be sure to change the Panel component's layout property to one of the standard Java layouts so that it will look nice on platforms other than the one on which it was designed.

Figure 6.24 shows what components placed in an XYLayout might look like.

FIGURE 6.24.

XYLayout *of various components in a* Panel.

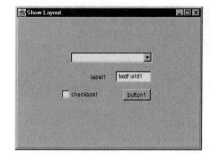

PaneLayout

The PaneLayout arranges components by splitting display space with existing selected components within the Panel. For example, if you added a TextField to a Panel and set the Panel component's layout property to PaneLayout, it would look as shown in Figure 6.25.

FIGURE 6.25.

A TextField *in a* Panel *set to* PaneLayout.

The TextField is automatically resized to take up the entire Panel's display space, so it just looks like an oversized TextField. Now add a second TextField and see what happens, as shown in Figure 6.26.

FIGURE 6.26.

Adding a second TextField *to the* Panel.

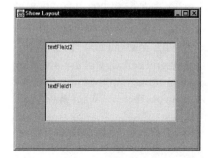

6

Adding a third, fourth, and fifth `TextField` produces the result in Figure 6.27.

FIGURE 6.27.

Adding three more
`TextField` *components*
to the `Panel`.

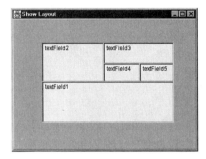

The `ScrollPane` layout simply splits the space of the currently selected component with the newly placed component.

Note   The way that the UI Designer splits the space of the currently selected component depends on where you click in the component to add new components. You can change the way JBuilder splits it up for you by dragging the splitter bars.

GridBagLayout

The `GridBagLayout` is a variation of the `GridLayout` which relies on `GridBagConstraints`. The number of constraint options that can be set for this layout make it the most complex layout available, but it gives you more control over layout.

When you have set the `layout` property of the `Panel` to `GridBagLayout`, you then set the `constraints` property for each container in the `Panel`. When this layout is in effect, the `constraints` property will display an ellipsis (...) button to the right of the property value. Clicking on that button will display the Constraints dialog for that component, as shown in Figure 6.28.

In this dialog, you can specify many aspects of how a component is positioned within the `Panel`:

- Grid Position options control the row and column position where the component will be placed and how many grid cells it will use as its display area. For example, a button in the second column of the third row would be X=1, Y=2 (indices begin at 0). A width of 2 would indicate that you want the component to take up two horizontal grid cells.

FIGURE 6.28.

The Constraints dialog for a Button *whose* Panel *has been set to* GridBagLayout.

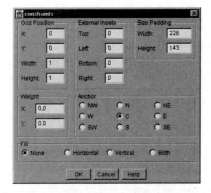

- External Insets options determine how much external padding a component will have between its border and the edge of its display area.

- Size Padding governs how many pixels are added to the component's minimum size as internal padding.

- Weight options specify what proportion of the row the component should receive for its display space when it is resized.

- Anchor options tell where the component should be positioned within its display area when the component is smaller than the area allowed.

- Fill options specify whether the component should expand itself to fill up its display area.

For a full explanation of how to use constraints, refer to the "GridBagLayout" topic in the User's Guide help file, listed under "Designing a User Interface, Layouts Provided by JBuilder."

Summary

Today, you learned more about the UI Designer and how you can use it to design your graphical user interface with drag-and-drop ease. You also learned about the components on the AWT page of the Component palette and their key properties, methods, and events. The AWT components form the basis of the other GUI components on the palette and are well worth studying. Tomorrow, you'll become acquainted with the advanced JavaBeans components that compose JBuilder's JavaBeans Component Library, or JBCL.

6

Q&A

Q You've mentioned a lot about the `Component` and `Container` classes, but it looks like the only `Container` objects that ever get created are `Panel` components. What do the `Component` and `Container` classes give me?

A Those classes factor out behavior for generic AWT components and containers. Although you don't necessarily create direct instances of these classes, you can create subclasses of them if you want to add behavior to the AWT that the default classes do not provide. When you begin to create your own JavaBeans components, these classes will become more valuable to you.

Q Can I put a UI component at a specific `x,y` position on the screen?

A By using the `XYLayout` manager provided by JBuilder, you can do so, but it is recommended only for the prototyping phase of creating your user interface. When you've decided which layout looks best, select the standard layout manager that corresponds with your final layout, and change over to that layout. That way, you'll be assured that your program will look its best on different platforms. You can't guarantee that with hard-coded layouts.

Q I was exploring the AWT package, and I saw this subpackage called `peer`. There are also references to the peer classes sprinkled throughout the API documentation. What do peers do?

A Peers are responsible for the platform-specific parts of the AWT. For example, when you create an AWT window, you have an instance of the `Window` class that provides generic window behavior, and then you have an instance of a class implementing `WindowPeer` that creates the very specific window for that platform—a Motif window under the X Window System, a Macintosh-style window on the Mac, or a MS Windows window under Windows 95 or Windows NT. These peer classes also handle communication between the window system and the Java window itself. By separating the generic component behavior (the AWT classes) from the actual system implementation and appearance (the peer classes), you can focus on providing behavior in your Java application and let the Java implementation deal with the platform-specific details.

Workshop

The Workshop provides two ways for you to affirm what you've learned in this chapter. The Quiz section poses questions to help you solidify your understanding of the material covered. You can find answers to the quiz questions in Appendix A, "Answers to Quiz Questions." The Exercises section provides you with experience in using what you have learned. Try to work through all these before continuing to the next day.

Quiz

1. What do you do to invoke UI Designer mode in the AppBrowser?

2. How do you switch between the Menu Designer and the UI Designer?

3. What are the differences between an exclusive and non-exclusive Checkbox? What component must be added, and what Checkbox property must be set to make a Checkbox act like a radio button?

4. True or False? It's okay to leave Panel components set to XYLayout when you are ready to distribute your program.

5. Which layout manager arranges your components according to the points of the compass?

Exercises

1. Create an application with a Frame component whose appearance mimics the layout of the dialog that appears when you select the Search | Browse Symbol menu item in the IDE. Begin the exercise by selecting File | New and double-clicking on the Application object.

2. Add one or more of each AWT component to a Panel and experiment with the different layout managers to see how they affect your design. Remember to first place a Panel component in the Frame, and then set the Panel component's layout property to change its effective layout manager. Experiment with the layout properties in each layout manager. Try nesting Panel components and selecting different layout managers for each level.

6

DAY 7

JavaBeans Component Library

JBuilder contains JavaBeans components that can be accessed through the Component Palette, each palette page containing a category of JavaBeans components.

NEW TERM A *Java bean*, or *bean*, is a Java-based component comprising a class with methods, properties, and events that defines an instantiable object.

In addition to the components provided with JBuilder, you can add third-party components that you've purchased, as well as your own custom components. Figure 7.1 shows the Component Palette as it appears in JBuilder's main window.

FIGURE 7.1.

The Component
Palette.

The items displayed on the palette are controlled by the currently loaded Palette .INI file. By maintaining different .INI files, you can switch among several component palettes, depending on your project's needs.

To configure the Component Palette, place the mouse over the palette and right-click. This displays a pop-up menu containing the Properties command. Selecting the Properties command displays the Palette Properties dialog box (see Figure 7.2), where you specify the page, class name, and icon image for the new component you want added to the Component Palette. The page name defaults to the currently selected palette page. You can select an existing page, or you can create a new page by specifying a name not currently on the palette. The class name must be fully qualified, and the icon image must be a GIF file. You can use the Shift+Ctrl keys to select multiple components.

FIGURE 7.2.

The Palette Properties
dialog box.

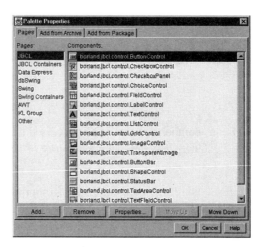

In its default configuration, the Component Palette presents tabbed pages containing AWT beans, JBuilder beans, and other JavaBeans components (such as you might create yourself). The sections that follow correspond to each Component Palette page and describe what the component's capabilities are after it is placed in the UI Designer.

Note On many of the palette pages, you'll notice that the components are data aware, which means that they can display fields of table data when used in conjunction with databases and the Data Express components (Pro and C/S only).

In the property descriptions that follow, the get*Xxxx*() method is used to obtain the property value, and the set*Xxxx*(*datatype*) method is used to set the property value. Occasionally, the data type of a method's return value or argument is different from the data type of the property; these exceptions are noted where they apply.

Using JBCL Components

The components on the JBCL page are defined in the borland.jbcl.control package and are data aware. In addition to being data aware, these components typically provide more special features than their AWT counterparts. For instance, the ButtonControl component is able to display images, whereas the Button component from the AWT is not. Figure 7.1 shows the JBCL page of components.

The components on this page are the ones you'll use most often in building your Java programs, and they are selected by default when you load JBuilder. The sections that follow give a brief description of each component, along with its key methods, properties, and events.

ButtonControl

The ButtonControl is a pushbutton to launch actions. It can include a graphical image as well as a text label. ButtonControl components have these key elements:

- label property—String representing the visible text on the ButtonControl; getLabel(), setLabel(String)

- image property—Image or URL value representing a GIF or JPEG image; getImage() returns an Image; setImage(Image); setImage(URL)

- imageFirst property—boolean value that controls whether the image is top/left of the button's label; isImageFirst()

- orientation property—int constant: Orientation.HORIZONTAL (image and label form a row) or Orientation.VERTICAL (image and label form a column); getOrientation(); setOrientation(int)

- actionPerformed event—names the method called when the ButtonControl is pressed

7

CheckboxControl

The CheckboxControl is a check box that enables the user to make on/off, true/false choices. It can also be used to set/display Boolean values in a table field. CheckboxControl components can be either non-mutually exclusive or mutually exclusive, just like AWT Checkbox components. CheckboxControl components have these key elements:

- label property—sets the visible text next to the Checkbox; getLabel(), setLabel(String)
- readOnly property—boolean value determines whether the check box is a read-only control (true) or a read-write control (false)
- checked property—boolean value determines whether the Checkbox is checked (true) or unchecked (false); getChecked(), setChecked(boolean)
- itemStateChanged event—names the method called when the state property of the Checkbox changes

Tip

CheckboxControl components in Java that are placed within a grouped CheckboxPanel container are radio buttons (exclusive check boxes).

CheckboxPanel

The CheckboxPanel is a BevelPanel with multiple check boxes that can be grouped. If the grouped property is true, all check boxes contained within the CheckboxPanel become exclusive (radio buttons). CheckboxPanel components have these key elements:

- grouped property—boolean value that determines whether the check boxes within are grouped and exclusive (true) or ungrouped and non-exclusive (false); isGrouped(), setGrouped(boolean)
- labels property—String array of labels for radio buttons; getLabels(), setLabels(String[]), addLabel(String)
- orientation property—int constant: Orientation.HORIZONTAL (check boxes form a row) or Orientation.VERTICAL (check boxes form a column); getOrientation(), setOrientation(int)
- selectedIndex property—int representing which radio button is selected in the group; getSelectedIndex(), setSelectedIndex(int)

- selectedLabel property—String of the selected radio button's text label; getSelectedLabel(), setSelectedLabel(String)

Note that check boxes within a CheckboxPanel that are not grouped are nonetheless contained within the CheckboxPanel and can be moved together as a unit.

ChoiceControl

The ChoiceControl is a drop-down selection list, also known as a combo box, which combines capabilities of a read-only TextFieldControl and ListControl components. ChoiceControl components combine the key elements of TextFieldControl and ListControl components.

FieldControl

The FieldControl is a type-controlled input and editing field of table data. FieldControl components have these key elements:

- columnName property—String representing the table column containing text to be displayed; getColumnName(), setColumnName(String)
- dataSet property—DataSet object containing the table data to be displayed; getDataSet(), setDataSet(DataSet)
- editInPlace property—boolean value that determines whether field is read-write (true) or read-only (false)
- text property—String for the default text; getText(), setText(String)
- modelContentChanged event—names the method called when the list content changes

LabelControl

The LabelControl component displays nonselectable, non-editable text. LabelControl components have these key elements:

- alignment property—int constant (LEFT, CENTER, RIGHT) representing the alignment of the Label; getAlignment(), setAlignment(int)
- columnName property—String representing the table column containing text to be displayed; getColumnName(), setColumnName(String)
- dataSet property—DataSet object containing the table data to be displayed; getDataSet(), setDataSet(DataSet)
- text property—String for the Label; getText(), setText(String)

7

TextControl

The TextControl component. TextControl components have these key elements:

- alignment property—int constant representing the alignment of the Label; getAlignment(), setAlignment(int)

- text property—String for the Label; getText(), setText(String)

The TextControl displays specified text over a transparent background. Your applications can dynamically change the text in a TextControl component.

ListControl

The ListControl displays a scrollable list of selectable text items, and it can be used to display/update a field of table data. You can limit selection to a single item or allow multiple selections by setting the multiSelect property. ListControl components have these key elements:

- columnName property—String representing the table column containing text to be displayed; getColumnName(), setColumnName(String)

- dataSet property—DataSet object containing the table data to be displayed; getDataSet(), setDataSet(DataSet)

- items property—String array of items in the list; getItems(), setItems(String[])

- boolean value that determines whether to allow multiple selections (true) or limit to single selection (false);

- multiSelect property—boolean value that determines whether to allow multiple selections (true) or limit to single selection (false); isMultiSelect(), setMultipleMode(boolean)

- setItems(DataSet, String) method—sets the contents of the specified column (String) in a DataSet to the list's current contents

- modelContentChanged event—names the method called when the list content changes

- selectionChanged event—names the method called when the single selection item changes

- selectionItemChanged event—names the method called when the noncontiguous multiple item selection changes

- selectionRangeChanged event—names the method called when the contiguous multiple item selection changes

If the items are too long to fit, either horizontally or vertically, scrollbars will be displayed automatically.

LocatorControl

The LocatorControl is used to select DataSet records by performing an incremental search of the current column if it is a character column. If the column is of some other type, the search is not incremental, and the locate occurs after the user presses the Enter key.

> **Tip**
>
> When the LocatorControl is used with another control sharing the same DataSet, such as a GridControl, the current match can be displayed in the GridControl as the incremental search proceeds. The locate can also generate messages, so it is a good idea to direct those messages to a StatusBar component.

LocatorControl components have these key elements:

- caseSensitive property—boolean value that determines whether the locate will not be case-sensitive (false) or will be case-sensitive (true); isCaseSensitive(), setCaseSensitive(boolean)
- columnName property—String value representing the table column containing text to be displayed; getColumnName(), setColumnName(String)
- columns property—int value representing limit for the number of characters that can be typed or displayed in the field; getColumns(), setColumns(int)
- dataSet property—DataSet object binds the control to a data set; getDataSet(), setDataSet(DataSet)
- echoChar property—char that is echoed to the screen for masking input; echoCharIsSet() returns a boolean, getEchoChar() returns a char, setEchoChar(char)
- text property—String for the component's default text; getText(), setText(String)
- modelContentChanged event—names the method called when the content in the related DataSet changes
- textValueChanged event—names the method called when the text property is modified or updated

7

GridControl

The GridControl displays table or query data in a grid format. Display properties can be set column-by-column and the grid can be used as a data-aware spreadsheet control. GridControl components have these key elements:

- columnCount property—int representing the number of columns in the grid's DataSet; getColumnCount()
- columnHeaderVisible property—boolean determining whether column headers should be displayed (true) or not displayed (false)
- dataSet property—DataSet object containing the table data to be displayed; getDataSet(), setDataSet(DataSet)
- editInPlace property—boolean value determining whether field is read-write (true) or read-only (false)
- items property—String array of items in the list; getItems(), setItems(String[])
- multiSelect property—boolean value determining whether to allow multiple selections (true) or limit to single selection (false); isMultiSelect(), setMultipleMode(boolean)
- navigateWithDataSet property—boolean indicating whether the current row in the GridControl should move in sync with the current row in the DataSet and vice-versa (true), or whether it should navigate independently (false); isNavigateWithDataSet(), setNavigateWithDataSet(boolean)
- rowCount property—int value representing the number of rows in the grid's DataSet; getRowCount()
- rowHeaderVisible property—boolean indicating whether row headers should be displayed (true) or not displayed (false)
- selectColumn property—boolean value determining whether the column is selected as you navigate the grid (true) or is unselected (false); isSelectColumn(), setSelectColumn(boolean)
- selectRow property—boolean value determining whether the row is selected as you navigate the grid (true) or is unselected (false); isSelectRow(), setSelectRow(boolean)
- toggleColumnSort(int) method—int value represents the column index whose sort order will be toggled (ascending or descending)
- modelContentChanged event—names the method called when the list content changes

- selectionChanged event—names the method called when the single selection item changes
- selectionItemChanged event—names the method called when the noncontiguous multiple item selection changes
- selectionRangeChanged event—names the method called when the range of items selected changes

ImageControl

The ImageControl displays a graphical image, optionally used to display an image-BLOB field of table data. ImageControl components have these key elements:

 Note | The ImageControl component works only with Java image types (GIFs, JPEGs).

- columnName property—String representing the table column containing the image to be displayed; getColumnName(), setColumnName(String)
- dataSet property—DataSet object containing the table data to be displayed; getDataSet(), setDataSet(DataSet)
- editInPlace property—boolean value determining whether field is read-write (true) or read-only (false)
- image property—Image or URL value representing a GIF or JPEG image; getImage() returns Image, setImage(Image), setImage(URL)
- imageName property—String value representing a GIF or JPEG image filename; getImageName(); setImageName(String)
- modelContentChanged event—names the method called when the list content changes

TransparentImage

The TransparentImage displays a transparent graphical image. TransparentImage components have these key elements:

- imageName property—String value representing a GIF or JPEG image filename; getImageName(); setImageName(String)
- transparent property—Boolean value sets whether or not the image is displayed as transparent

7

ButtonBar

The `ButtonBar` is a container for `ButtonControl` objects. Each button can have a text label, a graphic, or both. `ButtonBar` components have these key elements:

- `buttonType` property—int constant (`TEXT_ONLY`, `IMAGE_ONLY`, or `TEXT_AND_IMAGE`) that controls what appears on the button face; `getButtonType()`, `setButtonType(int)`

- `dataSet` property—`DataSet` object binds the component to a model; `getDataSet()`, `setDataSet(DataSet)`

- `hgap` property—int representing the gap (in pixels) between horizontal buttons; `getHgap()`, `setHgap(int)`

- `imageBase` property—`String` value representing the path prefix for button image filenames; `getImageBase()`, `setImageBase(String)`

- `imageNames` property—`String` array representing button image filenames; `getImageNames()`, `setImageNames(String[])`

- `labels` property—`String` array representing button text values (also implicitly sets each button's actionCommand); `getLabels()`, `setLabels(String[])`

- `layout` property—`LayoutManager` value for the layout of `ButtonBar`; `setLayout(LayoutManager)`

- `orientation` property—int constant: `Orientation.HORIZONTAL` (buttons form rows) or `Orientation.VERTICAL` (buttons form columns); `getOrientation()`, `setOrientation(int)`

- `vgap` property—int representing the gap (in pixels) between vertical buttons; `getVgap()`, `setVgap(int)`

- `addImageButton(Image, String, String)` method—adds a new `ButtonControl` to `ButtonBar` with the specified `Image`, text (`String`), and command (`String`)

- `addImageButton(String, String, String)` method—adds a new `ButtonControl` to `ButtonBar` with the specified image filename (`String`), text (`String`), and command (`String`)

- `addSpace()` method—adds four pixels to the existing `ButtonBar` gaps

- `addSpace(int)` method—adds int pixels to the existing `ButtonBar` gaps

- `addTextButton(String, String)` method—adds a new `ButtonControl` to `ButtonBar` with the specified text (`String`) and command (`String`)

- `setButtonEnabled(String, boolean)` method—button whose label matches `String` argument; enabled if boolean argument is `true`, and disabled if boolean is `false`

- setButtonEnabled(int, boolean) method—button whose index matches int argument is enabled if boolean argument is true, disabled if boolean is false
- actionPerformed event—names the method called when one of the buttons is pressed

NavigatorControl

The NavigatorControl is a descendant of ButtonBar that performs database record operations and database navigation. NavigatorControl components share the properties and methods of ButtonBar components, plus these additional key elements:

- buttonType property—int constant (TEXT_ONLY, IMAGE_ONLY, or TEXT_AND_IMAGE) that controls what appears on the button face; getButtonType(), setButtonType(int)
- dataSet property—DataSet object containing the table data to be displayed; getDataSet(), setDataSet(DataSet)
- labels property—String array (defaults: First, Prior, Next, Last, Insert, Delete, Post, Cancel, Ditto, Save, Refresh) that determines what text appears on navigator buttons when the buttonType property is set to TextOnly or TextAndImage

ShapeControl

The ShapeControl enables you to place shape objects, such as ellipses, lines, and rectangles, in your interface. ShapeControl components have these key elements:

- drawEdge property—boolean determining whether the shape's border is drawn (true) or not drawn (false); isDrawEdge(), setDrawEdge(boolean)
- edgeColor property—Color object for drawing the shape's edge; getEdgeColor(), setEdgeColor(Color)
- fill property—boolean value determining whether the shape is a filled (true) or an outlined (false) shape; isFill(), setFill(boolean)
- foreground property—Color object for drawing fill; setForeground(Color)
- type property—int constant (RECTANGLE, ROUND_RECT, SQUARE, ROUND_SQUARE, ELLIPSE, CIRCLE, HORZ_LINE, VERT_LINE, POS_SLOPE_LINE, NEG_SLOPE_LINE) representing what shape will be drawn; getType(), setType(int)

7

StatusBar

The StatusBar is a BevelPanel containing a java.awt.label component, on which messages can be displayed. It can also be used to display a database status messages by connecting to a DataSet. StatusBar components have these key elements:

- dataSet property—DataSet object binds the component to a model; getDataSet(), setDataSet(DataSet)
- text property—String for the java.awt.label text; getText(), setText(String)

TextAreaControl

The TextAreaControl accepts input and displays scrollable multiple-line text field or a text-BLOB field of table data. TextAreaControl components share the properties and methods of TextFieldControl and Scrollbar components, plus these additional key elements:

- columnName property—String representing the table column containing the text to be displayed; getColumnName(), setColumnName(String)
- dataSet property—DataSet object containing the table data to be displayed; getDataSet(), setDataSet(DataSet)
- rows property—int number of rows of text that the text window can display; getRows(), setRows(int)
- textValueChanged event—names the method called when the text property value is modified

TextFieldControl

The TextFieldControl displays a single line of editable text or field of data. In addition, you can use the TextFieldControl component to create a text field that obscures characters to implement password fields, by setting its echoChar property. Read-only fields are created by setting the editable property to false.

TextFieldControl components have these key elements:

- columnName property—String representing the table column containing text to be displayed; getColumnName(), setColumnName(String)
- columns property—int limit for the number of characters that can be typed or displayed in the field; getColumns(), setColumns(int)
- dataSet property—DataSet object containing the table data to be displayed; getDataSet(), setDataSet(DataSet)

- echoChar property—char that is echoed to the screen for masking input; echoCharIsSet() returns boolean, getEchoChar() returns char, setEchoChar(char)

- editable property—boolean value determining whether field is read-write (true) or read-only (false); isEditable(), setEditable(boolean)

- text property—String for the TextFieldControl component's default text; getText(), setText(String)

- textValueChanged event—names the method called when the text property is modified or updated

TreeControl

The TreeControl displays related data in a single-inheritance outline or hierarchy tree. A higher-level node is a *parent*, a same-level node is a *sibling*, and a lower-level node is a *child*. Individual nodes are LinkedTreeNode objects and can include graphical icons for each tree node. TreeControl components have these key elements:

- autoEdit property—boolean value determining whether a keypress automatically initiates an edit (true) for a selected node's label or not (false); getAutoEdit(), setAutoEdit(boolean)

- expandByDefault property—boolean value determining whether the tree will be expanded (true) or collapsed (false) when first displayed; getExpandByDefault(), setExpandByDefault(boolean)

- style property—int constant (STYLE_PLUSES, STYLE_ARROWS) representing the presentation style for node graphics; getStyle(), setStyle(int)

- removeChildren(GraphLocation) method—deletes the children of the specified parent node

- nodeCollapsed event—names the method called when a node is collapsed

- nodeExpanded event—names the method called when a node is expanded

- selectionChanged event—names the method called when the single selection item changes

- selectionItemChanged event—names the method called when the noncontiguous multiple item selection changes

Using JBCL Containers

The components on the JBCL Containers page are defined in the borland.jbcl.control package and are data aware. Figure 7.3 shows the JBCL Containers page of components.

7

FIGURE 7.3.

The JBCL Containers page of the Component Palette.

Containers are components in which you can place other components, and they can be nested as many levels deep as you desire. You can use them to group and arrange other UI components and to add visual depth to your interface. They also enable you to move nested components as a unit. Several container components are offered to you on the JBCL Containers page of the Component Palette. These are described in the following sections.

BevelPanel

The BevelPanel displays a rectangle, whose background color you can set, with beveled borders within which you can nest other components, including other container components. BevelPanel components have these key elements:

- background property—Color object for the background of BevelPanel; setBackground(Color)

- bevelInner property—int constant (FLAT, RAISED, LOWERED) representing the style of the inner bevel edge; getBevelInner(), setBevelInner(int)

- bevelOuter property—int constant (FLAT, RAISED, LOWERED) representing the style of the outer bevel edge; getBevelOuter(), setBevelOuter(int)

- layout property—LayoutManager that sets the arrangement of the components nested within; setLayout(LayoutManager)

- margins property—Insets object (defaults to 0,0,0,0 representing top, left, bottom, and right margins in pixels) which sets the width of the border that surrounds the nested objects when the layout property is applied; getMargins(), setMargins(Insets)

- soft property—boolean value that determines whether bevel edges are drawn as soft edge colors (true) or not (false); isSoft(), setSoft(boolean soft)

For an example of soft edges, click on an HTML file in the AppBrowser window's Navigation pane. The View tab of the Content pane displays soft edges, whereas the Source tab displays hard edges.

GroupBox

The GroupBox component is a rectangular container with an optional label that visually organizes and contains other components. GroupBox has these key elements:

- background property—Color object for background of GroupBox;
  setBackground(Color)

- label property—String representing the visible text on the ButtonControl;
  getLabel(), setLabel(String)

SplitPanel

The SplitPanel component is a multipaned container with splitters that divides its nested panels into panes. SplitPanel components have these key elements:

- background property—Color object for the background of SplitPanel;
  setBackground(Color)

- dividerColor property—Color object used for drawing pane dividers;
  getDividerColor(), setDividerColor(Color)

- gap property—int representing the gap (in pixels) between panes; getGap(),
  setGap(int)

- actionPerformed event—names the method called when the panel is clicked

TabsetControl

The TabsetControl is a set of horizontal tabs used to initiate actions (for example, to index the multiple cards or custom dialog pages). These exclusive tabs act like radio buttons in that only one tab can be selected at a time. TabsetControl components have these key elements:

- labels property—String array containing text for tab labels; getLabels(),
  setLabels(String[])

- readOnly property—boolean determining whether tab labels are read-only (true)
  or read-write (false) at runtime; isReadOnly(), setReadOnly(boolean)

- selectedIndex property—int representing the index of the selected tab (-1 if
  none selected); getSelectedIndex(), setSelectedIndex(int)

- tabsOnTop property—boolean determining whether tabs appear as top (true) or
  bottom (false) tabs; isTabsOnTop(), setTabsOnTop(boolean)

- addTab(String) method—adds new tab to the end of tabset with String as its
  label

- getLabel(int) method—returns String label of the tab at specified int index

- removeTab(String) method—deletes the tab with the specified String label

- renameTab(String, String) method—renames the tab with the specified String
  label (first argument) to the new String label (second argument)

7

- repaintTab(int) method—repaints the tab at the specified int index (call when a single tab has been updated)
- setLabel(int, String) method—renames the tab with the specified int index to the new String label
- keyPressed event—names the method called when one of the buttons is pressed; these four keypresses have special meaning in this component: Home selects the first tab, Left selects the tab to left, Right selects the tab to right, and End selects the last tab
- mouseClicked event—names the method called when one of the tabs is clicked

If not all the tabs can be displayed in the space provided, a scrollbar is automatically provided (similar to the one on the Component Palette in the JBuilder IDE). If an integrated page/tab solution is desired, use the TabsetPanel instead.

TabsetPanel

The TabsetPanel component is a multipaged container with tabs that combine the functionality of a panel and a TabsetControl. Each panel placed on this component becomes a separate page on which you can then place other components. These pages are exclusive in that only one page can be selected at a time. TabsetPanel components have these key elements:

- background property—Color object for the background of TabsetPanel; setBackground(Color)
- labels property—String array containing text for the page tab labels; getLabels(), setLabels(String[])
- itemMargins property—Insets object (defaults to 1,4,1,4 representing top, left, bottom, and right margins in pixels) which sets the width of the border that surrounds the nested objects; getItemMargins(), setItemMargins(Insets)
- selectedIndex property—int representing currently selected page (-1 if none selected); getSelectedIndex(), setSelectedIndex(int)
- addTab(int, String) method—adds a tab at the specified int index with the specified String as its label
- removeTab(String) method—deletes a tab with the specified String label
- actionPerformed event—names the method called when the panel is clicked
- modelContentChanged event—names the method called when the panel content changes
- selectionChanged event—names the method called when the single selection item changes

- selectionItemChanged event—names the method called when the noncontiguous multiple item selection changes

Dialog Boxes

Dialog boxes are containers, and the JBCL Containers page includes dialog box controls in its array of components. Dialog box components are nonvisual controls that display a dialog box when invoked via the show() method. When placed in the UI Designer, these components appear only in the Context Tree in the Structure pane of the AppBrowser window, in the Other folder. To display one of these dialog box components in your interface, you must call the show() method in another component's event handler. For example, to show a Filer dialog named filer1, you would add the line of code

```
filer1.show();
```

to an event handler. Which event handler you choose depends on the component that is intended to invoke the dialog. For example, if a button press or menu selection will invoke the dialog, you will put this line of code in that component's actionPerformed event handler. Also, you can have multiple components invoke a dialog by putting the show() method in more than one component's event handler or by using a shared handler that contains the show() method.

In addition to the event handler, you must also set the frame property to indicate the parent Frame to which the dialog component should return focus.

Filer

The Filer component displays a file-selection dialog box for opening and saving files. The Filer component has these key elements:

- frame property—Frame object parent of the dialog box, selected from a drop-down list; getFrame(), setFrame(Frame)
- directory property—String representing the default directory for the dialog box; getDirectory(), setDirectory(String)
- file property—String representing the default file for the dialog box; getFile(), setFile(String)
- filenameFilter property—FilenameFilter object for the Show Files of Type drop-down list; getFilenameFilter(), setFilenameFilter(FilenameFilter)
- mode property—int constant (LOAD, SAVE) for determining type of dialog box (File Open or File Save); getMode(), setMode(int)
- title property—String representing the title bar text (caption) of the dialog box; getTitle(), setTitle(String)

7

- show() method—displays the Filer dialog box

Figure 7.4 shows what the Filer dialog box looks like when invoked.

FIGURE 7.4.

The invoked Filer *dialog box with default settings.*

ColorChooser

The ColorChooser component is a wrapper component that displays the ColorChooser color selection dialog box for selecting colors. ColorChooser components have these key elements:

- frame property—Frame object parent of the dialog box, selected from a drop-down list; getFrame(), setFrame(Frame)
- result property—int constant (OK, CANCEL) representing the button chosen in the dialog; getResult(), setResult(int)
- title property—String representing the title bar text (caption) of the dialog; getTitle(), setTitle(String)
- value property—Color object that is active (default) in the dialog; getValue(), setValue(Color)
- show() method—displays the ColorChooser dialog box
- actionPerformed event—names the method called when the dialog is closed using the system Close command

Figure 7.5 shows what the ColorChooser dialog box looks like when invoked.

FIGURE 7.5.

The invoked ColorChooser *dialog box.*

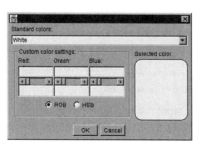

FontChooser

The `FontChooser` component is a wrapper component that displays the `FontChooser` font selection dialog box for setting font attributes and metrics. `FontChooser` components have these key elements:

- `frame` property—Frame object parent of the dialog box, selected from a drop-down list; `getFrame()`, `setFrame(Frame)`

- `result` property—int constant (`OK`, `CANCEL`) representing the button chosen in the dialog box; `getResult()`, `setResult(int)`

- `title` property—String representing the title bar text (caption) of the dialog box; `getTitle()`, `setTitle(String)`

- `value` property—Font object that is active (default) in the dialog; `getValue()`, `setValue(Font)`

- `show()` method—displays the `FontChooserDialog` dialog box

- `actionPerformed` event—names the method called when the dialog box is closed using the system Close command

Figure 7.6 shows what the `FontChooser` dialog box looks like when invoked.

FIGURE 7.6.

The invoked FontChooser *dialog box.*

Message

The `Message` component is a wrapper component which displays the `Message` dialog box that shows a text message to the user. `Message` components have these key elements:

- `frame` property—Frame object parent of the dialog, selected from a drop-down list; `getFrame()`, `setFrame(Frame)`

- `buttonSet` property—int constant (`OK`, `OK_CANCEL`, `YES_NO`, `YES_NO_CANCEL`) representing the default set of buttons for the dialog; `getButtonSet()`, `setButtonSet(int)`

- `labels` property—String array of labels for buttons in the dialog; `getLabels()`, `setLabels(String[])`

7

- message property—String representing the text of the message to be shown in the dialog; getMessage(), setMessage(String)
- result property—int constant (OK, OK_CANCEL, YES_NO, YES_NO_CANCEL) representing the button chosen in the dialog; getResult(), setResult(int)
- title property—String representing the title bar text (caption) of the dialog; getTitle(), setTitle(String)
- show() method—displays the FontChooser dialog box
- actionPerformed event—names the method called when the dialog box is closed using the system Close command

Figure 7.7 shows what the Message dialog box looks like when invoked.

FIGURE 7.7.

The invoked Message *dialog box with default settings.*

StringInput

The StringInput component displays the StringInput dialog box, which accepts a string typed by the user. Figure 7.8 shows what the StringInput dialog box looks like when invoked.

FIGURE 7.8.

The invoked StringInput *dialog box.*

StringInput components have these key elements:

- frame property—Frame object parent of the StringInput component, selected from a drop-down list; getFrame(), setFrame(Frame)
- result property—int constant (OK, OK_CANCEL, YES_NO, YES_NO_CANCEL) representing the button chosen in the dialog box; getResult(), setResult(int)
- title property—String representing the title bar text (caption) of the StringInput component; getTitle(), setTitle(String)
- show() method—displays the StringInput dialog box

Understanding Data Express Components

The components on the Data Express page are defined in the `borland.jbcl.dataset`, `borland.sql.dataset`, `borland.datastore`, and `borland.jbcl.control` packages. The JavaBeans components on this page are database access controls. Figure 7.9 shows the Data Express page of components.

FIGURE 7.9.

The Data Express page of the Component Palette.

> **Tip**
>
> The Data Express page of components is available in the Professional and Client/Server Editions only.

These components are discussed in greater depth on Day 14, "JBuilder Database Architecture," so some of the components are only briefly summarized here (from left to right):

- The `Database` component provides a persistent JDBC connection to a physical SQL database.
- The `TableDataSet` component represents data obtained from a file.
- The `TextDataFile` component holds properties used to import data from a text file.
- The `QueryDataSet` component uses a SQL query to acquire data from a physical database.
- The `QueryResolver` component saves changes to data using a SQL query.
- The `ProcedureDataSet` component runs a stored procedure against data stored in a SQL database.
- The `ProcedureResolver` component saves changes to data back to the data source by calling stored procedures in that data source.
- The `ParameterRow` component maps parameter values to columns.
- The `DataSetView` component provides an alternative view of data.
- The `DataStore` component provides the main access point to high-performance data caching and compact permanent storage.

7

dbSwing Components

The components on the dbSwing page are defined in the `borland.dbswing` package. The JavaBeans components on this page are database-aware Swing controls. Figure 7.10 shows the dbSwing page of components.

FIGURE 7.10.

The dbSwing page of the Component Palette.

Swing Components

The components on the Swing page are defined in the `com.sun.java.swing` package. The JavaBeans components on this page are Swing controls. Figure 7.11 shows the Swing page of components.

FIGURE 7.11.

The Swing page of the Component Palette.

Swing components are Java standard components that provide a wide range of options so that you can provide your Java applications with rich graphical user interfaces.

Swing Containers

The components on the Swing Containers page are defined in the `com.sun.java.swing` package. The JavaBeans components on this page are Swing containers. Figure 7.12 shows the Swing Containers page of components.

FIGURE 7.12.

The Swing Containers page of the Component Palette.

AWT Components

The components on the AWT page are defined in the `java.awt` package. Figure 7.13 shows the AWT page of components.

FIGURE 7.13.

The AWT page of the Component Palette.

These components are not part of the JBCL; rather, they are part of the Java Class Library (JCL). For more information on these components, refer to Day 6, "User Interface Design."

More Pages

Depending on which edition of JBuilder you have, you might have two additional pages on your Component Palette: KL Group and Other.

The KL Group page is populated with third-party JavaBeans components, which are supported directly by the KL Group. These components are defined in the `jclass.bwt`, `jclass.table`, and `jclass.chart` packages. Figure 7.14 shows the KL Group page of components.

FIGURE 7.14.

The KL Group page of the Component Palette.

To determine which component is what, place the mouse cursor over the icon and pause momentarily—this will reveal the component's class name so that you can investigate further. Refer to the KL Group documentation for details on these third-party components.

The Other page is provided as a place for you to put other third-party components or your own JavaBeans components. It is currently blank.

Tip

> One way to organize your new components is to create a new page for each third-party vendor that you buy them from.

Summary

Today you have had a look at the library of components that JBuilder provides for your use. You have learned about components in general, and you have learned about the key elements of specific components in the JavaBeans Component Library (JBCL). There is much more information about these components than can be covered in a single day.

7

Be sure to explore further by looking up individual components, properties, methods, and events in the JBCL Reference help files. Remember that these components are based, in part, on classes and interfaces in the AWT hierarchy, so follow the component tree back through those classes by using the hierarchy tree at the top of each component's help topic to find out more about what attributes and behaviors are inherited from the `java.awt` package.

Q&A

Q **If I change the `<name>` property of a component using the Inspector, JBuilder will automatically change all references to that component in my code, right?**

A Well, yes and no. It will change the component's identifier for all code generated by the JBuilder IDE, but it cannot track and will not change component identifiers in code you have manually written (in event handler method bodies, for example). This is why it is a good idea to rename components as soon as you have placed them in the UI Designer.

Q **The `Filer` component is obviously a visible component when it is invoked. Why is it called a nonvisual component?**

A It is a nonvisual component because it has no graphical representation at design time. It becomes visible only when the dialog box is actually invoked at runtime.

Q **I seem to be using properties more than methods when dealing with my components in code. Is that the right way to do it?**

A Yes, that's the way the components were designed. A well-written component makes maximum use of properties. For this reason, you might not use a component's methods very often. Use methods when necessary, but otherwise use properties to manipulate your components.

Workshop

The Workshop provides two ways for you to affirm what you've learned in this chapter. The Quiz section poses questions to help you solidify your understanding of the material covered. You can find answers to the quiz questions in Appendix A, "Answers to Quiz Questions." The Exercises section provides you with experience in using what you have learned. Try to work through all these before continuing to the next day.

Quiz

1. Can you change the `<name>` property of a component at runtime?

2. Which component presents a drop-down selection list? To what AWT component is it similar?

3. How are `TabsetControl` and `TabsetPanel` components similar to exclusive check boxes?

4. What does the term *data aware* mean?

5. What method is used to display a dialog box? Where should this method be called in your code?

Exercises

1. Create a user interface that mimics the layout of the File Properties dialog box in JBuilder. Don't worry about the event handling, just do the layout with JBCL components in a Frame.

2. Create an applet that displays two check box groups: one with six check boxes in two columns and another with a set of three radio buttons across the bottom of the applet's drawing space. Hint: use a `GroupBox` for the nonexclusive check boxes.

3. Explore the help topics for the dialog box components and find out how they are put together so that you can create your own dialog boxes later, using the same techniques.

7

WEEK 2

At a Glance

8

9

10

11

12

13

14

DAY **8**

Applets, Applications, and Wizards

Much of Java's current popularity has come about because of Java-enabled Web browsers and their support for Java applets—small routines that run inside a Web page and can be used to create dynamic, interactive Web page designs. Applets, as noted at the beginning of this book, are written in the Java language, and you can view them in any Web browser that supports Java, including Sun's HotJava, Netscape's Navigator, and Microsoft's Internet Explorer. Learning how to create applets is one of the most important topics on Java and probably the main reason you bought this book.

Note	Competition in the computer software industry has lead to various flavors of the Java Virtual Machine that don't necessarily conform to the official Java specification. You can be sure that all of your Java applications can run correctly when users run them in the Java Plug-in. Check the JavaSoft Web site at `http://splash.javasoft.com/products/plugin/` for more information and for downloading the Java Plug-in.

In addition, the Java language supports writing standalone programs, which are called applications. Last week, when you focused on learning about the Java language itself, most of the small programs you created were Java applications, albeit console applications that only wrote to the screen. Now that you have the basics down, you'll learn more about applications, including GUI applications.

The JBuilder IDE also provides both Applet and Application wizards to generate skeleton code for your Java programs. You'll also learn what these wizards can do for you and what information they require to do their magic.

Today, you'll cover a lot of ground:

- Reviewing the differences between Java applets and applications
- Getting started with applets: the basics of how an applet works and how to create your own simple applets
- Embedding an applet on a Web page by using the <APPLET> and </APPLET> tags, including the various features of the <APPLET> tag
- Passing parameters to applets and learning how to deal with those parameters inside your applet's code
- Creating Java applications, including how to pass arguments to a Java program from a command line
- Creating a dual-purpose program: one that can serve as both an applet and an application
- Using the Applet and Application wizards to set up your initial source code files

To create a new project for today's listings, select File | New Project and modify the File field so that it says this:

```
C:\jbuilder2\myprojects\AppletsAppsWizards.jpr
```

Then click the Finish button. All of today's listings will be added to this project via the Add to Project icon above the Navigation pane in the AppBrowser window.

Comparing Applets to Applications

Although you explored the differences between Java applications and Java applets in the early part of this book, let's review them again here.

In short, Java applications are standalone Java programs that can be run by using just the Java Virtual Machine from the command line, from within Windows, or from within JBuilder.

Java applets, however, cannot be run independently; they are run from inside a Web browser. A reference to an applet is embedded in a Web page using a special pair of HTML tags. When a Java-enabled browser loads a Web page with an applet in it, the browser downloads that applet's code from the Web server and executes it on the local system (the one on which the browser is also running).

Because Java applets run inside a Java-enabled Web browser, they have the advantage of the structure the Web browser provides: an existing window, an event-handling and graphics context, and the surrounding user interface (UI). Java applications can also create this structure, but they don't require it.

The convenience that applets have over applications in terms of structure and UI capabilities, however, is hampered by restrictions on what applets are allowed to do. Given the fact that Java applets can be downloaded from anywhere and run on a client's system, restrictions are necessary to prevent an applet from causing system damage or security breaches. Without these restrictions in place, Java applets could be written to contain viruses or Trojan horses (programs that seem friendly but can damage the system). These restrictions also don't allow applets to compromise the security of the system that runs them. The restrictions on what an applet can do include these:

- Applets can't have read/write access to the reader's file system except in specific directories (which are defined by the user through an access control list that, by default, is empty). Some browsers might not even allow an applet read/write access to the file system at all or at the same time as using the network.

- Applets usually can't communicate with a server other than the one that had originally stored the applet. (This might be configurable by the browser; however, your applet should not depend on having this behavior available to it.)

- Applets can't run any programs on the reader's system. For UNIX systems, this includes forking a process.

- Applets can't load programs native to the local platform, including shared libraries such as DLLs.

In addition, Java itself includes various forms of security and consistency checking in the Java compiler and interpreter to prevent unorthodox use of the language. This combination of restrictions and security features makes it more difficult for a rogue Java applet to damage the client's system.

Note
> These restrictions prevent all the traditional ways of causing damage to a client's system, but it's impossible to be absolutely sure that someone cannot somehow work around these restrictions, violate privacy, use CPU resources, and generally be annoying. To test Java's security, Sun has asked the Internet community at large to try to break Java's security and to create an applet that can work around the restrictions imposed upon it.

Creating Applets

For the most part, all the Java programs you've created up to this point have been Java applications—simple programs with a single `main()` method that created objects, set instance variables, and ran methods. Today, and in the days following, you'll be creating applets exclusively, so you'll need a good grasp of how an applet works, the features an applet has, and where to start when you first create your own applets.

To create an applet, you create a subclass of the class `Applet`, a member of the `java.applet` package. The `Applet` class provides behavior to enable your applet not only to work within the browser itself, but also to take advantage of the capabilities of AWT to include UI elements, to handle mouse and keyword events, and to draw to the screen. Although your applet can have as many "helper" classes as it needs, it's the main applet class that triggers the execution of the applet. That initial applet class always has a signature that looks like this:

```
public class myAppletClass extends java.applet.Applet {...}
```

Note the `public` keyword. Java requires that your applet subclass be declared `public`. This makes sense because the applet is intended to be run by the general public from the Internet. Again, this is true only of your main applet class; any helper classes you create can be either `public` or `private` as you want.

When a Java-enabled Web browser encounters your applet in a Web page, it loads your initial applet class over your Internet connection (modem, T1, LAN, and so on), as well as any other helper classes that the first class requires. With applications, Java calls the `main()` method directly on your initial class. In contrast, when your applet is loaded, Java creates an instance of that class, and a series of `Applet` methods are called on that instance. Different applets that use the same class use different instances, so each one can behave differently from the other applets running in the same Web browser.

Major Applet Activities

To create a basic Java application, your class has to have one method—main()—with a specific signature. Then, when your application starts, main() is executed, and from main() you can set up the behavior that your program needs. Applets are similar but more complicated. Applets have many different activities that correspond to various major events in the life cycle of the applet, such as initialization, painting, or mouse events. Each activity has a corresponding method. So when an event occurs, the browser or other Java-capable tool calls those specific methods.

The default implementations of these activity methods do nothing; to provide behavior for an event you must override the appropriate method in your applet's subclass. You don't have to override all of them, of course. Different applet behavior requires different methods to be overridden.

You'll learn about the various important methods to override as the week progresses. For now, the following sections discuss the five most important methods in an applet's execution: initialization, starting, stopping, destroying, and painting.

Initialization

Initialization occurs when the applet is loaded. Initialization might include creating the objects the applet needs, setting up an initial state, loading images or fonts, or setting parameters. To provide behavior for the initialization of your applet, override the init() method:

```
public void init() {...}
```

Starting

After an applet is initialized, it is started. Starting can also occur if the applet was previously stopped but not destroyed. For example, an applet is stopped if the reader follows a link to a different page, and it is started again when the reader returns to the applet's page. To provide startup behavior for your applet, override the start() method:

```
public void start() {...}
```

> **Note**
>
> Starting (and stopping) can occur several times during an applet's life cycle, whereas initialization happens only once.

Functionality that you might want to put in the start() method can include starting up a thread to control the applet, sending the appropriate messages to helper objects, or in some way telling the applet to begin running. You'll learn more about starting applets tomorrow.

Stopping

Stopping and starting go hand in hand. Stopping occurs when the reader leaves the page that contains a currently running applet, or you can stop the applet yourself by calling stop(). By default, when the reader leaves a page, any threads the applet has started will continue running. By overriding stop(), you can suspend execution of these threads and then restart them if the applet is viewed again (reloaded):

```
public void stop() {...}
```

Destroying

Destroying sounds rather more violent than it is. Destroying enables the applet to clean up after itself just before it is freed or the Web browser exits—for example, to kill any running threads or to release any other running objects. Generally, you won't want to override destroy() unless you have specific resources that need to be released, such as threads that the applet has created. To provide cleanup behavior for your applet, override the destroy() method:

```
public void destroy() {...}
```

 Note   The destroy() and finalize() methods are not the same. The destroy() method applies only to applets, whereas the finalize() method is a more general-purpose way for a single object of any type to clean up after itself.

Painting

Painting is how an applet actually draws something on the screen, be it text, a line, a colored background, or an image. Painting can occur many hundreds of times during an applet's life cycle. The following are some of the situations in which the paint() method is called:

- Browser is covered by another window and then uncovered
- Browser is moved to a new location
- Browser is minimized and then restored

> **Note**
>
> When an animation is being used, the paint() method is called each time the animation changes.

You override the paint() method for your applet to have a visual appearance on the screen. The paint() method looks like this:

```
public void paint(Graphics g) {...}
```

Note that unlike the other major methods in this section, paint() takes an argument, an instance of the class Graphics. This object is created and passed to the paint() method by the browser, so you don't have to worry about that part. However, you will have to make sure that the Graphics class (part of the java.awt package) gets imported by your applet code through an import statement at the top of your Java source code file:

```
import java.awt.Graphics;
```

Because your applet will not have a visible presence on the HTML page without overriding the paint() method, this import line is a virtual requirement in any applet source code you write.

Examining a Simple Applet

On Day 3, "Java Intermediate," you created a simple applet called HelloAgainApplet (the one that displayed the text Hello Again! in large red letters). There, you created and used that applet as an example of creating a subclass. Let's go over the code for that applet again, this time named HelloAgainApplet2, looking at it slightly differently in light of the things you just learned about applets. Listing 8.1 shows the code for this applet.

TYPE   **LISTING 8.1.** HelloAgainApplet2.java.

```
1:  import java.applet.*;
2:  import java.awt.*;
3:
4:  public class HelloAgainApplet2 extends Applet {
5:
6:    Font f = new Font("TimesRoman", Font.BOLD, 36);
7:
8:    public void paint(Graphics g) {
9:      g.setFont(f);
10:     g.setColor(Color.red);
11:     g.drawString("Hello again!", 5, 50);
12:   }
13: }
```

ANALYSIS This applet overrides the paint() method, one of the major methods described earlier today. Because the applet doesn't actually do much (it only prints two words to the screen), and there's not really anything to initialize; you don't need init(), start(), or stop() methods.

The paint() method is where the real work of this applet (what little work there is) goes on. The Graphics object passed into the paint() method holds the graphics state—that is, the current features of the drawing surface. Line 9 sets up the font for this graphics state (in the font object held in the f instance variable, created in line 6); line 10 sets up the color (from an object representing the color red that's stored in the Color class's variable red).

Line 11 then draws the string Hello Again! by using the current font and color at the x,y coordinates 5,50. Note that the coordinates 0,0 are at the top left of the applet's drawing surface, with positive x moving toward the right and positive y moving downward. Figure 8.1 shows how the applet's bounding box and the string are drawn on the page.

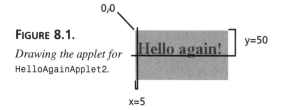

FIGURE 8.1.

Drawing the applet for HelloAgainApplet2.

Embedding an Applet on a Web Page

After you create a class or classes that contain your applet and compile them into class files as you would any other Java program, you have to create a Web page that will hold that applet by using HTML (Hypertext Markup Language). There is a special HTML tag pair for embedding applets in Web pages. Java-capable browsers use the information contained in that tag pair to locate the compiled class files and execute the applet itself. In this section, you'll learn about how to put Java applets in a Web page and how to serve those files to the Web at large.

Note   If you need help understanding and writing HTML pages, you might find *Teach Yourself Web Publishing with HTML in 14 Days*, Premier Edition, also available from Sams, useful.

To embed an applet on a Web page, use the <APPLET> and </APPLET> tag pair. This tag pair is a special extension to HTML for including applets in Web pages.

8

> **Note**
>
> You'll notice in this book that the terms "HTML page" and "Web page" are used somewhat interchangeably. However, you should be aware that not all Web pages are HTML-based. Web pages can also be based on Common Gateway Interface (CGI) scripts, which are often used to present form-based pages, such as order forms or surveys. For more information on CGI, you can refer to *Webmaster Expert Solutions*, available from Que (Macmillan).

Listing 8.2 shows a simple example of an HTML page with an applet embedded in it, similar to the one you used on Day 3, "Java Intermediate," to view the applet, with some additional HTML code added to it.

TYPE **LISTING 8.2.** HelloAgain2.html.

```
 1:  <HTML>
 2:  <HEAD>
 3:  <TITLE>Hello to Everyone!</TITLE>
 4:  </HEAD>
 5:  <BODY>
 6:  <P>My Java applet now says:
 7:  <BR>
 8:  <APPLET CODE="HelloAgainApplet2.class" WIDTH = 250 HEIGHT = 100>
 9:  The HelloAgainApplet2 applet would be running here
10:  in a Java-enabled browser.
11:  </APPLET>
12:  </BODY>
13:  </HTML>
```

>
> **Tip**
>
> When you create or modify an HTML file in the JBuilder IDE Editor, the new version of the source code is held in memory until you save it to disk. However, the appletviewer loads the referenced HTML file directly from the disk. JBuilder takes this into account and saves HTML files automatically before compiling code in your project. This way, the HTML file is always saved before the appletviewer utility is launched.

ANALYSIS There are several things to notice about the `<APPLET>` and `</APPLET>` tag pair on this page:

- The entirety of line 8 comprises the `<APPLET>` tag; line 11 contains the `</APPLET>` tag. Together, they delineate all the information that the Web page knows about the applet to be run.

- In the `<APPLET>` tag, the `CODE` attribute indicates the name of the class file that contains the applet to be run, including the `.class` filename extension. In this case, the class file must be in the same directory as this HTML file because no directory path is given. To indicate that applets are in a specific directory, use the `CODEBASE` attribute described later today.

- Also, in the `<APPLET>` tag, `WIDTH` and `HEIGHT` are optional and are used to indicate the bounding box of the applet—that is, how large a rectangular space to reserve, then draw, for the applet on the Web page. Be sure to set `WIDTH` and `HEIGHT` to an appropriate size for the applet because, depending on the browser, if your applet attempts to draw outside the boundaries of the space you've reserved for it, you might not be able to see or get to those parts of your applet.

- The text between the `<APPLET>` and `</APPLET>` tags, on lines 9 and 10, is displayed by browsers that do not understand the tag pair (which includes any browsers that are not Java-capable). Because your page might be viewed in many kinds of browsers (including WebTV), it is a very good idea to put alternate text here so that readers of your page who don't have Java will see something other than a blank space.

Here are some of the other additions to this HTML page:

- Lines 2 and 4 feature the `<HEAD>` and `</HEAD>` tag pair, which delineates a Web page's header area. Right now, it only encloses line 3 which contains the `<TITLE>` and `</TITLE>` tag pair you saw on Day 3.

- Line 6 adds the paragraph `<P>` tag followed by some text to be displayed on the Web page, outside the applet itself. The paragraph tag causes two linefeeds to be inserted at that point.

- On line 7, a break `<BR>` tag is placed, to insert a single linefeed just before the applet space is reserved.

Debugging and Testing the Applet

Now, with a compiled class file and an HTML file that refers to your applet, you should be able to load that HTML file into your Java-enabled browser (using either the Open File menu item or a file URL). The browser loads and parses your HTML file and then loads and executes your applet class.

8

Figure 8.2 shows the running applet in appletviewer.

FIGURE 8.2.

HelloAgainApplet2 *in appletviewer.*

Making Applets Available to the Web

After you have an applet and an HTML file and you've verified that everything is working correctly on your local system, the last step is making that applet available to the World Wide Web at large so that anyone with a Java-enabled browser can view it.

Java applets are served by a Web server the same way that HTML files, images, and other media are served. You don't need special server software to make Java applets available to the Web. You don't even need to configure your server to handle Java files. If you have a Web server up and running, or space on a Web server available to you (say, from your Internet Service Provider, or ISP), all you have to do is move your .html and compiled .class files to that server, as you would any other files.

If you don't already have a Web server, you can set one up yourself. (Web server setup and administration, as well as other facets of Web publishing in general, are outside the scope of this book, however.) The alternative for most of us is to rent space on someone else's server. Most ISPs, the folks who provide many of us with our Internet email accounts, will be more than happy to help you with setting up fee-based disk space on their server for your account. If you have a home page on your ISP account, you might already have some limited amount of server disk space available to you at no additional charge. So if you don't already have your own Web server, and aren't planning to get one, be sure to check with your ISP for more details.

Using Advanced <APPLET> Tag Features

In its simplest form, by using CODE, WIDTH, and HEIGHT, the <APPLET> tag merely creates a space of the appropriate size and then loads and runs the applet in that space. The <APPLET> tag, however, does include several attributes that can help you better integrate your applet into the overall design of your Web page. Among these are ALIGN, HSPACE, VSPACE, and CODEBASE.

ALIGN

The ALIGN attribute defines how the applet will be aligned on the page. This attribute can have one of nine values: LEFT, RIGHT, TEXTTOP, MIDDLE, ABSMIDDLE, BASELINE, BOTTOM, and ABSBOTTOM.

In the case of ALIGN=LEFT, the applet is placed at the left margins of the page, and all text following that applet flows in the space to the right of that applet. ALIGN=RIGHT does just the opposite, with the applet at the right margin and the text flowing in the space to the left. The text will continue to flow in that space until the end of the applet, or you can use a break <BR> tag with its CLEAR attribute set to start the line of text below that applet. The CLEAR attribute can have one of three values: CLEAR=LEFT starts the text at the next clear left margin; CLEAR=RIGHT starts the text at the next clear right margin; and CLEAR=ALL starts the text at the next line where both margins are clear.

For example, here's the body of an HTML file that aligns an applet against the left margin, has some text flowing alongside it, and then breaks at the end of the paragraph so that the next bit of text starts completely below the applet's drawing space:

```
<BODY>
<P>My Java applet now says: <BR>
<P><APPLET CODE="HelloAgainApplet2.class" WIDTH=200 HEIGHT=100>
HelloAgainApplet2</APPLET>
To the left of this paragraph is an applet. It's an unassuming
applet, in which a small string is printed in red type, set in 36 point
Times bold.
<BR CLEAR=ALL>
<P>In the next part of the page, we demonstrate how under certain
conditions,
what appear to be styrofoam peanuts can be used as a healthy snack.
</BODY>
```

Figure 8.3 shows how this applet and the text surrounding it might appear in a Java-enabled browser.

For smaller applets, you might want to include your applet within a single line of text. To do this, the other seven values for ALIGN determine how the applet is vertically aligned with the text:

- ALIGN=TEXTTOP aligns the top of the applet with the top of the tallest text in the line.

- ALIGN=TOP aligns the applet with the topmost item in the line (which might be another applet, an image, or the top of the text).

- ALIGN=ABSMIDDLE aligns the middle of the applet with the middle of the largest item in the line.

- `ALIGN=MIDDLE` aligns the middle of the applet with the middle of the baseline of the text.
- `ALIGN=BASELINE` aligns the bottom of the applet with the baseline of the text.
- `ALIGN=BOTTOM` is equivalent to `ALIGN=BASELINE`.
- `ALIGN=ABSBOTTOM` aligns the bottom of the applet with the lowest item in the line (which might be the baseline of the text, another applet, or an image).

FIGURE 8.3.

A left-aligned applet.

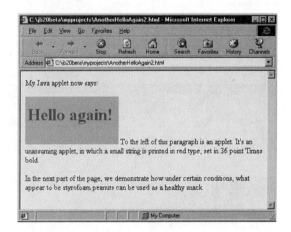

Figure 8.4 shows the various alignment options, where the line is an image and the arrowhead is a small applet named ArrowApplet.

FIGURE 8.4.

Applet alignment options in text.

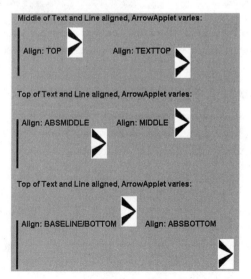

HSPACE and VSPACE

The HSPACE and VSPACE attributes are used to set the amount of space, in pixels, between an applet and its surrounding text. HSPACE controls the horizontal space (the space to the left and right of the applet). VSPACE controls the vertical space (the space above and below the applet). For example, here's the <APPLET> tag for the same sample of HTML you saw earlier, with vertical space of 30 and horizontal space of 30 added:

```
<P><APPLET CODE="HelloAgainApplet2.class" WIDTH=200 HEIGHT=100
ALIGN=LEFT VSPACE=30 HSPACE=30>
HelloAgainApplet2</APPLET>
```

The result in a typical Java-enabled browser might look as shown in Figure 8.5.

FIGURE 8.5.

Vertical and horizontal space.

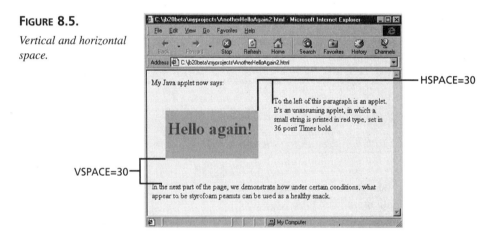

By comparing this to Figure 8.3, shown earlier, you can readily see that the applet's drawing space has both vertical and horizontal buffer zones between it and the surrounding text.

CODE and CODEBASE

CODE is used to indicate the name of the class file that holds the compiled Java code for the current applet. If CODE is used alone in the <APPLET> tag, the .class file is searched for in the same directory as the .html file that references it.

If you want to store your class files in a different directory than your HTML files, you have to tell the browser where to find those class files. To do this, you use the CODEBASE attribute. CODE contains only the name of the class file; CODEBASE contains an alternate pathname where the classes can be located. For example, say you have a directory where you keep your HTML files, and in that same directory you also have a subdirectory named `myapplets` where you keep the related class files. Here's what the `<APPLET>` tag might look like for the class file called `myclass.class`:

```
<APPLET CODE="myclass.class" CODEBASE="myapplets"
WIDTH=100 HEIGHT=100></APPLET>
```

Passing Parameters to Applets

With Java applications, you can pass parameters to your `main()` routine by using arguments on the command line. You can then parse those arguments inside the body of your class, and the application acts accordingly based on the arguments it is given.

Applets, however, don't have a command line because they are effectively subroutines run from the browser application. How, then, do you pass different arguments to an applet? Applets can get different input from the HTML file that contains the `<APPLET>` tag through the use of applet parameters. To set up and handle parameters in an applet, you need two things:

- A special parameter tag in the HTML file
- Code in your applet to parse those parameters

Applet parameters have two attributes: a `NAME` and a `VALUE`. The `NAME` is simply a name you pick, just like any other identifier in your code. The `VALUE` determines the value of that particular parameter. So, for example, for one HTML page, you can indicate the color of text in an applet by using a parameter with the name `color` and the value `red`, whereas for another HTML page, you can specify the value `blue`.

In the HTML file that contains the embedded applet, you indicate each parameter using the `<PARAM>` tag, which uses the `NAME` and `VALUE` attributes. The `<PARAM>` tag goes in between the `<APPLET>` and `</APPLET>` tag pair:

```
<APPLET CODE="MyApplet.class" WIDTH=100 HEIGHT=100>
<PARAM NAME=font VALUE="TimesRoman">
<PARAM NAME=size VALUE="36">
A Java applet appears here.
</APPLET>
```

This particular example defines two parameters to the MyApplet applet: one whose name is `font` and whose value is `TimesRoman` and another whose name is `size` and whose value is `36`.

Parameters are passed to your applet when it is loaded. In the `init()` method for your applet, you can then get hold of those parameters by using the `getParameter()` method. The `getParameter()` method takes one argument, a string representing the name of the parameter you're looking for, and returns a string containing the corresponding value of

8

that parameter. (Like arguments in Java applications, all the parameter values are returned as strings.) To get the value of the font parameter from the HTML file, you might have a line such as this in your init() method:

```
String theFontName = getParameter("font");
```

 Caution

> The names of the parameters as specified in <PARAM> and the names of the parameters in getParameter() must match, including case. In other words, just like everything else in Java, applet parameters are case-sensitive. Therefore, the line <PARAM NAME="name"> is different from <PARAM NAME="Name">. If your parameters are not being properly passed to your applet, the first thing to check is whether the parameter cases match.

Note that if a parameter you expect has not been specified in the HTML file, getParameter() returns null. Most often, you will want to test for a null parameter and supply a reasonable default:

```
if (theFontName == null)
  theFontName = "CourierNew";
```

Keep in mind that getParameter() returns strings. If you want a parameter to be some other object or type, you have to convert it yourself. To parse the size parameter from that same HTML file and assign it to an integer variable called theSize, you might use the following lines:

```
int theSize;
String s = getParameter("size");
if (s == null) theSize = 12;
else theSize = Integer.parseInt(s);
```

Got it? Not yet? Okay, let's create an example of an applet that uses these techniques. You'll modify the HelloAgainApplet2 code so that it says hello to a specific name, for example Fran or Chris. The name is passed into the applet through an HTML parameter. Start by copying the HelloAgainApplet2 class, renaming it to HelloAnybodyApplet:

```
import java.applet.*;
import java.awt.*;

public class HelloAnybodyApplet extends Applet {

  Font f = new Font("TimesRoman", Font.BOLD, 36);

  public void paint(Graphics g) {
    g.setFont(f);
    g.setColor(Color.red);
```

```
    g.drawString("Hello again!", 5, 50);
  }
}
```

The first thing you need to add to this class is a place for the name. Because you'll need that name throughout the applet, add an instance variable for the name, just after the variable for the font:

```
String helloName;
```

To set a value for `helloName`, you have to get the parameter. The best place to handle parameters to an applet is inside an `init()` method. The `init()` method is defined similarly to the `paint()` method (`public`, with a return type of `void`, but no arguments). Make sure when you get the parameter that you always test for a value of `null`. The default, in this case, if a name isn't indicated, is to say hello to `Chris`:

```
public void init() {
helloName = getParameter("name");
if (helloName == null)
  helloName = "Chris";
}
```

One last thing to do now that you have the name from the HTML parameters is to modify the name so that it's a complete string—that is, to tack `Hello` and a space onto the beginning and an exclamation point onto the end. You could do this in the `paint()` method just before printing the string to the screen; however, `paint()` is done every time the screen is repainted, so it's somewhat more efficient to put this line in the `init()` method instead:

```
helloName = "Hello " + helloName + "!";
```

And now, all that's left is to modify the `paint()` method. You want to replace the literal `Hello Again!` string in the original call to the `drawString()` method with the variable name:

```
g.drawString(helloName, 5, 50);
```

Listing 8.3 shows the final result of the `HelloAnybodyApplet` class.

Type   **Listing 8.3.** HelloAnybodyApplet.java.

```
1:  import java.applet.*;
2:  import java.awt.*;
3:
4:  public class HelloAnybodyApplet extends Applet {
5:
6:    Font f = new Font("TimesRoman", Font.BOLD, 36);
```

continues

LISTING 8.3. CONTINUED

```
 7:     String helloName;
 8:
 9:     public void init() {
10:       helloName = getParameter("name");
11:       if (helloName == null) helloName = "Chris";
12:       helloName = "Hello " + helloName + "!";
13:     }
14:
15:     public void paint(Graphics g) {
16:        g.setFont(f);
17:        g.setColor(Color.red);
18:        g.drawString(helloName, 5, 50);
19:     }
20:   }
```

Now, make a copy of the HelloAgain2.html file, name it HelloAnybodyApplet1.html, and edit the HTML file so that you can pass parameters to it and execute your newly created class. Listing 8.4 shows the new HTML code specifically designed for the HelloAnybodyApplet applet.

TYPE   **LISTING 8.4.** HelloAnybodyApplet1.html.

```
 1:   <HTML>
 2:   <HEAD>
 3:   <TITLE>Hello to Everyone!</TITLE>
 4:   </HEAD>
 5:   <BODY>
 6:   <P>
 7:   <APPLET CODE="HelloAnybodyApplet.class" WIDTH=300 HEIGHT=100>
 8:   <PARAM NAME=name VALUE="Fran">
 9:   Hello to whoever you are!
10:   </APPLET>
11:   </BODY>
12:   </HTML>
```

ANALYSIS   On line 7 is the <APPLET> tag, which points to the class file for the applet with the appropriate width and height (300 and 100). On line 8 is the <PARAM> tag, which you use to pass in the name. Here, the NAME parameter is simply name, and the VALUE is the string Fran.

To run this from within JBuilder, be sure you have added both the HelloAnybodyApplet.java and HelloAnybodyApplet1.html files to the AppletsAppsWizards.jpr project. Compile the HelloAnybodyApplet.java file, right-click on the HTML node in the Navigation pane, and then select the Run command. The appletviewer displays the results shown in Figure 8.6.

FIGURE 8.6.

HelloAnybodyApplet1.
html *as shown in*
appletviewer.

Now, let's try a second example. Remember that if no name is specified in the code for HelloAnybodyApplet.java, the default is the name Chris. Listing 8.5 shows an HTML page very similar to the HelloAnybodyApplet1.html file; however, HelloAnybodyApplet2.html has no parameter tag for name.

TYPE   **LISTING 8.5.** HelloAnybodyApplet2.html.

```
 1:  <HTML>
 2:  <HEAD>
 3:  <TITLE>Hello to Everyone!</TITLE>
 4:  </HEAD>
 5:  <BODY>
 6:  <P>
 7:  <APPLET CODE="HelloAnybodyApplet.class" WIDTH=300 HEIGHT=100>
 8:  Hello to whoever you are!
 9:  </APPLET>
10:  </BODY>
11:  </HTML>
```

Here, because no name is supplied by this HTML file, the applet will use the default. To run this from within JBuilder, be sure you have added HelloAnybodyApplet2.html to the project. Then, when you run this HTML file, the appletviewer displays the results shown in Figure 8.7.

FIGURE 8.7.

HelloAnybodyApplet2.
html *as shown in*
appletviewer.

Applet parameters, then, provide the same flexibility as application command-line parameters. They enable you to "reuse" the applet code in various HTML pages by allowing each HTML page to specify the parameters that it will provide to the applet.

Other Applet Tidbits

This section presents some miscellaneous applet hints that just didn't seem to fit anywhere else: using showStatus() to print messages in the Web browser's status window, providing applet information to others, and communicating among multiple applets on the same page.

Using the `showStatus()` Method

The `showStatus()` method, available in the applet class, enables you to display a string in the status bar of the Web browser that contains the applet. You can use this for printing error, link, help, or other status messages:

```
getAppletContext().showStatus("Changing the color.");
```

The `getAppletContext()` method enables your applet to access features of the Web browser that contains it.

> **Caution**
>
> The `showStatus()` method might not be supported in all Web browsers, so do not depend on it for your applet's functionality or interface. It is a useful way of communicating optional information to the user, but if you need a more dependable method of communication, set up a label in your applet and update it to reflect changes in the message.

Providing Applet Information

The `java.awt` class gives you a mechanism for associating information with your applet. Usually, there is a mechanism in the Web browser that's displaying the applet to view display information. You can use this mechanism either to sign your name or organization to your applet or to provide contact information so that users can reach you if they desire.

To provide information about your applet, override the `getAppletInfo()` method:

```
public String getAppletInfo() {
  return "AllClear copyright 1997 Triple-M Consulting";
}
```

When you've added this method to an applet and you display it using appletviewer, you can select Applet | Info to see what information your applet will display.

Communicating Among Applets

Sometimes you might want to have an HTML page with several applets on it. To do this, all you have to do is include several different instances of the <APPLET> tag. The browser will display the applet named in each <APPLET> tag in the HTML page, all at the same time. What if you want to communicate among those applets? What if you want a change in one applet to affect the other applets in some way?

8

The best way to approach this is to use the applet context to access different applets on the same page, using the getAppletContext().getApplets() method to find out which applets are out there, and getAppletContext().getApplet() method (note this is getApplet() singular) to address a particular applet.

For example, to call a method named sendMessage() on all the applets on a page, including the current applet, use the getAppletContext().getApplets() method and a for loop that looks like this:

```
for (Enumeration e = getAppletContext().getApplets();
     e.hasMoreElements(); ) {
    Applet current = (Applet)(e.nextElement());
    current.sendMessage();
}
```

The getApplets() method returns an Enumeration object with a list of the applets on the page. Iterating over the Enumeration object in this way enables you to access each element in the Enumeration in turn.

If you want to call a method in a specific applet, it's slightly more interesting. To do this, give your applets a name, and then refer to them by that name inside the body of code for that applet. To give the applet a name, use the NAME parameter in your HTML file:

```
<P>This applet sends information:
<APPLET CODE="AllClear.class" WIDTH=100 HEIGHT=150
                             NAME="sender"></APPLET>
<P>This applet receives information from the sender:
<APPLET CODE="RunIfClear.class" WIDTH=100 HEIGHT=150
                             NAME="receiver"></APPLET>
```

Use the getAppletContext().getApplet() method with the name of that applet, which gives you a reference to the named applet. You can then refer to that applet as if it were just another object: by using call methods, setting its instance variables, and so on:

```
// gain access to the receiver applet
applet receiver = getAppletContext().getApplet("receiver");
// tell it to update itself
receiver.update(text, value);
```

In this example, the getApplet() method gets a reference to the applet named receiver. Given that reference, you can then call methods in that applet as if it were just another object in your own environment. Here, for example, if receiver has an update() method, you can tell receiver to update itself by using the information the current applet has in the variables text and value.

Naming your applets and then referring to them by using the methods described in this section enables your applets to communicate and stay in sync with each other, providing uniform behavior for all the applets on your HTML page.

Creating Applications

Applications, unlike applets, do not require a Java-enabled browser to view them from within an HTML Web page. Applications are Java programs that run on their own. However, Java applications do require that the Java VM be installed on the client machine so that the applications have access to the runtime interpreter.

A Java application consists of one or more classes and can be as large or as small as you want it to be. HotJava is a good example of a large Java application. The only thing you need to make a Java application run is one class that serves as the "jumping-off" point for the rest of your Java program. If your program is small enough, it might need only that one class.

The jumping-off class for your program needs a main() method. When you run your compiled Java class (using the Java VM interpreter), the main() method is the first thing that gets called. None of this should be a surprise to you at this point; you've been creating Java applications with main() methods all along.

The signature for the main() method always looks like this:

```
public static void main(String args[]) {...}
```

Here are the parts of the main() method:

- public means that this method is available to other classes and objects. The main() method must always be declared public.
- static means that this is a class method.
- void means this method doesn't return a value.
- main() takes one argument: an array of strings. This argument is used for command-line arguments, which you'll learn about in the next section.

The body of the main() method contains any code you need to get your application started: initializing variables or creating instances of any classes you might have declared.

When Java executes the main() method, keep in mind that main() is a class method. The class that holds it is not automatically instantiated when your program runs. If you want to treat that class as an object, you have to instantiate it in the main() method yourself. (All examples up to this point have done just this.)

Passing Command-Line Arguments

Because Java applications are standalone programs, it's useful to be able to pass arguments or options to that program to determine how it will run or to enable a generic program to operate on different kinds of input. Command-line arguments can be used for many different purposes. For example, you can use them to turn on debugging input, to indicate a filename to read from or write to, or for any other information that you might want your Java program to know.

To pass arguments to a Java program, you merely append them to the command line when you run your Java program:

```
java myprogram argumentOne 2 three
```

On this command line, you have three arguments: `argumentOne`, `2`, and `three`. Note that a space separates arguments, so this command line produces three arguments also:

```
java myprogram Java is cool
```

To group arguments, surround them with double-quotes. This command line produces one argument:

```
java myprogram "Java is cool"
```

The double-quotes are stripped off before the argument gets to the `main()` method in your program, but they serve to keep the text between them intact as one argument until it gets there.

Parsing Arguments

How does Java handle arguments? It stores them as an array of strings, which is passed to the `main()` method in your Java program. Remember the signature for `main()`:

```
public static void main (String args[]) {...}
```

Here, `args` is the name of the array of strings that contains the list of arguments. You actually can call it anything you want. Inside your `main()` method, you can then handle the arguments your program was given by iterating through the array of arguments and handling those arguments as you want.

For example, examine the class named `EchoArgs` in Listing 8.6.

TYPE   **LISTING 8.6.** EchoArgs.java.

```
1:  class EchoArgs {
2:    public static void main(String args[]) {
3:      for (int i = 0; i < args.length; i++) {
4:        System.out.println("Argument " + i + ": " + args[i]);
5:      }
6:    }
7:  }
```

To pass arguments to a Java application from within the JBuilder IDE, select the Run |
Parameters menu item. Select the AppletAppsWizards.jpr Properties dialog box
Run/Debug page by clicking on the Run/Debug tab. Type the arguments that you want to
pass to the Java application in the Command line parameters text box. Do not enter `java`
or the program name; enter only the arguments to your program. For example, type the
following set of arguments into the Command line parameters text box to get the result
shown in Figure 8.8:

```
9 1 8 jump over the moon
```

FIGURE 8.8.

*The Parameters dialog
box with several argu-
ments entered.*

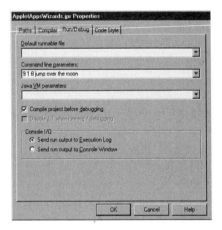

In the Default Runnable File field, click on the drop-down arrow and select the
`EchoArgs.java` program. Also, check to make sure that the radio button labeled Send run
output to Execution Log is selected, and then click OK. Now, select View | Execution
Log so that you can watch the output while you run this program, and then click the Run
button on the toolbar. With these command-line arguments, this program produces the
following output in the Execution Log window:

```
Argument 0: 9
Argument 1: 1
Argument 2: 8
Argument 3: jump
Argument 4: over
Argument 5: the
Argument 6: moon
```

Caution

In Java, args[0] is the first argument, *not* the program name as it is in C and
UNIX.

Now, enter this set of arguments in the Run/Debug page of the AppletAppsWizards.jpr Properties dialog box:

```
aOne "and aTwo" and aThree
```

With these arguments, this program produces the following output in the Execution Log window:

OUTPUT
```
Argument 0: aOne
Argument 1: and aTwo
Argument 2: and
Argument 3: aThree
```

An important thing to remember about the arguments you pass into a Java program is that those arguments are stored in an array of strings. To treat any of them as nonstrings, you have to convert them to whatever type you really wanted. For example, suppose you have a very simple Java program called SumAverage. This Java program can take any number of numeric arguments and returns the sum and the average of those arguments. Listing 8.7 shows a first pass at this program.

TYPE   **LISTING 8.7.** SumAverageNot.java.

```
 1:  class SumAverageNot {
 2:    // this listing doesn't compile
 3:    public static void main(String args[]) {
 4:      int sum = 0;
 5:      for (int i = 0; i < args.length; i++) {
 6:        sum += args[i];
 7:      }
 8:      System.out.println("Sum is: " + sum);
 9:      System.out.println("Average is: " +
10:        (float)sum / args.length);
11:    }
12:  }
```

ANALYSIS   At first glance, this program seems rather straightforward. A for loop iterates over the array of arguments and sums them, and then the sum and average are printed out as the last step. But what happens when you try to compile this? Go ahead and key in the listing and try it. You will be greeted with the following compiler error message (displayed in the Error pane of the AppBrowser window):

```
Error: (6) incompatible types; found: java.lang.String, required: int.
```

This error occurs because, in line 6, you are attempting to assign an element of the args array (which is an array of strings) to sum (which is an int). To solve this problem, you must convert the arguments to integers before assigning the values to sum. Fortunately, there's a handy method in the `Integer` class, called `parseInt()`, that does exactly that. Modify line 6 in `SumAverage` so that it looks like Listing 8.8.

Type   **Listing 8.8.** SumAverage.java.

```
 1:   class SumAverage {
 2:      // this listing compiles okay
 3:      public static void main(String args[]) {
 4:        int sum = 0;
 5:        for (int i = 0; i < args.length; i++) {
 6:          sum += Integer.parseInt(args[i]);
 7:        }
 8:        System.out.println("Sum is: " + sum);
 9:        System.out.println("Average is: " +
10:          (float)sum / args.length);
11:      }
12:   }
```

Now it should compile. Try out your program by selecting Run | Parameters to display the AppletAppsWizards.jpr Properties dialog box. Open the dialog box to the Run/Debug page by clicking on the Run/Debug tab. Select `SumAverage.java` as the Default Runnable File, and enter the following command-line arguments in the Command line parameters text box:

8 3 8 6 1

If you added `SumAverageNot.java` to the current project, your build will stop at that file's compiler error. Select the `SumAverageNot.java` node in the Navigation pane, and then click the Remove from Project icon (the folder with the minus) to unassociate that file with the project (it will remain on disk if you've saved it). Then do the build again; this time it should complete properly.

The following output appears in the Execution Log window:

Output   Sum is: 26
Average is: 5.2

Dual-Duty Programs

What if you wanted to write the same program and be able to use it as both an applet and an application? Java lets you do that by simply putting the code for both the applet's functionality and the application's functionality (including the `main()` method) in the same class. If the class is called from the `<APPLET>` tag in an HTML page, it will run as an applet (given that the appropriate code is present); if the class is called from the operating system, it will run as an application (given that the `main()` method is present). In other words, the Java VM interpreter is smart enough to be able to tell the context in which the class file is called and executes the appropriate part of the class.

As an example, Listing 8.9 shows the `HelloAnybodyApplet` converted so that it also functions as a standalone Java application and renamed to `HelloAnybody`.

TYPE   **LISTING 8.9.** `HelloAnybody.java`.

```
 1:   import java.applet.*;
 2:   import java.awt.*;
 3:
 4:   public class HelloAnybody extends Applet {
 5:
 6:      Font f = new Font("TimesRoman", Font.BOLD, 36);
 7:      String helloName;
 8:
 9:      public void init() {
10:        helloName = getParameter("name");
11:        if (helloName == null) helloName = "Chris";
12:        helloName = "Hello " + helloName + "!";
13:      }
14:
15:      public void paint(Graphics g) {
16:         g.setFont(f);
17:         g.setColor(Color.red);
18:         g.drawString(helloName, 5, 50);
19:      }
20:
21:      public static void main(String args[]) {
22:        System.out.print("Hello");
23:        if (args.length == 0) {
24:          System.out.print(" Chris");
25:        }
26:        else {
27:          for (int i = 0; i < args.length; i++) {
28:            System.out.print(" " + args[i]);
29:          }
30:        }
31:        System.out.println("!");
32:      }
33:   }
```

ANALYSIS   To make this a dual-duty program, you need to add the `main()` method, which does basically the same things that the applet code is doing.

- Line 22 prints the first part of the string, `Hello`.

- Lines 23 through 25 check to see whether any arguments have been provided and, if not, print a space and `Chris` as the default.
- Lines 26 through 30 execute when the `if` comparison is `false`—that is, there is at least one argument. The `for` loop iterates through the arguments and prints a space followed by the argument for each iteration.
- Line 31 prints the exclamation point at the end of the output string.

Listing 8.10 shows the HTML file associated with this program so that you can run it as an applet.

TYPE   **LISTING 8.10.** `HelloAnybody.html`.

```
 1:  <HTML>
 2:  <HEAD>
 3:  <TITLE>Hello to Everyone!</TITLE>
 4:  </HEAD>
 5:  <BODY>
 6:  <P>
 7:  <APPLET CODE="HelloAnybody.class" WIDTH=500 HEIGHT=100>
 8:  <PARAM NAME=name VALUE="JBuilder Fans">
 9:  Hello to whoever you are!
10:  </APPLET>
11:  </BODY>
12:  </HTML>
```

Now, you're all set. Select File | Save All, and then run your new program as an applet by right-clicking on the `HelloAnybody.html` node and selecting Run. The results will appear in the appletviewer window, as shown in Figure 8.9.

FIGURE 8.9.

The HelloAnybody applet displayed in the appletviewer.

Also, try running this as a standalone program by selecting the Run | Parameters command. Select the Run/Debug page by clicking on the Run/Debug tab. Select `HelloAnybody.java` in the Default Runnable File field. Finally, enter `Kristi` as the command-line argument in the Command line parameters text box. Click OK to dismiss the dialog box, and click on the Run toolbar button. The Execution Log window will display this:

OUTPUT   `Hello Kristi!`

8

The best approach to creating programs that can run as either an applet or an application is first to define the program as an applet, making sure that any output variables are defined as instance variables for accessibility. Then, create the HTML file and test the applet. When it's running properly, add the main() method so that your class file can also be run as a standalone application, and you've got it!

JBuilder Projects

A JBuilder project is any collection of files that you want to treat as an organized group, such as files that compose an application or an applet. In JBuilder, the project file that tracks all the pieces of a project is designated by the file extension .jpr. When you open an existing .jpr file in the Browser, all its elements are listed in the Navigation pane.

Creating a Project

You create a project file by selecting File | New Project, which displays the Project Wizard dialog box, shown in Figure 8.10.

FIGURE 8.10.

The Project Wizard dialog box.

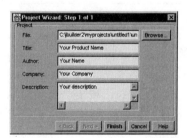

In this dialog box, the File field is the place where you enter information about the project name and the package to which it belongs. Remember that packages follow a directory hierarchy, so by entering the fully qualified path and filename for your project, you are telling JBuilder which package (directory) the project belongs in. In Figure 8.10, the package is untitled1, and the project is untitled1.jpr. You can either type the path and filename manually, as you have done in past days, or use the Browse button to find a particular directory (package) in which you want to locate your new project.

You can optionally enter a title, author, company, and description for your project as well. This information is inserted into an HTML file with the same root name as your project. By clicking the Finish button in this dialog, you instruct JBuilder to open the .jpr file in memory and prepare it to receive any files that you want to add to it to complete your project.

Dividing your packages into projects in this way is good practice. It enables you to partition your packages into sections that can be built and debugged independently, using the Build | Make Project or Build | Build Project command. For example, for today's lessons, you were instructed to add all the listing files to the `AppletAppsWizards` project. If you did so, you can build all the listings in today's lesson with just one command: Build | Build "AppletAppsWizards.jpr".

If you've added `SumAverageNot.java` to the project, your build will stop at that file's compiler error. Remove `SumAverageNot.java` and do the build again. This time it should complete properly if you've typed everything correctly.

Project File Extensions

Aside from the `.java` and `.html` files that you've added to projects so far, there are a number of other files that a project can comprise. Table 8.1 shows what types of files can be part of a JBuilder project and gives a brief explanation of the purpose of each type.

TABLE 8.1. JBUILDER PROJECT FILES.

Extension	Purpose
`.~jav, .~htm`	Backup files for `.java` and `.html` files; enable you to recover previous file contents after saving to disk.
`.au`	Audio file in AU (μ-law) format.
`.bmp`	Graphics file in Windows Bitmap format.
`.class`	Compiled source code file containing Java bytecodes.
`.gif`	Graphics file in GIF format.
`.html`	Hypertext Markup Language file; used to run applet class files in a Java-enabled Web browser.
`.jar`	Java ARchive file, a compressed collection of files.
`.java`	Source code file containing Java code for applets and/or applications; compiling this file creates a `.class` file.
`.jpg`	Graphics file in JPEG format.
`.jpr`	Project file; holds references to all other files in the project and project properties.
`.zip`	ZIP file, a compressed collection of files.

Tip

Any file can be added to a JBuilder 2 project. There's an option to treat custom extensions as text, such as .c or .cpp.

Using Wizards

8

You now have some experience with applets and applications, but with the JBuilder IDE, there's always an easier way! This section introduces you to the Applet and Application wizards, which generate skeleton code for your Java programs based on the answers you provide in the wizard dialog boxes.

You've already used one wizard, the Project Wizard, to create new projects to hold your files as you've been trying them out during the past week. (You *have* been trying them out, haven't you?) JBuilder also provides an Applet Wizard and an Application Wizard. These wizards present you with dialog boxes that step you through creating the source code for an applet or application. You specify some of the more common options while JBuilder generates the code for you.

Applet Wizard

First, make sure that today's project, AppletsAppsWizards, is open; you'll be adding this applet to it. Now, to create a Java applet using the Applet Wizard, select File | New to display the New dialog box. On the New page, click on the Applet icon and then click OK. The first page of the Applet Wizard dialog box appears, as shown in Figure 8.11.

FIGURE 8.11.

The first page of the Applet Wizard dialog box.

Creating the Source Files

The first page of the Applet Wizard dialog box asks you for the name of the applet's package and class. Keep the current package name, AppletsAppsWizards, displayed in the Package text box. In the Class text box, type GreenApplet. As you type this information, notice that the File field automatically reflects what you're typing, as shown in Figure 8.12.

FIGURE 8.12.

Applet Wizard: Step 1 of 3.

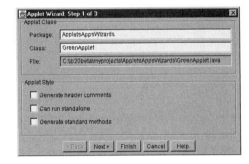

This page of the dialog box also enables you to decide whether to generate comments and methods and whether this applet will also be an application. Finish filling out the dialog as shown in Figure 8.12. After filling in this page, click the Next> button.

In the next page of the Applet Wizard dialog box, you're asked for the names and other details of the applet's parameters, as shown in Figure 8.13.

FIGURE 8.13.

Applet Wizard: Step 2 of 3.

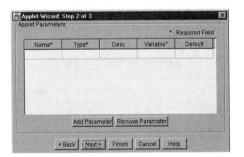

This applet doesn't take any parameters, so just click the Next> button again.

The third, and last, page of the Applet Wizard dialog box asks whether you want the wizard to generate an HTML page. You'll need one to run your applet in; so make sure that the Generate HTML Page check box is checked, and type `TestGreenApplet` in the Name field, as shown in Figure 8.14.

FIGURE 8.14.

Applet Wizard: Step 3 of 3.

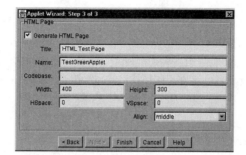

When you're done, click the Finish button. At this point, the JBuilder IDE generates the source code files, both .java and .html, needed to support your choices. You'll see that two files are added to the current project: an HTML file, GreenApplet.html, and a Java source code file, GreenApplet.java. When the IDE has completed the code generation, click on the GreenApplet.html entry in the Navigation pane, and click on the Source tab in the Content pane.

Modifying the HTML File

You might want to change some things in the HTML file to suit your needs. In this case, let's change the title and the width attributes. Click on the Contents pane, on the line below the <TITLE> tag that reads HTML Test Page. Press Home and then press Shift+End to select the entire line. Now type GreenApplet Is Alive! as the new title, which will appear as the caption of the HTML page's window. Press the down arrow until the cursor is on the WIDTH attribute line, press End and then Shift+Ctrl+left arrow to select the 400 value. Now type 600 as the new width. The applet will now appear in a rectangular area, 600 pixels by 300 pixels. Figure 8.15 shows the resulting HTML source file.

FIGURE 8.15.

GreenApplet.html.

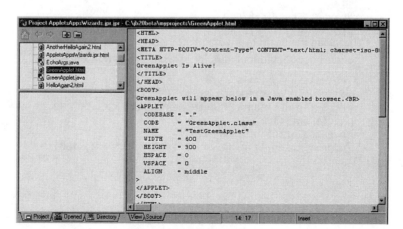

Select File | Save to preserve your changes. Next, you'll modify the skeleton applet file.

Modifying the Applet

Although the HTML page and the applet code have been generated for you, you will want to change a line of code in the jbInit() method and add a paint() method in the GreenApplet class.

To accomplish this in the JBuilder IDE, click on the GreenApplet.java entry in the Navigation pane. In the Structure pane, scroll down until you see a method named jbInit() and then click on that entry. The cursor in the Contents pane will automatically be positioned on that method, with its header highlighted, as shown in Figure 8.16.

FIGURE 8.16.

The AppBrowser with the jbInit() *method's signature highlighted.*

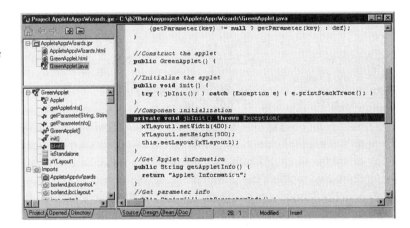

Click on the highlighted line and then move the cursor down and over to the offending 400 text. Change it to 600 so that the line reads as follows:

```
xYLayout1.setWidth(600);
```

Then add the paint() method listed next to your new applet. The GreenApplet.java file source code should look similar to what's shown in Figure 8.17.

```
//Paint the applet
public void paint(Graphics g) {
  Font f = new Font("TimesRoman", Font.ITALIC, 72);
  g.setFont(f);
  g.setColor(Color.green);
  g.drawString("I'm alive, I tell you!", 10, 150);
}
```

FIGURE 8.17.

The newly added `paint()` *method.*

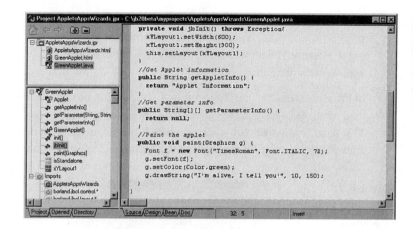

Select File | Save. Run the applet and see what happens! You'll also want to explore the generated .java file and see what different variables and methods JBuilder automatically provides for your applets. You'll learn more about how these work in the next few days.

Application Wizard

First, make sure today's project, AppletsAppsWizards, is open; you'll be adding this application to it. Now, to create a Java application using the Application Wizard, select File | New to display the New dialog box. On its New page, click on the Application icon and then click OK. The Application Wizard will display a series of pages with fields for you to fill in the blanks.

Creating the Source Files

The first page of the Application Wizard dialog box asks you for the name of the application class, which is `Hello`, and also allows you to decide whether to generate comments, as shown in Figure 8.18.

FIGURE 8.18.

Application Wizard: Step 1 of 2.

After filling in the first page, you can click the Finish button if your application is not going to have any UI components (in other words, it will be a command-line application only). However, most of the time, you will want to add UI components to your application, so click the Next> button.

In the second page of the Application Wizard dialog box, you'll be asked for the name of the Frame class. Remember that a Frame is a window that holds other UI components. This page also allows you to choose which generic methods and components will be generated automatically for you. Fill in the Name field as shown in Figure 8.19.

FIGURE 8.19.

Application Wizard:
Step 2 of 2.

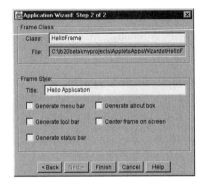

Notice once again that as you type HelloFrame in the Name field, the File field reflects your choice. When you're done, click the Finish button. At this point, the IDE generates the source code files needed to support your choices. When it's finished, click on the Hello.java entry in the Navigation pane of the AppBrowser window so that it looks as shown in Figure 8.20.

FIGURE 8.20.

Hello.java *in the*
AppBrowser window.

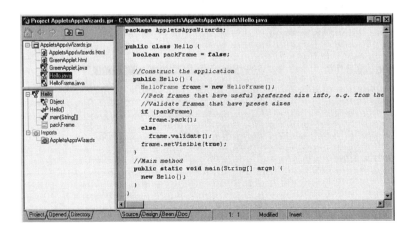

Modifying Source Files

You'll see that two Java source code files, `Hello.java` and `HelloFrame.java`, were generated. In a GUI application, such as this one, you'll add much of the functionality by putting components in the Frame and creating event handlers, just as you did on Day 6, "User Interface Design."

8

Summary

Applets are probably the most common use of the Java language today. Applets are more complicated than many Java applications because they are executed and drawn inline within Web pages, but they can access the graphics, user interface (UI), and event structure provided by the Web browser itself. Today, you learned the basics of creating applets, including the following:

- All applets you develop using Java inherit from the `Applet` class, which is part of the `java.applet` package. The `Applet` class provides basic behavior for how the applet will be integrated with and react to the browser and various forms of input from that browser and the person running it. By subclassing `Applet`, you have access to all that behavior.

- Applets have five major methods that are used for the basic activities an applet performs during its life cycle: `init()`, `start()`, `stop()`, `destroy()`, and `paint()`. Although you don't necessarily need to override all these methods, these are the most common ones you'll see repeated in many of the applets you create in this book and in other samples you might come across.

- The Applet Wizard can be used to generate foundation code for your Java Applets. You can invoke this code generator by selecting File | New from the JBuilder menu and then selecting Applet Wizard from the New page of the New dialog box. Fill in the requested information in the ensuing pages of the Applet Wizard dialog box to create an applet.

- To run a compiled applet class file, you embed it in an HTML Web page by using the `<APPLET>` and `</APPLET>` tag pair. When a Java-capable browser comes across `<APPLET>`, it loads and runs the applet described in that tag. If the browser is not Java-enabled, the text between the `<APPLET>` and `</APPLET>` tags (if any) is displayed instead. To publish Java applets on the World Wide Web in HTML files, you do not need special server software; any old Web server will do just fine.

- Unlike applications, applets do not have a command line on which to pass arguments, so those arguments must be passed into the applet through the HTML file in which the applet is embedded. You indicate parameters in the HTML file by placing the <PARAM> tag between the <APPLET> and </APPLET> tag pair. <PARAM> has two attributes: NAME for the name of the parameter (its identifier) and VALUE for its value. Inside the body of your applet (usually in the init() method), you can then gain access to those parameters using the getParameter() method; remember that all parameters are passed into the applet as strings, and you must convert values to other types if necessary.

You also learned about some miscellaneous applet tricks, such as how to use the showStatus() and getAppletInfo() methods and how to use named applets to facilitate communication among applets on the same HTML page.

You also learned about creating applications as well as dual-purpose programs that can serve as both applets and applications. Finally, you built both a GUI application project and an applet project by using the wizards in the JBuilder IDE.

Q&A

Q **In the first part of today's lesson, you say that applets are downloaded from random Web servers and run on the client's system. What's to stop an applet developer from creating an applet that deletes all the files on the client's system or in some other way compromises that system's security?**

A Recall that Java applets have several restrictions that make it difficult for all the more obvious malicious behavior to take place. For example, because Java applets cannot read or write files on the client system, they cannot delete or read system files that might contain private information. Because they cannot run programs on the client's system without your express permission, they cannot, for example, run system programs pretending to be you. Nor can they run so many programs that your system crashes.

In addition, Java's very architecture makes it difficult to circumvent these restrictions. The language itself, the Java compiler, and the Java Virtual Machine all have checks to make sure that no one has tried to sneak in bogus code or play games with the system itself. Of course, no system can claim to be 100 percent secure, and the fact that Java applets are run on your system *should* make you concerned. Being concerned is what makes you careful.

Q **Wait a minute—if I can't read or write files or run programs on the client system on which the applet is running, doesn't that mean that I basically can't do anything other than simple animations and flashy graphics? How can I save state in an applet? How can I create, say, a word processor or a spreadsheet as a Java applet?**

A For each person who doesn't believe that Java is secure enough, there is another who believes that Java's security restrictions are too severe for just these reasons. Yes, Java applets are limited because of the security restrictions. But given the possibility for abuse, the Java team believes that it's better to err on the side of being more cautious as far as security is concerned. Consider it a challenge!

Keep in mind, also, that Java applications have none of the restrictions that pertain to Java applets, but they are just as portable across platforms. It might be that the thing you want to create would make a much better application than an applet.

Q **I have an applet that takes parameters and an HTML file that passes values to those parameters. But when my applet runs, all I get are `null` values, so it always displays my defaults. What's going on here?**

A Check to make sure that your parameter identifiers (the strings following the `NAME` attributes) match the names you're testing for in your `getParameter()` statements. Remember that Java is case-sensitive, and this includes applet parameters. Make sure, also, that your `<PARAM>` tags are placed between the `<APPLET>` and `</APPLET>` tags and that you haven't misspelled anything.

Q **In the Browser, when my application project is open, I see that Java class files are sometimes imported into my project. What does this mean, and how can I find out more about these imported files?**

A Java class files are imported to add their functionality to your application. For example, if you used Java AWT controls in your project, the Imports node would show `java.awt.*` to indicate that those class files were used by your project. If you'd like to see what is in those imported files, just double-click on the entry in the Imports list, and JBuilder will load the import library and its files into the AppBrowser window so that you can examine them in detail.

Workshop

The Workshop provides two ways for you to affirm what you've learned in this chapter. The Quiz section poses questions to help you solidify your understanding of the material covered. You can find answers to the quiz questions in Appendix A, "Answers to Quiz Questions." The Exercise section provides you with experience in using what you have learned. Try to work through all these before continuing to the next day.

Quiz

1. What are the five major methods that an applet can override? Must an applet override all five of these methods to execute properly?

2. Plain text between the <APPLET> and </APPLET> tag pair serves what purpose? Is it a requirement, or is it optional?

4. What <APPLET> attribute can be used to tell the HTML page to look in some other directory for the applet's class files?

5. True or False? All applet parameters are passed as strings and must be converted within the applet body if they represent some other type of data.

Exercise

Using Listing 8.11 as a base, make the following changes to the HTML code, and name the resulting file HeyYouApplet2.html:

- Add a parameter named fname with a value of CourierNew.

- Add a parameter named fsize with a value of 12.

TYPE   **LISTING 8.11.** HeyYouApplet.html.

```
 1:  <HTML>
 2:  <HEAD>
 3:  <TITLE>Hey You!</TITLE>
 4:  </HEAD>
 5:  <BODY>
 6:  <P>
 7:  <APPLET CODE="HeyYouApplet.class" WIDTH=300 HEIGHT=150>
 8:  <PARAM NAME=name VALUE="Michelle">
 9:  Hey out there!
10:  </APPLET>
11:  </BODY>
12:  </HTML>
```

Then, using Listing 8.12 as a base, make the following changes to the Java code, and name the resulting file HeyYouApplet2.java:

- Get the fname parameter's value, and set fontName to that value; make the default value TimesRoman.

- Get the fsize parameter's value, and set fontSize to that value. Convert the fontSize to an integer fontSizeInt, and make the default value 36.

- In the paint() method, set the f variable's arguments using fontName and fontSizeInt.

- Also in the paint() method, pass f to the getSetFont() method.

TYPE **LISTING 8.12.** HeyYouApplet.java.

```java
1:  import java.awt.Graphics;
2:  import java.awt.Font;
3:  import java.awt.Color;
4:
5:  public class HeyYouApplet extends java.applet.Applet {
6:
7:    String heyName;
8:
9:    public void init() {
10:
11:      heyName = getParameter("name");
12:      if (heyName == null)
13:        heyName = "You";
14:      heyName = "Hey " + heyName + "!";
15:    }
16:
17:    public void paint(Graphics g) {
18:      Font f = new Font("TimesRoman", Font.BOLD, 36);
19:      g.setFont(f);
20:      g.setColor(Color.green);
21:      g.drawString(heyName, 5, 50);
22:    }
23:  }
```

DAY 9

Graphics, Fonts, and Multimedia

Yesterday, you gained a good understanding of how applets work. Now, you'll build on that understanding by learning the kinds of things you can do with applets with the Java and JBuilder class libraries and how to combine them to produce interesting effects. You'll start with how to draw to the screen—that is, how to produce lines and shapes with the built-in graphics primitives, how to print text using fonts, and how to use and modify color in your applets. Today, you'll learn the following:

- How the graphics system works in Java: the `Graphics` class, the coordinate system used to draw to the screen, and how applets paint and repaint

- Using the `Graphics` class primitives, including drawing and filling lines, rectangles, ovals, and arcs

- Creating and using fonts, including how to draw characters and strings and how to find out the metrics of a given font for better layout, using the `Font` and `FontMetrics` classes

- All about color in Java, including the `Color` class and how to set the foreground (drawing) and background color for your applet

Today, you'll also learn the fundamentals of animation in Java: how the various parts of the system all work together so that you can create moving figures and dynamically updatable applets. Specifically, you'll explore the following:

- How Java animations work—what the `paint()` and `repaint()` methods are, starting and stopping dynamic applets, and how to use and override these methods in your own applets

- Threads—a quick introduction to what they are and how they can make your applets more well behaved

- Using images—getting them from the server, loading them into Java, and displaying them in your applet

- Creating animations by using images, including an extensive example

- Using sounds—getting them and playing them at the appropriate times

- Sun's Animator applet—an easy way to organize animations and sounds in Java

- Reducing animation flicker, a common problem with animation in Java

- Double-buffering—advanced flicker avoidance

Animations are fun and easy to do in Java, but there's only so much you can do with the built-in Java methods for graphics, fonts and colors. For really interesting animations, you have to provide your own images for each frame of the animation. Having sounds is nice, as well. Today, you'll learn to create such animations, incorporating graphics, images, and sounds into Java applets.

To create a new project for today's listings, select File I New Project, and modify the File field so that it says

```
C:\jbuilder2\myprojects\GraphicsFontsEtc.jpr
```

Click the Finish button. You'll add all of today's listings to this project by selecting the Add to Project icon in the Navigation pane in the AppBrowser window.

Graphics

With Java's graphics capabilities, you can draw lines, shapes, characters, and images to the screen inside your applet. Most of the graphics operations in Java are methods defined in the `Graphics` class. You don't have to explicitly create an instance of `Graphics` in order to draw something in your applet. In fact, in one of your applets yesterday, you were given a `Graphics` object to work with simply by using the `Graphics` argument to the paint() method—in other words, the instance was created for you by the paint() method. By drawing on that object, you draw onto your applet, and the results appear on the screen.

The Graphics class is part of the java.awt package, so if your applet does any painting (as it usually will), make sure that you import the class at the beginning of your Java file (after the package statement, if any):

```
import java.awt.Graphics;

public class MyClass extends java.applet.Applet {...}
```

Graphics Coordinate System

To draw an object on-screen, you call one of the drawing methods available in the Graphics class. All the drawing methods have arguments representing endpoints, corners, or starting locations of the object as values in the applet's coordinate system. For example, a line starts at the point 10,10 and ends at the point 20,20.

Java's coordinate system has the origin (0,0) in the top-left corner. Positive x values go to the right, and positive y values are down. All pixel values are integers; there are no partial or fractional pixels. Figure 9.1 shows how you might draw a simple square by using this coordinate system.

FIGURE 9.1.

The Java graphics coordinate system.

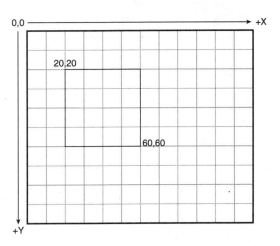

Java's coordinate system is different from some of the painting and layout programs that have their x and y origins in the bottom-left corner. If you're not used to working with this graphics coordinate system, it might take some practice to get familiar with it. Just remember that the numbers run the same way English is read, left to right, top to bottom.

Drawing and Filling

The Graphics class provides a set of simple built-in graphics primitives for drawing, including lines, rectangles, polygons, ovals, and arcs.

> **Note**
>
> Bitmap images, such as GIF files, can also be drawn by using the Graphics class. You'll learn about this tomorrow.

Lines

To draw straight lines, use the drawLine() method. This method takes four arguments: the x and y coordinates of the starting point and the x and y coordinates of the ending point.

```
public void paint(Graphics g) {
  g.drawLine(25,25,175,175);
}
```

Figure 9.2 shows the result of this snippet of code. Its starting point is 25,25 and the ending point is 175,175, so the line is drawn from upper-left to lower-right.

FIGURE 9.2.

Lines are drawn from one coordinate to another.

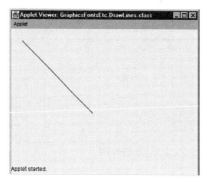

Rectangles

The Java graphics primitives provide not just one, but three kinds of rectangles:

- Plain rectangles with squared corners
- Rounded rectangles with rounded corners
- Three-dimensional rectangles, which are drawn with a shaded border

For each of these rectangles, you have two methods from which to choose: one that draws the rectangle in outline form and one that fills the rectangle with color.

To draw a rectangle with squared corners, use either the drawRect() or fillRect() methods. Both take four arguments: the x and y coordinates of the upper-left corner of the rectangle and the width and height of the rectangle to be drawn. For example, the following paint() method draws two squares; the left one is outlined, and the right one is filled:

```
public void paint(Graphics g) {
  g.drawRect(20,20,160,160);
  g.fillRect(200,20,160,160);
}
```

Figure 9.3 shows the resulting rectangles, which are actually squares because their width and height arguments are equal.

FIGURE 9.3.

The drawRect() *and* fillRect() *functions both create rectangles.*

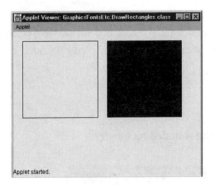

Rounded rectangles, are as you might expect, rectangles with rounded corners. The drawRoundRect() and fillRoundRect() methods are similar to the methods to draw regular rectangles except that rounded rectangles have two extra arguments, arcWidth and arcHeight, to specify the horizontal diameter and vertical diameter of the arc at the corners. Those two arguments determine how far along the edges of the rectangle that the arc for the corner will start: arcWidth for the arc along the horizontal (x dimension) and arcHeight for the vertical (y dimension).

In the first example in Figure 9.4, the arcWidth and arcHeight are both set to 5, which produces a nicely rounded corner. In the second example, the arcWidth is set to 30, and the arcHeight is set to 10. Larger values for arcWidth and arcHeight make the overall rectangle more rounded. Values equal to half the width and half the height of the rectangle itself produce a circle, as in the third example, although it's simpler to use ovals to create circles (see "Ovals" a bit later in this section).

FIGURE 9.4.

The arcWidth *and*
arcHeight *control the*
appearance of the
rounded corners.

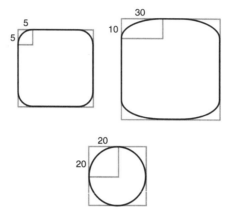

Here's a paint() method that draws two rounded rectangles: one as an outline with
rounded corners 10 pixels square; the other filled, with rounded corners 20 pixels square.

```
public void paint(Graphics g) {
    g.drawRoundRect(20,20,160,160,10,10);
    g.fillRoundRect(200,20,160,160,20,20);
}
```

Figure 9.5 shows the resulting rounded rectangles.

FIGURE 9.5.

Rounded corners
soften the appear-
ance of rectangles.

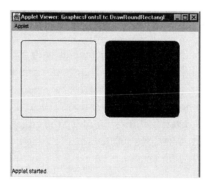

Finally, there are three-dimensional rectangles. These rectangles aren't really 3D.
Instead, they use a beveled border that makes them appear as if a light were shining from
the upper-left corner of the screen, so they look either raised or lowered from the surface
of the applet. Three-dimensional rectangles have five arguments: the starting x and y; the
width and height of the rectangle; and the fifth argument, a boolean, indicating whether
the 3D effect is raised (true) or indented (false). As with the other rectangles, there are
also different methods for drawing and filling: draw3DRect() and fill3DRect(). Here's

code to produce two outlined three-dimensional rectangles—the left one raised and the right one lowered.

```
public void paint(Graphics g) {
  g.draw3DRect(20,20,160,160,true);
  g.draw3DRect(200,20,160,160,false);
}
```

Figure 9.6 shows the resulting three-dimensional rectangles.

FIGURE 9.6.

*Three-dimensional
rectangles create the
appearance of depth.*

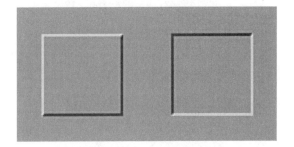

Note

Because you don't have any control over the width of the beveled border, it can be very difficult to see the 3D effect of 3D rectangles due to the fact that the default line width is only one pixel. (Actually, the borders on Figure 9.6 are enlarged to better show the effect.) If you are having trouble with 3D rectangles, this might be why. Drawing 3D rectangles in any color other than black makes them much easier to see.

Polygons

Polygons are shapes with an unlimited number of sides. To draw a polygon, you need a set of x,y coordinate pairs. The drawing method starts at the first pair of x,y coordinates and draws a line to the second pair, then a line to the third pair, and so on.

As with rectangles, you can draw an outline or a filled polygon with the drawPolygon() and fillPolygon() methods, respectively. Both of these methods automatically close the polygon for you if the starting and ending points are different. If you would rather have a series of connected lines, without automatically closing the outlined shape (an open polygon), you can use the drawPolyline() method. You also have a choice of how you want to list the coordinates—either as arrays of x and y coordinates or by passing them to an instance of the Polygon class.

Using the first technique, the drawPolyline(), drawPolygon(), and fillPolygon() methods take three arguments:

- An array of integers representing the x coordinates
- An array of integers representing the y coordinates
- An integer for the total number of points

The x and y arrays should, of course, have the same number of elements. Here's an example of drawing an open polygon's outline by using this technique:

```
public void paint(Graphics g) {
  int xCoordArr[] = { 78,188,194,284,106,116,52 };
  int yCoordArr[] = { 66,148,72,140,216,160,212 };
  int numPts = xCoordArr.length;
  g.drawPolyline(xCoordArr, yCoordArr, numPts);
}
```

Figure 9.7 shows the resulting open polygon.

FIGURE 9.7.

An open polygon.

The second technique uses a `Polygon` object to create the polygon and then passes it whole to the polygon drawing method. The `Polygon` class is useful if you intend to add points to the polygon or if you're building the polygon on-the-fly. The `Polygon` class enables you to treat the polygon as an object and use its methods to add points. To instantiate a polygon object, you can create an empty polygon:

```
Polygon poly = new Polygon();
```

After you have a polygon object, you can append points to the polygon as you need to, using the `Polygon` class `addPoint()` method. Here are the same seven points from the first polygon example specified as coordinate pairs passed to the `addPoint()` method:

```
poly.addPoint(78,66);
poly.addPoint(188,148);
poly.addPoint(194,72);
poly.addPoint(284,140);
poly.addPoint(106,216);
```

```
poly.addPoint(116,160);
poly.addPoint(52,212);
```

Then, to draw the polygon, just use the polygon object as an argument of the polygon drawing methods. Here's the previous example, rewritten using this second technique, including the last line which passes the `poly` object to the `g.drawPolygon()` method.

```
public void paint(Graphics g) {
  Polygon poly = new Polygon();
  poly.addPoint(78,66);
  poly.addPoint(188,148);
  poly.addPoint(194,72);
  poly.addPoint(284,140);
  poly.addPoint(106,216);
  poly.addPoint(116,160);
  poly.addPoint(52,212);
  g.drawPolygon(poly);
}
```

Figure 9.8 shows the resulting outlined polygon.

FIGURE 9.8.

An outlined polygon.

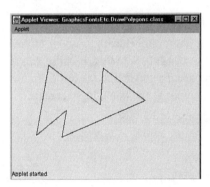

As you can see, if you have a lot of points to add, the arrays technique takes fewer lines of code. You can also combine the two techniques by defining the two arrays using one of the `Polygon` class's alternate constructors to create the polygon object with the coordinate arrays and finally passing the object to the desired polygon drawing method. Here's that same example using the two techniques combined, but this time you pass the object to the `fillPolygon()` method.

```
public void paint(Graphics g) {
  int xCoordArr[] = { 78,188,194,284,106,116,52 };
  int yCoordArr[] = { 66,148,72,140,216,160,212 };
  int numPts = xCoordArr.length;
  Polygon poly = new Polygon(xCoordArr, yCoordArr, numPts);
```

```
    g.fillPolygon(poly);
}
```

Figure 9.9 shows the resulting filled polygon.

FIGURE 9.9.

A filled polygon.

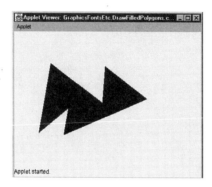

Ovals

You can use ovals to draw ellipses or circles. Ovals are just rectangles with overly rounded corners, drawn using four arguments: the x and y of the upper-left corner and the width and height of the oval itself. Note that, because you're drawing an oval, the starting coordinates are some distance up and to the left from the actual outline of the oval itself; it's the upper-left corner of the bounding rectangle.

As with other drawing operations, the drawOval() method draws an outline of an oval, and the fillOval() method draws a filled oval. Here's an example of two ovals: a circle and an ellipse.

```
public void paint(Graphics g) {
  g.drawOval(20,20,160,160);
  g.fillOval(200,20,200,160);
}
```

Figure 9.10 shows the resulting ovals. The first is a circle because its width and height are the same; the second is an ellipse whose width is a larger value than its height.

Arcs

Of all the drawing operations, arcs are the most complex to construct. An arc is a segment of an oval. In fact, the easiest way to think of an arc is as a section of a complete oval. Figure 9.11 shows some arcs.

FIGURE 9.10.

An outlined circle and a filled ellipse.

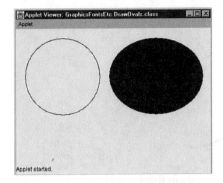

9

FIGURE 9.11.

Examples of arcs.

The arc drawing methods take six arguments: the starting corner x and y coordinates, the width and height of the bounding oval, the startAngle (degree at which to start the arc), and the arcAngle (degrees to draw before stopping). Once again, there is a drawArc() method to draw the arc's outline and a fillArc() method to draw a filled arc. Filled arcs are drawn as if they were sections of a pie; instead of joining the two endpoints, both endpoints are joined to the center of the oval.

The important thing to understand about arcs is that you're actually formulating the arc as an oval and then drawing only some of that oval. The starting x,y coordinates, width, and height, are not those of the actual arc as drawn on-screen; they're those of the full ellipse of which the arc is a part. The first four arguments determine the size and shape of the arc; the last two arguments (startAngle and arcAngle) determine the endpoints of the arc.

Let's start with a simple arc: a C-shaped arc based on a circle as shown in Figure 9.12.

FIGURE 9.12.

A circular arc.

To construct the list of arguments to draw this arc, the first thing you do is think of it as a complete circle. Then you find the x and y coordinates and the width and height of that circle. Those four values are the first four arguments to the drawArc() or fillArc() methods. The x and y coordinates are obtained by placing the upper-left corner of the bounding rectangle. Figure 9.13 shows how to obtain the width and height values from the circle's bounding rectangle.

FIGURE 9.13.

The width and height *arguments determine the length and position of the arc.*

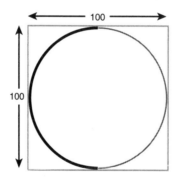

To get the last two arguments, think in degrees around the circle. Referring to Figure 9.14: 0 degrees is at 3 o'clock; 90 degrees is at 12 o'clock, 180 at 9 o'clock, and 270 at 6 o'clock. The start of the arc is the degree value of the starting point. In this example, the starting point is the top of the C at 90 degrees; therefore, 90 is the fifth argument, startAngle.

The sixth argument is another degree value indicating how far around the circle to sweep (*not* the ending degree value, as you might think) and the direction to go in (indicated by the integer's sign). In this case, because you're going halfway around the circle, you're sweeping 180 degrees. You're also sweeping in the direction that the degrees are increasing in number; therefore, the sign is positive. So the value of the sixth argument, arcAngle, is +180, or just 180. These particulars are shown in Figure 9.14.

FIGURE 9.14.

The arc begins at the value of the startAngle *argument and continues for the span of the value of the* arcAngle *argument.*

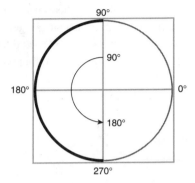

If you were drawing a backwards C, you would sweep 180 degrees in the negative direction, and the last argument would have been -180.

Here's the code for this example. You'll draw an outline of the C and a filled C.

```
public void paint(Graphics g) {
  g.drawArc(20,20,160,160,90,180);
  g.fillArc(200,20,160,160,90,180);
}
```

The arcs this code produces are shown in Figure 9.15.

FIGURE 9.15.

An outlined circular arc and a filled circular arc.

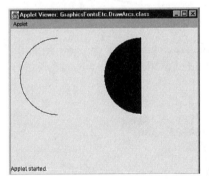

Visualizing arcs on circles is easy; arcs on ellipses are slightly more difficult. Let's go through this same process to draw the arc shown in Figure 9.16.

FIGURE 9.16.

An elliptical arc.

Like the arc on the circle, this arc is a piece of a complete oval—in this case, an elliptical oval. By completing the oval that this arc is a part of, you can get the four starting arguments for the `drawArc()` or `fillArc()` method: `x`, `y`, `width` and `height`. Figure 9.17 shows how these values are derived from the ellipse's bounding rectangle.

FIGURE 9.17.

The arc's `width` *and* `height` *arguments.*

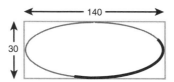

Then, all you need to do is figure out the starting angle and the angle to sweep to obtain the `startAngle` and `arcAngle` arguments. This arc doesn't start on a nice boundary such as 90 or 180 degrees, so you'll need to either use a protractor template or get the values by trial and error. This arc starts somewhere around 25 degrees and then sweeps clockwise about 130 degrees, as shown in Figure 9.18.

FIGURE 9.18.

The `startAngle` *and* `arcAngle` *arguments.*

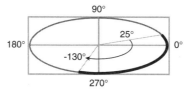

With all the arguments for the arc in hand, you can now write the code. Here's the code for this arc, both drawn and filled (notice that in the case of the filled arc, it is drawn as if it were a pie section):

```
public void paint(Graphics g) {
  g.drawArc(10,20,250,150,25,-130);
  g.fillArc(10,180,250,150,25,-130);
}
```

The arcs this code produces are shown in Figure 9.19.

A Simple Graphics Example

Here's an example of an applet that uses many of the built-in graphics primitives you've learned so far to draw a rudimentary shape. In this case, it's a lamp with a spotted shade (or a cubist mushroom, depending on your point of view). Listing 9.1 shows the complete code for the Lamp project; Figure 9.20 shows the resulting applet.

FIGURE 9.19.

An outlined elliptical arc and a filled elliptical arc.

9

TYPE **LISTING 9.1.** SpottedLamp.java.

```
 1:  package GraphicsFontsEtc;
 2:  import java.awt.Graphics;
 3:  public class SpottedLamp extends java.applet.Applet {
 4:
 5:    public void paint(Graphics g) {
 6:      // the lamp platform
 7:      g.fillRect(0,250,290,290);
 8:
 9:      // the base of the lamp
10:      g.drawLine(125,160,125,250);
11:      g.drawLine(175,160,175,250);
12:
13:      // the shade, top and bottom edges
14:      g.drawArc(85,87,130,50,62,58);
15:      g.drawArc(85,157,130,50,-65,312);
16:
17:      // the sides of the shade
18:      g.drawLine(119,89,85,177);
19:      g.drawLine(181,89,215,177);
20:
21:      // the spots on the shade
22:      g.fillArc(78,120,40,40,63,-174);
23:      g.fillOval(120,96,40,40);
24:      g.fillArc(173,100,40,40,110,180);
25:    }
26:
27:  }
```

Remember to create and save an .html file before attempting to run the applet.

The WIDTH and HEIGHT parameters for the HTML file are not specified here; that's left as an exercise. Experimenting with different parameters will give you a better feel for creating your own HTML files later.

FIGURE 9.20.

The SpottedLamp applet.

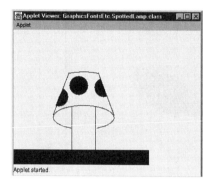

Copying and Clearing

After you've drawn a few things on-screen, you might want to move them around or clear the entire applet. The Graphics class provides methods for doing both of these things.

The copyArea() method copies a rectangular area of the screen to another area of the screen. This method takes six arguments: the x and y coordinates of the upper-left corner of the rectangle to copy, the width and height of that rectangle, and dx and dy, which represent the delta (change) in the x and y starting-point coordinates. For example, this line of code copies a rectangular area 90 pixels by 70 pixels with starting coordinates of 5,10 and copies it to a rectangle starting 100 pixels to the right of the original starting x coordinate with no change (0 pixels) to the starting y coordinate:

```
g.copyArea(5,10,90,70,100,0);
```

The dx and dy arguments can be either positive or negative, depending on which direction you want to copy the rectangle. Negative dx values copy the rectangle upward, and positive dx values copy downward; negative dy values copy the rectangle to the left, whereas positive dy values copy to the right.

To clear a rectangular area, use the clearRect() method, which takes the same four arguments as the drawRect() and fillRect() methods: starting x,y coordinates , width, and height. This method fills the specified rectangle with the current background color of the applet. (You'll learn how to set the current background color later today.)

To clear the entire applet's drawing area, use the Applet class getSize() method (inherited from the Component class), which returns a Dimension object representing the width and height of the applet. You can then get to the actual values for width and height by using the `Dimension` object's `width` and `height` instance variables and passing them to the `clearRect()` method:

```
g.clearRect(0,0,getSize().width,getSize().height);
```

Fonts and Text

The `Graphics` class also enables you to print text on-screen, in conjunction with the `Font` class and sometimes the `FontMetrics` class. The `Font` class represents a given font—its name, style, and point size. `FontMetrics` gives you information about that font (for example, the actual height or width of a given character) so you can precisely lay out text in your applet.

Note that graphics text is drawn to the screen once and intended to stay there. You'll learn about entering and displaying text from the keyboard later this week.

Creating Font Objects

To draw text to the screen, first you need to create an instance of the `Font` class. A Font object represents an individual font—that is, its font name, style, and point size. Font names are strings representing the family of the font, such as, `TimesRoman`, `Courier`, or `Arial`. Font styles are constants defined by the `Font` class; they are `Font.PLAIN`, `Font.BOLD`, or `Font.ITALIC`. Finally, the point size is the nominal size of the font, as defined by the font itself; the point size might or might not be the actual height of the characters. However, it is useful to know that, by typesetting convention, there are 72 points to a vertical inch of font height. So to specify 1/2-inch high characters, you would use 36 for the point size.

To create an individual font object, give three arguments to the `Font` class constructor:

```
Font f = new Font("TimesRoman", Font.BOLD, 24);
```

This example creates a font object in the Bold TimesRoman font, 24 points in height (1/3 inch high). Note that like most Java classes, you have to import this class before you can use it:

```
import java.awt.Font;
```

Font styles are actually integer constants that can be added to create combined styles. For example, the following statement produces a font that is both bold and italic:

```
Font f = new Font("TimesRoman", Font.BOLD + Font.ITALIC, 24);
```

The fonts you have available to you in your applets depend on which fonts are installed on the system where the applet is running. If you pick a font for your applet that isn't available on the client system, Java will substitute a default font (usually Courier). For best results, it's a good idea to stick with standard fonts such as TimesRoman or Courier.

You can also use the getFontList() method, defined in the java.awt.Toolkit class to get a listing of the current fonts available on the client system (returned as a String array). Then you can make choices on-the-fly about which fonts to use, based on this information. (Don't forget to import java.awt.Toolkit if you decide to use the getFontList() method in your code.)

Drawing Characters and Strings

With a font object in hand, you can draw text on-screen using the methods drawChars() and drawString(). First, though, you need to set the current font to your font object using the setFont() method.

The current font is part of the graphics state that is tracked by the Graphics object on which you're drawing. Each time you draw a character or a string to the screen, that text is drawn using the current font. To change the font of the text, first change the current font. Here's a paint() method that creates a new font, sets the current font to that font, and draws the string This is a big font., at the coordinates 10,100:

```
public void paint(Graphics g) {
  Font f = new Font("TimesRoman", Font.PLAIN, 72);
  g.setFont(f);
  g.drawString("This is a big font.", 10, 100);
}
```

This should all look very familiar to you—this is how the Hello applets throughout this book were produced.

The latter two arguments to drawString() determine the point where the string will start. The x value is the start of the leftmost edge of the text; y is the baseline for the entire string.

Similar to drawString() is the drawChars() method that, instead of taking a string as an argument, takes an array of characters. The drawChars() method takes five arguments. The first three arguments are the array of characters, an integer representing the first character in the array to draw, and another integer for the last character in the array to draw. All characters between the first and last, inclusive, are drawn. The last two arguments are the x,y starting coordinates.

Listing 9.2 shows an applet that draws several lines of text in different fonts; Figure 9.21 shows the result.

TYPE   **LISTING 9.2.** ManyFonts.java.

```
 1:  package GraphicsFontsEtc;
 2:  import java.awt.Font;
 3:  import java.awt.Graphics;
 4:  public class ManyFonts extends java.applet.Applet {
 5:
 6:    public void paint(Graphics g) {
 7:      Font f = new Font("TimesRoman", Font.PLAIN, 18);
 8:      Font fb = new Font("TimesRoman", Font.BOLD, 18);
 9:      Font fi = new Font("TimesRoman", Font.ITALIC, 18);
10:      Font fbi = new Font("TimesRoman", Font.BOLD + Font.ITALIC, 18);
11:
12:      g.setFont(f);
13:      g.drawString("This is a plain font.", 10, 25);
14:      g.setFont(fb);
15:      g.drawString("This is a bold font.", 10, 50);
16:      g.setFont(fi);
17:      g.drawString("This is an italic font.", 10, 75);
18:      g.setFont(fbi);
19:      g.drawString("This is a bold italic font.", 10, 100);
20:    }
21:
22:  }
```

FIGURE 9.21.

The ManyFonts applet.

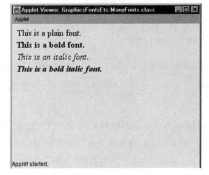

Getting Font Information

Sometimes, you might want to make decisions in your Java program based on the attributes of the current font—its point size or the total height of its characters. You can find out some basic information about fonts and font objects by creating a variable to hold the result and then assigning the attributes of the current font to that variable by using one of the methods shown in Table 9.1.

TABLE 9.1. FONT INFORMATION METHODS.

Method Name	Object	Returned Value
getFont()	Graphics	Current font object previously set by setFont()
getName()	Font	Current font name, a String
getSize()	Font	Current font size, an int
getStyle()	Font	Current font style, an int constant (0 is plain; 1 is bold; 2 is italic; 3 is bold italic)
isBold()	Font	true if font style is bold; else false
isItalic()	Font	true if font style is italic; else false
isPlain()	Font	true if font style is plain; else false

For example, to find out the name of the current font, you would declare a String variable to receive the information and then assign it the result of the getName() method. These methods, if not passed any arguments, return the current font's attributes. If you want to get information for a specific font, you can pass a font object to the method. Here's an example of both uses:

```
Font fcb = new Font("Courier", Font.BOLD, 12);
Font ftb = new Font("TimesRoman", Font.BOLD, 12);
g.setFont(fcp);
...
String currFontName = getName();
String ftbFontName = getFontName(ftb);
```

In this code snippet, currFontName is set to Courier because the current font object is fcp, whereas the ftbFontName is set to TimesRoman because the specified font object is ftb.

For more detailed information about the attributes of the current font, such as the length or height of given characters, you need to work with font metrics. The FontMetrics class methods describe information specific to a given font: the leading (pronounced "ledding") between lines, the height and width of each character, and so on. To work with these sorts of values, you create a FontMetrics object and then assign it the attributes of the current font by using the Graphics class getFontMetrics() method:

```
Font f = new Font("TimesRoman", Font.BOLD, 36);
g.setFont(f);
FontMetrics fmetrics = g.getFontMetrics();
```

The getFontMetrics() method, if not passed any arguments, returns the current font's metrics. If you want to get metrics for a specific font, you can pass a font object to the method:

```
g.getFontMetrics(fbi);
```

Table 9.2 shows some of the information you can find using font metrics by calling these methods on a `FontMetrics` object; all return values are in pixels.

TABLE 9.2. FONT METRICS METHODS.

Method Name	Returned Value
`charWidth(char)`	Width of the given character
`getAscent()`	Ascent of the font: the distance between the font's baseline and the top of the majority of the font's characters (such as b and d)
`getDescent()`	Descent of the font: the distance between the font's baseline and the bottom of the majority of the font's characters (such as p and q)
`getHeight()`	Total height of the font: the sum of the ascent, descent, and leading values
`getLeading()`	Leading of the font: the distance between the descent of one line and the ascent of the next
`getMaxAscent()`	Ascent of the font: the distance between the font's baseline and the top of the font's highest ascender
`getMaxDescent()`	Descent of the font: the distance between the font's baseline and the bottom of the font's deepest descender
`stringWidth(string)`	Width of the given string

As an example of the use of these font metrics methods, Listing 9.3 shows the Java code for an applet that automatically centers a string horizontally and vertically inside an applet. By using font metrics to find out the actual size of a string, you can determine the starting position of the string so that it is properly centered and displays in the appropriate place.

TYPE **LISTING 9.3.** CenterString.java.

```
1:  package GraphicsFontsEtc;
2:  import java.awt.Font;
3:  import java.awt.FontMetrics;
4:  import java.awt.Graphics;
5:  public class CenterString extends java.applet.Applet {
6:
7:    public void paint(Graphics g) {
8:      Font f = new Font("TimesRoman", Font.PLAIN, 36);
9:      g.setFont(f);
10:     FontMetrics fm = g.getFontMetrics();
11:
12:     String str = "Stuck in the middle with you.";
13:     int xStart = ( getSize().width - fm.stringWidth(str) ) / 2;
```

continues

LISTING 9.3. CONTINUED

```
14:        int yStart = ( getSize().height + fm.getHeight() ) / 2;
15:
16:        g.drawString(str, xStart, yStart);
17:    }
18:
19:  }
```

ANALYSIS Note the use of the `Applet` class `getSize()` method here, which returns the width and height of the overall applet area as a `Dimension` object. You then obtain the individual width and height by using the `Dimension` object's `width` and `height` instance variables. Figure 9.22 shows the result (which would be more interesting if you compiled and experimented with various applet and font sizes).

FIGURE 9.22.

The CenterString applet.

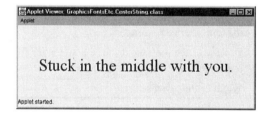

Using Color

Drawing black on a gray background is pretty dull; being able to use different colors is much more interesting. Java provides methods and behaviors for dealing with color in general through the `Color` class and also provides methods for setting the current foreground and background colors so you can draw with the colors you've created.

Java uses 24-bit color, wherein a color is represented as a combination of red, green, and blue values (also called the *RGB model*). Each component of the color can be a number between 0 and 255, inclusive. `0,0,0` is black, `255,255,255` is white, and this model can represent millions of colors in between, as well.

Note

Java's abstract color model maps onto the color model of the platform on which Java is running, which might have only 256 colors or fewer from which to choose. If a requested color in a color object is not available for display, the resulting color might be mapped to another color or dithered, depending on how the browser viewing the color implemented this feature and depending on the platform. In other words, although Java enables you to manage millions of colors, very few might actually be available to you in real life.

Color Objects

To draw an object in a particular color, you must create an instance of the Color class to represent that color. The Color class defines a set of standard Color objects, stored in class variables, that enable you to easily use some of the more common colors. For example, Color.red gives you a Color object representing red (RGB value 255,0,0). Table 9.3 shows the standard colors defined by Color class.

TABLE 9.3. STANDARD COLORS.

Color *Name*	*RGB Value*
Color.black	0,0,0
Color.blue	0,0,255
Color.cyan	0,255,255
Color.darkGray	64,64,64
Color.gray	128,128,128
Color.green	0,255,0
Color.lightGray	192,192,192
Color.magenta	255,0,255
Color.orange	255,200,0
Color.pink	255,175,175
Color.red	255,0,0
Color.white	255,255,255
Color.yellow	255,255,0

If the color you want to draw in is not one of the standard Color objects, you can create a Color object for any combination of red, green, and blue, as long as you know the values of the color you want. Just create a new color object:

```
Color c = new Color(140,140,140);
```

This line of Java code creates a Color object representing a shade of gray. Alternatively, you can create a Color object using three floats from 0.0 to 1.0, representing the percent of each color attribute you desire. This line of code produces the same color value as 140,140,140:

```
Color c = new Color(0.55,0.55,0.55);
```

Testing and Setting Colors

To draw an object or text using a color object, you have to set the current color to be that color object, just as you have to set the current font to the font you want to draw. Use the Graphics class setColor() method to do this:

```
g.setColor(Color.green);
```

After setting the current color, all drawing operations will occur in that color.

In addition to setting the current color for the graphics context, you can set the background and foreground colors for the applet itself by using the setBackground() and setForeground() methods. Both of these methods are defined in the java.awt.Component class, from which Applet is descended.

The setBackground() method sets the background color of the applet, which is usually gray. It takes a single argument, a Color object:

```
setBackground(Color.white);
```

The setForeground() method also takes a single Color object as an argument and affects everything that has been drawn on the applet to that point, regardless of the color in which it was originally drawn. You can use setForeground() to change the color of everything drawn in the applet at once, rather than having to redraw everything:

```
setForeground(Color.black);
```

There are also corresponding getColor(), getBackground(), and getForeground() methods that enable you to retrieve the current graphics color, background color, or foreground color. You can use these methods to choose colors based on existing colors in the applet:

```
setForeground(g.getColor());
```

A Simple Color Example

Listing 9.4 shows the code for an applet that fills the applet's drawing area with square boxes, each of which has a randomly chosen color in it. It's written so that it can handle any size of applet and automatically fills the area with the right number of boxes.

TYPE   **LISTING 9.4.** ColorBoxes.java.

```
1:    package GraphicsFontsEtc;
2:    import java.awt.Color;
3:    import java.awt.Graphics;
4:    public class ColorBoxes extends java.applet.Applet {
5:
```

```
 6:    public void paint(Graphics g) {
 7:      int rval, gval, bval;
 8:
 9:      for (int j = 30; j < (getSize().height - 25); j += 30)
10:        for (int i = 5; i < (getSize().width - 25); i += 30) {
11:          rval = (int)Math.floor(Math.random() * 256);
12:          gval = (int)Math.floor(Math.random() * 256);
13:          bval = (int)Math.floor(Math.random() * 256);
14:          g.setColor(new Color(rval,gval,bval));
15:          g.fillRect(i, j, 25, 25);
16:          g.setColor(Color.black);
17:          g.drawRect(i-1, j-1, 25, 25);
18:        }
19:
20:    }
21:
22:  }
```

ANALYSIS The two `for` loops are the heart of this example. The first one draws the rows, and the second draws the individual boxes within the rows. For each box, the random color is first calculated, and the rectangle is filled with that color. Then, a black outline is drawn around each box because some of the colors generated might blend into the background color of the applet.

Because this `paint()` method generates new colors each time the applet is painted, you can regenerate the colors by moving the window around or by covering the applet's window with another window. Figure 9.23 gives you an idea of what the finished applet would look like.

FIGURE 9.23.

The ColorBoxes applet.

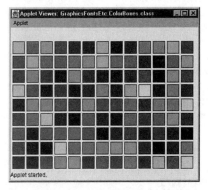

Creating Simple Animation

Animation in Java involves two steps: constructing a frame of animation and then asking Java to paint that frame. These two steps are repeated as necessary to create the illusion of movement on-screen. The basic static applets you created yesterday taught you how to construct a frame. Now you'll learn how to tell Java to paint a frame.

Painting and Repainting

The paint() method, as you learned yesterday, is called by Java whenever the applet needs to be painted—when the applet is initially drawn, when the window containing it is moved or restored, or when it is beneath another window and that covering window is removed. You can also, however, ask Java to repaint the applet any time you choose. So to change the appearance of what is on-screen, you construct the frame (image) you want to paint and then ask Java to paint this frame. If you do this repeatedly and quickly, with slightly varying images in each frame, you get animation inside your Java applet. That's really all there is to it.

Where does all this take place? Not in the paint() method itself—all paint() does is put dots on-screen. The paint() method, in other words, is responsible only for displaying the current frame of the animation. The real work of changing what paint() does, of modifying the frame for an animation, actually occurs somewhere else in the definition of your applet.

In that "somewhere else," you construct the frame (set variables and create Color, Font, or other objects that paint() will need), and then call the repaint() method. The repaint() method is the trigger that causes Java to call paint() and causes your frame to get drawn.

Note

A Java applet can contain many different components that all need to be painted, and applets are embedded inside a larger Java application (usually a browser) that also paints to the screen in similar ways. So when you call the repaint() method (and therefore the paint() method), you're not actually immediately drawing to the screen as you do in other window or graphics toolkits. Instead, repaint() is a request for Java to repaint your applet as soon as it can. Also, if too many repaint() requests are made in a short amount of time, the system might call repaint() only once for all of them. Much of the time, the delay between the call and the actual repaint is negligible.

Starting and Stopping

Remember the start() and stop() methods from Day 8, "Applets, Applications, and Wizards"? These are the methods that trigger your applet to begin and cease running. You didn't use start() and stop() yesterday because those applets did nothing except paint once. With animations and other Java applets that are actually processing and running over time, you'll need to make use of the `start()` and `stop()` methods to trigger the start of your applet's execution and to stop it from running when the reader leaves the page that contains that applet. For many applets, you'll want to override the `start()` and `stop()` methods for just this reason.

The `start()` method triggers the execution of the applet. You can either do all the applet's work inside that method or call other object's methods to perform tasks. Usually, `start()` is used to create and begin execution of a thread (more about threads momentarily in the section "Applets and Threads") so that the applet can run in its own time.

The `stop()` method, on the other hand, suspends an applet's execution so that when the reader moves off the page on which the applet is displaying, it doesn't keep running and using up system resources. Most of the time, when you create a `start()` method, you should also create a corresponding `stop()` method.

A Broken Digital Clock

Explaining how to do Java animation is more of a task than actually showing you how it works in code. Some examples will help make the relationship between all these methods clearer. Listing 9.5 shows a sample applet that attempts to use basic applet animation to display the date and time, updating it every second to create a very simple animated digital clock. A single frame from the working clock (which you'll soon create) is shown in Figure 9.24.

FIGURE 9.24.

A single frame from the working DigiClock applet.

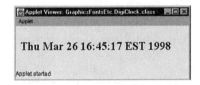

Thu Mar 26 16:45:17 EST 1998

> **Caution**
>
> The words "attempts to use" in the previous paragraph are very important: This applet, as described in Listing 9.5 does *not* work. However, despite the fact that it doesn't work, you can still learn a lot about basic animation from it, so working through the code will be a valuable exercise. In the following sections, you'll learn just what's wrong with it.

See whether you can figure out what's going on with this code before you go on to the analysis.

TYPE   **LISTING 9.5.** DigiClock.java (NONFUNCTIONAL VERSION).

```
 1:  package GraphicsFontsEtc;
 2:  import java.awt.Font;
 3:  import java.awt.Graphics;
 4:  import java.util.Date;
 5:  public class DigiClock extends java.applet.Applet {
 6:
 7:    Font theFont = new Font("TimesRoman", Font.BOLD, 24);
 8:    Date theDate;
 9:
10:    public void start() {
11:      while (true) {
12:        theDate = new Date();
13:        repaint();
14:        try { Thread.sleep(1000); }
15:        catch (InterruptedException e) { }
16:      }
17:    }
18:
19:    public void paint(Graphics g) {
20:      g.setFont(theFont);
21:      g.drawString(theDate.toString(), 10, 50);
22:    }
23:
24:  }
```

ANALYSIS Think you've got the basic idea? Let's go through it, line by line.

Lines 7 and 8 define two basic instance variables, theFont and theDate, which hold objects representing the current font and the current date, respectively. More about these later.

The start() method triggers the actual execution of the applet. Note the while loop inside this method; given that the test (true) always returns true, this loop never exits. A single animation frame is constructed inside that while loop, with the following steps:

- The Date class represents a date and time. (Date is part of the java.util package and was imported in line 3.) Line 12 creates a new instance of the Date class, which holds the system's current date and time, and assigns it to the instance variable, theDate.

- The repaint() method is called in line 13.

- Lines 14 and 15, as complex as they might look, do nothing except pause for 1000 milliseconds (one second) before the loop repeats. The sleep() method here, part of the Thread class, is what causes the applet to pause. Without a specific sleep()

method, the applet would run as fast as it possibly could, which, for most computer systems, would be too fast for the eye to see. Using sleep() enables you to control exactly how fast the animation takes place. The try and catch that surround it enable Java to manage errors if they occur. (The use of try and catch is covered on Day 11, "Compiling and Debugging.")

Now, on to the paint() method. Here, all that happens is that the current font is set to theFont (line 20), and the contents of theDate are printed to the screen (line 21). (Note that you have to call the toString() method to convert the Date object to a printable String. Most objects define this handy method.) Because paint() is called repeatedly (via repaint() in line 13) with whatever value happens to be in theDate, the string is updated every second to reflect the new date and time.

There is one other thing to note about this example. You might think it would be easier to create the new Date object inside the paint() method. That way you could use a local variable and not need an instance variable to pass the Date object around. Although doing things that way creates cleaner code, it also results in a less efficient program. The paint() method is called every time a frame needs to be changed. In this case, it's not that critical, but in an animation that needs to change frames very quickly, the paint() method would have to pause to create that new object each time. By leaving paint() to do what it does best—painting the screen—and calculating new objects beforehand, you can make painting as efficient as possible. This is precisely the same reason why the Font object is also in an instance variable.

So why doesn't the DigiClock applet work? The simple reason is it doesn't use threads. Instead, you put the while loop that cycles through the animation directly into the start() method so that when the applet starts running, it keeps going until you quit the appletviewer or the browser. Although this might seem like a good way to approach the problem, this applet won't work because the while loop in the start() method is monopolizing all the resources in the system—including the resources needed to do the repaint. If you try compiling and running the DigiClock.java in its current condition, all you'll get is a blank screen. You also won't be able to stop the applet normally because there's no way the inherited stop() method can ever be called.

The solution to this problem is to rewrite the applet to use threads. Threads enable this applet to animate on its own without interfering with other system operations, enable it to be started and stopped, and enable you to run it in parallel with other applets. So before you can fix the DigiClock applet, you need to have some understanding of how threads are used in applets.

Applets and Threads

Multithreading is a necessary part of animation in applets. Depending on your experience with operating systems and with environments within those systems, you might or might not have run into the concept of threads. What follows is a very brief introduction to simple threads.

When a typical program runs, it starts executing, runs its initialization code, calls methods, and continues running and processing either until it's complete or the program is stopped. This type of program uses a single thread, where the thread is a single locus of control for the program. Like a selfish child, it basically hogs the system until it's done playing. Multithreading, as in Java, enables several different execution threads to run at the same time inside the same program, in parallel, without interfering with each other. Like well-mannered children, threads share the system resources so that they can all play together.

Threads are especially useful if you have several applets on the same page. Without threads, each applet would have to run and finish before the next could begin execution. Using threads, you can have lots of applets running at once on the same page. Depending on how many you have, you might eventually tax the system so that they all run slower, but they will all run apparently simultaneously. (The word "apparently" is used because threads don't literally run in parallel; they trade control back and forth in time slices.

Even if you don't have lots of applets on the same page, using threads in your applets is good Java programming practice. The general rule of thumb for well-behaved applets is that whenever you have an animation loop, or anything that takes a long time to execute, put it in a thread.

How do you create an applet that uses threads? There are several things you need to do. Fortunately, none of them are particularly difficult. A lot of the basics of using threads in applets is just boilerplate code that you can copy and paste from one applet to another. Because it's so easy, there's almost no reason *not* to use threads in your applets, given the benefits.

There are five modifications you need to make to create an applet that uses threads:

- Change the signature of your applet class to include the words `implements Runnable`.
- Include an instance variable to hold this applet's thread.
- Modify your `start()` method to do nothing but spawn a thread and start it running.

- Create a run() method that contains the actual code that begins your applet's execution.

- Create a stop() method to kill the thread and release its memory.

The first change is to the first line of your class definition. You've already got something like this:

```
public class MyAppletClass extends java.applet.Applet {...}
```

You need to change it to the following:

```
public class MyAppletClass extends java.applet.Applet
                         implements Runnable {...}
```

What does this do? It includes support for the Runnable interface in your applet. If you think back to Day 4, "Java Advanced," in the "Interfaces" section, you'll remember that an interface was defined as a collection of abstract method declarations that can be implemented in whatever classes needing that particular behavior. Here, the Runnable interface defines the behavior your applet needs to run a thread; in particular, it gives you a default definition for the run() method. By implementing Runnable, you tell others that they can call the run() method on your instances.

The second step is to add an instance variable to hold this applet's thread. You can call it anything you like; it's a variable of type Thread. (Because Thread is a class in java.lang, you don't have to explicitly import it.) Because the thread will run the applet, let's name it runner:

```
Thread runner;
```

Third, add a start() method or modify the existing one so that it does nothing but create a new thread and start it running. Here's a typical example of a start() method:

```
public void start() {
  if (runner == null); {
    runner = new Thread(this);
    runner.start();
  }
}
```

This example assigns a new thread to the runner instance variable declared earlier and then calls the Thread class start() method to start the execution of the runner thread. This is called *spawning* a thread.

If you modify the applet's start() method to do nothing but spawn a thread, where does the body of your applet go? The fourth step, declaring the run() method, takes care of this:

```
public void run() {
    ...  // the body of your applet's working code
}
```

The `run()` method can contain anything you want to run in the newly-created thread: initialization code, the actual loop for your applet, or anything else that needs to run in its own thread. You can also create new objects and call methods from inside `run()`, and they'll also run inside that thread. The `run()` method is the real heart of your applet.

Finally, now that you have a thread running and a `start()` method to spawn it, you should add a `stop()` method to suspend execution of that thread (and, therefore, whatever the applet is doing at the time) whenever the reader leaves the page. The `stop()` method usually looks something like this:

```
public void stop() {
    if (runner != null); {
        runner.stop();
        runner = null;
    }
}
```

The `stop()` method here does two things: it stops the thread from executing and also sets the thread's variable `runner` to `null`. Setting the variable to `null` makes the `Thread` object available for garbage collection so that the applet can be removed from memory after a certain amount of time. If the reader comes back to this page and this applet, the `start()` method creates a new thread and starts up the applet once again.

And that's it! Five basic modifications, and now you have a well-behaved applet that runs in its own thread.

A Fixed Digital Clock

Now that you have a basic understanding of how to use threads in applets, let's fix `DigiClock.java` by making the five modifications outlined in the preceding section. Complete the following steps to do so:

1. Modify the class definition to include the `Runnable` interface:

   ```
   public class DigiClock extends java.applet.Applet
                           implements Runnable {
       ...
   }
   ```

2. Add an instance variable for the `Thread`:

   ```
   Thread runner;
   ```

3. Because the `start()` method already has the functionality you want in the `run()` method, just rename the existing `start()` method to `run()`:

```
public void run() {
  while (true) {
...
  }
}
```

4. Add the boilerplate `start()` and `stop()` methods for threads:

```
public void start() {
  if (runner == null) {
    runner = new Thread(this);
    runner.start();
  }
}

public void stop() {
  if (runner != null) {
    runner.stop();
    runner = null;
  }
}
```

You're finished! One applet converted to use threads in less than a minute flat. The resulting modified code is shown in Listing 9.6.

Type **Listing 9.6.** DigiClock.java (THREADED VERSION).

```
 1: package GraphicsFontsEtc;
 2: import java.awt.Font;
 3: import java.awt.Graphics;
 4: import java.util.Date;
 5: public class DigiClock extends java.applet.Applet
 6:                             implements Runnable {
 7:   Font theFont = new Font("TimesRoman", Font.BOLD, 24);
 8:   Date theDate = null;
 9:   Thread runner = null;
10:
11:   public void start() {
12:     if (runner == null) {
13:       runner = new Thread(this);
14:       runner.start();
15:     }
16:   }
17:
18:   public void stop() {
19:     if (runner != null) {
20:       runner.stop();
21:       runner = null;
```

continues

LISTING 9.6. CONTINUED

```
22:      }
23:    }
24:
25:    public void run() {
26:      while (true) {
27:        repaint();
28:        try { Thread.sleep(1000); }
29:        catch (InterruptedException e) { }
30:      }
31:    }
32:
33:    public void paint(Graphics g) {
34:      g.setFont(theFont);
35:        theDate = new Date();
36:      g.drawString(theDate.toString(), 10, 50);
37:    }
38:
39:  }
```

Retrieving and Using Images

When dealing with animation, you might already have a pre-constructed set of images that you want to use as frames in your applet. Using those images and basic image handling in Java is very easy. The Image class in java.awt provides abstract methods to represent common image behavior, and special methods defined in Applet and Graphics give you everything you need to load and display images in your applet as easily as drawing a rectangle. In this section, you'll learn how to get and draw images and how to implement images in Java-based animations.

 Note

Other formats might be supported later, for but now, Java supports images only in the GIF and JPEG formats. So be sure that your images are in one of these currently supported formats.

Getting Images

To display an image in your applet, you must first download that image over the Internet into your Java program. Images are stored as separate files from your Java class files, so you have to tell Java where to find them on the server.

> **Note**
>
> Just as your applet's class files must be downloaded from the server to the client system, so must your image files. Because the applet cannot write to the client's file system to store these image files locally, this means that *each time* your applet makes a call to paint(), the image must be downloaded over the Internet. Therefore, if you are dealing with large or high-quality images, your applet might experience an apparent loss of efficiency (that is, speed) while downloading these images. You'll want to keep that in mind when dealing with images in your Java applets.

The Applet class provides the getImage() method, which loads an image and automatically creates an instance of the Image class for you. To use it, all you have to do is import the java.awt.Image class and then give getImage() the URL of the image you want to load. There are two ways of doing the latter step:

- The getImage() method with a single argument (an object of type URL), which retrieves the image at that URL
- The getImage() method with two arguments: the base URL (also a URL object) and a String representing the path or filename of the actual image, relative to the base

Although the first way seems easier (just plug in the URL as a URL object), the second is more flexible. Because you're compiling .java files, remember that if you include a hard-coded URL of an image and then move your files to a different location on the server, you have to recompile those .java files.

The latter form is, therefore, usually the one to use. The Applet class also provides two methods that will help with the base URL argument to the getImage() method:

- The getDocumentBase() method returns a URL object representing the fully qualified directory location of the HTML document in which the applet is embedded.
- The getCodeBase() method returns a String representing the directory in which this applet is contained—which might or might not be the same directory as the HTML file, depending on whether the CODEBASE attribute in the <APPLET> tag is set or not.

Whether you use getDocumentBase() or getCodeBase() depends on whether your images are stored relative to your HTML files or relative to your Java class files. Use whichever one best applies to your situation. Note that either of these methods is more flexible than hard-coding a URL or pathname into the getImage() method; using either of these methods enables you to move your HTML files and applets, and Java will still be able find your images.

Here are a few examples of `getImage()`, to give you a better idea of how to use it. The first call to `getImage()` retrieves the file at a specific URL (`http://www.server.com/files/image.gif`). If any part of that URL changes, you would have to recompile your Java applet to take the new path into account:

```
Image img = getImage(new URL("http://www.server.com/files/image.gif"));
```

In the following form of `getImage()`, the `image.gif` file is in the same directory as the HTML files which refer to the applet that requires the image:

```
Image img = getImage(getDocumentBase(), "image.gif");
```

In this similar form, the file `image.gif` is in the same directory as the applet itself:

```
Image img = getImage(getCodeBase(), "image.gif");
```

If you have lots of image files, it's common to put them into their own subdirectory. This form of `getImage()` looks for the file `image.gif` in the directory named `myimages`, which in turn is a subdirectory in the directory where the Java applet resides:

```
Image img = getImage(getCodeBase(), "myimages/image.gif");
```

If `getImage()` can't find the file indicated, it returns `null`. Attempting to draw a `null` image will simply draw nothing. Using a `null` image in other ways will probably cause an error.

 Note

In URLs, you will see the forward slash (/) used in pathnames, which is the standard form on the World Wide Web. Even though the standard on Windows platforms is to use the backslash (\) character, JBuilder is smart enough to be able to use the forward slash (/) in the relative pathnames in Java code, so you won't have to change the pathnames for your code to run properly over the Internet.

Drawing Images

All those calls to `getImage()` do nothing except go off and retrieve an image and return it in an instance of the `Image` class. Now that you have an image, you'll want to do something with it. The most likely thing to do is to display it as you would a rectangle or a text string. The `Graphics` class provides six methods to do just this, all called `drawImage()`. Two of them are illustrated here.

The first form of `drawImage()` takes four arguments. The arguments are the instance of the image to be displayed, the x and y positions of the top-left corner, and `this`:

```
public void paint() {
  g.drawImage(img, 10, 10, this);
}
```

This first form does what you expect: it draws the image img in its original dimensions with the top-left corner at the given x,y coordinates. Listing 9.7 shows the code for a very simple applet that loads in an image called ladybug.gif and displays it; Figure 9.25 shows the resulting frame.

TYPE **LISTING 9.7.** Ladybug.java.

```
 1: package GraphicsFontsEtc;
 2: import java.awt.Graphics;
 3: import java.awt.Image;
 4: public class Ladybug extends java.applet.Applet {
 5:
 6:     Image bugImg;
 7:
 8:     public void init() {
 9:        bugImg = getImage(getCodeBase(), "myimages/ladybug.gif");
10:     }
11:
12:     public void paint(Graphics g) {
13:        g.drawImage(bugImg, 10, 10, this);
14:     }
15:
16: }
```

FIGURE 9.25.

The Ladybug applet.

ANALYSIS In this example, you have an instance variable bugImg to hold the ladybug image, which is loaded in the init() method. The paint() method then draws that image on-screen.

The second form of drawImage() takes six arguments: the image to draw, the x and y coordinates, a width and height of a rectangle with which to bound the image, and this. If the width and height arguments for the bounding rectangle are smaller or larger than the actual image, the image is automatically scaled to fit. Using those extra arguments enables you to squeeze and expand images into whatever space you need to fill. Keep in mind, however, that there might be some image degradation due to scaling it smaller or larger than its intended size.

One helpful hint for scaling images is to find out the actual size of the image you've loaded so you can then scale it to a specific percentage and avoid distortion in either dimension. Two methods defined for the Image class are provided to do this: getWidth() and getHeight(). Both take a single argument, an instance of ImageObserver, which is used to track the loading of the image (more about this in the analysis for Listing 9.8). Most of the time, you can just use this as an argument to either getWidth() or getHeight().

If you stored the ladybug image in a variable called bugImg, for example, this line of code returns the width of that image, in pixels:

```
theWidth = bugImg.getWidth(this);
```

Listing 9.8 shows multiple uses of the ladybug image, scaled to different sizes. Figure 9.26 shows the resulting screen images.

TYPE   **LISTING 9.8.** Ladybugs.java.

```
 1:  package GraphicsFontsEtc;
 2:  import java.awt.Graphics;
 3:  import java.awt.Image;
 4:  public class Ladybugs extends java.applet.Applet {
 5:
 6:    Image bugImg;
 7:
 8:    public void init() {
 9:      bugImg = getImage(getCodeBase(), "myimages/ladybug.gif");
10:    }
11:
12:    public void paint(Graphics g) {
13:
14:      int iWidth = bugImg.getWidth(this);
15:      int iHeight = bugImg.getHeight(this);
16:      int xPos = 10;
17:
18:      // 25%
19:      g.drawImage(bugImg, xPos, 10, iWidth/4, iHeight/4, this);
20:
21:      // 50%
22:      xPos += iWidth/4 + 15;
23:      g.drawImage(bugImg, xPos, 10, iWidth/2,
24:                               iHeight/2, this);
```

```
25:
26:        // 100%
27:        xPos += iWidth/2 + 15;
28:        g.drawImage(bugImg, xPos, 10, this);
29:
30:        // 150% x, 25% y
31:        g.drawImage(bugImg, 10, iHeight + 30,
32:                            (int)(iWidth*1.5), iHeight/4, this);
33:    }
34:
35: }
```

FIGURE 9.26.

The Ladybugs applet.

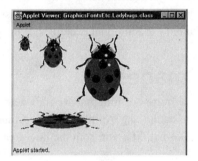

ANALYSIS What about that last argument to drawImage(), the mysterious this, which also appears as an argument to getWidth() and getHeight()? Why is it needed? Its official use is to pass in an object that functions as an ImageObserver (that is, an object that implements the ImageObserver interface). ImageObserver objects enable you to watch the progress of an image during the loading process and to make decisions when the image is only partially or fully loaded. The Applet class, which your applet inherits, contains default behavior for watching for images that should work in the majority of cases—hence, the this argument to the drawImage(), getWidth(), and getHeight() methods. The only reason you'll want to use an alternative argument is if you are tracking lots of images loading asynchronously. For more details, refer to the java.awt.image.ImageObserver interface documentation.

There are four other drawImage() method signatures. One does more advanced scaling operations and takes 10 arguments: the image, eight coordinate arguments, and this. The last three are duplicates of the first three, with an extra argument to specify an alternative background color for the non-opaque portions of the image. Be sure to read the Graphics class documentation for the details on these other forms of drawImage().

Modifying Images

In addition to loading and drawing images, the java.awt.Image package provides more classes and interfaces that enable you to modify images and their internal colors or to create bitmap images manually. Most of these classes require background knowledge in image processing, including a good grasp of color models and bitwise operations. All these things are outside the scope of an introductory book on Java, but if you have this background (or you're interested in investigating further), the classes in java.awt.Image will be helpful to you.

Take a look at the sample code for creating and using images that comes with the Java Development Kit (JDK) for examples of how to use the image classes. Also, check out the samples that came with JBuilder for additional examples of image processing.

Animation Using Images

Movies are made up of individual frames of film that are shown at a fast enough rate that the images they capture appear to be moving. Animations using images is basically the same process. Each image is somewhat different from the last, creating the illusion of movement.

In Java, creating animations with images uses the same methods as creating animations with graphics primitives. The difference is that you have a stack of images to flip through rather than a set of painting methods.

Probably the best way to show you how to use images for animation is simply to walk through an example. Here's an extensive one of an animation of a small cat called Neko.

Understanding the Neko Example Project

Neko was a small Macintosh animation/game written and drawn by Kenji Gotoh in 1989. "Neko" is Japanese for "cat," and the animation is of a small kitten that chases the mouse pointer around the screen, sleeps, scratches, and generally acts cute. The Neko program has since been ported to just about every possible platform and also has been reincarnated as a popular screen saver.

For this example, you'll implement a small animation based on the Neko graphics. The original Neko was autonomous—it could "sense" the edges of the window and turn and run off in a different direction, along with all its other antics. However, this applet merely causes Neko to enter stage-left, stop in the middle, yawn, scratch his ear, take a quick catnap, and then exit stage-right.

> **Note**
>
> This is by far the largest of the applets discussed in this book. So rather than build it up line by line, each part of the applet is discussed independently, leaving out the basic things you've already learned (such as stopping and starting threads, the run() method, and the like). At the end of this section, the entire Neko applet listing is printed for your reference.

Before you begin writing Java code to construct an animation, you should have all the images that form the animation itself. For this version of Neko there are nine of them (the original has 36), as shown in Figure 9.27.

FIGURE 9.27.

The images for the Neko applet.

I've stored these images in a directory called myimages. Where you store your images isn't all that important, just take note of that information because you'll need it later.

Building the Neko Example Project

The basic idea of animation by using images is that you have a set of images, and you display them rapidly one at a time so that they give the appearance of movement. The easiest way to manage this in Java is to store the images in an array of class Image and then to have a special variable that stores a reference to the current image.

> **Note**
>
> The java.util class contains the HashTable class which, oddly enough, implements a hash table. For large numbers of images, using a hash table to locate and retrieve images is faster and more efficient than an array. However, an array is used here because there's a small number of images and because arrays are better for fixed-length, repeating animations.

For the Neko applet, you'll include instance variables to implement both these things: an array to hold the images called nekopics and a variable of type Image to hold the current image.

```
Image nekopics[] = new Image[9];
Image currentimg;
```

Because you'll need to pass the position of the current image around between the methods in this applet, you'll also need to keep track of the current x and y positions. The y stays constant for this particular applet, but the x will vary. Let's add two instance variables for those positions:

```
int xpos;
int ypos = 50;
```

Next, the body of the applet. During the applet's initialization, you'll read in all the images and store them in the nekopics array. This is the sort of operation that works especially well in an init() method.

Given that you have nine images with nine different filenames, you could do a separate call to getImage for each one. You can save at least a bit of typing, however, by creating an array of the filenames (nekosrc, an array of strings) and then just using a for loop to iterate through them. Here's the init() method for the Neko applet that loads all the images into the nekopics array:

```
public void init() {
  Image
  String nekosrc[] =
    { "right1.gif", "right2.gif", "stop.gif",
      "yawn.gif", "scratch1.gif", "scratch2.gif",
      "sleep1.gif", "sleep2.gif", "awake.gif" };
  for (int i=0; i , nekopics.length; i++) {
    nekopics[i] = getImage(getCodeBase(), "myimages/" + nekosrc[i]);
  }
}
```

Note here in the call to getImage() that the directory where these images are stored is included as part of the path. With the images loaded, the next step is to start animating the individual images. You do this inside the applet thread's run() method. In this applet, Neko does five main things:

1. Enters stage-left running

2. Stops in the middle and yawns

3. Scratches four times

4. Takes a short catnap

5. Wakes up, runs stage-right, and exits

Although you could animate this applet by merely painting the right image to the screen at the right time, it makes more sense to write this applet so that many of Neko's activities are contained in individual methods. This way, you can reuse some of the activities (running, in particular) if you want Neko to do things in a different order.

Actually, given that during this animation there will be a lot of sleeping of various intervals, it also makes sense to create a method that does the sleeping for the appropriate time interval. Call it pause()—here's its definition:

```
void pause(int time) {
  try { Thread.sleep(time); }
  catch (InterruptedException e) { }
}
```

With that out of the way, let's create a method to make Neko run. Because you're going to be using this one at least twice, making it generic is a good plan. Let's create the nekorun() method, which takes two arguments: the x position to start and the x position to end. Neko then runs between those two positions (the y remains constant).

There are two images that represent Neko running, so to create the running effect, you need to alternate between those two images (stored in positions 0 and 1 of the image array), as well as move them across the screen. The moving part is a simple for loop from the start to the end position, setting x to the current loop value. Swapping the images means merely testing to see which one is active at each turn of the loop and assigning the other one to the current image. Finally, at each new frame, you'll call repaint() and then pause() for a bit. Here's the definition of nekorun():

```
void nekorun(inst start, int end) {
  currentimg = nekopics[0];
  for (int i = start; i < end; i+=10) {
    xpos = i;
    // swap images
    if (currentimg == nekopics[0])
      currentimg = nekopics[1];
    else currentimg = nekopics[0];
    repaint();
    pause(150);
  }
}
```

Note in that second line you increment the loop by 10, which increments the x position by 10 pixels. Why 10 pixels, and not, say, 5 or 8? Ten simply seems to work best for this animation. When you write your own animations, you will have to play with both the distances and the sleep times until you get the effect you want.

Next, let's cover the paint() method that paints each frame. Here the paint() method is trivially simple. All paint() is responsible for is painting the current image at the current x and y positions. All this information is stored in instance variables. But before you can call the drawImage() method, you have to have a current image to draw, so add a check to ensure that currentimg isn't null:

```
public void paint(Graphics g) {
    if currentimg != null
      g.drawImage(currentimg, xpos, ypos, this);
  }
```

Now, on to the run() method, where the main processing of this animation will be happening. You've created the nekorun() method, so in run() you'll call that method with the appropriate values to make Neko run from the left edge of the screen to the center:

```
// run from left side of the screen to the middle
nekorun(0, getSize().width / 2);
```

The second major thing Neko does in this animation is stop and yawn. You have a single frame for each of these things (in positions 2 and 3 of the array), so you don't really need a separate method for them. All you need to do is set the appropriate image, call repaint(), and pause for the right amount of time. This example pauses for a full second each time for both stopping and yawning (again, using trial and error to determine the time). Here's that code:

```
// stop and pause
currentimg = nekopics[2]
repaint();
pause(1000);

// yawn
currentimg = nekopics[3]
repaint();
pause(1000);
```

The third part of the animation is Neko scratching. There's no horizontal movement for this part of the animation. You simply alternate between the two scratching images (stored in positions 4 and 5 of the array). Because scratching is a repeatable action, however, let's create a separate method for it.

The nekoscratch() method takes a single argument: the number of times to scratch. With that argument, you can then iterate in a loop, alternate between the two scratching images, and repaint() each time.

```
void nekoscratch(int numtimes) {
  for (int i = numtimes; i > 0; i--) {
    currentimg = nekopics[4];
    repaint();
    pause(150);
    currentimg = nekopics[5];
    repaint();
    pause(150);
  }
}
```

Inside the run method, you then can call nekoscratch() with an argument of 4:

```
// scratch 4 times
nekoscratch(4);
```

After scratching, Neko settles in for a short catnap. Again, you have two images for sleeping (in positions 6 and 7 of the array), which you'll alternate a certain number of times. Here's the `nekosleep()` method, which takes a single number argument and animates for that many "turns":

```
void nekosleep(int numtimes) {
  for (int i = numtimes; i > 0; i--) {
    currentimg = nekopics[6];
    repaint();
    pause(250);
    currentimg = nekopics[7];
    repaint();
    pause(250);
  }
}
```

Call `nekosleep()` in the body of the `run()` method like this:

```
// sleep for 5 "turns"
nekosleep(5);
```

Finally, to complete the animation, Neko wakes up and runs off. The `wakeup()` method uses the last image in the array (position 8), and you can reuse the `nekorun()` method to finish:

```
// wake up and run off
currentimg = nekopics[8];
repaint();
pause(500);
nekorun(xpos, getSize().width + 10);
```

There's one more thing left to do to finish the applet. The images for the animation all have white backgrounds. Drawing those images on a Web browser's default applet background (a medium gray) means an unsightly white box around each image. To get around this problem, set the applet's background to white at the start of the `run()` method:

```
setBackground(Color.white);
```

You might not notice the difference in appletviewer (depending on your Windows color scheme), but it will make a big difference when you view the applet in your Web browser. Setting the applet background to the same color as your images' base background color is always a good idea.

Well, that's all of it. There's a lot of code in this applet and there are a lot of individual methods to accomplish a rather simple animation, but it's not all that complicated. The heart of it, as in the heart of all Java animations, is to set up the frame and then call `repaint()` to enable the screen draw. Listing 9.9 shows the complete code for the Neko applet.

TYPE   **LISTING 9.9.** Neko.java.

```java
1:  package GraphicsFontsEtc;
2:  import java.applet.*;
3:  import java.awt.*;
4:  public class Neko extends Applet implements Runnable {
5:
6:    Image nekopics[] = new Image[9];
7:    Image currentimg;
8:    Thread runner;
9:    int xpos;
10:   int ypos = 50;
11:
12:   public void init() {
13:     String nekosrc[] = { "right1.gif", "right2.gif",
14:                          "stop.gif", "yawn.gif",
15:                          "scratch1.gif", "scratch2.gif",
16:                          "sleep1.gif", "sleep2.gif",
17:                          "awake.gif" };
18:     for (int i=0; i < nekopics.length; i++) {
19:       nekopics[i] = getImage(getCodeBase(),
20:                     "myimages/" + nekosrc[i]);
21:     }
22:     setBackground(Color.white);
23:   }
24:
25:   public void start() {
26:     if (runner == null) {
27:       runner = new Thread(this);
28:       runner.start();
29:     }
30:   }
31:
32:   public void stop() {
33:     if (runner != null) {
34:       runner.stop();
35:       runner = null;
36:     }
37:   }
38:
39:   public void run() {
40:
41:     // run from one side of the screen to the middle
42:     nekorun(0, getSize().width / 2);
43:
44:     // stop and pause
45:     currentimg = nekopics[2];
46:     repaint();
47:     pause(1000);
48:
```

```
49:        // yawn
50:        currentimg = nekopics[3];
51:        repaint();
52:        pause(1000);
53:
54:        // scratch four times
55:        nekoscratch(4);
56:
57:        // sleep for 5 seconds
58:        nekosleep(5);
59:
60:        // wake up and run off
61:        currentimg = nekopics[8];
62:        repaint();
63:        pause(500);
64:        nekorun(xpos, getSize().width + 10);
65:
66:    }
67:
68:    void nekorun(int start, int end) {
69:        currentimg = nekopics[0];
70:        for (int i = start; i < end; i+=10) {
71:          xpos = i;
72:          // swap images
73:          if (currentimg == nekopics[0])
74:            currentimg = nekopics[1];
75:          else currentimg = nekopics[0];
76:          repaint();
77:          pause(150);
78:        }
79:    }
80:
81:    void nekoscratch(int numtimes) {
82:        for (int i = numtimes; i > 0; i--) {
83:          currentimg = nekopics[4];
84:          repaint();
85:          pause(150);
86:          currentimg = nekopics[5];
87:          repaint();
88:          pause(150);
89:        }
90:    }
91:
92:    void nekosleep(int numtimes) {
93:        for (int i = numtimes; i > 0; i--) {
94:          currentimg = nekopics[6];
95:          repaint();
96:          pause(250);
97:          currentimg = nekopics[7];
```

continues

LISTING 9.9. CONTINUED

```
98:         repaint();
99:         pause(250);
100:     }
101:   }
102:
103:   void pause(int time) {
104:     try { Thread.sleep(time); }
105:     catch (InterruptedException e) { }
106:   }
107:
108:   public void paint(Graphics g) {
109:     if (currentimg != null)
110:       g.drawImage(currentimg, xpos, ypos, this);
111:   }
112:
113: }
```

Reducing Animation Flicker

If you've been trying the examples in this book as you go along, you might have noticed that when the CurrentDate program runs, every once in a while, there's an annoying flicker in the animation. This isn't an error in the program; it's a side effect of creating animations. However, there are ways of reducing flicker so that your animations run cleaner and look better on-screen, after you understand how flicker is actually caused.

Flicker is a result of the way Java paints and repaints each frame of an applet. At the beginning of today's lesson, you learned that when you request a repaint, the repaint() method calls paint(). That's not precisely the case. What actually happens is this:

1. The call to repaint() results in a call to the method update().

2. The update() method clears the applet of any existing contents (in essence, it fills it with the current background color).

3. The update() method then calls paint().

4. The paint() method draws the contents of the current frame to the applet.

It's step 2, the call to update(), that causes animation flicker. Because the screen is cleared between frames, the parts of the screen that don't change alternate rapidly between being painted and being cleared. Hence, you have flicker. There are three main ways to avoid flickering:

- Override `update()` so it doesn't clear the screen and just paints over what's already there.
- Override `update()` so it clears only the parts of the screen that are changing.
- Override both `update()` and `paint()`, and use double-buffering.

If the third way sounds complicated, that's because it is. Double-buffering involves drawing to an offscreen graphics surface and then copying that entire surface to the screen. Because it's more complicated, you'll look at it last. For now, let's begin with overriding just the `update()` method.

Here's the default version of the `update()` method that you'll be overriding:

```
public void update(Graphics g) {
  g.setColor(getBackground());
  g.fillRect(0, 0, width, height);
  g.setColor(getForeground());
  paint(g);
}
```

Overdrawing: Don't Clear the Applet

The first solution to reducing flicker is not to clear the applet at all. This works only for some applets, of course. Here's an example of an applet of this type. The `ColorSwirl` applet prints a single string to the screen, but that string is presented in different colors that fade into each other dynamically. This applet flickers terribly when it's run. Listing 9.10 shows the source for this applet, and Figure 9.28 shows one frame of the result.

TYPE **LISTING 9.10.** `ColorSwirl.java`.

```
1:   package GraphicsFontsEtc;
2:
3:   import java.applet.*;
4:   import java.awt.*;
5:
6:   public class ColorSwirl extends Applet implements Runnable {
7:
8:     Font f = new Font("TimesRoman",Font.BOLD,48);
9:     Color colors[] = new Color[50];
10:    Thread runner;
11:
12:    public void start() {
13:      if (runner == null) {
14:        runner = new Thread(this);
15:        runner.start();
```

continues

LISTING 9.10. CONTINUED

```
16:        }
17:    }
18:
19:    public void stop() {
20:      if (runner != null) {
21:        runner.stop();
22:        runner = null;
23:      }
24:    }
25:
26:    public void init() {
27:      // initialize the color array
28:      float c = 0;
29:      for (int i = 0; i < colors.length; i++) {
30:        colors[i] = Color.getHSBColor(c,(float)1.0,(float)1.0);
31:        c += .02;
32:      }
33:    }
34:
35:    public void run() {
36:      // cycle through the colors
37:      int i = 0;
38:      while (true) {
39:        setForeground(colors[i]);
40:        repaint();
41:        i++;
42:        try { Thread.currentThread().sleep(50); }
43:        catch (InterruptedException e) { }
44:        if (i == (colors.length)) i = 0;
45:      }
46:    }
47:
48:    public void paint(Graphics g) {
49:      g.setFont(f);
50:      g.drawString("Swirling Colors", 15, 50);
51:    }
52:
53: }
```

FIGURE 9.28.

The ColorSwirl applet.

ANALYSIS There are some new things in this applet that require explaining:

- In the init() method (lines 26 through 33), you initialize the array of Color objects, so that you then can just draw text by accessing each color using the array subscripts.

- To create the different colors, a method in the Color class named getHSBColor() (line 30) creates a Color object based on the HSB (hue, saturation, brightness) color model rather than RGB (red, green, blue). This enables you to deal with the colors as floating-point values so you can easily control the shades of the colors mathematically (line 31).

- In the run() method (lines 35 through 46), the applet cycles through the array of colors, setting the foreground to each in turn and calling repaint(). When it gets to the end of the array, it resets the color to the first entry in the array (line 44) and starts over.

- The flicker results each time the applet is painted. Of course, line 40 is the culprit here because it calls the repaint() method, which calls update(), which causes the applet to "blank out" momentarily between each color change—not at all the effect you desired.

Because the flicker is caused by the update() method clearing the applet, the solution is easy. Simply override update() and remove the part where the applet is cleared. It doesn't really need to get cleared anyway because nothing is redrawn—only the color is changing. With the applet-clearing behavior removed from update(), all that's left for update()to do is call paint(). Here's what the update() method looks like for this type of applet:

```
public void update(Graphics g) {
  paint(g);
}
```

With this small three-line addition—no more flicker! Wasn't that easy? Add this code to the ColorSwirl applet and see how much better it looks.

Clipping: Redraw Only When Necessary

Of course, for some applets, it won't be quite that easy. Here's a different example. In this applet, called Checkers, a red oval (checker piece) moves from a black square to a white square, as if on a checkerboard. Listing 9.11 shows the code for this applet.

TYPE   **LISTING 9.11.** Checkers.java.

```java
1:  package GraphicsFontsEtc;
2:  import java.applet.*;
3:  import java.awt.*;
4:  public class Checkers extends Applet implements Runnable {
5:
6:    Thread runner;
7:    int xpos;
8:
9:    public void start() {
10:     if (runner == null); {
11:       runner = new Thread(this);
12:       runner.start();
13:     }
14:   }
15:
16:   public void stop() {
17:     if (runner != null) {
18:       runner.stop();
19:       runner = null;
20:     }
21:   }
22:
23:   public void init() {
24:     setBackground(Color.blue);
25:   }
26:
27:   public void run() {
28:
29:     while (true) {
30:
31:       for (xpos = 5; xpos <= 105; xpos+=4) {
32:         repaint();
33:         try { Thread.sleep(100); }
34:         catch (InterruptedException e) { }
35:       }
36:
37:       for (xpos = 105; xpos > 5; xpos -=4) {
38:         repaint();
39:         try { Thread.sleep(100); }
40:         catch (InterruptedException e) { }
41:       }
42:
43:     }
44:
45:   }
46:
47:   public void paint(Graphics g) {
48:     // Draw background
```

```
49:        g.setColor(Color.black);
50:        g.fillRect(0, 0, 100, 100);
51:        g.setColor(Color.white);
52:        g.fillRect(101, 0, 100, 100);
53:        // Draw checker
54:        g.setColor(Color.red);
55:        g.fillOval(xpos, 5, 90, 90);
56:    }
57:
58: }
```

9

Figure 9.29 shows one frame of the Checkers applet.

FIGURE 9.29.

The Checkers applet.

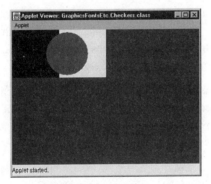

ANALYSIS Here's a quick run-through of what this applet does:

- An instance variable, xpos, keeps track of the current starting position of the checker. (Because it moves horizontally, the y stays constant.)
- In the run() method (lines 27 through 43), you change the value of x and repaint, waiting 100 milliseconds between each move.
- The checker moves from one side of the screen to the other (lines 31 through 35) and then moves back (lines 37 through 41).
- In the actual paint() method (lines 47 through 56), the background squares are painted (one black and one white), and then the checker is drawn at its current position.
- This applet also has a terrible flicker. The applet's background color is set to blue (line 24) in the init() method to emphasize it, so when you run this applet, you'll definitely see the flicker.

The solution to the flicker problem for this applet is more difficult than for the ColorSwirl applet because in this instance, you actually do want to clear the applet before the next frame is drawn. Otherwise, the red checker won't have the appearance of leaving one position and moving to another; it'll just leave a red smear as it crosses the applet's space.

How do you get around this? You still want the animation effect, but rather than clearing the entire applet area, you clear only the part you actually are changing. By limiting the redraw to only a small area, you can eliminate much of the flicker you would get from redrawing the entire applet space.

To limit what gets redrawn, you need a couple of things. First, you need a way to restrict the drawing area so that each time paint() is called, only the part that needs to redraw does so. Fortunately, this is easy by using a mechanism called clipping.

NEW TERM   *Clipping*, as implemented in the Graphics class, enables you to restrict the drawing area to a small portion of the full applet area. Although the entire applet area might get instructions to redraw, only the portions defined as being inside the clipping area are actually redrawn.

The second thing you need is a way to keep track of the actual area to redraw. Both the left and right edges of the redrawing area change for each frame of the animation (the left side to erase the bit of oval left over from the previous frame, and the right side to draw the new oval). So to keep track of those two x values, you need instance variables for both the left side and the right.

With those two concepts in mind, let's start modifying the Checkers applet to redraw only what needs redrawing. First, you'll add instance variables for the left and right edges of the redrawing area. Let's call them ux1 and ux2 (u for update), where ux1 is the left side of the area to redraw, and ux2 is the right.

```
int ux1, ux2;
```

Now let's modify the run() method so that it keeps track of the redraw area. You would think this is easy—just update each side for each iteration of the animation. Here, however, is where things get complicated because of the way Java uses paint() and repaint().

The problem with updating the edges of the redraw area with each frame of the animation is that for every call to repaint(), there might not be an individual corresponding paint(). If system resources get tight (because of other programs running on the system or for any other reason), paint() might not be immediately executed, and several calls to paint() might queue up waiting for their turn to change the pixels on-screen. In that case, rather than trying to make all those calls to paint() in order (and be potentially behind all the time), Java catches up by executing only the *most recent call* to paint() and flushes the queue (skipping all the other calls to the paint() method).

If you update the edges of the redraw area with each `repaint()` and a couple of calls to `paint()` are skipped, you end up with bits of the redraw area not being updated, and bits of the oval are left behind. There's a way around this: Update the leading edge of the oval each time the frame updates, but update the trailing edge only if the most recent `paint()` has actually occurred. This way, if some calls to `paint()` get skipped, the drawing area will get larger for each frame, and when `paint()` finally catches up, everything will get repainted correctly.

Yes, this is horribly complex and not terrifically elegant. But alas, without this mechanism, the applet will not get repainted correctly. Let's step through it in the code, so you can get a better grasp of what's going on at each step.

Let's start with `run()`, where each frame of the animation takes place. Here's where you calculate each side of the drawing area based on the old position of the oval and the new position of the oval. When the oval is moving toward the right side of the screen, this is easy. The value of ux1 (the left side of the redraw area) is the previous oval's x position (xpos), and the value of ux2 is the x position of the current oval plus the width of that oval (90 pixels, in this example).

Here's what the original `run()` method looks like, for reference:

```
public void run() {
  while (true) {
    for (xpos = 5; xpos <= 105; xpos+=4) {
      repaint();
      try { Thread.sleep(100); }
      catch (InterruptedException e) { }
    }
    for (xpos = 105; xpos > 5; xpos -=4) {
      repaint();
      try { Thread.sleep(100); }
      catch (InterruptedException e) { }
    }
  }
}
```

In the first `for` loop, where the oval is moving toward the right, you want to update ux2 (the right edge of the redraw area):

```
ux2 = xpos + 90;
```

After the `repaint()` has occurred, you update ux1 to reflect the old x position of the oval. However, you want to update this value only if the `paint()` has actually happened. How can you tell? You can reset ux1 at the end of the `paint()` method to a given value (0) and then test to see whether you can update that value or whether you are still waiting for the `paint()` to occur:

```
if (ux1 == 0) ux1 = xpos;
```

Here's the new for loop when the oval is moving toward the right:

```
for (xpos = 5; xpos <= 105; xpos+=4) {
  ux2 = xpos + 90;
  repaint();
  try { Thread.sleep(100); }
  catch (InterruptedException e) { }
  if (ux1 == 0) ux1 = xpos;
}
```

When the oval is moving toward the left, everything flips. The left side (ux1) is the leading edge of the oval that gets updated every time, and the right side (ux2) has to wait to make sure it gets updated. So in the second for loop, first update ux1 to be the x position of the current oval:

```
ux1 = xpos;
```

After the repaint() is called, test to make sure that the paint() method has executed, and update ux2:

```
if (ux2 == 0) ux2 = xpos + 90;
```

Here's the new version of the second for loop in the run() method:

```
for (xpos = 105; xpos > 5; xpos -=4) {
  ux1 = xpos;
  repaint();
  try { Thread.sleep(100); }
  catch (InterruptedException e) { }
  if (ux2 == 0) ux2 = xpos + 90;
}
```

Those are the only modifications the run() method needs. But you still need to override update() to limit the region that is being painted to the left and right edges of the drawing area that you set inside run(). To clip the drawing area to a specific rectangle, use the clipRect() method. This method is defined in the Graphics class and takes four arguments: x and y starting coordinates and the width and height of the region.

Here's another place where ux1 and ux2 come into play. The ux1 variable represents the x point of the top corner of the region; use ux2 to get the width of the region by subtracting ux1. The y values are constant for the top and height of the oval, so they are entered as such (5 and 95). Then, to complete the overridden update() method, call paint().

```
public void update(Graphics g) {
  g.clipRect(ux1, 5, ux2-ux1, 95);
  paint(g);
}
```

Note that with the clipping region in place you don't have to do much to the actual paint() method to control the redraw area. The paint() method attempts to redraw the entire applet area each time, but only the areas inside the clipping region defined inside the update() method actually are redrawn. The only modification you need to make to paint() is to reset ux1 and ux2 to 0 at the end so that you can test when the paint() method has actually been executed (in case some calls to paint() get skipped) in the two for loops:

```
ux1 = ux2 = 0;
```

Although it seems like a lot of work, that's only because you needed to step through the explanation of each change. Actually, there are only six new lines of code inserted plus four more lines for overriding the update() method. This doesn't totally eliminate flickering in the animation, but it does reduce it a great deal—try it and see. Listing 9.12 shows the updated code for the applet, renamed to Checkers2.

TYPE **LISTING 9.12.** Checkers2.java.

```
 1:  package GraphicsFontsEtc;
 2:  import java.applet.*;
 3:  import java.awt.*;
 4:  public class Checkers2 extends Applet implements Runnable {
 5:
 6:     Thread runner;
 7:     int xpos;
 8:     int ux1, ux2;
 9:
10:     public void start() {
11:        if (runner == null); {
12:           runner = new Thread(this);
13:           runner.start();
14:        }
15:     }
16:
17:     public void stop() {
18:        if (runner != null) {
19:          runner.stop();
20:          runner = null;
21:        }
22:     }
23:
24:     public void init() {
25:        setBackground(Color.blue);
26:     }
27:
28:     public void run() {
```

continues

LISTING 9.12. CONTINUED

```
29:
30:      while (true) {
31:
32:        for (xpos = 5; xpos <= 105; xpos+=4) {
33:          ux2 = xpos + 90;
34:          repaint();
35:          try { Thread.sleep(100); }
36:          catch (InterruptedException e) { }
37:          if (ux1 == 0) ux1 = xpos;
38:        }
39:
40:        for (xpos = 105; xpos > 5; xpos -=4) {
41:          ux1 = xpos;
42:          repaint();
43:          try { Thread.sleep(100); }
44:          catch (InterruptedException e) { }
45:          if (ux2 == 0) ux2 = xpos + 90;
46:        }
47:
48:      }
49:
50:    }
51:
52:    public void update(Graphics g) {
53:      g.clipRect(ux1, 5, ux2-ux1, 95);
54:      paint(g);
55:    }
56:
57:    public void paint(Graphics g) {
58:      // Draw background
59:      g.setColor(Color.black);
60:      g.fillRect(0, 0, 100, 100);
61:      g.setColor(Color.white);
62:      g.fillRect(101, 0, 100, 100);
63:      // Draw checker
64:      g.setColor(Color.red);
65:      g.fillOval(xpos, 5, 90, 90);
66:      ux1 = ux2 = 0;
67:    }
68:
69:  }
```

> **Tip**
>
> By drawing only the parts of the screen that need to be redrawn, you not only make your applet flicker less, but you also conserve system resources. A well-behaved applet should always endeavor to use as few system resources as possible. So using clipping regions is good practice to follow in general, not just when you have a problem with flicker.

Double-Buffering: Drawing Offscreen

In addition to the two flicker-reduction techniques you've seen so far, there is one other way to reduce flicker in an application: double-buffering.

With double-buffering, you create a second surface (offscreen, so to speak), do all your painting to that surface, and then draw the whole surface at once onto the actual applet area at the end. Because all the work actually goes on behind the scenes, there's no opportunity for interim parts of the drawing process to appear accidentally and disrupt the smoothness of the animation.

Double-buffering isn't always the best solution. If your applet is suffering from flicker, try one of the first two solutions first—they might solve your problem and for a lot less overhead. Double-buffering is less efficient than regular buffering and also takes up more memory and space, so if you can avoid it, make an effort to do so. In terms of nearly eliminating animation flicker, however, double-buffering works exceptionally well.

To create an applet that uses double-buffering, you need two things: an offscreen image to draw on and a graphics context for that image. Those two together mimic the effect of the applet's drawing surface: the graphics context that provides the drawing methods and the Image to hold the dots that get drawn.

There are five major steps to adding double-buffering to your applet:

1. Add instance variables to hold the image and graphics contexts for the offscreen buffer.
2. Create an image and a graphics context when your applet is initialized.
3. Do all your applet painting to the offscreen buffer, not the applet's drawing area.
4. At the end of your paint() method, draw the offscreen buffer to the real applet drawing area onscreen.
5. Override the update() method so that it doesn't clear the drawing area each time.

First, your offscreen image and graphics context need to be stored in instance variables so that you can pass them to the paint() method. Declare the following instance variables in your class definition:

```
Image offscreenImage;
Graphics offscreenGraphics;
```

Second, during the initialization of the applet, create an `Image` and a `Graphics` object and assign them to these variables. (You have to wait until initialization occurs so you know how big they'll be.) The `createImage()` method gives you an instance of `Image`, which you can then send the `getGraphics()` method to get a new graphics context for that image:

```
offscreenImage = createImage(getSize().width, getSize().height);
offscreenGraphics = offscreenImage.getGraphics();
```

Third, whenever you have to draw to the screen (usually in your `paint()` method), rather than drawing to the applet's drawing area, draw to your offscreen graphics. For example, use this line of code to fill a square of 100 pixels by 100 pixels with the current color:

```
offscreenGraphics.fillRect(0, 0, 100, 100);
```

Fourth, at the end of your `paint()` method, after all the drawing to the offscreen image is completed, add the following line to draw the offscreen buffer to the applet's actual drawing area:

```
g.drawImage(offscreenImage, 0, 0, this);
```

Finally, of course, you'll want to override `update()` so that it doesn't clear the drawing area between paintings:

```
public void update(Graphics g) {
  paint(g);
}
```

That's it—and it's a whole lot more elegant than the second solution. But remember, it takes more system resources to do double-buffering, so use it only when really necessary. Listing 9.13 shows the Checkers3 applet, which is the Checkers2 applet rewritten to add double-buffering, so that you can compare the effect.

TYPE **LISTING 9.13.** Checkers3.java.

```
1:  package GraphicsFontsEtc;
2:  import java.applet.*;
3:  import java.awt.*;
4:  public class Checkers3 extends Applet implements Runnable {
5:
6:      Thread runner;
7:      int xpos;
8:      int ux1, ux2;
9:      Image offscreenImage;
10:     Graphics offscreenGraphics;
```

```
11:
12:    public void start() {
13:      if (runner == null); {
14:        runner = new Thread(this);
15:        runner.start();
16:      }
17:    }
18:
19:    public void stop() {
20:      if (runner != null) {
21:        runner.stop();
22:        runner = null;
23:      }
24:    }
25:
26:    public void init() {
27:      setBackground(Color.blue);
28:      offscreenImage = createImage(getSize().width,
29:                                   getSize().height);
30:      offscreenGraphics = offscreenImage.getGraphics();
31:    }
32:
33:    public void run() {
34:
35:      while (true) {
36:
37:        for (xpos = 5; xpos <= 105; xpos+=4) {
38:          ux2 = xpos + 90;
39:          repaint();
40:          try { Thread.sleep(100); }
41:          catch (InterruptedException e) { }
42:          if (ux1 == 0) ux1 = xpos;
43:        }
44:
45:        for (xpos = 105; xpos > 5; xpos -=4) {
46:          ux1 = xpos;
47:          repaint();
48:          try { Thread.sleep(100); }
49:          catch (InterruptedException e) { }
50:          if (ux2 == 0) ux2 = xpos + 90;
51:        }
52:
53:      }
54:
55:    }
56:
57:    public void update(Graphics g) {
58:      g.clipRect(ux1, 5, ux2-ux1, 95);
59:      paint(g);
```

continues

LISTING 9.13. CONTINUED

```
60:    }
61:
62:    public void paint(Graphics g) {
63:        // Draw background
64:        offscreenGraphics.setColor(Color.black);
65:        offscreenGraphics.fillRect(0, 0, 100, 100);
66:        offscreenGraphics.setColor(Color.white);
67:        offscreenGraphics.fillRect(101, 0, 100, 100);
68:        // Draw checker
69:        offscreenGraphics.setColor(Color.red);
70:        offscreenGraphics.fillOval(xpos, 5, 90, 90);
71:        ux1 = ux2 = 0;
72:        g.drawImage(offscreenImage, 0, 0, this);
73:    }
74:
75: }
```

ANALYSIS Notice that you're still clipping the main graphics rectangle in the update() method, just as you did earlier. You could just redraw the entire screen, but that would not be nearly as efficient, and remember that you always want your applet to use as few system resources as possible.

As you can see, each successive technique for reducing flicker builds on the earlier techniques, so it really does make sense to try the three solutions in order, stopping when you're satisfied with the way your applet paints. That way, you'll be assured you're using the most efficient solution that gives the desired results.

Making It Multimedia

Multimedia generally refers to the use of more than one medium of expression through which information is communicated, including both sights and sounds. Earlier today, you learned how to draw and use images in your animations. Now, you'll learn how to add sounds to make multimedia animations.

Java has built-in support for playing sounds in conjunction with running animations and for using sounds on their own. Currently, the only sound format that Java supports is Sun's AU format, sometimes called the μ-law format. The AU files tend to be smaller than sound files in other formats, but the sound quality is not very good. If you're especially concerned with sound quality, you might want your sound clips to be references in the traditional HTML way (as links to external files) rather than included in a Java applet.

> **Note** The JavaSoft multimedia Application Programming Interfaces will greatly improve Java's sound capabilities.

However, for some purposes, applet sounds might be quite sufficient. First, you'll see how to add sounds to your applets, and then you'll review Sun's Animator applet.

Adding Sounds

The simplest way to retrieve and play a sound is through the `play()` method, part of the `Applet` class and therefore available to you in your applets. The `play()` method is similar to the `getImage()` method in that it takes one of two forms:

- With one argument (a URL object), `play()` loads and plays the given audio clip at that URL.
- With two arguments (a base URL and a pathname), `play()` loads and plays that audio file. The first argument can be either a call to `getDocumentBase()` or `getCodeBase()`.

For example, the following line of code retrieves and plays the sound `meow.au`, which is contained in the `mysounds` directory that, in turn, is located in the same directory as this applet:

```
play(getCodeBase(), "mysounds/meow.au");
```

The `play()` method retrieves and plays the given sound as soon as possible after it is called. If it can't find the sound, you won't get an error; you just won't get any sound when you expect it.

If you want to play a sound repeatedly or to start and stop the sound clip, things get slightly more interesting. In this case, you use the applet method `getAudioClip()` to load the sound clip into an instance of the class `AudioClip` (defined in `java.applet`) and then operate directly on that `AudioClip` object.

Suppose, for example, that you have a sound loop you want to play in the background of your applet. In your initialization code, you can use this line of code to get the audio clip:

```
AudioClip clip = getAudioClip(getCodeBase(), "mysounds/loop.au");
```

To play the clip once, use the `play()` method:

```
clip.play();
```

To stop a currently playing sound clip, use the stop() method:

```
clip.stop();
```

To loop the clip (play it repeatedly), use the loop() method:

```
clip.loop();
```

In your applet, you can play as many audio clips as you need; all the sounds you use will mix together properly as they are played by your applet. If the getAudioClip() method can't find the sound you indicate or can't load it for some reason, it returns null. You should always test for this case in your code before trying to play the audio clip because attempting to call the play(), stop(), and loop() methods on a null object results in an exception being thrown.

If you use a background sound—a sound clip that repeats—that sound clip will not stop playing automatically when you suspend the applet's thread. This means that even if your reader moves to another page, the first applet's sounds will continue to play, even if a second applet gets loaded. You can fix this problem by adding this line of code in your stop() method to stop the applet's background sound:

```
if (bgsound != null) bgsound.stop();
```

Basically, anywhere you use runner.stop() to stop a thread, you should also have an accompanying bgsound.stop() to stop the sound.

Listing 9.14 shows the AudioLoop applet, a simple framework for an applet that plays two sounds. The first, a background sound (loop.au), plays repeatedly. The second, a horn honking (beep.au), plays once every five seconds. The graphic is unimportant, so it's not shown here; it just displays the name of the applet to the screen.

TYPE **LISTING 9.14.** AudioLoop.java.

```
 1: package GraphicsFontsEtc;
 2: import java.applet.*;
 3: import java.awt.*;
 4: public class AudioLoop extends Applet implements Runnable {
 5:
 6:    AudioClip bgsound;
 7:    AudioClip beep;
 8:    Thread runner;
 9:
10:    public void start() {
11:      if (runner == null) {
12:        runner = new Thread(this);
13:        runner.start();
14:      }
```

```
15:    }
16:
17:    public void stop() {
18:      if (runner != null) {
19:        if (bgsound != null) bgsound.stop();
20:        runner.stop();
21:        runner = null;
22:      }
23:    }
24:
25:    public void init() {
26:      bgsound = getAudioClip(getCodeBase(),
27:              "mysounds/loop.au");
28:      beep = getAudioClip(getCodeBase(),
29:              "mysounds/beep.au");
30:    }
31:
32:    public void run() {
33:      if (bgsound != null) bgsound.loop();
34:      while (runner != null) {
35:        try { Thread.sleep(5000); }
36:        catch (InterruptedException e) { }
37:        if (bgsound != null) beep.play();
38:      }
39:    }
40:
41:    public void paint(Graphics g) {
42:      g.drawString("AudioLoop Applet", 10, 10);
43:    }
44:
45:  }
```

Sun's Animator Applet

Because most Java animations have a lot of code in common, being able to reuse all that code as much as possible makes creating animations with images and sounds much easier. For this reason, Sun provides an Animator class as part of the standard JDK.

The Animator applet provides a simple, general-purpose animation interface. You compile the code and create an HTML file with the appropriate parameters for the animation. Using the Animator applet, you can do the following:

- Create an animation loop—an animation that runs repeatedly.
- Add a soundtrack to the applet.
- Add sounds to be played for individual frames.
- Indicate the speed at which the animation is to occur.

9

- Specify the order of frames in the animation—which means you can reuse frames that repeat during the course of the animation.

Even if you don't intend to use Sun's `Animator`, it's a great example of how animations work in Java and the sorts of clever tricks you can use in a Java applet. The `Animator` class is part of the JDK, and in the standard JBuilder installation, it will be located at

`C:\jbuilder2\samples\java\demo\Animator`

In this directory, there is also an `Animator.jpr` project, which you can open and run in the JBuilder IDE, along with several sample HTML files, audio files, and image files. Documentation for the applet is in the `index.html` file. You can find more information about this handy applet on Sun's Java home page at `http://www.javasoft.com`.

Summary

You present something on-screen by painting inside your applet: shapes, graphics, text, or images. Today, you learned the basics of how to paint by using graphics primitives to draw rudimentary shapes, using fonts and font metrics to draw text, and using `Color` objects to change the color of what you are drawing on-screen. It's this foundation in painting that enables you to do animation inside an applet (iterative painting to the screen) and to work with images.

You learned quite a bit about animation today, including which methods to use and override: `start()`, `stop()`, `paint()`, `repaint()`, `run()`, and `update()`. You were introduced to creating and using threads. You also learned how to locate, load, and display images in your applets and how to create animations using images.

You mastered the three major techniques for reducing flicker: overdrawing, clipping, and double-buffering. You also had an opportunity make your animations multimedia by adding audio, either as background sounds or stopping and starting sound clips as needed. Sun's Animator applet was also introduced, which serves as a template for further animation development and as an example of some of the more advanced things you can do with animation applets.

Q&A

Q In all the examples you show and in all the tests I've made, the graphics primitives, such as `drawLine()` and `drawRect()`, produce lines that are one pixel wide. How can I draw thicker lines?

A In the current implementation of the `Graphics` class, you can't set the line thickness; there are no methods for changing the default width of the line. If you need a thicker line, you have to draw multiple lines one pixel apart to produce that effect.

Q I tried out `ColorBoxes`, but each time it draws, a lot of the boxes are the same color. The same occurs when running `ColorSwirl`. Why is this?

A The most likely reason is that there probably aren't enough colors available in your browser or on your system to draw all the colors that the applet is actually generating. If your system can't produce the wide range of colors available using the `Color` class, or if the browser has allocated too many colors for other things, you might end up displaying duplicate colors in the applet, depending on how the browser and system have been set up to handle such things. Usually your applet won't use quite so many colors, so you won't run into this problem so often in your real programs.

Q. Why all the indirection with `paint()`, `repaint()`, and `update()`? Why not have a simple `paint()` method that just puts stuff on-screen when you want it there?

A. The reason is that Java allows you to nest drawable surfaces within other drawable surfaces. When a repaint occurs, all parts of the system are redrawn, starting from the outermost surface and moving on to the most nested surface. Because the drawing of your applet takes place at the same time everything else is drawn, your applet doesn't get any special treatment—it will be painted with everything else. Although you sacrifice some immediacy, this enables your applet to coexist cleanly with the rest of the system.

Q. When an applet uses threads, is it true that I just tell the thread to start and it starts, and tell it to stop and it stops? I don't have to test anything in my loops or keep track of the thread's state?

A. That's true. When you put your applet into a thread, Java can control the execution of your applet much more readily. By causing the thread to stop, your applet just stops running and then resumes when the thread starts up again. It's all automatic. Neat, eh?

Workshop

The Workshop provides two ways for you to affirm what you've learned in this chapter. The Quiz section poses questions to help you solidify your understanding of the material covered. You can find answers to the quiz questions in Appendix A, "Answers to Quiz Questions." The Exercises section provides you with experience in using what you have learned. Try to work through all these before continuing to the next day.

Quiz

1. True or False? The following line of code draws a filled rectangle whose upper-left corner is at 20,20 and whose lower-right corner is at 60,60:

   ```
   g.fillRect(20,20,60,60);
   ```

2. True or False? You can draw an outline of a circle using either the drawRoundRect() or the drawOval() method.

3. There is no isBoldItalic() method defined in the Font class. What method could you use to help you find out whether the font object was both bold and italic?

4. Describe the effect of the following line of code in an applet:

   ```
   setForeground(getBackground());
   ```

Exercises

1. Write an applet named PacIsBack that draws the graphic (in blue) and text in Figure 9.30 to the applet's drawing surface (TimesRoman Bold Italic, 24 points, in red). Also, create an HTML file to display the applet; be sure to size the applet appropriately to display the entire the applet.

FIGURE 9.30.

The PacIsBack applet.

2. Add sound to the Neko applet.

DAY 10

Streams and I/O

Today, you'll explore the topic of Java's streams and files, including the differences and similarities between an input stream and an output stream. You'll learn how to do the following:

- Create, use, and detect the end of input streams
- Use and nest filtered input streams
- Create, use, and close output streams
- Read and write typed streams
- Use utility classes to access the file system

Caution	None of the examples in today's lessons will work unless you remember to add the following line at the top of each source code file you create: `import java.io.*` If you forget, you'll get a compiler error because Java won't know where the `java.io` classes and methods you're using are defined.

Let's begin with a little history behind the invention of streams and their precursors, pipes.

NEW TERM A *pipe* is a mechanism for passing data from one item in a system to another. The item sending information through the pipe is the *source*; the item receiving information is the *destination*.

NEW TERM A *stream* is a path of communication between the source of some information and its destination. The item sending information through the stream is the *producer*; the item receiving information is the *consumer*.

NEW TERM A *processor* is a filter that manipulates the data in some way while it is in transit—that is, between the producer and the consumer.

One of the early inventions of the UNIX operating system was the pipe. By unifying many disparate ways of communicating into a single metaphor, UNIX paved the way for a whole series of related inventions, culminating in the abstraction now known as streams.

An uninterpreted stream of bytes can come from any pipe source, which might include files, programs, peripherals, a computer's memory, or even the Internet. In fact, the source and destination of a stream are completely arbitrary producers and consumers of bytes, respectively. Therein lies the power of the abstraction. You don't need to know about the source of the information when reading from a stream, and you don't need to know about the final destination when writing to one.

General-purpose methods that can read from any source will accept a stream argument to specify that source; general methods for writing will accept a stream to specify the destination. Arbitrary processors of data have two stream arguments. They read from the first argument, process the data, and write the results to the second argument. These processors have no idea of either the source or the destination of the data they are processing. Sources and destinations can vary widely—from a memory buffer on a local computer to a NASA deep-space probe's real-time data streams.

Decoupling the producing, processing, and consuming of data from the sources and destinations of that data enables you to mix and match combinations at will as you write your program. In the future, when new forms of sources and destinations are introduced, they can be used within the same framework, without changing your classes. In addition, new stream abstractions, supporting higher levels of interpretation, can be written completely independently of the underlying transport mechanism for the data bytes themselves.

The main foundations of this stream framework are the two abstract classes InputStream and OutputStream. You'll begin with these two superclasses and work your way down in the hierarchy.

> **Tip**
> The methods you will explore today are declared to throw an IOException object. The IOException class is a subclass of the Exception class and conceptually embodies all the possible input/output errors that might occur while using streams. Several subclasses define even more specific exceptions that can be thrown as well. For now, just know that your code must either catch an IOException or pass the exception back up the hierarchy to be considered a well-behaved user of streams.

Understanding Input Streams

10

Input streams read data from various sources of input, such as keyboard input, a byte at a time. Data that is read by an input stream can be directed, in many different ways, to any valid consumer of data. These are the input stream classes discussed in this section:

- InputStream (the abstract class)
- ByteArrayInputStream
- FileInputStream
- FilterInputStream
- ObjectInputStream
- PipedInputStream
- SequenceInputStream
- StringBufferInputStream

InputStream Abstract Class

InputStream is an abstract class that defines the fundamental ways in which a consumer reads a stream of bytes from some source. The identity of the source and the manner of the creation and transport of the bytes are irrelevant. The input stream is simply the destination of those bytes, and that's all that is necessary for your program to know.

All input streams descend from the abstract class InputStream. All share the few methods described in this section. Thus, stream s in the following examples can be any of the more complex streams described later in this section. The read() and skip() methods provide basic default functionality in the abstract class; the available(), close(), `markSupported()`, `mark()`, and `reset()` methods are simply skeletons and must all be overridden in a stream subclass to do anything useful.

read()

The most important method to the consumer of an input stream is the one that reads bytes from the source. The `read()` method comes in three flavors, and each of these `read()` methods is defined to block (wait) until all the input requested becomes available.

> **Tip**
>
> Don't worry about the blocking limitation; due to multithreading, your program can do as many other things as you like while this one thread is waiting for input. In fact, it is common to assign a thread to each stream of input or output that is solely responsible for reading or writing the stream. These threads might then hand off the information to other threads for processing, overlapping your program's I/O time with its compute time. However, we'll forgo that small pleasure for the time being and just pretend we have to be concerned only with input and output.

The first form of the `read()` method simply reads a single byte of data:

```
InputStream s = getAnInputStream ();
System.out.println("Bytes read: " + s.read());
```

If the `read()` method is successful, it returns 1 (an `int` representing the number of bytes read). If it is unsuccessful, it will return -1. This indicates either that you are already at the end of the input stream or that there were no bytes in the stream at all.

Here's an example of the second form of the `read()` method, which takes a buffer name as its only argument:

```
byte[] myBuff = new byte[1024];   // any size will do
System.out.println("Bytes read: " + s.read(myBuff));
```

This form of the `read()` method attempts to fill the entire buffer given to it. If it can't, it returns the actual number of bytes that were read into the buffer. After that, any further calls to the `read()` method return -1, indicating that you are at the end of the stream. It also returns -1 if there are no bytes in the stream.

Because a buffer is an array of bytes, you can specify an offset into the buffer and the number of bytes as arguments to the `read` method:

```
s.read(myBuff, 101, 300);
```

This example tries to fill in bytes 101 through 400 and otherwise behaves exactly the same as the second `read()` method just presented. In fact, the default implementation of that `read()` method does exactly this, using 0 as the offset and `b.length` (buffer length) as the number of bytes to read.

skip()

What if you want to skip over some of the bytes in a stream or start reading a stream from some point other than its beginning? The `skip()` method is similar to the `read` method and does the trick nicely:

```
if (s.skip(1024) != 1024)
  System.out.println("I skipped less than I anticipated.");
```

This would skip over the next 1,024 bytes in the input stream, and if the `skip` method doesn't return 1024 as the number of bytes skipped, the message is printed. The `skip()` method takes and returns a `long` value because streams are not required to be limited to any particular size. The implementation of the `skip` method simply uses the `read()` method without storing the bytes anywhere; it just throws them in the bit bucket!

available()

If, for some reason, you need to know how many bytes are in the stream right now, you can ask:

```
if (s.available() < 1024)
  System.out.println("Too few bytes are in there just now.");
```

This tells you the number of bytes that you can read by using the `read()` method without blocking. Due to the abstract nature of the source of these bytes, streams might or might not be able to provide a reasonable answer to such a direct question. For example, some streams always return 0. Unless you use specific subclasses of `InputStream` that you know will provide a reasonable answer to this question, it's not a good idea to rely on this method. Remember, multithreading eliminates many of the problems associated with blocking while waiting for a stream to fill again. Thus, one of the strongest rationales for the use of the `available()` method is considerably weakened.

Note

In `InputStream`, the `available()` method is set to always return 0. To make it do something useful, you must override it in a stream subclass.

10

markSupported(), mark(), and reset()

Some streams support the notion of marking a position in the stream, reading some bytes, and then resetting the stream to the marked position so you can re-read the bytes. Clearly, the stream would have to "remember" all those bytes, so there is a limitation on how far apart in a stream the mark and its subsequent reset can occur. There is also a method that asks whether the stream supports the notion of marking at all. Here's an example:

```
InputStream s = getAnInputStream();
if (s.markSupported()) {  //does s support mark and reset?
  ...                // read the stream for a while
  s.mark(1024);
  ...                // read a limit of 1024 more bytes
  s.reset();
  ...                // now we can re-read those bytes
}
else {...}  // no mark/reset support, so do something else
```

The markSupported() method checks to see whether this particular stream supports the mark() and reset() methods. Because InputStream is an abstract class, the markSupported() method returns false. The markSupported method must be overridden in the stream subclass and set to return true to indicate support.

The mark() method takes an argument that specifies how many bytes you intend to allow the read() method to look at before resetting. If the program reads further than this self-imposed limit, the mark is invalidated, and a call to the reset() method throws an exception; otherwise, the reset() method repositions the stream to the previously marked position. These methods are only skeletons in the InputStream abstract class; they must be overridden and defined in a subclass, although the reset() method can throw an exception if you should call it directly from InputStream.

Tip

> For an example of a subclass in which the markSupported() method is true and in which the mark() and reset() methods are well defined, look at the java.io.BufferedInputStream.java source code. The easiest way to do this is to select File | Open / Create from the JBuilder menu and click the Packages tab to open the Packages page in the File Open / Create dialog box. Type java.io.BufferedInputStream into the Name text box or select the BufferedInputStream class from the java.io package in the tree, and click OK.

Marking and resetting a stream is most valuable when you are attempting to identify the type of data coming through the stream, but to make a positive identification you must consume a significant piece of it in the process. Often, this is because you have several proprietary parsers that you can hand the stream to, but they will consume some (unknown to you) number of bytes before deciding whether the stream is of their type. Set a large size for the read limit, and let each parser run until it either throws an error or completes a successful parse. If an error is thrown, call the `reset()` method and try the next parser.

close()

Because you don't necessarily know what resources an open stream represents, or how to deal with them properly when you're finished reading the stream, you should explicitly close down a stream so that it can release those resources. Of course, garbage collection and a `finalization()` method can do this for you, but what if you need to reopen that stream or those resources before they have been freed by this asynchronous process? At best, this is annoying or confusing; at worst, it introduces an unexpected, obscure, and difficult-to-find bug. Because you're interacting with external resources, it's safer to be explicit about when you're finished using them:

```
InputStream s = alwaysMakesANewInputStream();
if (s != null) {
  try {
    ...    // use s until you're through
  }
  finally {
    s.close();
  }
}
```

Using the `finally` block makes sure that closing the stream always gets done. To avoid closing a stream that's not open or wasn't successfully created, this example checks to make sure that `null` is not assigned to the s variable before attempting the `try` block.

Note

> In `InputStream`, the `close()` method does nothing; it should be overridden in a stream subclass to be made functional.

ByteArrayInputStream

The inverse of some of the previous examples would be to create an input stream from an array of bytes. This is exactly what `ByteArrayInputStream` does:

```
byte[] myBuff = new byte[1024];
fillWithUsefulData(myBuff);
InputStream s = new ByteArrayInputStream(myBuff);
```

Readers of the new stream s see a stream 1,024 bytes long, containing the bytes in the array myBuff. Just as the read() method has a form that takes an offset and a length, so does this class's constructor:

```
InputStream s = new ByteArrayInputStream(myBuff, 101, 300);
```

Here, the stream is 300 bytes long and consists of bytes 101 through 400 from the byte array assigned to the myBuff variable.

> **Note**
>
> At last, you've seen an example of the creation of a stream. These new streams are attached to the simplest of all possible sources of data, an array of bytes in the memory of the local computer.

The ByteArrayInputStream class simply implements the standard set of methods that all input streams can implement. Here, the available() method has an especially simple job—it returns 1024 and 300, respectively, for the two instances of the ByteArrayInputStream class you created earlier because it knows exactly how many bytes are available by definition. Calling the reset() method in the ByteArrayInputStream object resets the position to the beginning of the stream assigned to the myBuff variable if no mark has previously been set (rather than throwing an exception). A ByteArrayInputStream object can also use the skip method.

FileInputStream

One of the most common uses of streams is to attach them to files in the file system. Here, for example, is the creation of such an input stream:

```
InputStream s = new FileInputStream("/some/path/and/filename");
```

> **Caution**
>
> Although reading and writing files is not a problem for standalone Java applications, attempting to open, read, or write streams based on files from an applet can cause security violations (depending on the safety level set by the browser's user). When creating applets, don't depend on files, but rather use servers to hold shared information.

You can also create the stream from a previously opened file descriptor:

```
int fd = openInputFile();
InputStream s = new FileInputStream(fd);
```

In either case, because this type of stream is based on an actual (finite length) file, the `FileInputStream` object can implement the `available()` method precisely, and it can call the `skip()` method, as well. In addition, `FileInputStream` objects know a few more tricks:

```
FileInputStream aFIS = new FileInputStream("aFileName");
int myFD = aFIS.getFD();
/* close() will automatically be called by garbage collection */
```

> **Caution**
> You must declare the stream variable aFIS to be of type `FileInputStream` because the `InputStream` class doesn't know about these new methods.

`10`

The second line of the preceding code fragment includes the `getFD()` method. The `getFD()` method returns the file descriptor of the file on which the stream is based. The second new thing is that you don't need to do finalization or call the `close()` method directly. The garbage collector will call the `close()` method automatically when it notices that the stream is no longer in use but before actually destroying the stream. Thus, you can go merrily along reading the stream, never explicitly closing it, and all will be well.

You can get away with this because streams based on files tie up very few resources, and these resources cannot be accidentally reused before garbage collection. (These were the issues raised in the earlier discussion of finalization and the `close()` method.) However, if you were also writing to the file, you would have to be more careful. Just because you don't have to close the stream doesn't mean that you might not want to do so anyway. For clarity, or if you don't know precisely what type of an `InputStream` object you were handed, you might choose to call the `close()` method yourself and leave the stream in a known state.

FilterInputStream

This class simply provides a pass-through for all the standard methods of the `InputStream` abstract class. It holds inside itself another stream, by definition one further down the chain of filters, to which it forwards all method calls. It implements nothing new but allows itself to be nested:

```
InputStream s = getAnInputStream();
FilterInputStream s1 = new FilterInputStream(s);
FilterInputStream s2 = new FilterInputStream(s1);
```

```
FilterInputStream s3 = new FilterInputStream(s2);
... s3.read() ...
```

Whenever a `read()` method is performed on the filtered stream `s3`, it passes along the request to `s2`, then `s2` does the same to `s1`, and lastly `s` is asked to provide the bytes. Subclasses of the `FilterInputStream` class should, of course, do some nontrivial processing of the bytes as they flow past. The rather verbose form of chaining in the preceding example can be made more elegant because this style clearly expresses the nesting of chained filters:

```
s3 = new FilterInputStream
   (new FilterInputStream
   (new FilterInputStream(s)));
```

Although this class does not do much on its own, it is declared `public`, not `abstract`. This means that as useless as they are by themselves, you actually can instantiate them directly. However, to do anything really useful, you should use one of the subclasses presented in the following subsections.

BufferedInputStream

The `BufferedInputStream` class is one of the most valuable of all the stream classes. It implements the full complement of the `InputStream` class methods, but it does so by using a buffered array of bytes that acts as a cache for future reading. This decouples the rate and size of the chunks you're reading from the larger block sizes in which streams are read (for example, from peripherals, files, or networks). It also allows smart streams to read ahead when they expect that you will want more data soon.

Because the buffering mechanism of the `BufferedInputStream` class is so valuable, and it's also the only subclass to fully implement the `mark()` and `reset()` methods, you might wish that every input stream could somehow share its valuable capabilities. Normally, you would be out of luck because they don't descend from this `InputStream` subclass. However, you already have seen a way that filter streams can wrap themselves around other streams. The following is a buffered version of the `FileInputStream` class that can handle marking and resetting properly:

```
InputStream s = new BufferedInputStream(new FileInputStream("myfile"));
```

This gives you a buffered input stream based on `myfile` that can use the `mark()` and `reset()` methods. Now you can begin to see the power of nesting streams. Any capability provided by a filter input stream (or output stream, as you see later today) can be used by any other basic stream through nesting.

DataInputStream and DataInput

All the DataInputStream class methods are overrides of abstract methods defined in the DataInput interface. This interface is general-purpose enough that you might want to use it yourself in the classes you create.

When you begin using streams, you quickly discover that byte streams are not a terrific format to force all your data into. In particular, the primitive types of the Java language embody a rather nice way of looking at data, but with the streams you've been defining thus far today, you could not read data of these types. The DataInput interface defines a higher-level set of methods that, when used for both reading and writing, can support a more complex, typed stream of data. Here are the method signatures that this interface defines:

```
void    readFully(byte buf[])                        throws IOException;
void    readFully(byte buf[], int off, int len) throws IOException;
int     skipBytes(int n)                             throws IOException;
boolean readBoolean()         throws IOException;
byte    readByte()            throws IOException;
int     readUnsignedByte()    throws IOException;
short   readShort()           throws IOException;
int     readUnsignedShort()   throws IOException;
char    readChar()            throws IOException;
int     readInt()             throws IOException;
long    readLong()            throws IOException;
float   readFloat()           throws IOException;
double  readDouble()          throws IOException;
String  readLine()            throws IOException;
String  readUTF()             throws IOException;
```

The first three methods are simply new names for forms of the read() and skip() methods that you've seen previously. Each of the next 10 methods reads in either a primitive type or its unsigned counterpart. These last 10 methods must return an integer of a wider size because integers are always signed in Java, and so the unsigned value will not fit in anything smaller. The final two methods read a newline-terminated string of characters (ending in \r, \n, or \r\n) from the stream. The readLine() method reads ASCII characters; the readUTF() method reads Unicode.

The DataInputStream class implements the DataInput interface—that is, the DataInputStream class provides concrete definitions for the DataInput interface abstract methods. Now that you know what that interface looks like, let's see it in action. In this example, the first item in the stream is a long value that contains the size of the stream:

```
DataInputStream s = new DataInputStream(getNumericInputStream());
long size = s.readLong();  // the number of items in the stream
```

10

```
while (size-- > 0) {
  if (s.readBoolean()) {  // should I process this item?
    int    anInteger    = s.readInt();
    int    magicBitFlags = s.readUnsignedShort();
    double aDouble      = s.readDouble();
    if ((magicBitFlags & 010000) != 0) {
      ... // high bit set, do something appropriate
    }
    ... // process anInteger and aDouble
  }
}
```

A point about most of the methods provided by the `DataInputStream` class: When the end of a stream is reached, most methods throw an `EOFException` object. This is actually quite useful because you can catch the exception and do any end-of-stream processing you need to do:

```
try {
  while (true) {
    byte b = (byte) s.readByte();
    ... // process the byte b
  }
}
catch (EOFException e) {  // reached end of stream
... // do end-of-stream cleanup here
}
```

This works just as well for all the methods in this class except for the `skipBytes()` and `readUTF()` methods. The `skipBytes()` method does nothing when it reaches the end of the stream. As for the `readUTF()` method, it might throw a `UTFDataFormatException` object, if it notices the problem at all.

PushbackInputStream

The filter stream provided by the `PushbackInputStream` class is handy for "unreading" data by pushing it back into the stream whence it came. You can have a one-byte push-back buffer or specify the size of pushback buffer that you want. In addition to its `read()` methods, the `PushbackInputStream` class provides three `unread()` methods and uses a simplified version of marking and resetting to keep track of its position. Listing 10.1 is a simple custom implementation of a `readLine()` method using the `PushbackInputStream` class. The new class created in the listing can be imported by other classes wanting to use the features of your custom implementation.

TYPE **LISTING 10.1** SimpleLineReader.java.

```
1: package IO;
2: import java.io.*;
```

```
 3:  public class SimpleLineReader {
 4:    private FilterInputStream s;
 5:
 6:    public SimpleLineReader(InputStream anIS) {
 7:      s = new DataInputStream(anIS);
 8:    }
 9:
10:    // ... other read() methods using stream s
11:
12:    public String readLine() throws IOException {
13:      char[] buffer = new char[100];
14:      int offset = 0;
15:      byte thisByte;
16:
17:      try {
18: lp:    while (offset < buffer.length) {
19:          switch (thisByte = (byte) s.read()) {
20:            case '\n':
21:              break lp;
22:            case '\r':
23:              byte nextByte = (byte) s.read();
24:              if (nextByte != '\n') {
25:                if (!(s instanceof PushbackInputStream)) {
26:                  s = new PushbackInputStream(s);
27:                }
28:                ((PushbackInputStream)s).unread(nextByte);
29:              }
30:              break lp;
31:            default:
32:              buffer[offset++] = (char) thisByte;
33:              break;
34:          }
35:        }
36:      }
37:
38:      catch (EOFException e) {
39:        if (offset == 0)
40:          return null;
41:      }
42:
43:      return String.copyValueOf(buffer, 0, offset);
44:    }
45:
46:  }
```

ANALYSIS   The SimpleLineReader class demonstrates various things. For the purpose of this example, the readLine() method is restricted to reading the first 100 characters of the line (see lines 12 and 13), rather than reading any size line, as it would in a general-purpose line processor. It also reminds you how to break out of a loop (lines 18 to 35) and how to produce a `String` object from an array of characters (line 43). This example also includes standard uses of the `InputStream` class `read()` method (line 19) for reading bytes one at a time and for determining the end of the stream by enclosing it in a `DataInputStream` object (line 7) and catching thrown `EOFException` objects (lines 38 to 41).

One of the more unusual aspects of the example is the way in which the `PushbackInputStream` class is used. To be sure that `\n` is ignored following `\r`, you have to look ahead one character; but if the character is not `\n` you must push it back (lines 22 to 30). Take a closer look at lines 25 and 26. First, the object assigned to the s variable is checked to see whether it's already an instance of a `PushbackInputStream` class (line 25). If it is, the program uses the object. Otherwise, the current object is enclosed inside a new `PushbackInputStream` object, which is then used (line 26).

Following this, the `unread()` method is called (line 28). This presents a problem because the s variable has a `FilterInputStream` object compile-time data type, so the compiler doesn't recognize the `unread` method. However, the previous lines of code (lines 25 and 26) have ensured that the s variable is assigned the `PushbackInputStream` object runtime data type, so you can safely cast it to that type and then call the `unread()` method without any problem. The `SimpleLineReader` class also supports the `mark` and `reset` methods; the `markSupported()` method returns `true`.

Note

This example was written in an unusual way for demonstration purposes. You could have simply declared a `PushbackInputStream` variable and always assigned the `DataInputStream` enclosed object to it. Conversely, the `SimpleLineReader` class constructor could have checked whether its argument was already of the right class—the way that the `PushbackInputStream` class did—before creating a new `DataInputStream` object. The interesting thing about the approach of "wrapping a class only as needed" as demonstrated here is that it works for any `InputStream` class that you hand it, and it does additional work only if it needs to. Both are good general design principles.

java.security.DigestInputStream

Although implemented in the `java.security` package, the `DigestInputStream` class is descended from the `FilterInputStream` class found in the `java.io` package. This stream class creates the input required by the `java.security.MessageDigest` object, which is a byte array and can be turned on and off. When the stream is turned on, a `read()` method will update the digest; when off, the digest is not updated. Its constructor takes the form

DigestInputStream(*anInputStream*, *aMessageDigest*)

where the *anInputStream* parameter takes an InputStream object or descendant, and the *aMessageDigest* parameter takes the MessageDigest object to be updated by this stream. For more information about the MessageDigest class, refer to the Java API documentation for the java.security package.

java.util.zip.CheckedInputStream

Although implemented in the java.util.zip package, the CheckedInputStream class is descended from the FilterInputStream class found in the java.io package. Its purpose is to create a stream that also can maintain a checksum of the data being read. Its constructor takes the form

CheckedInputStream(*anInputStream*, *aChecksum*)

where the *anInputStream* parameter takes any InputStream object, and the *aChecksum* parameter takes either a CRC32 or an Adler32 object. For more information on these checksum classes, refer to the Java API documentation for the java.util.zip package.

java.util.zip.InflaterInputStream

Although implemented in the java.util.zip package, the InflaterInputStream class is descended from the FilterInputStream class found in the java.io package. Its purpose is to create a stream for uncompressing data that is in the deflate compression format. The InflaterInputStream class has three constructors, two of which take the forms

InflaterInputStream(*anInputStream*, *anInflater*)
InflaterInputStream(*anInputStream*, *anInflater*, *theSize*)

where the *anInputStream* parameter takes any InputStream object, and the *anInflater* parameter takes an Inflater object. The first constructor creates a stream with a default buffer size; the second enables you to specify the buffer size by passing an integer to the *theSize* parameter. The InflaterInputStream class also has two subclasses: java.util.zip.GZIPInputStream, which reads data compressed in the GZIP format, and java.util.zip.ZipInputStream, which reads data compressed in the ZIP file format (and implements java.util.zip.ZipConstants). Here are their constructors:

GZIPInputStream(*anInputStream*)
GZIPInputStream(*anInputStream*, *theSize*)
ZIPInputStream(*anInputStream*)

As you can see, these constructors do not have *anInflater* parameters. This is because these classes manipulate data in particular compression formats and therefore they're automatically set to the correct Inflater objects (the first two to GZIP, and the last to

ZIP). The ZIPInputStream class does not have a constructor that enables you to specify the buffer size.

For more information on inflaters, refer to the Java API documentation for the java.util.zip package.

ObjectInputStream

The ObjectInputStream class implements both the java.io.ObjectInput and java.io.ObjectStreamConstants interfaces and is used to deserialize (restore) primitive data and graphs of objects that were previously stored using the ObjectOutputStream class. These two classes are used to provide your application with persistent storage of objects when used with the FileInputStream and FileOutputStream classes. Examples of how the ObjectInputStream and ObjectOutputStream classes work in tandem are presented later today in the "ObjectOutputStream" section.

PipedInputStream

The PipedInputStream class and its sibling, the PipedOutputStream class, are used together to create a simple, two-way communication conduit between threads. These two classes are covered later today in the "PipedOutputStream" section so that they can be demonstrated together.

SequenceInputStream

Suppose that you have two separate streams and you would like to make a composite stream that consists of one stream followed by the other, similar to concatenating two String objects. This is exactly what the SequenceInputStream class was created to do:

```
InputStream s1 = new FileInputStream("theFirstPart");
InputStream s2 = new FileInputStream("theRest");
InputStream s = new SequenceInputStream(s1, s2);
... s.read() ...  // reads from each stream in turn
```

You could have read each file in turn; but some methods expect to be handed a single InputStream object, and using a SequenceInputStream object is the easiest way to provide the single stream required.

If you want to string together more than two streams, you could try the following:

```
Vector v = new Vector();
... // set up all the streams and add each to the Vector
/* now concatenate the vector elements into a single stream */
InputStream s1 = new SequenceInputStream(v.elementAt(0),
                                         v.elementAt(1));
```

```
InputStream s2 = new SequenceInputStream(s1, v.elementAt(2));
InputStream s3 = new SequenceInputStream(s2, v.elementAt(3));
...
```

 Note

> A Vector object is a dynamic array of objects that can be filled, referenced (using the elementAt() method), and enumerated.

However, here's an alternative, which uses a different constructor that the SequenceInputStream class provides:

```
Vector v = new Vector();
... // set up all the streams and add each to the Vector
/* now concatenate the vector elements into a single stream */
InputStream s = new SequenceInputStream(v.elements());
...
```

This constructor takes an enumeration of all the streams you wish to combine and returns a single stream that reads through the data of each in turn.

Output Streams

Output streams are, in almost every case, paired with a sibling input stream that you already have learned about. If an InputStream class performs a certain operation, its sibling OutputStream class performs the inverse operation. These are the output stream classes discussed in this section:

- OutputStream (the abstract class)
- ByteArrayOutputStream
- FileOutputStream
- FilterOutputStream
- ObjectOutputStream
- PipedOutputStream

OutputStream Abstract Class

OutputStream is an abstract class that defines the fundamental ways in which a producer writes a stream of bytes to some destination. The identity of the destination and the manner of the transport and storage of the bytes are irrelevant. When using an output stream, it is the source of those bytes, and that's all that is necessary for your program to know.

10

All output streams descend from the abstract class OutputStream. All share the few methods described in this section. The write() method provides basic default functionality in the abstract class; the flush() and close() methods are skeletons and must be overridden in an OutputStream subclass to do anything useful.

write()

The most important method to the producer of an output stream is the one that writes bytes to the destination. The write() method comes in three flavors, and each of these write() methods is defined to block (wait) until the first byte is written.

The first form of the write() method writes a single byte of data:

```
OutputStream s = getAnOutputStream ();
while (thereAreMoreBytesToOutput()) {
  byte b = getNextByteForOutput();
  s.write(b);
}
```

Here's an example of the second form of the write() method, which takes a buffer name as its only argument:

```
byte[] outBuff = new byte[1024];  // any size will do
fillInData(outBuff):  // the data to be output
s.write(outBuff);
```

This form of the write() method attempts to output the entire buffer given to it. Because a buffer is an array of bytes, you can specify an offset into the buffer and the number of bytes as arguments to the write method:

```
s.write(outBuff, 101, 300);
```

This example writes bytes 101 through 400 and otherwise behaves exactly the same as the second write() method just presented. In fact, the default implementation of that write() method does exactly this, using 0 as the offset and b.length (buffer length) as the number of bytes to write.

flush()

Because you don't necessarily know what an output stream is connected to, you might be required to flush your output through some buffered cache to get it written in a timely manner (or at all). The OutputStream class version of the flush() method does nothing, but it is expected that subclasses that require this functionality (for example, the BufferedOutputStream and PrintStream classes) will override this method to something useful.

close()

Just as for objects created from the InputStream class, you should explicitly close down an OutputStream object so that it can release any resources it might have reserved. The notes and the example listed under the InputStream class close() method also apply here. The InputStream class close() method does nothing; it should be overridden in a stream subclass to be made functional.

ByteArrayOutputStream

The ByteArrayOutputStream class is the inverse of the ByteArrayInputStream class. The following example uses a ByteArrayOutputStream object to write output to an array of bytes:

```
OutputStream s = new ByteArrayOutputStream();
s.write(123);
...
```

The size of the internal byte array grows as needed to store a stream of any length. You can provide an initial capacity to the class, if you like:

```
OutputStream s = new ByteArrayOutputStream(1024 * 1024);  // one MB
```

> **Note**
>
> Now you've seen an example of the creation of an output stream. These new streams are attached to the simplest of all possible data destinations, an array of bytes in the memory of the local computer.

After the ByteArrayOutputStream object assigned to the s variable has been filled, it can be sent to another output stream using the writeTo() method:

```
OutputStream secondOutputStream = getFirstOutputStream();
ByteArrayOutputStream s = new ByteArrayOutputStream();
fillWithUsefulData(s);
s.writeTo(secondOutputStream);
```

It can also be extracted as a byte array or converted to a String object:

```
byte[] buffer = s.toByteArray();
String bufferString = s.toString();
String bufferEncodedString = s.toString(charEncoding);
```

This last method enables you to convert data to a String object by using the character encoding specified by the String object passed to the charEncoding parameter.

The ByteArrayOutputStream class has two utility methods as well. The size() method returns the number of bytes stored in the internal byte array; the reset() allows the stream to be reused without reallocating the memory:

```
int sizeOfMyByteArray = s.size();  // returns current size
s.reset();  // s.size() would now return 0
s.write(123);
...
```

FileOutputStream

One of the most common uses of streams is to attach them to files in the file system. Here, for example, is the creation of such an output stream on a UNIX system:

```
OutputStream s = new FileOuputStream("/some/path/and/filename");
```

You can also create the stream from a previously opened file descriptor:

```
int fd = openOutputFile();
OutputStream s = new FileOutputStream(fd);
```

Because the FileOutputStream class is the inverse of the FileInputStream class, it knows the same tricks:

```
FileOutputStream aFOS = new FileOutputStream("aFileName");
int myFD = aFOS.getFD();
/* close() will automatically be called by garbage collection */
```

 Caution

> To call the new methods, you must declare the stream variable aFOS to be a FileOutputStream class data type because the OutputStream class doesn't know about these new methods.

The first part, the getFD() method returns the file descriptor of the file on which the stream is based. Also, you don't need to do finalization or call the close() method directly. The garbage collector will call the close() method automatically when it notices that the stream is no longer in use but before actually destroying the stream. (See the "FileInputStream" section for more details on how this works.)

FilterOutputStream

The FilterOutputStream class simply provides a pass-through for all the standard methods of the OutputStream class. It holds inside itself another stream, by definition one further down the chain of filters, to which it forwards all method calls. It implements nothing new but allows itself to be nested:

```
OutputStream s = getAnOutputStream();
FilterOutputStream s1 = new FilterOutputStream(s);
FilterOutputStream s2 = new FilterOutputStream(s1);
FilterOutputStream s3 = new FilterOutputStream(s2);
... s3.write(123) ...
```

Whenever a write() method is performed on the filtered stream s3, it passes along the request to s2, then s2 does the same to s1, and lastly s is asked to output the bytes. Subclasses of FilterOutputStream should, of course, do some nontrivial processing of the bytes as they flow past. (See its sibling class "FilterInputStream" for more details.)

Although the FilterOutputStream class does not do much on its own, it is declared public, not abstract. This means that, as useless as they are by themselves, you can actually use FilterOutputSteam objects directly. However, to do anything really useful, you should use one of the subclasses listed in the following sections.

BufferedOutputStream

The BufferedOutputSteam class is one of the most valuable of all the stream classes. It implements the full complement of the OutputStream class methods, but it does so by using a buffered array of bytes that acts as a cache for future writing. This decouples the rate and size of the chunks you're writing from the larger block sizes in which streams are written (for example, to peripherals, files, or networks). It also enables smart streams to read ahead when they expect that you will want more data soon.

Because the buffering of the BufferedOutputStream class is so valuable, and it's also the only subclass to fully implement the flush() method, you might wish that every output stream could share its capabilities. Fortunately, you can surround any output stream with a BufferedOutputStream object to do just that:

```
OutputStream s = new BufferedOutputStream(new FileOutputStream("myfile"));
```

This gives you a buffered input stream based on myfile that can use the flush() method properly. As with filtered input streams, any capability provided by a filter output stream can be used by any other basic stream through nesting.

DataOutputStream and DataOutput

All the DataOutputStream class methods are overrides of abstract methods defined in the DataOutput interface. This interface is general-purpose enough that you might want to use it yourself in the classes you create.

In cooperation with its sibling inverse interface DataInput, the DataOutput interface provides a higher-level set of methods that, when used for both reading and writing, can support a more complex, typed stream of data. Here are the method signatures that the DataOutput interface defines:

```
void write(int i)                         throws IOException;
void write(byte buf[])                    throws IOException;
void write(byte buf[], int off, int len) throws IOException;

void writeBoolean(boolean b)  throws IOException;
void writeByte(int i)         throws IOException;
void writeShort(int i)        throws IOException;
void writeChar(int i)         throws IOException;
void writeInt(int i)          throws IOException;
void writeLong(long l)        throws IOException;
void writeFloat(float f)      throws IOException;
void writeDouble(double d)    throws IOException;
void writeBytes(String s)     throws IOException;
void writeChars(String s)     throws IOException;
void writeUTF(String s)       throws IOException;
```

Most of these methods have counterparts in the DataInput interface. The first three methods mirror the write() methods that you've seen previously. Each of the next eight methods writes out a primitive type. The final three methods write a string of bytes or characters to the stream. The writeBytes() method writes 8-bit bytes; the writeChars() method writes 16-bit Unicode characters; the writeUTF() method writes a special Unicode stream (readable by the DataInput interface readUTF() method).

The DataOutputStream class implements the DataOutput interface—that is, DataOutputStream provides concrete definitions for DataOutput's abstract methods. Now that you know what the interface that the DataOutputStream class implements looks like, let's see it in action:

```
DataOutputStream s = new DataOutputStream(getNumericOutputStream());
long size = getNumberOfItemsInNumbericStream);
s.writeLong();  // the number of items in the stream
for (int i = 0; i < size; ++i) {
  if (shouldProcessNumber(i)) {  // should I process this item?
    s.writeBoolean(true);
    s.writeInt(theIntegerForItemNumber(i));
    s.writeShort(theMagicBitFlagsForItemNumber(i));
    s.writeDouble(theDoubleForItemNumber(i));
  }
  else
    s.writeBoolean(false);
}
```

This is the inverse of the example that was given to demonstrate the DataInput interface. Together they form a pair that can communicate a particular array of structured primitive types across any stream (or transport layer). Use the pair of examples as a jumping-off point whenever you need to do something similar.

In addition to the interface just presented, the class implements one utility method that returns the number of bytes written at that point in time:

```
int theNumberOfBytesWrittenSoFar = s.size();
```

java.security.DigestOutputStream

Although implemented in the `java.security` package, the `DigestOutputStream` class is descended from the `FilterOutputStream` class found in the `java.io` package. This stream class creates the output required for the `java.security.MessageDigest` object and can be turned on and off. When the stream is turned on, a `write()` method will update the digest; when off, the digest is not updated. The form is

```
DigestOutputStream(anOutputStream, aMessageDigest)
```

where the *anOutputStream* parameter takes an `OutputStream` object, or descendant, and the *aMessageDigest* parameter takes a `MessageDigest` object associated with this stream. For more information about the `MessageDigest` class, refer to the Java API documentation for the `java.security` package.

java.util.zip.CheckedOutputStream

Although implemented in the `java.util.zip` package, the `CheckedOutputSteam` class is descended from the `FilterOutputStream` class found in the `java.io` package. Its purpose is to create a stream that can also maintain a checksum of the data being read. Its constructor takes the form

```
CheckedOutputStream(anOutputStream, aChecksum)
```

where the *anOutputStream* parameter takes any `OutputStream` object, and the *aChecksum* parameter takes either a `CRC32` or an `Adler32` object. For more information on these checksum classes, refer to the Java API documentation for the `java.util.zip` package.

java.util.zip.DeflaterOutputStream

Although implemented in the `java.util.zip` package, the `DeflaterOutputStream` class is descended from the `FilterOutputStream` class found in the `java.io` package. Its purpose is to create a stream for compressing data into the deflate compression format. The class provides three constructors, two of which take the forms

```
DeflaterOutputStream(anOutputStream, aDeflater)
DeflaterOutputStream(anOutputStream, aDeflater, theSize)
```

where the *anOutputStream* parameter takes any `OutputStream` object, and the *aDeflater* parameter takes a `Deflater` object encapsulating the compressor to be used. The first constructor creates an output stream with a default buffer size; the second enables you to specify the size by passing an integer value to the *theSize* parameter.

10

This class also has two subclasses: java.util.zip.GZIPOutputStream, which writes compressed data in the GZIP format, and java.util.zip.ZipOutputStream, which writes compressed data in the ZIP file format (and implements java.util.zip.ZipConstants). Here are their constructors:

```
GZIPOutputStream(anOutputStream)
GZIPOutputStream(anOutputStream, theSize)
ZIPOutputStream(anOutputStream)
```

As you can see, these constructors do not have *aDeflater* as a parameter because they are specific to a particular compression format and default to that deflater automatically (the first two to GZIP, and the last to ZIP). The ZIPOutputStream class does not have a constructor that enables you to specify the buffer size.

For more information on inflaters, refer to the Java API documentation for the java.util.zip package.

ObjectOutputStream

The ObjectOutputStream class implements both the java.io.ObjectOutput and java.io.ObjectStreamConstants interfaces and is used to serialize primitive data and graphs of objects that can later be deserialized (restored) by an ObjectInputStream object. Serialization causes the class and class signature of the object and all its nontransient and nonstatic fields to be written, and any objects referenced are also traversed and written. Used together, the ObjectOutputStream and ObjectInputStream classes can provide your application with persistent storage of objects when used with the FileOutputStream and FileInputStream classes. For example:

```
FileOutputStream FOS = new FileOutputStream("myfile");
ObjectOutputStream OOS = new ObjectOutputStream(FOS);
OOS.writeObject("Today is: ");
OOS.writeObject(new Date());
OOS.flush()
FOS.close();
```

Here, the ObjectOutputStream object writes the phrase "Today is: " and the system date to myfile. When these data are read by an ObjectInputStream object, the date retains its original format and is recognized as a Date object:

```
FileInputStream FIS = new FileInputStream("myfile");
ObjectInputStream OIS = new ObjectInputStream(FIS);
String today = (String).OIS.readObject();
Date date = (Date)OIS.readObject();
FIS.close();
```

PipedOutputStream

The `PipedOutputStream` class (along with the `PipedInputStream` class) supports a UNIX-like pipe connection between two threads implementing all the careful synchronization that allows this sort of shared queue to operate safely. To set up the connection, use this code:

```
PipedInputStream   sIn = PipedInputStream();
PipedOutputStream sOut = PipedOutputStream(sIn);
```

One thread writes to the object assigned to the sOut variable, and the other reads from the object assigned to the sIn variable. By setting up two such pairs, the threads can communicate safely in both directions.

Reader

10

The `Reader` class accomplishes the same goals as the `InputStream` class, but instead of dealing with bytes, this class is optimized to deal with characters. There are three `read()` methods that parallel those of the `InputStream` class:

```
read();
read(cBuff[]);
read(cBuff[], offset, length);
```

The first reads a single character; the second reads a character array *cBuff*; and the third reads part of the character array *cBuff*, beginning at *offset* for *length* characters. The `skip()` method for this class takes a `long` data type as its argument.

In addition, there is a new method added, the `ready()` method. This method returns `true` if the next call by the `read()` method is guaranteed not to block for input; otherwise, it returns `false` if the next call by the `read()` method isn't guaranteed not to block.

BufferedReader

The `BufferedReader` subclass is similar to the `BufferedInputStream` class in functionality and includes the `ready()` method inherited from the `Reader` superclass.

LineNumberReader

In an editor or a debugger, line numbering is crucial. To add this capability to your programs, use the `LineNumberReader` class, which keeps track of line numbers as its stream flows through the `LineNumberReader` object. This class is even smart enough to remember a line number and later restore it, through calls by the `mark()` and `reset()` methods. You might use this class like this:

```
LineNumberInputStream aLNIS;
aLNIS = new LineNumberInputStream(new FileInputStream("source"));
```

```
DataInputStream s = newDataInputStream(aLNIS);
String line;
while ((line = s.readLine()) != null) {
  ... // process the line
  System.out.println("Just did line " + aLNIS.getLineNumber());
}
```

Here, two streams are nested around the `FileInputStream` object actually providing the data—one to read lines one at a time and another to track the line numbers as they go by. You must explicitly assign the intermediate stream object to the `aLNIS` variable, because if you did not, you wouldn't be able to call the `getLineNumber()` method later. Note that if you invert the order of the nested streams, reading from the `DataInputStream` object does not cause the `LineNumberReader` object to track the lines. The stream pulling in the data must be nested outside the `LineNumberReader` object for it to successfully monitor the incoming data.

The `LineNumberReader` class can also call the `setLineNumber()` method for those few times when it is necessary for you to do so explicitly.

CharArrayReader

The `CharArrayReader` class reads from a character array, similarly to the way that the `ByteArrayInputStream` class works. It can read either the entire array or from a specified section of the array:

```
CharArrayReader(cBuff[]);
CharArrayReader(cBuff[], offset, length);
```

Here, the *cBuff* argument takes the character array from which to read, the *offset* argument takes the index of the first character to be read, and the *length* argument takes an integer value that sets the number of characters to read. The `CharArrayReader` class also implements the full complement of `Reader` class methods, including the `mark()`, `reset()`, and `ready()` methods.

FilterReader

`FilterReader` is an abstract class for reading filtered character streams that supports the `mark()` and `reset()` methods. Currently, the only subclass implemented is `PushbackReader`.

The `PushbackReader` class is used for "unreading" data by pushing it back into the stream whence it came, which is commonly useful in parsers. You can have a one-character pushback buffer or specify the size of pushback buffer that you want. In addition to its `read()` methods, this subclass provides three `unread()` methods and uses a simplified version of marking and resetting to keep track of its position.

InputStreamReader

The InputStreamReader class provides the connection between byte streams and character streams. An InputStreamReader object reads each byte and translates it into a character based on the character encoding specified. If no character encoding is specified, the platform's default encoding is used. It's best to wrap it within a buffered reader:

```
BufferedReader myBuffRead = new BufferedReader
                      (new InputStreamReader(System.in));
```

The InputStreamReader class, in addition to the other standard Reader class methods, implements the getEncoding() method which returns the name of the encoding that the stream is currently using.

FileReader

The FileReader class reads character files using the default character encoding and the default buffer size. It has three constructors:

```
FileReader(aFileName);
FileReader(aFile);
FileReader(aFD);
```

Pass the aFileName argument a filename of type String, pass the aFile argument a filename of type File, and pass the aFD argument a FileDescriptor object.

PipedReader

PipedReader and its sibling class PipedWriter are used together to create a simple, two-way communication conduit between threads. These two classes are very similar to the PipedInputStream and PipedOutputStream classes, and they are covered later today in the "PipedWriter" section so that they can be demonstrated together.

StringReader

The StringReader class reads from a String object. It can read either the entire string encapsulated in a String object, or it can read a section of the string:

```
StringReader(aStr);
StringReader(aStr, offset, length);
```

Here, the aStr argument takes the String object to read from, the offset argument takes the index of the first character to be read, and the length argument takes the number of characters to read. The StringReader class also implements the mark(), reset(), ready(), and skip() methods.

Writer

The Writer class is the companion to the Reader class and accomplishes the same goals as the OutputStream class. However, rather than using bytes, this class is optimized to use characters. There are five write() methods, three that parallel those of the OutputStream class and two more for dealing with String objects.

The following write() method will write the entire character array assigned to the *cBuff* variable:

```
write(cBuff[]);
```

This write() method is declared abstract and is overridden in Writer subclasses (such as the BufferedWriter class in the next subsection) to have a useful function:

```
write(cBuff[], offset, length);
```

In this version of the write() method, the *anInt* argument takes an integer argument whose low-order 16 bits are written as a single character (the high-order 16 bits are ignored):

```
write(anInt);
```

In this write() method, the *aStr* argument takes the String object to be written:

```
write(aStr);
```

String objects can also be accessed as arrays. The following version of the write() method's *offset* argument takes an integer value that specifies the first character in the String object passed to the *aStr* argument to be written, and a *length* argument takes an integer value that sets the number of characters that are to be written:

```
write(aStr, offset, length);
```

The close() and flush() methods are declared abstract and must be overridden by those subclasses that need to implement their functionality. Now take a look at subclasses of the Writer class.

BufferedWriter

The BufferedWriter subclass is similar to BufferedOutputStream class in functionality. It also overrides three of the write() methods inherited from its Writer superclass to merge their functionality with the buffering that this class provides:

```
write(cBuff[], offset, length);
write(anInt);
write(aStr, offset, length);
```

The first `write()` method also provides basic functionality for writing a portion of the character array because it is declared abstract in the `Writer` superclass.

In addition, this subclass overrides the `flush()` and `close()` methods to deal with buffering. The output buffer will automatically grow to accommodate the characters written.

CharArrayWriter

The `CharArrayWriter` class writes a character array, similarly to the way that the `ByteArrayOutputStream` class works. It can write either the entire array or a specified section of the array:

```
CharArrayWriter(cBuff[]);
CharArrayWriter(cBuff[], offset, length);
CharArrayWriter(aStr, offset, length);
```

Here, either the *cBuff* argument takes the character array to write or the *aStr* argument takes the `String` object to write; the *offset* argument takes the index of the first character to be written; and the *length* argument takes the number of characters to write. Again, the output buffer grows automatically as needed.

The `CharArrayWriter` class implements an additional method:

```
writeTo(aWriter);
```

Here, the *aWriter* argument takes another `Writer` class character stream to which the characters are to be written.

FilterWriter

`FilterWriter` is an abstract class for writing filtered character streams. Currently, no subclasses are implemented. However, it declares a single variable `out`, which enables you to define your own filtered stream subclasses using this variable to refer to the underlying output stream. It overrides the `flush()` and `close()` methods and the following three `write()` methods:

```
write(cBuff[], offset, length);
write(anInt);
write(aStr, offset, length);
```

OutputStreamWriter

The `OutputStreamWriter` class provides the output connection between character streams and byte streams. This class reads each character and translates it into a byte based on the character encoding specified. If no character encoding is specified, the platform's default encoding is used. It's best to wrap an OutputStreamWriter object in a buffered writer:

```
BufferedWriter myBuffWrite = new BufferedWriter
                         (new OutputStreamWriter(System.out));
```

The OutputStreamWriter class implements an additional method, the getEncoding() method, which returns the name of the encoding that the stream is currently using.

FileWriter

The FileWriter class writes character files using the default character encoding and the default buffer size. It has four constructors,

```
FileWriter(aFile);
FileWriter(aFD);
FileWriter(aStr);
FileWriter(aStr, aBool);
```

where the aFile argument takes a filename of type File, the aFD argument takes a file descriptor, and the aStr argument takes a String object that represents a filename. The aBool argument of the fourth constructor takes a boolean value; true directs the stream to append; false directs it to overwrite.

PipedWriter

The PipedWriter class (along with the PipedReader class) supports a UNIX-like pipe connection between two threads, carefully synchronized to safely operate this shared queue. To set up the connection, use this code:

```
PipedReader sRead = PipedReader();
PipedWriter sWrite = PipedWriter(sRead);
```

One thread writes to the PipedWriter object assigned to the sWrite variable, and the other reads from the PipedReader object assigned to the sRead variable. By setting up two such pairs, the threads can communicate safely in both directions.

PrintWriter

The PrintWriter class supersedes the deprecated PrintStream class and implements all its methods. Because it is usually attached to a screen output device of some kind, it provides an implementation of the flush() method. It also provides the familiar write() and close() methods, as well as many choices for outputting primitive types and String objects:

```
public void write(char buf[]);
public void write(char buf[], int off, int len);
public void write(int c);
public void write(String s);
public void write(String s, int off, int len);

public void close();
public void flush();

public void print(boolean b);
public void print(char c);
public void print(char s[]);
public void print(double d);
public void print(float f);
public void print(int i);
public void print(long l);
public void print(Object obj);
public void print(String s);

public void println();   // outputs a newline character only
public void println(boolean x);
public void println(char x);
public void println(char x[]);
public void println(double x);
public void println(float x);
public void println(int x);
public void println(long x);
public void println(Object x);
public void println(String x);
```

The first `println()` method simply outputs a newline character; the rest of the
`println()` methods call the corresponding `print()` method and then output a newline
character. `PrintWriter` objects can be wrapped around any output stream, just like a filter class:

```
PrintWriter s = new PrintWriter(new FileOutputStream("myfile"));
s.println("Here's the first line of the text to write to myfile.");
```

There are four constructors for this class:

```
public PrintWriter(Writer out);
public PrintWriter(Writer out, boolean autoFlush);
public PrintWriter(OutputStream out);
public PrintWriter(OutputStream out, boolean autoFlush);
```

The first constructor creates a new `PrintWriter` object without automatic line flushing.
The second constructor creates a new `PrintWriter` object by specifying, through the
boolean argument `autoFlush`, whether its `println` methods should flush the output
buffer. The third creates a new `PrintWriter` object from an existing `OutputStream`

object, which is passed to the out argument. The object is created without automatic line flushing. The fourth creates a new PrintWriter object from an existing OutputStream object, which is passed to the out argument. The autoFlush argument is passed a boolean data type, which tells the object whether its println() methods should flush the output buffer.

The PrintWriter class does not throw exceptions, so to find out the error state, you must invoke the checkError() method. This method flushes the stream and then returns true if an error was found on this or any previous call.

StringWriter

The StringWriter class writes a String object, character, or character array. It can write either an entire string or a section of a string:

```
StringWriter(aStr);
StringWriter(aStr, offset, length);
```

Here, the aStr argument takes the String object to write, the offset argument takes the index of the first character to be written, and the length argument takes the number of characters to write. It can also write a single character,

```
StringWriter(anInt);
```

where the anInt argument takes an integer whose low-order 16 bits are written as a single character (the high-order 16 bits are ignored). Additionally, it can write a section of a character array,

```
StringWriter(cBuff[], offset, length);
```

where the cBuff argument takes the character array to write, the offset argument takes the index of the first character to be written, and the length argument takes the number of characters to write.

File Classes

The java.io package implements three classes that give Java an abstract definition, which is intended to handle various aspects of platform-dependent file naming conventions. These include the following:

- File (implements Serializable)
- FileDescriptor
- RandomAccessFile (implements DataOutput and DataInput)

File

The File class has three constructors:

```
File(aFile, aStr);
File(bStr);
File(cStr, dStr);
```

The first constructor creates a File object assigned the name encapsulated in a String object passed to the *aStr* argument and assigned the directory file encapsulated in the File object passed to the *aFile* argument. The second constructor creates a File object assigned the name encapsulated in a String object passed to the *bStr* argument. The third constructor creates a File object assigned the name encapsulated in a String object passed to the *dStr* argument and assigned the directory encapsulated in the String object passed to the *cStr* argument.

The File class defines four variables: separator, assigned a filename separator string; separatorChar, assigned a filename separator character; pathSeparator, assigned a pathname separator string; and pathSeparatorChar, assigned a pathname separator character. These variables enable you to handle system-specific separators.

The File class also defines a wide variety of methods that enable you to manipulate file and pathnames. The canRead() and canWrite() methods are boolean methods that tell you whether a file is readable or writable, respectively. The equals() method does an object-level comparison. The exists() method is a boolean method that tells whether a file exists, and the isDirectory() method tells whether a directory exists.

There are several methods that return pieces of file and pathnames, whose names are self-explanatory: the getAbsolutePath(), getCanonicalPath(), getName(), getParent(), and getPath() methods. There are other methods that return attributes of the file: the isAbsolute() method tells whether the filename is absolute; the isFile() method returns true if a normal file exists; the lastModified() method returns the modification time stamp; and the length() method returns the length of the file.

Utility methods also abound. The mkDir() and mkDirs() methods create a directory or several levels of directories, respectively. The renameTo() method attempts to rename a file and returns a boolean value indicating whether it succeeded. The list() method lists the files in a directory. The delete() method deletes a specified file from the system. The hashCode() method computes the hashcode for the file. Lastly, the toString() method returns a String object encapsulating the file's pathname.

To redefine any of these methods or to provide additional methods, simply subclass the File class, and override its methods or define your own.

10

FileDescriptor

The FileDescriptor class provides a mechanism for referring to an underlying system-specific structure that represents an open file or socket. The Java documentation emphasizes that your application should not create its own file descriptors; the Java Virtual Machine does this for you automatically. This class has one constructor,

```
FileDescriptor();
```

which is used by the Java interpreter to initialize the class variables in a system-dependent manner. The four variables it initializes are fd, the file descriptor handle; in, the standard input stream handle; out, the standard output stream handle; and err, the standard error stream handle.

There are also two methods: the valid() method, which returns true if the file descriptor references an actual open file or socket, and the sync() method, which forces all down-stream buffers to synchronize with the physical storage medium, enabling you to put the file system into a known state.

RandomAccessFile

The RandomAccessFile class's main function is to provide a way to specify access to read-write or read-only files along with the capability to skip around in the file by manipulating a file pointer. It implements both the DataInput and the DataOutput interfaces described earlier today and their myriad read() and write() methods.

This class has two constructors,

```
RandomAccessFile(aStr, alaMode);
RandomAccessFile(aFile, alaMode);
```

where the aStr argument takes a String object encapsulating a filename; the aFile argument takes a File object; and the alaMode argument takes a String object encapsulating either rw, indicating a read-write file, or r, indicating a read-only file.

Besides the read and write methods provided by its implementation of the DataInput and DataOutput interfaces, the RandomAccessFile class implements several utility methods: the getFD() method returns the file descriptor; the skipBytes() method specifies the number of bytes to skip ahead in the file; the getFilePointer() method returns the current location of the file pointer; the seek() method sets the location of the file pointer to a specified position; the length() method returns the length of the file; and the close() method closes the file. Interestingly, there is no open() method; the getFD() method serves the purpose because it returns the file descriptor of an already open file.

Related Classes

There are a few interfaces and classes in the java.io package that have not been covered yet, such as the Serializable class, which has been mentioned several times already. In this section, the Serializable, Externalizable, FilenameFilter, and ObjectInputValidation interfaces are discussed. Also, the ObjectStreamClass and StreamTokenizer classes are covered.

Interfaces

The Serializable interface, as was implied earlier, has to do with preserving the state of objects and data while streaming. If a class implements this interface, that class's objects and data will be serialized when streamed and deserialized when restored from a stream. Any subclasses will also inherit this functionality. This interface specifies that classes wanting to handle their own serialization and deserialization should implement two private methods with these signatures:

```
void writeObject(ObjectOutputStream out)
   throws IOException; {...}

void readObject(ObjectInputStream in)
   throws IOException, ClassNotFoundException; {...}
```

The ObjectInput interface extends the DataInput interface and defines the readObject() method so that it can read objects. The ObjectOutput interface extends the DataOutput interface and defines the writeObject() method so that it can write objects. Together, these interfaces provide functionality for the next interface, Externalizable.

The Externalizable interface extends the Serializable interface and defines two methods of its own. The writeExternal() method saves the contents of its ObjectOutput interface type argument by using ObjectOutput interface's writeObject() method for objects or DataOutput interface's methods (which are inherited by the ObjectOutput interface) for primitive data. The readExternal() method restores the contents of its ObjectOutput interface type argument by using ObjectOutput interface's readObject() method for objects or DataOutput interface's methods for primitive data, which accomplishes the inverse of the writeExternal() method. Because strings and arrays are implemented in Java as objects, they are treated as such by this interface.

ObjectInputValidation is a callback interface that allows validation of graphed objects, and it allows an object to be called when the graphed object has completed deserialization. It defines a single abstract method, validateObject(), which throws an InvalidObjectException object if the object cannot validate itself.

`FilenameFilter` is an interface whose purpose is to provide a filter interface for file-names. It defines an abstract `boolean` method:

`accept(aFile, aStr);`

This returns `true` if the filename assigned to the `aStr` variable is in the file list assigned to the `aFile` variable.

Classes

There are two `java.io` classes that you haven't seen yet: the `ObjectStreamClass` and `StreamTokenizer` classes.

The `ObjectStreamClass` class implements the `Serializable` interface and enables your application to determine whether or not a specified class is serializable by using the `lookup` method. If an instance of a class is serialized, you can use the `ObjectStreamClass` class `getSerialVersionUID()` method to obtain the `serialVersionUID` for the class that identifies in what format the class was serialized.

The `StreamTokenizer` class takes an `InputStream` or `Reader` object and converts it into a stream of tokens. Each token can have any (or none) of five attributes: whitespace, numeric, character, string (single- or double-quoted), and comment character.

Each `StreamTokenizer` instance has four flags indicating whether the instance returns line terminators as tokens or whitespace, whether it recognizes C-style (`/*`) comments, whether it recognizes C++-style (`//`) comments, and whether identifiers are converted to all lowercase characters. You can create powerful lexical parsers by subclassing this class and defining additional functionality of your own.

Summary

Today, you learned about the `InputStream` class and its subclasses that provide byte-based input streams based on byte arrays, files, pipes, sequences of other streams, objects, and string buffers, as well as input filters for buffering, typed data, and pushing back characters. You also were introduced to the `OutputStream` class and its subclasses that define byte-based output streams for byte arrays, files, pipes, and objects, and output filters for buffering and typed data.

You saw how the `Reader` and `Writer` classes provide optimized handling for character-based streams, including the unique output filter used for printing and many methods and subclasses analogous to those of the `InputStream` and `OutputStream` classes.

Along the way, you became familiar with the fundamental methods all streams understand, such as the `read()` and `write()` methods, as well as the unique methods many streams add to this repertoire. You learned about catching IOException objects—especially the most useful of them, EOFException, for determining when you've reached the end of a stream.

You are now familiar with the three file classes in the java.io package, and you've been introduced to the interfaces defined in the package, including the twice-useful DataInput and DataOutput interfaces, which form the heart of operations for the DataInputStream, DataOutputStream, and RandomAccessFile classes. Others allow objects and data to be serialized (stored) and deserialized (restored) so that their state can be preserved and restored. Last, but not least, you saw that the StreamTokenizer class enables you to create lexical parsers.

Java streams provide a powerful base on which you can build multithreaded, streaming interfaces of the most complex kind and the programs (such as HotJava) to interpret them. The higher-level Internet protocols and future services that your applications and applets can build upon this base are almost unlimited.

10

Q&A

Q **What input streams in `java.io` actually implement the `mark()`, `reset()`, and `markSupported()` methods?**

A These methods are first implemented as public methods in the InputStream and Reader classes; however, the markSupported() method returns false, the mark() method does nothing, and the reset() method simply throws an IOException object with the message mark/reset not supported.

Of InputStream's subclasses, BufferedInputStream and ByteArrayInputStream implement the mark() and reset() methods, and the markSupported() method returns true for instances of these subclasses. Also, the markSupported() method returns true for an instance of the FilterInputStream class if its underlying input stream supports it; however, FilterInputStream's subclass, PushbackInputStream, overrides the markSupported() method and returns false.

Of Reader's subclasses, BufferedReader and CharArrayReader implement the mark() and reset() method, and the markSupported() method returns true for instances of these subclasses. Also, the markSupported() method returns true for an instance of the FilterReader class if its underlying reader stream supports it; however, FilterReader's subclass, PushbackReader, overrides the markSupported() method and returns false.

Q Why is the `available()` method useful if it sometimes gives the wrong answer?

A First, for many streams, it does give the correct answer. Second, for some network streams, its implementation might be sending a special query to discover some information you couldn't get any other way (for example, the size of a file being transferred by `ftp`). If you were displaying a progress bar for network or file transfers, for example, the `available()` method often will give you the total size of the transfer, and when it doesn't (usually returning 0), it will be obvious enough to you and your users.

Q I didn't see any mention of the `LineNumberInputStream` subclass, which was implemented in JDK 1.0. Is it still available? If not, what should I use instead?

A Yes, it is still defined, but it is not covered here because it is a deprecated class. Java provides this class strictly for backward compatibility with JDK 1.0-based applications, and it should not be used in new programs. Instead, use the `LineNumberReader` class.

Workshop

The Workshop provides two ways for you to affirm what you've learned in this chapter. The Quiz section poses questions to help you solidify your understanding of the material covered. You can find answers to the quiz questions in Appendix A, "Answers to Quiz Questions." The Exercise section provides you with experience in using what you have learned. Try to work through all these before continuing to the next day.

Quiz

1. True or False? Streams can make use of the methods in the `DataInput` and `DataOutput` interfaces, but files cannot.

2. What does the term *deprecated* mean?

3. Which of the following classes are byte-based, and which are character-based: `InputStream`, `OutputStream`, `Reader`, `Writer`, and `RandomAccessFile`.

4. Which class should you use for screen output and printing, `PrintStream` or `PrintWriter`?

Exercise

Create a program named `Cat.java` that echoes lines of keyboard input to the screen using a `DataInputStream` with standard input (`System.in`) and the `readLine()` and `System.out.println()` methods.

DAY 11

Compiling and Debugging

Compiling your programs, resolving errors, and testing your logic must be completed before you can distribute your programs. Although no development product can guarantee you bug-free code, JBuilder provides you with the tools to do your best to wring every last error out of your program.

Debugging is one of the more advanced topics, which is why it has not been discussed until today. In this section, you'll be introduced to the process of debugging your Java programs from the JBuilder IDE using JBuilder's integrated debugger. You'll also learn about the various debugger views available in the JBuilder IDE and how they assist you in creating bug-free code.

Today, you'll take a look at these topics:

- Using the Build menu commands, Make and Rebuild, to compile your Java programs in the JBuilder IDE

- How to get context-sensitive help for correcting errors in your code

- Examples that have been rigged with bugs so you can see what types of errors they produce and how JBuilder responds to these errors
- JBuilder's integrated debugger and the debugging views available in the AppBrowser and other JBuilder IDE windows

To create a new project for today's listings, select File | New Project, and modify the File field so that it contains the following:

```
C:\JBUILDER2\myprojects\CompileDebug.jpr
```

Click the Finish button. All of today's listings will be added to this project by selecting the Add to Project icon above the Navigation pane in the AppBrowser.

Compiling

After your application files are created, the user interface modified, and the files saved, you're ready to compile the application. In the JBuilder IDE, this is accomplished by selecting one of the choices on the Build menu: Make or Rebuild. You can also use commands on the selected node's pop-up menu in the AppBrowser window. For example, if you have a .java node selected in the Navigation pane, right-clicking will display the pop-up menu shown in Figure 11.1.

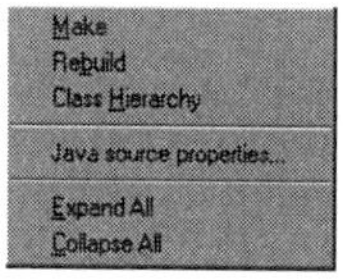

FIGURE 11.1.

Pop-up menu for a .java file in the Navigation pane.

These commands are available for both the individual selected node in the AppBrowser window and for entire packages and projects, by selecting their nodes. The filename and project name are dynamically added to the menu items for your convenience. If there are no errors during compilation, the message Compiling successful. will appear in the main window's status bar.

In addition, the Run and Debug commands (both are available on the Run menu and the pop-up menu for runnable nodes) will do an implicit Make before attempting to run or debug the selected node by default.

Make

The Make menu item will compile any nodes that either don't have a .class file yet or whose .class file is older than the source file. This is known as a *conditional compilation.*

In the case of a new project, either Build command will work because none of the `.class` files has been created yet. However, you will normally use the Make command to ensure that all your `.class` files for the project are up-to-date.

By selecting the Build|Make Project "*ProjectName*.jpr" command, you are instructing the JBuilder IDE to conditionally compile, or make, any source files in the current project. Alternatively, by selecting the Build|Make "*FileName*.java", you are instructing the JBuilder IDE to make only the currently selected source file. If there are no source files with outdated or missing `.class` files, no compilation will occur.

> **Tip**
>
> Typically, you frequently compile the individual .java file that you're working on to let the compiler catch any syntax errors that you inadvertently added to the code. Less frequently, and only after the code forms a complete and runnable application, you compile the entire project so that you can run it and catch any runtime bugs that it might have.

Selecting a node and then choosing Make from the pop-up menu causes a conditional compile of that node and of any source files on which it depends, such as imported class files or packages.

Rebuild

The Rebuild menu item will compile all project files regardless of their status, doing unconditional compilation. Rebuild is especially useful when you are getting ready to distribute your application and you want to rebuild the entire project without debugging information.

By selecting the Build|Rebuild Project "*ProjectName*.jpr" command, you are instructing the JBuilder IDE to unconditionally compile, or rebuild, any source files in the current project. Alternatively, by selecting the Build|Rebuild "*FileName*.java" you are instructing the JBuilder IDE to rebuild only the currently active source file. No matter what the state of the associated `.class` files (or lack thereof), compilation will occur.

This command also causes all imported files and packages, for which source is available, to be recursively compiled (excluding any packages that are marked as stable or "libraried").

11

> **Note**
>
> Packages that are marked as stable or "libraried" include the Java, JBCL, JGL, and Swing packages.

Project Options

JBuilder provides a number of compiler options that enable you to control how your executable files are created. These options can be set either for all projects as IDE-wide options or for the current project as project-specific options. You can also set options for Run and Debug sessions, which can affect your compilation because, by default, these commands invoke Make.

Compiler Options

With a project open, select File | Project Properties to display the *ProjectName*.jpr Properties dialog box. Figure 11.2 shows this dialog box for the Welcome project.

FIGURE 11.2.

Project properties for the Welcome project.

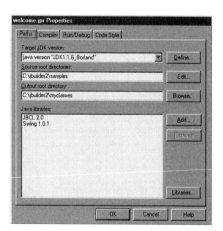

In this dialog box, you can set options that will affect all the files in your project. All the drop-down lists in this dialog are history lists that enable you to select from previously entered options.

The Paths page contains pathname settings for the compiler. You can either type pathnames manually or use the Browse button associated with each combo box to navigate to the pathname that you want to include.

The Source Root Directory tells the compiler where to look for source files when you compile the project. The Output Root Directory tells the compiler where to look for the .class files during a Make so that it can determine which files need to be compiled. The compiler can look in multiple paths for source files, so the Source Root Directory accepts multiple pathnames separated by semicolons. The compiler can look in only one path for .class files, so the Output Root Directory text box accepts only one path entry. The Output Root Directory also tells the compiler where to deposit the compiled .class files when the compilation has successfully been completed.

The Compiler page settings control how the executable file itself is created. The Include Debug Information check box controls whether or not symbolic debug information is added to the executable file. This must be checked for you to be able to use the integrated debugger (covered later today).

The Show Warnings check box controls whether nonfatal warning messages are displayed during compilation. Your project will compile successfully even if it contains errors at the warning level (such as deprecated methods). This check box controls only the display of such warnings in the Message view.

The Check Stable Packages check box controls whether so-called "stable" packages should be checked by the compiler to determine whether they should be included in a Make. Packages such as java or jbcl are considered stable (rarely changed) by the compiler and so are not normally checked during a Make; this saves time during regular compiles. If you want to force the compiler to check stable packages, check this check box.

The Exclude Class combo box enables you to list any .class files that you do not want the compiler to compile. This can be useful if you are in the midst of changing the source code for a class, rendering it uncompilable. A Make normally would include this modified file, halting at compiler errors that you haven't yet fixed. However, by entering the filename of that class in this combo box, you can compile all the rest of the nodes by selecting the Make command for the whole project, and the compiler will ignore the listed class. You can also use the Browse button to interactively locate the class to exclude.

The Encoding combo box gives you the option to specify an alternate encoding, controlling the way non-ASCII characters are interpreted. If this option is set to None, the default platform encoding will be used.

11

Caution

Setting the encoding option might limit the platforms on which your program will properly work, so use this option with care.

The default pathnames that you see in a new project are originally determined during the JBuilder installation. You also can set IDE-wide project options by selecting the Tools | Default Project Properties menu item and making your choices in the Default Project Properties dialog box, which forms the basis for what appears in the *ProjectName*.jpr Properties dialog box.

Compiler option settings in a project override the compiler option settings in the Default Project Properties dialog box. You can think of the settings in the Default Project Properties dialog box Compiler page as the starting point for all projects. Then customize each project in the Compiler page of the *ProjectName*.jpr Properties dialog box.

Run/Debug Options

Click on the Run/Debug tab to open the Run/Debug page of the *ProjectName*.jpr Properties dialog box. This page is shown in Figure 11.3.

FIGURE 11.3.

Run/Debug properties for the Welcome *project.*

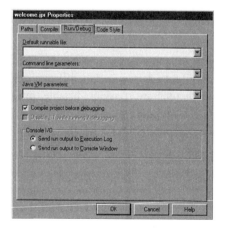

In the Run/Debug page, you can set property-specific options that will control how the program will be executed when you use the Run or Debug commands. In this page of the *ProjectName*.jpr Properties dialog box, you can set options that will affect all the files in your project. All the drop-down lists in this dialog are history lists that enable you to select from previously entered options. In the default configuration, you can implicitly Make a project by selecting either the Run or the Debug command.

The Run/Debug page contains several items that control which files are run, what parameters are provided to your program's command line, and whether a node is compiled before debugging.

The Default Runnable File option enables you to specify which file in the project will be run by default when you select the Run command. If you use the Run command and a file other than what you expected attempts to run, this is the place to check! If there is an entry in this combo box and you select the Run command from the Run menu (or its iconic representation on the toolbar), this option controls what file is run. However, if this combo box is empty, or if you use the Run command from a node's pop-up menu, this option is ignored, and the selected node is run instead.

The Command Line Parameters combo box gives you a place to specify what your program's arguments will be for the current run. This enables you to try different arguments when testing your program in the JBuilder IDE. If this combo box is empty, no arguments will be passed to your program, which can be useful for testing how your program handles a `null` parameter list.

The Java VM Parameters combo box enables you to specify command-line options to be passed to the Java Virtual Machine itself. The valid parameters are platform-specific. The easiest way to learn which parameters are valid on a platform is to go to a command prompt, type `java` with no arguments, and press Enter. This will display a usage statement that lists all the command-line options available for that platform. Options might include setting heap size, setting stack size, and turning garbage collection on or off.

The Compile project before debugging check box controls whether invoking the Run or Debug command does an implicit Make before attempting to run the program. This check box is checked by default, but if you would rather the JBuilder IDE didn't perform a conditional compilation every time you choose the Run or Debug commands, uncheck this option.

The Console I/O group of options control where standard output and standard error messages are displayed. The Send run output to Execution Log radio button will direct your command-line program's output to the Execution Log window, which you can view by selecting View|Execution Log. The Send run output to Console Window radio button will direct your program's output to a console window, a DOS window in Microsoft Windows.

Syntax Errors

When you make or build your project, unless you are a lot more careful than most of us, you will have the occasional compiler error. One of the JBuilder Editor features, syntax highlighting, can help you spot syntax errors before you compile your program, but other errors are more subtle. In this section, you'll look at a program that has been rigged with errors so that you can see how these errors appear in both the AppBrowser window Content pane Editor and in the Message view, a subpane of the Content pane.

11

With the `CompileDebug.jpr` project open, click the Add to Project button above the Navigation pane in the AppBrowser window. Type `HelloDebug.java` in the File name text box and then click the Open button. In the Content pane, enter the code including syntax errors shown in Listing 11.1. The applet in Listing 11.1 will not compile without errors.

TYPE **LISTING 11.1.** HelloDebug.java (WITH SYNTAX ERRORS).

```
1:   import java.awt.*;
2:
3:   public class HelloDebug extends java.applet.Applet {
4:
5:     public void init() {
6:       Font f = new Font("Helvetica, Font.BOLD, 36);
7:       setFont(f);
8:     }
9:
10:    public void paint(Graphics g) {
11:      g.drawString("Hello!", 50, 50)
12:    }
13:
14:  }
```

Code Editor Options

In looking at Listing 11.1, you might already have spotted the two syntax errors. In line 6, the declaration of the Font object is missing the terminating double-quote at the end of the font name. In line 11, the ending semicolon is missing—a common mistake.

However, the Editor's syntax highlighting feature can be used to help you spot some syntax errors. You can customize the syntax highlighting feature settings. Select the HelloDebug.java node, then right-click on the Content pane and select the Properties command from the pop-up menu. The Editor Properties dialog box appears. Click on the Colors tab and then click on String in the Element list so that the dialog box looks as shown Figure 11.4.

Assuming that you are using the default color scheme, the dialog has an FG in the upper-left color box, which is black, and the Background check box is checked in the Use Defaults For area. Left-click on the lower-left color box, which is bright blue, and click the OK button. Back in the Content pane, it will be immediately obvious that the Helvetica string isn't terminated properly because the rest of the line is the same color as the string.

FIGURE 11.4.

The String *element selected in the Colors page of the Editor Properties dialog box.*

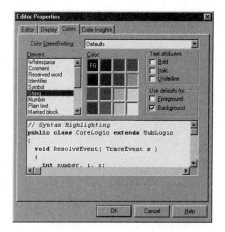

Experiment with coloring different syntax elements. In addition to the text's foreground color, you can also change the background color. For example, you can make comments appear as blue text on a yellow background to make them stand out. You can also change font attributes (bold, italic, and underline).

At the top of the Color page of the Editor Properties dialog box you can select from four Color SpeedSetting options that provide you with predefined color combinations. You can use these as defined or use them as a starting point to create your own special color scheme. The scroll box at the bottom of the Color page of the Editor Properties dialog box displays each code element in a sample program. This enables you to click on an element to choose it. That way, even if you don't know what an element is called, you can still change its syntax highlighting attributes. For example, clicking on void in the sample box will show you that it is a reserved word which, by default, is displayed in black bold text on the default background.

Compiler Errors

Other syntax errors are not so easily exposed. These syntax errors will show up when you attempt to compile your program. Select the HelloDebug.java node in the Navigation pane, right-click and select the Make command on the pop-up menu.

In theory, you might expect that one syntax error would produce one compiler error. However, no one has yet devised a compiler with that much intelligence, as you will see in just a moment—yet the JBuilder compiler is more intelligent than most.

When the compiler is finished, you should see three errors in the Message view, as shown in Figure 11.5.

FIGURE 11.5.

Errors produced by the `HelloDebug.java` *compilation.*

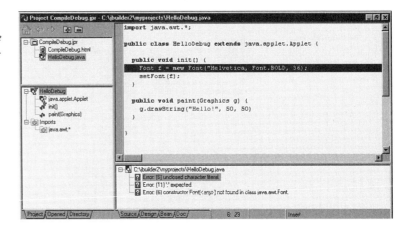

If you have typed each example perfectly in the first 10 days, this might be the first time you've seen an error message in the JBuilder IDE. The first part `Error:` identifies this message as a syntax error rather than a warning. Errors are fatal—that is, your program will not compile properly until the problem is fixed. The next part in parentheses tells you which line of source code caused the problem. After the line number is the actual error message itself, which gives you a brief explanation of the problem that needs to be corrected. The first error message, in this case

```
Error: (6) unclosed character literal.
```

is telling you that there is a fatal error on line 6 and the problem is that there is an `unclosed character literal` on that line.

There are several other things to note about Figure 11.5:

- In the Message view, the first error is highlighted.
- In the Content pane, the line of code referenced by that error is highlighted.
- The cursor is positioned at the origin of the problem in that line.
- The Status Bar in the main window is displaying the message `Compiler: Failed, with errors`.

Now, back to the Message view. The first error message is saying that you forgot to put a double-quote at the end of `Helvetica` to close the string. The cursor is positioned at the beginning of the string, ready for you to review the problem. Why is it telling you that you have an unclosed character literal when what you have is an unclosed string? The compiler sees the first double-quote and a character, so it knows that it should expect another double-quote. It doesn't know whether you want a character literal or a string, it just knows there is no closing double-quote. This is the type of deduction you need to be able to make in order to interpret some error messages.

Let's look at the other two error messages. To do so, you can either click on the next message with the mouse or use the View|Next Error Message command. The second error message,

```
Error: (11) ';' expected.
```

tells you that a semicolon was expected on line 11 and that the cursor is positioned at the end of the line. This seems straightforward enough. The third and final error message is

```
Error: (6) constructor Font (<any>) not found in class java.awt.Font.
```

But why is there a third message when there are only two errors? This message is caused by the fact that, after the syntax check, the compiler also does a referential check of classes and methods. Because of the missing double-quote on line 6 (the first error), the compiler cannot resolve the Font constructor statement because it is improperly formed, and outputs another error.

Let's go back and correct the first error. To do so, you can either double-click on the first error with the mouse or use the View|Previous Error Message command twice. Position the cursor at the end of the string Helvetica, and insert a double-quote before the comma. Don't fix anything else at this point. With the HelloDebug.java node selected, right-click and then choose the Make command. The result is shown in Figure 11.6.

FIGURE 11.6.

The remaining error produced by the HelloDebug.java *compilation.*

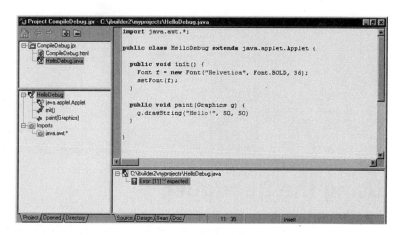

Notice that two of the errors were resolved with this one fix. Now that the string Hello! is properly terminated, the Font constructor resolves properly, too. The cursor is now positioned at the point in the source code where the missing semicolon should go. Insert the semicolon, and recompile. The program should now compile without errors.

Getting Help with Errors

When an error is displayed in the Message view, note the line number and type (either error or warning). To obtain more information on that error, select Help | Help Topics, and refer to the "Error and warning messages" topic in the online Getting Started with JBuilder book.

Let's go back and take out the ending double-quote on line 6 and then make the file to recreate the error message. Select Help | Help Topics. When the Help viewer appears, select Getting Started with JBuilder from the Available books drop-down list. Expand the Error and warning messages node, then click on the Error messages entry to display that topic. Use either the links at the top of the page or scroll down to the error you want to know more about. Figure 11.7 shows the help for the unclosed character literal syntax error.

FIGURE 11.7.

Help for errors.

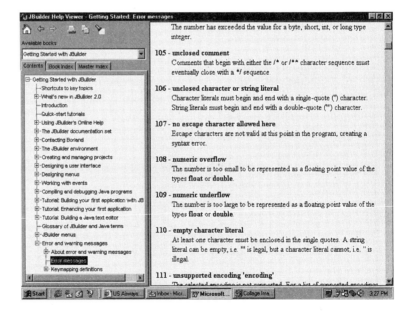

Using the Debugger

With a completed and successfully compiled application, you are ready to test your program. Although all the different types of tests you can perform on an application are outside the scope of this book, you will want to perform certain basic tests to ensure that your application can be run by all the users for whom it is intended.

Basic tests include exercising each menu item, entering different values into input fields, checking for proper display of graphical items, and testing output to various devices. You can perform most of these tests from within the JBuilder IDE by running your application. To run your project, select Run | Run, which will load your program and let you interact with it as a user would. If something doesn't work properly or you receive a run-time error, you'll want to debug your program using the JBuilder IDE integrated debugger.

To debug your project, select Run | Debug, which will load your project into the inte-grated debugger, allowing you to step, trace, pause, and examine values and states of your variables and objects.

The integrated debugger enables you to manipulate your code in a controlled manner. It also enables you to try out different scenarios, find obscure bugs, and otherwise examine values at any point in your program's execution, enabling you to completely debug your Java programs. You can go through your code line by line, stepping conditionally into and over parts of your source code. You will use many of the Run menu and View menu items during a debug session, both to set up the session and to control the execution of your program during the session.

Debugging Options

Before you can begin debugging with the integrated debugger, ensure that certain pro-ject options are enabled. Remember that the debugging options are specified in the *ProjectName*.jpr Properties dialog box. When debugging, you'll want to set your project options to the values shown in Table 11.1.

TABLE 11.1. DEBUGGING PROJECT OPTIONS.

Dialog Page	Compiler Option	Setting
Compiler	Include Debug Information	Checked
Run/Debug	Compile project before debugging	Checked
Run/Debug	Send run output to Execution Log	Selected

Before you begin your debug session, you might also want to modify the parameters in the Run/Debug page of the *ProjectName*.jpr Properties dialog box to try out different sets of arguments to see how your program parses and uses those arguments.

Invoking the Debugger

To begin using the integrated debugger, select the Debug command, either from the selected node's pop-up menu, the Run menu, or by clicking its iconic representation on the JBuilder toolbar (lightening bolt with a bug). If you have breakpoints set (which you'll learn about in the "Breakpoints" section), you can use the Run command to invoke a debug session.

Invoking the debugger causes an implicit make to be performed on the selected node, which can be a file, a package, or a project node. If the compile is successful, your program will begin to run. As soon as any procedural code is called, the execution point is displayed in the Editor pane, as shown in Figure 11.8.

FIGURE 11.8.

The execution point.

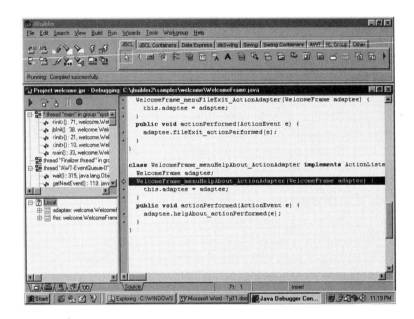

 NEW TERM   The *execution point* is the line of code about to be executed during a debug session.

The execution point is highlighted by a line of color and an arrowhead in the left margin of the Editor pane. If you have yet to set any breakpoints or watches, you can do so any time an execution point is displayed and your program is paused.

> **Tip**
>
> If you have clicked on some other line of code and want to reposition the cursor at the execution point, you can do so by selecting Run | Show Execution Point.

Pausing and Resuming

Whenever your program is awaiting user input, you can select the Run | Program Pause command to temporarily stop the execution of the program in the integrated debugger. This also will enable you to change debugging settings, such as breakpoints and watches. To resume program execution, use one of four commands on the Run menu: Trace Into, Step Over, Run to Cursor, or Run to End of Method.

Tracing into the code using the Trace Into command causes the debugger to execute each line of code in turn, including all executable lines in called methods. When this command is used and the debugger encounters a method call, it executes the method call and positions the execution point at the next line of code in the method itself.

Stepping over code using the Step Over command causes the debugger to execute each line of code in turn, except in the case of called methods. When the debugger encounters a line of code that calls a method, it executes all the statements in that method as a group and then positions the execution point at the statement immediately following the method call.

To use the Run to Cursor command, position the cursor in the Editor on the line of code where you want to begin (or continue) debugging. This command will run your program straight through until it reaches the source code line where your cursor is. When it reaches that point, the execution point is positioned on that line of code, and you can proceed by stepping or tracing from there.

The Run to End of Method command causes the debugger to run from the point where the command is invoked through the rest of the current method, positioning the execution point at the line immediately following the method call. This command is especially useful if you have traced into a method and don't want to trace through all its remaining lines of code.

Breakpoints

When you run your program in the debugger, it runs at full speed unless you tell it to stop at a particular point. Breakpoints tell the debugger that you want to pause execution when it gets to the line of code that contains a breakpoint.

NEW TERM
A *breakpoint* is a line of source code marked so that the debugger will pause program execution when that point in the program is reached.

Breakpoints are useful for pausing the program at a predetermined point, enabling you to examine the state of variables (using watches or the Evaluate/Modify dialog box), the call stack, and thread status. To set a breakpoint, right-click on the source code line in

the Content pane where you want the program execution to pause and select Toggle
Breakpoint from the pop-up menu.

Note

> A breakpoint can be set only on a line that generates actual executable
> code. Breakpoints are not valid if set on blank lines, comments, or declara-
> tions. You are not prevented from setting a breakpoint on these types of
> lines, but the debugger will warn you that you have set a breakpoint on a
> line that contains no code, producing an invalid breakpoint. Invalid break-
> points will simply be ignored by the debugger. Breakpoints are valid, how-
> ever, on return statements or on the closing brace of a method.

To indicate a breakpoint, a red sphere is placed in the Editor's left margin adjacent to the
line of code, as shown in Figure 11.9.

FIGURE 11.9.

*A breakpoint in the
Editor pane.*

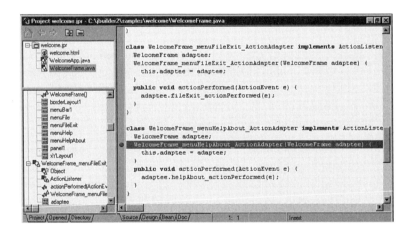

In addition to setting breakpoints from the Editor, you can also use the Run | Add
Breakpoint command to display the Breakpoint Options dialog box. In JBuilder, there
are two types of breakpoints: source and exception. Source breakpoints are those that are
set on a particular line in the source code, and they cause execution to pause when that
line of code is the next to be executed. Exception breakpoints are invoked and pause execution whenever a listed exception is thrown.

Setting Source Breakpoints

Figure 11.10 shows the Breakpoint Definition page for Source Breakpoint.

FIGURE 11.10.

The Breakpoint Definition page for Source Breakpoint.

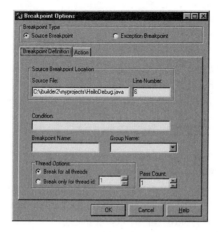

Source breakpoints have a number of options that control how they are invoked. You can set the filename and source code line for which the breakpoint is effective. The Condition is an expression which, if satisfied, will cause the program to pause. On the Action page, you can also name the breakpoint and assign it to a group of breakpoints. The thread options control whether this particular breakpoint will stop the execution of all threads or only a specified thread ID. The pass count controls how many times the breakpoint will be ignored before pausing execution. For example, if you have a breakpoint in a loop that executes 20 times, you might want the breakpoint to stop only the last time through the loop. The pass count is decremented each time it encounters the breakpoint during execution, pausing only when it reaches 1.

Setting Exception Breakpoints

Figure 11.11 shows the Breakpoint Definition page for Exception Breakpoint.

FIGURE 11.11.

The Breakpoint Definition page for Exception Breakpoint.

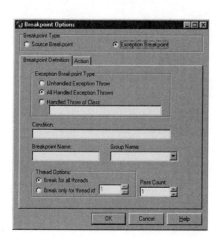

11

As you can see, for exception breakpoints, some of the options are different. Instead of filename and line number, you specify for which type of exception you want the breakpoint to pause. The default is All Handled Exception Throws, but you can alternatively set it to stop for only an Unhandled Exception Throw, or for only Handled Throw of Class and name a specific class. The rest of the options on this page are the same as for a source breakpoint, except that they apply to the specified type of exception.

Performing an Action at a Breakpoint

Figure 11.12 shows the Action page. This page contains the same options for both types of breakpoints. You can specify any combination of actions that you want to occur when a particular breakpoint is reached. One of the options, interestingly enough, allows you to disable the Halt Execution option, which can be useful if you use some of the other Enable/Disable options. The Dialog on breakpoint occurrence check box enables the display of a dialog when a breakpoint is reached. The Log breakpoint occurrence check box causes a message to be written to the debug log; an Expression causes it to be written only when the expression evaluates to true. The Enable/Disable another breakpoint check boxes cause the named breakpoints to be enabled/disabled when the current breakpoint is reached; the Enable/Disable a group of breakpoints check boxes cause a named group of breakpoints to be enabled or disabled when the current breakpoint is reached. These four options rely on the Name and Group Name options selected in the Breakpoint Definition page for the current breakpoint.

FIGURE 11.12.

The Action page for both types of breakpoints.

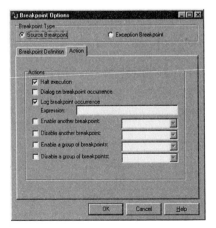

Viewing Breakpoints

To see what breakpoints are set in the current debug session, use the View|Breakpoints command to display the Breakpoints window, shown in Figure 11.13.

FIGURE 11.13.

The Breakpoints window and its pop-up menu.

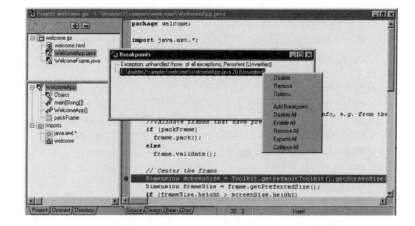

The Breakpoints window's pop-up menu gives you easy access to the most commonly used commands without your having to invoke the Breakpoints Options dialog box. Figure 11.13 shows the pop-up menu commands that appear when a particular breakpoint is selected. Most of the commands, such as Disable or Remove, are self-explanatory. The Options command displays the Breakpoints Options dialog box with the currently selected breakpoint's information. The Add Breakpoint command invokes the Breakpoints Options dialog box with the current execution point's information displayed.

Watches

Watches are those identifiers, or expressions containing one or more identifiers, for which you want to see the current value when the program pauses. The watch can "see" only identifiers that are in the current scope. If an individual identifier or any identifier in an expression goes out of scope, the watch will be undefined.

Caution

> An expression can contain almost anything a regular assignment statement can contain. The one exception is that a watch expression cannot contain a method call on the right side of the assignment operator.

To examine watches while your program is running, choose the Watch tab in the AppBrowser to put it into Watch mode. The left pane becomes the Watch pane and will display the currently defined watches. To set a watch, select the Run | Add Watch command, which displays the Add Watch dialog box.

Threads and Stack

When the AppBrowser window is in Debug mode, clicking on the Debug tab reveals two debugging views: the Threads and Stack pane and the Data pane.

The Threads and Stack pane appears in the upper-left pane, and displays the threads, methods, and parameters called up to the current execution point. The Stack displays the name of the currently executing method and all the methods that were called in prior sequence. Each item lists the method names and the values of its calling parameters. Threads are subprocesses in your application. Even if you haven't designed your application to be multithreaded, the default single thread for your program will be shown in this window and its progress followed.

The Data pane in the lower-left pane lets you see what the current value is of an object's data. This enables you to examine the state of an object whenever your program is paused.

You can also customize what types of information are shown in these panes. Right-click in either the Thread and Stack pane or the Data pane, and select Properties to display the Context Tree Properties dialog box, shown in Figure 11.14.

FIGURE 11.14.

The Context Tree Properties dialog box.

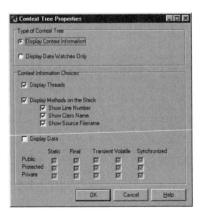

In this dialog box, you can determine exactly what types of data are displayed in these panes. Most of the choices are self-explanatory, but worth noting are the choices presented by the array of check boxes under the Display Data check box. These check boxes control whether the associated data types are hidden from view or are displayed in the pane.

Other Debug Views

There are three other views and windows that are available to give you additional information about your program during a debug session. The following sections give a brief explanation of each.

Inspector Window

In the Inspector window you can examine a data element, such as a property value or program data. The value will be updated as you step through your program in the debug session. Invoke this window through the Inspect dialog box by selecting the Run I Inspect command.

Evaluate/Modify Dialog Box

The Evaluate/Modify dialog box enables you to evaluate an expression or temporarily change data elements, such as property values, while debugging. This dialog box is invoked by selecting the Run I Evaluate/Modify command. In the Expression combo box, either type the identifier, constant, or expression that you want to evaluate or choose a previously evaluated expression from its history list. Click the Evaluate button to display the result of the evaluation in the Result field. To modify a value, type the desired value in the New Value combo box, and click the Modify button. This enables you to input a desired value and continue debugging, either correcting a wrong value or specifying an incorrect value in order to test your code to see whether it will handle the error correctly.

Loaded Classes Window

The Loaded Classes window displays a list of all the classes associated with the current program in the debug session. This window is invoked by selecting the View I Loaded Classes command.

Summary

Today, you've learned how to prepare your code for compilation, including using the Editor's syntax highlighting to spot errors prior to doing a syntax check. You should now be able to decide whether to do a Make or a Rebuild, and you know how to invoke those commands in a number of ways. You also learned that invoking Run or Debug does an implicit Make and that you can use F1 to get help with those pesky compiler errors.

You've learned how to invoke the debugger, how to pause and reset, and the difference between stepping and tracing. In addition, you've learned about breakpoints, watches, how to examine thread status, the method call stack, and other program data during a

11

debug session. You've seen that you can look at which classes are loaded by the current class and inspect the current value of data elements. Finally, you now know how to use the Evaluate/Modify dialog box to see what values an identifier represents and to change the current value of an identifier while debugging, to perform "what if" execution.

Q&A

Q What are some common errors that programmers new to Java should look for?

A There are three common mistakes that result in compiler errors. Always check for these things while entering your source code:

- Make sure that braces are balanced, matching opening braces with closing braces. One technique that ensures this is to type the line of code and the beginning brace, press the Enter key, and type the ending brace. Then insert the code for that block between the two balanced braces—that way, you won't forget the one at the end. Also, because of the Editors "smart tabbing" feature, entering the braces this way will automatically place the ending brace at the proper level of indentation for you.

- Don't forget the semicolon at the end of each statement. Remember that semicolons are *not* required after an ending brace. Also, if a block statement doesn't ever seem to get executed, one of the first things to look for is an extraneous semicolon before the block's first brace.

- Case-sensitivity is the one mistake that gets all new Java programmers. If the compiler claims that something isn't declared, and you know that it is, check the case and make sure that all occurrences of the identifier are identically spelled and that the uppercase and lowercase characters match.

Workshop

The Workshop provides two ways for you to affirm what you've learned in this chapter. The Quiz section poses questions to help you solidify your understanding of the material covered. You can find answers to the quiz questions in Appendix A, "Answers to Quiz Questions." The Exercise section provides you with experience in using what you have learned. Try to work through all the sections before continuing to the next day.

Quiz

1. What is the difference between a Make and a Rebuild?

2. How do you set a breakpoint on a particular line of source code?

3. What command enables you to execute each line of a method while debugging?

4. How can you change the value of a variable during execution?

5. True or False? The execution point indicates the line of code that was just executed.

6. To make the debugger run your code until it encounters the line of code in which the cursor is positioned in the Editor, what command would you use?

Exercise

Take any of the projects you've worked on earlier this week and set various types of source code breakpoints. Try all the debug commands on the Run menu and see whether they work like you think they will. Make a new project, and copy some working code into it; then create syntax errors and see what types of error messages they produce. Experiment with the syntax highlighting to see what combinations will show syntax errors the best.

11

DAY 12

Handling Events

Event handling is where most of the action in your application takes place. So far, this book has concentrated on the graphical interface between your application and its user. Now, it's time to make that beautiful and carefully crafted interface earn its keep.

Handling events is how your Java application responds to messages sent to it by the system. When a user clicks on a button, selects a menu item, or types text, the system transmits a message to your application.

NEW TERM An *event* occurs when the system transmits a message to your program.

Messages can also be transmitted in response to system events, such as another program closing or a top-level window being minimized and exposing your window. All these events must be handled, either implicitly or explicitly, by your program. The methods in which you write the code to handle these events are called event-handling methods, or event handlers.

NEW TERM An *event handler* is a method that contains code to respond to a system event message.

Today, you'll learn how to handle events and how to write event handlers using JBuilder. In particular, you'll learn how to respond to these user actions:

- Mouse clicks
- Mouse movements, including dragging
- Keypresses

The project for today is named HandlingEvents.jpr, to which all of today's listings will be added.

Creating Event Handlers

Creating event handlers, as you've seen in previous days, is simplicity itself. First, in UI Designer mode, select the component in the UI Designer or Menu Designer for which you want to handle an event—a menu-command item, a button, or the like.

To create a new event handler, click on the Events tab of the Inspector window, and then select the event for which you want to write a method. Click once in the right column to name a new method, and then double-click to transfer focus to the Source tab of the AppBrowser window. The cursor will be positioned in the source code at your new event-handling method, awaiting your commands. You first saw an example of how to do this on Day 6, "User Interface Design," when you created the menuFileSayHello's actionPerformed event-handling method.

If you want to use an existing event handler, click on the Events tab, and then select the event for which you want to reuse the existing event-handler. Click on the right column and type the existing method's name. That's it! Your component or menu-command item will now reuse that method for its own events. You saw an example of how to do this on Day 6 when you re-used the menuFileSayHello's actionPerformed method for the Button's actionPerformed event. Both the menu item and the button performed exactly the same action in response to the user's action (selecting the menu item or clicking on the button), so they were able to share the same event handler.

A quick way to create the default event handler for a component is to double-click the component in the UI Designer. The event that is considered the default event is defined for most components. For example, the default event for a Button component is actionPerformed, and its default event handler is actionPerformed_buttonName. The actionPerformed event is also the default for those components that don't explicitly define one.

When you create an event handler, in addition to the method stub, the JBuilder IDE automatically generates all the code necessary to connect that method with the component that needs to use it to respond to events. These include an `EventAdapter` and an `EventListener`, which are created as new classes in your source code—be sure not to edit this generated code. Explaining the how and why of these classes is beyond the scope of this book, but they are mentioned here as another example of the ways in which the JBuilder IDE simplifies the task of writing Java code. In addition, whenever you add a `Frame` class to your project, the JBuilder IDE automatically adds the appropriate import line,

```
import java.awt.event.*;
```

to your source code so that it can handle events properly when you add event-handling code.

To delete an event handler, select the handler's name in the right column of the event. Then, with the entire method name highlighted, press the Delete key. This disconnects the named event handler from that particular event but does not remove the event-handling method itself. This is a safety feature so that a method is not erased simply because you've momentarily removed the last reference to it. (Perhaps you intended to connect it to some other component later.)

To remove the event-handling method from your source code entirely, remove the body of the method, leaving the empty method signature. The next time your code is compiled, all the code related to that handler (including the `EventAdapter` and `EventListener` generated code) will be removed from your source code file.

Managing Simple Events

12

Java events are part of the Abstract Windowing Toolkit package. An event is the way that components communicate to you, as the programmer, and to other components that something has happened. That something can be input from the user (mouse clicks, mouse movements, keypresses), changes in the system environment (a window opening or closing, the window being scrolled up or down), or a host of other things that might, in some way, be relevant to the operation of the program.

In other words, whenever just about anything happens to a component, including an applet, an event is generated. Some events are handled implicitly without your needing to do anything. For example, `paint` method calls are generated and handled by the browser—all you have to do is say what you want painted when it gets to your part of the window. Some events, however, such as a mouse click inside the boundaries of your applet, you will need to handle explicitly by writing code in an event-handling method. Writing your Java programs to handle these kinds of events enables you to get input from the user and have your program change its behavior based on that input.

Mouse Events

Mouse events come in two basic flavors, mouse clicks and mouse movements. Mouse click events occur when a user presses and releases one of the mouse buttons; mouse movement events occur when the mouse is moved from one position to another. If one of the mouse buttons is pressed while the mouse is being moved, the movement is called dragging.

Handling mouse events in your applet is easy; just select the appropriate event in the Inspector pane; then double-click. When you do, a method stub is inserted into your source code which looks something like this:

```
void this_mouseClicked(MouseEvent e) {...}
```

All the mouse events have as their argument an object of type MouseEvent, whose constructor method header is

```
public MouseEvent(Component source, int id, long when,
                  int modifiers, int x, int y,
                  int clickCount, boolean popupTrigger)
```

The source parameter is passed the Component object that triggered the event, such as a Button or a MenuItem object. The id parameter is passed an integer defining the type of mouse event that occurred (int constants: MOUSE_CLICKED, MOUSE_PRESSED, MOUSE_RELEASED, MOUSE_MOVED, MOUSE_ENTERED, MOUSE_EXITED, or MOUSE_DRAGGED). Each event has a unique when time stamp. The modifiers parameter is passed information on whether or not one or more modifier keys (Shift, Alt, or Ctrl) were pressed while the mouse event occurred. The x and y parameters are passed the x,y coordinate of the mouse event relative to the source component. The clickCount parameter is passed the number of mouse-button clicks (if any) that occurred. For example, a double-click would result in 2 being passed to the clickCount parameter. The popupTrigger parameter is passed true if the mouse event causes pop-up menus to occur on the platform, such as a right-click in the Windows environment.

The MouseEvent object has several methods associated with it, which give you access to its nonpublic instance variables:

- The getX() and getY() methods each return an int value containing the x and y coordinates, respectively, which are relative to the source component generating the event.
- The getPoint() method returns the same x,y coordinate in a Point object, whereas the translatePoint(x, y) method adds the specified x and y values to the x,y coordinate encapsulated by the Point object.

- The `getClickCount()` method returns the `int` value passed to the `clickCount` parameter.

You can use these methods to obtain information about the `MouseEvent` instance in your own mouse event-handling methods. Because the standard event handler generated by JBuilder assigns `MouseEvent` objects to the e variable, you can refer to these methods as `e.getX()` or `e.getClickCount()` in your event handler.

Mouse Clicks

Mouse click events occur when a user clicks the mouse somewhere in the body of your applet, or within the boundaries of your application's windows. You can intercept mouse clicks to do very simple things—to toggle the sound on and off in your application, to move to the next slide in a presentation, or to clear the screen and start over. Or you can use mouse clicks in conjunction with mouse movements to perform more complex actions in your program.

When you click the mouse, several events are generated. A `mouseClicked` event signals that the mouse was pressed and released. But what about those times when you need to discriminate between pressing the mouse button and releasing it? For example, consider a pull-down menu. Pressing the mouse button extends the menu, and releasing the mouse button selects a menu item (with mouse drags in between, which you'll learn about in the "Mouse Motions" section). If you had only one event for both, you could not implement that sort of user interaction. So in addition to the `mouseClicked` event, clicking the mouse also generates a `mousePressed` event as the mouse button is pressed and a `mouseReleased` event as the mouse button is released.

For example, here is a trio of simple `Button` component event handlers that print coordinate information (relative to the `Button` component's x,y origin) whenever a `mouseClicked`, `mousePressed`, or `mouseReleased` event occurs:

```
void button1_mouseClicked(MouseEvent e) {
  System.out.println("A mouseClicked event occurred at "
                     + e.getX() + "," + e.getY());
}

void button1_mousePressed(MouseEvent e) {
  System.out.println("A mousePressed event occurred at "
                     + e.getX() + "," + e.getY());
}

void button1_mouseReleased(MouseEvent e) {
  System.out.println("A mouseReleased event occurred at "
                     + e.getX() + "," + e.getY());
}
```

12

Remember, to create the handler, select the event in the Events tab. Click in the right column to name the handler, and then double-click to create the method stub (or you can just triple-click to do these two steps at once); then add the two lines of code for the body of each method. Also, note that the `MouseEvent` instance variables are not public and are accessible only through the `MouseEvent` methods described in the "Mouse Events" section earlier.

If you try this out, you'll see that for a simple mouse click, three lines are printed:

```
A mousePressed event occurred at 31,5
A mouseReleased event occurred at 31,5
A mouseClicked event occurred at 31,5
```

This looks fairly straightforward: The mouse button is pressed, it's released, and so a mouse click has been completed. However, if you click and then drag before releasing, only two lines are printed:

```
A mousePressed event occurred at 9,8
A mouseReleased event occurred at 42,10
```

Why not a mouse click? The system knows that something happened (a mouse drag) in between the press and release of the mouse button, so it cannot resolve the two into a simple mouse click, and it doesn't generate a `mouseClicked` event.

Spots Applet

In this section, you'll create an applet that makes use of the `mousePressed` event. The Spots applet starts with a blank screen and then sits and waits. When you click the mouse on that screen, a blue dot is drawn.

Start by building the basic applet with the Applet Wizard. With the `HandlingEvents.jpr` project open and active in the JBuilder IDE, select File | New to open the New dialog box. Make sure that the New dialog box is open to the New page by clicking on the tab; then double-click the Applet icon to start the Applet Wizard. When the Applet Wizard: Step 1 of 3 dialog box appears, erase the text in the Package field, and type `Spots` in the Class field. Then click the Finish button. This will generate skeleton code for the `Spots.java` applet and also the `Spots.html` file with which to test your applet.

In the Structure pane, click on the `Applet` node (just below the `Spots` node) which will highlight the `Spots` class declaration. Insert these lines of code just below that line in the Content pane:

```
int x;
int y;
```

This code defines the class's two instance variables: the x and y coordinates where the current spot will be drawn.

Note

> This class doesn't need to include `implements Runnable` in its class definition. As you'll see later as you build this applet, it also doesn't have a `run()` method. Why not? Because it doesn't actually do anything on its own—all it does is wait for input and then respond when input happens. There's no need for threads if your applet isn't actively doing something all the time.

Next, you want to set the `background` property for the applet to `white`. Click on the Design tab to put the AppBrowser window into UI Design mode. The `this(XYLayout)` object should be selected in the Structure pane, as shown in Figure 12.1. The `this(XYLayout)` object represents your applet's drawing area.

FIGURE 12.1.

The `this(XYLayout)` *object is highlighted in the AppBrowser window Structure pane.*

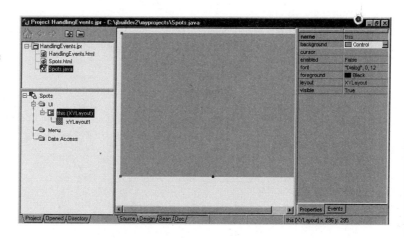

Click on the Properties tab of the Inspector pane, double-click on the `background` property, and then click the ellipses button to display the background dialog box, shown in Figure 12.2.

Click the drop-down arrow in the choice box at the top of the dialog and scroll up all the way to the top of the list to select `White`, and then click OK. If you look at your source code, in the `jbInit()` method, you will see that a new line of code has been added:

```
this.setBackground(Color.white);
```

You want to set the `background` property here, instead of in the `paint()` method, because the `paint()` method is called each time a new spot is added. Because you really only need to set the background once, putting it in the `paint()` method unnecessarily slows down that method. Setting it here improves performance.

FIGURE 12.2.

The background dialog box.

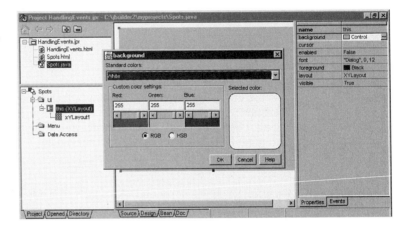

The main action of this applet occurs in the `this_mousePressed()` method. To add the event handler, click on the Events tab in the Inspector pane, and then triple-click in the `mousePressed` event's right column to place the method stub in your source code. Add these lines of code to the body of the newly created `this_mousePressed` method:

```
x = e.getX();
y = e.getY();
repaint();
```

When the mouse click occurs, the `this_mousePressed()` method sets the x and y variables to the coordinates returned by the `MouseEvent` object's `getX()` and `getY()` methods. Then it calls the `repaint()` method.

Tip

Why respond to the `mousePressed` event instead of the `mouseClicked` event? You really only care about the coordinates where the mouse button was pressed, not where it was released. Consider what happens if the user is a little "heavy-handed" and clicks and drags the mouse slightly before releasing the mouse button, instead of making a nice discrete mouse click. If your method responded only to `mouseClicked` events, you'd be out of luck; since a mouse drag occurred, only a `mousePressed` and `mouseReleased` event would be generated, so your method would not respond properly. By responding to the `mousePressed` rather than the `mouseClicked` event, you eliminate that potential problem in your code.

You also need to override the `update()` method to eliminate its internal call to the `repaint()` method. Add the following code to your `Spot.java` source file:

```
public void update(Graphics g) {
  paint(g);
}
```

This isn't an animation, so why override the update() method? If you didn't, you would have to keep track of all the past spots in addition to the current spot so that you could redraw them after the update() method's internal call to the repaint() method cleared your applet's screen.

Now, on to your paint() method, in which you'll draw the current spot in response to your call to the repaint() method initiated by the mousePressed event:

```
public void paint(Graphics g) {
  g.setColor(Color.blue);
  g.fillOval(x - 10, y - 10, 20, 20);
}
```

Because the oval's point of origin is the upper-left corner of the bounding rectangle, in this paint() method, you paint the current spot a little to the left and upward so that the spot is painted around the mouse pointer's hotspot, rather than below and to the right of it. Listing 12.1 shows the code for the Spots applet.

TYPE   **LISTING 12.1.** Spots.java.

```
 1:   import java.awt.*;
 2:   import java.awt.event.*;
 3:   import java.applet.*;
 4:   import borland.jbcl.layout.*;
 5:   import borland.jbcl.control.*;
 6:
 7:   public class Spots extends Applet {
 8:       int x;
 9:       int y;
10:       XYLayout xYLayout1 = new XYLayout();
11:       boolean isStandalone = false;
12:
13:       //Construct the applet
14:
15:       public Spots() {
16:       }
17:       //Initialize the applet
18:
19:       public void init() {
20:       try {
21:         jbInit();
22:       }
23:       catch (Exception e) {
24:         e.printStackTrace();
25:       }
26:       }
```

continues

12

LISTING 12.1. CONTINUED

```
27:     //Component initialization
28:
29:     private void jbInit() throws Exception {
30:       this.setBackground(Color.white);
31:       this.addMouseListener(new java.awt.event.MouseAdapter() {
32:         public void mousePressed(MouseEvent e) {
33:           this_mousePressed(e);
34:         }
35:       });
36:       xYLayout1.setWidth(400);
37:       xYLayout1.setHeight(300);
38:       this.setLayout(xYLayout1);
39:     }
40:     //Get Applet information
41:
42:     public String getAppletInfo() {
43:       return "Applet Information";
44:     }
45:     //Get parameter info
46:
47:     public String[][] getParameterInfo() {
48:       return null;
49:     }
50:
51:     void this_mousePressed(MouseEvent e) {
52:       x = e.getX();
53:       y = e.getY();
54:       repaint();
55:     }
56:
57:     public void update(Graphics g) {
58:       paint(g);
59:     }
60:
61:     public void paint(Graphics g) {
62:       g.setColor(Color.blue);
63:       g.fillOval(x - 10, y - 10, 20, 20);
64:     }
65:   }
66: }
```

That's all you need to create an applet that can handle mouse clicks. Everything else is handled for you. Figure 12.3 shows what the Spots applet looks like running in the appletviewer after you've added numerous spots.

FIGURE 12.3.

The Spots applet in action.

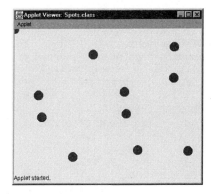

To clear the drawing area, just minimize and restore the appletviewer window to restart the applet. You might notice that one circle remains in the upper-left corner of the applet, even after you've minimized and restored the appletviewer. This is because the fillOval() method is in the paint() method, which is called whenever the applet's user interface is refreshed.

Mouse Motions

Every time the mouse is moved, mouse move events are generated. Just how many events are generated depends on the type of mouse move, of which there are four:

mouseMoved event	The mouse is moved, but no buttons are pressed.
mouseDragged event	The mouse is moved while a mouse button is pressed.
mouseEntered event	The mouse is moved over the boundary going into the specified object.
mouseExited event	The mouse is moved over the boundary leaving the specified object.

Consider the following four event handlers, based on these events:

```
void button1_mouseMoved(MouseEvent e) {
  System.out.println("A mouseMoved event occurred at "
                  + e.getX() + "," + e.getY());
}

void button1_mouseDragged(MouseEvent e) {
  System.out.println("A mouseDragged event occurred at "
                  + e.getX() + "," + e.getY());
```

12

```
}

void button1_mouseEntered(MouseEvent e) {
  System.out.println("A mouseEntered event occurred at "
                     + e.getX() + "," + e.getY());
}

void button1_mouseExited(MouseEvent e) {
  System.out.println("A mouseExited event occurred at "
                     + e.getX() + "," + e.getY());
}
```

When you run an applet with these event handlers, you'll see that for a mouse move of five pixels, five mouseMoved events are generated, one for each pixel the mouse flies over:

OUTPUT
```
A mouseMoved event occurred at 31,5
A mouseMoved event occurred at 31,6
A mouseMoved event occurred at 31,7
A mouseMoved event occurred at 31,8
A mouseMoved event occurred at 31,9
```

A mouse drag over five pixels fires off five mouseDragged events, again, one for each pixel. In addition, a mouse drag involves a mousePressed event at the beginning and a mouseReleased event at the end, so the output for a mouse drag of five pixels would look like this:

OUTPUT
```
A mousePressed event occurred at 48,7
A mouseDragged event occurred at 46,7
A mouseDragged event occurred at 45,8
A mouseDragged event occurred at 44,8
A mouseDragged event occurred at 43,8
A mouseDragged event occurred at 42,8
A mouseReleased event occurred at 42,8
```

Whenever the mouse crosses the border into an object, a mouseEntered event occurs. Conversely, a mouseExited event occurs when the mouse crosses the border leaving the object. For example, a slow vertical flyover of our sample button1 component produces this output:

OUTPUT
```
A mouseEntered event occurred at 112,78
A mouseMoved event occurred at 16,0
A mouseMoved event occurred at 16,1
A mouseMoved event occurred at 16,2
A mouseMoved event occurred at 16,2
A mouseMoved event occurred at 16,3
A mouseMoved event occurred at 16,4
A mouseMoved event occurred at 16,5
```

```
A mouseMoved event occurred at 16,6
A mouseMoved event occurred at 16,7
A mouseMoved event occurred at 16,8
A mouseMoved event occurred at 16,9
A mouseMoved event occurred at 16,10
A mouseMoved event occurred at 16,11
A mouseMoved event occurred at 16,12
A mouseMoved event occurred at 16,13
A mouseMoved event occurred at 16,14
A mouseMoved event occurred at 16,15
A mouseMoved event occurred at 16,16
A mouseMoved event occurred at 16,17
A mouseMoved event occurred at 16,18
A mouseMoved event occurred at 16,19
A mouseMoved event occurred at 16,20
A mouseMoved event occurred at 16,21
A mouseMoved event occurred at 16,22
A mouseExited event occurred at 16,23
```

And that's just for a small 23-pixel tall button—imagine all the events that occur as the mouse traverses a 400×300 applet! Note that the mouseEntered event occurred at 112,78, which is clearly not within the button's coordinate space. The entry coordinates are those of the surrounding Frame object, at the point where the mouse leaves the Frame object and enters the Button component assigned to the button1 variable. Handling mouseEntered and mouseExited events is useful if you need to change the mouse cursor when the mouse flies over a particular area of the screen, for example, or any time you need to know when the mouse has entered your applet screen's airspace.

All the previous examples assume that you are moving the mouse in a slow deliberate manner. But what happens when you quickly fly over a component? Does the system actually track the movement pixel by pixel? Here's the output produced by a speedy flyover of the same button1 component:

```
A mouseEntered event occurred at 133,89
A mouseMoved event occurred at 38,11
A mouseExited event occurred at 38,29
```

This demonstrates that the mouseMoved events are detected in discrete increments of system time, not actually pixel by pixel.

Lines Applet

Examples always help to make concepts more concrete. In this section, you'll create an applet that enables you to draw up to 10 straight lines on the screen by dragging from the startpoint to the endpoint. Figure 12.4 shows the Lines applet hard at work.

FIGURE 12.4.

The Lines applet.

With the `HandlingEvents.jpr` project open and active in the JBuilder IDE, select File | New, and double-click the Applet icon in the New page of the New dialog box. When the Applet Wizard: Step 1 of 3 dialog box appears, erase the text in the Package field, and type `Lines` in the Class field. Then click the Finish button. This will generate the skeleton `Lines.java` applet source code and a `Lines.html` file.

In the Structure pane, click on the `Applet` node (just below the `Lines` node) which will highlight the `Lines` class declaration. Insert these lines of code just below that line in the Content pane:

```
int MAXLINES = 10;
Point starts[] = new Point[MAXLINES];  // startpoints
Point ends[] = new Point[MAXLINES];    // endpoints
Point anchor = null;                   // start of current line
Point currPoint = null;                // current end of line
int currLine = 0;                      // number of lines
```

This code defines the `Lines` class instance variables:

- `starts` array holds the startpoints of lines already drawn.
- `ends` array holds the endpoints of the same lines.
- `anchor` holds the startpoint of the line being drawn, initialized to `null`.
- `currPoint` holds the current endpoint of the line being drawn, initialized to `null`.
- `currLine` holds the total number of lines drawn so far (to test against the constant `MAXLINES`), initialized to `0`.

Next, click the Design tab of the AppBrowser window, click the Properties tab of the Inspector pane, and then set the `background` property to `pink`, which generates this line of code in the `jbInit()` method:

```
this.setBackground(Color.pink);
```

The three main events in this applet are mousePressed to set the anchor point for the current line, mouseDragged to animate the current line as it's being drawn, and mouseReleased to set the endpoint for the new line. Given the instance variables that you've just created, it's merely a matter of plugging the right variables into the right methods and testing to see whether you've exceeded MAXLINES along the way.

Click on the Design tab, click on the Events tab of the Inspector pane, and then triple-click in the mousePressed event's right column to place the method stub in your source code. Add these lines of code to the body of the this_mousePressed method:

```
if (currLine <= MAXLINES)
  anchor = new Point(e.getX(), e.getY());
```

When the mouse click occurs, the this_mousePressed method sets the Point object anchor to the x and y variables to the coordinates returned by the getX() and getY() methods.

Next, you want to create an animated rubber-banding effect so that the line follows the mouse as the line is being drawn. Click the Design tab to switch back to Design mode, triple-click the mouseDragged event, and add these lines of code to the this_mouseDragged method stub:

```
if (currLine <= MAXLINES) {
  currPoint = new Point(e.getX(), e.getY());
  repaint();
}
```

The mouseDragged event contains the current point each time the mouse is dragged, so use that event handler to keep track of the current point and repaint for each movement so that the line animates.

The startpoint and endpoint for the new line don't get added to the arrays until the mouse button is released. You'll do this in the addLine() method in a moment. Click on the Design tab, triple-click on mouseReleased, and then add these lines of code to the body of the this_mouseReleased method:

```
if (currLine <= MAXLINES)
  addLine(e.getX(), e.getY());
```

When you've reached the maximum number of lines, you'll see the white line when drawing, but it won't get added to the current list of lines. Here's the addLine() method, which you can add just after the this_mouseReleased() method:

```
void addLine(int x, int y) {
  starts[currLine] = anchor;
  ends[currLine] = new Point(x, y);
  currLine++;
```

12

```
  currPoint = null;
  repaint();
}
```

This adds the anchor Point to the starts array, adds the Point object passed to the addLine() method in the mouseReleased() method to the ends array, and increments the number of lines assigned to the currLine variable. Setting the currPoint variable to null indicates that you are finished drawing the current line, so you can test this variable in the paint() method. Lastly, you call the repaint() method.

Painting the applet means drawing all the old lines whose endpoints are stored in the starts and ends arrays, as well as drawing the current line in process, whose endpoints are assigned to the anchor and currPoint variables. To show the animation of the current line, draw it in white. Here's the paint() method (add this code just below the addLine() method):

```
public void paint(Graphics g) {

  // draw existing lines
  for (int i = 0; i < currLine; i++) {
    g.drawLine(starts[i].x, starts[i].y, ends[i].x, ends[i].y);
  }

  // draw current line
  g.setColor(Color.white);
  if ((currLine <= MAXLINES) & (currPoint != null))
      g.drawLine(anchor.x, anchor.y, currPoint.x, currPoint.y);
}
```

In the paint() method, when you're drawing the current line, in addition to the test for MAXLINES, you test first to see whether the currPoint variable is assigned null. If it is, the applet isn't in the middle of drawing a line, so there's no reason to repaint. By testing the currPoint variable, you can paint only when you actually need to. By adding a few lines of code to each event handler, and writing a few basic methods, you now have a very basic drawing applet. Listing 12.2 contains the entire Lines applet code.

TYPE   **LISTING 12.2.** Lines.java.

```
1:  import java.awt.*;
2:  import java.awt.event.*;
3:  import java.applet.*;
4:  import borland.jbcl.layout.*;
5:  import borland.jbcl.control.*;
6:
7:  public class Lines extends Applet {
```

```
 8:     int MAXLINES = 10;
 9:     Point starts[] = new Point[MAXLINES]; // startpoints
10:     Point ends[] = new Point[MAXLINES];   // endpoints
11:     Point anchor = null;                  // start of current line
12:     Point currPoint = null;               // current end of line
13:     int currLine = 0;                     // number of lines
14:     XYLayout xYLayout1 = new XYLayout();
15:     boolean isStandalone = false;
16:
17:     //Construct the applet
18:     public Lines() {
19:     }
20:     //Initialize the applet
21:
22:     public void init() {
23:       try {
24:         jbInit();
25:       }
26:       catch (Exception e) {
27:         e.printStackTrace();
28:       }
29:     }
30:     //Component initialization
31:
32:     public void jbInit() throws Exception{
33:       this.setBackground(Color.pink);
34:       this.addMouseMotionListener(new
    ➥java.awt.event.MouseMotionAdapter() {
35:         public void mouseDragged(MouseEvent e) {
36:           this_mouseDragged(e);
37:         }
38:       });
39:       this.addMouseListener(new java.awt.event.MouseAdapter() {
40:         public void mousePressed(MouseEvent e) {
41:           this_mousePressed(e);
42:         }
43:         public void mouseReleased(MouseEvent e) {
44:           this_mouseReleased(e);
45:         }
46:       });
47:       xYLayout1.setWidth(400);
48:       xYLayout1.setHeight(300);
49:       this.setLayout(xYLayout1);
50:     }
51:     //Get Applet information
52:
53:     public String getAppletInfo() {
```

continues

12

LISTING 12.2. CONTINUED

```
54:        return "Applet Information";
55:      }
56:      //Get parameter info
57:
58:      public String[][] getParameterInfo() {
59:        return null;
60:      }
61:
62:      void this_mousePressed(MouseEvent e) {
63:        if (currLine <= MAXLINES)
64:          anchor = new Point(e.getX(), e.getY());
65:      }
66:
67:      void this_mouseDragged(MouseEvent e) {
68:        if (currLine <= MAXLINES) {
69:          currPoint = new Point(e.getX(), e.getY());
70:          repaint();
71:        }
72:      }
73:
74:      void this_mouseReleased(MouseEvent e) {
75:        if (currLine <= MAXLINES)
76:          addLine(e.getX(), e.getY());
77:      }
78:
79:      void addLine(int x, int y) {
80:        starts[currLine] = anchor;
81:        ends[currLine] = new Point(x, y);
82:        currLine++;
83:        currPoint = null;
84:        repaint();
85:      }
86:
87:      public void paint(Graphics g) {
88:
89:        // draw existing lines
90:        for (int i = 0; i < currLine; i++) {
91:          g.drawLine(starts[i].x, starts[i].y, ends[i].x, ends[i].y);
92:        }
93:
94:        // draw current line
95:        g.setColor(Color.white);
96:        if ((currLine <= MAXLINES) & (currPoint != null))
97:            g.drawLine(anchor.x, anchor.y, currPoint.x, currPoint.y);
98:      }
99:  }
100:  }
```

Testing Modifiers

There are three modifiers variables defined in the MouseEvent class's parent class InputEvent that apply specifically to mouse events. They are BUTTON1_MASK, BUTTON2_MASK, and BUTTON3_MASK. Because these constants are stored as int values, you can use them in a switch statement, after obtaining the value by calling the getModifiers method, also inherited from the InputEvent class:

```
switch (e.getModifiers()) {
  case BUTTON1_MASK:
    // handle left-button press
    break;
  case BUTTON2_MASK:
    // handle middle-button press
    break;
  case BUTTON3_MASK:
    // handle right-button press
    break;
}
```

If you don't explicitly handle the button press, the left mouse button will be assumed. In addition to these mouse-related constants, there are four additional constants: ALT_MASK, CTRL_MASK, META_MASK, and SHIFT_MASK. To test for these modifier keys, use the isAltDown(), isCtrlDown(), isMetaDown(), and isShiftDown() Boolean methods, respectively (also defined in the InputEvent class). These last four modifiers can also be used with keyboard events.

Key Events

Key events are generated whenever a user presses a key, or combination of keys, on the keyboard. By using key events, you can grab the values of the keys pressed to perform an action or merely to get character input from the users of your program.

Handling key events is just as easy as handling mouse events. Just create the appropriate event handler. The method stub inserted in your source code will look something like this:

```
void textField1_keyPressed(KeyEvent e) {...}
```

All the key events have as their argument an object of type KeyEvent, whose constructor method header is

```
public KeyEvent(Component source, int id, long when,
                int modifiers, int keyCode, char keyChar)
```

12

The source parameter is passed the Component object that triggered the event, such as a TextField or TextArea object. The id parameter is passed an integer data type representing the kind of mouse event that occurred (int constants: KEY_PRESSED, KEY_RELEASED, or KEY_TYPED). Each event has a unique time stamp passed to the when parameter. The modifiers parameter is passed an integer value that indicates whether one or more modifier keys (Shift, Alt, or Ctrl) were pressed at the same time that the key event occurred. The keyCode parameter is passed the key's ASCII value, whereas the keyChar parameter is passed the Unicode character corresponding to the key.

The KeyEvent class defines methods that give you access to its nonpublic instance variables:

- getKeyCode() returns the current int value of the keyCode instance variable; setKeyCode(int) sets the keyCode.

- getKeyChar() returns the current char value of the keyChar instance variable; setKeyChar(char) sets the keyChar.

- getKeyText(int) returns the String object that corresponds to the keyCode associated with int, such as ENTER or F12.

- getKeyModifiers(int) returns the String object that corresponds to the modifiers associated with int, such as Ctrl+Shift.

- getModifiers() (inherited from the InputEvent class) returns the int associated with the modifiers variable; setModifiers(int) sets the modifiers variable to int.

These methods can be used in your key event-handling methods to use the variables instantiated when a KeyEvent object is created. Just as for MouseEvent objects, JBuilder assigns KeyEvent objects to the e variable, so you can refer to these methods as e.getKeyCode() or e.getKeyChar() in your event handler code.

As you can see from these method summaries, the keyCode variable is defined as an integer. Because this value is stored as an int value, it can be used in a switch statement, just like the modifiers discussed in the "Testing Modifiers" section earlier. Table 12.1 gives a quick overview of the most often used keyCode constants.

TABLE 12.1. keyCode CONSTANTS.

Category	Constant	Corresponding Keyboard Key
Alphanumerics	VK_0 through VK_9	0 through 9
	VK_A through VK_Z	a through z
	CHAR_UNDEFINED	[Returned when there is no corresponding Unicode character]

Category	Constant	Corresponding Keyboard Key
Numeric Keypad	VK_NUM_LOCK	NumLock
	VK_ADD	+
	VK_SUBTRACT	-
	VK_MULTIPLY	*
	VK_DIVIDE	/
	VK_DECIMAL	.
	VK_NUMPAD0 through VK_NUMPAD9	0 through 9
Cursor Keypad	VK_INSERT	Insert
	VK_DELETE	Delete
	VK_HOME	Home
	VK_PAGE_UP	Page Up
	VK_PAGE_DOWN	Page Down
	VK_END	End
	VK_UP	Up [cursor arrow key]
	VK_LEFT	Left [cursor arrow key]
	VK_DOWN	Down [cursor arrow key]
	VK_RIGHT	Right [cursor arrow key]
Function Keys	VK_ESCAPE	Esc
	VK_F1 through VK_F12	F1 through F12
	VK_PRINTSCREEN	Print Screen/SysRq
	VK_SCROLL_LOCK	Scroll Lock
	VK_PAUSE	Pause/Break
	VK_ALT	Alt
	VK_BACK_SLASH	\
	VK_BACK_SPACE	Backspace
	VK_CAPS_LOCK	Caps Lock
	VK_ENTER	Enter
	VK_META	Meta
	VK_SHIFT	Shift
	VK_SLASH	/
	VK_SPACE	Spacebar
	VK_TAB	Tab
	VK_UNDEFINED	[Returned by keyTyped event]

12

For a full list including symbol and punctuation constants, refer to the
`java.awt.event.KeyEvent` topic in the Java Reference help file.

Handling Key Events

To capture keypresses, there are three events, analogous to those for mouse clicks: the
`keyPressed`, `keyReleased`, and `keyTyped` events. Here is a trio of simple event handlers
which handle events that happen to a `TextArea` object. The event handlers print out the
event that occurred and the key that was pressed for each event, using the `KeyEvent`
object's `getKeyCode()` and `getKeyText()` methods:

```
void textArea1_keyPressed(KeyEvent e) {
  System.out.println("A keyPressed event occurred.");
  System.out.println("Keyboard Key: " + e.getKeyText(e.getKeyCode()));
}

void textArea1_keyReleased(KeyEvent e) {
  System.out.println("A keyReleased event occurred.");
  System.out.println("Keyboard Key: " + e.getKeyText(e.getKeyCode()));
}

void textArea1_keyTyped(KeyEvent e) {
  System.out.println("A keyTyped event occurred.");
  System.out.println("Keyboard Key: " + e.getKeyText(e.getKeyCode()));
}
```

If you try this out, you'll see that each time you press a character key, all three events are
generated: first a `keyPressed` event, followed by a `keyTyped` event, and finally a
`keyReleased` event:

```
A keyPressed event occurred.
Keyboard Key: A
A keyTyped event occurred.
Keyboard Key: Unknown keyCode: 0x0
A keyReleased event occurred.
Keyboard Key: A
```

The keyTyped event returns `VK_UNDEFINED` to the `getKeyCode()` method, which translates
as "Unknown keyCode: 0x0" when the `getKeyText()` method is called. This is because
the `keyTyped` event is used simply to say whether an alphanumeric key has been typed. If
you don't care what the alphanumeric key itself is, you can simply handle the `keyTyped`
event, and you're done.

If pressing a key always generates both a `keyPressed` and a `keyReleased` event, why have two separate events? This is so that you can detect the order of keys pressed in multiple key combinations. Say, for example, you wanted to indent a block of text in a text editor applet by allowing the user to use the key combination Ctrl+B+I. However, your applet requires that the Ctrl key remain pressed while the B and I keys are pressed in sequence because Ctrl+B by itself performs a different action. Assuming a block of text was selected in the applet, the sequence would be as follows:

1. A `keyPressed` event for the Ctrl key

2. A `keyPressed` event for the B key

3. A `keyReleased` event for the B key

4. A `keyPressed` event for the I key

5. A `keyReleased` event for the I key

6. A `keyReleased` event for the Ctrl key

If those six events don't happen in that sequence, the indent would not be performed. Here's what happens when you type the following sequence of keys in a program containing our test methods:

TYPE   Up+Down+Enter

OUTPUT
```
A keyPressed event occurred.
Keyboard Key: Up
A keyReleased event occurred.
Keyboard Key: Up
A keyPressed event occurred.
Keyboard Key: Down
A keyReleased event occurred.
Keyboard Key: Down
A keyPressed event occurred.
Keyboard Key: Enter
A keyTyped event occurred.
Keyboard Key: Unknown keyCode: 0x0
A keyReleased event occurred.
Keyboard Key: Enter
```

This demonstrates that although all alphanumeric keys fire a `keyTyped` event, not all keypresses do so. For example, the Up and Down keys do not, but the Enter key does. So be careful about relying on `keyTyped` events when handling nonalphabetic keypresses.

12

KeyTest Applet

This section examines an applet that deals with keyboard events. This applet enables you
to type a character and display that character in the center of the applet's window. You
can then move that character around on the screen by using the arrow cursor keys.
Typing another character at any time restarts the cycle.

This applet is actually less complicated than other applets you've built previously. This
one only requires a `keyPressed` event handler, a `paint()` method, two additions to the
`init` method, and two property settings.

With the `HandlingEvents.jpr` project open and active in the JBuilder IDE, select File |
New, and double-click the Applet icon in the New page of the New dialog box. When the
Applet Wizard: Step 1 of 3 dialog box appears, erase the text in the Package field, and
type `KeyTest` in the Class field. Then click the Finish button. This generates the skeleton
`KeyTest.java` applet and a `KeyTest.html` file. Insert these lines of code just below the
`KeyTest` class declaration:

```
char currKey = 'A';
int currX;
int currY;
```

This code defines the `KeyTest` class instance variables: `currKey` to track when the character changes (initialized to `A`), and `currX` and `currY` for the character's `x,y` coordinate.

Next, click on the Design tab of the AppBrowser window, click on the Properties tab in
the Inspector pane, and set the `background` property to `Green`. Double-click on the `font`
property, and then click on its ellipses button to display the font dialog box (see Figure
12.5).

FIGURE 12.5.

The font dialog box.

Select `Helvetica`, `Bold`, and `36`, and then click OK. These property settings generate the
following two lines of code in the `jbInit()` method:

```
this.setFont(new Font("Helvetica", 1, 36));
this.setBackground(Color.green);
```

You also need to add this next line of code to the very end of the jbInit() method, so that the keypresses will be intercepted by your applet:

```
this.requestFocus();
```

Click on the Source tab to return to Project Browser mode, and set the beginning position for the character (approximately the middle of the screen) by adding these lines to the end of the init() method:

```
currX = (getSize().width / 2);
currY = (getSize().height / 2);
```

Because this applet's behavior is based on keyboard input, the keyPressed event handler is where most of the work of the applet takes place. Click on the Design tab, click on the Events tab, and then triple-click the keyPressed event to insert the this_keyPressed method stub and then add these lines of code to it:

```
switch (e.getKeyCode()) {
  case e.VK_UP:
    currY -= 5;
    break;
  case e.VK_DOWN:
    currY += 5;
    break;
  case e.VK_LEFT:
    currX -= 5;
    break;
  case e.VK_RIGHT:
    currX += 5;
    break;
  default:
    currKey = e.getKeyChar();
}
repaint();
```

This moves the character's position five pixels each time an arrow key is pressed and changes the character if any other key is pressed, ignoring any keys that are not characters or arrow keys. All that's left now is to create the paint() method, which is fairly trivial:

```
public void paint(Graphics g) {
  g.drawString(String.valueOf(currKey), currX, currY);
}
```

It just paints the current character at the current position. Listing 12.3 contains the entire KeyTest applet code.

12

TYPE   **LISTING 12.3.** KeyTest.java.

```
1:   import java.awt.*;
2:   import java.awt.event.*;
3:   import java.applet.*;
4:   import borland.jbcl.layout.*;
5:   import borland.jbcl.control.*;
6:
7:   public class KeyTest extends Applet {
8:     char currKey = 'A';
9:     int currX;
10:    int currY;
11:    XYLayout xYLayout1 = new XYLayout();
12:    boolean isStandalone = false;
13:
14:    //Construct the applet
15:
16:    public KeyTest() {
17:    }
18:    //Initialize the applet
19:
20:    public void init() {
21:      try {
22:        jbInit();
23:      }
24:      catch (Exception e) {
25:        e.printStackTrace();
26:      }
27:      currX = (getSize().width / 2);
28:      currY = (getSize().height / 2);
29:    }
30:    //Component initialization
31:
32:    private void jbInit() throws Exception{
33:      this.setFont(new Font("Helvetica", 1, 36));
34:      this.addKeyListener(new java.awt.event.KeyAdapter() {
35:        public void keyPressed(KeyEvent e) {
36:          this_keyPressed(e);
37:        }
38:      });
39:      this.setBackground(Color.green);
34:      xYLayout1.setWidth(400);
35:      xYLayout1.setHeight(300);
36:      this.setLayout(xYLayout1);
37:      this.requestFocus();
38:    }
39:    //Get Applet information
40:
41:    public String getAppletInfo() {
42:      return "Applet Information";
```

```
43:    }
44:    //Get parameter info
45:
46:    public String[][] getParameterInfo() {
47:      return null;
48:    }
49:
50:    void this_keyPressed(KeyEvent e) {
51:      switch (e.getKeyCode()) {
52:        case e.VK_UP:
53:          currY -= 5;
54:          break;
55:        case e.VK_DOWN:
56:          currY += 5;
57:          break;
58:        case e.VK_LEFT:
59:          currX -= 5;
60:          break;
61:        case e.VK_RIGHT:
62:          currX += 5;
63:          break;
64:        default:
65:          currKey = e.getKeyChar();
66:      }
67:      repaint();
68:    }
69:
70:    public void paint(Graphics g) {
71:      g.drawString(String.valueOf(currKey), currX, currY);
72:    }
73:  }
```

12

Standard Events

In addition to keyboard and mouse events, the Abstract Windowing Toolkit has various other standard events to which you can respond in your interface. Most of the event handlers for these events can be set through the Events tab of the Inspector pane, just as you did for the mouse and keyboard events. Figure 12.6 shows a partial hierarchy of the java.awt.AWTEvent class, corresponding to the categories these events fall into.

As you can see, the InputEvent subclasses form only a small part of the AWTEvent class hierarchy. In each subsection that follows, you'll see which event handlers in JBuilder correspond to the events in each of these subclass categories. The methods defined in these subclasses are also summarized, but keep in mind that each subclass also inherits methods from its superclass. As before, the event handler generated by JBuilder assigns the event object to the e variable; so, for example, you can refer to the getModifiers() method as e.getModifiers() in your event handler.

FIGURE 12.6.

Selected AWTEvent *sub-classes.*

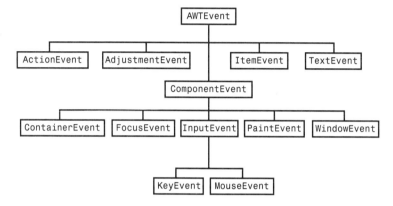

> **Tip**
>
> For full coverage of a class and its methods, be sure to explore the class documentation in the Java Reference help file, and use the links in the inheritance tree at the top of the help topic to further explore its superclasses and their method definitions.

Action Events

User interface components produce a special type of event known as an action event. In JBuilder, to intercept an action by any user interface component, you define the actionPerformed event handler. Here's what the method header for an actionPerformed event handler would look like for a component assigned to the myButton variable:

```
void myButton_actionPerformed(ActionEvent e) {...}
```

These event handlers take as their argument an ActionEvent object. Here's its constructor method header:

```
public ActionEvent(Object source, int id,
                   String command, int modifiers)
```

The source parameter is passed the user interface component object that triggered the event. The id parameter is passed an integer that defines the type of action that was performed (int constant: ACTION_PERFORMED). The modifiers parameter takes an integer that indicates whether one or more modifier keys were also pressed when the event occurred. The command parameter is passed the value of the component's actionCommand property.

The ActionEvent object's methods include the following:

- getActionCommand() returns the String value of the actionCommand property.
- getModifiers() returns the int associated with the modifiers variable.

Say you want to create a simple applet that has six buttons labeled with the colors of the rainbow. You could create an event handler for each button individually; however, in this example you'll create the actionPerformed() event handler method for the first button and then reuse it for the other five buttons. In the event handler, the background color of the applet is changed based on which button was clicked.

Add a new applet to today's project named ActionTest. In Design mode, with this(XYLayout) selected in the Structure pane, change the background property to Gray, the layout property to FlowLayout, and then add six Button components. Select flowLayout1 in the Structure pane and enter 4 for the hgap property and enter 2 for the vgap property.

Select button1, and change its <name> property to redBtn and its label property to Red. Note that as soon as you press Enter to complete the label property change, the actionCommand property also changes to Red. By default, the actionCommand for a Button component is the same as its label property. This makes it easy to test which button was pressed using the getActionCommand() method later.

Select each button in turn, and change its <name> and label properties as shown in Table 12.2. Figure 12.7 shows the ActionTest applet user interface after these changes have been made.

TABLE 12.2. PROPERTY CHANGES FOR ACTIONTEST APPLET.

Component	<name> property	label property
button1	redBtn	Red
button2	orangeBtn	Orange
button3	yellowBtn	Yellow
button4	greenBtn	Green
button5	blueBtn	Blue
button6	purpleBtn	Purple

12

FIGURE 12.7.

The ActionTest applet displays several buttons for users to interact with.

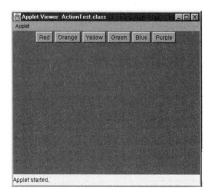

To create the event handler for these six buttons, select the redBtn component, and then click on the Events tab. If you triple-click to create a handler now, it would be named redBtn_actionPerformed, based on the selected component. But you want to create a handler that will deal with all six buttons—a shared handler—so it's a good idea to name it more generically. To do so, click once on the actionPerformed event, which inserts redBtn_actionPerformed as the tentative method name. Press Home to move the cursor to the beginning of the method name, and change red to color. Now, double-click to create the method stub in the source code for your event handler.

In this event handler, you want to know which button caused the event to occur. By testing the String object returned by the getActionCommand() method, you can set the applet's background to the appropriate color and then call the repaint() method. Because the getActionCommand method returns a String object and not a primitive type, you'll have to use a set of nested if-else statements rather than a switch. Here's the body of the colorBtn_actionPerformed() event handler method:

```
String btnColor = e.getActionCommand();
if (btnColor.equals("Red"))
  this.setBackground(Color.red);
else if (btnColor.equals("Orange"))
  this.setBackground(Color.orange);
else if (btnColor.equals("Yellow"))
  this.setBackground(Color.yellow);
else if (btnColor.equals("Green"))
  this.setBackground(Color.green);
else if (btnColor.equals("Blue"))
  this.setBackground(Color.blue);
else if (btnColor.equals("Purple"))
  this.setBackground(Color.magenta);
repaint();
```

Well, magenta is as close as you're going to get to purple! Remember that because you're dealing with a String object, you have to use the equals() method for object comparison. Now, all that's left is to hook up the other buttons to this same event handler. Click on each of the five remaining button components in the Structure pane in turn, and set the actionPerformed event handler to colorBtn_actionPerformed. Every time you click one of the six color buttons in this applet, this shared event handler will be executed, and the applet's drawing space will change color. Listing 12.4 shows the code listing for the entire ActionTest applet.

TYPE **LISTING 12.4.** ActionTest.java.

```
 1: import java.awt.*;
 2: import java.awt.event.*;
 3: import java.applet.*;
 4: import borland.jbcl.layout.*;
 5: import borland.jbcl.control.*;
 6:
 7: public class ActionTest extends Applet {
 8:   boolean isStandalone = false;
 9:   FlowLayout flowLayout1 = new FlowLayout();
10:   Button redBtn = new Button();
11:   Button orangeBtn = new Button();
12:   Button yellowBtn = new Button();
13:   Button greenBtn = new Button();
14:   Button blueBtn = new Button();
15:   Button purpleBtn = new Button();
16:
17:   //Construct the applet
18:
19:   public ActionTest() {
20:   }
21:   //Initialize the applet
22:
23:   public void init() {
24:   try {
25:     jbInit();
26:   }
27:   catch (Exception e) {
28:     e.printStackTrace();
29:   }
30:   //Component initialization
31:
32:   private void jbInit() throws Exception{
33:     this.setBackground(Color.gray);
34:     flowLayout1.setHgap(4);
35:     flowLayout1.setVgap(2);
36:     redBtn.setLabel("Red");
37:     redBtn.addActionListener(new java.awt.event.ActionListener() {
```

continues

LISTING **12.4.** CONTINUED

```
38:          public void actionPerformed(ActionEvent e) {
39:            colorBtn_actionPerformed(e);
40:          }
41:        });
42:        orangeBtn.setLabel("Orange");
43:        orangeBtn.addActionListener(new java.awt.event.ActionListener() {
44:          public void actionPerformed(ActionEvent e) {
45:            colorBtn_actionPerformed(e);
46:          }
47:        });
48:        yellowBtn.setLabel("Yellow");
49:        yellowBtn.addActionListener(new java.awt.event.ActionListener() {
50:          public void actionPerformed(ActionEvent e) {
51:            colorBtn_actionPerformed(e);
52:          }
53:        });
54:        greenBtn.setLabel("Green");
55:        greenBtn.addActionListener(new java.awt.event.ActionListener() {
56:          public void actionPerformed(ActionEvent e) {
57:            colorBtn_actionPerformed(e);
58:          }
59:        });
60:        blueBtn.setLabel("Blue");
61:        blueBtn.addActionListener(new java.awt.event.ActionListener() {
62:          public void actionPerformed(ActionEvent e) {
63:            colorBtn_actionPerformed(e);
64:          }
65:        });
66:        purpleBtn.setLabel("Purple");
67:        purpleBtn.addActionListener(new java.awt.event.ActionListener() {
68:          public void actionPerformed(ActionEvent e) {
69:            colorBtn_actionPerformed(e);
70:          }
71:        });
72:        this.setLayout(flowLayout1);
73:        this.add(redBtn, null);
74:        this.add(orangeBtn, null);
75:        this.add(yellowBtn, null);
76:        this.add(greenBtn, null);
77:        this.add(blueBtn, null);
78:        this.add(purpleBtn, null);
79:      }
80:      //Get Applet information
81:
```

```
82:     public String getAppletInfo() {
83:       return "Applet Information";
84:     }
85:     //Get parameter info
86:
87:     public String[][] getParameterInfo() {
88:       return null;
89:     }
90:
91:     void colorBtn_actionPerformed(ActionEvent e) {
92:       String btnColor = e.getActionCommand();
93:       if (btnColor.equals("Red"))
94:         this.setBackground(Color.red);
95:       else if (btnColor.equals("Orange"))
96:         this.setBackground(Color.orange);
97:       else if (btnColor.equals("Yellow"))
98:         this.setBackground(Color.yellow);
99:       else if (btnColor.equals("Green"))
100:        this.setBackground(Color.green);
101:      else if (btnColor.equals("Blue"))
102:        this.setBackground(Color.blue);
103:      else if (btnColor.equals("Purple"))
104:        this.setBackground(Color.magenta);
105:      repaint();
106:    }
107:  }
```

MenuBar and PopupMenu components also use the label property to set the default
actionCommand value. Be sure to check the Java Reference documentation for the details
on actionCommand values for other Abstract Windowing Toolkit components.

Adjustment Events

The adjustmentValueChanged event is defined in the Abstract Windowing Toolkit for
increment and decrement adjustments for adjustable objects, such as Scrollbar. The
method header for an adjustmentValueChanged event handler might look like this:

```
void scrollbar1_adjustmentValueChanged(AdjustmentEvent e) {...}
```

These event handlers take as their argument an AdjustmentEvent object. Here's its constructor method header:

```
public AdjustmentEvent(Adjustable source, int id,
                       int type, int value)
```

The source parameter takes the Adjustable object that triggered the event. The id parameter takes an integer value that indicates the type of adjustment event that occurred
(int constant: ADJUSTMENT_VALUE_CHANGED). The type parameter is passed an integer

value which indicates the kind of adjustment that caused the event, one of five constants: UNIT_INCREMENT, UNIT_DECREMENT, BLOCK_INCREMENT, BLOCK_DECREMENT, or TRACK. (Unit adjustments are triggered by arrow clicks, block adjustments by shaft clicks, and track adjustments by moving the thumb.) The value parameter takes an integer representing the number of units of the adjustment.

The AdjustmentEvent object's methods include the following:

- getAdjustable() returns the Adjustable object that caused the event.
- getValue() returns the int value of the adjustment.
- getAdjustmentType() returns the int value of the constant representing the type of adjustment (UNIT_INCREMENT, UNIT_DECREMENT, BLOCK_INCREMENT, BLOCK_DECREMENT, or TRACK).

To see this event in action, create an applet named ScrollTest. Add a Label and a Scrollbar, and then change properties as indicated in Table 12.3.

TABLE 12.3. PROPERTY CHANGES FOR THE SCROLLTEST APPLET.

Component	Property	Value(s)	Notes
label1	text	0	
label1	font	TimesRoman, Bold, 24	Use dialog
label1	alignment	2	Right aligned
label1	<name>	valueLbl	
scrollbar1	orientation	0	Horizontal
scrollbar1	<name>	valueSbar	
this(XYLayout)	background	Cyan	

When you're done setting the properties, click on valueSbar, click on the Events tab, and triple-click the adjustmentValueChanged event. Then add the following lines to the method stub in your source code:

```
int v = e.getValue();
valueSbar.setValue(v);
valueLbl.setText(String.valueOf(v));
```

The first line gets the value of the adjustment from the AdjustmentEvent object. The second line then sets the value property of the valueSbar component. The third sets the text of the valueLbl to String representation of that value. When you run the ScrollTest applet, the current value of the scrollbar will be reflected in the valueLbl component, as shown in Figure 12.8.

FIGURE 12.8.

The ScrollTest applet.

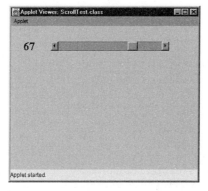

The interesting thing to note about this applet is that because the thumb is 10 units wide, the value can't actually go all the way up to the maximum of 100. This shows that the value is actually designated by the trailing edge of the thumb, so you need to take that into account when designing such scrollbars. The complete source code for ScrollTest is shown in Listing 12.5.

TYPE   **LISTING 12.5.** ScrollTest.java.

```
 1: import java.awt.*;
 2: import java.awt.event.*;
 3: import java.applet.*;
 4: import borland.jbcl.layout.*;
 5: import borland.jbcl.control.*;
 6:
 7: public class ScrollTest extends Applet {
 8:    XYLayout xYLayout1 = new XYLayout();
 9:    boolean isStandalone = false;
10:    Label valueLbl = new Label();
11:    Scrollbar valueSbar = new Scrollbar();
12:
13:    //Construct the applet
14:
15:    public ScrollTest() {
16:    }
17: //Initialize the applet
18:
19:    public void init() {
20:      try {
21:      jbInit();
22:      }
23:      catch (Exception e) {
```

continues

12

LISTING 12.5. CONTINUED

```
24:      e.printStackTrace();
25:      }
26:   }
27: //Component initialization
28:
29:   private void jbInit() throws Exception {
30:      this.setBackground(Color.cyan);
31:      xYLayout1.setWidth(400);
32:      xYLayout1.setHeight(300);
33:      valueSbar.setOrientation(0);
34:      valueSbar.addAdjustmentListener(new
   ➥java.awt.event.AdjustmentListener() {
35:         public void adjustmentValueChanged(AdjustmentEvent e) {
36:            valueSbar_adjustmentValueChanged(e);
37:         }
38:      });
39:      valueLbl.setFont(new Font("TimesRoman", 1, 24));
40:      valueLbl.setAlignment(2);
41:      valueLbl.setText("0");
42:      this.setLayout(xYLayout1);
43:      this.add(valueLbl, new XYConstraints(192, 123, -1, -1));
44:      this.add(valueSbar, new XYConstraints(215, 194, -1, -1));
45:   }
46: //Get Applet information
47:
48:   public String getAppletInfo() {
49:      return "Applet Information";
50:   }
51: //Get parameter info
52:
53:   public String[][] getParameterInfo() {
54:      return null;
55:   }
56:
57:   void valueSbar_adjustmentValueChanged(AdjustmentEvent e) {
58:      int v = e.getValue();
59:      valueSbar.setValue(v);
60:      valueLbl.setText(String.valueOf(v));
61:   }
```

Component Events

Component events are defined in the Abstract Windowing Toolkit so that you can tell whether a component has been hidden, shown, moved, or resized. The Abstract Windowing Toolkit automatically handles the moving, resizing, and display of components, but there are times when you might want to create additional functionality based on these events. The ComponentEvent class constructor is simple:

```
public ComponentEvent(Component source, int id)
```

Here, the source parameter is passed the source Component object of the event, and the id parameter is passed an integer identifying the event (int constants: COMPONENT_ HIDDEN, COMPONENT_MOVED, COMPONENT_RESIZED, COMPONENT_SHOWN). The ComponentEvent class has a getComponent() method that returns the object t hat created the event (the value passed to the source parameter).

All components have these four events listed on their Events page which are self-explanatory: the componentHidden, componentMoved, componentResized, and componentShown events, which correspond to the id parameter constants of the ComponentEvent object. When you create an event handler method in your source code, the method signature will look something like this:

```
void textarea1_ComponentResized(ComponentEvent e) {...}
```

So, as before, you can access ComponentEvent object methods (including inherited methods by using the e.*methodName* syntax.

Focus Events

Focus events are defined in the Abstract Windowing Toolkit so that you can tell whether a component has gained focus (is the active component) or lost focus (becomes inactive). Here is the FocusEvent class constructor:

```
public FocusEvent(Component source, int id,
                  boolean temporary)
```

The source parameter is passed the Component object that created the event, and the id parameter is passed an integer value that identifies the event (int constants: FOCUS_GAINED and FOCUS_LOST). In addition, the FocusEvent class constructor has a temporary parameter that is passed true or false depending on whether the FocusEvent object was created due to a temporary change. Temporary changes occur when components get momentary focus during other operations. Permanent focus is gained, for example, when a user tabs to a component in a dialog box.

Most components list the focusGained and focusLost events on their Events page, which correspond to the id constants for the FocusEvent object. When you create an event handler method in your source code, the method signature might look like this:

```
void checkbox1_focusGained(FocusEvent e) {...}
```

12

Once again, you can access ComponentEvent class methods (including inherited methods) by using the e.*methodName* syntax.

Item Events

The itemStateChanged event is defined in the Abstract Windowing Toolkit to indicate whether an object is selected, such as items in a List or Choice component. The method header for a List component's itemStateChanged event handler would be

```
void list1_ itemStateChanged(ItemEvent e) {...}
```

These event handlers take as their argument an ItemEvent object. Here's its constructor method header:

```
public ItemEvent(ItemSelectable source, int id,
                 Object item, int stateChange)
```

The source parameter is passed the ItemSelectable object that triggered the event. The id parameter is passed an int constant, ITEM_STATE_CHANGED, which corresponds to the identity of the particular itemStateChanged event. The item parameter is passed the object that caused the event by being selected or deselected. The stateChange parameter is passed one of two integer constants: SELECTED or DESELECTED. The ItemEvent object's methods include the following:

- getItemSelectable() returns the ItemSelectable component (source) that caused the event.
- getItem() returns the Object that was selected or deselected.
- getStateChange() returns the int value of the constant representing the current state (SELECTED, or DESELECTED).

Method access is via the e.*methodName* syntax.

Window Events

Window events let you monitor the current state of your interface's Frame object. Here is the WindowEvent class constructor:

```
public WindowEvent(Window source, int id)
```

The source parameter is passed the Window object where the event originated, and the id parameter is passed one of the following integer constants:

- WINDOW_ACTIVATED happens when the window gains focus.
- WINDOW_CLOSED occurs when the window has been closed due to a call to hide() or destroy().

- WINDOW_CLOSING occurs by selecting "Quit" from the window's system menu.
- WINDOW_DEACTIVATED happens when the window loses focus.
- WINDOW_DEICONIFIED happens when the window is restored.
- WINDOW_ICONIFIED happens when the window is minimized.
- WINDOW_OPENED occurs the first time a window becomes visible.

These constants correspond to the Frame object events, windowActivated, windowClosed, windowClosing, windowDeactivated, windowDeiconified, windowIconified, and windowOpened. The WindowEvent class defines a getWindow() method that returns the Window object assigned to the source instance variable.

Summary

Handling events in JBuilder is easy, particularly because the Events tab of the Inspector pane lists all the relevant events for any selected component. Triple-click on the event, and a method stub is inserted for you, ready for you to add your event-handling code. With the event handler method in place, your program automatically intercepts and handles the event using the appropriate method.

All events in the Abstract Windowing Toolkit generate an instance of one of the AWTEvent class's descendants, such as a MouseEvent object for mouse events and an AdjustmentEvent object for scrollbar adjustment events. Each object has accessor methods that enable you to obtain information about the event, such as x,y coordinate or which key was pressed. For mouse and key events, you can also test for modifier keys such as which button on the mouse was pressed or which of the Ctrl, Alt, Meta, or Shift keys were being held down when the event occurred.

You also learned about the other Abstract Windowing Toolkit standard event categories:

- Action
- Adjustment
- Component
- Focus
- Item
- Window

Each category defines additional methods and constants that enable you to obtain information about a wide variety of events in your Java programs. Tomorrow, you'll learn about an unanticipated type of event, called an exception, and how to handle those occurrences.

12

Q&A

Q **In the Lines applet, the startpoint and endpoint coordinates are stored in arrays, which have a limited size. How can I modify this applet so that it will draw an unlimited number of lines?**

A You can use the `Vector` class. The `Vector` class, part of the `java.util` package, implements an array that is automatically growable—sort of like linked lists in other languages. The disadvantage of the `Vector` class is that it requires its members to be objects. This means you have to cast `int` values to `Integer` objects to add them to the `Vector` object and then extract their values from the `Integer` objects to treat them as `int` values once again. You can access and change elements encapsulated by a `Vector` object easily through its methods. If you need an array of indeterminate size, consider using the `Vector` class.

Q **What's a Meta key?**

A The Meta key is popular in UNIX systems and is mapped to Alt on most keyboards. Because Alt, Shift, and Ctrl are much more widespread, it's probably a good idea to base your interfaces on those modifier keys instead, if you can.

Workshop

The Workshop provides two ways for you to affirm what you've learned in this chapter. The Quiz section poses questions to help you solidify your understanding of the material covered. You can find answers to the quiz questions in Appendix A, "Answers to Quiz Questions." The Exercises section provides you with experience in using what you have learned. Try to work through all these before continuing to the next day.

Quiz

1. How do you create an event handler in the JBuilder IDE?

2. True or False? A `MouseClicked` event object is not generated when the mouse button is pressed and released, if a `MouseDragged` event object occurred in between.

3. For what event does the `getKeyCode()` method return the `VK_UNDEFINED` integer constant?

4. What do you do to share an event handler method?

5. For what event would you create a handler to detect and do something whenever a particular component receives focus?

6. What class is the superclass for all the Abstract Windowing Toolkit events?

Exercises

1. Take some of the sample applets you created today and add other components to them so you can try out all the event handlers listed in their Events pages. Experiment with shared handlers.

2. Explore the Java Reference for the `java.awt.event` package. Start with the topic for a particular type of event listed, and then work your way up the hierarchy, noting which methods are defined or overridden in the subclass and which methods are inherited as defined in the superclasses.

12

Day 13

Exception Handling

Sometimes, even in debugged and tested applications, things can go wrong that are beyond the control of the program. Problems can be caused by the environment in which your program is being run, or the user will do something your program didn't anticipate. Whatever the problem, a well-designed application should be capable of either handling the unexpected or at least exiting gracefully.

NEW TERM An *exception* is an event or condition that, if it occurs, breaks the normal flow of program execution.

Before exception handling was added to programming languages, programmers were forced to try to anticipate every type of possible user error and environmental condition. This led to the ubiquitous "error-handling function," which looked something like this:

```
int status = callSomethingThatAlmostAlwaysWorks();
if (status == ABNORMAL_RETURN_VALUE) {
  . . . // something unusual happened, handle it
  switch(someGlobalErrorIndicator) {
    . . . // handle potential problem #1
    . . . // handle potential problem #2
```

```
    . . .    // handle potential problem #3
    . . .
    . . .    // handle potential problem #n
  }
  else {
    . . .    // all is well, go your merry way
  }
}
```

This could be a rather lengthy section of code, depending on how thorough the developers felt they needed to be. Aside from having to do a lot of work to handle what was probably the rare case, it also plunked down the error-handling logic right in the middle of the code in which the error was produced, creating readability and maintainability problems. Handling multiple errors was difficult, if not impossible. Many times, the only thing to be done was to attempt to shut down the program and make the user reload the program and start over.

With exception handling, most of this has been solved. Exceptions allow your program to deal with the exceptional case easily, and many times, your program can execute alternate code instead of simply shutting down. The error-handling logic is segregated into an exception-handling method and is replaced in your code by a simple method call, improving readability and maintainability. Multiple errors can be dealt with efficiently, and you have the opportunity to do cleanup tasks before closing down.

Today, you'll learn about exceptions in Java, which are instances of the class `Throwable` (or any of its subclasses):

- Declaring exceptions when you are expecting one, with the `throws` keyword
- Handling them in your code, using the `try` and `catch` keywords
- Using the `throw` keyword to create new exceptions
- Cleaning up afterward with the `finally` keyword
- Creating custom exception subclasses by extending the `Throwable` class
- What limitations are created by exceptions and how they increase your program's robustness
- The differences between runtime errors and exceptions

Exceptions by Design

When you begin to build complex programs in Java, you will discover that after designing the classes and interfaces, and their method descriptions, you still have not defined all the behaviors of your objects. After all, an interface describes the normal way to use an object and doesn't include any strange, exceptional cases. In many systems, the documentation takes care of this problem by explicitly listing the distinguished values used in error-handling methods, like the example in today's introduction. Because the system knows nothing about these methods, it cannot check them for consistency. In fact, the compiler can do nothing at all to help you with these exceptional conditions, in contrast to the helpful warnings and errors it produces if a method defined in the language is used incorrectly.

More important, you have not captured in your design this crucial aspect of your program. Instead, you are forced to make up a way to describe it in the documentation and hope you have not made any mistakes when you implemented it. What's worse, this results in not having a standard way of handling these exceptional cases, which means that each Java programmer would have to make up his own way of describing the same circumstances. Clearly, you need some uniform way of declaring the intentions of classes and methods with respect to these exceptional conditions.

Think of a method's description as a contract between the designer of that method (or class) and the caller of the method. Usually, this description tells the types of a method's arguments, what it returns, and the general semantics of what it normally does. It can now also notify the caller, as well, what abnormal things it can do. Just like when a method is designed to return a value of a certain type, this helps to make explicit all the places where exceptional conditions should be handled in your program, making large-scale design easier.

Because exceptions are instances of classes, they can be put into a hierarchy that naturally describes the relationships among different types of exceptions. If you look at the class hierarchy in the Help (Java Reference), you will see that the Throwable class actually has two large hierarchies of classes beneath it, called Error and Exception. These hierarchies embody the rich set of relationships that exist between exceptions and errors in the Java runtime environment.

Understanding the throws Keyword

When you know that a particular kind of error or exception can occur in your method, you are supposed to either handle it yourself or explicitly warn potential callers (classes or other methods that might call your method) about the possibility through the throws clause. Here is a brief example of using the throws keyword:

```
public class MyFileClass {
  . . .
  public void aClassyMethod() throws EOFException,
                              FileNotFoundException {
    FileInputStream aFIS = new FileInputStream("IDoNotExist.txt");
```

```
    . . .
  }
}
```

Here, you notify the compiler (and readers of your code) that the code in the aClassyMethod() method might result in the creation (throwing) of predefined Java exception objects named EOFException and FileNotFoundException. For example, the FileNotFoundException object is required because this method attempts to create a new FileInputStream object by naming a particular file, which might or might not exist. By declaring that this method throws FileNotFoundException, you tell the compiler that your method uses code that might throw that type of exception object.

When code is written that calls the aClassyMethod method, this mechanism ensures that the code will either catch the exception, or it, too, throws the exception. If it does not, the compiler will complain that nothing is handling the exception that the code is liable to throw.

Because exceptions are objects in a class hierarchy, you can also group exceptions by their superclasses in throws clauses. In the previous example, because both EOFException and FileNotFoundException are subclasses of the IOException class, you could have done this:

```
public void aClassyMethod() throws IOException {...}
```

and covered both types of exceptions at once with their IOException superclass. However, this prevents you from handling each type of exception discretely in the code that called the aClassyMethod() class.

Understanding `Error` and `RuntimeException`

Not all errors and exceptions must be listed; instances of either class Error or RuntimeException (or their subclasses) do not have to be listed in your throws clause. They get special treatment because they can occur anywhere within a Java program and are usually conditions that your code did not cause. One good example is the OutOfMemoryError exception object, which can happen anywhere, at any time, and for any number of reasons.

> **Note**
>
> You can choose to list these errors and runtime exceptions in your throws clause if you want, but callers of your methods will not be forced to deal with them; only non-runtime exceptions *must* be handled.
>
> Whenever you see the word "exception" by itself, it almost always means "exception or error"—that is, an instance of the Throwable class. The previous discussion makes it clear that the Exception and Error classes actually form two separate hierarchies, but except for the throws clause rule, they act exactly the same.

Bearing in mind the exemption for errors and runtime exceptions, there are six top-level types of exceptions in the java.lang package that must be listed in a throws clause:

- java.lang.ClassNotFoundException
- java.lang.CloneNotSupportedException
- java.lang.IllegalAccessException
- java.lang.InstantiationException
- java.lang.InterruptedException
- java.lang.NoSuchMethodException

There are exceptions declared in other packages as well. In the java.io package, for example, the IOException class is defined, whose exception subclasses belong to several different packages:

- java.io.EOFException
- java.io.FileNotFoundException
- java.io.InterruptedIOException
- java.net.MalformedURLException
- java.net.ProtocolException
- java.net.SocketException
- java.net.UnknownHostException
- java.net.UnknownServiceException
- java.lang.UTFDataFormatException

Also, in the java.awt package, the AWTException class is defined. Any time you use a Java method that is defined as throwing one of these exceptions, you must include that exception in the throws clause of your method.

13

The Java Class Library uses exceptions everywhere and to good effect. If you examine the detailed API documentation in the JBuilder Help (Java Reference), you'll see that many of the methods in the library have throws clauses, and some even document (when they believe it will clarify the situation) when they might throw one of the implicit errors or runtime exceptions. This is just a nicety on the documenter's part because you are not required to catch those implicit conditions. If it wasn't obvious that such a condition could happen in that particular location and for some reason you really cared about catching it, this would be useful information.

Handling Exceptions

Now that you have a feeling for how exceptions can help you design a program and a class library better, how do you actually use exceptions? Let's create a new class that contains a method that throws a custom exception:

```
public class MyFirstClass {
  . . .
  public void aSpecialMethod() throws MyFirstException {
    . . . // do something significant here
  }
}
```

Somewhere else, you define another method:

```
public void anotherSpecialMethod() throws MyFirstException {
  MyFirstClass aMFEC = new MyFirstClass()
  . . .
  aMFEC.aSpecialMethod();
}
```

Let's examine this code more closely. Assuming that MyFirstException is a subclass of the Exception class, it means that if you don't handle it in the code of the anotherSpecialMethod() method, you must warn callers of the anotherSpecialMethod() method about it. Because your code simply calls the aSpecialMethod() method without doing anything explicit about the fact that it might throw a MyFirstException object, you must add that exception to the throws clause of the anotherSpecialMethod() method. This is perfectly legal, but it does defer to the caller something that perhaps you should be responsible for doing yourself. It depends on the circumstances, of course.

Suppose that you feel responsible today and decide to handle the exception yourself. So, you now declare the method without a throws clause, which means that you must do something useful with the expected exception:

```
public void aResponsibleMethod() {
  MyFirstClass aMFEC = new MyFirstClass()
  . . .
  try {
    aMFEC.aSpecialMethod();
  }
  catch (MyFirstException mfe) {
    . . .  // do something terribly responsible
  }
}
```

Two new keywords are introduced here: `try` and `catch`. The `try` statement says basically, "Try running the code in this block, and if exceptions are thrown, we'll handle them." The `catch` statement says, "I'll grab this particular exception and do something about it." You can have as many `catch` statements as you need.

Using `try` and `catch`

In the `try` block, you should put any code that might throw an exception. When using a Java method for the first time, look up its definition in the Help or in the source code (if it's available). Look for the `throws` clause in the method signature. If the method `throws` an exception, you must decide whether to include it in your method's `throws` clause or handle it. If you decide to handle it, enclose the call to that method in a `try` block.

In the `catch` block, you can handle all exceptions referred to in its argument list. These include any instance of a named class or any of its subclasses and any class that implements a named interface. In the `catch` statement in the previous example, exceptions of the class `MyFirstException` (or any of its subclasses) will be handled.

Using the `throw` Keyword

What if you want to combine both of the approaches shown so far? You want to handle the exception yourself but also reflect it up to your method's caller. This can be done by explicitly rethrowing the exception, using the `throw` keyword:

```
public void responsibleExceptMethod() throws MyFirstException {
MyFirstClass aMFEC = new MyFirstClass()
  . . .
  try {
    aMFEC.aSpecialMethod();
  }
  catch (MyFirstException mfe) {
    . . .          // do something responsible
    throw mfe;  // rethrow the exception
  }
}
```

13

This works because exception handlers can be nested. Suppose that you handle the exception by doing something responsible with it but decide that it is important to give an exception handler that might be in your caller the chance to handle it as well. Exceptions percolate all the way up the chain of method callers this way (usually not being handled by most of them) until, at last, the system itself handles any uncaught ones by aborting your program and printing an error message. In a standalone program, this is not necessarily a bad idea, but in an applet, it can cause the Web browser to crash. Most Web browsers protect themselves from this disaster by catching all applet-generated exceptions themselves whenever they run an applet, but you cannot rely on that to be the case. If it's possible for you to catch an exception and do something intelligent with it, you definitely should do so.

You can also use the `throw` keyword to instantiate a new exception. Let's take the `MyFirstClass` class definition and flesh it out a bit more:

```
public class MyFirstClass {
  . . .
  public void aSpecialMethod() throws MyFirstException {
    . . .
    if (someUnusualThingHappened()) {
      throw new MyFirstException();
      // execution never gets past here
      . . .
    }
  }
}
```

> **Note**
>
> The `throw` keyword acts like a `break` keyword—nothing beyond the `break` keyword within the method is executed.

This is the fundamental way in which all exceptions are generated—someone, somewhere, has to create an exception object and `throw` it. In fact, the whole hierarchy under the class `Throwable` would be worth much less if `throw` statements were not scattered throughout the code in the Java library at just the right places. Because exceptions propagate up from any depth inside methods, any method call you make might generate a plethora of possible errors and exceptions. Luckily, only the ones listed in the `throws` clause of a method need be considered; the rest travel silently past on their way to becoming an error message (or being caught and handled higher up in the system).

Here's an unusual demonstration of this, in which the exception that is thrown and the handler that catches it are very close together:

```
System.out.print("Now ");
try {
  System.out.print("is ");
  throw new MyFirstException();
  System.out.print("a ");
}
catch (MyFirstException m) {
  System.out.print("the ");
}
System.out.println("time.");
```

The output from this snippet shows the flow of control through the code:

OUTPUT   `Now is the time.`

Falling Through

Exceptions are really a powerful way of partitioning the space of all possible error conditions into manageable pieces. Because the first `catch` block that matches is executed, you can build chains such as the following:

```
try {
  someReallyExceptionalMethod();
}
catch (NullPointerException n) {
  . . . // subclass of RuntimeException
}
catch (RuntimeException r) {
  . . . // subclass of Exception
}
catch (MyFirstException m) {
  . . . // your subclass of Exception
}
catch (IOException i) {
  . . . // subclass of Exception
}
catch (Exception e) {
  . . . // subclass of Throwable
}
catch (Throwable t) {
  . . . // Error class errors, plus anything else
  . . . // not yet caught by the previous catch blocks
}
```

By listing subclasses before their parent classes and custom exceptions before standard exceptions, you create a hierarchy of error-handling that allows the more specific exceptions to have first crack at handling the problem and the more general classes of exceptions to grab whatever falls through the cracks. By juggling chains like these, you can express almost any combination of tests. If there's some really obscure case you can't handle, perhaps you can use an interface to handle it instead. That would enable you to design your peculiar exceptions hierarchy simulating multiple inheritance. Catching an interface rather than a class can also be used to test for a property that many exceptions share but that cannot be expressed in the single-inheritance tree alone.

Suppose, for example, that a scattered set of your exception classes require a reboot after being thrown. You create an interface called `NeedsReboot`, and all these classes implement the interface. (None of them needs to have a common parent exception class.) Then, the highest level of exception handler simply catches classes that implement the `NeedsReboot` interface and performs the task:

```
public interface NeedsReboot { }  // needs no contents at all

try {
  someMethodThatGeneratesExceptionsThatImplementNeedsReboot();
}
catch (NeedsReboot n) {  // catch an interface
  . . .                     // cleanup
  SystemClass.reboot();   // reboot using a made-up system class
}
```

By the way, if you need truly unusual behavior during an exception, you can place the behavior into the exception class itself! Remember that an exception is also a normal class, so it can contain instance variables and methods. Although using them is a bit unusual, it might be valuable on a few occasions. Here's what this might look like:

```
try {
  someExceptionallyStrangeMethod();
}
catch (ComplexException e) {
  switch (e.internalState()) { // may return an instance variable
    case e.COMPLEX_CASE:  // class variable of exception's class
      e.performComplexBehavior(myState, theContext, ...);
      break;
    . . . // the rest of the switch
  }
}
```

Using a `finally` Block

Last of all, consider the `finally` block. Suppose there is some action that you absolutely must do, no matter what happens. Usually, this is to free up some external resource after acquiring it, to close a file after opening it, or something similar. To be sure that "no matter what" includes exceptions as well, you use the `finally` block designed for exactly this sort of thing:

```
SomeFileClass f = new SomeFileClass();
if (f.open("/a/path/name/file")) {
  try {
    someReallyExceptionalMethod();
  }
  finally {
    f.close();
  }
}
```

This use of the finally keyword behaves much as though you had written the following:

```
SomeFileClass f = new SomeFileClass();
if (f.open("/a/path/name/file")) {
  try {
    someReallyExceptionalMethod();
  }
  catch (Throwable t) {
    f.close();
    throw t;
  }
}
```

The only difference is that the finally keyword can also be used to clean up not only after exceptions but also after return, break, and continue statements. Listing 13.1 is a complex (and rather convoluted) demonstration.

TYPE **LISTING 13.1.** MyExceptionalClass.java.

```
 1:  public class MyExceptionalClass {
 2:    public static void main(String args[]) {
 3:      int mysteriousState = Integer.parseInt(args[0]);
 4:      while (true) {
 5:        System.out.print("Who ");
 6:        try {
 7:          System.out.print("is ");
 8:          if (mysteriousState == 1)
 9:            return;
10:          System.out.print("that ");
11:          if (mysteriousState == 2)
12:            break;
13:          System.out.print("strange ");
14:          if (mysteriousState == 3)
15:            continue;
16:          System.out.print("but kindly ");
17:          System.out.print("not at all ");
18:        }
19:        finally {
```

13

continues

LISTING 13.1. CONTINUED

```
20:             System.out.print("amusing man?\n");
21:         }
22:         System.out.print("I'd like to meet the man.");
23:       }
24:       System.out.print("Please tell me.\n");
25:     }
26:   }
```

ANALYSIS   The output produced depends on the value assigned to the mysteriousState variable. When mysteriousState = 1, the output is as follows:

OUTPUT   Who is amusing man?

Here, the output reflects the print() method statement before the return statement. The return statement is put on "hold" while the print() method statement in the finally block is executed. Then the main() method is exited. When mysteriousState = 2:

OUTPUT   Who is that amusing man?
             Please tell me.

The print() method statements before the break statement are executed—the print() method statement in the finally block, followed by the print() method statement after the end of the while loop. When mysteriousState = 3:

OUTPUT   Who is that strange amusing man?
             Who is that ...

The print() method statements before the continue statement are executed and then the print() method statement in the finally block. Because the continue statement causes execution to begin again at the top of the while loop, this is an unending cycle, and you must press Ctrl+C to break the output. When mysteriousState = 4:

OUTPUT   Who is that strange but kindly amusing man?

The print() method statements before the throw statement are executed and then the print() method statement in the finally block. In fact, when mysteriousState = 5 (or any integer value other than 1 through 3):

OUTPUT   Who is that strange but kindly not at all amusing man?
             I'd like to meet the man. Who is that strange but kindly not ...

The print() method statements before the finally block are all executed and then the print() method statement in the finally block. Because the while loop always evaluates to true, this is an unending cycle, and you must press Ctrl+C to break the output.

Although this is a rather contrived example, it does illustrate how the `finally` block can be used by all these statements to perform housekeeping tasks.

Limitations

As powerful as this all sounds, isn't it a little limiting? For example, suppose that you want to override one of the standard methods of the `Object` class, the `toString()` method, to be smarter about how the `Object` object and its class prints:

```
public class MyIllegalClass {
  public String toString() {
    someReallyExceptionalMethod();
    . . . // returns some String
  }
}
```

Because the superclass `Object` defined the method declaration for the `toString()` method without a `throws` clause, any implementation of it in any subclass must obey this restriction. In other words, you cannot use a `throws` clause in your method definition that overrides the `toString()` method because the original method definition didn't have one.

In particular, you cannot just call the `someReallyExceptionalMethod()` method within the overriding definition as you just did because it will generate a host of errors and exceptions, some of which are not exempt from being listed in a `throws` clause (such as `IOException` and `MyFirstException` exception classes). If all the exceptions thrown were exempt, you would have no problem. However, as it is, you cannot use `throws` to pass them on, so you have to catch at least those few exceptions for this to be legal Java:

```
public class MyLegalClass {
  public String toString() {
    try {
      someReallyExceptionalMethod();
    }
    catch (IOException e) {
    }
    catch (MyFirstException m) {
    }
    . . . // returns some String
  }
}
```

13

In both cases, you elect to catch exceptions and do absolutely nothing with them. Although this is legal, it is not always the right thing to do. You might need to think for a while to come up with the best, nontrivial behavior for any particular `catch` block. The `toString()` method of the `MyIllegalClass` class would produce a compiler error to remind you to reflect on these issues. This extra care will reward you richly as you reuse your classes in later projects and in larger and larger classes. It will make your programs more robust, better able to handle unusual input, and more likely to work correctly when used by multiple threads. Of course, the Java Class Library has been written with this same degree of care, which is one of the reasons it's robust enough to be used in constructing all your projects.

Creating Custom Exceptions

Sometimes you will need to create your own classes of exceptions. This is a straightforward task in Java. Simply extend the `Exception` class and define the behavior that you want your exception to have:

```
class MyFirstException extends Exception {
  MyFirstException() {
    super();
    . . . // error-handling here
  }
  MyFirstException(String errMsg) {
    super(errMsg);
    . . . // error-handling here
  }
}
```

In this example, `MyFirstException` is defined as a subclass of the `Exception` class, inheriting all its attributes and behaviors. This exception can be called without arguments, or it can be supplied a `String` argument. Call the superclass's constructor and add your error-handling code. It's just that simple.

Summary

Today, you learned about how exceptions improve your program's design and robustness. This knowledge, coupled with the information on Day 8, "Applets, Applications, and Wizards," in which exceptions were first introduced, gives you a solid understanding of exceptions.

You also learned about the vast collection of exceptions defined and thrown in the Java Class Library, how to use the `throws` clause to defer exception handling, how to `throw` a new exception, and how to rethrow a handled exception. You also know how to use the `try` block to attempt to execute methods while using `catch` blocks to handle any of a hierarchically ordered set of possible exceptions and errors. The `finally` block is used to unconditionally perform cleanup tasks, and you saw that it can be used for the same purpose with `return`, `break`, and `continue` statements, as well.

Java's reliance on strict exception handling does place some restrictions on the programmer, but you learned that these restrictions are light compared to the rewards: more resilient and robust programs. You also learned that you can create your own hierarchies of error-handling exceptions by extending the Exception class.

Q&A

Q **I'm still a bit unsure about the differences between the Error, Exception, and RuntimeException classes. Could you explain it another way?**

A Error faults are caused by dynamic linking or virtual machine problems and are thus too low-level for most programs to care about (although sophisticated development libraries and environments probably care a great deal about them).

RuntimeException faults are generated by the normal execution of Java code and usually reflect a coding mistake by the programmer. Thus they simply need to print an error message to help flag that mistake.

Exception faults that are not RuntimeException faults (IOException, for example) are conditions that should be explicitly handled by any robust and well-thought-out program. The Java Class Library has been written using only a few of these, but those few are extremely important to using the system safely and correctly. The compiler reminds you to handle these exceptions properly through its throws clause checks and restrictions.

Q **Is there a way to get around the strict restrictions placed on methods by the throws clause being present?**

A Yes. Suppose that you thought long and hard and then decided that you need to circumvent this restriction. This is almost never the case because the right solution is to go back and redesign your methods to reflect the exceptions that you need to throw. Imagine, however, that for some reason a system class has you in a straightjacket. Your first solution is to subclass RuntimeException to make up a new, exempt exception of your own. Now you can throw it to your heart's content because the throws clause that was annoying you does not need to include this new exception.

If you need a lot of such exceptions, an elegant approach is to mix in some novel exception interfaces to your new RuntimeException classes. You're free to choose whatever subset of these new interfaces you want to catch (because they're subclasses of RuntimeException), and any leftover RuntimeException errors can go through that otherwise annoying standard method in the library.

13

Q **Given how annoying it can sometimes be to handle exceptional conditions properly, what's to stop me from surrounding any method as follows and simply ignoring all exceptions?**

```
try { anyAnnoyingMethod(); } catch (Throwable t) { }
```

A Nothing, other than your own conscience. In some cases, you *should* do nothing because it's the right thing to do given your method's implementation. Otherwise, you should work through the annoyance and gain experience. Good style can sometimes be a struggle even for the best of programmers, but the rewards are rich indeed.

Workshop

The Workshop provides two ways for you to affirm what you've learned in this chapter. The Quiz section poses questions to help you solidify your understanding of the material covered. You can find answers to the quiz questions in Appendix A, "Answers to Quiz Questions." The Exercises section provides you with experience in using what you have learned. Try to work through all these before continuing to the next day.

Quiz

1. How many catch blocks can legally follow a try statement?
2. Can you have both catch blocks and finally blocks following a try block?
3. What keyword do you use when you want to do something no matter what else happens?
4. Explain the difference between the throws and throw keywords.
5. True or False? When you catch an exception, you must always do something to handle it.

Exercise

Create a hierarchy of custom exceptions to go with the project that you completed as the exercise for Day 6, "User Interface Design."

DAY 14

JBuilder Database Architecture

Today, you'll explore JBuilder's database architecture, the JDBC architecture, and the database component hierarchy. You'll learn about the classes and interfaces that form the basis of these architectures and see what each has to offer. Specifically, you'll learn about the following topics:

- Different database models, types, and their purposes
- JBuilder's database architecture
- JDBC and how it affects applet and application development
- Four types of JDBC drivers and a brief introduction to RMI and CORBA
- JDBC's classes and interface and its Application Programming Interface (API)
- JBuilder's data-aware components and an introduction to the DataBroker

> **Note** The JBuilder data-aware components discussed today are located on the Data Express tab of the Component Palette. This tab is available only in the Professional (Pro) and Client/Server (C/S) Editions of JBuilder. However, the JDBC classes are included in the standard Java Development Kit, so even if you have the Standard Edition, most of today's information will still be of interest.

Database Basics

Spend a few moments reviewing database terminology and some information about different database models and types before you begin to learn about JBuilder's database architecture. Read this section if you haven't yet worked much with databases or if you'd like a brief refresher on database technology. (If you do database development every day, you can skip this section.)

Tables and Terms

Throughout the day, you'll be inundated by database terminology, so let's begin by defining how those terms are used in this book. Some of these terms are specific to JBuilder or Java; some are general database terms. Table 14.1 summarizes these terms and gives a brief explanation of each.

TABLE 14.1. SELECTED DATABASE TERMS.

Term	Description
Client	A program that is asking for access
Client/Server	A system that distributes its processing between server and client machines
Column	A field or an attribute containing a vertical column of data
Concurrency	The capability to prioritize and process multiple access requests
Data-access control	A control that connects other controls to database tables
Data-aware control	A control that has the capability of displaying and modifying data by way of data access controls
Database	One or more tables of data
DBMS	Database Management System, such as Sybase, Oracle, or InterBase
DBMS Driver	An executable that connects with a DBMS platform
Field	A discrete piece of data, such as a name or customer ID
Multiuser	Enabled to handle concurrency
Row	A single record containing a horizontal row of one or more columns (fields) of data

Term	Description
SQL	Structured Query Language, a standard language used for interrogating databases
Server	A program that provides access
Table	A collection of rows (records) and columns (fields) in a database

With these terms defined, let's move on to the types of databases and database models.

Database Models

There are many applications that use databases, but which database model should your programs use? That depends on the type of program you're developing.

Relational Model

Most databases today are relational databases. A relational database stores information in logical tables made up of rows and columns. The tables can have columns in common that relate the information in one table to the information in another. Suppose you've just opened a wholesale photography supply, and you have one table with information about a customer and another table with customer invoices. After the first month, your tables might look something like Tables 14.2 and 14.3.

TABLE 14.2. THE CUSTOMERS TABLE.

ID	Customer	City	State	ZipCd
2345	Diamond Head Photography	Honolulu	HI	96815
3458	Deep-Sea Cameras	Hilo	HI	96721
7857	Pretty as a Picture	Lahaina	HI	96761

TABLE 14.3. THE INVOICES TABLE.

ID	TransDate	InvDate	Qty	Item	Price
2345	19970404	19970531	1	34756	43.99
7857	19970406	19970531	2	38756	19.99
2345	19970412	19970531	1	14333	48.99
7857	19970414	19970531	2	38756	19.99
2345	19970416	19970531	10	38756	19.99
7857	19970423	19970531	2	32875	562.99
3458	19970428	19970531	7	12387	5.55

14

Well, business is kind of slow, but you get the idea. The ID field relates these two tables. This is an example of a one-to-many relationship. In other words, for every one record in the Customers table, there can be many related records in the Invoices table.

Flat-File Model

Unlike a relational database, a flat-file database has all its information within each record. For example, in the example just given, if the same information were to be kept in a flat-file database table, there would be no customer table, and the invoice table would have to include the customer's name and address in each record. This wastes a tremendous amount of space because of the redundancy of the information. For this reason, most databases today are relational.

 Tip

> If you've ever used the term "database" when you meant "table," it's probably because in the days when only flat-file databases existed, there could be only one table to a database. People who learned about databases often used the terms interchangeably. However, this is incorrect when you're referring to relational tables. In the relational world, tables that are related to one another form a database.

Database Types

In addition to the two basic database models, flat-file and relational, there are various other types of databases from which you can choose. Again, the decision depends on the type of application you're developing and how it will be used.

Standalone

A standalone database has its tables stored on the local file system, and the program to access it also resides on the same machine. This type of database might be appropriate for Java programs that are meant for single-user access. That is, only one person (the one using the local machine) is accessing the data at any one time. This is the simplest scenario because you don't have to worry about multiuser access (concurrency), network traffic, or other client/server issues. For example, if you want to create a program to track your personal business expenditures and don't intend to share this information with anyone else, a standalone database program might meet your requirements.

File-Share

A file-share database is a distributed form of database that enables multiple users to access the same tables. Generally, the users have a program to access the tables on their local machine on the network, and the database itself is on a central machine. The type of network is unimportant because the local machine simply accesses the database as a shared file on the network. When a user accesses the file, it is locked until that user is finished with the query, update, or other processing. Each user, therefore, must wait his or her turn to access the file, so this solution is best reserved when there is not a large number of potential users of the database's tables.

Client/Server

A client/server database (also known as a two-tier system) is one that has been optimized to handle many concurrent requests. Part of the processing is done on the local machine (client), and part is done on the central machine (server). Although the file access is still one request at a time, the client can do something else while the server is processing the client's request (via SQL queries or stored procedures). Other clients can also queue up their requests instead of receiving a "Tabled Locked" message.

How much processing does the client do, and how much is done by the server? That is a balancing act that requires detailed work up front when designing the solution, taking into account the number of potential users, network traffic, and the types of requests and their frequency, among other considerations. Client/server systems also require a protocol (unlike file-sharing systems), such as TCP/IP, creating additional configuration and administrative tasks. Although client/server is typically a more expensive solution, when there are many potential concurrent users, it might be the one you need.

Multitier

Multitier systems are client/server systems that split up the processing even further, sometimes adding a middle layer called "middleware" that does additional processing and takes some of the load from the server. This frees the server to handle more requests, increasing capacity and throughput. The middleware is usually multithreaded to handle multiple concurrent requests and can be configured to handle requests to multiple databases.

JDBC Architecture

The JDBC opens up a whole new world in client/server technology. If you thought configuring client/server on the local network was interesting, you can now work with clients and servers thousands of miles apart, and you'll also have to consider traffic on the Internet!

NEW TERM *JDBC* is a JavaSoft trademark and not an acronym. However, it is usually associated with Java Database Connectivity. JDBC is JavaSoft's standard API, which uses SQL statements to access databases in Java programs.

14

JDBC might sound familiar if you have done any work with ODBC. ODBC is Open Database Connectivity, a standard promulgated by Microsoft to provide a way to access the multitude of databases that exist with a single API. So why didn't Java just use ODBC? The major reason is that ODBC is C-centric and uses lots of pointers. Also, ODBC is mainly implemented only for Microsoft platforms. So, keeping their goals in mind (simplicity, robustness, and portability), the Java team decided to create an API that would work with databases no matter what the native language of their platform.

Like ODBC, JDBC is based on the X/Open SQL CLI (Call Level Interface), but unlike ODBC, the JDBC is an all-Java API that is cross-platform and vendor-neutral. The JDBC API uses SQL (Structured Query Language) to access data across the Internet and so can access almost any data your application needs to use. The JDBC is also object-oriented and so is easier to learn and implement. Finally, JDBC supports client/server and multi-tier systems.

Using JDBC with Applets

Applets have made a big splash on the Internet, and just as there are security concerns with applets, so there are with database access across the Internet. In this section, you'll learn about the processes, the issues, and some of the security concerns that are dealt with by JDBC.

When you develop an applet with access to a database on the Internet, there are some obvious security concerns. As you learned in Week 1, a Java applet is restricted in almost every way, from accessing the client's hard disk to making network connections other than to its own server. For many businesses, data is their most important asset, so when you're considering database access across the Internet, security concerns are multiplied. So how does the JDBC address these concerns?

JDBC-enabled applets cannot access data from a local database unless they are digitally signed. Due to applet security, calls to files on the machine aren't allowed unless the applet is signed. The JDBC applet will be able to connect only to a database that resides on the server from which it was downloaded. However, if the applet is trusted by the Java Virtual Machine (by using an encoded password, or if the client specifies that applets from a particular site are considered safe), the applet is treated just like an application as far as security is concerned.

Using JDBC with Applications

Java applications are now being used as solutions for more than just the Internet. Corporate intranets and extranets are growing exponentially, and JDBC enables you to create applications that take full advantage access of them.

NEW TERM An *intranet* is a network that takes advantage of Internet-related technology to give access to corporate data and can involve local area networks (LANs), wide area networks (WANs), and remote access (via modems or ISDN lines). In essence, an intranet is a private version of the Internet, allowing access from clients on different platforms.

NEW TERM An *extranet* is an intranet that has been expanded to include the corporation's business partners, such as suppliers and customers. An extranet connects several corporations with mutual interests and data that they want to share.

Unlike groupware, intranets and extranets are using the ubiquitous Web browser as a familiar user interface that requires little training. This interface makes use of legacy data without requiring conversion to a proprietary format; it also allows users to access data from a mixture of Windows, Macintosh, and UNIX machines. It's no wonder this technology is becoming increasingly popular with corporations.

With Java applications, because of firewall technology, security is not as much of a concern. Applications that are loaded locally are assumed to be trusted. Another solution is to use a multitiered system, in which the middleware is responsible for security and access, and acts as a security enforcer between the client and server. As you'll see shortly, JDBC supports all these security answers.

Database Connectivity

JDBC provides an API that supports drivers for Informix, InterBase, Microsoft SQL Server, Oracle, Paradox, Sybase, and Xbase, among others. It provides this support through four types of connectivity:

- **JDBC-ODBC Bridge:** This driver, provided in the Java Development Kit by JavaSoft, allows existing ODBC drivers to be used. However, this is not the best solution because it requires the installation of ODBC drivers and client libraries. ODBC drivers are also implemented natively, which compromises cross-platform support and applet security.

 Note
> The JDBC-ODBC Bridge is win32 only and usually can't be used in applets due to applet security.

- **Native API to Java:** This type of driver translates the JDBC calls into native API calls to the DBMS. It also requires native C-language code on the client machine and so does not provide cross-platform support. However, if your target environment is homogeneous with respect to the platform being used, it might provide some performance enhancements.

14

- **Neutral Network Protocol:** This type of driver uses DBMS-neutral network proto-cols to translate the JDBC calls into native DBMS API calls. This driver is typi-cally used with middleware to facilitate access from pure Java clients to DBMS servers, and it might be provided as part of the middleware package.

- **Native Network Protocol:** This type of driver translates JDBC calls into DBMS-proprietary network protocol calls that the DBMS can use directly. This driver is typically used for intranet access and, being DBMS-proprietary, is obtained from the database vendor.

The last two protocol solutions are recommended by JavaSoft as the preferred ways to access databases from JDBC.

> For the latest information from JavaSoft regarding JDBC drivers, connect to
> http://www.javasoft.com/products/jdbc/.

JDBC Classes

To understand more about how the JDBC works, let's explore the interfaces and classes that the JDBC comprises, which are all located in the java.sql package. (Don't forget to import this package in your code when using these classes.) Retrieving data with the JDBC is based on four simple steps:

1. Obtain a driver from those drivers that are currently instantiated.

2. Using the driver, establish a connection to the database.

3. Send a SQL statement to the database.

4. Assign the results to local variables.

The first step is usually done automatically by a DriverManager object, which you'll look at in the next section.

> This section is not meant to be an exhaustive coverage of the JDBC methods; rather, it is meant to highlight the most commonly used methods. For more detailed information on the JDBC classes, interfaces, and methods, be sure to select Help | Java Reference and read the full documentation online.

Understanding the `DriverManager` Class

The `DriverManager` class contains various methods for managing, registering, and deregistering drivers. However, most of the time, you will only need to call the `getConnection` method, and the `DriverManager` object will automatically load the most appropriate driver for the database being accessed. Table 14.4 gives a summary of the key methods defined in this class.

TABLE 14.4. `DriverManager` CLASS METHODS.

Method Signature	Summary
`deregisterDriver(Driver)`	Removes specified `Driver` object from the `DriverManager` object's list of registered drivers
`getConnection(String)`	Returns a `Connection` object that encapsulates a connection to the database located at the URL encapsulated in the `String` object passed to the method
`getConnection(String, Properties)`	Returns a `Connection` object that encapsulates a connection to the database located at the URL encapsulated by the `String` object passed to the method, with the connection properties encapsulated in the `Properties` object
`getConnection(String, String, String)`	Returns a `Connection` object that encapsulates a connection to the database located at the URL encapsulated by the first `String` object passed to the method and logs in using the login encapsulated in the second `String` object and the password encapsulated in the third `String` object
`getDrivers()`	Returns an `Enumeration` object encapsulating a list of the available drivers
`registerDriver(Driver)`	Adds the `Driver` object passed to the method to the `DriverManager` object's registered drivers list

The `registerDriver()` and `deregisterDriver()` methods allow the calling class to add or delete drivers from the class loader's `Driver` object list; the `getDrivers()` method returns a list of all the drivers available to the calling class.

The overloaded `getConnection()` method gives you several ways to establish the connection, all requiring the use of a URL. For databases, the URL syntax might look a bit different than what you're used to seeing. The basic format is this:

```
protocol:subprotocol:subname
```

14

The most common protocols are `http:` and `ftp:`, and subnames usually look like `//www.microsoft.com/` or `//www.javasoft.com/`. When you're using JDBC, the *protocol* is `jdbc:`, the *subprotocol* represents a particular type of database mechanism, and the *subname* is the information actually used to connect to the database (including port). Here are some typical JDBC URLs:

```
jdbc:odbc:mydata
jdbc:odbc:mydata;UID=mylogin;PWD=mypasswd
jdbc:dbprot://testsite:321/mytables/mydata
```

The first example listed shows how to connect to a database named `mydata` by using the JDBC-ODBC bridge via the `odbc` subprotocol. The second example shows the same connection with ODBC login (`UID`) and password (`PWD`) attributes added. The third example shows how to use a particular database subprotocol (`dbprot:`) logging in to port `:321` on a Web site named `testsite`, where the database `mydata` is located in the `mytables` directory.

 Tip

> Typically, connection URLs are documented and provided as part of the JDBC driver.

To use the `getConnection()` method, simply assign the appropriate URL to a `String` variable and then call the `getConnection()` method using that `String` object:

```
String myURL = ("jdbc:dbprot://testsite:321/mytables/mydata");
getConnection(myURL, "myUID", "myPWD");
```

 Note

> In URLs, you will see the forward slash (/) used in pathnames, the standard form on the World Wide Web. Even though the Windows platforms use the backslash (\) character, JBuilder allows you to use the forward slash (/) in Java code, so you don't have to change your URLs before your code will run properly over the Internet.

After you've made a successful connection, a `Connection` object is returned. Here's a line of code showing how this is usually done:

```
Connection dbConn = DriverManager.getConnection
  ("jdbc:odbc:dbname", "mylogin", "mypasswd");
```

Next, you'll look at the `Connection` interface.

Understanding the `Connection` Class

A class that implements the `java.sql.Connection` interface can override methods that deal with locking tables, committing and rolling back changes, and closing connections. It also has methods for preparing certain types of calls and statements. Table 14.5 summarizes some of this interface's more commonly overridden methods.

TABLE 14.5. `java.sql.Connection` INTERFACE METHODS.

Method Signature	Summary
`close()`	Provides a way to immediately close a connection and release JDBC resources
`commit()`	Permanently updates the table with all modifications made since the last commit/rollback; releases connection locks on the database
`createStatement()`	Returns a new `Statement` object
`getAutoCommit()`	Returns `boolean`: `true` if the `AutoCommit` object is enabled; `false` if the `AutoCommit` object is disabled
`getMetaData()`	Returns a `DatabaseMetaData` object that contains information about the tables, stored procedures, and supported SQL grammar for the current connection database
`isClosed()`	Returns `boolean`: `true` if the connection is closed; `false` if the connection is open
`prepareCall(String)`	Returns a new `CallableStatement` object with optional `OUT` or `INOUT` parameters; the `String` object passed to the method encapsulates a SQL statement
`prepareStatement(String)`	Returns a new `PreparedStatement` object containing a precompiled simple SQL statement or one with `IN` parameters; the `String` object passed to the method encapsulates a SQL statement
`rollback()`	Drops all modifications made to the table since the last commit/rollback; releases connection locks
`setAutoCommit(boolean)`	Passes the `boolean` argument `true` to enable the `AutoCommit` object; passes `false` to disable

You can use the `isClosed()` method to determine whether the connection is still open; if it is, use the `Close()` method to immediately release the connection, if desired.

The `getMetaData()` method returns all the information that is available about the properties of the current connection's database in a `DatabaseMetaData` object. This information includes a list of the database's stored procedures, the SQL grammar that it supports,

14

access rights for the table columns, primary and foreign keys, indexes, the database product name and version number, the driver version number, schema, and literally dozens of pieces of information about the database itself. For a complete list of all the methods in the `DatabaseMetaData` class that return information about the `DatabaseMetaData` object, be sure to look in the Java Reference online help.

What a transaction comprises depends on the state of the auto-commit mode. By default, the auto-commit mode is set to `true`, which means that each statement is a transaction that will get committed as soon as the statement is executed. If the auto-commit mode is set to `false`, all statements since the last commit/rollback are grouped together into a single transaction.

The `getAutoCommit()` method tells you whether the connection's auto-commit mode is currently set to true. To group statements, pass a `false` value to the `setAutoCommit` method, and use the `commit()` and `rollback()` methods to manage the transactions.

The `createStatement()` method creates a new `Statement` object; the `prepareCall()` and `prepareStatement()` methods create `CallableStatement` and `PreparedStatement` objects. These objects are used to store simple and precompiled SQL statements, which the connection can then execute. JDBC statements form the core of database transactions, and you'll examine them next.

Understanding the `Statement` Class

The class that implements the `Statement` interface can override methods, which enable you to handle and execute several types of SQL statements. Table 14.6 summarizes some of this interface's more commonly overridden methods.

TABLE 14.6. `java.sql.Statement` INTERFACE METHODS.

Method Signature	Summary
cancel()	Cancels a statement being executed in another thread
close()	Provides a way to immediately close the connection and release JDBC resources
execute(String)	Executes the SQL statement encapsulated in the `String` object passed to the method; returns `true` if the first result is a `ResultSet` object and `false` if the result is an `int` value
executeQuery(String)	Executes the SQL statement encapsulated in the `String` object passed to the method; returns the `ResultSet` object containing the query results

Method Signature	Summary
executeUpdate(String)	Executes the SQL UPDATE, INSERT, DELETE, or no-return statement (such as the DDL statement) encapsulated by the String object passed to the method; returns an int value representing the number of rows that were affected (0 for no-return statements)
getCursorName()	Returns a String object containing the identifier of the current row (set by a SQL UPDATE or DELETE statement)
getMoreResults()	Returns a true value if the next result is a ResultSet object and false value if the next result is an int value
getQueryTimeout()	Returns an int value representing the number of seconds the Driver object will wait for a SQL statement to execute
getResultSet()	Returns a ResultSet object if there are current results; if no more results or an update count, returns null
setCursorName(String)	Sets the identifier of the current row (set by a SQL UPDATE or DELETE statement) to the value encapsulated by the String object passed to the method
setQueryTimeout(int)	Sets the number of seconds the Driver object will wait for a SQL statement to execute to the int value passed to the method

There are many other methods in the Statement interface. For details, be sure to study the "Statement Interface" topic in the Java Reference online help.

Note

A SQL statement is the actual instruction that enables you to communicate with the database. A formal introduction to SQL is definitely beyond the scope of this book, but the Sams book *Teach Yourself SQL in 14 Days, Premier Edition*, gives you an excellent introduction to the SQL language.

In addition to the Statement interface, there are two other interfaces to be considered. The CallableStatement interface inherits from the PreparedStatement interface, which, in turn, inherits from the Statement interface. At each level, additional abstract methods specific to the type of SQL statement being handled are provided.

The PreparedStatement interface is used when you want to precompile a simple SQL statement to execute it multiple times or when the SQL statement has IN parameters and has to be precompiled. This provides a more efficient way of calling the precompiled statement.

14

The CallableStatement interface is usually a precompiled stored procedure statement that must be used with stored database procedures containing OUT or INOUT parameters.

Here's a typical code snippet that shows a query to myTable:

```
Connection dbConn = DriverManager.getConnection
  ("jdbc:odbc:dbname", "mylogin", "mypasswd");
Statement sqlStmt = dbConn.createStatement();
ResultSet rSet = sqlStmt.executeQuery
  ("SELECT xInt, yString FROM myTable");
```

This example uses an instance of the Connection interface assigned to the dbConn variable and creates an instance of the Statement interface assigned to the sqlStmt variable. Then, using sqlStmt, it executes the SQL query using the Statement interface's executeQuery() method and returns it to an instance of the ResultSet interface assigned to the rSet variable. The ResultSet abstract class is the final piece of the JDBC architecture, which you'll examine next.

Understanding the ResultSet Class

Implementation of the java.sql.ResultSet abstract class methods controls access to the row results from a given SQL statement. It is through this class that you are able to access the results of all your queries. Table 14.7 summarizes some of this interface's key methods.

TABLE 14.7. java.sql.ResultSet abstract METHODS.

Method Signature	Summary
close()	Provides a way to immediately close a Connection object and release JDBC resources
findColumn(String)	Returns an int value representing the column index corresponding to the column name encapsulated in the String object passed to the method
getAsciiStream(int)	Returns an InputStream object containing the ASCII values in the LONGVARCHAR value from the current row; the int value passed to the method represents the column index
getAsciiStream(String)	Returns an InputStream object encapsulating the ASCII values in the LONGVARCHAR value from the current row; the String object passed to the method encapsulates the column name
getBinaryStream(int)	Returns an InputStream object containing the ASCII values in the LONGVARBINARY value from the current row; the int value passed to the method represents the column index

Method Signature	Summary
getBinaryStream(String)	Returns an InputStream object containing the ASCII values in the LONGVARBINARY value from the current row; the String object passed to the method encapsulates the column name
getCursorName()	Returns a String object containing the identifier of the current row (set by a SQL UPDATE or DELETE statement)
getMetaData()	Returns a ResultSetMetaData object containing the number of columns, data types, and other properties of the rows in the current ResultSet object
getUnicodeStream(int)	Returns an InputStream object containing the ASCII values in the LONGVARCHAR value from the current row; the int value passed to the method represents the column index
getUnicodeStream(String)	Returns an InputStream object containing the ASCII values in the LONGVARCHAR value from the current row; the String object passed to the method represents the column name
getXxxx(int)	Returns a data type represented by Xxxx (for example, int, long, String, Object, and so on) containing the value in the current row; the int value passed to the method represents the column index
getXxxx(String)	Returns a data type represented by Xxxx (for example, int, long, String, Object, and so on) containing the value in the current row; the String object passed to the method encapsulates the column name
setCursorName(String)	Sets the identifier of the current row (set by a SQL UPDATE or DELETE statement) to the value encapsulated by the String object passed to the method
next()	Returns true if the next row is a valid row and false if there are no more rows
wasNull()	Returns true if the value just read was null and false if the value wasn't null

There are two getXxxx() methods for each Java type, one that uses a column index and one that uses a column name. For example, to get a String object from the second column of the current row, you would use the following statement:

```
getString(2);
```

This statement returns the value in that field encapsulated in a String object. To get a character value from the column named Gender, you would use the following statement:

```
getChar(Gender);
```

14

> **Caution** Unlike Java indices, SQL column indexes begin at 1, not 0. Also unlike Java, SQL column names are not case-sensitive. If you use column names to access fields in the current row, there might be more than one column with the same name due to case-insensitivity. If that happens, the first matching column name will be used.

The findColumn() method returns the column number associated with the specified column name.

The cursor in a ResultSet object is positioned just before the first row when the ResultSet object is created. To iterate the cursor through the ResultSet object, call the next() method. Before attempting to read the data in the row, however, you should test the next() method's returned value to see whether you have landed on a valid row or whether there are no more rows left to examine. The following code snippet combines the previous sample snippets with a while loop that iterates through the ResultSet object assigned to the rSet variable:

```
Connection dbConn = DriverManager.getConnection
  ("jdbc:odbc:dbname", "mylogin", "mypasswd");
Statement sqlStmt = dbConn.createStatement();
ResultSet rSet = sqlStmt.executeQuery
  ("SELECT xInt, yString FROM myTable");
while (rSet.next()) {
  int xIntVal = getInt("xInt");
  String yStrVal = getString("yStr");
}
```

The getMetaData() method returns a ResultSetMetaData object that contains information about the ResultSet object, such as the number of columns. It also returns information about individual columns (fields) such as the name, label (for headers), maximum width, data types, precision (decimal digits), scale (decimal points), and other pertinent information. For a complete list of all the methods in the ResultSetMetaData class that return information about the ResultSetMetaData object, be sure to look in the Java Reference online help.

Mapping Types

Simply stated, there are data types specific to SQL that need to be mapped to Java data types if you expect Java to be able to handle them. This conversion falls into three categories:

- Certain SQL types have direct equivalents in Java and can be read directly into Java types. For example, a SQL INTEGER is a direct equivalent of the Java int data type.

- Several SQL types can be converted to a Java equivalent. For example, the SQL CHAR, VARCHAR, and LONGVARCHAR can all be converted to the Java String data type. This means that it is not necessary for Java to have a data type for every SQL data type.

- A few SQL data types are unique and require a special Java data object to be created specifically for their SQL equivalents. For example, the SQL DATE is converted to the Java Date object that is defined in the java.sql package especially for this purpose.

> **Caution**
>
> Don't confuse java.sql.Date used for converting SQL DATE information with the internal java.util.Date that is used as a Java Date object. The latter will *not* accept a SQL DATE field.

There are tables in the Java API Documentation online Help file that explicitly define the conversions that occur, going in both directions (from SQL to Java, from Java to SQL). To locate this topic, select Help|Java Reference. Choose JDK 1.x.x Documentation from the Help viewer's "Available books" drop-down list. Click the JDK Guide to New Features link, and then click the JDBC-Connecting Java and Databases link. In that topic, click the Getting Started link; scroll down to the 8 Mapping SQL and Java Types link and click it. Be sure to examine this topic for exact details on how types are mapped.

The DECIMAL and NUMERIC data types need to be converted using a special class because absolute precision is necessary (as in dealing with currency values). Before the JDBC, there were no data types for exactly what was needed. So the JDBC API includes the java.sql.Numeric class, which enables you to convert the SQL DECIMAL and NUMERIC values to Java.

The SQL DATE consists of day, month, and year; TIME is hours, minutes, and seconds; TIMESTAMP combines DATE and TIME and adds a nanosecond field. Because the java.util.Date does not have a one-to-one correspondence with these SQL types, the java.sql.Date class is defined to handle the SQL DATE and TIME values, whereas java.sql.Timestamp is defined to handle the SQL TIMESTAMP.

A JDBC API Example

Building on the earlier examples, here is a complete listing showing a typical JDBC connection, querying a database, pulling results from a ResultSet object, and printing the data. Although you can't actually run Listing 14.1 (unless you happen to have a table

14

named myTable with the required data), it is here to give you a complete example of what such a program would look like using the JDBC API.

TYPE **LISTING 14.1.** QueryMyTable.java.

```
 1: import java.net.URL;
 2: import java.sql.*;
 3:
 4: public class QueryMyTable {
 5:
 6:   public static void main(String args[]) {
 7:
 8:     try {
 9:
10:       // connect to the database
11:       String theUrl = "jdbc:odbc:dbname";
12:       Connection dbConn = DriverManager.getConnection
13:         (theUrl, "mylogin", "mypasswd");
14:
15:       // execute the SELECT statement
16:       Statement sqlStmt = dbConn.createStatement();
17:       ResultSet rSet = sqlStmt.executeQuery
18:         ("SELECT xInt, yString FROM myTable");
19:
20:       // iterate through the result rows and
21:       // print out the values obtained
22:       System.out.println("Return results");
23:       while (rSet.next()) {
24:         int xIntVal = rSet.getInt("xInt");
25:         String yStrVal = rSet.getString("yStr");
26:         System.out.print("xIntVal = " + xIntVal);
27:         System.out.print("yStrVal = " + yStrVal);
28:         System.out.print("/n");
29:       }
30:
31:       sqlStmt.close();
32:       dbConn.close();
33:     }
34:
35:     catch (Exception e) {
36:       System.out.println("EXCEPTION: " + e.getMessage());
37:     }
38:
39:   }
40:
41: }
```

ANALYSIS Most of this code should look familiar by now. However, a few bits of it warrant explanation:

- In line 11, the URL is a `String` object assigned to the `theUrl` variable, and then in line 13, the `String` object is passed to the `getConnection()` method. This is a useful device for uncluttering the `getConnection()` method that makes it easier to read. You can either do it this way or insert the URL as an argument directly in the `getConnection()` method, as you saw in the earlier code snippets.
- The entire connection is in a `try` block because many of the methods presented up to this point throw exceptions. In particular, a `SQLException` object is thrown if a database access error occurs.
- The `catch` block uses the `getMessage()` method (defined in the `java.lang.Throwable` class), which returns a `String` object containing the exception's detail message (if any). Line 36 prints this `String`.

Now that you have a good grounding in the JDBC API, it's time to look at the data-aware components in JBuilder that provide you with higher-level access to the JDBC classes and methods.

JBCL and DataBroker

In JBuilder, the DataBroker approach to data access and update of JDBC data sources uses three phases:

- The first phase is called *providing*, in which the data from a JDBC `ResultSet` object is provided as input to a JBCL `DataSet` component.
- In the second phase, you can navigate through the rows of data in the `DataSet` object and edit the data.
- The third phase is called *resolving*, in which the data in the `DataSet` object is posted back to the originating database.

Potential edit conflicts are automatically reconciled. This approach, as implemented in the DataBroker architecture, enables you to deal with data access at a very high level using drag-and-drop JBCL components and hooking them up to JBCL data-aware components in your user interface.

NEW TERM · A *data-access* component is one that you can attach (via properties) to a data source, such as a database.

NEW TERM · A *data-aware* component is one that can accept data using a data-access component as its conduit.

The DataBroker architecture is based on the `DataSet` class hierarchy in the JBCL. This enables you to use already-tested components, ready to customize by setting properties

14

and creating event handlers. This architecture also includes `Resolver` and `DataFile` interfaces (which you'll learn about a bit later). Figure 14.1 shows the DataBroker architecture.

FIGURE 14.1.

JBuilder's DataBroker architecture.

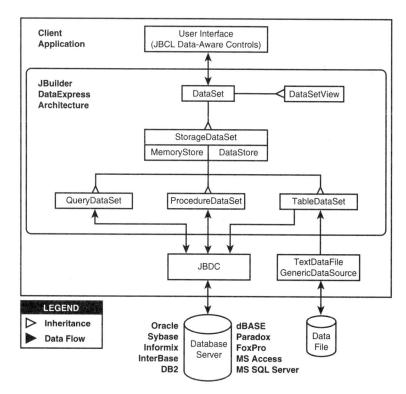

The `DataSet` and `StorageDataSet` classes are `abstract`, whereas `DataSetView`, `QueryDataSet`, `ProcedureDataSet`, `TableDataSet`, and `TextDataFile` are components on the Data Express tab of the Component Palette that you can use in your Java programs. Figure 14.2 shows the Data Express tab with each component called out.

No special driver installation or Registry settings are required with an all-Java JDBC driver. This allows applications built with the DataBroker to be run as an application or as an applet.

DataBroker handles type mapping through the use of `Variant` data types. `Variant` is a class that has static `int` identifiers that enumerate the data types supported. For the most part, the mapping from JDBC types to `Variant` types is one-to-one and is documented in the JBCL Reference.

borland.sql.dataset.QueryResolver ─┐

borland.jbcl.dataset.TextDataFile ─┐   ┌─ borland.sql.dataset.ProcedureResolver

borland.sql.dataset.Database ─┐   ┌─ borland.jbcl.dataset.DataSetView

FIGURE 14.2.

*The Data Express tab
of the Component
Palette.*

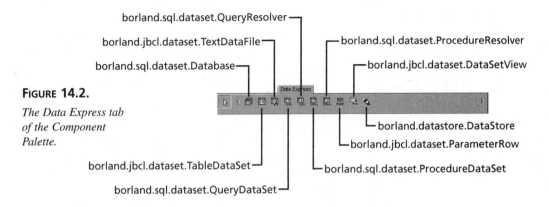

└─ borland.datastore.DataStore

└─ borland.jbcl.dataset.ParameterRow

borland.jbcl.dataset.TableDataSet ─┘

└─ borland.sql.dataset.ProcedureDataSet

borland.sql.dataset.QueryDataSet ─┘

In the area of error handling, all DataBroker exception classes are either a
`DataSetException` or a subclass. DataBroker exceptions can also catch other types of
exceptions (such as `IOException` and `SQLException` objects).

Data Access

Now, let's look at each of the classes and components that you'll use to create database
applications in JBuilder.

DataSet

`DataSet` is an `abstract` class, and all navigation, data access, and update methods for a
`DataSet` object are provided in this class, as well as support for master-detail relationships, ordering, and filtering. Data-aware JBCL controls have a `DataSet` property that
allows those controls to set their `DataSet` properties to any of the components derived
from `DataSet`, such as `DataSetView`, `QueryDataSet`, `ProcedureDataSet`, and
`TableDataSet`.

StorageDataSet

`StorageDataSet` is an `abstract` class that manages the storage of `DataSet` data and view
indices. It also provides methods for adding, deleting, changing, and moving data, and it
is where all row updates, inserts, and deletes are automatically recorded.

DataSetView

`DataSetView` is used to provide a cursor with ordering and filtering, by setting the
`StorageDataSet` property. You can also use this component to switch multiple
`DataSetView` components to a new `DataSet` by changing their `StorageDataSet` properties.

14

QueryDataSet

QueryDataSet is a JDBC-specific subclass of DataSet, which manages a JDBC data provider, as specified in the Query property (a SQL statement).

ProcedureDataSet

ProcedureDataSet (C/S only) is also a JDBC-specific subclass of DataSet, which manages a JDBC data provider, as specified in the Procedure property (a stored procedure).

QueryResolver

A QueryResolver is used to control how updates occur and how conflicts are resolved by setting a DataSet component's Resolver property to your QueryResolver component.

TableDataSet

TableDataSet is a DataSet component without any built-in provider; however, it can still resolve its changes back to a data source.

DataModule

The DataModule is a nonvisual container for components, such as DataSet and Database components, and is available from the New page of the New dialog box (File | New). Although other containers such as frames and applets can contain data-access components, it is usually better to gather them into a DataModule object. This enables you to separate application logic from the user interface components (such as frames and data-aware controls). If you use the following line of code as a template for how you should refer to the DataModule object in your code,

```
DataModule myDMod = DataModule.getDataModule();
```

you can reference the DataModule object you just created in other frames or applets, enabling you to reuse its components as a group.

Database

Multiple DataSet components (such as QueryDataSet and ProcedureDataSet objects) can share the same Database object by setting their Database properties. The Database Connection property specifies the URL, login name, password, and optional JDBC driver.

Providing Data

DataSet components can obtain data from any JDBC data source. The Database property is used to specify what Connection to run the query against. The Query property is a String object encapsulating the SQL statement. The ParameterRow property is where you can set optional query parameters. The executeOnOpen event causes the QueryDataSet object to execute the query when it is first opened, which is useful for presenting live data at design time. The AsynchronousExecution property causes DataSet object rows to be obtained in a separate thread, allowing the data to be accessed and displayed while the QueryDataSet object is obtaining rows from the Connection.

The QueryDataSet component can be used in three ways to get data:

- **Unparameterized Query:** The query is executed, and rows are retrieved into the QueryDataSet object.

- **Parameterized Query:** The ParameterRow property is used to set the Query parameters, and there is a getParameterRow method as well. If named parameters are used, name matching will be used to set parameters; if question markers are used, setting is left-to-right.

- **Dynamic Retrieval of Detail Groups:** The MasterLinkDescriptor property of a DataSet object contains a FetchAsNeeded property. If this property is set for a QueryDataSet object, the first time a new master row is navigated, the Detail query is executed.

In general, by setting the Query property and calling the executeQuery() method of a QueryDataSet object, the query is executed.

Navigating and Editing Data

After data has been retrieved into a DataSet object, it can be navigated. Navigation can be relative (next, prior, first, and last) either by position using the goToRow() method or by value using the locate() or lookup() methods. If the DataSet object is connected to a data-aware control in the user interface, that control will track the current row in the DataSet object. If this is not desired, you can use a DataSetView object instead, which has an independent cursor, row ordering, and filtering.

A DataSet object also has methods for adding, deleting, and updating rows inside itself. Posting a new row to an unordered DataSet object sends the row to the end of the DataSet; if the DataSet object is ordered, the row goes to its properly sorted position. There is also a getStatus() method in the DataSet object that returns a bit mask indicating status information. The bit settings are defined in the RowStatus class.

Sorting and Filtering

Each DataSet object can have its own column ordering, specified by its Sort property. The SortDescriptor object also specifies non–case-sensitive and descending orderings, maintained with indexes. Indexes are freed by calling the freeAllIndexes() method

14

(defined in the StorageDataSet class). Filtering is accomplished by defining the DataSet component's RowFilter event. If a RowFilter event handler is parameterized, the DataSet object can be forced to recalculate the filter by calling its recalc() method.

Master-Detail Support

You enable master-detail support by setting the detail DataSet component's MasterLink property, linking column values from the master DataSet object to the detail DataSet object. As the master is navigated, the detail will show only the associated group of details that have matching link column values. A master row cannot be deleted, and a master link column cannot be modified if it has detail rows associated with it. A master DataSet object can have multiple detail DataSet components associated with it, and a detail DataSet object can be a master for another detail DataSet object.

There are two approaches to using master-detail functionality with QueryDataSet components:

- Set the MasterLink property, and then execute the queries for all DataSet objects that have master-detail relationships in the same transaction, which provides a consistent view of all the related DataSet objects.

- If the detail DataSet object is parameterized, you can set the fetchAsNeeded property in the MasterLink property. However, because detail groups are retrieved in separate transactions, they might be inconsistent in relation to each other.

Resolving a DataSet

The DataBroker architecture has extensive built-in support for saving DataSet object changes to a JDBC data source and resolving any conflicts that might occur. Automatic resolution calls the saveChanges() method (defined in the Database class) for the DataSet objects (or any DataSet subclass), causing all the inserts, deletes, and updates to be saved to the JDBC data source in a single transaction by default. Custom resolution involves using the DataSet component's Resolver property. (Any DataSet object that descends from the StorageDataSet class has this property.) You can also instantiate a QueryResolver class, set its properties and event handlers, and then set the DataSet component's Resolver property to your QueryResolver component. By using a Resolver in this way, you can control how updates occur and how conflicts are resolved (using error handlers).

The saveChanges() method delegates the work of actually saving changes to a subclass called SQLResolutionManager. Here is a code snippet that shows what the saveChanges() method actually does:

```
SQLResolutionManager resolutionManager = new SQLResolutionManager();
resolutionManager.setDatabase(this);
resolutionManager.setDoTransactions(true);
resolutionManager.savechanges(DataSets);
```

Data-Aware Controls

In this section, each data-aware control is listed with a brief explanation of how it relates to underlying data-access components. To connect each of these components to its related data-access component, click the drop-down arrow in the `DataSet` property, and simply select one of the `DataSet` subclass components available in the list.

GridControl

When a grid column header is clicked, data will be sorted in ascending order by that column. If clicked a second time, the column will be sorted in descending order. The grid notifies the `DataSet` object when it switches columns, and the `LocatorControl` object uses the information so that it knows what column to search.

StatusBar

When the `StatusBar` object's `DataSet` property is set, it makes the `StatusBar` a `StatusListener` of the `DataSet`. This causes the `StatusBar` to show information about `DataSet` navigation, editing, query execution progress, and other status messages.

NavigatorControl

If this component's `DataSet` property is set, the `NavigatorControl`'s buttons can control navigation, row replication, refresh (providing), and save (resolving) of the related `DataSet`. Refresh and save buttons are enabled only for `QueryDataSet` and `ProcedureDataSet` components.

LocatorControl

The `LocatorControl` component has `DataSet` and `ColumnName` properties to bind an interactive locator to a column. If the column is not specified, the first column in the `DataSet` will be located. If connected to a `GridControl`, the last column visited will be located. Incremental search is supported for columns of `String` type, which is not case-sensitive if all lowercase characters are typed.

ChoiceControl

Setting this control's `DataSet` property allows use of the `ColumnComponent`'s `PickListDescriptor` property to fill in its choice list and so can be used as a simple pick list control.

14

Summary

Today, you learned about the JDBC as a low-level solution for connecting to a SQL database, noting that performance and security can become an issue when you're connecting your Java programs to a SQL back end. Also, you had a chance to look at the JDBC API and an example of how a Java program might connect to a SQL database, query information, and return the results.

You also learned about the JBuilder data-access components as a high-level solution for connecting to SQL databases and using the underlying JDBC API. The DataBroker architecture was also introduced. Each data-access component's key properties were reviewed. The data-aware components were also discussed as they relate to the data-access components.

This is only an introduction to the overall capabilities of the JDBC and JBuilder's data-access components. Tomorrow, you'll look at how to design and build a large database application using these concepts. Day 15, "Building Database Applications," begins Week 3, which will also cover multithreading, persistence, building JavaBeans, deploying Java programs, network communications, and, on the final day, called "Inside Java," bytecodes and garbage collection.

Q&A

Q Might the JDBC pose any new security risks to the current Java security structure as described earlier in this book?

A The JDBC has been painstakingly designed to conform to the same security model that Java follows. One added security risk that might pose a problem, however, involves dealing with BLOBs (Binary Large Objects). The BLOB, also known as data type LONG RAW in SQL, is typically used to store binary data, including graphics and sounds. This could pose a potential loophole for passing viruses or native code to the client's system.

Q By using the ODBC, I am able to execute a SQL statement asynchronously. Does Java have something equivalent?

A Actually, Java has something better: multithreading. The DriverManager can have several connections to a database at one time, and each of these connections can execute more than one statement as well. Just like when you created animations, you can use put SQL statements in their own threads.

Workshop

The Workshop provides two ways for you to affirm what you've learned in this chapter. The Quiz section poses questions to help you solidify your understanding of the material covered. You can find answers to the quiz questions in Appendix A, "Answers to Quiz Questions." The Exercise section provides you with experience in using what you have learned. Try to work through all these before continuing to the next day.

Quiz

1. What are the four major types of JDBC connectivity?
2. What are the advantages of using a `DataModule`?
3. What property links a master `DataSet` to a detail `DataSet`?
4. Which property must be set in a data-aware component to connect it to its underlying data-access component?

Exercise

Using Listing 14.1 as a base, experiment with a table of your own, accessing and printing various rows of data based on a SQL query.

14

WEEK 3

At a Glance

15

16

17

18

19

20

21

DAY 15

Building Database Applications

Yesterday you were introduced to the underlying architecture that JBuilder implements to support building Java database applications. Today you'll create several database applications using the data-aware components and the DataBroker components. These components are found on the JBCL and the Data Express pages of the Component Palette, respectively.

Today, you'll learn about various aspects of creating a database application, such as these:

- Setting up Local InterBase and data sources
- Creating, updating, and deleting tables
- Designing the database application's user interface
- Handling dataset exceptions
- Building and testing the database application

You'll explore these topics by creating a simple table-editing utility application.

Today's project will be a member of a package. To create a new project for this application, select File|New Project. In the Project Wizard dialog box, select `untitled\untitled1.jpr` in the File field and type `DBApps\TableEdit.jpr` in its place. Click the Finish button to close the dialog box and generate the project files.

Installing and Configuring Local InterBase

Before you work with any of today's examples, you'll want to be sure that Local InterBase is properly installed and configured. It's best if you install Local InterBase after installing JBuilder so that you can set up the data source easily.

To install Local InterBase, click the Local InterBase 5.11 button in the Borland JBuilder 2.0 Installation dialog box, shown in Figure 15.1.

FIGURE 15.1.

The Borland JBuilder 2.0 Installation dialog box.

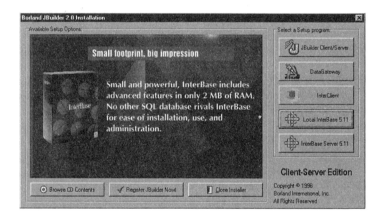

The InterBase Server Setup prepares the InstallShield Wizard, and then the InterBase Server Setup dialog box appears, as shown in Figure 15.2.

Click the Next> button and read the software license agreement in the Software License Agreement dialog box. Click the Yes button (if you click No, you abort the installation process), and the Important Installation Information dialog box appears.

Read last-minute installation information in the Important Installation Information dialog box, and then click the Next> button. The License Certificate dialog box appears, as shown in Figure 15.3.

Enter your Certificate ID and Certificate Key into the appropriate text boxes, and then click the Next> button. The Select InterBase Components dialog box appears, as shown in Figure 15.4.

FIGURE 15.2.

The InterBase Server Setup dialog box.

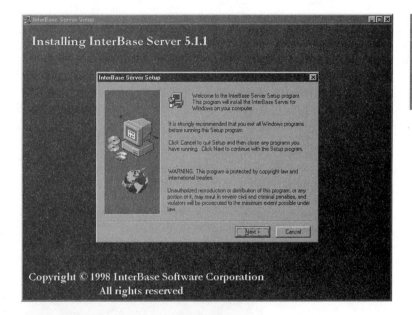

15

FIGURE 15.3.

The License Certificate dialog box requests an ID and a Key value.

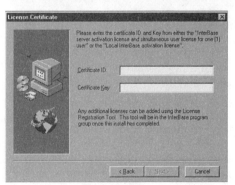

It's recommended that you install most of the components listed for working through this. Make sure that the InterBase ODBC Driver option is checked. Also, be sure to check the InterBase SQL Tutorial, InterBase Example Programs, and InterBase Example Database components. You use a database provided in the SQL tutorial and example components in this chapter. These components are also helpful if you're a SQL novice. You don't need the InterBase SDK Support component for this chapter. Use the InterBase SDK Support component for developing native InterBase applications in C or C++. After you've selected the components that you want installed, click the Next> button, and the InterBase TCP/IP Support dialog box appears, as shown in Figure 15.5.

FIGURE 15.4.

Select the InterBase components to install.

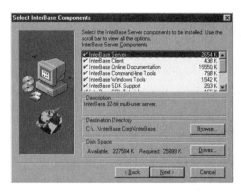

FIGURE 15.5.

InterBase TCP/IP support can be completed automatically.

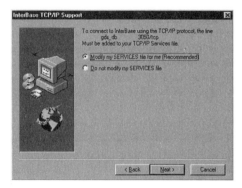

Select one of the two options provided in the InterBase TCP/IP Support dialog box. It's recommended that you let the installation program modify your TCP/IP services file for you. Then click the Next> button and the Ready to Copy Files dialog box appears, as shown in Figure 15.6.

FIGURE 15.6.

The ODBC Configuration dialog box.

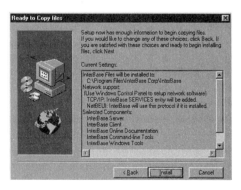

If you're happy with the list of files that will be installed, click the Install button. Otherwise, you can go back and make modifications by clicking the <Back button.

15

After the files are copied to disk, the ODBC Configuration dialog box shown in Figure 15.7 appears.

FIGURE 15.7.

The ODBC Configuration dialog box.

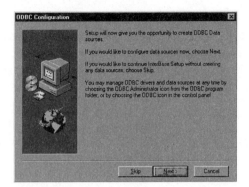

Click the Next> button to display the ODBC Data Source Administrator dialog box, shown in Figure 15.8.

FIGURE 15.8.

Use the ODBC Data Source Administrator dialog box to add and remove data sources.

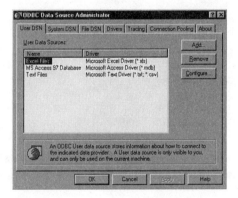

Add an InterBase data source to the User Data Sources list on the User DSN page of the ODBC Data Source Administrator dialog box. Click the Add button to open the Create New Data Source dialog box, shown in Figure 15.9.

FIGURE 15.9.

The Create New Data Source dialog box lists the available drivers.

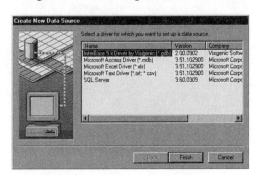

Select InterBase 5.x Driver by Visigenic (*.gdb) from the list on the Create New Data
Source dialog box, and then click the Finish button. The InterBase ODBC Configuration
dialog box appears. Type `DataSet Tutorial` into the Data Source Name text box. Make
sure that `<local>` is selected from the Network Protocol drop-down list. Type
`C:\Program Files\InterBase Corp\InterBase\Examples\employee.gdb` into the
Database text box. Enter `SYSDBA` into the Username text box and `Masterkey` into the
Password text box. The InterBase ODBC Configuration dialog box should look as shown
in Figure 15.10. Click the OK button.

Note

C:\Program Files\InterBase Corp\InterBase\Examples\employee.gdb is the
most common place to find the file when you use the default InterBase
installation. Nevertheless, the folder where you find the employee.gdb file
might vary depending on where you installed InterBase.

FIGURE 15.10.

*The InterBase ODBC
Configuration dialog
box with your database
information entered.*

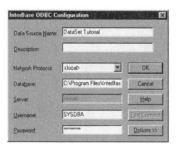

DataSet Tutorial should now be included in the User Data Sources list on the ODBC
Data Source Administrator dialog box, as shown in Figure 15.11.

FIGURE 15.11.

*The ODBC Data
Source Administrator
dialog box with your
new data source added
to the list.*

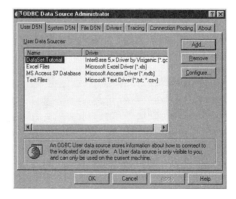

Click the OK button. The InterBase Server setup complete dialog box appears, as shown in Figure 15.12. Click the Finish button to complete the InterBase setup.

FIGURE 15.12.

The InterBase Server setup complete dialog box.

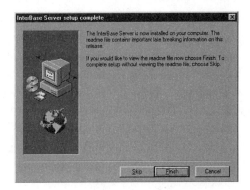

Basic Requirements

To introduce you to some of the most basic database components on the Data Express page of the Component Palette, this section shows you how to create a table editing utility application. The focus of this exercise is to demonstrate how easy it is to create, update, and delete tables using JBuilder. You'll also design the utility application's user interface using data-aware components from the JBCL page of the palette.

To create the main source files for the application, select File | New. In the New page of the New dialog box, double-click the Application icon. The Application Wizard dialog box appears. In the Application Wizard: Step 1 of 2 dialog box, type `TableEditor` in the Class field and check the Generate header comments option. Click the Next> button.

In the Application Wizard: Step 2 of 2 dialog, type `TEFrame` in the Class field and `Table Editor` in the Title field. Click the options Center frame on-screen and Generate status bar, and then click the Finish button. Select File | Save All.

To create your table-editing application, you will need to provide the following:

- A table connection to access data, called *providing*
- A display of existing and modified data
- A device for navigating the rows
- A mechanism for saving changes, called *resolving*

Some of these elements involve visual data-aware JBCL components, and some rely on nonvisual Data Express components. Let's look at each element in turn.

Providing Data

In the Navigation pane, select TEFrame.java and then click the Content pane's Design tab. In the UI Designer, a Frame object containing a BevelPanel object and a StatusBar object is displayed.

The first item you want to add is a Database component, which supplies the JDBC connection to the SQL server. Choose the Data Express tab of the Component Palette, and then click the Database component. Because this is a nonvisual component (it has no runtime representation, and it is represented only by an icon during design time), you can place it into the project by clicking anywhere in the Content pane or Structure pane. The entry for this component will appear as a member of the Data Access folder in the Structure pane, so click there. An entry for database1 will appear.

With database1 selected in the Structure pane, click on the Properties tab to open the Inspector pane to the Properties page. Click the connection property in the Properties page of the Inspector pane, and then click its ellipsis (...) button to display the connection property's editor. Figure 15.13 shows the connection dialog box that appears.

FIGURE 15.13.

The connection dialog box.

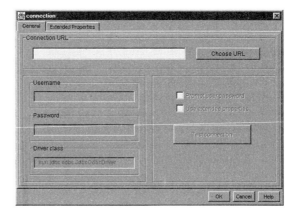

On the General page of the connection dialog box, click the Choose URL button. The Choose a Connection URL dialog box appears, as shown in Figure 15.14.

Click the Show Data Sources button in the ODBC Drivers area of the Choose a Connection URL dialog box. Scroll down in the list created in the dialog box to the following entry:

```
jdbc:odbc:Dataset Tutorial <sun.jdbc.odbc.JdbcOdbcDriver>
```

FIGURE 15.14.

*The Choose a
Connection URL
dialog box.*

Select this entry and then click the OK button. Back in the connection dialog box, type
SYSDBA in the Username field and masterkey in the Password field, and then click the
Test Connection button.

Just below the Test Connection button, a message should appear: Connecting. This
should be followed by another message: Success. If not, go back through the preceding
steps, rechecking everything carefully. When you have successfully connected, click the
OK button to close the property editor. Your connection is now established, giving you
access to all the InterBase tables in that database data source.

In addition to a database connection, you need to add a component that can read the data
from a table and provide the rows to the visual components of your user interface. For
this, you'll need to add a QueryDataSet component from the Component palette's Data
Express page. Click the QueryDataSet component and then drop it onto the Structure
pane to add queryDataSet1 to your program.

With queryDataSet1 selected, click its query property, and then click the ellipsis button
to display its property editor, the query dialog box shown in Figure 15.15.

FIGURE 15.15.

*Modify database
queries in the query
dialog box.*

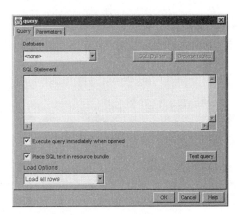

In the Database choice menu on the Query page of the query dialog box, select database1 from the drop-down list. In the SQL Statement edit field, type this:

```
select * from COUNTRY
```

Now click the Test Query button. Below the button will appear the text Running... and then Success. Click OK to close the dialog box. The Create ResourceBundle dialog box appears, as shown in Figure 15.16.

FIGURE 15.16.

The Create ResourceBundle dialog box.

Use the Create ResourceBundle dialog box to create a ResourceBundle object encapsulating special-purpose text, in this case SQL statements.

You have two choices for the type of resource bundle—you can select the ListResourceBundle or PropertyResourceBundle class. Each is a subclass of the ResourceBundle class. A ListResourceBundle object provides the better performance, and a PropertyResourceBundle object provides easier access to and modification of the data. Select ListResourceBundle this time from the Type drop-down list. Click the OK button.

The following new class, SqlRes, is added to your project:

```java
package DBApps;

import java.util.*;

public class SqlRes extends java.util.ListResourceBundle {
  static final Object[][] contents = {
    { "COUNTRY", "select * from COUNTRY" }};

  public Object[][] getContents() {
    return contents;
  }
}
```

The SqlRes class is the resource bundle—a SQL resource bundle to be exact—and it's extended from the ListResourceBundle class. Your connection and query are completed and ready to provide data to the data-aware components that you will use in your user interface.

User Interface

For your user interface, you already have a Frame object that displays a bordered window, a StatusBar object on which to display messages, and a BevelPanel object as a background for the rest of your user interface. You still need to display the data to provide a way for users to navigate through the data and to provide a way to load other tables.

On the Control palette's JBCL page, click the NavigatorControl component and drop it onto bevelPanel1. The navigatorControl1 will appear in its default size in the upper-left corner of the panel, but you can use the grab handles to stretch it across the top of the panel. Also, you should move it down about the same distance as the control is thick. You'll be adding a couple of controls at the top later. Next, click the GridControl component (also on the JBCL page) and click just below the left side of the navigatorControl1 component. Hold down the left mouse button while you drag the mouse cursor to the lower-right corner of the panel, and then let go to create gridControl1. If it didn't come out quite the right size, use the grab handles to resize. Arrange these components as shown in Figure 15.17.

To connect your user interface elements to the query object, click navigatorControl1, Shift+click gridControl1, and Shift+click statusBar. As you do this, note that the properties these controls have in common are displayed in the Inspector pane. Now, click the dataset property and select queryDataSet1 from the list. When you do, you should see the grid populate with records from the COUNTRY table, and the status bar will display Record 1 of 14, as shown in Figure 15.17.

FIGURE 15.17.

The user interface is connected with the query.

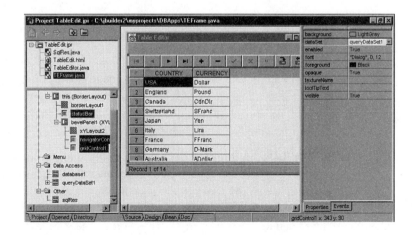

This takes care of displaying the data and navigation, but you still need to have a way to load other tables. You will use a `ChoiceControl` component with a `Label` component to indicate its purpose. Choose the AWT tab of the Component Palette, click the `Label` component, and then click the upper-left portion of `bevelPanel1`. Change its `text` property to `Currently Editing:` and its `alignment` property to 2.

Click the `ChoiceControl` component on the palette's JBCL page and drop it on `bevelPanel1` just to the right of `label1`. Double-click `choiceControl1`'s `items` property. Click the ellipsis button. The items dialog box appears, as shown in Figure 15.18.

FIGURE 15.18.

The items dialog box.

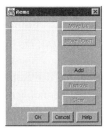

Add the following list of items to the items dialog box:

```
COUNTRY
CUSTOMER
DEPARTMENT
EMPLOYEE
EMPLOYEE_PROJECT
JOB
PROJECT
PROJ_DEPT_BUDGET
SALARY_HISTORY
SALES
PHONE_LIST
```

This is a list of all the tables in the `employee.gdb` database. You add each item by clicking the Add button and then double-clicking on the newly added item. Type the name of the item from the list. Repeat this procedure until you've added all 11 items. Click the OK button to save the list of selectable items.

The last item for the user interface is a message dialog to confirm that you want to load the new table selection. Choose the Control palette's JBCL Containers tab, click the Message component, and click anywhere on the Structure pane to add `message1` to the Component Tree. Select `message1` in the Structure pane, and set its `buttonSet` property to `OkCancel` and its `frame` property to `this`. Type `Load new table?` into its message property field, and type `Load Confirmation` into its title property field. Click the

15

Inspector pane's Events tab to change to the Events page, and then triple-click the `actionPerformed` event and add the code shown in Listing 15.1.

Type   **LISTING 15.1** THE switch STATEMENT.

```
 1: switch (message1.getResult()) {
 2:   case Message.OK:
 3:     try {
 4:       String newSelect = (String)choiceControl1.get();
 5:       queryDataSet1.close();
 6:       queryDataSet1.setQuery(new
    ➥borland.sql.dataset.QueryDescriptor(database1,
 7:         "select * from " + newSelect, true));
 8:       queryDataSet1.executeQuery();
 9:       statusBar.setDataSet(queryDataSet1);
10:       navigatorControl1.setDataSet(queryDataSet1);
11:       gridControl1.setDataSet(queryDataSet1);
12:       prevSelect = newSelect;
13:     }
14:     catch (Exception me) {
15:       borland.jbcl.dataset.DataSetException.handleException(me);
16:     }
17:     break;
18:   case Message.CANCEL:
19:     choiceControl1.select(prevSelect);
20:   default:
21:     // just close dialog
22: }
```

Analysis   If the user clicks the OK button in the message dialog box, you need to handle the table selection. This should always be done inside a `try` block because query operations can throw a `DataSetException` object, which must be handled or rethrown. In the `try` block, `newSelect` is set to the `choiceControl1` selection by calling the `get()` method (which returns the int index of the selection) and then casting it to a `String` object. Then you close the current query and set the new query using code similar to that inserted for the original query. This sets up the SQL statement by concatenating `"select * from "` and `newSelect`. Execute the query by calling `queryDataSet1.executeQuery()` and set your three data-aware controls to the newly updated `queryDataSet1`. The last line in this block sets the variable `prevSelect` to the current selection. The `catch` block calls the `handleException()` method to handle the `DataSetException` object.

If the user clicks the Cancel button in the message dialog box, you need only reset the selection in `choiceControl1` to its original selection, keeping it in sync with the loaded table. You do this by selecting the value preserved in `prevSelect`.

Well, you've used `prevSelect` twice, so you'd better declare it somewhere! You'll want to declare it as a variable in the `TEFrame` class, so add this line of code just under the class declaration:

```
String prevSelect = "COUNTRY";
```

It is set to `"COUNTRY"` to match the original table loaded by the query in the `jbInit()` method. Now, if the user cancels his selection, you can do the reset. If he selects a new table, this variable is updated to reflect the currently loaded table. You also want `choiceControl1` to display `"COUNTRY"` as its initial selection, so add this line of code to the `jbInit()` method:

```
choiceControl1.select("COUNTRY");
```

There's one last piece to tie all this together, because you want the message dialog to be displayed whenever the user makes a selection in `choiceControl1`. Switch back to UI Designer mode, select the `choiceControl1` object in the Structure pane, and then click the Events page of the Inspector pane. Triple-click the `itemStateChanged` event. Type this line of code in the method stub:

```
message1.show();
```

That should do it. Be sure to save your work by selecting File | Save All. Click the Run button in the toolbar to compile and run the new application. Figure 15.19 shows the completed application user interface.

FIGURE 15.19.

The user interface for Table Editor.

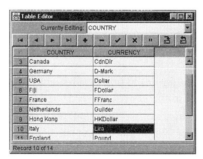

Resolving Changes

Because of the built-in features of the grid, you can resize the columns by dragging their left and right borderlines, reorder (sort) the entries by clicking a column header, and scroll both horizontally and vertically to display more columns and rows. Because it is hooked to the same dataset as the grid, the navigator control is fully functional. The status bar, also hooked to the same dataset, displays messages as you navigate through the rows. The status bar also displays messages when you insert or delete rows using the navigator control buttons. So, much of the functionality you need for your table editor is already here.

This includes saving changes, called *resolving*. The next-to-last button on the navigator control, the Save button, saves your changes to the database when it is clicked. You can also explicitly save changes to the table by adding this line of code where necessary:

```
database1.saveChanges(queryDataSet1);
```

This should always be done inside a `try` block, just like the earlier query-related operations.

Listing 15.2 shows the completed source code for TEFrame.

TYPE   **LISTING 15.2.** TEFrame.java.

```
 1: //Title:        Your Product Name
 2: //Version:
 3: //Copyright:    Copyright (c) 1998
 4: //Author:       Your Name
 5: //Company:      Your Company
 6: //Description:Your description
 7: package DBApps;
 8:
 9: import java.awt.*;
10: import java.awt.event.*;
11: import borland.jbcl.control.*;
12: import borland.jbcl.layout.*;
13: import borland.sql.dataset.*;
14: import java.util.*;
15:
16: public class TEFrame extends DecoratedFrame {
17:     String prevSelect = "COUNTRY";
18:     ResourceBundle sqlRes = ResourceBundle.getBundle("DBApps.SqlRes");
19:
20:     //Construct the frame
21:     BorderLayout borderLayout1 = new BorderLayout();
22:     XYLayout xYLayout2 = new XYLayout();
23:     BevelPanel bevelPanel1 = new BevelPanel();
24:     StatusBar statusBar = new StatusBar();
25:     Database database1 = new Database();
26:     QueryDataSet queryDataSet1 = new QueryDataSet();
27:     NavigatorControl navigatorControl1 = new NavigatorControl();
28:     GridControl gridControl1 = new GridControl();
29:     Label label1 = new Label();
30:     ChoiceControl choiceControl1 = new ChoiceControl();
```

continues

LISTING 15.2. CONTINUED

```
31:    Message message1 = new Message();
32:
33:    public TEFrame() {
34:      try  {
35:        jbInit();
36:      }
37:      catch (Exception e) {
38:        e.printStackTrace();
39:      }
40:    }
41: //Component initialization
42:
43:    private void jbInit() throws Exception  {
44:      this.setLayout(borderLayout1);
45:      this.setSize(new Dimension(400, 300));
46:      this.setTitle("Table Editor");
47:      statusBar.setDataSet(queryDataSet1);
48:      database1.setConnection(new
   ➥ borland.sql.dataset.ConnectionDescriptor(
   ➥ "jdbc:odbc:DataSet Tutorial", "SYSDBA", "masterkey", false,
   ➥ "sun.jdbc.odbc.JdbcOdbcDriver"));
49:      queryDataSet1.setQuery(new borland.sql.dataset.QueryDescriptor(
   ➥ database1, sqlRes.getString("COUNTRY"), null, true, Load.ALL));
50:      navigatorControl1.setDataSet(queryDataSet1);
51:      gridControl1.setDataSet(queryDataSet1);
52:      gridControl1.setDefaultColumnWidth(1000);
53:      label1.setAlignment(2);
54:      label1.setText("Currently Editing:");
55:      choiceControl1.setItems(new String[] {"COUNTRY", "CUSTOMER",
   ➥ "DEPARTMENT", "EMPLOYEE", "EMPLOYEE_PROJECT", "JOB", "PROJECT",
   ➥ "PROJ_DEPT_BUDGET", "SALARY_HISTORY", "SALES", "PHONE_LIST"});
56:      choiceControl1.addItemListener(new java.awt.event.ItemListener() {
57:        public void itemStateChanged(ItemEvent e) {
58:          choiceControl1_itemStateChanged(e);
59:        }
60:      });
61:      choiceControl1.select("COUNTRY");
62:      message1.setFrame(this);
63:      message1.setMessage("Load new table?");
64:      message1.setTitle("Load Confirmation");
65:      message1.addActionListener(new java.awt.event.ActionListener() {
66:        public void actionPerformed(ActionEvent e) {
67:          message1_actionPerformed(e);
68:        }
69:      });
70:      message1.setButtonSet(Message.OK_CANCEL);
71:      bevelPanel1.setLayout(xYLayout2);
```

```
72:     this.add(statusBar, BorderLayout.SOUTH);
73:     this.add(bevelPanel1, BorderLayout.CENTER);
74:     bevelPanel1.add(navigatorControl1, new XYConstraints(0, 25, 390,
➥-1));
75:     bevelPanel1.add(gridControl1, new XYConstraints(0, 51, 390,
➥197));
76:     bevelPanel1.add(label1, new XYConstraints(48, 1, -1, -1));
77:     bevelPanel1.add(choiceControl1, new XYConstraints(160, 0, 227,
➥19));
78:   }
79:
80:   void message1_actionPerformed(ActionEvent e) {
81:     switch (message1.getResult()) {
82:       case Message.OK:
83:         try {
84:           String newSelect = (String)choiceControl1.get();
85:           queryDataSet1.close();
86:           queryDataSet1.setQuery(new
➥borland.sql.dataset.QueryDescriptor(
87:             database1, "select * from " + newSelect, true));
88:           queryDataSet1.executeQuery();
89:           statusBar.setDataSet(queryDataSet1);
90:           navigatorControl1.setDataSet(queryDataSet1);
91:           gridControl1.setDataSet(queryDataSet1);
92:           prevSelect = newSelect;
93:         }
94:         catch (Exception me) {
95:           borland.jbcl.dataset.DataSetException.handleException(me);
96:         }
97:         break;
98:       case Message.CANCEL:
99:         choiceControl1.select(prevSelect);
100:      default:
101:        // just close dialog
102:     }
103:   }
104:
105:   void choiceControl1_itemStateChanged(ItemEvent e) {
106:     message1.show();
107:   }
108: }
```

Creating Tables

In any project where you have a QueryDataSet component, you can use it to create a
new SQL table. Now, let's create one using today's project.

With `queryDataSet1` selected, click its `query` property, and then click the ellipsis button to display its property editor. In the Database choice menu, select `database1` from the drop-down list. In the SQL Statement edit field, type the following:

```
create table SAMPLETABLE (
  firstField char(10),
  nextField numeric(5));
```

Now click the Test Query button. Below the button will appear the text `Running...` and then `Failed`. The error is caused by the fact that the query doesn't return a result set, which is actually the desired behavior. An Error dialog box states:

```
Execution of query failed.
```

Click the Next> button, and a second message appears:

```
No ResultSet was produced.
```

This is what you expected, so dismiss this dialog by clicking OK. Now, click the Browse Tables button. You should see `SAMPLETABLE` in the list of tables. When you click `SAMPLETABLE` in the left list box, the right list box displays two columns: `FIRSTFIELD` and `NEXTFIELD`. Click Cancel. Now you can use your table editor to add records to your new table.

To delete this table from `employee.gdb`, use this SQL query:

```
drop table SAMPLETABLE
```

Summary

Today you created a simple utility application that demonstrated some of the very basic operations needed to create a database application. You learned about setting up the Local InterBase Server, and you connected to its sample `employee.gdb` database. You also saw how JBuilder makes it easy to create and test new queries using the `QueryDataSet` component's `query` property.

By using data-aware JBCL components and hooking their `dataset` properties to the appropriate `QueryDataSet` component, you were able to provide data to these components. This allowed you to display the data in a grid, navigate through the table rows, and automatically show table-related messages in a status bar. Resolving changes was also briefly discussed. You saw that by using the `NavigatorControl` component's Save button, changes were saved to the table's disk file, and you learned about the `saveChanges()` method as well.

15

This chapter only scratched the surface of what you can do with Java database programming, but hopefully it has whetted your appetite to explore this area of programming.

Q&A

Q **Where can I learn more about SQL statements?**

A The Local InterBase Server installation includes an excellent tutorial that will teach you about SQL statements. To go through this tutorial, load the InterBase Help file. On the Contents page, double-click Getting Started, and then double-click Windows ISQL Tutorial.

Q **I keep trying to get my Data Sources set up, but I keep getting Connection Failed. I've installed both JBuilder and InterBase. What could be wrong?**

A For the connection to be made, the Local InterBase Server must be running. Normally, when you complete the installation, you should restart your machine or manually load the Local InterBase Server. After the Local InterBase Server is loaded, you should see a graphic in the Windows system tray that looks like a server with a green wedge behind it (the Local InterBase Server logo). Try your connection again; it should work correctly now.

Workshop

The Workshop provides two ways for you to affirm what you've learned in this chapter. The Quiz section poses questions to help you solidify your understanding of the material covered. You can find answers to the quiz questions in Appendix A, "Answers to Quiz Questions." The Exercises section provides you with experience in using what you have learned. Try to work through all of these before continuing to the next day.

Quiz

1. Where is the icon for configuring the Local InterBase Server data sources?
2. Where do nonvisual components appear at design time?
3. Which property of a data-aware component needs to be hooked up to the data-providing component?
4. What one thing must you do before attempting to set and execute a new query?
5. Why do query-related operations need to be put inside a try block?
6. What method can you use to resolve changes to a database?

Exercises

1. Explore the sample database applications in the `c:\jbuilder2\samples\` `borland\samples\tutorial\dataset` subdirectory. Go through the tutorials in Part I of the Programmer's Guide (paper manual) and create some of these samples from scratch.

2. Convert an existing database application that you have programmed in some other language (such as C++ or Pascal).

DAY 16

Multithreading

Today, you'll look at threads—what they are and how they can make your programs work better with other programs and with the Java system in general. You'll see how to:

- Think multithreaded thoughts
- Protect your methods and variables from unintended thread conflicts
- Create, start, and stop threads and threaded classes

You'll also learn how the scheduler works in Java.

Let's begin by understanding the motivation for threads, which are a relatively recent innovation in the world of computer science.

Why Use Threads?

Although processes have been around for decades, threads have only recently been adopted and accepted into the mainstream. This is odd because threads are extremely valuable, and programs written with them have better performance, noticeable even to the casual user. In fact, some of the best individual efforts over the years have involved implementing a threadlike facility by hand to give a program a friendlier feel.

Imagine that you're using your favorite editor on a large file. When it starts up, does it need to examine the entire file before it lets you edit? Does it need to make a backup copy of the file first? If the file is huge, this can make the file load seem to take forever. Wouldn't it be better for your editor to show you the first page, let you begin editing, and somehow (in the background) complete the slower tasks necessary for initialization? Threads allow exactly this kind of parallelism within a program.

Perhaps the best example of threading (or the lack thereof) is a Web browser. Can your browser download an indefinite number of files and Web pages at one time while still letting you continue browsing? While pages are downloading, can your browser download all the pictures and sounds in parallel, interleaving the fast and slow download times of multiple Internet servers? HotJava can do all these things—and more—by using the built-in threading features of the Java language.

When a nonmultithreaded program runs, it begins by executing its initialization code, and then it calls methods and continues processing until it's either complete or the program has exited. This program comprises a single thread, which is the program's locus of control. On the other hand, a multithreaded program allows several different execution threads in a program to run in parallel by trading timeslices so that the threads appear to be running simultaneously. Whenever you have a complex calculation, anticipate a lengthy load time, or have anything that takes a long time to execute, it's a good candidate for a new thread.

Applet Threads

You were first introduced to simple threads on Day 9, "Graphics, Fonts, and Multimedia," as a necessary part of creating animations. Let's review those basic concepts as they relate to applets. You need to make five modifications to create an applet that uses threads:

- Change the signature of your applet class to include the words `implements Runnable`.
- Include an instance variable to hold this applet's thread.
- Modify your `start()` method to do nothing but spawn a thread and start it running.
- Create a `run()` method that contains the actual code that begins your applet's execution.
- Create a `stop()` method to kill the thread and release its memory.

First, change the first line of your class definition to implement the Runnable interface:

```
import java.applet.*;
public class MyAppletClass extends Applet implements Runnable {...}
```

Remember that the Runnable interface defines the behavior your applet needs to run a thread, giving you a default definition for the run() method. By implementing the Runnable interface, you notify others that they can call the run() method on your instances.

Second, add an instance variable of type Thread to hold this applet's thread. In this example, the instance variable is named runner:

```
Thread runner;
```

Third, add a start() method or modify the existing one so that it does nothing but create and spawn a new thread. For example:

```
public void start() {
  if (runner == null); {
    runner = new Thread(this);
    runner.start();
  }
}
```

This example assigns a new thread to the runner instance variable declared earlier and then calls the Thread class's start() method to spawn the runner thread.

Fourth, declare the run() method to hold the body of your applet, containing anything that needs to run in its own thread:

```
public void run() {
    ...  // the body of your applet's working code
}
```

Finally, add a stop()method to suspend execution of that thread whenever the reader leaves the page. For example:

```
public void stop() {
  if (runner != null); {
    runner.stop();
    runner = null;
  }
}
```

The stop() method stops the thread from executing and sets the thread's variable runner to null to make the Thread object available for garbage collection.

That's it! With five basic modifications, you have an applet that runs in its own thread.

16

Parallelism Problems

If threading is so wonderful, why doesn't every system have it? Many modern operating systems have the basic primitives needed to create and run threads, but they are missing a key ingredient. The rest of the environment is not thread-safe.

NEW TERM   *Thread-safe* denotes a system that can automatically handle potential conflicts among running threads.

Imagine that you're running a thread, one of many, and each of these threads is sharing some important data managed by the system. If your thread were managing the data, it could take steps to protect it (as you'll see later today in the "Thinking Multithreaded" section), but the system is managing it. Now imagine a piece of code in the system that reads some crucial value, considers what to do for a while, and then increments the value:

```
if (crucialValue < 10) {
  . . .  // consider what to do for a while
  crucialValue += 1;
}
```

Remember that any number of threads might be calling this part of the system at once. The disaster occurs when two threads have both executed the `if` test before either has incremented the value. In this case, the value is clobbered by both threads with the same increment, so one increment is lost in the process. In this way, mouse or keyboard events can be dropped, database commits or rollbacks can be lost, and screen displays can be updated incorrectly.

This is known as the *synchronization problem*, and it's inescapable if any significant part of the system hasn't been written with threads in mind. Therein lies the barrier to a threaded environment—the great effort required to rewrite existing libraries for thread safety. Luckily, Java was written from scratch with thread safety in mind, and every Java class in its library is thread-safe. Thus, you now have to worry only about your own synchronization and thread-ordering problems because you can assume that the Java system will do the right thing.

> **Note**
>
> You might be wondering about the fundamental synchronization problem. Can't you just make the "consider what to do" area in the example smaller and smaller to reduce or eliminate the problem? Without atomic operations, the answer is no. (*Atomic operations* are a series of instructions that can't be interrupted by another thread. They make the operations appear to happen instantaneously, as if they were a single operation.) Even if the "consider what to do" took zero time, it's still at least two operations: First, look at some variable to make a decision, and then change something to reflect that decision. These two steps can never be made to happen "at the same time" without an atomic operation. To use an atomic operation, you must be provided with one by the system; it's literally impossible to create one on your own.

16

Consider the single line that follows:

```
crucialValue += 1;
```

This line involves three steps: Get the current value, add 1 to it, and store it. (Using `++crucialValue` doesn't help.) All three steps need to happen "all at once" (atomically) to be safe. Special Java primitives, and the lowest levels of the language, provide you with the basic atomic operations you need to build safe, threaded programs.

In addition to Java's thread-safe methods, however, you must also think about how to make your own methods thread-safe. This requires a new way of thinking.

Thinking Multithreaded

Getting used to threads takes a little while and a new way of thinking. Rather than imagining that you always know exactly what's happening when you look at a method you've written, you have to ask yourself some additional questions. What will happen if more than one thread calls into this method at the same time? Do you need to protect it in some way? What about your class as a whole? Are you assuming that only one of its methods is running at a time?

Often such assumptions are made without really being considered, and a local instance variable gets corrupted as a result. Let's make a few mistakes and then try to correct them. First, examine Listing 16.1, which shows the simplest case.

Type **LISTING 16.1.** `ThreadCounter.java.`

```
 1: public class ThreadCounter {
 2:   int crucialValue;
 3:
 4:   public void countMe() {
 5:     crucialValue += 1;
 6:   }
 7:
 8:   public int getCount() {
 9:     return crucialValue;
10:   }
11: }
```

This code suffers from the purest form of the synchronization problem: The += takes more than one step, and you might miscount the number of threads as a result. (Don't be too concerned about the thread specifics at this point. Just imagine that a whole bunch of threads can call countMe() at slightly different times.) Java lets you fix this, as shown in Listing 16.2.

Type **LISTING 16.2.** `SafeThreadCounter.java.`

```
 1: public class SafeThreadCounter {
 2:   int crucialValue;
 3:
 4:   public synchronized void countMe() {
 5:     crucialValue += 1;
 6:   }
 7:
 8:   public int getCount() {
 9:     return crucialValue;
10:   }
11: }
```

The synchronized keyword tells Java to make the block of code in the method thread-safe. Only one thread will be allowed inside this method at any one time; others must wait until the currently running thread is finished with it before they can begin running it. Basically, this atomizes the method, making it appear to happen instantaneously.

However, this implies that synchronizing a large, long-running, commonly called method is almost always a bad idea. All your threads would end up stuck in a queue at this bottleneck, waiting single-file to get their turn at this one slow method. So be sure to break the parts that really need protecting into small, atomizable methods.

The synchronization problem is even worse than you might think for unsynchronized variables. Because the interpreter can keep them around in registers during computations, and because a thread's registers can't be seen by other threads (especially if they're on another processor in a true multiprocessor computer), a variable can be corrupted in such a way that *no possible order* of thread updates could have produced the result. To avoid this bizarre case, you can label a variable volatile, meaning that you know it will be updated asynchronously by multiprocessor-like threads. Java then loads and stores the variable each time it's needed instead of using registers. This forces the program to use the "master copy" of the variable each time the variable's value is requested.

16

> **Note**
>
> In earlier releases of Java, variables that were safe from these odd effects were labeled threadsafe. Because most variables are safe to use, they are now assumed to be thread-safe unless you mark them volatile. Using the volatile keyword is such a rare event, however, that it was not used anywhere in the Java Class Library.

Points About Points

The howMany() method in Listing 16.2 doesn't need to be synchronized because it simply returns the current value of the instance variable. A method higher in the call chain might need to be synchronized, though—one that uses the value returned from the called method. Listing 16.3 shows an example.

TYPE   **LISTING 16.3.** Point.java.

```
 1: public class Point {  // redefines Point from java.awt package
 2:   private float x, y;  // OK since this is a different package
 3:
 4:   public float getX() {  // needs no synchronization
 5:     return x;
 6:   }
 7:
 8:   public float getY() {  // needs no synchronization
 9:     return y;
10:   }
11:   . . .  // methods to set and change x and y
12: }
13:
14: public class UnsafePointPrinter {
15:   public void print(Point p) {
16:     System.out.println("The point's x is " + p.getX()
17:                         + " and y is " + p.getY() + ".");
18:   }
19: }
```

The howMany() method is analogous to the getX() and getY() methods shown previously. They don't require synchronization because they just return the values of instance variables. It is the responsibility of the caller of the getX() and getY() methods to decide whether the caller needs to synchronize itself—and in this case, it does. Although the print() method simply reads values and prints them, it reads *two* values. This means that there is a chance that some other thread, running between the call to p.getX() and p.getY(), could have changed the values assigned to the x and y variables encapsulated in Point p. Remember, you don't know how many other threads have a way to reach and call methods on this Point object! "Thinking multithreaded" comes down to being careful anytime you make an assumption that something has *not* happened between two parts of your program (even two parts of the same line, or the same expression, such as the string + concatenation in this example).

Understanding the TryAgainPointPrinter Class

You could try to make a safe version of the print() method by simply adding the synchronized keyword modifier to it, but instead, let's try a slightly different approach, which is shown in Listing 16.4.

TYPE   **LISTING 16.4.** TryAgainPointPrinter.java.

```
 1: public class TryAgainPointPrinter {
 2:   public void print(Point p) {
 3:     float safeX, safeY;
 4:
 5:     synchronized(this) {
 6:       safeX = p.getX();  // these two lines now
 7:       safeY = p.getY();  // occur atomically
 8:     }
 9:     System.out.println("The point's x is " + safeX
10:                         + " and y is " + safeY + ".");
11:   }
12: }
```

The synchronized statement takes an argument that says what object you want to lock to prevent more than one thread from executing the enclosed block of code at the same time. Here, you use this (the instance itself), which is exactly the object that would have been locked if you had modified the whole print() method by adding the synchronized keyword. You have an added bonus with this new form of synchronization: You can specify exactly what part of a method needs to be protected, and the rest can be left alone.

Notice that you took advantage of this freedom to make the protected part of the method as small as possible while leaving the string creations, concatenations, and printing (which together take a small but nonzero amount of time) outside the "safe" area. This is both good style (as a guide to the reader of your code) and more efficient because fewer threads get stuck waiting to execute the protected area.

Understanding the `SafePointPrinter` Class

You might still be concerned about the `TryAgainPointPrinter` example. It seems as if you made sure that nothing executes internal calls to the getX() and getY() methods out of order; but have you prevented Point p from changing out from under you? The answer is no. You still haven't solved that part of the problem because between the time that the `TryAgainPointPrinter()` method is called (and grabs the current Point object assigned to the p variable) and its synchronized statement method is executed, another thread could have changed Point p. You really need the full power of the synchronized statement here. Listing 16.5 shows how to provide this.

16

> **TYPE** **LISTING 16.5.** SafePointPrinter.java.

```
 1: public class SafePointPrinter {
 2:   public void print(Point p) {
 3:     float safeX, safeY;
 4:
 5:     synchronized(p) {    // nothing can change p
 6:       safeX = p.getX();  // while these two lines
 7:       safeY = p.getY();  // occur atomically
 8:     }
 9:     System.out.println("The point's x is " + safeX
10:                        + " and y is " + safeY + ".");
11:   }
12: }
```

Now you've got it. You actually needed to protect the Point object assigned to the p variable from changes, so you lock it by giving it as the argument to your synchronized statement. Now when the getX() and getY() methods are executed at the same time, they can be sure to get the current values assigned to the x and y variables encapsulated by the Point object assigned to the p variable when the synchronized statement executes.

A Safe `Point` Class

You're still assuming, however, that the Point object assigned to the p variable has properly protected *itself*. You can always assume this about system classes, but you redefined the `Point` class, so now it's your worry. You can make sure by writing and synchronizing the only method that can change the values assigned to the x and y variable inside the `Point` object yourself, as shown in Listing 16.6.

TYPE   **LISTING 16.6.** `Point.java`.

```
 1: public class Point {
 2:   private float x, y;
 3:
 4:   public float getX() {
 5:     return x;
 6:   }
 7:
 8:   public float getY() {
 9:     return y;
10:   }
11:
12:   public synchronized void setXandY(float newX, float newY) {
13:     x = newX;   // these two lines
14:     y = newY;   // occur atomically
15:   }
16: }
```

By making the only set method in the `Point` object synchronized, you guarantee that any other thread trying to grab a `Point` object and change it out from under you has to wait. You've locked the `Point` object assigned to the p variable with your `synchronized(p)` statement, and any other thread has to try to lock the same `Point` object (the same instance) via the implicit `synchronized(this)` statement that the `Point` object now executes upon entering the `setXandY()` method. Thus, at last you are thread-safe.

Note   If Java had some way of returning more than one value at a time, you could write a `synchronized getXandY()` method for the `Point` class that returned both values safely. In the current Java language, such a method could return a new, unique `Point` object to guarantee to its callers that no one else has a copy that might be changed. This sort of trick could then be used to minimize the parts of the system that needed to be concerned with synchronization.

Understanding the `ReallySafePoint` Class

An added benefit of the use of the `synchronized` modifier on methods (or of `synchronized(this) {...}`) is that only one of these methods (or blocks of code) can run at a time. You can use that knowledge to guarantee that only one of several crucial methods in a class will run at a time. Consider Listing 16.7.

TYPE **LISTING 16.7.** ReallySafePoint.java.

```
 1: public class ReallySafePoint {
 2:    private int x, y;
 3:
 4:    public synchronized Point getUniquePoint() {
 5:       // replaces getX and getY methods
 6:       return new Point(x,y);   // can be less safe because
 7:    }                          // only the caller has it
 8:
 9:    public synchronized void setXandY(int newX, int newY) {
10:       x = newX;
11:       y = newY;
12:    }
13:
14:    public synchronized void scale(int scaleX, int scaleY) {
15:       x *= scaleX;
16:       y *= scaleY;
17:    }
18:
19:    public synchronized void add(ReallySafePoint aRSP) {
20:       Point p = aRSP.getUniquePoint();
21:
22:       x += p.x;
23:       y += p.y;
24:       // Point p is soon thrown away by GC; no one else ever saw it
25:    }
26: }
```

This example combines several ideas mentioned earlier. To avoid callers having to synchronize(p) whenever getting the values assigned to the x and y variables, you've given them a synchronized way to get a unique Point object (such as returning multiple values). Each method then modifies the object's instance variables and is also synchronized to prevent the methods from running between the references to the values assigned to the x and y variables in the getUniquePoint() method and from stepping on each other as they modify the values assigned to the local x and y variables. Note that the add() method itself uses the getUniquePoint() method to avoid having to say synchronized(aRSP).

Classes that are this safe are a little unusual. It is more often your responsibility to protect yourself from other threads using a commonly held object (such as a Point object). You can only fully relax if you created the object yourself and nothing else has access to it. Otherwise, always consider thread safety.

Class Variable Protection

Suppose that you want a class variable to collect some information across all of a class's instances, as shown in Listing 16.8.

TYPE   **LISTING 16.8.** StaticCounter.java.

```
1: public class StaticCounter {
2:   private static int crucialValue;
3:
4:   public synchronized void CountMe() {
5:     crucialValue += 1;
6:   }
7: }
```

Is this safe? If crucialValue were an instance variable, it would be. Because it's a class variable, however, and there is only one copy of it for all instances, you can still have multiple threads modifying it by using different instances of the class. (Remember, the synchronized modifier locks the object this—an instance.) Luckily, you already have the tools you need to solve the problem. Listing 16.9 shows the solution.

TYPE   **LISTING 16.9.** StaticCounter.java.

```
1: public class StaticCounter {
2:   private static int crucialValue;
3:
4:   public void CountMe() {
5:     syncrhonized(getClass()) { // can't directly name StaticCounter
6:       crucialValue += 1;       // the (shared) class is now locked
7:     }
8:   }
9: }
```

The trick is to lock on a different object—not on an instance of the class, but on the class itself. Because a class variable is "inside" a class, just as an instance variable is inside an instance, this shouldn't be all that surprising. Similarly, classes can provide global resources that any instance (or other class) can access directly using the class name and lock using that same class name. In the preceding example, the crucialValue variable was used from within an instance of the StaticCounter class, but if the crucialValue variable were declared public instead, from anywhere in the program, it would be safe to say this:

```
synchronized(Class.for.Name("StaticCounter")) {
  StaticCounter.crucialValue +=1;
}
```

Note

> The direct use of another class's (or object's) variable is really not good style. It's used here simply to demonstrate something quickly. The StaticCounter class would normally provide a countMe()-like class method of its own to do this sort of dirty work.

16

You can now begin to appreciate how much work the Java team has done for you by considering all these eventualities for each and every class (and method) in the Java class library to make it thread-safe.

Creating and Using Threads

Now that you understand the power (and dangers) of having many threads running simultaneously, you'll see how those threads are actually created.

Caution

> The system itself always has a few so-called *daemon* threads running, one of which is constantly doing the tedious task of garbage collection for you in the background. There is also a main user thread that listens for events from your mouse and keyboard. If you're not careful, you can sometimes lock up this main thread. If you do, no events are sent to your program, and it appears to be dead. A good rule to keep in mind is that whenever you're doing something that *can* be done in a separate thread, it probably *should* be. Threads in Java are relatively cheap to create, run, and destroy, so don't use them too sparingly.

Because there is a class java.lang.Thread, you might guess that you can create a thread of your own by subclassing it—and you're right:

```
public class MyFirstThread extends Thread {  // i.e. java.lang.Thread
  public void run() {
    . . .  // do something useful
  }
}
```

You now have a new type of Thread class called MyFirstThread, which does something useful (unspecified) when its run() method is called. Of course, no one has created this thread or called its run() method, so it does absolutely nothing at the moment. To actually create and run an instance of your new thread class, you write the following:

```
MyFirstThread aMFT = new MyFirstThread();

aMFT.start();  // calls the run() method
```

You create a new instance of your thread class and then ask it to start running. What could be simpler? Stopping a thread:

```
aMFT.stop();
```

Besides responding to the start() and stop() methods, a thread can also be temporarily suspended and later resumed:

```
Thread t = new Thread();
t.suspend();
. . .  // do something special while t isn't running
t.resume();
```

A thread will automatically call the suspend() method when it's first blocked at a synchronized statement, and then it'll call the resume() method when it's later unblocked (when it's that thread's turn to execute the statement).

The Runnable Interface

This is all well and good if every time you want to create a thread you have the luxury of being able to place it under the Thread class in the single-inheritance class tree. What if it more naturally belongs under some other class, from which it needs to get most of its implementation? Interfaces come to the rescue:

```
public class ImportantThreadedSubclass extends ImportantClass implements
➥Runnable {
  public void run() {
    . . .  // do something useful
  }
}
```

By implementing the Runnable interface, you declare your intention to run in a separate thread. In fact, the Thread class itself implements the Runnable interface. As you also might guess from this example, the Runnable interface specifies only one method: the run() method. As in the MyFirstThread class, you expect something to create an instance of a thread and somehow call your run() method. Here's how that is accomplished:

```
ImportantThreadedSubclass anITS = new ImportantThreadedSubclass();
. . .
Thread aThread = new Thread(anITS);
. . .
aThread.start();  // calls the run() method indirectly
```

First you create an instance of the ImportantThreadedSubclass class. Then, by passing this instance to the constructor making the new Thread object, you assign the thread to the aThread variable. Whenever the Thread object assigned to the aThread variable starts up, its run() method calls the run() method of the target it was given (assumed by the Thread object to be an object that implements the Runnable interface). Therefore, when aThread.start() is executed, it indirectly calls your run() method. You can stop the thread assigned to the aThread variable by calling the stop() method, of course.

Tip

> If you don't need to talk to the Thread object explicitly or to the instance of the ImportantThreadedSubclass class, here's a one-line shortcut:
>
> new Thread(new ImportantThreadedSubclass()).start();

Understanding the ThreadTester Class

Listing 16.10 shows a longer, more involved example.

TYPE **LISTING 16.10.** SimpleRunnable.java.

```
 1: public class SimpleRunnable implements Runnable {
 2:   public void run() {
 3:     System.out.println("Currently in thread named '"
 4:                     + Thread.currentThread().getName() + "'.");
 5:   } // any other methods run() calls are in current thread as well
 6: }
 7:
 8: public class ThreadTester {
 9:   public static void main(String args[]) {
10:     SimpleRunnable aSR = new SimpleRunnable();
11:
12:     while (true) {
13:       Thread t = new Thread(aSR);
14:       System.out.println("new Thread() "
15:                     + (t == null ? "fail" : "succeed")
16:                     + "ed.");
17:       t.start();
18:       try {
19:         t.join();
20:       }
21:       catch (InterruptedException ignored) {}
22:       // waits for thread to finish its run() method
23:     }
24:   }
25: }
```

16

You might be concerned that only one instance of the class SimpleRunnable is created, but many new threads are using it. Don't they get confused? Remember to separate in your mind the instance (and the methods it understands) from the various threads of execution that can pass through it. The methods provide a template for execution, and the multiple threads created share that template. Each remembers where it is executing and whatever else it needs to make it distinct from the other running threads. They all share the same instance and the same methods. That's why, when adding synchronization, you need to imagine numerous threads running rampant over each of your methods.

The currentThread() class method can be called to get the thread in which a method is currently executing. If the SimpleRunnable class were a subclass of Thread, its methods would know the answer already (*it* is the running thread). Because the SimpleRunnable class implements the Runnable interface, however, and counts on something else (the ThreadTester class main() method) to create the thread, its run() method needs an alternative way to get its hands on that thread. Often you'll be deep inside methods called by your run() method when suddenly you need to get the current thread. The class method shown in the example works, no matter where you are.

Caution

> You can do some reasonably dangerous things with your knowledge of threads. For example, suppose that you're running in the main thread of the system and, because you think you're in a different thread, you accidentally do this:
>
> ```
> Thread.currentThread().stop();
> ```
>
> This has unfortunate consequences for your soon-to-be-deceased program!

The example then calls the getName() method on the current thread to get the thread's name (usually something helpful, such as Thread-23) so that it can tell the world in which thread the run() method is running.

The final thing to note is the use of the join() method, which, when sent to a thread, means "I'm planning to wait forever for you to finish your run() method." You don't want to do this lightly. If you have anything else important you need to get done in your thread anytime soon, you can't count on how long the joined thread might take to complete. In the example, the run() method is short and finishes quickly, so each loop can safely wait for the previous thread to die before creating the next one. (Of course, in this example, you didn't have anything else you wanted to do while waiting for the join() method anyway.)

Here's the output produced:

OUTPUT
```
new Thread() succeeded.
Current in thread named 'Thread-1'.
new Thread() succeeded.
Current in thread named 'Thread-2'.
new Thread() succeeded.
Current in thread named 'Thread-3'.
^C
```

Ctrl+C was pressed to interrupt the program because otherwise it would continue forever.

16

Understanding the NamedThreadTester Class

If you want your threads to have specific names, you can assign them yourself by using a two-argument form of the Thread class constructor, as shown in Listing 16.11.

TYPE   **LISTING 16.11.** NameThreadTester.java.

```
 1: public class NamedThreadTester {
 2:   public static void main(String args[]) {
 3:     SimpleRunnable aSR = new SimpleRunnable();
 4:
 5:     for (int i = 1; true; ++i) {
 6:       Thread t = new Thread(aSR, "" + (100 - i)
 7:                           + " threads on the wall...");
 8:       System.out.println("new Thread() "
 9:                        + (t == null ? "fail" : "succeed")
10:                        + "ed.");
11:       t.start();
12:       try {
13:         t.join();
14:       }
15:       catch (InterruptedException ignored) {}
16:       // waits for thread to finish its run() method
17:     }
18:   }
19: }
```

This constructor takes a target object, as before, and a String object, which names the new thread. Here's the output produced:

OUTPUT
```
new Thread() succeeded.
Current in thread named '99 threads on the wall...'.
new Thread() succeeded.
Current in thread named '98 threads on the wall...'.
new Thread() succeeded.
Current in thread named '97 threads on the wall...'.
^C
```

Naming a thread is one easy way to pass it some information. This information flows from the parent thread to its new child. It's also useful, for debugging purposes, to give threads meaningful names (such as `networkInput`) so that when they appear during an error—in a stack trace, for example—you can easily identify which thread caused the problem.

Thread Groups

You might also think of using names to help group or organize your threads, but Java actually provides a `ThreadGroup` class to perform this function. To set up the `ThreadGroup` object itself, two constructors are provided:

```
public ThreadGroup(aThreadGroupNameString)

public ThreadGroup(parentThreadGroup, aThreadGroupNameString)
```

The first constructor creates a new thread group named `aThreadGroupNameString`, and its parent is the currently running thread's `ThreadGroup` object. The second constructor creates a new thread group named `aThreadGroupNameString`, and its parent is the `parentGroupThread`.

A `ThreadGroup` object lets you organize threads into named groups and hierarchies, to control them all as a unit, and to keep them from being able to affect other threads (useful for security). Here are the three constructors with which you can assign a new thread to a `ThreadGroup` object:

```
Thread(aThreadGroup, aRunnableTarget)

Thread(aThreadGroup, aThreadNameString)

Thread(aThreadGroup, aRunnableTarget, aThreadNameString);
```

The first constructor creates the thread as a member of `aThreadGroup` and has as its target `aRunnableTarget`. The second constructor creates the thread as a member of `aThreadGroup` and names the thread `aThreadNameString`. The third constructor does it all.

Knowing When a Thread Has Stopped

Let's imagine a different version of the `NamedThreadTester` example, one that creates a thread and then hands the thread off to other parts of the program. Suppose that it would then like to know when that thread is killed (the `stop` method is called) so that it can perform a cleanup operation. If `SimpleRunnable` were a subclass of the `Thread` class, you might try to catch the stop method whenever it's sent—but look at the Thread class declaration of the stop method:

```
public final void stop() {...}
```

The final keyword means that you can't override this method in a subclass. In any event, SimpleRunnable isn't a subclass of the Thread class, so how can this imagined example possibly catch the untimely death of its thread? The answer is in Listing 16.12.

TYPE   **LISTING 16.12.** SingleThreadTester.java.

```
 1: public class SingleThreadTester {
 2:   public static void main(String args[]) {
 3:     Thread t = new Thread(new SimpleRunnable());
 4:     try {
 5:       t.start();
 6:       someMethodThatMightKillTheThread(t);
 7:     }
 8:     catch (ThreadDeath aTD) {
 9:       . . . // do some required cleanup
10:       throw aTD;  // re-throw the error
11:     }
12:   }
13: }
```

All you need know is that if the thread created in the example is killed, it throws an error of class ThreadDeath. The code catches that error and performs the required cleanup. It then rethrows the error, allowing the thread to finally die. The cleanup code isn't called if the thread dies a natural death (its run() method completes), but that's fine; the example asserted that cleanup was needed only when the stop() method was used on the thread.

Threads can die in other ways—for example, by throwing uncaught exceptions. In these cases, the stop() method is never called, and the code in Listing 16.12 wouldn't be sufficient. (If the cleanup must occur no matter how the thread dies, you can always put it in a finally clause.) Because unexpected exceptions can come out of nowhere to kill a thread, multithreaded programs that carefully handle all their exceptions are more predictable, robust, and easier to debug.

Thread Scheduling

You might be wondering in exactly what order your threads are run by the Java system scheduler.

NEW TERM   The *scheduler* is the part of the system that decides the real-time ordering of
threads.

The scheduler orders threads based on default and assigned priorities, requirements of
other running threads, current availability of system resources, and a number of other
considerations, so there's no way to precisely answer this question in advance. On the
other hand, if you're wondering how you can control that order, although it's a lot of
work, it can certainly be done.

Preemptive Versus Nonpreemptive

Normally, any scheduler has two fundamentally different ways of looking at its job: preemptive scheduling and nonpreemptive timeslicing.

NEW TERM   In *preemptive timeslicing,* the scheduler runs the current thread until it has used
up a set amount of time. Then the scheduler interrupts the thread, suspends it,
and resumes the next thread in line for another set amount of time. The set amount of
time is usually a tiny fraction of a second—so tiny that as each thread uses its slice of
time in turn, all threads appear to be running simultaneously.

NEW TERM   In *nonpreemptive scheduling*, the scheduler runs the current thread forever,
requiring that the thread tell the scheduler when it's safe to start a different
thread. Each thread appears to have control of the system until it explicitly gives up that
control.

Nonpreemptive scheduling always asks for permission to schedule and is valuable in
time-critical real-time applications in which being interrupted at the wrong moment, or
for too long, could have dire consequences. However, most modern schedulers use preemptive timeslicing because, except for a few time-critical cases, it has turned out to
make writing multithreaded programs much easier. For example, it doesn't force each
thread to decide exactly when it should yield control to another thread. Instead, every
thread can just run on blindly, knowing that the scheduler will be judicious about giving
all the other threads their chance to run.

This approach is still not the ideal way to schedule threads. You've given up a bit too
much control to the scheduler. The final touch that many modern schedulers add is to
allow you to assign each thread a priority. This creates a total ordering of all threads,
making some threads more "important" than others. Being higher priority might mean
that a thread gets a timeslice more often (or gets more time in its timeslice), but this
always means that the thread can interrupt other, lower-priority threads, even before their
timeslice has expired.

Java doesn't precisely specify scheduler behavior. Threads can be assigned priorities, and when a choice is made between several threads that all want to run, the highest-priority thread wins. However, Java doesn't specify what happens when threads of the same priority want to run. In fact, tugs-of-war between threads with the same priority are resolved differently, depending on the underlying platform. Some platforms cause Java to behave more like preemptive timeslicing, and others more like a nonpreemptive scheduler.

16

Note

Not knowing the fine details of how scheduling occurs is perfectly all right, but not knowing whether equal-priority threads must explicitly yield or face running forever is not a good thing. For example, all the threads you've created so far are equal-priority threads, so you don't know their cross-platform scheduling behavior.

Testing Your Scheduler

To find out what kind of scheduler you have on your system, try the code in Listing 16.13 and Listing 16.14.

TYPE **LISTING 16.13.** RunningInIdaho.java.

```
1: public class RunningInIdaho implements Runnable {
2:    public void run() {
3:       while (true)
4:          System.out.println(Thread.currentThread().getName());
5:    }
6: }
```

TYPE **LISTING 16.14.** PotatoThreadTester.java.

```
1: public class PotatoThreadTester {
2:    public static void main(String args[]) {
3:       RunningInIdaho aRII = new RunningInIdaho();
4:       new Thread(aRII, "one potato").start();
5:       new Thread(aRII, "two potato").start();
6:    }
7: }
```

For a nonpreemptive scheduler, the output will look like this:

OUTPUT
```
one potato
one potato
...
one potato
^C
```

This would go on forever, until you interrupted the program by pressing Ctrl+C. For a preemptive timeslicing scheduler, this program alternates between the two threads:

OUTPUT
```
one potato
one potato
...
one potato
two potato
two potato
...
two potato
one potato
^C
```

It will keep alternating like this until you once again interrupt it using Ctrl+C. What if you want to ensure that the two threads will take turns, no matter what the system scheduler wants to do? You can rewrite the `RunningInIdaho` class to match Listing 16.15.

TYPE **LISTING 16.15.** RunningInIdaho.java.

```
1: public class RunningInIdaho implements Runnable {
2:   public void run() {
3:     while (true)
4:       System.out.println(Thread.currentThread().getName());
5:       Thread.yield();  // let another thread run for a while
6:   }
7: }
```

Tip

Normally, you would have to write:

`Thread.currentThread().yield()`

to get your hands on the current thread and then yield. However, because this usage is so common, the Thread class provides the method call:

`Thread.yield()`

as a shortcut alternative to the longer method call.

The `Thread.yield()` method explicitly gives any other threads that are waiting a chance to begin running. If no other threads are waiting to run, the thread that called the `yield()` method simply regains control and continues running. In the current example, another thread is just *dying* to run. So when you now execute the class `ThreadTester`, it should output the following:

OUTPUT

```
one potato
two potato
one potato
two potato
one potato
two potato
one potato
^C
```

16

Even if your system scheduler is nonpreemptive and would never normally run the second thread, calling the `yield()` method will do the trick.

Understanding the `PriorityThreadTester` Class

To see whether priorities are working on your system, try the code in Listing 16.16.

TYPE   **LISTING 16.16.** `PriorityThreadTester.java`.

```
 1: public class PriorityThreadTester {
 2:   public static void main(String args[]) {
 3:     RunningInIdaho aRII = new RunningInIdaho();
 4:     Thread t1 = new Thread(aRII, "one potato");
 5:     Thread t2 = new Thread(aRII, "two potato");
 6:
 7:     t2.setPriority(t1.getPriority() + 1);
 8:     t1.start();  // at priority Thread.NORM_PRIORITY
 9:     t2.start();  // at priority Thread.NORM_PRIORITY + 1
10:   }
11: }
```

Tip

The values representing the lowest, normal, and highest priorities that threads can be assigned are stored in class variables of the `Thread` class: `MIN_PRIORITY`, `NORM_PRIORITY`, and `MAX_PRIORITY`. By default, the system assigns new threads the priority `NORM_PRIORITY`. Priorities in Java are currently defined in a range from 1 to 10, with 5 being normal, but you shouldn't depend on these numerical values. Always use the class variables or some expression that relies on the class variables.

If two potato shows up as the first line of output, your system preempts using priorities. What actually happens here? Imagine that the first thread (t1) has just begun to run. Before it has a chance to print anything, along comes a higher-priority thread (t2) that wants to run right away. That higher-priority thread preempts (interrupts) the first and prints two potato before t1 prints anything. In fact, if you use the RunningInIdaho class from Listing 16.13, t2 stays in control forever, printing two potato lines, because it has higher priority than t1 and never yields control. If you use the RunningInIdaho class from Listing 16.15, the output consists of alternating lines as before, but always starting with two potato.

Understanding the ComplexThread Class

Listing 16.17 is a good example of how complex threads behave.

TYPE   **LISTING 16.17.** ComplexThread.java.

```
 1: public class ComplexThread extends Thread {
 2:   private int delay;
 3:
 4:   ComplexThread(String name, float seconds) {
 5:     super(name);
 6:     delay = (int) seconds * 1000;   // delays are in milliseconds
 7:     start();                        // start your engines!
 8:   }
 9:
10:   public void run() {
11:     while (true) {
12:       System.out.println(Thread.currentThread().getName());
13:       try {
14:         Thread.sleep(delay);
15:       }
16:       catch (InterruptedException e) {
17:         return;
18:       }
19:     }
20:   }
21:
22:   public static void main(String args[]) {
23:     new ComplexThread("one potato",   1.1F);
24:     new ComplexThread("two potato",   1.3F);
25:     new ComplexThread("three potato", 0.5F);
26:     new ComplexThread("four",         0.7F);
27:   }
28: }
```

This example combines the thread and its tester into a single class. Its constructor takes care of naming and starting itself because it is now a Thread object. The main() method creates new instances of its own class because that class is a subclass of `Thread`. The `run()` method is also more complicated because it now uses, for the first time, a method that can throw an unexpected exception.

The `Thread.sleep()` method forces the current thread to call the `yield()` method and then waits for at least the specified amount of time to elapse before allowing that thread to run again. However, another thread might interrupt the sleeping thread. In such a case, it throws an `InterruptedException` object. Now, because the `run()` method isn't defined as throwing this exception, you must "hide" this fact by catching and handling it yourself. Because interruptions are usually requests to stop, you should exit the thread, which you can do by simply returning from the `run()` method.

16

This program should output a repeating but complex pattern of four different lines, where every once in a great while you see the following:

OUTPUT
```
...
one potato
two potato
three potato
four
...
^C
```

Study the pattern output to prove to yourself that true parallelism is going on inside Java programs. You might also begin to appreciate that, if even this simple set of four threads can produce such complex behavior, many more threads must be capable of producing near chaos if not carefully controlled. Luckily, Java provides the synchronization and thread-safe libraries you need to control this chaotic but powerful feature.

Summary

Today, you saw that although parallelism is desirable and powerful, it introduces many new problems that must be considered and controlled. For example, methods and variables need to be protected from thread conflicts.

By "thinking multithreaded," you can detect the places in your programs that require synchronization (statements or modifiers) to make them thread-safe. A series of `Point` object examples demonstrated the various levels of safety you can achieve, and thread tester examples showed how subclasses of `Thread` or classes that implement the `Runnable` interface are used to create multithreaded programs.

You also learned how to use the `yield()`, `start()`, `stop()`, `suspend()`, and `resume()` methods in your threads and how to catch the dreaded `ThreadDeath` object whenever it happens. You were also introduced to thread naming and thread grouping.

Finally, you learned about preemptive timeslicing and nonpreemptive scheduling, both with and without priorities. Several examples showed you how to test the Java system to see which type of scheduling it performs on a particular platform.

You now know enough to begin writing the most complex type of programs: multi-threaded. As you get more comfortable with threads, you may begin to use the `ThreadGroup` class or the enumeration methods of the `Thread` class to get your hands on all the threads in the system and manipulate them. Don't be afraid to experiment; you can learn only by trying.

Q&A

Q If threads are so important to Java, why haven't they appeared throughout the entire book?

A Actually, they have. Every standalone program written so far has created at least one thread—the one in which it is running. Of course, in those instances, the system created that thread automatically. Now you have learned how to create your own threads explicitly.

Q Exactly how do these system-created threads get created and run? What about applets?

A When a simple standalone Java program starts up, the system creates a main thread, and its `run()` method calls your application's `main()` method to execute your program—you do nothing to get that thread. Similarly, when a simple applet loads into a Java-capable browser, a thread has already been created by the browser, and that thread's `run()` method calls your applet's `init()` and `start()` methods to start your program—again, you do nothing to get that thread. In both cases, a new thread was created by the Java system itself.

Q The `ThreadTester` class has an infinite loop that creates threads and then joins with them. Is it really infinite?

A In theory, yes. In actuality, how far the loop runs is determined by the resource limits (and the stability) of the threads package and garbage collector in your Java system.

Q I know Java is still a bit fuzzy about the scheduler's behavior, but can you tell me more?

A Here are the details, relayed by Arthur van Hoff at Sun: How Java schedules threads "...depends on the platform. It is usually preemptive, but not always time-sliced. Priorities are not always observed, depending on the underlying implementation." This last clause gives you a hint that, in some future release, the design and implementation might be made clearer with regard to scheduling behavior.

Q Does Java support more complex multithreaded concepts, such as semaphores?

A The Object class in Java provides methods that can be used to build up condition variables, semaphores, and any higher-level parallel construct you might need. The wait() method (and its two variants with time-outs) causes the current thread to wait until some condition has been satisfied. The notify() (or notifyAll()) method, which must be called from within a synchronized method or block, tells the thread (or all threads) to wake up and check that condition again because something has changed. By carefully combining these two primitive methods, any data structure can be manipulated safely by a set of threads, and all the classical parallel primitives needed to implement published parallel algorithms may be built.

Q My parallel friends tell me I should worry about something called "deadlock." Should I?

A Not for simple multithreaded programs. However, in more complicated programs, one of the biggest concerns is avoiding a situation in which one thread has locked an object and is waiting for another thread to finish, while that other thread is waiting for the first thread to release the *same* object before *it* can finish. That's a deadlock—both threads are stuck forever. Mutual dependencies like this involving multiple threads can be intricate, convoluted, and difficult to locate—much less rectify. They are one of the primary challenges in writing complex multithreaded programs.

Workshop

The Workshop provides two ways for you to affirm what you've learned today. The Quiz section poses questions to help you solidify your understanding of the material covered. You can find answers to the quiz questions in Appendix A, "Answers to Quiz Questions." The Exercises section provides you with experience in using what you have learned. Try to work through all these before continuing to the next day.

16

Quiz

1. With what keyword can you atomize a block or method?

2. True or false: The word `synchronized` can be used as both a method and a keyword in Java.

3. What method call takes place as the implicit first statement in any `synchronized` method?

4. When you subclass a class other than `Thread`, what interface must be implemented to make that new subclass capable of running threads?

5. What is the difference between preemptive and nonpreemptive timeslicing?

Exercises

1. Create an applet that displays a digital clock with the system time (HH:MM) using multiple threads and the `sleep` method to update its display once a minute.

2. Write an application that simulates a bank account whose current balance is being updated with withdrawals and deposits from multiple ATMs.

DAY 17

Persistence

Today, you'll explore the topic of Java object persistence through serialization and deserialization. Specifically, you'll learn about:

- Creating serializable and externalizable objects
- Writing and reading object streams
- Using object input and output streams
- Catching persistence-related exceptions
- Dealing with persistence security issues

> **Caution**
>
> For today's examples to work, you must remember to add the following line at the top of each source code file you create:
>
> ```
> import java.io.*
> ```
>
> If you forget, you'll get a compiler error because Java won't know where classes that belong to the `java.io` package are defined.

Let's begin with some term definitions:

NEW TERM *Persistence* is a mechanism for preserving object states across program sessions. It is also used when transmitting or receiving objects from one system to another across a network using streams.

NEW TERM *Serialization* is the process by which object state information is preserved when writing data out to a stream.

NEW TERM *Deserialization* is the process by which object state information is restored when reading data in from a stream.

Normally, when you close a Java program, the objects in that program cease to exist. You could save the data to a file, but that would only save the data bytes and wouldn't preserve the object states. In fact, unless your object implements either the `Serializable` or `Externalizable` interface, there is no way to preserve those states.

This same problem occurs when you attempt to transmit objects from one Java Virtual Machine to another—for example, when objects are used as arguments to a remote object's method. Normally, an object's state would cease to exist when its data was transmitted to a second Java Virtual Machine. However, with persistence, the object's state can be transmitted as well, allowing the object to be restored in the destination Java Virtual Machine's memory space. Without this capability, Remote Method Invocation (RMI) wouldn't be possible. (You'll learn more about RMI on Day 20, "Java Network Communications.")

With persistence, Java provides automated mechanisms for preserving the current state of objects. This important information can then be restored the next time the program is invoked, or, in the case of network operations, it can be restored to or from a remote system after transmission via object streams.

The main foundations of the persistence framework comprise four interfaces: the `Serializable`, `Externalizable`, `ObjectOutput`, and `ObjectInput` interfaces. In addition, you'll learn about the `ObjectOutputStream` and `ObjectInputStream` classes, which are based on `OutputStream` and `InputStream` abstract classes, respectively. (You learned about these two abstract classes on Day 10, "Streams and I/O.")

Note Because the classes used in serialization and deserialization depend on classes defined in the `java.io` package, the methods you will explore today are declared to throw an `IOException` object. There are also persistence-specific exceptions, and we'll examine them later today in the section "Persistence Exceptions."

In addition to encoding objects, serialization recursively searches the object for references to other objects and preserves them as well. The structure of the encoded object and its supporting objects is called an object's *graph*.

NEW TERM   An object's *graph* is the structure created by recursively mapping out that object's dependencies on other objects. The graph is preserved with the objects and is then used to assist in restoring the objects in the graph.

So in addition to preserving the objects explicitly named in your program, persistence preserves all the objects (and their states) that your object depends on to reconstitute itself. For all this to work, the object must implement either the `Serializable` or `Externalizable` interface, as do many classes that form the core of the Java Class Library.

The `Externalizable` Interface

By implementing the `Externalizable` interface, a class can specify the methods for writing and reading objects. The `Externalizable` interface defines two such methods: the `writeExternal()` and `readExternal()` methods. You can implement these methods in your class to manage the contents of objects and their graphs, saving and restoring this information. The class must also contain a default (no-argument) constructor to implement the `Externalizable` interface.

When an object implementing the `Externalizable` interface is being saved, the `writeExternal()` method is called, and the object is saved to the output stream. When an object implementing the `Externalizable` interface is being restored, the default constructor is used to initialize the object instance, and then the `readExternal()` method is called to restore the data from the input stream.

Although some of the work of saving and restoring your objects is handled for you, unless you really need to micromanage your objects, you will be better off using the `Serializable` interface instead. Objects implementing the `Externalizable` interface also present some security concerns, which are discussed in the later section "Security Issues."

The `writeExternal()` Method

If your object's class implements the `Externalizable` interface, it must also implement the `writeExternal()` method to preserve the state of the object. This method takes an object implementing the `ObjectOutput` interface as its argument.

The `ObjectOutput` interface provides the `writeObject()` method, which is used by the `writeExternal()` method to preserve arrays, strings, and objects. (This method is discussed later today.) For primitive data types, your `writeExternal()` method implementation can call any of the following methods provided by the `DataOutput` class:

```
void writeBoolean(boolean b)   throws IOException;
void writeByte(int i)          throws IOException;
void writeShort(int i)         throws IOException;
void writeChar(int i)          throws IOException;
void writeInt(int i)           throws IOException;
void writeLong(long l)         throws IOException;
void writeFloat(float f)       throws IOException;
void writeDouble(double d)     throws IOException;
```

These methods were discussed on Day 10, but their signatures are listed here for your reference.

The `readExternal()` Method

If your object's class implements the `Externalizable` interface, it must also implement the `writeInternal()` method to restore the state of the object. This method takes an object implementing the `ObjectInput` interface as its argument.

The `ObjectInput` interface provides the `readObject()` method, which is used by the `readExternal()` method to restore arrays, strings, and objects. (This method is discussed later today.) For primitive data types, your `readExternal()` method implementation can call any of the following methods provided by the `DataInput` class:

```
boolean readBoolean()         throws IOException;
byte    readByte()            throws IOException;
int     readUnsignedByte()    throws IOException;
short   readShort()           throws IOException;
int     readUnsignedShort()   throws IOException;
char    readChar()            throws IOException;
int     readInt()             throws IOException;
long    readLong()            throws IOException;
float   readFloat()           throws IOException;
double  readDouble()          throws IOException;
```

These methods were discussed on Day 10, but their signatures are listed here for your reference.

The `Serializable` Interface

For Java to know that an object instance of your class can be serialized, it must implement the `Serializable` interface:

```
public class MyClass implements Serializable {...}
```

The `Serializable` interface doesn't define any methods. It's used by Java to designate classes that can be serialized. If your class extends a superclass that doesn't implement the `Serializable` interface, that superclass must have a default (no-argument) constructor available to initialize the state of the superclass during restoration. If the superclass doesn't have such a default constructor, you can't serialize any of its subclasses. If you attempt to do so, an `InvalidClassException` object will be thrown.

When the object is being serialized, all its dependencies are checked recursively. In other words, if the object depends on other objects, those objects are added to the object graph and serialized as well. However, if during this process one of the objects farther down in the graph is discovered to be nonserializable, a `NotSerializableException` object will be thrown.

Serialization takes place using a special output stream class, `ObjectOutputStream`, which implements the `ObjectOutput` interface. When it's time to restore the object graph, deserialization takes place using the `ObjectInputStream` class, which implements the `ObjectInput` interface. These stream classes provide methods for writing and reading the objects to and from the streams for serialization and deserialization.

17

The `ObjectOutput` Interface

The `ObjectOutput` interface extends the `DataOutput` interface by defining an abstract method for writing out arrays, strings, and objects called the `writeObject()` method. The `ObjectOutputStream` class implements the `ObjectOutput` interface, which is responsible for writing out the serialized data. The serialized data can then be read back in using an `ObjectInputStream` object.

The `ObjectOutputStream` Class

The `ObjectOutputStream` class descends from the `OutputStream` class and implements both the `ObjectOutput` and `ObjectStreamConstants` interfaces. It is used to serialize primitive data and object graphs that can later be restored using an `ObjectInputStream` object. This class can preserve data to an instance of `FileOutputStream`, making it persistent. It can also preserve objects passed as parameters to an output stream during a Remote Method Invocation.

For primitive data, `DataOutput` class methods are overridden, but they perform essentially the same operations:

```
void close()                        throws IOException
void flush()                        throws IOException
void write(int data)                throws IOException
void write(byte b[])                throws IOException
```

```
void write(byte b[], int off, int len) throws IOException
void writeBoolean(boolean data)         throws IOException
void writeByte(int data)                throws IOException
void writeShort(int data)               throws IOException
void writeChar(int data)                throws IOException
void writeInt(int data)                 throws IOException
void writeLong(long data)               throws IOException
void writeFloat(float data)             throws IOException
void writeDouble(double data)           throws IOException
void writeBytes(String data)            throws IOException
void writeChars(String data)            throws IOException
void writeUTF(String data)              throws IOException
```

This stream class also defines a number of additional serialization-specific methods, including the writeObject() method, which is described next.

The writeObject() Method

The writeObject() method writes an object's nontransient and nonstatic members to an ObjectOutputStream object. (Static members don't change, so it only makes sense not to serialize them. Transient members are so marked to prevent them from being serialized.) For example, assuming that you had assigned an ObjectOutputStream object to the anOOS variable, you could write a Date object assigned to the someDate variable to the ObjectOutputStream object with this method call:

```
anOOS.writeObject(someDate);
```

If static or transient fields are in the object's class, they are ignored because these fields can't be serialized. Any objects referenced by the object being preserved are then traversed recursively until the entire object graph is written to the output stream.

Here is the writeObject() method's signature:

```
void writeObject(Object obj) throws IOException
```

The IOException is needed because this method writes to a stream.

The ObjectInput Interface

The ObjectInput interface extends the DataInput interface by defining an abstract method for reading in arrays, strings, and objects called the readObject() method. The ObjectInputStream class implements the ObjectInput interface, and it is responsible for reading in serialized data that had previously been written out by an ObjectOutputStream object.

The `ObjectInputStream` Class

The `ObjectInputStream` class descends from the `InputStream` class and implements both the `ObjectInput` and `ObjectStreamConstants` interfaces. It is used to deserialize primitive data and object graphs that were previously serialized using an `ObjectOutputStream` object. This class can restore persistent data from an instance of `FileInputStream`. It can also restore objects used as parameters, which are obtained from an input stream during a Remote Method Invocation.

During restoration of the persistent objects, the `ObjectInputStream` instantiates each object in the graph as a new object. In other words, it doesn't overwrite any existing objects in memory but creates new instances based on the persistent data in the stream. As each new object is instantiated, the appropriate classes required are loaded by the Java Virtual Machine. If the required class can't be found, an `InvalidClassException` object is thrown.

For primitive data, the familiar methods from the `DataInput` interface are overridden in this class, but they perform essentially the same operations:

```
int      available()                                throws IOException
void     close()                                    throws IOException
int      read()                                     throws IOException
int      read(byte data[], int offset, int length)  throws IOException
boolean  readBoolean()                              throws IOException
byte     readByte()                                 throws IOException
char     readChar()                                 throws IOException
double   readDouble()                               throws IOException
float    readFloat()                                throws IOException
void     readFully(byte data[], int offset, int size) throws IOException
void     readFully(byte data[])                     throws IOException
int      readInt()                                  throws IOException
String   readLine()                                 throws IOException
long     readLong()                                 throws IOException
short    readShort()                                throws IOException
int      readUnsignedByte()                         throws IOException
int      readUnsignedShort()                        throws IOException
String   readUTF()                                  throws IOException
int      skipBytes(int len)                         throws IOException
```

This stream class also defines a number of additional serialization-specific methods, the most important of which is the `readObject()` method, described next.

The `readObject()` Method

The `readObject()` method reads an object from an `ObjectInputStream` object. Because arrays and strings are treated as objects for purposes of serialization, you must use casting to specify which object type you expect from the stream. For example, assuming that you had assigned an `ObjectInputStream` object to the `anOIS` variable, you could restore a `Date` object with this method call:

```
Date restoredDate = (Date)anOIS.readObject();
```

When the object is read, a new instance is created, as if you had called the object's class constructor. The default constructors of the object's superclasses are called first, and then down the chain of inheritance to the object's constructor.

After memory is allocated for the object by calling this chain of constructors, the object's state and data are read from the stream. Fields are restored starting with the highest-level serializable superclass, working down through the inheritance chain to the current serializable object's fields.

If static or transient fields are in the object's class, they are initialized to their default values because these fields aren't serialized. Any objects referenced by the object being restored are themselves restored until the entire object graph is reconstituted.

Here is the `readObject()` method's signature:

```
Object readObject() throws OptionalDataException,
                ClassNotFoundException, IOException
```

The `IOException` is necessary, of course, when dealing with streams. The `ClassNotFoundException` object is thrown when the `readObject()` method attempts to instantiate the object and it can't find a matching class in the Java Virtual Machine or the client machine's `CLASSPATH` environmental variable. The `OptionalDataException` object is thrown when you try to read an object, but there is still primitive data in the stream.

A Serialized Example

Used together, the `ObjectOutputStream` and `ObjectInputStream` classes can provide your application with persistent storage of objects when used with the `FileOutputStream` and `FileInputStream` classes. For example:

```
FileOutputStream aFOS = new FileOutputStream("myfile.ser");
ObjectOutputStream anOOS = new ObjectOutputStream(aFOS);
anOOS.writeObject("This data was preserved on: ");
anOOS.writeObject(new Date());
anOOS.flush()
aFOS.close();
```

Here, the `ObjectOutputStream` object writes the phrase `This data was preserved on:` and the current system date to `myfile.ser`. When an `ObjectInputStream` object reads these data, the date retains its original format:

```
FileInputStream aFIS = new FileInputStream("myfile.ser");
ObjectInputStream anOIS = new ObjectInputStream(aFIS);
String theStr = (String).anOIS.readObject();
Date preserveDate = (Date)anOIS.readObject();
aFIS.close();
```

 Caution Remember that although reading or writing files isn't a problem for stand-alone Java applications, attempting to open, read, or write streams based on files from an applet can cause security violations (depending on the browser's current user safety level). Of course, applets can open URL streams and pull objects from the server that the applets were served from.

Persistence Exceptions

17

Most persistence-related exceptions descend from the IOException class and its subclass ObjectStreamException. Some of these exceptions were mentioned earlier today, but they are all summarized in Table 17.1 for easy reference.

TABLE 17.1. PERSISTENCE-RELATED EXCEPTIONS.

Exception	Purpose
InvalidClassException	Thrown if the class of the object being restored isn't public or doesn't have a default (no-argument) constructor.
InvalidObjectException	Thrown if the restored object can't be validated.
NotSerializableException	Thrown by serialization methods when they encounter an object in the graph that doesn't implement the Serializable interface.
OptionalDataException	Thrown when the readObject() method finds a primitive but was expecting an object in the stream.
SecurityException	The class being restored is not a trusted class.
StreamCorruptedException	Thrown when the stream data or stream header is invalid.
WriteAbortedException	Thrown when reading a stream that had an exception thrown when it was written.

In addition, any of the DataInput or DataOutput class exceptions can be thrown by using the primitive read and write methods descended from those classes.

Security Issues

The purpose of serialization is to preserve an object outside the Java system. However, this also means that serialized data are preserved outside the boundaries of Java's security system. In particular, because the readExternal() method is public, Externalizable classes are vulnerable to being overwritten. This section addresses ways that you can protect your sensitive data, either by marking it so that it isn't preserved externally or by encrypting it.

The transient Keyword

When data are serialized, only nonstatic and nontransient object class members are written out. When you mark class members with the transient keyword, you prevent those members from being serialized, keeping them safe from the outside world.

In addition, references to system-specific items (such as file handles) that refer to the object's current address in memory should never be serialized. When the object is deserialized, it is allocated new memory even if it is restored to the same system from which it came, so file handle information would be redundant at best. At worst, it could give the new object access to system resources that it shouldn't be given.

Using Encryption

Of course, there are times when sensitive data must be written out for one reason or another. For these circumstances, encryption is the answer. Because serialization is accomplished using streams, you can direct the output of serialization streams to encryption streams, which were introduced on Day 10. This process can then be reversed when the sensitive data must be restored. First, push the data through the de-encryption stream and then pass the data to a deserialization stream.

Summary

Today, you were introduced to the Externalizable interface and its two methods, the writeExternal() and readExternal() methods. You were also introduced to the Serializable interface, which, when implemented by a class, can be serialized. The ObjectOutput and ObjectInput interfaces are implemented by the ObjectInputStream and ObjectOutputStream classes. These classes provide the writeObject() and readObject() methods with which an object's state is preserved and restored. You also learned that many of the methods defined in the DataInput and DataOutput interfaces are implemented by these classes to handle the preservation and restoration of primitive data during serialization and deserialization.

Persistence-related exceptions were summarized, and you learned that your serializable objects must also handle any input/output exceptions that can be thrown by primitive methods. Security issues were briefly explored, and you learned that sensitive information should either be marked `transient` so that it can't be serialized or encrypted using streams.

Without persistence, after your program ended, the object state information would be lost. Object state information would also be lost when the object was used as a parameter to a remote method invocation because the destination system wouldn't have access to the sender's memory address space. Persistence in Java gives your programs a way to preserve necessary object state information across program sessions and across the network and then restore that state information in a new program session or on a destination system.

Q&A

Q When should I use `Externalizable` rather than `Serializable`?

A The `Externalizable` interface should be implemented only when you need to do special handling of your data, for two reasons: 1) It requires you to implement the `writeExternal()` and `readExternal()` methods, defining exactly how your data should be preserved and restored. 2) The `writeExternal()` method is public, which, as mentioned earlier, presents a security concern. You're really much better off using `Serializable` if at all possible, but `Externalizable` is there if you really need it.

Q Can't I just write my own methods for preserving my data to a file? Why should I bother with serialization?

A You *could* write out all the information necessary to save an object's state to a file yourself. You would need to write methods to write each object and data type out to the file. Then you would need to manually create the object's graph and preserve all the objects that it relied on, and all the objects those objects relied on, and so on,. Then you also would have to write methods to restore all the data and objects from your homemade graph, restoring each object's state, keeping track of all the objects you had restored so far so that you didn't duplicate objects. When you think about it, serialization is much less troublesome than doing all this yourself!

Q What happens if I decide to use one of the JBCL classes to derive my own beans? Can I serialize my subclasses?

A Yes, as long as the JBCL classes that you subclass (and all of their superclasses) have default (no-argument) constructors, you will be able to implement the `Serializable` interface in your subclasses.

Workshop

The Workshop provides two ways for you to affirm what you've learned today. The Quiz section poses questions to help you solidify your understanding of the material covered. You can find answers to the quiz questions in Appendix A, "Answers to Quiz Questions." The Exercises section provides you with experience in using what you have learned. Try to work through all these before continuing to the next day.

Quiz

1. True or false: Streams can make use of the methods in the `ObjectInput` and `ObjectOutput` interfaces, but files can't.

2. Which interface requires you to define your object's external format: `Externalizable` or `Serializable`?

3. Which method is used for serializing objects? Which method is used for deserializing objects?

Exercise

Create a drawing application that lets the user click and drag the mouse to draw rectangles on the screen. When the user closes the program, save the rectangles already drawn on the screen to a file and then restore those rectangles the next time the drawing program is invoked.

DAY **18**

Building JavaBeans

JavaBeans is the specification for Java components, which are known as *beans*. Beans are reusable components that application developers use to build their applications. For example, all the controls on the Component Palette are beans. Beans allow you as a component writer to distribute the functionality of your code without distributing the source code itself. For developers working in teams, beans are a handy way to provide all members of the team with standardized project pieces without having multiple copies of the underlying source code lying around. You can create both visual and nonvisual beans in JBuilder.

Not only can you reuse a bean without having its source code available, but you also can modify the bean's behavior. Beans provide properties and events that can be modified at design time. In other words, they allow these elements to be read by a visual development environment, such as JBuilder. A properly constructed bean displays modifiable properties and events in the JBuilder Inspector pane during Design mode.

Borland was one of the companies that closely participated in creating the JavaBeans specification that Sun published. This specification gives guidelines on how beans should be constructed and how properties and events should be displayed in visual tools, such as JBuilder.

| Tip | Current JavaBeans information is available from the Sun Web site at http://java.sun.com/beans/. |

Today you'll learn how JBuilder helps you create beans that conform to the JavaBeans specification, Sun's specifications for cross-platform reusable Java components. Specifically, you'll explore these topics:

- Basic bean requirements
- BeansExpress components
- Creating beans using the JavaBean Wizard

In JBuilder, beans expect to be created as members of a package, so for today's project, you'll use BuildBeans\NewBeans.jpr and then add each class to that package or project as you create your new beans. The basic steps for creating a bean are simple:

1. Open a project and add a bean class or classes. Each must have a default (no-argument) constructor.

2. Design your new bean's user interface if it is a visual bean. (Of course, this is unnecessary for nonvisual beans.)

3. Add properties, methods, and events to your bean to define its design time and runtime functionality.

4. If needed, add a BeanInfo class for each bean to assist your bean in presenting itself to visual tools such as JBuilder.

5. Choose an icon to represent your bean (or use JBuilder's default icon), add the bean to the Component Palette, and test it. (After the bean is added to the palette, if you change it, you'll need to restart JBuilder to have the changes take effect.)

After testing your bean, you can deploy it in an archive, just like any other Java program. (You'll learn about archives on Day 19, "Deploying Java Programs.")

Before getting into the details of each step, let's examine some of the requirements and guidelines for creating beans.

Meeting Bean Requirements

The JavaBean component model specifies several requirements for a component to qualify as a bean. There are also several guidelines that help make your bean easier to use in visual environments:

- A bean must be written as a `public` class.
- A bean's class must declare a `public` default (no-argument) constructor.

That's it! If your bean does these two things, it will work in the JBuilder Integrated Development Environment. However, without specifying properties and events, the developer using your bean will be unable to modify any of the bean's attributes or tell it to react to any events. This isn't usually what you want, so there are other guidelines you must follow to create a bean's properties and events. Also, you will probably want to specify methods that developers can call in their own source code to manipulate your bean at runtime.

Properties and events are displayed in visual tools automatically, if they follow certain naming conventions, through *introspection*.

NEW TERM *Introspection* is a process that allows JBuilder to recognize appropriately named accessor and registration methods so that when a bean is installed on the Component Palette and subsequently used in Java program design, those properties and events will be displayed in the AppBrowser window Design mode Inspector pane.

These naming requirements are straightforward. The property get and set accessor method names must be of the form `getProperty()` and `setProperty()`. For `boolean` properties, the get accessor method is named `isProperty()`, where `Property` represents the property's identifier. For events, the registration methods are named `addEventListener()` and `removeEventListener()`, where `Event` represents the event's identifier. Being aware of these naming conventions will help you read the code that is generated by JBuilder when creating beans using BeansExpress.

Using BeansExpress

The JBuilder IDE, in an effort to make building beans easier, provides some basic starter beans and code snippets. To access these, select File | New to display the New dialog box, and then click on the BeansExpress tab to open the BeansExpress page, shown in Figure 18.1.

On this page are several sample beans and code snippets to help you on your way to creating your first bean.

New Bean

The `NewBean` component is a very simple skeleton bean that has sample placeholders where the properties, events, and their methods belong. To add a `NewBean` to today's project, select File | New. In the New dialog box, choose the BeansExpress tab and double-click the New Bean icon.

FIGURE 18.1.

The BeansExpress page of the New dialog box.

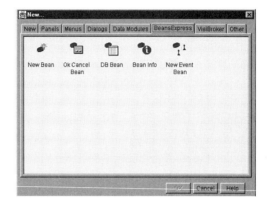

Note

When you're creating a bean with the NewBean component, the generated filename, its class name, and its default constructor are all named NewBean by default. To change these default names, you need to do two things: re-name the file itself, and search and replace to rename the class and con-structor.

First, click NewBean.java in the Navigation pane, select File | Rename, and give it a new name. In the Save As dialog box, type MyNewBean.java in the File name field and click the Save button. Next, click the Content pane and select Search | Replace. In the Replace Text dialog box, type NewBean in the Text to find field and type MyNewBean in the Replace with field. In the Origin radio-button group, click the Entire scope radio button. The Replace Text dialog box should look as shown in Figure 18.2.

FIGURE 18.2.

The filled-out Replace Text dialog box.

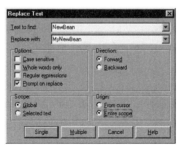

After you've filled in the Replace Text dialog box correctly, click the Multiple button so that multiple text replacements are performed. The Confirm dialog box appears, as shown in Figure 18.3.

FIGURE 18.3.

*The Confirm dialog
box.*

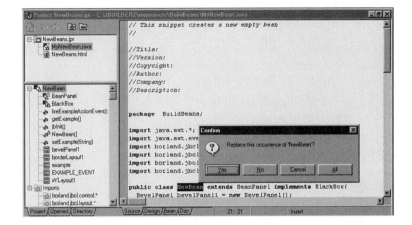

Click the All button in the Confirm dialog box to tell JBuilder to automatically carry out
all the text replacements without asking for conformation each time. This operation
changes both the class-name declaration and the default-constructor declaration to the
new bean name. Be sure to save your changes.

Listing 18.1 shows the source code for MyNewBean.java after the search-and-replace operation and file renaming have been completed.

18

TYPE   **LISTING 18.1.** MyNewBean.java.

```
 1:  // This snippet creates a new, empty bean
 2:  //
 3:  //Title:
 4:  //Version:
 5:  //Copyright:
 6:  //Author:
 7:  //Company:
 8:  //Description:
 9:
10:  package BuildBeans;
11:
12:  import java.awt.*;
13:  import java.awt.event.*;
14:  import borland.jbcl.layout.*;
15:  import borland.jbcl.control.*;
16:  import borland.jbcl.view.*;
17:  import borland.jbcl.util.BlackBox;
18:
19:  public class MyNewBean extends BeanPanel implements BlackBox {
20:     BevelPanel bevelPanel1 = new BevelPanel();
```

continues

LISTING **18.1.** CONTINUED

```
21:    BorderLayout borderLayout1 = new BorderLayout();
22:    XYLayout xYLayout1 = new XYLayout();
23:
24:    public MyNewBean() {
25:      try {
26:        jbInit();
27:      }
28:      catch (Exception e) {
29:        e.printStackTrace();
30:      }
31:    }
32:
33:    public void jbInit() throws Exception {
34:      bevelPanel1.setLayout(xYLayout1);
35:      this.setLayout(borderLayout1);
36:      this.add(bevelPanel1, BorderLayout.CENTER);
37:    }
38:
39:    // Example properties
40:    private String example = "Example1";
41:
42:    public void setExample(String s) {
43:      example=s;
44:    }
45:    public String getExample(){
46:      return example;
47:    }
48:
49:    // Example event
50:    public static final String EXAMPLE_EVENT = "ExampleEvent";
51:    protected void fireExampleActionEvent() {
52:      //Args: event source, event ID, event command
53:      processActionEvent(new ActionEvent(this,
                           ➥ActionEvent.ACTION_PERFORMED,
                           ➥EXAMPLE_EVENT));
54:    }
55:  }
```

ANALYSIS   Lines 1 through 8 are comments that identify the generated code and allow you to fill in some internal documentation for the bean. Line 10 declares the project's package affiliation.

Lines 12 through 17 declare imports for the bean. A bean inherits from a number of classes, most of which you've seen or used already. However, two imports warrant further explanation. The borland.jbcl.view.* import is necessary because your class extends the BeanPanel class, which resides in that package. The `borland.jbcl.util.BlackBox` import is required because your class implements the important `BlackBox` interface, which prevents developer users of your bean from messing around with your bean's design. In other words, this is the class that ensures that the bean is modified only by changing properties, creating event handlers, and using public methods, as its designer intended. No matter how many widgets you add to your bean, it will always be selected and treated as a unit.

Line 19 is the `public` class declaration, which every bean requires. Your bean's class implements the `BlackBox` interface that was imported on line 17. It also extends the `BeanPanel` class that was imported on line 16. The `BeanPanel` class itself extends the `Panel` class and handles focus, key, and mouse events, as well as managing action listeners. Lines 20 through 22 set up the initial user interface for the new bean.

Lines 24 through 31 declare the `public` default (no-argument) constructor, which is required of every bean. (This body of this constructor should look familiar to you from working with previous generated project code.) Lines 33 through 37 do the required user interface initialization.

Lines 39 through 47 pertain to properties and their methods. On line 40, a property named `example`, which can be assigned a `String` object, is declared. Note that the `example` property is declared `private`, which prevents users from changing the property variable directly. Access to properties is intended to be accomplished only through the accessor methods. The `setExample()` accessor method declared in lines 42 through 44 shows how you might create set accessor methods for the `example` property. The `getExample()` accessor method declared in lines 45 through 47 outlines a get accessor method for the `example` property. You can copy and paste these sample lines of code to create various properties of all data types and use the accessor method examples as templates for your own accessor methods.

Lines 49 through 54 form a template for an action event. The `EXAMPLE_EVENT` event command is declared `public`, but the method is declared `protected`. The `fireExampleActionEvent()` method calls the `processActionEvent()` method, which takes three parameters: the event source `this`, the event ID `ActionEvent.ACTION_PERFORMED`, and the event command `EXAMPLE_EVENT`. This is the information necessary to notify event listeners that this bean's action event has occurred. (The `processActionEvent()` method and the listener registration methods are declared in the `BeanPanel` superclass.) If your bean needs to generate more than one event, you can use the `NewEventBean` object, which you'll learn about later today.

That was quite a whirlwind tour of a bean, but the point is that this skeleton code is almost all you need to create a basic user interface bean. To modify the bean's user interface, choose the Design tab of the Content pane in the AppBrowser window and make

18

the necessary changes, and then fill out the skeleton code for the properties and events. After you have everything filled in, save your changes and compile the code. After debugging, you can add the bean to the Component Palette and test your new design. (You'll learn about adding beans to the Component Palette later today in the section "Testing Beans.")

Ok Cancel Bean

The OkCancelBean component is a bean that has OK, Cancel, and Help buttons on a panel. To add an OkCancelBean to today's project, select File | New. In the New dialog box, choose the BeansExpress tab and double-click the Ok Cancel Bean icon.

The generated filename and all references to the class in the source code are named OkCancelBean by default, so you'll need to rename these references and the file. Do a search-and-replace to change all instances of OkCancelBean to MyOkCancelBean in the source code, save your changes, and rename the file MyOkCancelBean.java. Listing 18.2 shows the source code for MyOkCancelBean.java after all the renaming has been done.

TYPE   **LISTING 18.2.** MyOkCancelBean.java.

```
 1:  // This snippet creates a bean with OK, Cancel, and Help buttons
 2:  // The listener responds to a single action event and checks the
 3:  // event object to determine which button was pressed.
 4:  // Additional behavior for each button can be added if desired.
 5:  // For example: the Help button can launch help without firing an
 6:  // action event.
 7:  //
 8:  //Title:
 9:  //Version:
10:  //Copyright:
11:  //Author:
12:  //Company:
13:  //Description:
14:
15:  package BuildBeans;
16:
17:  import java.awt.*;
18:  import java.awt.event.*;
19:  import borland.jbcl.layout.*;
20:  import borland.jbcl.control.*;
21:  import borland.jbcl.view.*;
22:  import borland.jbcl.util.BlackBox;
23:
24:  public class MyOkCancelBean extends BeanPanel implements BlackBox{
25:     // Use these constants in the event listener.
26:     public final static String OK_EVENT = "OkEvent";
```

```
27:     public final static String CANCEL_EVENT = "CancelEvent";
28:     public final static String HELP_EVENT = "HelpEvent";
29:
30:     private BorderLayout borderLayout1 = new BorderLayout();
31:     private Panel panel1 = new Panel();
32:     private FlowLayout flowLayout1 = new FlowLayout();
33:     private Button ok = new Button();
34:     private Button cancel = new Button();
35:     private Button help = new Button();
36:
37:     public MyOkCancelBean() {
38:       try {
39:         jbInit();
40:       }
41:       catch (Exception e) {
42:         e.printStackTrace();
43:       }
44:     }
45:
46:     public void jbInit() throws Exception{
47:       ok.setLabel("   OK   ");
48:       ok.addActionListener(new
              ➥MyOkCancelBean_ok_actionAdapter(this));
49:       cancel.setLabel("Cancel");
50:       cancel.addActionListener(new
              ➥MyOkCancelBean_cancel_actionAdapter(this));
51:       help.setLabel(" Help ");
52:       help.addActionListener(new
              ➥MyOkCancelBean_help_actionAdapter(this));
53:       panel1.setLayout(flowLayout1);
54:       this.setLayout(borderLayout1);
55:       this.add(panel1, BorderLayout.CENTER);
56:       panel1.add(ok, null);
57:       panel1.add(cancel, null);
58:       panel1.add(help, null);
59:     }
60:
61:     // The action listener for this bean should check the ActionEvent
62:     // to determine which button was pressed.
63:     // The Help button could be handled entirely inside this bean
64:     // if desired.
65:     void ok_actionPerformed(ActionEvent e) {
66:       //Args: event source, event ID, event command
67:       processActionEvent(new ActionEvent(this,
              ➥ActionEvent.ACTION_PERFORMED, OK_EVENT));
68:     }
69:     void cancel_actionPerformed(ActionEvent e) {
70:       processActionEvent(new ActionEvent(this,
              ➥ActionEvent.ACTION_PERFORMED, CANCEL_EVENT));
```

18

continues

LISTING 18.2. CONTINUED

```
71:     }
72:     void help_actionPerformed(ActionEvent e) {
73:       processActionEvent(new ActionEvent(this,
              ➥ActionEvent.ACTION_PERFORMED, HELP_EVENT));
74:     }
75:   }
76:
77:   class MyOkCancelBean_ok_actionAdapter
              ➥implements java.awt.event.ActionListener {
78:     MyOkCancelBean adaptee;
79:
80:     MyOkCancelBean_ok_actionAdapter(MyOkCancelBean adaptee) {
81:       this.adaptee = adaptee;
82:     }
83:
84:     public void actionPerformed(ActionEvent e) {
85:       adaptee.ok_actionPerformed(e);
86:     }
87:   }
88:
89:   class MyOkCancelBean_cancel_actionAdapter
              ➥implements java.awt.event.ActionListener {
90:     MyOkCancelBean adaptee;
91:
92:     MyOkCancelBean_cancel_actionAdapter(MyOkCancelBean adaptee) {
93:       this.adaptee = adaptee;
94:     }
95:
96:     public void actionPerformed(ActionEvent e) {
97:       adaptee.cancel_actionPerformed(e);
98:     }
99:   }
100:
101:  class MyOkCancelBean_help_actionAdapter
              ➥implements java.awt.event.ActionListener {
102:    MyOkCancelBean adaptee;
103:
104:    MyOkCancelBean_help_actionAdapter(MyOkCancelBean adaptee) {
105:      this.adaptee = adaptee;
106:    }
107:
108:    public void actionPerformed(ActionEvent e) {
109:      adaptee.help_actionPerformed(e);
110:    }
111:  }
```

ANALYSIS Lines 1 through 13 are internal documentation. Line 15 declares the package. Lines 17 through 22 import the same classes as the NewBean class.

Line 24 declares the MyOkCancelBean class that extends the BeanPanel class and implements the BlackBox interface. Lines 26 through 28 declare constants that are used later when the processActionEvent() method is called. Lines 30 through 35 contain the declarations for this bean's standard user interface elements, including its three buttons.

Lines 37 through 44 declare this bean's default (no-argument) constructor. Lines 46 through 59 do the user interface initialization. In the case of the MyOkCancelBean class, labels are set for the three buttons in lines 47, 49, and 51. (An interesting trick used here is the extra spaces in the shorter labels to center them on the buttons and make them closer to the same size.) The buttons' action listeners are added to the bean in lines 48, 50, and 52. Also, in lines 56 through 58, the buttons themselves are added to the bean's panel. Any user interface additions you make to this bean will show up in this section as well.

Lines 65 through 68 define the ok_actionPerformed() method, a listener method that is invoked whenever the OK button is pressed. This method is just like the stub methods created when you're creating a program and you triple-click the actionPerformed event to create a new event handler. In this case, the event handler called the processActionEvent() method using the previously defined constant, OK_EVENT, to identify the event command to be processed. Also, in lines 77 through 87, this listener's actionAdapter is created. Again, this is similar to the adapter created each time you generate a new event handler in your own programs. This set of functionality is repeated for the Cancel button in lines 69 through 71 for the event handler and in lines 89 through 99 for its adapter, and for the Help button in lines 72 through 75 for the event handler and lines 101 through 111 for its adapter.

The bean is now ready for you to make any additions or changes that you might want. Perhaps you would like to add or remove a button or have the Help button do some additional processing (such as launch a Help topic in a viewer). When you're done with this bean's user interface and have added whatever additional functionality you wish, remember that you can use the NewEventBean object to create additional events. Save your changes, compile your code, and add the bean to the Component Palette as described in the "Testing Beans" section. Then test your new design.

DB Bean

The DBBean component is a bean that provides a status bar, a grid, and a navigator so that it can be used as the basis for database operation beans. To add a DBBean to today's project, select File|New. In the New dialog box, click on the BeansExpress tab and double-click the DB Bean icon.

18

The generated filename and all references to the class in the source code are named DBBean by default, so be sure to rename these references and the file. Do a search and replace to change all instances of DBBean to MyDBBean in the source code, save your changes, and rename the file MyDBBean.java. Listing 18.3 shows the source code for MyDBBean.java after all the renaming has been done.

TYPE   **LISTING 18.3.** MyDBBean.java.

```
 1:  // This snippet creates a sample database bean
 2:  // that has a grid, navigator, and status bar.
 3:  // Properties for userName, password, etc are surfaced.
 4:  // An entirely new dataset can also be specified.
 5:  //
 6:  //Title:
 7:  //Version:
 8:  //Copyright:
 9:  //Author:
10:  //Company:
11:  //Description:
12:
13:  package BuildBeans;
14:
15:  import java.awt.*;
16:  import java.awt.event.*;
17:  import borland.jbcl.layout.*;
18:  import borland.jbcl.control.*;
19:  import borland.jbcl.view.*;
20:  import borland.jbcl.dataset.*;
21:  import borland.jbcl.util.BlackBox;
22:
23:  public class MyDBBean extends BeanPanel implements BlackBox {
24:    private BorderLayout borderLayout1 = new BorderLayout();
25:    private NavigatorControl navigatorControl1 = new
      ➥NavigatorControl();
26:    private GridControl gridControl1 = new GridControl();
27:    private Database database1 = new Database();
28:    private QueryDataSet queryDataSet1 = new QueryDataSet();
29:    private StatusBar statusBar1 = new StatusBar();
30:    private String userName = "SYSDBA";
31:    private String password = "masterkey";
32:    private String query = "select * from employee";
33:    private String connectionURL = "jdbc:odbc:dataset tutorial";
34:
35:    public MyDBBean() {
36:      try {
37:        jbInit();
38:      }
39:      catch (Exception e) {
40:        e.printStackTrace();
```

```
41:    }
42:  }
43:
44:  public void jbInit() throws Exception{
45:    navigatorControl1.setDataSet(queryDataSet1);
46:    gridControl1.setDataSet(queryDataSet1);
47:    database1.setConnection(new
➥borland.jbcl.dataset.ConnectionDescriptor(
48:      connectionURL, userName, password, false,
➥"sun.jdbc.odbc.JdbcOdbcDriver"));
49:    queryDataSet1.setQuery(new borland.jbcl.dataset.QueryDescriptor(
50:      database1, query, null, true, false));
51:    statusBar1.setDataSet(queryDataSet1);
52:    this.setLayout(borderLayout1);
53:    this.add(navigatorControl1, BorderLayout.NORTH);
54:    this.add(gridControl1, BorderLayout.CENTER);
55:    this.add(statusBar1, BorderLayout.SOUTH);
56:  }
57:
58:  // Example properties
59:
60:  public void setPassword(String s) {
61:    password=s;
62:    database1.getConnection().setPassword(s);
63:  }
64:
65:  public String getPassword() {
66:    password=database1.getConnection().getPassword();
67:    return password;
68:  }
69:
70:  public void setUserName(String s) {
71:    userName=s;
72:    database1.getConnection().setUserName(s);
73:  }
74:
75:  public String getUserName() {
76:    userName=database1.getConnection().getUserName();
77:    return userName;
78:  }
79:
80:  //!To do: Trigger update of other prop when qds changes
81:  public void setQueryDataSet(QueryDataSet qds) {
82:    navigatorControl1.setDataSet(qds);
83:    gridControl1.setDataSet(qds);
84:    statusBar1.setDataSet(qds);
85:    queryDataSet1 = qds;
86:  }
87:
88:  public QueryDataSet getQueryDataSet() {
```

18

continues

LISTING 18.3. CONTINUED

```
89:         return queryDataSet1;
90:      }
91:
92:      public void setQuery(String s) {
93:         try {
94:            query=s;
95:            queryDataSet1.close();
96:            queryDataSet1.setQuery(new
               ➥borland.jbcl.dataset.QueryDescriptor
               ➥(database1, query));
97:            queryDataSet1.open();
98:         }
99:         catch (Exception e) {
100:           e.printStackTrace();
101:        }
102:     }
103:
104:     public String getQuery() {
105:        query=queryDataSet1.getQueryString();
106:        return query;
107:     }
108:
109:     public void setConnectionURL(String s) {
110:        connectionURL=s;
111:        database1.getConnection().setConnectionURL(s);
112:     }
113:
114:     public String getConnectionURL() {
115:        connectionURL=database1.getConnection().getConnectionURL();
116:        return connectionURL;
117:     }
118:
119:     // Example events
120:     public static final String EXAMPLE_EVENT = "ExampleEvent";
121:     protected void fireExampleActionEvent() {
122:        //Args: event source, event ID, event command
123:        processActionEvent(new ActionEvent(this,
               ➥ActionEvent.ACTION_PERFORMED, EXAMPLE_EVENT));
124:     }
125:  }
```

ANALYSIS Lines 1 through 11 are the internal documentation. Line 13 declares the package. Lines 15 through 21 import the same classes as previous beans, with one new addition. On line 20, `borland.jbcl.dataset.*` is imported to support the database functionality of this bean.

Line 23 declares the class, which extends the BeanPanel class and implements the BlackBox interface. The declarations for this bean's private variables are found in lines 24 through 33.

Lines 35 through 42 are the default constructor, and lines 44 through 56 do the initialization. Note that the accessor methods are used to set the initial values for the bean's controls.

Various property accessor methods are predefined for this bean. Lines 60 through 68 define the setPassword() and getPassword() methods. Lines 70 through 78 define the setUserName() and getUserName() methods. Lines 80 through 90 deal with the setQueryDataSet() and getQueryDataSet() methods. Lines 92 through 107 define the setQuery() and getQuery() methods, which deal with query strings. Lines 109 through 117 declare the setConnectionURL() and getConnectionURL() methods.

The last section of code, lines 119 through 124, provides a sample event identical to the one provided by the NewBean class.

To use the DBBean bean, you will need to have installed a JDBC-accessible database. By default, the grid attaches to the default data source available when you follow the normal instructions for installing Local InterBase with JBuilder. Because of this requirement, you might get this error when you click the Design tab for this bean:

```
[Microsoft][ODBC Driver Manager] Data source name not found and no
default driver specified.
```

If this happens, it means that you didn't set up a data source when you installed Local InterBase. Click the OK button to clear the error and make sure you've saved everything in the current project. Close JBuilder, and then follow these steps to rectify the situation:

1. Double-click the 32bit ODBC icon in the Windows Control Panel.

2. In the ODBC Data Source Administrator dialog box, click the Add button. The Create New Data Source dialog box appears.

3. Choose InterBase 5.x Driver by Visigenix (*.gdb) from the list of installed ODBC drivers, and then click the Finish button.

4. In the InterBase ODBC Configuration dialog box, fill out the fields as shown here:

18

Field	Value
Data Source Name	`DataSet Tutorial`
Network Protocol	`<local>`
Database	`C:\Program Files\InterBase Corp\InterBase\ Examples \employee.gdb`
Username	`SYSDBA`
Password	`masterkey`

5. To test the connection, click the Test Connect button. When you receive the `Connection Successful` message, click OK to close the InterBase ODBC Configuration dialog box. Click the OK button in the ODBC Data Source Administrator dialog box.

After you've completed these steps, reload JBuilder and reopen your project. Click `MyDBBean` in the Structure pane and choose the Design tab to switch your AppBrowser window to Design mode. JBuilder will take a minute or two to load the user interface and make the database connection. When it is finished loading, you should see data from the `employee.gdb` database file populating the grid. You now have a live connection to the InterBase database in your bean, and developers who use it will experience the same thing when using this bean in their designs.

Bean Info

Bean information is provided to visual environments such as JBuilder through introspection. For elements that don't follow the naming conventions, and therefore can't be surfaced using introspection, you can use the code in the `BeanInfo` class to manually expose these elements. The bean information code can also hide elements that are properly named and that would normally be exposed by introspection in visual development environments, such as runtime-only methods.

To add the `BeanInfo` class to today's project, select File|New, click on the BeansExpress tab, and double-click the Bean Info icon. The `BeanInfo` class is provided as a code snippet. The Paste Snippet [Bean Info] dialog box appears, as shown in Figure 18.4.

The Paste Snippet [Bean Info] dialog box gives you the opportunity to change the name of the `MyComponentBeanInfo` class extended from the `BeanInfo` class and also, therefore, to change the name of the `MyComponentBeanInfo.java` file.

Click the Parameters button and the Parameters dialog box appears, as shown in Figure 18.5.

FIGURE 18.4.

The Paste Snippet [Bean Info] dialog box.

FIGURE 18.5.

The Parameters dialog box.

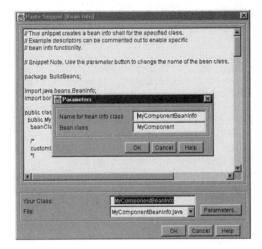

18

Change the name of the bean information class in the Name for bean info class text box to MyDBBeanInfo, and change the name of the bean class in the Bean class text box to MyDBBean. Click the OK button to return to the Paste Snippet [Bean Info] dialog box. Note that references to MyComponentBeanInfo have been changed to MyDBBeanInfo, and references to MyComponent have been changed to MyDBBean. Click the OK button to add this new class to today's project.

Listing 18.4 shows the resulting source code for MyDBBeanInfo.java.

TYPE   **LISTING 18.4.** MyDBBeanInfo.java.

```
 1: // This snippet creates a bean info shell for the specified class.
 2: // Example descriptors can be commented out to enable specific
 3: // bean info functionality.
 4: //
 5: // Snippet Note: Use the parameter button to change the name
      ➥of the bean class.
 6:
 7: package BuildBeans;
 8:
 9: import java.beans.BeanInfo;
10: import borland.jbcl.util.BasicBeanInfo;
11:
12: public class MyDBBeanInfo extends BasicBeanInfo {
13:   public MyDBBeanInfo() {
14:     beanClass = MyDBBean.class;
15:
16:     /*
17:     customizerClass=null; //Optional customizer class
18:     */
19:
20:     /**
21:      * The event information for your JavaBean.
22:      * Format:  {{"EventSetName", "EventListenerClass",
          ➥"AddMethod", "RemoveMethod"}, ...}
23:      * Example: {{"ActionListener", "java.awt.event.ActionListener",
          ➥"addActionListener", "removeActionListener"}, ...}
24:      */
25:     /*
26:     eventSetDescriptors = new String[][] {
27:       {"ActionListener", "java.awt.event.ActionListener",
           ➥"addActionListener", "removeActionListener"},
28:     };
29:     */
30:
31:     /**
32:      * The names of each event set's listener methods.
33:      * Format:  {{"listener1Method1", "listener1Method2",
          ➥"listener1Method3", ...}, ...}
34:      * Example: {{"actionPerformed"}, ...}
35:      */
36:     /*
37:     eventListenerMethods = new String[][] {
38:       {"actionPerformed"},
39:     };
40:     */
41:
42:     /**
43:      * The index of the default event for your JavaBean.
44:      */
```

```
45:        defaultEventIndex = -1;
46:
47:        // Property Info
48:
49:        /**
50:         * The property information for your JavaBean.
51:         * Format: {{"PropertyName", ""PropertyDescription",
                ➥"ReadMethod", "WriteMethod"}, ...}
52:         * Example: {{"fontSize", "Get the font size (points)",
                ➥"getFontSize", "setFontSize"}, ...}
53:         */
54:        /*
55: propertyDescriptors = new String[][] {
56:         {"fontSize", "Get the font size (points)",
                ➥"getFontSize", "setFontSize"},
57:        };
58:        */
59:
60:        /**
61:         * The index of the default property for your JavaBean.
62:         */
63:        defaultPropertyIndex = -1;
64:
65:        // Method Info
66:
67:        /**
68:         * The method names (nonproperties) for your JavaBean.
69:         * Format:  {"method1", "method2", "method3", ...}
70:         * Example: {"fillRect", "eraseRect", "close", "open"}
71:         */
72:        methodNames = new String[] {"fillRect", "eraseRect",
                ➥"close", "open"};
73:
74:        /**
75:         * The method parameters for each of your JavaBean's methods.
76:         * Format:  {{"method1Parameter1", "method1Parameter2", ...},
                ➥...}
77:         * Example: {{"java.awt.Graphics", "java.awt.Rectangle", ...},
                ➥...}
78:         */
79:        /*
80:        methodParameters = new String[][] {
81:          {"java.awt.Graphics", "java.awt.Rectangle"},
82:        };
83:        */
84:
85:        // Icon Info
86:
87:        /**
88:         * A 16x16 color icon for your JavaBean.
```

18

continues

LISTING **18.4.** CONTINUED

```
 89:        */
 90:        iconColor16x16 = null;
 91:
 92:        /**
 93:         * A 32x32 color icon for your JavaBean.
 94:         */
 95:        iconColor32x32 = null;
 96:
 97:        /**
 98:         * A 16x16 monochromatic icon for your JavaBean.
 99:         */
100:        iconMono16x16 = null;
101:
102:        /**
103:         * A 32x32 monochromatic icon for your JavaBean.
104:         */
105:        iconMono32x32 = null;
106:
107:        // Additional Info
108:
109:        /**
110:         * Any additional BeanInfo for this JavaBean.
111:         */
112:        /*
113:        additionalBeanInfo = new BeanInfo[0];
114:        */
115:    }
116: }
```

ANALYSIS Lines 1 through 5 form the internal documentation for this class. Line 7 declares the package. Lines 9 and 10 import the java.beans.BeanInfo and borland.jbcl.util.BasicBeanInfo classes necessary to support this class, which inherits its initial values from the BasicBeanInfo class. Line 12 declares the MyDBBeanInfo class, which extends the BasicBeanInfo class.

The remainder of this listing comprises the declaration for the MyDBBeanInfo() class constructor (lines 13 through 115). Note that most of the lines of code defining the MyDBBeanInfo class constructor are commented out, as often as javadoc comments. There are, however, several default values and a statement that sets the association to the underlying bean (line 14) that aren't commented out.

By uncommenting and modifying the lines you need to expose your bean's properties and events, you can use this class to provide nonstandard bean information to any visual environment that can handle the JavaBeans standard. There is also a method available to hide properties and events that follow the standard naming conventions that would normally be exposed through introspection. To use this method, simply write

```
propertyName.setHidden(true);
```

```
eventName.setHidden(true);
```

where *propertyName* represents a property's identifier, and *eventName* represents an event's identifier. This will keep the property or event from being accessible in visual design environments such as JBuilder. For example, a property or event that called setHidden() would not be displayed in the Inspector pane at design time. This is especially useful if the property should be changed only at runtime, or if the event shouldn't be handled by developers using your bean.

New Event Bean

There is a code snippet called NewEventBean that you can use to create new events. To add one to today's project, select File I New, click the BeansExpress tab, and double-click the New Event Bean icon. The Paste Snippet [New Event Bean] dialog box appears. Click the Parameters button to open the Parameters dialog box. Change the event class name in the Name for new event class text box to MyCustomEvent. Click the OK button. The appropriate references in the code snippet are renamed. Click the OK button in the Paste Snippet [New Event Bean] dialog box.

The MyCustomEvent.java file, as generated, actually contains three classes that have to be separated into three separate files before compilation: the MyCustomEventExampleBean.java, MyCustomEventListener.java, and MyCustomEvent.java files.

To create the first file, click the Add to Project icon in the Navigation pane. In the File name field of the File page in the File Open / Create dialog box, type MyCustomEventExampleBean.java and click the Open button. Click MyCustomEvent.java in the Navigation pane. Click the Content pane, select lines 37 through 80 (remember, the selected line number is displayed in the status bar at the bottom of the AppBrowser window), and select Edit I Cut. Click MyCustomEventExampleBean.java in the Navigation pane and then click in the Content pane. Select Edit I Paste. You will also need to add the following lines of code near the top of the file (just after the opening comments):

```
package BuildBeans;
import java.util.*;
```

The resulting file is shown in Listing 18.5.

LISTING 18.5. MyCustomEventExampleBean.java.

```
 1:  // This is an example of a nonvisual bean that fires the new events
 2:  //
 3:
 4:  package BuildBeans;
 5:
 6:  import java.util.*;
 7:
 8:  public class MyCustomEventExampleBean {
 9:    MyCustomEventExampleBean() {
10:    }
11:
12:    // The add/remove methods provide the signature for the IDE to
         ➥recognize
13:    // these events and show them in the event list
14:    public synchronized void addMyCustomEventListener
         ➥(MyCustomEventListener l) {
15:      listenerList.addElement(l);
16:    }
17:    public synchronized void removeMyCustomEventListener
         ➥(MyCustomEventListener l){
18:      listenerList.removeElement(l);
19:    }
20:
21:    // A single process method keeps all event dispatching in one place.
22:    // Separate processEVENT1, processEVENT2 methods could also be used.
23:    protected void processMyCustomEvent(MyCustomEvent e) {
24:      switch (e.getID()) {
25:        case MyCustomEvent.EVENT1:
26:          for (int i=0; i<listenerList.size(); i++)
27:            //Send event to all registered listeners
28:            ((MyCustomEventListener)listenerList.elementAt(i)).event1(e);
29:          break;
30:        case MyCustomEvent.EVENT2:
31:          for (int i=0; i<listenerList.size(); i++)
32:            ((MyCustomEventListener)listenerList.elementAt(i)).event2(e);
33:          break;
34:        case MyCustomEvent.EVENT3:
35:          for (int i=0; i<listenerList.size(); i++)
36:            ((MyCustomEventListener)listenerList.elementAt(i)).event3(e);
37:          break;
38:      }
39:    }
40:
```

```
41:     // A test method to fire all three example events
42:     public void testMyCustomEvent () {
43:        processMyCustomEvent (new MyCustomEvent
               ➥(this, MyCustomEvent.EVENT1));
44:        processMyCustomEvent (new MyCustomEvent
               ➥(this, MyCustomEvent.EVENT2));
45:        processMyCustomEvent (new MyCustomEvent
               ➥(this, MyCustomEvent.EVENT3));
46:     }
47:
48:     private Vector listenerList = new Vector();
49:  }
```

To create the second file, click the Add to Project icon in the Navigation pane. In the File
name field of the File page in the File Open / Create dialog box, type
MyCustomEventListener.java and then click the Open button. Click
MyCustomEvent.java in the Navigation pane. Click the Content pane, select lines 29
through 37, and select Edit I Cut. Click MyCustomEventListener.java in the Navigation
pane and then click in the Content pane. Select Edit I Paste. Again, you must add these
lines near the top of the file:

```
package BuildBeans;
import java.util.*;
```

The resulting file is shown in Listing 18.6.

18

TYPE **LISTING 18.6.** MyCustomEventListener.java.

```
1:   // This defines a listener interface for the set of events that
2:   // are generated by MyCustomEvent
3:   //
4:
5:   package BuildBeans;
6:
7:   import java.util.*;
8:
9:   public interface MyCustomEventListener extends EventListener {
10:     public void event1(MyCustomEvent e);
11:     public void event2(MyCustomEvent e);
12:     public void event3(MyCustomEvent e);
13:  }
```

The remainder can stay in MyCustomEvent.java, as shown in Listing 18.7.

TYPE   **LISTING 18.7.** MyCustomEvent.java.

```
 1:   // This snippet takes advantage of JBuilder's ability to define
 2:   // multiple public classes in a single source file.  This is not
 3:   // recommended, and is only used here as an example.
 4:   // Each class should be pasted into its own .java file.
 5:   // You will see warnings to remind you when you compile.
 6:   //
 7:   // Snippet Note: Use the parameter button to change the name of the
      ➥event class.
 8:
 9:   package BuildBeans;
10:
11:   import java.util.*;
12:
13:   // This defines a new event, with minimum state.
14:   public class MyCustomEvent extends EventObject {
15:      static final int EVENT1=1;
16:      static final int EVENT2=2;
17:      static final int EVENT3=3;
18:      private int id=0;
19:
20:      public int getID() {return id;};
21:
22:      MyCustomEvent(Object source,int i) {
23:        super(source);
24:        id=i;
25:        }
26:   }
```

After making all these changes, be sure to select File | Save All and File | Save Project. These three files present you with an event object class, event registration methods, an event notification mechanism, and a method for sending event notifications to listeners.

After modifying these classes and methods to suit your needs and compiling them, you will need to import the MyCustomEventExampleBean class into the bean class that needs to use its functionality.

JavaBean Wizard

You can create a bean by using the JavaBean Wizard. Create a bean using the JavaBean Wizard named DigiTime that displays the time digitally. Start by selecting File | New to open the New dialog box, click on the New tab to open the New page of the New dialog box if it's not already open, and double-click the JavaBean icon. The JavaBean Wizard dialog box appears, as shown in Figure 18.6.

FIGURE 18.6.

The JavaBean Wizard dialog box.

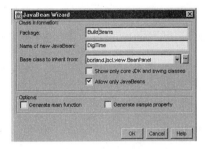

Type the name of the bean, `DigiTime`, into the Name of new JavaBean text box. Leave all the other settings with their default values. Click the OK button to create the `DigiTime` class.

First, add a component to display the output of your bean—the date and time. Click on the AppBrowser window Design tab to switch to the Design mode. Select the JBCL tab in the Component Palette and click on the TextControl icon. Click in the `DigiTime` user interface in the Content Pane to add the `TextControl` component. Select the `TextControl` component in the Structure pane (most likely named `textControl1`). Click on the `text` property in the Property page of the Inspector pane. Type the name of your new bean, `The DigiTime Bean`, in the `text` property text box. Now you're ready to add some code to your new bean. Switch back into Edit mode by clicking on the AppBrowser window Source tab. Modify the `DigiTime` class declaration so that it implements the `Runnable` interface. Change the class declaration to the following:

```
public class DigiTime extends BeanPanel implements Runnable{
```

The `Runnable` interface allows you to run the class in its own thread. Add the following statement after the first import statement to import the `Date` class into your bean:

```
import java.util.Date;
```

Declare the `thread`, `running`, and `theDate` variables by adding the following three lines of code just under the `textControl1` variable definition:

```
Thread thread = null;
private boolean running = false;
private Date theDate = null;
```

The `running` variable is the `running` property for the `DigiTime` bean. Add a getter method for the Boolean `running` property. The `isRunning()` getter method is as follows:

```
public boolean isRunning() {
  return running;
}
```

18

Use the `isRunning()` getter method to retrieve the state of the `running` property. If the bean's thread is running, the `isRunning()` method returns `true`. Otherwise, it returns `false`.

Now you're ready to create a setter method for the `DigiTime` bean. Add the setter method, `setRunning()`, to the `DigiTime` class as shown here:

```
public void setRunning( boolean running ) {
  this.running = running;
  if( running && thread == null ) {
    thread = new Thread( this );
    thread.start( );
  }
  else if( !running && thread != null ) {
    thread.stop();
    thread = null;
  }
}
```

You or another programmer can set the `DigiTime` bean's `running` property programmatically through the `setRunning()` method. Pass `true` or `false` to the method depending on whether you want to start or stop the bean's clock. The method checks the Boolean value that was passed and whether or not a thread is already running. Based on this information, the method either creates a new thread and starts it running, or stops an existing thread and assigns `null` to the `thread` variable.

Finally, it's time to create the clock's engine, which is located in the `run()` method. Add the following `run()` method to your `DigiTime` class:

```
public void run() {
  while (true) {
    theDate = new Date();
    textControl1.setText(theDate.toString());
    try {
      Thread.sleep(1000);
    }
    catch (InterruptedException e) {
    }
  }
}
```

You're finished coding your `DigiTime` bean. The complete `DigiTime` bean source code is provided in Listing 18.8. Build your `DigiTime` bean so that you can test it in the next section.

LISTING 18.8. DigiTime.java.

```
 1: //Title:         Your Product Name
 2: //Version:
 3: //Copyright:     Copyright (c) 1998
 4: //Author:        Your Name
 5: //Company:       Your Company
 6: //Description:   Your description
 7:
 8: package BuildBeans;
 9:
10: import java.awt.*;
11: import java.util.Date;
12: import borland.jbcl.view.BeanPanel;
13: import borland.jbcl.control.*;
14:
15: public class DigiTime extends BeanPanel implements Runnable{
16:    BorderLayout borderLayout1 = new BorderLayout();
17:    TextControl textControl1 = new TextControl();
18:    Thread thread = null;
19:    private boolean running = false;
20:    private Date theDate = null;
21:
22:    public DigiTime() {
23:      try  {
24:        jbInit();
25:      }
26:      catch (Exception ex) {
27:        ex.printStackTrace();
28:      }
29:    }
30:
31:    private void jbInit() throws Exception {
32:      textControl1.setText("The DigiTime Bean");
33:      this.setLayout(borderLayout1);
34:      this.add(textControl1, BorderLayout.CENTER);
35:    }
36:
37:    public boolean isRunning() {
38:      return running;
39:    }
40:
41:    public void setRunning( boolean running ) {
42:      this.running = running;
43:      if( running && thread == null ) {
44:        thread = new Thread( this );
45:        thread.start( );
46:      }
47:      else if( !running && thread != null ) {
```

continues

LISTING 18.8. CONTINUED

```
48:        thread.stop();
49:        thread = null;
50:      }
51:    }
52:
53:    public void run() {
54:      while (true) {
55:        theDate = new Date();
56:        textControl1.setText(theDate.toString());
57:        try {
58:          Thread.sleep(1000);
59:        }
60:        catch (InterruptedException e) {
61:        }
62:      }
63:    }
64:  }
```

Testing Beans

To test your bean, you must first add it to the Component Palette. After you have successfully compiled your bean's class file (and any auxiliary files it requires), you're ready
to install your new bean for testing. Select Tools | Configure Palette to display the Palette
Properties dialog box, shown in Figure 18.7.

FIGURE 18.7.

*The Palette Properties
dialog box.*

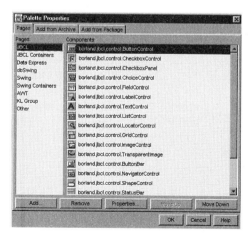

Open the Palette Properties dialog box to the Pages page by clicking on the Pages tab. In
the Pages list, click Other and then click on the Add from Package tab to display the Add
from Package page of the Palette Properties dialog box, shown in Figure 18.8.

FIGURE 18.8.

The Add from Package page of the Palette Properties dialog box.

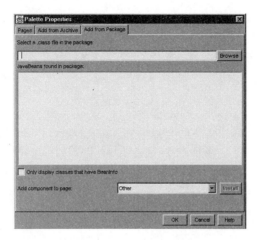

Click the Browse button to display the Select File dialog box. Navigate to the myclasses\BuildBeans package subdirectory, select a bean to install—in this case, DigiTime.class—and click the Open button.

Back on the Add from Package page, with BuildBeans.DigiTime selected, click the Install button. When you see the message Installation Complete, click the Pages tab. You should see the BuildBeans.DigiTime component listed in the Components list box, as shown in Figure 18.9.

18

FIGURE 18.9.

The BuildBeans.DigiTime bean is listed in the Components list box.

Click the OK button in the Palette Properties dialog box. Your DigiTime bean should be added to the Other page of the Component Palette.

Caution   Changes made to beans that have been placed on the palette do not take effect until JBuilder has been closed and restarted.

Now that you have the new bean on the palette, you can try it out. Start a new project and create a new application. When Frame1.java appears in the Navigation pane, click the Design tab and then click bevelPanel1. Click the DigiTime bean and then click in the Content pane. The DigiTime bean is added to your application interface. Change the bean's font size in the font property editor. (Change the font size to 24, for instance.) Then click and drag the handles surrounding the DigiTime bean's graphical representation to resize it in the user interface. Finally, click on the bean's running property on the Property page in the Inspector pane and select True from the drop-down list. You should see your digital clock hard at work, as shown in Figure 18.10.

FIGURE 18.10.

The DigiTime bean shows the date and time in an application displayed in the AppBrowser window Design mode.

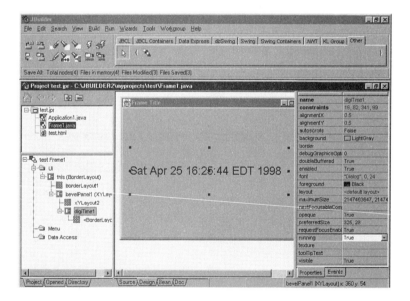

That's it for this bean. It has been added to the palette, and you've used it in a new application. With other beans, you might want to try setting properties, creating event handlers—all the things you would want to do with the bean. After it's fully tested, you can deploy the bean using an archive file. (You'll learn more about archiving tomorrow.)

If you decide to deploy your bean as an archive (a JAR or ZIP file), first select Tools | Configure Palette and select the unarchived bean that you tested. Click the Remove button to remove the test bean. Archive the bean's class file(s) and then select Tools |

Configure Palette to install the archived bean. Click Other in the Pages list box, and then choose the Add from Archive tab. Navigate to the subdirectory where the archive resides (which must be on your CLASSPATH), and click the Install button. Your archived bean is now installed on the Component Palette. Other developers in your group (or customers) can install it in their visual environments and use your bean as well.

Summary

Today you became familiar with developing JavaBeans components, reusable components that you can create and distribute for use in any compliant visual development environment, such as JBuilder. Bean requirements were discussed, and some guidelines were introduced. You got a thorough overview of JBuilder's BeansExpress and its various beans and code snippets, including NewBean, OkCancelBean, DBBean, BeanInfo, and NewEventBean. You also learned how to create beans using the JavaBean Wizard.

Testing beans is an important last step toward ensuring that your beans work properly, that properties can be set, that event handlers can be created, and that all the kinks are worked out before deployment. You also learned how to add beans to your development environment.

Q&A

Q What about dialog boxes? There are some on JBuilder's Component Palette, but I didn't read anything about creating dialog box beans.

A Creating dialog boxes as beans is a somewhat advanced topic, because the Dialog subclass requires a parent Frame object as a parameter. However, recall that one of the requirements of beans is that they have a parameterless default constructor. Because of this conflict, dialog boxes must be wrapped, but this process is difficult. For a solid introduction to accomplishing this task, check out the BeansExpress help topic "Making a Bean from a Dialog."

Q I've added my bean to the Component Palette and used it in an applet, but I keep getting Cannot instantiate xxx.class errors. What's going on here?

A When you run applets locally (on your client machine), all the class files on which they depend must be available on your browser's CLASSPATH for testing. You'll learn more about the details of why this is true tomorrow. For now, just be aware that either the class files must be on the existing CLASSPATH or you must add the subdirectory to the CLASSPATH. If you're using archived beans, the archive's fully qualified pathname and filename must be added to the CLASSPATH.

18

Workshop

The Workshop provides two ways for you to affirm what you've learned in this chapter. The Quiz section poses questions to help you solidify your understanding of the material covered. You can find answers to the quiz questions in Appendix A, "Answers to Quiz Questions." The Exercises section provides you with experience in using what you have learned. Try to work through all these before continuing to the next day.

Quiz

1. What are the two basic requirements for creating beans?
2. How should accessor methods be named in order for JBuilder to expose them using introspection?
3. You've added a DBBean to your project, but when you choose the Design tab, you get an ODBC Driver Manager error. What is probably wrong?
4. What are the two main uses of the BeanInfo class?
5. What method is used to hide bean elements?

Exercises

1. Create new beans from some of the applets you created during the first two weeks.
2. Explore the BeansExpress tutorials accessible from the Help menu by selecting Help | BeansExpress.

DAY 19

Deploying Java Programs

After you've created and tested your Java programs on your computer, you'll want to deploy them in such a way that users have access to the files necessary to run the program.

NEW TERM *Deployment* is the preparation and placement of program files so that the program will work properly in its intended environment. Often, deployment involves the optimization of file sizes so that the programs load rapidly across networks and other information traffic bottlenecks.

For applications, deployment can be on individual machines or across Local Area Networks (LANs). For applets, deployment will usually be to a Web server, although you can also deploy applets locally, perhaps on an intranet or extranet.

Note Internet Service Providers (ISPs) have differing requirements for uploading applets and associated files to their Web servers, so be sure to check with yours before attempting to do so.

For Java programs created with JBuilder, you will generally need your project's class files and auxiliary files (HTML, image, audio, and so on). Before you can distribute your program to end users or customers, you need to learn about the following to make sure that the proper files are deployed:

- Preparing your projects for deployment
- Creating JAR and ZIP archive files
- Using the Deployment Wizard
- Deploying applets and applications

In addition to your program files, you might need to include the JBCL or JGL archives, which are located in the `c:\jbuilder2\redist\` subdirectory. Today, you'll learn when these files need to be redistributed. To follow the examples in this chapter, create a project file named `DeployJava.jpr`.

Caution   Java is backward compatible so the Java 1.1 virtual machine runs applications developed using Java 1.0. However, the Java 1.0 virtual machine does not necessarily run applications developed using Java 1.1. Different browser versions implement different versions of the Java Virtual Machine. Check into the compatibility of the browsers that you want to use your Java program. Make sure that the browser supports Java 1.1 applications if that's the version of Java you developed the application in. Using the Java Plug-in, available from the Java Web site at `http://www.javasoft.com`, can solve much of the browser compatibility problem.

Project Preparation

Before bundling up your program files, you need to prepare your JBuilder project so that it is in its final form. There are various considerations you should take into account:

- Directory structure and relative paths
- Adding auxiliary files
- Resourcing strings
- Doing a final build

Let's look at each aspect of project preparation in turn.

Directories and Paths

Typically, you'll want to keep auxiliary files in separate subdirectories. On Day 9, "Graphics, Fonts, and Multimedia," for example, the images were kept in a subdirectory named `myimages`, and the sounds were deposited in a subdirectory names `mysounds`. If you use this type of structure, be sure to use relative pathnames to these subdirectories in your program source.

For example, say you have a line of code like this in your source:

```
play(getCodeBase(), "mysounds/meow.au");
```

Your program will then look for the `meow.au` file in the `mysounds` subdirectory. Therefore, for proper execution of your program, you must make sure that this exact same subdirectory structure is in place, with the proper files deposited in it, when deploying your program.

> **Caution**
>
> Java is a case-sensitive language. Directory names, for instance, must exactly match the string in the code.

You'll be using the `Neko` applet created on Day 9 as your sample deployment project, so copy the `Neko.java` and `Neko.html` files into your `myprojects` subdirectory. In the `myprojects` directory, create a subdirectory named `myimages`, and then copy the nine Neko images (`*.gif`) into the new `myimages` subdirectory.

With these files in place, you're ready to begin adding them to today's project. With the AppBrowser window open to `DeployJava.jpr`, click the Add to Project icon in the Navigation pane. Select both the `Neko.java` and `Neko.html` files, and click the Open button. Select File | Save Project. At this point, you should test the applet by selecting `Neko.html` in the Structure pane, clicking your right mouse button, and selecting the Run command.

Auxiliary Files

If you will be creating an archive file, such as a JAR or ZIP archive file, you will need to add any auxiliary files to the project before archiving. To make these files members of the project, use the Add to Project icon in the AppBrowser window Navigator pane. You'll learn how to make an archive file later today, so let's prepare the `DeployJava` project for archiving by adding the files in the `myimages` subdirectory to the project.

Click the Add to Project icon in the AppBrowser window Navigation pane. When the File Open / Create dialog box appears, open it to the File page by clicking on the File tab and then double-click on the `myimages` folder. Select all nine Neko images in the `myimages` folder and then click the Open button. The project's Navigation pane should now include a list of the nine Neko images, as shown in Figure 19.1.

FIGURE 19.1.

*The DeployJava pro-
ject AppBrowser win-
dow with the Neko
images added.*

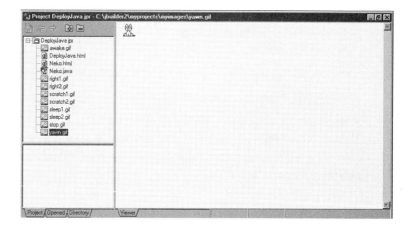

Any other files that you might want to include in your archive should also be added to the project, such as audio or text files. When you're finished adding files, be sure to select File | Save Project.

Accessing Auxiliary Files

You must use special methods for accessing auxiliary files from Java archives. The methods available from the classes in the `java.io` package typically don't work, and the `Applet` class `getImage()` method doesn't work. Use the `getResource()` method in the `Class` class instead.

Currently, your Neko applet loads images in its `init()` method with the following lines of code:

```
for (int i=0; i < nekopics.length; i++) {
  nekopics[i] = getImage(getCodeBase(), "myimages/" + nekosrc[i]);
}
```

When you put all of your applet's auxiliary files into a JAR file, everything that applet needs is stored in one place. This makes finding the files needed by the applet (or other Java program) relatively easy because you know they're in the applet's JAR. The `getResource()` method, shown here, takes advantage of this fact:

```
public URL getResource(String name)
```

The `getResource()` method was added to the `Class` class for accessing auxiliary files from a JAR. When you call the `getResource()` method from your program, it returns a `URL` object encapsulating the URL to your program's resources or, in other words, the URL to your program's JAR file. The `Class` class is part of the `java.lang` package, which is automatically imported into all Java programs. You get a class's `Class` object through the `Object` class's `getClass()` method, shown here:

```
public final Class getClass()
```

You can get the `Class` object for any Java class using the `getClass()` method because all Java classes are ultimately derived from the `Object` class. In the Neko applet's `init` method, add the following line of code just before the `for` loop that loads the applet's images:

```
Class myClass = getClass();
```

This statement gets the Neko applet's `Class` object and assigns it to the `myClass` variable. Next, you need to modify the body of the `for` loop so that it uses the `getResource()` method to load the Neko images. First, create a new variable that you can assign `URL` objects to and place the declaration, shown next, just before the `for` loop:

```
URL url = null;
```

Caution

Don't forget to import `java.net.URL` into your code.

Note

It's good practice to initialize all new variables. Assign object variables a `null` value if there is no initial object assigned to them. Likewise, numeric variables should be assigned a `0`; string variables, an empty string (`""`).

19

The body of the `for` loop should be changed so that the statement is identical to the following:

```
for (int i=0; i < nekopics.length; i++) {
  url = myClass.getResource("myimages/" + nekosrc[i]);
  try{
    nekopics[i] = createImage((ImageProducer) url.getContent());
  }
  catch (IOException ioe) {
    System.out.print( ioe.toString() );
  }
}
```

Caution

Don't forget to import `java.awt.image.ImageProducer` and `java.io.IOException` into your code.

The first statement in the body of the `for` loop, reproduced in the following code line, gets the URL object encapsulating the URL to the Neko applet's image resource using the `getResources()` method, and assigns it to the `url` variable:

```
url = myClass.getResource("myimages/" + nekosrc[i]);
```

The Neko applet can load and create an image for display now that it has the location of its image file resource. The image file is zipped together into the same JAR file as `Neko.class`, which is at the location encapsulated by the URL object held by the `url` variable. Using the line of code reproduced next, the Neko applet gets the data contained in the image file and calls the `Component` class's `createImage()` method to create an image from the data:

```
nekopics[i] = createImage((ImageProducer) url.getContent());
```

The call to the URL class `getContent()` method gets the data from the image file located in the Neko applet JAR file. The `getContent()` method signature is shown here:

```
public final Object getContent() throws IOException
```

The `getContent()` method returns an `Object` object. This means that any class of data can be loaded through the `getContent()` method because the `Object` class is the superclass for all Java classes. The Toolkit `createImage()` method takes an `ImageProducer` object. The `createImage()` method signature is shown here:

```
public abstract Image createImage(ImageProducer producer)
```

You need to cast the object returned from a call to the `getContent()` method to an `ImageProducer` object. `ImageProducer` is an interface found in the `java.awt.image` package. The data are run through the `createImage()` method and are returned as an `Image` object, which is assigned to the `nekopics[i]` variable array. Now the Neko applet can load images from a JAR file. Use the same methods for loading any kind of auxiliary file into all of your Java programs that use Java archives. The modified source code for the Neko applet is shown in Listing 19.1.

LISTING 19.1. Neko.java.

```
1:  package GraphicsFontsEtc;
2:  import java.applet.*;
3:  import java.awt.*;
4:  import java.net.URL;
5:  import java.awt.image.ImageProducer;
6:  import java.io.IOException;
7:
8:  public class Neko extends Applet implements Runnable {
9:
```

```
10:      Image nekopics[] = new Image[9];
11:      Image currentimg;
12:      Thread runner;
13:      int xpos;
14:      int ypos = 50;
15:
16:      public void init() {
17:        String nekosrc[] = { "right1.gif", "right2.gif",
18:                             "stop.gif", "yawn.gif",
19:                             "scratch1.gif", "scratch2.gif",
20:                             "sleep1.gif", "sleep2.gif",
21:                             "awake.gif" };
22:        Class myClass = getClass();
23:        URL url = null;
24:        for (int i=0; i < nekopics.length; i++) {
25:          url = myClass.getResource("myimages/" + nekosrc[i]);
26:          try {
27:            nekopics[i] = createImage((ImageProducer) url.getContent());
28:          }
29:          catch (IOException ioe) {
30:            System.out.print( ioe.toString() );
31:          }
32:        }
33:        setBackground(Color.white);
34:      }
35:
36:      public void start() {
37:        if (runner == null) {
38:          runner = new Thread(this);
39:          runner.start();
40:        }
41:      }
42:
43:      public void stop() {
44:        if (runner != null) {
45:          runner.stop();
46:          runner = null;
47:        }
48:      }
49:
50:      public void run() {
51:
52:        // run from one side of the screen to the middle
53:        nekorun(0, getSize().width / 2);
54:
55:        // stop and pause
56:        currentimg = nekopics[2];
57:        repaint();
58:        pause(1000);
```

19

continues

LISTING 19.1. CONTINUED

```
59:
60:        // yawn
61:        currentimg = nekopics[3];
62:        repaint();
63:        pause(1000);
64:
65:        // scratch four times
66:        nekoscratch(4);
67:
68:        // sleep for 5 seconds
69:        nekosleep(5);
70:
71:        // wake up and run off
72:        currentimg = nekopics[8];
73:        repaint();
74:        pause(500);
75:        nekorun(xpos, getSize().width + 10);
76:
77:    }
78:
79:    void nekorun(int start, int end) {
80:        currentimg = nekopics[0];
81:        for (int i = start; i < end; i+=10) {
82:          xpos = i;
83:          // swap images
84:          if (currentimg == nekopics[0])
85:            currentimg = nekopics[1];
86:          else currentimg = nekopics[0];
87:          repaint();
88:          pause(150);
89:        }
90:    }
91:
92:    void nekoscratch(int numtimes) {
93:        for (int i = numtimes; i > 0; i--) {
94:          currentimg = nekopics[4];
95:          repaint();
96:          pause(150);
97:          currentimg = nekopics[5];
98:          repaint();
99:          pause(150);
100:       }
101:   }
102:
103:   void nekosleep(int numtimes) {
104:       for (int i = numtimes; i > 0; i--) {
105:         currentimg = nekopics[6];
106:         repaint();
107:         pause(250);
```

```
108:        currentimg = nekopics[7];
109:        repaint();
110:        pause(250);
111:      }
112:    }
113:
114:    void pause(int time) {
115:      try { Thread.sleep(time); }
116:      catch (InterruptedException e) { }
117:    }
118:
119:    public void paint(Graphics g) {
120:      if (currentimg != null)
121:        g.drawImage(currentimg, xpos, ypos, this);
122:    }
123:
124:  }
```

Resource Wizard

If you're planning on deploying your program in more than one language or locale, you'll want to consider using the Resource Wizard to convert any hard-coded strings into identifiers. To do this, select the .java source code file for which you want to bundle resource strings, and then select Wizards | Resource Strings. The Resource Wizard dialog box appears, as shown in Figure 19.2.

FIGURE 19.2.

The Resource Wizard dialog box.

19

Create a new resource bundle by clicking the New button. The Create ResourceBundle dialog box appears, as shown in Figure 19.3.

FIGURE 19.3.

The Create ResourceBundle dialog box.

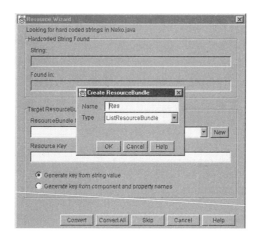

By default, the resource file is named Res.java, but you can change this name if you like in the Name text box of the Create ResourceBundle dialog box. (The name without the .java extension is displayed in the Name text box. Don't enter the extension.) Select the bundle type in the Type drop-down list. When you're satisfied with the entries, click the OK button.

As the Resource Wizard finds each hard-coded string in your source code, that string is shown under the For String label, and the block that contains it appears under the Found in: label. As each string is presented, you have the opportunity to assign it an identifier called a *key*. If you then click the Convert button, the identifier replaces the string in your source code, and the string is pulled out into the resource file. Alternatively, you can skip the string if it isn't one you intend to localize later (such as a product name).

After you've gone through all the strings presented, the Res.java file is automatically added to the current project. The resource strings are now bundled in the resource file, which can be translated and relinked with your project as required to create localized versions of your project.

Final Build

Now that you've added all the auxiliary files and bundled your hard-coded strings, you're ready to do the final build of your project. First, select File | Project Properties to open the DeployJava.jpr Properties dialog box. Open the Compiler page by clicking on the Compiler tab, and uncheck the Include Debug Information check box, which is checked by default. This will create a class file without the extra symbolic information that the integrated debugger requires but that your program doesn't require when running on its own. This also makes the class files smaller and faster to load.

You might also need to uncheck Show Warnings if you've purposely used any deprecated methods. (Using deprecated methods is not recommended.) Select Build|Rebuild Project to create all new class files for your project, and then test-run your project one more time. If you don't intend to archive, your project is now ready to deploy.

Unarchived Projects

To deploy an unarchived project, all you really need to do is duplicate your basic directory structure on your intended platform. For example, say you have a subdirectory on your Web server directory at `http://www.mysite.org/homepage/applets/` where you want to put `Neko`. Copy `Neko.html` to that directory. Recall that the `Neko.class` is part of the `GraphicsFontsEtc` package. You need to put the `Neko.class` file in a subdirectory named after the package. Create a subdirectory named `GraphicsFontsEtc` and place the `Neko.class` inside it. Finally, create a subdirectory named `myimages` inside the `GraphicsFontsEtc` subdirectory, and deposit the Neko images into the new `applets/GraphicsFontsEtc/myimages` subdirectory.

That's it! Test-run the applet from the Web site, and `Neko` is off and running. If you have many class files associated with an applet, you could create a `myclasses` subdirectory and deposit the class files there. If you do this, just be sure that you adjust the `CODEBASE` attribute in the `<APPLET>` tag of the HTML file so that it reflects that relative path. If you used packages in your program, be sure to duplicate that directory structure as well.

Another aspect of this simple deployment is that it involves an applet that didn't make use of any beans from the JavaBeans Class Library, so therefore it doesn't require the JBCL classes to be present to run. If your program uses any of the components on the Component Palette, you've used JBuilder beans, so if your Web site or user doesn't already have access to the JBCL class archives, your program won't run. You'll need to copy the `jbcl2.0-rt.jar` file from the `c:\jbuilder2\redist\` directory to your user's machine or your Web site to make the archives available in order for your program to run properly.

 Note

> Many JBCL classes rely on classes and interfaces in the Java Generic Library (JGL). In addition to deploying the JBCL archive, it might be necessary to include the JGL archive, the `jgl3.1.0.jar` file residing in the `c:\jbuilder2\redist\` directory, when you deploy applications using the JBCL class.

If you've used any of the KL Group beans or any of the Java Generic Library (JGL) classes, you might also need to copy one or more of the `jcbwt.jar`, `jcchart.jar`,

19

jctable.jar, or jgl3.1.0.jar files from the c:\jbuilder2\redist\ directory. These redistributable Java Archive (JAR) files contain the dependency classes that the KL Group beans and JGL methods require in order to run in Java.

Run the deployed application by using the Java Runtime Environment utility program, jre.exe and jrew.exe under Windows. You can find both in the C:\JBuilder2\java\bin\, or equivalent, directory. Be sure to use the -cp option so that the utility knows the path and filename of each archive needed to run your application. The command line should look something like the following:

```
jre -cp MyJar.jar;OtherJar.jar;YetAnotherJar.jar myPackage.myClass
```

Note Your applets run in browsers, which provide their own Java runtime environment. Your applet users don't need to worry about including directory and filenames to necessary archive files because you provide the appropriate archive files available to the Web server on which you place your applets. The user's browser downloads the archive files specified in the HTML file.

Archives

Archiving your project isn't absolutely necessary, but it's highly recommended. It's probably okay to deploy small applets (such as Neko) as unarchived projects. However, when users download your applet into their browsers, the associated unarchived files (class, audio, image, and so on) are downloaded separately, each causing an additional http connection to be made for the download. If your Internet Service Provider charges you by the connection, or *hit,* this can add up to a lot of money in no time. An archived program, on the other hand, downloads all its files in a single HTTP connection.

Four types of archives are supported in Java:

- JAR uncompressed
- JAR compressed
- ZIP uncompressed
- ZIP compressed

Tip If you are deploying an applet that you know will be distributed only to users of Microsoft's Internet Explorer, you can also compress files using the .CAB cabinet file format.

NEW TERM *JAR* stands for *Java Archive,* a portable ziplike archive that contains the files and directory structure of a Java program.

JAR files can be created as compressed or uncompressed archives. In an uncompressed archive, the files are stored in a single archive but remain their original size. Compression decreases the size of the archive file and therefore decreases download time and increases performance. JAR files also automatically preserve the subdirectory structure of the program being archived. They are the cross-platform solution of choice for creating archives.

For example, the Microsoft Internet Explorer supports JAR and CAB file formats for applets, with JAR support in the ARCHIVE attribute and CAB support in the CABBASE attribute of the <APPLET> tag. (CAB is Microsoft's proprietary file compression scheme, used by Microsoft's installation programs.) However, the Netscape Navigator supports both JAR and ZIP files in the ARCHIVE attribute. It appears that only the JAR file format will be universally available to browser users, so you might want to eschew ZIP files unless your program will be run exclusively on a platform that supports them (perhaps on your company intranet, for example).

In addition to program files, a JAR file must contain a manifest file listing its contents and signature files for authentication. For more information on manifest (.MF) and signature (.SF) files, select Help | Java Reference and choose the JDK Documentation node. Under the JDK Guide to New Features topic, locate and click the JAR File Format link, and then click the Manifest Format Specification link to view the details.

You can create JAR files manually by using the JAR.EXE command-line utility (see Appendix B, "JBuilder and Java Utilities"). ZIP files can be created with any one of a number of ZIP creation utilities, such as PKZIP.EXE and WinZip32. However, the easiest way to create your program's archive is by using JBuilder's Deployment Wizard.

19

Note Be sure that you are using a recent version of PKZIP.EXE or WinZip. They must be the 32-bit versions that allow long filenames.

Deployment Wizard

The JBuilder IDE provides a wizard to automate the task of archiving your program files. After you've prepared your project, select Wizards | Deployment Wizard to invoke this utility, which is shown in Figure 19.4.

FIGURE **19.4.**

*The Deployment
Wizard dialog box.*

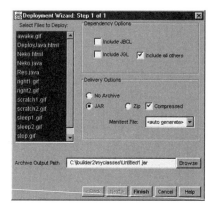

The Deployment Wizard dialog box's Select Files to Deploy list box automatically displays all the files that are members of the current project. The .class files are implicitly referenced by the .java source code files that are members. All other file types must be explicitly selected. (This is why it is necessary to add the auxiliary files to the project before attempting to archive.)

In this list box, be sure to deselect any of the HTML files, because they shouldn't be part of the archive. Note that the JPR isn't listed; it should never be deployed because it has significance only in the JBuilder development environment. Also, the JDK should never need to be deployed; your users should already have the Java VM installed on their client machine.

The Dependency Options section has three check boxes. The Include JBCL and Include JGL check boxes control whether the JBCL and JGL class files are included in the archive. If you know that the user already has these files available on his client machine, or if you already have them available on your Web site for your applet, you can keep these options unchecked to exclude these files. Check the Include all others check box if you want the Deployment Wizard to review the current project to determine whether it requires any additional class files in order to run. If others are found, they are included in the archive.

Caution

It's recommended that you deploy both JBCL and JGL all the time. This prevents conflicts if an older or a newer version conflicts with the version you built your application with.

The Delivery Options area includes mostly radio buttons because most options in the area are mutually exclusive. Choose one of the three formats offered: No Archive, Zip, or JAR. If you select a Zip or a JAR format, you can choose between having the file compressed or uncompressed by checking or clearing the Compressed check box. Selecting a JAR format will cause the Deployment Wizard to generate a manifest file if necessary. If you've already created a manifest file and want that one used instead, you should add it to the project before invoking the wizard and then select it in the Manifest File list box. The generated manifest file is deposited in the `meta-inf` subdirectory (also created by the wizard as needed) and is always named `manifest.mf`.

The Archive Output Path edit box contains the pathname specified in the project's Out Path option by default. The archive filename is set to either `Untitled1.jar` or `Untitled1.zip`, depending on the archive format chosen. You can change the pathname and filename manually or use the Browse button to locate an appropriate path or existing archive to replace.

When you click the Finish button, the wizard creates the JAR or ZIP file. Both JAR and ZIP archive files can then be viewed using WinZip32 or another zip file viewer. When you examine the archive, you'll see that the subdirectory structures are included in the Path column, including the `meta-inf` subdirectory for the `manifest.mf` manifest.

Applets and Applications

Because applets are run in a browser and applications are standalone programs, they have slightly different deployment requirements. For example, it isn't necessary to create an install procedure for applets, but it's a necessity for applications. Also, there are differences in distributing archived and unarchived programs. These differences are discussed in the following sections.

However, for all Java programs, if you have used any of the JBuilder beans, KL Group beans, or JGL classes, you will need to deploy one or more of the JAR files in the `c:\jbuilder2\redist\` subdirectory. Your license agreement allows these files to be redistributed, but be sure to read the agreement for all the details. Where these files are placed changes depending on whether your program is deployed as an applet on a server or as an application on a client machine or network. These differences are discussed in the following sections.

Deploying Applets

Deploying applets is fairly straightforward. It's accomplished mainly by copying the applet's project files to your Web server. Some requirements must be fulfilled for your ap-

19

plet to run correctly. For applets, some of these requirements have already been mentioned, but let's review them here.

If you deploy an unarchived applet project, you will need to duplicate the project's directory structure on the Web server, including any subdirectories containing auxiliary files (images, audio, and so on) and any package subdirectory structures. If you keep your class files in a directory separate from your HTML file, you must also be sure to include this relative pathname in the <APPLET> tag's CODEBASE attribute where the class file is called.

For archived applets, in addition to copying the archive files to the Web server, you will also need to specify their relative location in the ARCHIVE attribute of the <APPLET> tag in your HTML file. For example, let's assume that you have archived your classes and sound files in separate JAR files. Your <APPLET> tag's ARCHIVE attribute might look something like this:

```
ARCHIVE="myclasses.jar, mysounds.jar"
```

Note that each archive must be listed individually in a comma-delimited list enclosed in double quotation marks. If the JAR files are kept in a subdirectory relative to your HTML file, you must include the relative pathname in the ARCHIVE attribute. For example, if you decided to keep myclasses.jar and mysounds.jar in a subdirectory named archives. Here's how the ARCHIVE attribute would need to be adjusted:

```
ARCHIVE="archives/myclasses.jar, archives/mysounds.jar"
```

 Caution

> When placed on a Web server, an archive's directory is located relative to the current directory that the .html file is served from.

If your applet uses any of the JBuilder beans, KL Group beans, or JGL classes, their respective archive files must be deposited on your Web server. They must also be specified in the ARCHIVE attribute. Continuing with the preceding example, let's surmise that you have used components from both the JBCL and the KL Group pages of the Component Palette and have also used several of the JGL classes to create an optimized hash table. Because your applet depends on redistributable JAR files, they must be mentioned in the ARCHIVE attribute as well:

```
ARCHIVE="archives/myclasses.jar, archives/mysounds.jar,
        archives/jbcl2.0-rt.jar, archives/jctable.jar,
        archives/jgl3.1.0.jar"
```

> **Caution** Remember that JBCL depends on JGL in many places. Sometimes you need both.

Be sure to copy the archives from `c:\jbuilder2\redist\` to the `archives` subdirectory on your Web server so that the HTML file will be able to find them when the applet is run. Although each archive is downloaded as a separate HTTP connection, this is still preferable to downloading each of their constituent files individually.

Even if the main applet class file is in `myclasses.jar`, you must still include the `CODE` attribute naming that main applet class:

```
CODE="myApplet.class"
```

> **Note** When you deploy code that is in a package, the package must be indicated in the `CODE` parameter: `CODE="myPackage.myApplet.class"`.

Because you've specified the `ARCHIVE` attribute, the browser will look in the `myclasses.jar` file for that class, but it must still be named explicitly as a starting point for the execution of your applet program. The completed `<APPLET>` tag for this example might look like this:

```
<APPLET CODE="myApplet.class"
        ARCHIVE="archives/myclasses.jar, archives/mysounds.jar,
                 archives/jbcl2.0-rt.jar, archives/jctable.jar,
                 archives/jgl3.1.0.jar"
        WIDTH=400 HEIGHT=300>
</APPLET>
```

After you're satisfied that all the files and archives have been copied to your Web server location and that the appropriate entries have been made to the `<APPLET>` tag, you should once again test your applet as a "live" program. Be sure to try it from several popular browsers. Sun HotJava, Microsoft Internet Explorer, and Netscape Communicator are highly recommended. You may also want to try it from different types of net connections, such as modem and T1, and from behind a firewall to expose any performance problems that these connections might uncover.

19

Deploying Applications

For applications, you need to add a few niceties to make the deployment complete: an install procedure and run instructions. For the install procedure, you can use an installation program generator for your target platforms, or you can simply create a platform-specific batch file. Creating an install procedure that works properly (that doesn't overwrite existing files without asking, that allows the user to restore original settings, and so on) is a lot of work but worth the effort in reduced technical support costs. Your install procedure will need to create the duplicate subdirectory structure that your program requires and deposit the files in those subdirectories.

Once again, you will need to make the `jbcl2.0-rt.jar`, `jctable.jar`, and `jgl3.1.0.jar` archive files available to the user if you have used any of the JBCL beans, KL Group beans, or JGL classes. When you run a Java application, use the Java Runtime Environment utility program, `jre.exe` and `jrew.exe` under Windows. Be sure to use the `-cp` option so that the utility knows the path and filename of each archive needed to run your application. The command line should look something like the following:

```
jre -cp MyJar.jar;OtherJar.jar;YetAnotherJar.jar myPackage.myClass
```

You should create a README file to instruct your users how to run the Java application. If your users are running your program in a windowed environment, perhaps you've provided an icon for them to double-click to execute your program. If so, be sure to include this information in your README. If your users will be running your program from a command prompt, they should be instructed to run the `jre.exe` or `jrew.exe` program from the prompt with your program's class name as its argument:

```
jre -cp archive.jar myPackage.newprog
```

Note

> The Java Runtime Environment (JRE) is available for a wide variety of platforms. Different platforms have different file-naming conventions, so executables might not end in `.exe` as they do on the Windows platforms. Con-sult your operating system's documentation for the appropriate form of its executable filenames.

In this example, your program's class name is `newprog.class`, and the Java `jre.exe` utility is in the user's path. Your program depends on the `archive.jar` archive.

Note   Although you have used `java.exe` to run programs during development, it isn't part of the standard redistributable Java VM that your users should have installed on their machines. Therefore, instruct your users to run your programs using the `jre.exe` or `jrew.exe` utility instead, which is the standard Java VM redistributable runtime environment.

Summary

Although there are several requirements for deploying your Java programs, none of them is particularly difficult. Create a checklist and carefully test each step of the way.

Today you learned that both applets and applications require that their subdirectory structures are exactly duplicated or preserved in archive files in order for your Java programs to run properly when deployed. In addition, archives present several of their own requirements.

For applets, archives must be named in the ARCHIVE attribute of the <APPLET> tag. In contrast, you provide archive information for your Java applications by using the Java Runtime Environment utility's -cp flag.

You saw how archives can save your users time when downloading and improve your programs' performance. They might also save you money if your Internet Service Provider charges you by the hit, because archives can download multiple files in a single HTTP connection.

You learned how to prepare your programs for archiving and deployment, including how to add auxiliary files such as images, sounds, and text files to your project before archiving. The Resource Wizard was demonstrated as an automated way to substitute identifiers for hard-coded strings in your programs, making them easier to localize. You should now be able to do a final build to produce class files without symbolic debugging information. In addition, you were introduced to the Deployment Wizard—JBuilder's easy-to-use utility that helps you select the appropriate files for your project archives.

Finally, you examined some of the differences between deploying applets and applications. You were introduced to the requirements of installation programs and how to instruct your users to execute your Java programs.

19

Q&A

Q **Where can I get more information on deploying Java programs?**

A Inprise promises to put updates concerning deployment on its Web site at `http://www.inprise.com/jbuilder/` as needed. Be sure to check there for additional tips and techniques. Other places to check are the various browser Web sites for browser-specific information on the `<APPLET>` tag and its attributes, as well as which archive formats are supported by the browser. Those sites are listed here:

HotJava (by Sun)	`http://java.sun.com/products/hotjava/`
Microsoft Internet Explorer	`http://www.microsoft.com/ie/`
Netscape Communicator	`http://www.netscape.com/communicator/`

Q **How many archives can I list in the ARCHIVE attribute? Is there a limit?**

A There isn't a hard limit, but remember that the more archives you list, the more connections your user's browser will need to make to download all your files. However, depending on which version of HTML your user's browser supports, there might be a limit on how long the `<APPLET>` tag itself can be. Check the browser Web sites for more information on their HTML support.

Q **I'm not absolutely certain which class files I may use in my applets. Can I just mention all the redistributables in the ARCHIVE attribute to be safe?**

A As long as you've put them up on your Web server where your applets can locate them, this will work. However, if your program doesn't actually require those archives, your applet will take the performance hit for downloading files that are unnecessary for its operation. You might also be charged for those additional hits each time your applets are executed. This isn't recommended as a standard practice.

It's fairly simple to know which archive files you've used. If you added any of the beans from the Component Palette from the standard JBCL pages, add `jbcl2.0-rt.jar` and `jgl3.1.0.jar` to the ARCHIVE tag. If you've used beans from the KL Group page, add the `jcbwt.jar`, `jcchart.jar`, or `jctable.jar` archive. If you've used any of the JGL optimized data structures or methods, add the `jgl3.1.0.jar` archive. The best way to remember to do this is to update your HTML file when you add the first bean or method that requires it to your program. Then check the HTML file to see which archives you need to upload to your Web site, and you're done.

Q **I forgot to do a final build before archiving my project, and now my program still has debugging information in it. Do I have to go through the whole process of archiving again?**

A Yes. You will need to re-archive and replace the old archive files. The archive doesn't simply reference the file; it also includes the compressed or uncompressed files themselves.

Workshop

The Workshop provides two ways for you to affirm what you've learned in this chapter. The Quiz section poses questions to help you solidify your understanding of the material covered. You can find answers to the quiz questions in Appendix A, "Answers to Quiz Questions." The Exercise section provides you with experience in using what you have learned. Try to work through all these before continuing to the next day.

Quiz

1. Which option do you need to uncheck before doing a final build?

2. True or false: You always need to add auxiliary files to your project.

3. True or false: Although you can't create JAR files with a zip utility, you can use a zip utility to view a JAR file's contents.

4. How can you include the `jbcl2.0-rt.jar` and/or `jgl3.1.0.jar` archive files in your own archives? Under what circumstances is this necessary?

5. True or false: If you include your applet's main class file in an archive referenced by the `ARCHIVE` attribute, you don't need to use the `CODE` attribute in the `<APPLET>` tag.

6. What is the one semantic difference between adding archive files to the `<APPLET>` tag's `ARCHIVE` attribute and adding them to the `CLASSPATH`?

19

Exercise

Take one of the multimedia projects created on Day 9, "Graphics, Fonts, and Multimedia," and deploy it (using a JAR file) on another machine that has the Java VM installed. Don't forget to add image and/or audio files to the project.

WEEK 3

DAY 20

Java Network Communications

Networking is the capability to make connections from your applet or application to a system over the network, perhaps a Local Area Network (LAN) or the Internet. You'll need to know how to load HTML files, how to retrieve files from Web sites, and how to work with generic sockets in Java. Today's networking topics include the following:

- Creating networking links in applets
- Locating and opening Web connections (URLs)
- How the URLConnection class is used
- Using the Socket and SocketServer classes
- How to handle network-related exceptions

Remote Method Invocation (RMI) is also an important part of Java networking that allows your applet or application to call methods on objects that reside on another system on the network. Today, you'll learn about these RMI topics:

- How Remote Method Invocation works
- Defining interface and implementation classes
- Stubs, skeletons, servers, and clients
- Registering the server and testing the client
- Where to find additional RMI documentation

To create a new project, select File | New Project, and then modify the File field so that it says this:

```
C:\jbuilder2\myprojects\JavaNetworking.jpr
```

Click the Finish button. You'll add today's listings to this project.

Networking

Networking in Java involves classes in the `java.net` package that provide cross-platform abstractions for simple networking operations, including connecting and retrieving files by using common web protocols and creating basic UNIX-like sockets. When these classes are used in conjunction with input and output streams, reading and writing to files over the network becomes as easy as reading and writing to files on the local disk.

Of course, some restrictions apply. Java applets can't read or write to the disk on the client machine that's running the applets without its express permission—or, depending on the browser, perhaps not at all. In most situations, Java applets might not be able to connect to systems other than the server from which they were originally invoked. But even given these restrictions, you can accomplish a great deal and take advantage of the Web to read and process information over the Internet.

Creating Links in Applets

Probably the easiest way to use networking inside an applet is to tell the browser running the applet to load a new page. For example, you can create animated image maps by telling the browser to load a particular page when a certain location is clicked.

To link to a new page, you create a new instance of the URL class. You might remember some of this from your work with images on Day 9, "Graphics, Fonts, and Multimedia." The URL class represents a Uniform Resource Locator that lets you access particular sites and files on the web. To create a new URL object, you can use one of the following four constructors:

- `URL(String, String, int, String)`: This constructor takes four arguments and creates a new URL object. The first argument (`String`) takes a String object encapsulating a protocol name such as `http`, `ftp`, `gopher`, or `file`. The second argument

(String) takes a String object encapsulating a hostname such as www.borland.com or ftp.netcom.com. The third argument (int) takes an integer value representing a port number—80 for http. The fourth argument (String) takes a String object encapsulating a filename or pathname.

- URL(String, String, String): This constructor takes three arguments and performs the same function as the preceding constructor, minus the port number (int) argument.

- URL(URL, String): This constructor creates a URL object given a base path (URL) encapsulated in a URL object and a relative path (String) encapsulated in a String object. For the base path argument, you can use the getDocumentBase() method to return the URL of the current HTML file, or the getCodeBase() method to return the URL of the Java applet class file. The relative path (String) argument is concatenated onto the last directory in the base URL (just as was done when you worked with images and sounds).

- URL(String): This constructor creates a URL object from a String object that encapsulates a fully-qualified URL name (one that includes the protocol, hostname, optional port number, and pathname or filename).

When creating a URL object using String arguments, you must catch the exception that occurs when there is a typo or error in the name of the URL, so be sure to surround the URL class constructor call with try...catch blocks:

```
String someURLString = "http://www.microsoft.com/";
try {
  theURL = new URL(someURLString);
}
catch (MalformedURLException e) {
  System.out.println("Bad URL: " + someURLString);
}
```

This way, if the value of the String object doesn't pass as a fully-qualified URL address, the catch block handles the error and prints the offending string.

Getting the URL object is the hard part. After you have a valid one, all you have to do is pass it to the browser. This is done using a single line of code, in which theURL is assigned the URL object encapsulating the URL you want the applet to link to:

```
getAppletContext().showDocument(theURL);
```

The browser that contains your applet and then loads and displays the document that resides at that URL address. To try this out, in JBuilder, select File | New. In the New page of the New dialog box, double-click the Applet icon. In the Applet Wizard: Step 1 of 3 dialog box, erase the Package: field, change the Class: field to Bookmarks, and click the Finish button.

20

You want to add several buttons to this new applet, but before you do, you need to make some property changes to the applet's drawing area. With Bookmarks.java selected in the Navigation pane, choose the Design tab in the AppBrowser window under the Content pane and make the changes outlined in Table 20.1.

TABLE 20.1. INITIAL PROPERTY CHANGES.

Component	Property	Value
this(XYLayout)	layout	GridLayout
gridLayout1	rows	3

Click on this(GridLayout) in the Structure pane, and then add three Button components from the AWT page of the Component Palette. Your AppBrowser window should currently look something like what's shown in Figure 20.1.

FIGURE 20.1.

The AppBrowser window after three Button components have been added to the Bookmarks applet.

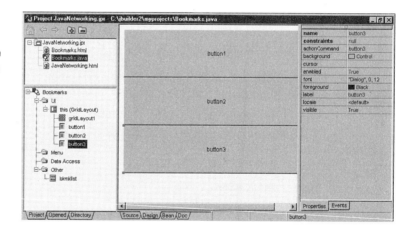

Change the labels and names of the three buttons. Table 20.2 shows the property changes needed for these buttons.

TABLE 20.2. ADDITIONAL PROPERTY CHANGES.

Component	Property	Value
button1	name	btnJBuilder
button1	label	JBuilder
button2	name	btnSamsnet
button2	label	Sams.net
button3	name	btnJavaSoft
button3	label	JavaSoft

Now you're ready to create event handlers for each button. Click `btnJBuilder` in the Structure pane. Then, in the Events page of the Inspector pane, triple-click on the right column of the `actionPerformed` event row to create a method stub, and add the following code:

```
linkTo("JBuilder");
```

Choose the Design tab, click `btnSamsnet`, triple-click its `actionPerformed` event, and add this line of code:

```
linkTo("Sams.net");
```

Repeat this process for `btnJavaSoft`, adding this line of code:

```
linkTo("JavaSoft");
```

If you don't think you've seen the `linkTo` method before, you're right. Now that the Bookmarks applet user interface is complete, it's time to add the Java code that performs the central functions of the applet, including the `linkTo` method and a private class named `Bookmark`.

First, create the new `Bookmark` class at the end of the source code in the `Bookmarks.java` file. A `Bookmark` object encapsulates the name and address of a web site. The `Bookmark` class constructor takes the web site name encapsulated in a `String` object and passed to the `theName` parameter, and it takes the Web site address encapsulated in a `String` object and passed to the `theURL` parameter. As you can see in the following code listed, the `Bookmark` class is made up of just its class constructor and two class variables. The class constructor assigns the web name to the `name` class variable, and it assigns the web address to the `url` class variable.

```
class Bookmark {
  String name;
  URL url;
  Bookmark(String theName, String theURL) {
    this.name = theName;
    try {
      this.url = new URL(theURL);
    }
    catch (MalformedURLException e) {
      System.out.println("Bad URL: " + theURL);
    }
  }
}
```

20

The Bookmarks applet uses classes from the `java.io` package. Therefore, add the following line of code to the import statements already listed at the top of the `Bookmarks.java` file:

```
import java.net.*;
```

Three bookmarks are hard-coded into the Bookmarks applet, one for each button. Therefore, the applet needs an array of three Bookmark objects. Add the following line of code under the existing Bookmarks class variables:

```
Bookmark bkmklist[] = new Bookmark[3];
```

This declares the bkmklist variable as a Bookmark object array and assigns the variable three new Bookmark objects. Each Bookmark object in this array must be initialized. A good place for initialization is in the jbInit method. Add the following lines of code to the jbInit method:

```
bkmklist[0] = new Bookmark("JBuilder",
                           "http://www.inprise.com/jbuilder/");
bkmklist[1] = new Bookmark("Sams.net",
                           "http://www.mcp.com/sams/");
bkmklist[2] = new Bookmark("JavaSoft",
                           "http://www.javasoft.com/");
```

Each statement assigns a Bookmark object encapsulating one of the three web sites to one of the three spaces in the bkmklist array.

Finally, you need to add code to the Bookmarks class that will perform the connections between the Bookmarks applet and the Web sites encapsulated in the Bookmark objects. The linkTo method in the Bookmarks applet uses Bookmark objects to connect with Web sites. Add the following code to the Bookmarks class:

```
void linkTo(String name) {
  URL theURL = null;
  for (int i = 0; i < bkmklist.length; i++) {
    if (name.equals(bkmklist[i].name))
      theURL = bkmklist[i].url;
  }
  if (theURL != null)
    getAppletContext().showDocument(theURL);
}
```

The linkTo method takes the name passed to the name parameter and checks it against the names assigned to the name variables encapsulated in the three Bookmark objects. When the names match, the URL encapsulated in the Bookmark object is extracted and passed to the showDocument method.

The complete class source is shown in Listing 20.1. Compile and run the Bookmarks applet. Figure 20.2 shows the applet's user interface. Clicking the buttons in this applet causes the document to be loaded from the locations to which the buttons refer.

| Note | The appletviewer can't load web pages. Nothing happens when you click on the Bookmarks applet buttons in the appletviewer window. Load the Bookmarks applet into your web browser to see it in action. |

FIGURE 20.2.

The Bookmarks applet.

TYPE **LISTING 20.1.** Bookmarks.java.

```
 1: import java.awt.*;
 2: import java.awt.event.*;
 3: import java.applet.*;
 4: import java.net.*;
 5: import borland.jbcl.layout.*;
 6: import borland.jbcl.control.*;
 7:
 8: //import com.sun.java.swing.UIManager;
 9: public class Bookmarks extends Applet {
10:    boolean isStandalone = false;
11:    GridLayout gridLayout1 = new GridLayout();
12:    Button btnJBuilder = new Button();
13:    Button btnSamsnet = new Button();
14:    Button btnJavaSoft = new Button();
15:    Bookmark bkmklist[] = new Bookmark[3];
16:
17:    //Construct the applet
18:
19:    public Bookmarks() {
20:    }
21: //Initialize the applet
22:
23:    public void init() {
24:      try {
25:        jbInit();
```

continues

20

LISTING 20.1. CONTINUED

```
26:     }
27:     catch (Exception e) {
28:       e.printStackTrace();
29:     }
30:   }
31: //static {
32: //   try {
33: //     //UIManager.setLookAndFeel(new
     ➥com.sun.java.swing.plaf.metal.MetalLookAndFeel());
34: //     //UIManager.setLookAndFeel(new
     ➥com.sun.java.swing.plaf.motif.MotifLookAndFeel());
35: //     UIManager.setLookAndFeel(new
     ➥com.sun.java.swing.plaf.windows.WindowsLookAndFeel());
36: //   }
37: //   catch (Exception e) {}
38: //}
39: //Component initialization
40:
41: private void jbInit() throws Exception {
42:   gridLayout1.setRows(3);
43:   btnJBuilder.setLabel("JBuilder");
44:   btnJBuilder.addActionListener(new java.awt.event.ActionListener() {
45:     public void actionPerformed(ActionEvent e) {
46:       btnJBuilder_actionPerformed(e);
47:     }
48:   });
49:   btnSamsnet.setLabel("Sams.net");
50:   btnSamsnet.addActionListener(new java.awt.event.ActionListener() {
51:     public void actionPerformed(ActionEvent e) {
52:       btnSamsnet_actionPerformed(e);
53:     }
54:   });
55:   btnJavaSoft.setLabel("JavaSoft");
56:   btnJavaSoft.addActionListener(new java.awt.event.ActionListener() {
57:     public void actionPerformed(ActionEvent e) {
58:       btnJavaSoft_actionPerformed(e);
59:     }
60:   });
61:   this.setLayout(gridLayout1);
62:   this.add(btnJBuilder, null);
63:   this.add(btnSamsnet, null);
64:   this.add(btnJavaSoft, null);
65:   bkmklist[0] = new Bookmark("JBuilder",
     ➥"http://www.inprise.com/jbuilder/");
66:   bkmklist[1] = new Bookmark("Sams.net", "http://www.mcp.com/sams/");
```

```
 67:     bkmklist[2] = new Bookmark("JavaSoft", "http://www.javasoft.com");
 68: }
 69: //Get Applet information
 70:
 71:  public String getAppletInfo() {
 72:    return "Applet Information";
 73:  }
 74: //Get parameter info
 75:
 76:  public String[][] getParameterInfo() {
 77:    return null;
 78:  }
 79:
 80:  void linkTo(String name) {
 81:    URL theURL = null;
 82:    for ( int i = 0; i < bkmklist.length; i++ ) {
 83:      if ( name.equals( bkmklist[i].name ) )
 84:        theURL = bkmklist[i].url;
 85:    }
 86:    if ( theURL != null )
 87:      getAppletContext().showDocument( theURL );
 88:  }
 89:
 90:  void btnJBuilder_actionPerformed(ActionEvent e) {
 91:    linkTo("JBuilder");
 92:  }
 93:
 94:  void btnSamsnet_actionPerformed(ActionEvent e) {
 95:    linkTo("Sams.net");
 96:  }
 97:
 98:  void btnJavaSoft_actionPerformed(ActionEvent e) {
 99:    linkTo("JavaSoft");
100:  }
101: }
102:
103: class Bookmark {
104:    String name;
105:    URL url;
106:    Bookmark(String theName, String theURL) {
107:      this.name = theName;
108:      try {
109:        this.url = new URL(theURL);
110:      }
111:      catch (MalformedURLException e) {
112:        System.out.println("Bad URL: " + theURL);
113:      }
114:    }
115:  }
```

20

ANALYSIS Let's go over the manually added lines of code:

- Line 4 gives your applet access to the URL and MalformedURLException classes needed for its networking functionality by importing the java.net classes.
- Line 15 declares an array to hold three Bookmark objects.
- Lines 65 through 67 initialize the array by calling the Bookmark constructor for each of the three bookmarks.
- Lines 80 through 88 compose the linkTo() method, which takes a String object as an argument. This method is called from each button's event handler method. It compares the String object passed by the event handler to the list of bookmark names. If it finds one that matches, it sets the URL address to the corresponding URL object, and then it calls the getAppletContext() method (in line 87) to load the address referenced in the URL object into the browser.
- Lines 103 through 115 declare the Bookmark class. (Note that this is not a public class, so it's allowed here.) This class defines the constructor that creates bookmarks from fully qualified URL addresses. (This is the constructor that is called in lines 65 through 67.) Notice that this class couches the creation of the URL object in a try block and that the catch block handles the MalformedURLException object if necessary.

This applet could easily be modified to accept bookmarks as parameters.

Opening Web Connections

Instead of asking the browser to just load the contents of a file, sometimes you might want to get hold of that file's contents so your applet can use them. If the file you want to grab is stored on the Web and can be accessed using the more common URL forms (HTTP, FTP, and the like), your applet can use the URL class to get it.

Note that, for security reasons, applets can by default connect back only to the same host from which they were originally loaded. This means that if you have your applets stored on a system called www.myhost.com, the only machine your applet can open a connection to is that same host (and that same *hostname,* so be careful with host aliases). If the file that the applet wants to retrieve is on the same system, using a URL connection is the easiest way to access it.

The URL class defines the openStream() method, which opens a network connection using the given URL address and returns an instance of the class InputStream (part of the java.io package). If you convert that stream to a BufferedReader object (with an InputStreamReader object inside for better performance), you can then read characters and lines from that stream. For example, the following lines open a connection to the

URL address assigned to the theURL variable and then read and echo each line of the file to standard output:

```
try {
  InputStream in = theURL.openStream();
  BufferedReader data =
    new BufferedReader(new InputStreamReader(in));

  String line;
  while ((line = data.readLine()) != null) {
    System.out.println(line);
  }
}

catch (IOException e) {
  System.out.println("IO Error: " + e.getMessage());
}
```

> **Note**
>
> Remember to wrap these lines in try...catch blocks to handle any IOException object that might get thrown.

Listing 20.2 is an example of an applet that uses the openStream() method to open a connection to a web site, read a file from that connection, and display the result in a text area. To create this applet in today's project, select File | New and double-click the Applet icon. In the Applet Wizard: Step 1 of 3 dialog box, erase the Package: field, change the Class: field to GetRaven, and click the Finish button.

The user interface is very simple. Click the Design tab below the Content pane in the AppBrowser window, and then select this(XYLayout) in the Structure pane. Change the layout property to BorderLayout. Add a TextArea component from the AWT page of the Component Palette and change its text property to Getting text.... The rest must be added manually.

20

TYPE **LISTING 20.2.** GetRaven.java.

```
1:  import java.awt.*;
2:  import java.awt.event.*;
3:  import java.applet.*;
4:  import java.io.*;
5:  import java.net.*;
6:  import borland.jbcl.layout.*;
7:  import borland.jbcl.control.*;
8:
```

continues

LISTING 20.2. CONTINUED

```
 9:  public class GetRaven extends Applet implements Runnable {
10:     boolean isStandalone = false;
11:     BorderLayout borderLayout1 = new BorderLayout();
12:     TextArea textArea1 = new TextArea();
13:     URL theURL;
14:     Thread runner;
15:
16:     //Construct the applet
17:     public GetRaven() {
18:     }
19:     //Initialize the applet
20:
21: public void init() {
22:   try {
23:     jbInit();
24:   }
25:   catch (Exception e) {
26:     e.printStackTrace();
27:   }
28: }
29: //static {
30: //   try {
31: //     //UIManager.setLookAndFeel(new
    ⮞com.sun.java.swing.plaf.metal.MetalLookAndFeel());
32: //     //UIManager.setLookAndFeel(new
    ⮞com.sun.java.swing.plaf.motif.MotifLookAndFeel());
33: //     UIManager.setLookAndFeel(new
    ⮞com.sun.java.swing.plaf.windows.WindowsLookAndFeel());
34: //   }
35: //   catch (Exception e) {}
36: //}
37: //Component initialization
38:
39:   private void jbInit() throws Exception{
40:     this.setLayout(borderLayout1);
41:     this.add(textArea1, BorderLayout.CENTER);
42:     textArea1.setText("Getting text...");
43:     String urlString = "http://www.lne.com/Web/Java/raven.txt";
44:     try {
45:       this.theURL = new URL(urlString);
46:     }
47:     catch (MalformedURLException e) {
48:       System.out.println("Bad URL: " + urlString);
49:     }
50:   }
51:   //Get Applet information
52:
53:   public String getAppletInfo() {
54:     return "Applet Information";
55:   }
```

```
56:    //Get parameter info
57:
58:    public String[][] getParameterInfo() {
59:      return null;
60:    }
61:
62:    public Insets insets() {
63:      return new Insets(10,10,10,10);
64:    }
65:
66:    public void start() {
67:      if (runner == null) {
68:        runner = new Thread(this);
69:        runner.start();
70:      }
71:    }
72:
73:    public void stop() {
74:      if (runner != null) {
75:        runner.stop();
76:        runner = null;
77:      }
78:    }
79:
80:    public void run() {
81:      InputStream conn;
82:      BufferedReader data;
83:      String line;
84:      StringBuffer buf = new StringBuffer();
85:
86:      try {
87:        conn = theURL.openStream();
88:        data = new BufferedReader(new InputStreamReader(conn));
89:        while ((line = data.readLine()) != null) {
90:          buf.append(line + "\n");
91:        }
92:        textArea1.setText(buf.toString());
93:      }
94:      catch (IOException e) {
95:        System.out.println("IO Error: " + e.getMessage());
96:      }
97:    }
98:  }
```

20

ANALYSIS Because it might take some time to load the file over the network, put that routine into its own thread and use the familiar start(), stop(), and run() methods to control that thread. Other than those three methods, here's what else must be added manually:

- Lines 4 and 5 import the necessary classes from the java.io and java.net packages.

- On line 9, `implements Runnable` must be added so that you can use the thread.
- Lines 13 and 14 contain declarations for the URL and `Thread` variables.
- Lines 43 through 49 set up the URL address `String` object and assign it to the URL object, encased in a set of `try...catch` blocks. It could just as easily have been passed in as an applet parameter, but it's hard-coded here for simplicity.
- Lines 62 through 64 simply put a nice border around the applet.
- Lines 66 through 78 are the standard `start()` and `stop()` applet methods.
- Lines 80 through 97 represent the `run()` method, where all the real work takes place. Here, you initialize variables and then open a connection to the URL (using the `openStream()` method in line 87). After the connection is opened, in lines 88 through 90, you set up an input stream and read from it line-by-line, depositing the results into an instance of `StringBuffer`.
- Also in the `run()` method, in line 92, the buffer is converted to a `String` object, and the result is put into the text area.

Another thing to note about this example is that the part of the code that opens a network connection, reads from the file, and creates a string is in a `try` block, so you can `catch` any `IOException` object that might be generated by all this activity. If any errors do occur while you're attempting to read or process the file, these blocks let you recover from them without the entire program's crashing. (In this case, the program exits with an error, because there's little else to be done if the applet can't read the file.)

Remember that both this applet and the file it addresses must be on the same host (or the applet must reside on the client, as it does when you're testing it on your machine). Figure 20.3 shows the applet as it appears in Internet Explorer.

The `URLConnection` Class

The URL class's `openStream()` method is actually a simplified use of the `URLConnection` class. The `URLConnection` class provides a way to retrieve files using URLs, web sites, or FTP sites, for example. It also lets you create output streams if the protocol allows it.

To use a URL connection, you first create a new instance of the `URLConnection` class, set its parameters (whether it enables writing, for example), and then use the `connect()` method to open the connection. Keep in mind that with a URL connection, the class handles the protocol for you based on the first part of the URL. You therefore don't have to make specific requests to retrieve a file; all you have to do is read it.

Client and Server Sockets

For networking applications beyond what the URL and `URLConnection` classes offer (for example, for other protocols or for more general networking applications), Java provides the `Socket` and `SocketServer` classes as an abstraction of standard socket programming techniques.

FIGURE 20.3.

The GetRaven applet.

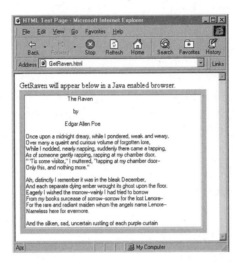

> **Note**
>
> Although a full explanation of how socket programming works is beyond the scope of this book, a number of good books discuss it in depth. If you haven't worked with sockets before, see whether the `openStream()` method will meet your needs first. Then, if you really need to do more, dive into one of the heftier socket programming tomes.

The `Socket` class provides a client-side socket interface similar to standard UNIX sockets. To open a connection, create a new instance of `Socket`; pass the *hostname* parameter a `String` object encapsulating the name of the host to connect to, and pass the *portnum* parameter an integer value representing the port number:

```
Socket clientConn = new Socket(hostname, portnum);
```

20

> **Caution**
>
> If you use sockets in an applet, you are still subject to the same security restrictions about where you can connect that apply to accessing files.

After the socket is open, you can use input and output streams to read to and write from that socket:

```
BufferedReader in = new BufferedReader
  (new InputStreamReader(clientConn.getInputStream()));
BufferedWriter out = new BufferedWriter
  (new InputStreamWriter(clientConn.getOutputStream()));
```

When you're done with the socket, don't forget to close it. This also closes all the input and output streams you might have set up for that socket:

```
connection.close();
```

Server-side sockets work similarly, with the exception of the `accept()` method. A server socket listens on a TCP port for a connection from a client. When a client connects to that port, the `accept()` method accepts the connection from that client. By using both client and server sockets, you can create applications that communicate with each other over the network (such as Dial-Up Networking).

To create a server socket and bind it to a port, create a new instance of the `ServerSocket` class with the port number:

```
ServerSocket serverConn = new ServerSocket(8080);
```

To listen on that port (and to accept a connection from any clients, should one be requested), use the `accept()` method:

```
serverConn.accept();
```

After the socket connection is made, you can use input and output streams to read from and write to the client.

Network Exceptions

You've seen one of the exceptions that networking can produce—the `MalformedURLException` object when you're attempting to construct a fully-qualified URL address. But there are several other networking-related exceptions you should be aware of:

- `BindException`: Occurs when there is an error trying to bind a socket to a port.
- `ConnectException`: Typically, there is no server socket listening for the connection request, so the connection is refused.
- `NoRouteToHostException`: Usually happens because there is a firewall between the client and the server, or a router is out.
- `ProtocolException`: A protocol (such as TCP) error has been received.
- `SocketException`: Indicates that there is a problem with the socket itself.
- `UnknownHostException`: Means that the host's IP address could not be determined.
- `UnknownServiceException`: Received when trying to write to a read-only connection, or the MIME type returned is nonsense.

As you saw earlier, whenever you're dealing with code that might throw one of these exceptions, you must enclose it in a try block and catch the exception. The try...catch blocks enable you to handle and recover from the errors. If you're using streams, don't forget about catching the IOException object.

Remote Method Invocation

Remote Method Invocation (RMI) gives you a way to access Java objects on another host and call its methods remotely. Your program's object is the client, and the remote object is the server. The remote object can also be a client of another remote server object, and so on. By using persistence (serialization and deserialization), local objects can be passed as arguments to the methods of remote objects, as well as primitive values. These features allow Java programs to take advantage of distributed computing to spread the workload out over a number of Java Virtual Machines.

How Does It Work?

The architecture consists of several layers on both the client side and server side of the RMI system, as shown in Figure 20.4.

FIGURE 20.4.

The RMI architecture.

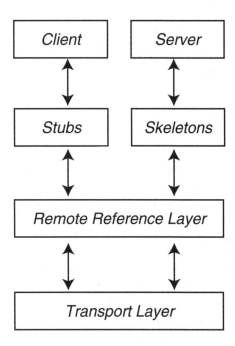

20

The method call travels down from the client object through the stub, remote reference layer, and transport layer. It is then transmitted to the host, where it travels back up through the transport layer, remote reference layer, and skeleton to the server object.

The stub acts as a surrogate for the remote server object so that it can be invoked by the client. The remote reference layer deals with object semantics and manages communications with single and replicated objects, deciding whether the call must be sent to one server or many. The transport layer manages the actual connection and tracks remote objects to which it can dispatch method calls. The skeleton on the server side makes the actual method to the server object and obtains the return value. The return value is then sent back through the remote reference layer and transport layer on the server side and transmitted back to the client, where it travels back through the transport layer and remote reference layer. Finally, the stub receives the return value.

A special *marshaling stream* is used to handle the transmission of information between client and server. For primitive method arguments, the stream could simply send the bytes back and forth. However, for method calls that require object arguments, persistence is used to transmit the object's characteristics, serializing the object on the client side and then deserializing it on the server side. Then the deserialized object argument is passed to the skeleton as part of the method invocation. (This was discussed in detail on Day 17, "Persistence.")

To make all this activity happen, you need to know how to do the following:

- Create a remote interface
- Implement the remote object
- Create the stub and skeleton
- Write the server program
- Write the client program
- Register your remote object

In the following sections, you'll learn how to implement these various pieces in your Java programs.

Remote Interface

To create a remote object, you must first define a remote interface. The interface must be a member of a package, and it must be public so that the client will be able to call its methods. It must extend `java.rmi.Remote` so that the Java system will be aware that it is a remote object. Each of its methods must have `java.rmi.RemoteException` in its throws clause.

For example, if you wanted to declare a remote object with a method that returned a string, you could write the following interface:

```
package LetsTalk;
public interface SaySomething extends java.rmi.Remote {
  String talkToMe() throws java.rmi.RemoteException;
}
```

This interface lets you implement the talkToMe() method in a remote server object and have that method called by a client on another system.

Implementation Class

To write a remote object, write a class that implements one or more remote interfaces. In the implementation, you define the remote object's constructor and implement the method(s) that can be invoked by a client, as is shown Listing 20.3.

LISTING 20.3. SaySomethingImpl.java.

```
package LetsTalk;
import java.rmi.*;
import java.rmi.server.UnicastRemoteObject;

public class SaySomethingImpl extends UnicastRemoteObject
                             implements SaySomething {
  private String name;

  public SaySomethingImpl(String str) throws RemoteException {
    super();
    name = str;
  }

  public String talkToMe() throws RemoteException {
    return "Far and Away!";
  }
}
```

20

By extending the UnicastRemoteObject class, you get its default sockets behavior for your transport layer and define your remote object as a nonreplicated (single) remote object.

Stubs and Skeletons

After the implementation class has been created, run the rmic command-line compiler to create the stub and skeleton class files. For this example, from the MS-DOS command prompt, type this:

```
rmic LetsTalk.SaySomethingImpl
```

This produces the skeleton class file SaySomethingImpl_Skel.class and the stub class file SaySomethingImpl_Stub.class. These files are then used by your client and server programs.

Server Program

In the main() method, you need to install a security manager. This ensures that your program abides by Java's security.

| | Without a security manager, RMI won't work at all. This means that you must either use the one provided by RMI or install one of your own creation. |

Finally, the implementation needs to create at least one instance of the remote object and register it with the RMI object registry (see Listing 20.4).

LISTING 20.4. A MAIN METHOD.

```
package LetsTalk;
import java.rmi.*;
import java.rmi.security.*;

  public static void main(String args[]) {
    // Create and install a security manager
    System.setSecurityManager(new RMISecurityManager());
    try {
      SaySomethingImpl theObj = new SaySomethingImpl("SaySomeServer");
      Naming.rebind("//anyhost/SaySomeServer", theObj);
      System.out.println("SaySomeServer bound in registry");
    }
    catch (Exception e) {
      System.out.println("SaySomethingImpl err: " + e.getMessage());
    }
  }
}
```

The Naming.rebind() method does the registration with RMI's object registry, and it requires a URL like this:

//hostname/objectname

hostname is the host where the remote object resides, and objectname is the string that was passed to the remote object's constructor. This object registry serves as a lookup table for method calls, translating object name to object reference and invoking the method. The remote object is restricted to binding and unbinding on its own host for security reasons.

Client Program

For this example, let's create an applet that calls the remote object's `talkToMe()` method, as shown in Listing 20.5.

LISTING 20.5. TalkingApplet.java.

```
package LetsTalk;
import java.applet.*;
import java.awt.*;
import java.rmi.*;

public class TalkingApplet extends Applet {
  String localStr = "";
  public void init() {
    try {
      SaySomething theObj = (SaySomething)Naming.lookup("//" +
      ➥getCodeBase().getHost() + "/SaySomeServer");
      localStr = theObj.talkToMe();
    }
    catch (Exception e) {
      System.out.println("TalkingApplet exception: " + e.getMessage());
    }
  }

  public void paint(Graphics g) {
    g.drawString(localStr, 10, 50);
  }
}
```

The applet does the method lookup on the remote host and then invokes the method on the remote object. If all goes well, the message `Far and Away!` should appear on the client system. (Don't forget to write the HTML page from which to run the applet.) If the host isn't named, the applet will try to access the local system and throw an exception.

Start Registry and Server

To start the RMI registry, use this command:

```
start rmiregistry [portnum]
```

Here, *portnum* is an optional port number on the host (`1099` by default). If you use a port number other than the default, you will also need to specify that port number wherever the hostname is required, such as in the `Naming.rebind` command:

```
Naming.rebind("//hostname:portnum/objectname", obj);
```

20

Also, the applet will require an additional parameter:

```
<PARAM name="url" value="//hostname:portnum/objectname">
```

To start the server, use the following command:

```
java -Djava.rmi.server.codebase=http://hostname/codebase/
LetsTalk.SayHelloImpl
```

The `codebase` property (with a trailing /) is required so that the stub class will be dynamically loaded into a client's Java VM. Now you are finally ready to run the applet.

RMI Documentation

For more details on RMI, select Help|Java Reference, click New Feature Summary, and then click Remote Method Invocation. On that page, in addition to direct links to the RMI API docs, you'll find topics and links for further exploration, such as the following:

- RMI Tools: Links to pages documenting the RMI command-line tools `rmic` and `rmiregistry`. These utilities aren't listed in the index, so these links are the only access to their online manual pages.
- RMI Specification: Links to a document that details Java's Distributed Object Model (DOM) and RMI system architecture.
- Release Notes: Links to information and last-minute notes regarding RMI, serialization, firewalls, CGI, and known problems.

In addition to the documentation, two RMI sample packages are provided in the `c:\jbuilder2\doc\java\guide\rmi\examples` subdirectory.

Summary

Today you were introduced to Java networking through some of the classes in the `java.net` package. Applet networking includes things as simple as pointing the browser to another page from inside your applet, but it can also include retrieving files from the Web by using standard Web protocols (HTTP, FTP, and so on). For additional networking capabilities, Java provides socket interfaces that can be used to implement many basic network-oriented applets, such as client/server interactions, chat sessions, and so on.

You were also introduced to Remote Method Invocation (RMI), which lets you do Java-to-Java programming, calling methods on remote objects. It also lets you use both primitives and objects as method arguments through serialization and deserialization (persistence). RMI follows Sun's Distributed Object Model (DOM), and lets you put Java objects on the machines that are appropriate to their tasks while giving your Java programs to those objects and their methods.

Q&A

Q How can I mimic an HTML form submission in a Java applet?

A Currently, applets make it difficult to do this. You can submit HTML forms in two ways: by using the GET request or by using POST. The best (and easiest) way is to use GET notation to get the browser to submit the form contents for you. If you use GET, your form information is encoded in the URL itself, something like this:

```
http://www.blah.com/cgi-bin/myscript?foo=1&bar=2&name=Kilroy
```

Because the form input is encoded in the URL, you can write a Java applet to mimic a form, get input from the user, then construct a new URL object with the form data included on the end. Then pass that URL to the browser using this:

```
getAppletContext().showDocument();
```

The browser submits the form results itself. For simple forms, this is all you need.

Q How can I do POST form submissions?

A You'll have to mimic what a browser does to send forms using POST: Open a socket to the server and send the data. For example:

```
POST /cgi-bin/mailto.cgi HTTP/1.0
Content-type: application/x-www-form-urlencoded
Content-length: 36
```

The exact format is determined by the HTTP protocol. This is only a subset.

If you've done this right, you'll get the CGI form output back from the server. It's then up to your applet to handle that output properly. Note that if the output is in HTML, there really isn't a way yet to pass that output to the browser that is running your applet. If you get back a URL, however, you can redirect the browser to that URL.

Q It looks as though the openStream() method and the socket classes implement TCP sockets. Does Java support UPD (datagram) sockets?

A The JDK provides two classes, DatagramSocket and DatagramPacket, that implement UDP sockets. The DatagramSocket class operates much like the Socket class. Use instances of DatagramPacket for each packet you send or receive over the socket. See the Java Reference in the Help documentation on java.net for more details.

20

Q You mentioned that I need to use several command-line utilities when creating RMI programs. Where are those utilities found?

A The `rmic` and `rmiregistry` command-line utilities are located in the `c:\jbuilder2\java\bin` subdirectory (assuming a default installation). Also, if the command `start rmiregistry` doesn't work on one of the platforms you're using, `javaw` can be used instead. It is also located in the `java\bin` subdirectory.

Q RMI seems like a lot of work. Is it worth all the trouble?

A Definitely! Remote Method Invocation is a very powerful mechanism that allows you to use persistence to pass objects as arguments and invoke methods on remote systems. This is the essence of client/server systems. Today's example implemented only a single method, so the overhead might seem like a lot, but if you were designing and implementing a full-fledged client/server program, the overhead would shrink to a small percentage of the whole.

Workshop

The Workshop provides two ways for you to affirm what you've learned in this chapter. The Quiz section poses questions to help you solidify your understanding of the material covered. You can find answers to the quiz questions in Appendix A, "Answers to Quiz Questions." The Exercise section provides you with experience in using what you have learned. Try to work through all these before continuing to the next day.

Quiz

1. What package(s) do you need to import in order to write networked Java programs?
2. What is the `MalformedURLException` for?
3. What method in the `URL` class opens a network connection using the supplied URL address and returns an instance of the class `InputStream`?
4. After a server socket is bound to a port, which method should you use to get the server socket to listen on the port for a client connection request?
5. When creating an RMI server, what is the circumstance under which you can leave out `RMISecurityManager`?

Exercise

Convert the ATM program you created as an exercise on Day 16, "Multithreading," so that it runs as a client/server program using RMI.

DAY 21

Inside Java

Today, the final day, the inner workings of the Java system will be revealed. You'll find out all about the vision of Java's developers, the Java Virtual Machine, those bytecodes you've heard so much about, that mysterious garbage collector, and why you might worry about security but don't have to. We'll begin, however, with the big picture.

The Big Picture

The Java team is ambitious. Their ultimate goal is nothing less than a revolution in the way software is written and distributed. They've started with the Internet, where they believe much of the interesting software of the future will live.

To achieve such an ambitious goal, a large faction of the Internet programming community itself must be marshaled behind a similar goal and given the tools to help achieve it. The Java language, with its goals of being small, simple, safe, and secure, along with its flexible Internet-oriented environment, is intended to become the focal point for the rallying of a new legion of programmers.

To this end, Sun Microsystems has done something gutsy. What was originally a secret, multimillion-dollar research and development project, and 100 percent proprietary, has become an open and relatively unencumbered technology standard upon which anyone can build. Sun sells licenses to other companies to create their own Java Virtual Machines while retaining the rights to maintain and grow the Java standard.

Any truly open standard must be supported by at least one excellent, freely available "demonstration" implementation. In parallel, several universities, companies, and individuals have already expressed their intention to duplicate the Java environment, based on the open Application Programming Interface (API) that Sun has created. Several software companies, including Inprise, have implemented development environments based on Java.

One reason this brilliant move on Sun's part has a real chance of success is the pent-up frustration of a whole generation of programmers who want to share their code to be usable on many machines regardless of platform. Right now, the computer science world is splintered into factions at universities and companies all over the world, with hundreds of languages, dozens of them widely used, dividing and separating us all. It's the worst sort of Tower of Babel. Java hopes to build some bridges and help tear down that tower. Because Java's so simple, because Java's so useful for programming over the Internet, and because the Internet is so hot right now, this confluence of forces has propelled Java to center stage.

This new vision of software is one in which the Internet becomes a heterogeneous grouping of objects, classes, and components and the open Application Programming Interfaces (APIs) between them. Traditional applications have vanished, replaced by skeletal components, such as JavaBeans components, that can be fitted with any parts from this and grouped together, on demand, to suit any purpose. Java component technology supports entertainment, business, and the social cyberspaces of today, and will do so even more in the near future.

The Java Virtual Machine

To make visions such as this possible, Java must be ubiquitous. It must be capable of running on any computer on any operating system, now and in the future. To achieve this level of portability, Java must be precise not only about the language itself but also about the environment in which the language lives. You can see from earlier in this book that the Java environment includes a generally useful set of packages of classes and a freely available implementation of them. This takes care of a portion of what is needed, but it is also crucial to specify exactly how the runtime environment of Java behaves.

This final requirement has stymied many attempts at ubiquity in the past. If you base your system on any assumptions about what is "beneath" the runtime system, you lose. If you depend in any way on the computer or the operating system below, you lose. Java solves this problem by inventing an abstract computer of its own and running on that.

NEW TERM The *Java Virtual Machine,* or *Java VM,* provides a layer of abstraction between the physical machines on which the Java environment is designed to run and the Java interpreter. A separate Java VM is created for each platform (UNIX, Windows 95, Windows NT, and so on) that knows how to deal with the idiosyncrasies of that operating system and the physical machine on which it runs. Although the Java VM presents a "native" face to the platform, it always presents the same abstraction to the interpreter, allowing the Java-compiled bytecodes to run on any and all instances of the Java VM.

The Java VM runs a special set of instructions called *bytecodes* that are simply a stream of formatted bytes, each of which has a precise specification that defines exactly what each bytecode does to the Java VM. The Java VM is also responsible for certain fundamental capabilities of Java, such as object creation and garbage collection.

> **Note**
>
> The Java Virtual Machine is backward compatible. Java applications created using older versions of Java run in newer instances of the Java VM. However, the reverse isn't true. Older instances of the Java VM, created for earlier versions of Java, do not always run applications created using newer versions of Java.

Finally, to be able to move bytecodes safely across the Internet, you need a bulletproof security model—and the know-how to maintain it—and a precise format for how this stream of bytecodes can be sent from one Java VM to another.

Each of these requirements is addressed in this chapter.

> **Note**
>
> This discussion blurs the distinction between the terms *Java runtime* and *Java VM*. This is intentional but a bit unconventional. Think of the Java VM as providing all the capabilities, even those conventionally assigned to the Java runtime. This book generally uses *Java runtime* (or *runtime*) and *Java VM* interchangeably. Equating the two highlights the single environment that must be created to support Java.
>
> Much of the following description is based closely on the latest "Java Virtual Machine Specifications" documents (and the bytecodes), so if you delve more deeply into the details online at Sun's Web site http://www.javasoft.com, you should cover some familiar ground.

21

An Overview

It is worth quoting the introduction to the original Java VM documentation here because it is so relevant to the vision outlined earlier:

> "The Java virtual machine specification has a purpose that is both like and unlike equivalent documents for other languages and abstract machines. It is intended to present an abstract, logical machine design free from the distraction of inconsequential details of any implementation. It does not anticipate an implementation technology or an implementation host. At the same time it gives a reader sufficient information to allow implementation of the abstract design in a range of technologies.

> "However, the intent of the…Java project is to create a language…that will allow the interchange over the Internet of executable content, which will be embodied by compiled Java code. The project specifically does not want Java to be a proprietary language and does not want to be the sole purveyor of Java language implementations. Rather, we hope to make documents like this one, and source code for our implementation, freely available for people to use as they choose.

> "This vision…can be achieved only if the executable content can be reliably shared between different Java implementations. These intentions prohibit the definition of the Java virtual machine from being fully abstract. Rather, relevant logical elements of the design have to be made sufficiently concrete to allow the interchange of compiled Java code. This does not collapse the Java virtual machine specification to a description of a Java implementation; elements of the design that do not play a part in the interchange of executable content remain abstract. But it does force us to specify, in addition to the abstract machine design, a concrete interchange format for compiled Java code."

The Java VM specification consists of the following:

- The bytecode syntax, including opcode and operand sizes, values, and types, and their alignment and endianness

> **NEW TERM** *Endianness* is the arrangement of bytes inside a value. The value must contain more than one byte for endianness to apply.

- The values of any identifiers (for example, type identifiers) in bytecodes or in supporting structures
- The layout of the supporting structures that appear in compiled Java code (for example, the constant pool)
- The Java .class file format

Each of these is covered today. Despite this degree of specificity, several elements of the design remain purposely abstract, including the following:

- The layout and management of the runtime data areas
- The particular garbage-collection algorithms, strategies, and constraints used
- The compiler, development environment, and runtime extensions (apart from the need to generate and read valid Java bytecodes)
- Any optimizations performed after valid bytecodes are received

These are places where the creativity of a Java VM implementor has full rein.

Fundamental Parts

The Java VM can be divided into five fundamental pieces:

- A bytecode instruction set
- A set of registers
- A stack
- A garbage-collected heap
- An area for storing methods

Some of these might be implemented by using an interpreter, a native binary code compiler, or even a hardware chip—but all these logical, abstract components of the Java VM must be supplied in some form in every Java system.

 Note

> The memory areas used by the Java VM are not required to be at any particular place in memory, to be in any particular order, or even to use contiguous memory. However, all but the method area must be able to represent aligned 32-bit values (for example, the Java stack is 32 bits wide).

The Java VM and its supporting code are often referred to as the runtime environment. When this book refers to something being done at runtime, the Java VM is doing it.

Java Bytecodes

The Java VM instruction set is optimized to be small and compact. It is designed to travel across the Internet, and therefore has traded speed of interpretation for space. (Given that both Internet bandwidth and mass storage speeds increase less rapidly than CPU speed, this seems like an appropriate trade-off.)

21

Java source code is compiled into bytecodes and stored in a .class file. On Sun's Java system, this is performed using the javac tool. It is not exactly a traditional compiler because javac translates source code into bytecodes, a lower-level format that can't be run directly but must be further interpreted by the Java VM on each computer. Of course, it is exactly this level of indirection that buys you the power, flexibility, and extreme portability of Java code.

A bytecode instruction consists of a one-byte opcode that serves to identify the instruction involved and zero or more operands, each of which may be more than one byte long, that encode the parameters that the opcode requires.

Note

When operands are more than one byte long, they are stored in *big-endian* order—high-order byte first. These operands must be assembled from the byte stream at runtime. For example, a 16-bit parameter appears in the stream as two bytes so that its value is first_byte * 256 + second_byte. The bytecode instruction stream is only byte-aligned, and the alignment of any larger quantities is not guaranteed (except for within the special bytecodes lookupswitch and tableswitch, which have special alignment rules of their own).

Bytecodes interpret data in the runtime memory areas as belonging to a fixed set of types:

- The primitive types you've seen several times before, consisting of several signed integer types (8-bit byte, 16-bit short, 32-bit int, 64-bit long)
- One unsigned integer type (16-bit char)
- Two signed floating-point types (32-bit float, 64-bit double)
- The object reference type (a 32-bit pointer-like type)

Some special bytecodes (for example, the dup instructions) treat runtime memory areas as raw data, without regard to type. This is the exception, however, not the rule.

These primitive types are distinguished and managed by the compiler, javac, not by the Java runtime environment. These types are not "tagged" in memory and thus can't be distinguished at runtime. Different bytecodes are designed to handle each of the various primitive types uniquely, and the compiler carefully chooses from this palette based on its knowledge of the actual types stored in the various memory areas. For example, when adding two integers, the compiler generates an iadd bytecode; for adding two floating-point values, fadd is generated. (You'll see all this in more detail later.)

Registers

The registers of the Java VM are just like the registers inside a real computer.

 Registers hold the machine's state, affect its operation, and are updated after each bytecode is executed.

The following are the Java registers:

- pc, the program counter, which indicates what bytecode is being executed
- optop, a pointer to the top of the operand stack, which is used to evaluate all arithmetic expressions
- frame, a pointer to the execution environment of the current method, which includes an activation record for this method call and any associated debugging information
- vars, a pointer to the first local variable of the currently executing method

The Java VM defines these registers to be 32 bits wide.

> **Note**
>
> Because the Java VM is primarily stack-based, it doesn't use any registers for passing or receiving arguments. This is a conscious choice skewed toward bytecode simplicity and compactness. It also aids efficient implementation on register-poor architectures, which includes most of today's computers. Perhaps when the majority of CPUs are a little more sophisticated, this choice will be reexamined—although simplicity and compactness might still be reason enough to keep it the way it is.

By the way, the pc register is also used when the runtime handles exceptions; catch clauses ultimately are associated with ranges of the pc within a method's bytecodes.

Stack

The Java VM is stack-based. A Java stack frame is similar to the stack frame of a conventional programming language in that it holds the state for a single method call. Frames for nested method calls are stacked on top of this frame.

 The *stack* is used to supply parameters to bytecodes and methods and to receive results from them.

Each stack frame contains three possibly empty sets of data: the local variables for the method call, its execution environment, and its operand stack. The sizes of these first two are fixed at the start of a method call, but the operand stack varies in size as bytecodes are executed in the method.

21

Local variables are stored in an array of 32-bit slots, indexed by the register vars. Most types take up one slot in the array, but the long and double types each take up two slots.

 Note

> The long and double values, stored or referenced through an index N, take up the 32-bit slots N and N + 1. These 64-bit values are therefore not guaranteed to be 64-bit-aligned. Implementors are free to decide the appropriate way to divide these values between the two slots.

The execution environment in a stack frame helps to maintain the stack itself. It contains a pointer to the previous stack frame, a pointer to the local variables of the method call, and pointers to the stack's current "base" and "top." Additional debugging information can also be placed into the execution environment.

The operand stack, a 32-bit first-in-first-out (FIFO) stack, is used to store the parameters and return values of most bytecode instructions. For example, the iadd bytecode expects two integers to be stored on the top of the stack. It pops them, adds them together, and pushes the resulting sum back onto the stack.

Each primitive data type has unique instructions that tell how to extract, operate, and push back operands of that type. For example, long and double operands take two slots on the stack, and the special bytecodes that handle these operands take this into account. It is illegal for the types on the stack and the instruction operating on them to be incompatible (javac outputs bytecodes that always obey this rule).

 Note

> The top of the operand stack and the top of the overall Java stack are almost always the same. Thus, the phrase "the stack" refers to both stacks collectively.

Heap

The heap is often assigned a large, fixed size when the Java runtime system is started, but on systems that support virtual memory, it can grow as needed, in a nearly unbounded fashion.

New Term The *heap* is that part of memory from which newly created instances (objects) are allocated.

Because objects are automatically garbage-collected in Java, programmers do not have to (and, in fact, *cannot*) manually free the memory allocated to an object when they are finished using it.

Java objects are referenced indirectly in the runtime, through handles, which are a kind of pointer into the heap. Because objects are never referenced directly, parallel garbage collectors can be written that operate independently of your program, moving around objects in the heap at will. You'll learn more about garbage collection later today.

Method Area

Like the compiled code areas of conventional programming language environments, or the TEXT segment in a UNIX process, the method area stores the Java bytecodes that implement almost every method in the Java system. (Remember that some methods might be `native`, and thus implemented—for example, in C.) The method area also stores the symbol tables needed for dynamic linking, as well as any additional information that debuggers or development environments might want to associate with each method's implementation.

Note

> A *native* method is just like anything else that is called *native* in Java. It means that the code outside the Java language is involved. The term *native method call* refers to a method call from your Java applications to code written in other languages (usually C).
>
> Because bytecodes are stored as byte streams, the method area is aligned on byte boundaries. (The other areas all are aligned on 32-bit word boundaries.)

Constant Pool

In the heap, each class has a constant pool "attached" to it. Usually created by `javac`, these constants encode all the names (of variables, methods, and so on) used by any method in a class. The class contains a count of how many constants there are and an offset that specifies how far into the class description itself the array of constants begins. These constants are typed through specially coded bytes and have a precisely defined format when they appear in the `.class` file for a class. A little of this file format is covered later today, but everything is fully specified by the Java VM specifications in your Java release.

21

Limitations

The Java VM, as currently defined, places some restrictions on legal Java programs by virtue of the choices it has made (some were described earlier, and more will be detailed later today).

Here are the limitations and their implications:

- 32-bit pointers, which imply that the Java VM can address only 4GB of memory (this might be relaxed in later releases)
- Unsigned 16-bit indexes into the exception, line number, and local variable tables, which limit the size of a method's bytecode implementation to 64KB
- Unsigned 16-bit indices into the constant pool, which limits the number of constants in a class to 64KB (a limit on the complexity of a class)

In addition, Sun's implementation of the Java VM uses so-called _quick bytecodes, which further limit the system. Unsigned 8-bit offsets into objects might limit the number of methods in a class to 256 (this limit might not exist in future releases), and unsigned 8-bit argument counts limit the size of the argument list to 255 32-bit words. (Although this means that you can have up to 255 arguments of most types, you can have only 127 of them if they're all long or double.)

All About Bytecodes

One of the main tasks of the Java VM is the fast, efficient execution of the Java bytecodes in methods. Unlike in the previous discussions about generality versus efficiency, this is a case where speed is of the utmost importance. Every Java program suffers from a slow implementation here, so the runtime must use as many tricks as possible to make bytecodes run fast. The only other goal (or limitation) is that Java programmers must not be able to notice these tricks in the behavior of their programs. A Java runtime implementor must be extremely clever to satisfy both of these goals.

The Bytecode Interpreter

A bytecode interpreter examines each opcode byte (bytecode) in a method's bytecode stream in turn and executes a unique action for that bytecode. This might consume further bytes for the operands of the bytecode and might affect which bytecode will be examined next. It operates like the hardware CPU in a computer, which examines memory for instructions to carry out in exactly the same manner. It is the software CPU of the Java VM.

Your first, naive attempt to write such a bytecode interpreter will almost certainly be disastrously slow. The inner loop, which dispatches one bytecode each time through the loop, is notoriously difficult to optimize. In fact, smart people have been thinking about this problem, in one form or another, for more than 20 years. Luckily, they've gotten results, all of which can be applied to Java.

The final result is that the interpreter shipped in the current release of Java has an extremely fast inner loop. In fact, on even a relatively slow computer, this interpreter can perform more than 590,000 bytecodes per second! This is really quite good because the CPU in that computer does only about 30 times better using *hardware*.

This interpreter is fast enough for most Java programs (and those requiring more speed can always use `native` methods), but what if a smart implementor wants to do better?

Just-In-Time Compiler

About a decade ago, Peter Deutsch discovered a really clever trick while he was trying to make the object-oriented programming language SmallTalk run faster. He called it "dynamic translation" during interpretation. Sun calls it *just-in-time compiling*.

The trick is to notice that the really fast interpreter you've just written—in C, for example—already has a useful sequence of native binary code for each bytecode it interprets: *the binary code that the interpreter itself is executing.* Because the interpreter has already been compiled from C into native binary code, for each bytecode it interprets, it passes through a sequence of native code instructions for the hardware CPU on which it's running. By saving a copy of each binary instruction as it goes by, the interpreter can keep a running log of the binary code that it *itself* has run to interpret a bytecode. It can just as easily keep a log of the set of bytecodes that it ran to interpret an entire method.

You take that log of instructions and "peephole-optimize" it, just as a smart compiler does. This eliminates redundant or unnecessary instructions from the log and makes it look just like the optimized binary code that a good compiler might have produced. This is where the "compiler" part of the phrase "just-in-time compiler" comes from, but it's really only the back-end of a traditional compiler—the part that generates native machine code. By the way, the front-end compiler here is javac.

Here's where the trick comes in. The next time that method is run (in exactly the same way), the interpreter can directly execute the stored log of binary native code. Because this optimizes the inner-loop overhead of each bytecode, as well as any other redundancies between the bytecodes in a method, it can gain a factor of 10 or more in speed. In fact, an early version of this technology at Sun showed that Java programs using it can run as fast as compiled C programs.

21

Note The preceding paragraph said "in exactly the same way" because if anything is different about the input to the method, it takes a different path through the interpreter and must be relogged. (Sophisticated versions of this technology solve this, and other, difficulties.) The cache of native code for a method must be invalidated whenever the method has changed, and the interpreter must pay a small cost up front each time a method is run for the first time. However, these small bookkeeping costs are far outweighed by the amazing gains in speed that are possible.

java2c Translator

Another, simpler, trick, which works well whenever you have a good, portable C compiler on each system that runs your program, is to translate the bytecodes into C and then compile the C into binary native code. If you wait until the first use of a method or class and then perform this as an "invisible" optimization, it gains you an additional speed-up over the approach outlined earlier without the Java programmer needing to know about it.

Of course, this does limit you to systems that have a C compiler. In theory, your Java code might be capable of traveling with its own C compiler, or know where to pull one from the Internet as needed, for each new computer and operating system it faced. (Because this practice violates some of the rules of normal Java code movement over the Internet—which is to not have native code on a user's system—it should be used sparingly.)

If you're using Java, for example, to write a server that lives only on your computer, it might be appropriate to use Java because of its flexibility in writing and maintaining the server (and for its capability to dynamically link new Java code on-the-fly) and then run java2c manually to translate the basic server itself entirely into native code. You'd link the Java runtime environment into that code so that your server would remain a fully capable Java program, but it's now an extremely fast one. In fact, an experimental version of the java2c translator at Sun has shown that it can reach the speed of compiled and optimized C code. This is the best that you can hope to do.

Note Unfortunately there still is no publicly available java2c tool.

The .class File Format

You won't be given the entire .class file format here, only a taste of what it's like. (You can read all about it in the release documentation.) It's mentioned here because it is one part of Java that needs to be specified carefully if all Java implementations are to be compatible with one another, and if Java bytecodes are expected to travel across arbitrary networks—to and from arbitrary computers and operating systems—and yet arrive safely.

The rest of this section paraphrases, and extensively condenses, the latest release of the .class documentation.

.class files are used to hold the compiled versions of both Java classes and Java interfaces. Compliant Java interpreters must be capable of dealing with all .class files that conform to the following specification.

A Java .class file consists of a stream of 8-bit bytes. All 16-bit and 32-bit quantities are constructed by reading in two or four 8-bit bytes, respectively. The bytes are joined together in big-endian order. (Use java.io.DataInput and java.io.DataOutput to read and write class files.)

The class file format is presented as a series of C-struct-like structures. However, un like a C struct, there is no padding or alignment between pieces of the structure. Each field of the structure may be of variable size, and an array may be of variable size (in this case, some field prior to the array gives the array's dimension). The types u1, u2, and u4 represent an unsigned one-, two-, or four-byte quantity, respectively.

Attributes are used at several different places in the .class format. All attributes have the following format:

```
GenericAttribute_info {
  u2 attribute_name;
  u4 attribute_length;
  u1 info[attribute_length];
}
```

The attribute_name is a 16-bit index into the class's constant pool; the value of constant_pool[attribute_name] is a string giving the name of the attribute. The field attribute_length gives the length of the subsequent information in bytes. This length doesn't include the four bytes needed to store attribute_name and attribute_length. In the following text, whenever an attribute is required, names of all the attributes currently understood are listed. In the future, more attributes will be added. Class file readers are expected to skip over and ignore the information in any attributes that they do not understand.

21

The following pseudo-structure gives a top-level description of the format of a class file:

```
ClassFile {
  u4 magic;
  u2 minor_version;
  u2 major_version;
  u2 constant_pool_count;
  cp_info constant_pool[constant_pool_count - 1];
  u2 access_flags;
  u2 this_class;
  u2 super_class;
  u2 interfaces_count;
  u2 interfaces[interfaces_count];
  u2 fields_count;
  field_info fields[fields_count];
  u2 methods_count;
  method_info methods[methods_count];
  u2 attributes_count;
  attribute_info attributes[attribute_count];
}
```

Here's one of the smaller structures used:

```
method_info {
  u2 access_flags;
  u2 name_index;
  u2 signature_index;
  u2 attributes_count;
  attribute_info attributes[attribute_count];
}
```

Finally, here's a sample of one of the later structures in the .class file description:

```
Code_attribute {
  u2 attribute_name_index;
  u2 attribute_length;
  u1 max_stack;
  u1 max_locals;
  u2 code_length;
  u1 code[code_length];
  u2 exception_table_length;
  {
    u2 start_pc;
    u2 end_pc;
    u2 handler_pc;
    u2 catch_type;
  }
  exception_table[exception_table_length];
  u2 attributes_count;
  attribute_info attributes[attribute_count];
}
```

None of this is meant to be completely comprehensible (although you might be able to guess at what many structure members are), just suggestive of the sort of structures that live inside .class files. Because the compiler and runtime sources are available, you can always begin with them if you actually have to read or write .class files yourself. Thus, you don't need to have a deep understanding of the details, even in that case.

Method Signatures

Because method signatures are used in .class files, now is an appropriate time to explore them in the detail promised on earlier days. They're probably most useful to you when writing the native methods.

NEW TERM   A *signature* is a string representing the type of method, field, or array.

A field signature represents the value of an argument to a method or the value of a variable and is a series of bytes in the following grammar:

```
<field signature>      := <field_type>
<field type>           := <base_type> : <object_type> : <array_type>
<base_type>            := B ¦ C ¦ D ¦ F ¦ I ¦ J ¦ S ¦ Z
<object_type>          := L <full.className>
<array_type>           := [ <optional_size> <field_type>
<optional_size>        := [0-9]*
```

Here are the meanings of the base types:

B	byte
C	char
D	double
F	float
I	int
J	long
S	short
Z	boolean

A return-type signature represents the return value from a method and is a series of bytes in the following grammar:

```
<return signature>     := <field type> ¦ V
```

21

The character V (void) indicates that the method returns no value. Otherwise, the signature indicates the type of the return value. An argument signature represents an argument passed to a method:

```
<argument signature>  := <field type>
```

Finally, a method signature represents the arguments that the method expects and the value that it returns:

```
<method_signature>    := (<arguments signature>) <return signature>
<arguments signature> := <argument signature>*
```

Let's try out the new rules: A method called complexMethod() in the class a.package.name.ComplexClass takes three arguments—a long, a boolean, and a two-dimensional array of short values—and returns this. Therefore, this is its method signature:

```
(JZ[[S)La.package.name.ComplexClass;
```

A method signature is often prefixed by the name of the method or by its full package (using underscores in the place of dots) and its class name followed by a slash (/) and the name of the method, to form a complete method signature. Now at last you have the full story! Thus, the following is the full, complete method signature of complexMethod() (Whew!):

```
a_package_name_ComplexClass/complexMethod(JZ[[S)La.package.name.ComplexClass;
```

Garbage Collection

Java programmers are able to ignore memory deallocation. Memory allocation is fundamental. However, memory deallocation is typically forced on the programmer by the laziness of the system. Not in Java. Java can figure out what is no longer useful and remove it from your computer memory. This capability makes it relatively easy to write programs using Java, avoiding both design time and runtime bugs.

The Problem

Software engineering estimates indicate that for every 55 lines of production C-like code in the world, there is one bug. This means that your electric razor has about 80 bugs, and your TV has about 400. Soon they will have even more because the size of this kind of embedded computer software is growing exponentially. When you begin to think of how much C-like code is in your car's engine, it should give you pause.

Many errors are due to the misuse of difficult memory management language features such as pointers and the deallocation of objects in computer memory. Java addresses both of these issues—the former by eliminating explicit pointers from the Java language altogether, and the latter by including, in every Java system, a garbage collector that solves the problem.

The Solution

Imagine a runtime system that tracks each object you create, notices when the last reference to it has vanished, and frees the object for you. How could such a thing actually work?

One brute-force approach, tried early in the days of garbage collection, is to attach a reference counter to every object. When the object is created, the counter is set to 1. Each time a new reference to the object is made, the counter is incremented; and each time such a reference disappears, the counter is decremented. Because all such references are controlled by the language—as variables and assignments, for example—the compiler can tell whenever an object reference might be created or destroyed, just as it does in handling the scoping of local variables, and thus it can assist with this task. The system itself holds onto a set of root objects that are considered too important to be freed. The class Object is one example of such a VIO (Very Important Object). Finally, all that's needed is to test, after each decrement, whether the counter has hit 0. If it has, the object is freed.

If you think carefully about this approach, you will soon convince yourself that the system is definitely correct when it decides to free anything. It is so simple that you can immediately tell it will work. The low-level hacker in you also might feel that if it's *that* simple, it's probably not fast enough to run at the lowest level of the system—and you'd be right.

Think about all the stack frames, local variables, method arguments, return values, and local variables created in the course of even a few hundred milliseconds of a program's life. For each of these tiny nanosteps in the program, an extra increment (at best) or decrement, test, and deallocation (at worst) will be added to the program's running time. In fact, the first garbage collectors were slow enough that many predicted they could never be used at all!

Luckily, a whole generation of smart programmers has invented a big bag of tricks to solve these overhead problems. One trick is to introduce special "transient object" areas that don't need to be reference counted. The best of these generational scavenging garbage collectors today can take less than 3 percent of the total time of your program—

21

a remarkable feat if you realize that many other language features, such as loop over-heads, can be as large or larger!

There are other problems with garbage collection. If you're constantly freeing and re-claiming space in a program, won't the heap of objects soon become fragmented, with small holes everywhere and no room to create new, large objects? Because programmers are now free from the chains of manual deallocation, won't they create even more objects than usual?

What's worse, there is another way that this simple reference counting scheme is ineffi-cient—in space rather than time. If a long chain of object references eventually comes full circle, back to the starting object, each object's reference count remains at least 1 *forever*. None of these objects will ever be freed!

Together, these problems imply that a good garbage collector must, every once in a while, step back to compact or clean up wasted memory.

NEW TERM   *Compaction* occurs when a garbage collector steps back and reorganizes mem-ory, eliminating the holes created by fragmentation. Compacting memory is sim-ply a matter of repositioning objects one by one into a new, compact grouping that places them all in a row, leaving all the free memory in the heap in one big piece.

NEW TERM   Cleaning up the circular garbage still lying around after reference counting is called *marking and sweeping*. A mark and sweep of memory involves first mark-ing every root object in the system and then following all the object references inside those objects to new objects to mark, and so on, recursively. Then, when you have no more references to follow, you "sweep away" all the unmarked objects and then compact memory as before.

The good news is that this solves the space problems you were having. The bad news is that when the garbage collector "steps back" and does these operations, a nontrivial amount of time passes, during which your program is unable to run—all its objects are being marked, swept, rearranged, and so forth, in what *seems* like an uninterruptible pro-cedure. Your first hint to a solution is the word "seems."

Garbage collecting actually can be done a little at a time, between or in parallel with nor-mal program execution, thus dividing the large time needed to "step back" into numerous so-small-you-won't-notice-them chunks of time that happen between the cracks. (Of course, years of smart thinking went into the intricate algorithms that make all this possi-ble!)

One final problem that might worry you a little has to do with these object references. Aren't these "pointers" scattered throughout your program and not just buried in objects?

Even if they're only in objects, don't they have to be changed whenever the object they point to is moved by these procedures? The answer to both of these questions is a resounding *yes,* and overcoming them is the final hurdle to making an efficient garbage collector.

There are really only two choices. The first, brute force, assumes that all the memory containing object references needs to be searched regularly. Whenever the object references found by this search match objects that have moved, the old reference is changed. This approach assumes that there are "hard" pointers in the heap's memory—ones that point directly to other objects. By introducing various kinds of "soft" pointers, including pointers that are like forwarding addresses, the algorithm improves greatly. Although these brute-force approaches sound slow, it turns out that modern computers can perform them fast enough to be useful.

Note

> You might wonder how brute-force techniques identify object references. In early systems, references were specially tagged with a "pointer bit" so that they could be located unambiguously. Now, so-called "conservative" garbage collectors simply assume that if it looks like an object reference, it is—at least for the purposes of the mark and sweep. Later, when actually trying to update it, they can find out whether it really is an object reference.

The final approach to handling object references, and the one Java currently uses, is also one of the very first ones tried. It involves using 100-percent "soft" pointers. An object reference is actually a handle to the real pointer, and a large object table exists to map these handles into the actual object reference. Although this does introduce extra overhead on almost every object reference (some of which can be eliminated by clever tricks, as you might guess), it's not too high a price to pay for this incredibly valuable level of indirection.

This indirection allows the garbage collector, for example, to mark, sweep, move, or examine one object at a time. Each object can be independently "moved out from under" a running Java program by changing only the object table entries. This not only allows the "step back" phase to happen in the tiniest steps, but it also makes a garbage collector that runs literally in parallel with your program much easier to write. This is what the Java garbage collector does.

21

Probably the only time you will need to be very careful about garbage collection is when your application involves critical, real-time programs (such as those that legitimately require native methods). But how often will your Java code be flying a commercial jetliner in real time, anyway?

Parallel Garbage Collector

Java applies almost all these advanced techniques to give you a fast, efficient, parallel garbage collector. Running in a separate thread, it clears the Java environment of almost all trash (it is conservative), silently and in the background; it's efficient in both space and time; and it never steps back for more than a small amount of time. You should never need to know it's there.

By the way, if you want to force a full mark-and-sweep garbage collection to happen soon, you can do so simply by calling the System.gc() method. You might want to do this if you just freed up a majority of the heap's memory in circular garbage and want it all taken away quickly. You might also call this whenever you're idle, as a hint to the system about when it would be best to come and collect the garbage. This "meta knowledge" is rarely needed by the system, however.

Ideally, you will never notice the garbage collector, and all those decades of programmers beating their brains out on your behalf will simply let you sleep better at night—and what's wrong with that?

The Security Story

Speaking of sleeping well at night, if you haven't stepped back yet and said, "My goodness! You mean that Java programs will be running rampant on the Internet?" you better do so now, because this is a legitimate concern. In fact, it is one of the major technical stumbling blocks to achieving the dream of ubiquity and code sharing mentioned earlier.

Why You Should Worry

Any powerful, flexible technology can be abused. As the Internet becomes mainstream and widespread, it too will be abused. Already there have been many blips on the security radar screens of people who worry about such things, warning that, at least until recently, the computer industry (or the media) hasn't paid enough attention to solving some of the problems that this new world brings with it. One of the benefits of constructively solving security once and for all will be a flowering unseen before in the virtual communities of the Internet. Whole new economies based on people's attention and creativity will spring to life, rapidly transforming our online world in new and positive ways.

The downside of all this new technology is that we (or someone) must worry long and hard about how to make our online playgrounds of the future safe for everyone. Fortunately, Java is a big part of the answer.

Why You Might Not Have to Worry

Java protects you from potentially "nasty" Java code through a series of interlocking defenses that together form an imposing barrier to all such attacks.

Java's powerful security mechanisms act at four different levels of the system architecture. First, the Java language itself was designed to be safe, and the Java compiler ensures that source code doesn't violate these safety rules. Second, all bytecodes executed by the runtime are screened to be sure that they also obey these rules. (This layer guards against having an altered compiler produce code that violates the safety rules.) Third, the class loader ensures that classes don't violate namespace or access restrictions when they're loaded into the system. Finally, API-specific security prevents applets from doing destructive things. This final layer depends on the security and integrity guarantees from the other three layers.

Let's now examine each of these layers in turn.

The Language and Its Compiler

The Java language and its compiler are the first line of defense. Java was designed to be a safe language.

Most other C-like languages have facilities to control access to objects but also have ways to forge access to objects (or to parts of objects), usually by using and misusing pointers. This introduces two fatal security flaws to any system built on these languages. One is that no object can protect itself from outside modification, duplication, or "spoofing" (others pretending to be that object). Another is that a language with powerful pointers is more likely to have serious bugs that compromise security. These pointer bugs, in which a runaway pointer starts modifying some other object's memory, were responsible for most of the public (and not-so-public) security problems on the Internet this past decade.

Java gets rid of these threats in one stroke by eliminating pointers from the language altogether. There are still pointers of a kind—object references—but these are carefully controlled to be safe. They are unforgeable, and all casts are checked for legality before being allowed. In addition, powerful new array facilities in Java not only help offset the

21

loss of pointers but also offer additional safety by strictly enforcing array bounds, catching more bugs for the programmer (bugs that, in other languages, might lead to unexpected and thus bad-guy-exploitable problems).

The language definition and the compilers that enforce it create a powerful barrier to any nasty Java programmer.

Because an overwhelming majority of the "Internet-savvy" software on the Internet might soon be written in Java, its safe-language definition and compilers help guarantee that most of this software has a solid, secure base. With fewer bugs, Internet software will be more predictable—a property that thwarts attacks.

Verifying the Bytecodes

What if some nasty programmer rewrites the Java compiler to suit his nefarious purposes? The Java runtime, getting the lion's share of its bytecodes from the Internet, can never tell whether a "trustworthy" compiler generated those bytecodes. Therefore, it must verify that they meet all the safety requirements.

Before running any bytecodes, the runtime subjects them to a rigorous series of tests that vary in complexity from simple format checks all the way to running a theorem prover to make certain that they are playing by the rules. These tests verify that the bytecodes don't do the following:

- Forge pointers
- Violate access restrictions
- Access objects as other than what they are (InputStream objects are always used as InputStream objects and never as anything else)
- Call methods with inappropriate argument values or types
- Overflow the stack

Consider the following Java code sample:

```
public class VectorTest {
  public int array[];
  public int sum() {
    int[] localArray = array;
    int sum = 0;
    for (int  i = localArray.length; -i >= 0;  )
      sum += localArray[i];
    return sum;
  }
}
```

Here are the bytecodes generated when this code is compiled:

aload_0	Load `this`
getfield #10	Load `this.array`
astore_1	Store in `localArray`
iconst_0	Load `0`
istore_2	Store in sum
aload_1	Load `localArray`
arraylength	Gets its `length`
istore_3	Store in `i`
A:iinc_3 -1	Subtract 1 from `i`
iload_3	Load `i`
iflt B	Exit loop if < `0`
iload_2	Load sum
aload_1	Load `localArray`
iload_3	Load j
iaload	Load `localArray[i]`
iadd	Add sum
istore_2	Store in sum
goto A	Do it again
B:iload_2	Load sum
ireturn	Return it

Note The excellent examples and descriptions in this section are paraphrased from the tremendously informative security paper in the Java release. You are encouraged to read whatever the latest version of this document is in newer releases if you want to follow the ongoing Java security story. You can find it on Sun's Java site: http://www.javasoft.com.

21

Extra Type Information and Requirements

Java bytecodes encode more type information than is strictly necessary for the interpreter. Even though, for example, the `aload` and `iload` opcodes do exactly the same thing, `aload` is always used to load an object reference, and `iload` is used to load an integer. Some bytecodes (such as `getfield`) include a symbol table reference—and that symbol table has even *more* type information. This extra type information allows the runtime system to guarantee that Java objects and data aren't manipulated illegally.

Conceptually, before and after each bytecode is executed, every slot in the stack and every local variable has some type. This collection of type information—all the slots and local variables—is called the type *state* of the execution environment. An important requirement of the Java type state is that it must be able to be determined statically by induction—that is, before any program code is executed. As a result, as the runtime system reads bytecodes, each is required to have the following inductive property: given only the type state before the execution of the bytecode, the type state afterward must be fully determined.

Given straight-line bytecodes (no branches), and starting with a known stack state, the state of each slot in the stack is therefore always known. For example, starting with an empty stack, the following is true:

`iload_1`	Load integer variable. Stack type state is I.
`iconst_5`	Load integer constant. Stack type state is II.
`iadd`	Add two integers, producing an integer.
	Stack type state is I.

Note

> SmallTalk and PostScript bytecodes don't have this restriction. Their more dynamic type behavior does create additional flexibility in those systems, but Java needs to provide a secure execution environment. Therefore, it must know all types *at all times* to guarantee a certain level of security.

Another requirement made by the Java runtime is that when a set of bytecodes can take more than one path to arrive at the same point, all such paths must arrive with exactly the same type state. This is a strict requirement, and it implies, for example, that compilers can't generate bytecodes that load all the elements of an array onto the stack. (Because each time through such a loop the stack's type state changes, the start of the loop—the same point in multiple paths—would have more than one type state, which isn't allowed.)

The Verifier

Bytecodes are checked for compliance with all these requirements, using the extra type information in a .class file, by a part of the runtime called the *verifier*. It examines each bytecode in turn, constructing the full type state as it goes, and verifies that all the types of parameters, arguments, and results are correct. Thus, the verifier acts as a gatekeeper to your runtime environment, letting in only those bytecodes that pass muster.

Caution The verifier is the *crucial piece* of Java's security, and it depends on your having a correctly implemented runtime system (no bugs, intentional or otherwise). Your runtime is the base on which all the rest of Java's security is built, so make sure that it's a good, solid, secure base. (The runtime that comes with JBuilder is provided by Sun.)

When bytecodes have passed the verifier, they are guaranteed not to do the following:

- Cause any operand stack underflows or overflows
- Use parameter, argument, or return types incorrectly
- Illegally convert data from one type to another (from an integer to a pointer, for example)
- Access any object's fields illegally (in other words, the verifier checks that the rules for public, package, protected, private protected, and private are obeyed)

As an added bonus, because the interpreter can now count on all these facts being true, it can run much faster than before. All the required checks for safety have been done up front, so the interpreter can run at full throttle. In addition, object references now can be treated as capabilities because they are unforgeable. Capabilities allow, for example, advanced security models for file input/output and authentication to be safely built on top of Java.

Note Because you can now trust that a private variable really is private, and that no bytecode can perform magic with casts to extract information (such as your credit card number) from the variable, many of the security problems that might arise in other, less safe environments simply vanish! These guarantees also make erecting barriers against destructive applets possible and easier. Because the Java system doesn't have to worry about "nasty" bytecodes, it can get on with creating the other levels of security it wants to give you.

21

The Class Loader

The class loader is another kind of gatekeeper, albeit a higher-level one. The verifier was the security of last resort. The class loader is the security of first resort.

When a new class is loaded into the system, it is placed into (lives in) one of several different realms. The current release has three possible realms: your local computer, the firewall-guarded local network on which your computer is located, and the Internet (the global Internet and the World Wide Web). The class loader treats each of these realms differently.

Actually, there can be as many realms as your desired level of security (or paranoia) requires. This is because the class loader is under your control. As a programmer, you can make your own class loader that implements your own peculiar brand of security. (This is a radical step: You might have to give the users of your program many classes—and they give you a lot of trust—to accomplish this.)

> **Tip**
>
> As a user, you can tell your Java-capable browser, or Java system, what realm of security (of the three) you want it to implement for you right now or from now on.

If you're a system administrator, Java has global security policies that you can set up to help prevent your users from giving away the store. In other words, even if users set all their preferences to be unrestricted, global security will override those settings to provide more restrictive security for your site as a whole.

In particular, the class loader never allows a class from a "less protected" realm to replace a class from a "more protected" realm. The file system's input/output primitives, about which you should be very worried (and rightly so), are all defined in a local Java class, which means that they all live in the local-computer realm. Thus, no class from outside your computer (from either the supposedly trustworthy local network or from the Internet) can take the place of these classes and "spoof" Java code into using "nasty" versions of these primitives. In addition, classes in one realm can't call upon the methods of classes in other realms unless those classes have explicitly declared those methods `public`. This implies that classes from other than your local computer can't even *see* the file system I/O methods, much less call them, unless you or the system wants them to do so.

In addition, every new applet loaded from the network is placed into a separate package-like namespace. This means that applets are protected even from each other. No applet can access another's methods (or variables) without its cooperation. Applets from inside the firewall can even be treated differently from those outside the firewall if you want.

Actually, it's all a little more complex than that. In the current release, an applet is in a package namespace along with any other applets from that *source.* This source, or origin, is most often a host (domain name) on the Internet. Depending on where the source is located, outside the firewall or inside, further restrictions might apply (or be removed entirely). This model is likely to be extended in future releases of Java, providing an even finer degree of control over which classes get to do what.

The class loader essentially partitions the world of Java classes into small, protected little groups, about which you can safely make assumptions that will *always* be true. This type of predictability is the key to well-behaved and secure programs.

You've now seen the full lifetime of a method. It starts as source code on some computer, is compiled into bytecodes on possibly a different computer, and then can travel (as a .class file) into any file system or network anywhere in the world. When you run an applet in a Java-capable browser (or download a .class file and run it manually using java), the method's bytecodes are extracted from its .class file and carefully looked over by the verifier. After they're declared safe, the interpreter can execute them for you (or a code generator can generate native binary code for them using either the "just-in-time" compiler or java2c and then run that native code directly).

At each stage, more and more security is added. The final level of that security is the Java class library itself, which has several carefully designed classes and Application Programming Interfaces (APIs) that add the final touches to the system's security.

The Security Manager

SecurityManager is an abstract class added to the Java system to collect, in one place, all the security policy decisions that the system has to make as bytecodes run. You learned earlier that you could create your own class loader. In fact, you might not have to because you can subclass SecurityManager to perform most of the same customizations.

An instance of some subclass of SecurityManager is always installed as the current security manager. It has complete control over which of a well-defined set of "dangerous" methods are allowed to be called by any given class. It takes into account the considerations discussed in the preceding section. It also takes into account the class's source (origin) and type (standalone or loaded by an applet). Each of these can be configured separately to have the effect that you (the programmer) want on your Java system. For nonprogrammers, the system provides several levels of default security policies from which you can choose.

21

What is this "well-defined set" of methods that are protected?

File input/output is a part of the set, for obvious reasons. Applets, by default, can open, read, or write files only with the permission of the user—and even then, only in certain restricted directories.

Also in this protected set are the methods that create and use Internet network connections, both incoming and outgoing.

The final members of the set are the methods that allow one thread to access, control, and manipulate other threads. (Of course, you can protect additional methods as well by creating a new subclass of SecurityManager that handles them.)

For both file and network access, the user of a Java-capable browser can choose between three realms of protection (and one subrealm):

- Unrestricted (allows applets to do anything)
- Firewall (allows applets within the firewall to do anything)
- Source (allows applets to do things only with their originating Internet host or with other applets from that same host)
- Local (disallows all file and network access)

For file access, the *source* subrealm isn't meaningful, so it really has only three realms of protection. (As a programmer, of course, you have full access to the security manager and can set up your own peculiar criteria for granting and revoking privileges to your heart's content.)

For network access, you can imagine wanting many more realms. For example, you might specify different groups of trusted domains (companies), each of which is given added privileges when applets from that group are loaded. Some groups can be more trusted than other groups, and you might even allow groups to grow automatically by allowing existing members to recommend new members for admission (with the Java seal of approval?).

In any case, the possibilities are endless, as long as there is a secure way of recognizing the original creator of an applet.

You might think that this problem has already been solved because classes are tagged with their origins. In fact, the Java runtime goes far out of its way to be sure that that origin information is never lost. Any executing method can be dynamically restricted by this information anywhere in the call chain. So why *isn't* this enough?

Because what you really want to be able to do is permanently "tag" an applet with its original creator (its true origin), and no matter where it has traveled, a browser could verify the integrity and authenticate the creator of that applet. Just because you don't know the company or individual who operates a particular server machine doesn't mean that you *want* to mistrust every applet stored on that machine. It's just that, currently, to be really safe, you *should* mistrust those applets.

If somehow those applets were tagged irrevocably with the digital signature of their creator, and that signature could also guarantee that the applet hadn't been tampered with, you'd be golden. Currently, you can use digital signing to secure your Java applets and JavaBeans components.

One final note about security. Despite the best efforts of the Java team, there is always a trade-off between useful functionality and absolute security. For example, Java applets can create windows, an extremely useful capability, but a "nasty" applet could use this to trick the user into typing private password information by showing a familiar program window (or operating system window) and then asking an expected, legitimate-looking question in it. This is why Java adds a banner at the bottom that says `Untrusted Applet`.

Flexibility and security can't both be maximized. Thus far on the Internet, people have chosen maximum flexibility and have lived with the minimal security that the Internet now provides. Let's hope that Java can help tip the scales a bit, enabling much better security while sacrificing only a minimal amount of the flexibility that has drawn so many to the Internet.

Summary

Today, you learned about the grand vision that some people have for Java and about the exciting future it promises.

The following were all revealed: the inner workings of the Java Virtual Machine (Java VM), the bytecode interpreter, the garbage collector, the class loader, the verifier, the security manager, and Java's powerful security model.

You now know *almost* enough to write a Java runtime environment of your own—but luckily, you don't have to. You can simply use the latest release of Java provided with JBuilder—or use a Java-capable browser to enjoy most of the benefits of Java right away.

21

Q&A

Q I'm still a little unclear about why the Java language and compiler make the Internet safer. Can't they just be "side-stepped" by "nasty" bytecodes?

A Yes, they can. But don't forget that the whole point of using a safe language and compiler is to make the Internet safer *as a whole* as more Java code is written. Ethical Java programmers will write an overwhelming majority of the Java code resulting in safe bytecodes. This makes the Internet more predictable over time, and thus more secure.

Q I know you said that garbage collection is something I don't have to worry about, but what if I want (or need) to?

A So you *are* planning to fly a plane with Java! Cool! For just such cases, there is a way to ask the Java runtime, during startup (java -noasyncgc), *not* to run garbage collection unless forced to, either by an explicit call (System.gc()) or by running out of memory. (This can be useful if you have multiple threads that are messing each other up and you want to get the gc thread out of the way while testing them.) Don't forget that turning off garbage collection means that any object you create will live a long, *long* time. If you're real-time, you never want to step back for a full gc—so be sure to reuse objects often, and don't create too many of them!

Q I like the explicit control as you explained it in the preceding answer. Can I do anything else to the garbage collector?

A You can also force the finalize methods of any recently freed objects to be called immediately through System.runFinalization(). You might want to do this if you're about to ask for some resources that you suspect might still be tied up by objects that are gone but not forgotten (waiting for the finalize method). This is even rarer than starting a gc by hand, but it's mentioned here for completeness.

Q What's the last word on Java?

A Java adds much more than it can ever take away. It has certainly done so for me, and now I hope it will do the same for you.

The future of the Internet is filled with as-yet-undreamed-of horizons. The road is long and hard, but Java is a great traveling companion.

APPENDIX A

Answers to Quiz Questions

This appendix provides the answers to the quiz questions at the end of each day.

Day 2

1. a. False. The `boolean` variables cannot be assigned numeric values in Java. They can only take on the values of `true` or `false`.

   b. False. The add operator does not have precedence over the multiply operator. When using Table 2.6 to determine operator precedence, be sure not to confuse the unary plus (+) and minus (-) operators with the binary infix add (+) and subtract (-) operators.

   c. False. The elements of an array must contain identical data types.

   d. False. An `if-else` conditional can return only a `boolean` value.

   e. True. As long as you can cast the resulting value to an `int`, you can use an expression as a `switch` statement's `condition`.

2. The symbols used to enclose statements to be treated as a group are the braces ({ }).

3. Subscripts in Java begin with 0.

4. It throws a `NegativeArraySizeException` object at runtime because the integer expression in the subscript evaluates to -2, which is not a valid subscript.

5. It is 8 because the `wwwStr` variable is assigned the value assigned to the `chArr` variable, which contains eight characters.

6. It creates only two actual strings in memory. It creates one `String` object in memory with the contents `Here I am!`, and a second `String` object in memory with the contents `No, I'm over here!!`. This is due to optimization of strings in Java. Therefore, both the `firstStr` and `thirdStr` variables point to the same `String` object in memory.

7. Because you've declared a variable inside a block of statements, it's defined only in the block's local scope. After the block has finished executing, the variable's value is undefined (it no longer exists).

8. It will iterate seven times but will output nothing. After the `for` loop exits on the eighth test, the `println` statement will execute.

   Did you miss the extraneous semicolon (;) at the end of the first line of code? It causes the `println` statement to be outside the `for` loop's scope.

9. If you want to execute the body of a loop and then re-execute the loop body as long as a specified condition is `true`, you should use a `do-while` loop.

Day 3

1. Avoid creating too many custom classes to use with your applets because it can take longer to download. Otherwise, just be sure to deploy the custom classes so that your applet has access to them.

2. If you don't specify a superclass, your class will inherit from the `Object` class by default.

3. False. Java does not support multiple inheritance; it supports only single inheritance. That is, a subclass can have only one superclass.

4. The first line of code initializes a primitive `boolean` variable named `aBoolean` to the value `true`. The second line of code instantiates a `Boolean` object named `boolObj` and assigns it the current value of `aBoolean`, which is `true`.

5. When a class takes advantage of method overloading and contains several methods with the same name, the method that gets called is determined by the method's

A

signature. The method's signature comprises the type and number of arguments in its definition.

6. To declare a class variable, you would use the `static` keyword.

7. The `this` keyword refers to the current object instance. The `super` keyword refers to the superclass of the current class.

8. The `this()` method calls the current class's constructor. If there is more than one constructor (that is, the class contains overloaded constructors), the `this()` method calls whichever one matches the method signature, based on the argument list.

   The `super()` method calls the superclass's constructor. If there is more than one constructor in the superclass (that is, it has overloaded constructors), the `super()` method calls whichever one matches the method signature, based on the argument list.

Day 4

1. The answers are as follows:

   a. True. To declare a constant, you only need to use the final modifier. However, if you want the constant to be available as a global value to all instances of the class in which it is declared, you must use the static modifier as well.

   b. False. In fact, each `public` class should be in a separate `.java` source file so that they will compile properly into separate `.class` files. To ensure that a class is a member of a package, put the appropriate `package` statement at the top of each `.java` source file.

   c. False. Interfaces that do not extend another interface become top-level interfaces and do not automatically extend `Object`.

   d. False. A class can implement any number of interfaces and is not limited to implementing only one interface.

2. Well, this was a trick question. You cannot declare a class method and allow subclasses to override it. Remember that class methods are `final` by default and therefore cannot be overridden in subclasses. To declare the class method, use the `static` keyword before the method's return type.

3. To create a variable that is read-only, use the convention of accessor methods to get and set the variable, making the set method `private` and the get method `public`. This is also good practice for your own use within the class because accessor methods indirectly modify the variable, thus protecting you from changes in its representation.

4. The only part of an abstract method you need to declare in the abstract class is the method signature. In other words, you need only declare the modifier(s), return type, method name, and arguments (if any). You do not declare the body of an abstract method; its body is defined when the subclass implements the abstract method.

5. To import all the `java.util` classes and subclasses, you would add this statement to your source code file:

```
import java.util.*
```

To import `java.util`'s subpackage `zip`, you would add this statement to your source code file:

```
import java.util.zip.*
```

Remember that the asterisk (`*`) that enables you to import a whole package of classes and subclasses does *not* import that package's subpackages. Each package and subpackage must be declared in its own `import` statement, as shown here.

6. The `package` statement belongs at the top of the source code file (not counting comments and whitespace). Your `import` statements follow directly after the `package` statement (if any).

Day 5

1. You can get context-sensitive help in the JBuilder IDE by pressing F1.

2. When you select a `.java` file in the AppBrowser window Navigation pane, its classes, objects, methods, resources, and import files are displayed in the Structure pane, and the source code is displayed in the Content pane when the Source tab is selected.

3. The UI Designer is invoked when you have a Frame object, applet, or other visual object node selected in the Navigation pane, by clicking on the Design tab located below the Content pane in the AppBrowser window. The Menu Designer is invoked either by double-clicking on a menu item in the Component Tree pane or by right-clicking and selecting Activate Designer from the pop-up menu.

4. The `Make` command compiles the files in a project if the `.class` file is older than the `.java` source code file or if there is no `.class` file yet.

Day 6

1. To invoke UI Designer mode in the AppBrowser window, click on the Design tab of the Content pane when a `Frame` object node is selected in the Navigation pane.

A

2. To switch between the Menu Designer and the UI Designer, double-click on one of the components under the Menu or UI node in the Context Tree (in the Structure pane), respectively.

3. An exclusive Checkbox component is not programmatically related to and does not depend on other Checkbox components. A non-exclusive Checkbox component is one that has its checkboxGroup property set, which makes it a member of a group of Checkbox components. To create a group of non-exclusive Checkbox components so that they will become radio buttons, you must add a CheckboxGroup component and set the Checkbox components' checkboxGroup property to that CheckboxGroup component.

4. True. It's okay to leave Panel components set to XYLayout when you are ready to distribute your program. However, it is definitely not recommended. Always set your layout to one of the standard Java layouts before final distribution.

5. The BorderLayout manager arranges your components according to the points of the compass: North, South, East, West, and Center.

Day 7

1. You cannot change the <name> property of a component at runtime because it's not a true property. It is a pseudoproperty that enables you to globally change the component's identifier in all JBuilder generated code.

2. The ChoiceControl component presents a drop-down selection list. It is similar to the Choice component on the AWT page.

3. TabsetControl and TabsetPanel components are similar to exclusive check boxes in that they all act as radio buttons; only one exclusive tab/page/check box can be selected at a time.

4. A *data-aware* component has the capability (usually through its dataSet property) to display and sometimes edit data in a database table.

5. The show() method is used to display a dialog box. This method should be called in the event handler of the component that is to invoke the dialog box, such as a button or menu item.

Day 8

1. The five major methods that an applet can override are the init(), start(), stop(), destroy(), and paint() methods. The only one that your applet is really required to override is the paint() method because if it doesn't, it will have no visible presence on the Web page.

2. Plain text between the <APPLET> and </APPLET> tag pair serves as an alternative message when your applet is encountered by a browser that is not Java-capable. That way, the reader isn't presented with a blank space. It's optional but certainly recommended.

3. The CODEBASE attribute can be used in the <APPLET> tag to tell the HTML page to look in some other directory for the applet's class files. The directory is specified as a string, and the pathname is relative to the HTML file's directory.

4. True. All applet parameters are passed into the applet as strings. If you want them to be some other data type, you must write code in the applet body to convert them to the desired type.

Day 9

1. False. This line of code draws a filled rectangle whose upper-left corner is at 20,20 and whose lower-right corner is at 79,79:

```
g.fillRect(20,20,60,60);
```

Remember that the last two arguments are width and height, not coordinates. Also, don't forget to count the starting coordinates as one of the pixels in the filled rectangle (pixels 20 through 79 give a total of 60 pixels).

2. True. You can draw an outline of a circle using either the drawRoundRect() or the drawOval() method. Here's an example of the paint() method that uses both of these methods to draw a circle 60 pixels by 60 pixels:

```
public void paint(Graphics g) {
  g.drawRoundRect(20,20,60,60,30,30);
  g.drawOval(120,20,60,60);
}
```

Of course, it's simpler to use the drawOval() method because it takes fewer arguments.

3. It's true that there is no isBoldItalic() method defined in the Font class. However, you can use the getStyle() method and test the integer constant it returns. If it returns 3, the style of the Font object is bold italic.

4. The effect of the following line of code in an applet is to erase all that has been drawn on it to this point:

```
setForground(getBackground());
```

By getting the background color and setting the foreground color equal to it, you color in all the drawn graphics with the background color, effectively wiping them clean. If what you wanted to do was set the current drawing color to the background color (as painting programs do when they implement an eraser tool), you could use this line of code:

```
g.setColor(getBackground());
```

This sets the current drawing color without disturbing any existing graphics.

Day 10

1. False. Both streams and files make use of the `DataInput` and `DataOutput` interfaces because they are implemented by the `DataInputStream`, `DataOutputStream`, and `RandomFileAccess` classes.

2. A *deprecated* class is one that is obsolete but that remains defined for purposes of backward compatibility.

3. The `InputStream`, `OutputStream`, and `RandomAccessFile` classes are byte-based; the `Reader` and `Writer` classes are character-based.

   Although the text doesn't say so explicitly, you can easily tell that the `RandomAccessFile` class is byte-based because it implements the `DataInput` and `DataOutput` interfaces, with methods that are also implemented in the `DataInputStream` and `DataOutputStream` classes (subclasses of `InputStream` and `OutputStream`).

4. Even though some methods still depend on the existence of the `PrintStream` class (most notably, the `System.out.println()` method), it has been superseded by the `PrintWriter` class. This means that your programs should use the `PrintWriter` class rather than the deprecated `PrintStream` class.

Day 11

1. `Make` does a conditional compilation, compiling only those source code files that do not have up-to-date `.class` files. `Rebuild` compiles everything regardless of the state of the `.class` files.

2. There are several ways to set a breakpoint on a particular line of source code. First, with the cursor position on the source code line, you can right-click on the line of source code in the Content pane and select the Toggle Breakpoint command from the Editor's pop-up menu. Second, select View|Breakpoints to display the Breakpoints window, and then right-click and select the Breakpoints Options dialog box

and set the desired breakpoint. Third, select Run I Add Breakpoints to display the Breakpoints Options dialog box and set the desired breakpoint.

3. The Trace Into command lets you execute each line of a method while debugging. (If you trace into a method and then change your mind, you can select the Run to End of Method menu item to execute the remaining lines of code in the method as a group.)

4. To change a variable's value during execution, select Run I Evaluate/Modify to display the Evaluate/Modify dialog box, specify the new value, and then click the Modify button.

5. False. The execution point indicates the line of code that will be executed next.

6. To make the debugger run your code until it encounters the line of code in which the cursor is positioned in the Editor, select Run I Run to Cursor.

Day 12

1. To create an event handler in the JBuilder IDE, first select the component in the UI Designer pane of the AppBrowser window. Click on the Events tab in the Inspector pane, and triple-click the event in question. This will insert the method stub, ready for your event-handling code.

2. True. A MouseClicked event is not generated when the mouse button is pressed and released if a MouseDragged event occurred in between.

3. The getKeyCode() method returns VK_UNDEFINED for the keyTyped event.

4. To share an event handler, after it is created, you need only put the event handler's method name in the right column of the event that you want to share the handler.

5. The event for which you would create a handler to detect and do something whenever a particular component receives focus is the focusGained event.

6. The AWTEvent class is the superclass for all the AWT events.

Day 13

1. You can have as many catch blocks as you need following a try statement.

2. No; you can have either catch blocks or a finally block following a try block, but not both.

A

3. Use the `finally` keyword when you want to do something no matter what else happens.

4. The `throws` keyword in a method signature alerts the compiler that the caller of that method must either catch the exceptions listed in the `throws` clause or must also list those exceptions in its own `throws` clause. The `throw` keyword is used to throw or rethrow an exception during execution.

5. False. When you catch an exception, you can handle it by doing nothing at all.

Day 14

1. The four major types of JDBC connectivity are JDBC-ODBC Bridge, native API partly-Java driver, net-protocol all-Java driver, and native-protocol all-Java driver.

2. By using a `DataModule` class, you can reuse the components within as a group.

3. The detail `DataSet` component's `MasterLink` property is what links it to the master `DataSet` component.

4. In a data-aware component, the `DataSet` property must be set to the underlying data-access component to make the connection.

Day 15

1. The icon for configuring the Local InterBase Server data sources is installed on the Windows Control Panel—it's the 32-bit ODBC icon.

2. At design time, nonvisual components appear on the Component Tree in the AppBrowser window's Structure pane. You can place them by clicking either in the Structure pane or in the Content pane, but they'll display on the Component Tree nevertheless.

3. The `dataset` property of a data-aware component needs to be hooked up to the data-providing component. To do this, select the data-providing component from the `dataset` property's drop-down list.

4. Before attempting to set and execute a new query, you must close the existing query using its `close()` method.

5. Query-related operations need to be put inside a `try` block because they can throw a `DataSetException` object, which must be either handled or rethrown.

6. You can use the `saveChanges()` method to resolve changes to a database.

Day 16

1. You use the `synchronized` keyword to atomize a block or method—that is, make its statements appear to happen all at once and protect them from interruptions.

2. True. The word `synchronized` can be used as both a method and a keyword in Java. As a keyword, it serves to atomize the block or method it modifies. As a method, it locks the instance of the object that is contained in its argument.

3. The method call that takes place as the implicit first statement in any `synchronized` method is:

   `synchronized(this);`

4. When you subclass a class other than `Thread`, the `Runnable` interface must be implemented to make that new subclass capable of running threads.

5. Preemptive timeslicing allows threads to run (according to their priorities) in small incremental units of time, yielding to one another so that all have a chance to use system resources. Nonpreemptive scheduling requires that a program ask for permission to run, and after it receives that permission, it runs until it is finished; no other program can use the resources until it has completed its mission.

Day 17

1. False. Both streams and files can make use of the methods in the `ObjectInput` and `ObjectOutput` interfaces. Streams can read and write other streams, including RMI marshaling streams; files can be written to and read from within security restrictions. (Applets can read and write files only on their host systems.)

2. The `Externalizable` interface requires you to define your object's external format, so you must define this class's abstract `writeExternal()` and `readExternal()` methods in your object's class.

3. For serializing objects, use the `writeObject()` method. For deserializing objects, use the `readObject()` method.

Day 18

1. The two basic requirements for creating beans are that the bean class must be declared `public` and the bean musst have a `public` default constructor that takes no arguments.

2. For JBuilder to expose properties and events, their methods must follow certain conventions. Property accessor methods should be named get*Property*() and set*Property*() for most property types. For boolean values, the get accessor method should be named is*Property*(). Event methods are named add*Event*Listener() and remove*Event*Listener.

3. If you get an ODBC Driver Manager error when you choose the Design tab for a DBBean, you probably didn't create the necessary Data Source when you installed Local InterBase. Refer to the instructions in the section "Making Connections" to correct the problem.

4. The two main uses of the BeanInfo class are to describe bean elements that don't follow the naming conventions so that they can be found by introspection and to hide elements from introspection.

5. The method used to hide bean elements is called setHidden(), and it takes a boolean argument.

Day 19

1. You need to uncheck the Include Debug Information check box in the Compiler page of the Project Properties dialog box before doing a final build. This will create class files without the symbolic debugging information and create smaller, faster class files.

2. False. You do not always need to add auxiliary files to your project. This is required only if you're planning to archive your project using the Deployment Wizard.

3. True. You can't create JAR files with a zip utility, but you can use a zip utility to view the contents of a JAR file.

4. To include the jbcl2.0-rt.jar and/or jgl3.1.0.jar archive files in your own archives, uncheck the appropriate check boxes in the Deployment Wizard dialog box. This is necessary if you're planning to deploy your program on a machine that you know won't contain these files. This might be the case if you were going to deploy an applet on a friend's web site as a demo, for instance.

5. False. If you include your applet's main class file in an archive referenced by the ARCHIVE attribute, you must still reference that class file in the <APPLET> tag's CODE attribute so that the browser will know which class file contains the main method.

6. The semantic difference between adding archive files to the <APPLET> tag's ARCHIVE attribute and adding them to the CLASSPATH is that the ARCHIVE attribute is

comma-delimited, and the CLASSPATH is semicolon-delimited. If your archives aren't being loaded properly, this is one of the things to check. (The other thing to check is that each archive filename contains its fully qualified pathname.)

Day 20

1. To write networked Java programs, you must import the `java.net` package.

2. `MalformedURLException` is used to signal that the URL you tried to instantiate is not correctly specified (for example, it has a typo).

3. The `openStream()` method in the URL class opens a network connection using the supplied URL address and returns an instance of the class `InputStream`.

4. When a server socket is bound to a port, use the `accept()` method to get the server socket to listen on the port for a client connection request.

5. When creating an RMI server, the only circumstance under which you can leave out `RMISecurityManager` is if you create and install your own security manager. RMI won't run without a security manager installed; this is a Java security feature.

APPENDIX B

JBuilder and Java Utilities

This appendix briefly describes each utility provided with JBuilder. Table B.1 alphabetically lists each utility by its executable name and cross-references the utility's category (Java or JBuilder) and its full name. Utilities in the JDK category are provided by Sun as part of the Java Development Kit, and Borland provides those in the JBuilder category.

 Note — The JBuilder Standard edition includes only the JDK utilities provided by JavaSoft. The JBuilder Professional and Enterprise editions provide Borland command-line tools.

TABLE B.1. EXECUTABLES CROSS-REFERENCED BY UTILITY NAMES.

Executable	Category	Utility Name
appletviewer	JDK	Java AppletViewer
bcj	JBuilder	Borland Compiler for Java
bmj	JBuilder	Borland Make for Java

continues

TABLE B.1. CONTINUED

Executable	Category	Utility Name
Grep	JBuilder	Turbo GREP
jar	JDK	Java Archive Tool
java	JDK	Java Interpreter
javac	JDK	Java Compiler
javadoc	JDK	Java Documentation Generator
javah	JDK	C Header and Stub File Generator
javakey	JDK	Digital Signing Tool
javap	JDK	Class File Disassembler
jdb	JDK	Java Debugger
jre	JDK	Java Runtime Loader
Make	JBuilder	MAKE
native2ascii	JDK	Native-to-ASCII Converter
rmic	JDK	Java RMI Stub Converter
rmiregistry	JDK	Java Remote Object Registry
serialver	JDK	Serial Version Command

To find a utility's description, go to the section of this appendix that corresponds to its category. The programs in both categories are listed alphabetically by utility name.

These programs are command-line utilities that must be run from the DOS prompt or your console window. In Windows, there are two ways to run a DOS session:

- From Windows, choose Start | Programs | MS-DOS Prompt or Start | Programs | Command Prompt. Choose the latter option if you're running Windows NT. Invoking DOS in this way treats the session as a windowed application, allowing you to switch to other applications in Windows by clicking the Windows taskbar or by using Alt+Tab. However, this method usually gives you less available memory in the session. When you've completed your work and want to close the session, right-click the taskbar's MS-DOS icon and choose Close, or type exit at the DOS command prompt and press Enter. You will be returned to the Windows desktop.

- From Windows 95 or Windows 98, choose Start | Shut Down. Choose the radio button that's labeled Restart the computer in MS-DOS mode? and then click the Yes button. This method usually gives you more available memory than the windowed DOS session, but you won't be able to use any Windows applications until you exit the session. To close the session, type exit and press Enter. Windows will be restarted.

For these utilities to find the classes needed for your program, the SOURCEPATH and CLASSPATH environment variables must be set. To run the batch file that sets the appropriate DOS environment variables while in a DOS session, type the following at the command prompt:

```
c:\jbuilder2\bin\setvars.bat c:\jbuilder2
```

This assumes the default installation pathnames. If you installed JBuilder to a different directory, you'll need to modify this command accordingly. You can also put this command in your AUTOEXEC.BAT file.

Each of the descriptions in the following sections includes the syntax and usage information describing the allowable parameters and options for the utility (if any). In most cases, you can view this information during a DOS session by entering the utility's executable name at the command prompt. For example, to see the usage screen for the Java Compiler, type javac and press Enter.

Java Utilities

These utilities, which are provided by Sun as part of the JDK, are found in the c:\jbuilder2\java\bin directory unless otherwise indicated.

C Header and Stub File Generator (javah)

The C Header and Stub File Generator utility is used for attaching native methods to Java code.

```
Usage: JAVAH.EXE [-v] [-options] classes...

where options include:
    -help     print out this message
    -o        specify the output file name
    -d        specify the output directory
    -jni      create a JNI-style header file
    -td       specify the temporary directory
    -stubs    create a stubs file
    -trace    adding tracing information to stubs file
    -v        verbose operation
    -classpath <directories separated by colons>
    -version  print out the build version
```

Class File Disassembler (javap)

The Class File Disassembler utility disassembles compiled .class files and prints a representation of the bytecodes.

```
Usage: javap <options> <classes>...

where options include:
    -b          Backward compatibility with javap in JDK 1.1
    -c          Disassemble the code
    -classpath <directories separated by colons>
                List directories in which to look for classes
    -l          Print line number and local variable tables
    -public     Show only public classes and members
    -protected  Show protected/public classes and members
    -package    Show package/protected/public classes
                and members (default)
    -private    Show all classes and members
    -s          Print internal type signatures
    -verbose    Print stack size, number of locals and args for methods
                If verifying, print reasons for failure
    -version    Print the javap version string
    -verify     Run the verifier
```

To use the last option to run the verifier, you must also have `javaverify.exe` in the same directory as the utility (where it is installed by default as part of the JDK).

Digital Signing Tool (`javakey`)

The Digital Signing Tool utility manages security for Java programs, such as keys, certificates, and the level of trust associated with them.

```
javakey
        l       list of the identities in the database.
        c       create a new identity.
        r       remove an identity from the database.
        i       import a public key, a key pair, etc.
        g       generate a key pair, a certificate, etc.
        d       display a certificate.

for more information, see documentation.
```

Java AppletViewer (`appletviewer`)

The Java AppletViewer utility is used to test and run applets.

```
usage: appletviewer [-debug] [-J<runtime flag>] url¦file ...
```

Java Archive Tool (`jar`)

The Java Archive Tool utility combines `.class` files and other resources into a single JAR file. Using JAR files allows your applet to cause all its supporting members to be accessed in a single download, improving your program's performance.

```
Usage: jar {ctx}[vfm0M] [jar-file] [manifest-file] files ...
```

```
Options:
 -c  create new archive
 -t  list table of contents for archive
 -x  extract named (or all) files from archive
 -v  generate verbose output on standard error
 -f  specify archive file name
 -m  include manifest information from specified manifest file
 -0  store only; use no ZIP compression
 -M  Do not create a manifest file for the entries
```

```
If any file is a directory then it is processed recursively.
Example: to archive two class files into an archive called classes.jar:
  jar cvf classes.jar Foo.class Bar.class
Note: use the '0' option to create a jar file that can be put in your
CLASSPATH
```

Java Compiler (javac)

The Java Compiler utility compiles .java files containing source code into .class files containing bytecodes.

```
use: javac [-g][-O][-debug][-depend][-nowarn][-verbose]
           ➥[-classpath path][-nowrite][-deprecation]
           ➥[-d dir][-J<runtime flag>] file.java...
```

Java Debugger (jdb)

The Java Debugger utility helps you find bugs in Java programs. To view the help screen outlined here, invoke the jdb utility and then type help at its prompt after it initializes.

```
threads [threadgroup]       -- list threads
thread <thread id>          -- set default thread
suspend [thread id(s)]      -- suspend threads (default: all)
resume [thread id(s)]       -- resume threads (default: all)
where [thread id] ¦ all     -- dump a thread's stack
threadgroups                -- list threadgroups
threadgroup <name>          -- set current threadgroup

print <id> [id(s)]          -- print object or field
dump <id> [id(s)]           -- print all object information

locals                      -- print all local variables in current stack
frame

classes                     -- list currently known classes
methods <class id>          -- list a class's methods

stop in <class id>.<method> -- set a breakpoint in a method
stop at <class id>:<line>   -- set a breakpoint at a line
up [n frames]               -- move up a thread's stack
down [n frames]             -- move down a thread's stack
```

```
clear <class id>:<line>      -- clear a breakpoint
step                         -- execute current line
cont                         -- continue execution from breakpoint

catch <class id>             -- break for the specified exception
ignore <class id>            -- ignore when the specified exception

list [line number¦method]    -- print source code
use [source file path]       -- display or change the source path

memory                       -- report memory usage
gc                           -- free unused objects

load classname               -- load Java class to be debugged
run <class> [args]           -- start execution of a loaded Java class
!!                           -- repeat last command
help (or ?)                  -- list commands
exit (or quit)               -- exit debugger
```

Java Documentation Generator (javadoc)

The Java Documentation Generator utility is used to extract documentation comments from your source code. It parses the declarations and documentation comments in a set of .java source files and produces a set of HTML pages that can be viewed with a browser. Also, after the HTML files are generated and placed in the same directory as the .java source files, you can load and select the .java source file in a JBuilder AppBrowser window and then select the Content pane's Doc tab to view the HTML page from within the JBuilder IDE.

```
usage: javadoc flags* [class ¦ package]*
        -sourcepath <path>  Colon-separated list of source-file
                            directories
        -classpath <path>   Synonym for -sourcepath
        -d <directory>      Destination directory for output files
        -version            Include @version paragraphs
        -nodeprecated       Exclude @deprecated paragraphs
        -author             Include @author paragraphs
        -noindex            Do not generate method and field index
        -notree             Do not generate class hierarchy
        -public             show only public classes and members
        -protected          show protected/public classes and members
                            (default)
        -package            show package/protected/public classes and
                            members
        -private            show all classes and members
        -J<flag>            Pass <flag> directly to the runtime system
        -encoding <name>    Source file encoding name
        -docencoding <name> Output encoding name
```

Java Interpreter (`java`)

The Java Interpreter utility executes Java applications—that is, those Java `.class` files that were compiled from source code containing a `main` function.

```
usage: java [-options] class

where options include:
    -help               print out this message
    -version            print out the build version
    -v -verbose         turn on verbose mode
    -debug              enable remote JAVA debugging
    -noasyncgc          don't allow asynchronous garbage collection
    -verbosegc          print a message when garbage collection occurs
    -noclassgc          disable class garbage collection
    -ss<number>         set the maximum native stack size for any thread
    -oss<number>        set the maximum Java stack size for any thread
    -ms<number>         set the initial Java heap size
    -mx<number>         set the maximum Java heap size
    -classpath          <directories separated by semicolons>
                        list directories in which to look for classes
    -prof[:<file>]      output profiling data to .\java.prof or .\<file>
    -verify             verify all classes when read in
    -verifyremote       verify classes read in over the network [default]
    -noverify           do not verify any class
```

Java Remote Object Registry (`rmiregistry`)

The Java Remote Object Registry utility creates and starts a remote object registry on the specified port of the current host, enabling communications.

```
Syntax: rmiregistry portnumber
```

Java RMI Stub Converter (`rmic`)

The Java RMI Stub Converter utility generates objects from the identifiers in compiled `.class` files that contain remote object implementations.

```
use: rmic [-g][-O][-debug][-depend][-nowarn][-verbose][-classpath path]
        ➥[-nowrite][-d dir][-dstub dir][-dskel dir][-show]
        ➥[-keepgenerated] classname...
```

Java Runtime Loader (`jre`)

The Java Runtime Loader is the version of the JDK runtime that end users can employ to run your Java programs. The `jre` is a slimmed-down version of the `java` utility, which doesn't include support for development tools and command-line utilities, so it takes up less space on end users' machines.

```
Usage: jre [-options] classname [arguments]
Options:
    -?, -help          print out this message
    -v, -verbose       turn on verbose mode
    -verbosegc         print a message when garbage collection occurs
    -noasyncgc         disable asynchronous garbage collection
    -noclassgc         disable class garbage collection
    -ss<number>        set the maximum native stack size for any thread
    -oss<number>       set the maximum Java stack size for any thread
    -ms<number>        set the initial Java heap size
    -mx<number>        set the maximum Java heap size
    -D<name>=<value>   set a system property
    -classpath <path>  set class path to <path>
    -cp <path>         prepend <path> to base class path
    -verify            verify all classes when loaded
    -verifyremote      verify classes loaded from the network (default)
    -noverify          do not verify any classes
    -nojit             disable JIT compiler
```

Native-to-ASCII Converter (`native2ascii`)

The Native-to-ASCII Converter utility converts a native encoding file (platform-specific) to an ASCII file that is formatted using \udddd Unicode notation.

```
syntax: native2ascii nativefilename asciifilename
```

Serial Version Command (`serialver`)

The Serial Version Command utility returns the serialVersionUID in a form that can be used in your source code.

```
use: serialver [-show] [classname...]
```

JBuilder Utilities

The JBuilder utilities, which are provided by Borland as part of the JBuilder Professional and JBuilder Client/Server packages, are found in the c:\jbuilder2\bin directory. All of them have the .EXE extension.

Borland Compiler for Java (`bcj`)

The Borland Compiler for Java utility does an unconditional compilation. Dependencies are not checked.

```
Usage: bcj [-g][-verbose][-quiet][-nowarn][-obfuscate][-encoding name]
       ➡[-d dir][-classpath path] {file.java}
```

For a full discussion of this utility's options, refer to the User's Guide online documentation (select Help | Help Topics).

Borland Make for Java (bmj)

The Borland Make for Java utility does a conditional compilation and checks dependencies on the current CLASSPATH.

```
Usage: bmj [-g][-verbose][-quiet][-nowarn][-obfuscate][-encoding name]
       ➥[-d dir][-classpath path][-sourcepath path][-rebuild]
       ➥[-nocompile][-nocheckstable][-nomakestable]
       ➥{[-s] {source.java} ¦ -p {package} ¦ -c {class}}
```

For a full discussion of this utility's options, refer to the User's Guide online documentation (select Help | Help Topics).

MAKE (Make)

The MAKE utility does a conditional compilation of the named target files but doesn't do the dependency checking that the bmj utility performs.

```
Syntax: MAKE [options ...] target[s]
    -B               Builds all targets regardless of dependency dates
    -Dsymbol[=string] Defines symbol [equal to string]
    -Idirectory      Names an include directory
    -K               Keeps (does not erase) temporary files created by
                     MAKE
    -N               Increases MAKE's compatibility with NMAKE
    -Wfilename       Writes MAKE to filename updating all non-string
                     options
    -Usymbol         Undefine symbol
    -ffilename       Uses filename as the MAKEFILE
    -a               Performs auto-dependency checks for include files
    -c               Caches auto-dependency information
    -e               Ignores redefinition of environment variable macros
    -i               Ignores errors returned by commands
    -l+              Enables use of long command lines
    -m               Displays the date and time stamp of each file
    -n               Prints commands but does not do them
    -p               Displays all macro definitions and implicit rules
    -q               Returns zero if target is up-to-date and nonzero
                     if it is not (for use in batch files)
    -r               Ignores rules and macros defined in BUILTINS.MAK
    -s               Silent, does not print commands before doing them
    -? or -h         Prints this message
       Options marked with '+' are on by default. To turn off a default
       option follow it by a '-', for example: -a-
```

Turbo GREP (Grep)

The Turbo GREP utility is a global regular expression printer that is used to search for text in a file. It prints to standard output (by default) or to a specified file (by redirection). For example, if you wanted to find all occurrences of the word java in thisfile, and you wanted the results to be deposited in results.txt, you would use the following syntax:

```
grep java thisfile > results.txt
```

Here is the syntax that is displayed when you enter the utility name at the command prompt:

```
Syntax:  GREP [-rlcnvidzuwo] searchstring file[s]
         GREP ? for help
```

In addition, typing grep ? at the command prompt causes the following help screen to be displayed:

```
Syntax:  GREP [-rlcnvidzuwo] searchstring file[s]
Options are one or more option characters preceeded by "-", and optionally
followed by "+" (turn option on), or "-" (turn it off).  The default is
"+".
   -r+  Regular expression search      -l-  File names only
   -c-  match Count only               -n-  Line numbers
   -v-  Non-matching lines only        -i-  Ignore case
   -d-  Search subdirectories          -z-  Verbose
   -u-  NewFileName Update options      -w-  Word search
   -o-  UNIX output format                  Default set: [0-9A-Z_]

A regular expression is one or more occurrences of:  One or more
characters
optionally enclosed in quotes.  The following symbols are treated
specially:
      ^  start of line          $  end of line
      .  any character          \  quote next character
      *  match zero or more      +  match one or more
      [aeiou0-9]   match a, e, i, o, u, and 0 thru 9 ;
      [^aeiou0-9]  match anything but a, e, i, o, u, and 0 thru 9
```

APPENDIX C

Additional Resources

This appendix lists some of the innumerable resources available to the JBuilder user and Java programmer on the World Wide Web, CompuServe, and elsewhere.

Inprise International

You'll want to check Borland resources regularly at the Inprise International Web site. The JBuilder Product Team posts white papers, competitive analyses, answers to frequently asked questions (FAQ), sample applications, updated software, and information about upgrades. TeamB (volunteer users) answers questions on the Inprise newsgroups.

World Wide Web

General information and Inprise product home page links:

`http://www.inprise.com`

List of Inprise offices and distributors worldwide:

`http://www.inprise.com/bww/`

Electronic newsletter listserv subscription forms:

`http://www.inprise.com/feedback/listserv.html`
`http://www.inprise.com/feedback/intlist.html`

Lists of user-supported Inprise newsgroups:

`http://www.inprise.com/newsgroups/`

JBuilder home page:

`http://www.inprise.com/jbuilder/`

JBuilder Developer Support:

`http://www.inprise.com/devsupport/jbuilder/`

JBuilder documentation updates and miscellaneous files:

`http://www.inprise.com/techpubs/jbuilder/`

Newsgroups

Newsgroups hosted by `forums.inprise.com`:

`borland.public.install.jbuilderborland.public.jbuilder.announce`

`borland.public.jbuilder.applet-issues`

`inprise.public.as400.jbuilder`

`borland.public.jbuilder.compiler`

`borland.public.jbuilder.corba-rmi`

`borland.public.jbuilder.database`

`borland.public.jbuilder.debugger`

`borland.public.jbuilder.deployment`

`borland.public.jbuilder.documentation`

`borland.public.jbuilder.ide`

`borland.public.jbuilder.java`

`borland.public.jbuilder.java.api`

`borland.public.jbuilder.java.language`

`borland.public.jbuilder.javabeans`

```
borland.public.jbuilder.javabeans.using

borland.public.jbuilder.javabeans.writing

borland.public.jbuilder.jbcl

borland.public.jbuilder.jobs

borland.public.jbuilder.multi-lingual-apps

borland.public.jbuilder.non-technical

borland.public.jbuilder.thirdpartytools
```

CompuServe

Although Inprise no longer officially supports CompuServe forums, there is still a large user community that gathers and discusses Inprise products on CompuServe.

Inprise's top level:

```
GO INPRISE
```

JBuilder forum:

```
GO JBUILDER
```

Mail, Phone, Fax

Comments or questions can be emailed to

```
feedback@corp.inprise.com
```

Inprise's street address:

> Inprise International
> World Wide Headquarters
> 100 Enterprise Way
> Scotts Valley, CA 95066-3249
> USA

Telephone switchboard:

> (408) 431-1000

Technical documents available by fax in North America:

> (800) 822-4269

C

Sun Microsystems

Sun Microsystems, the developer of Java, offers support and information via its Web sites, anonymous FTP, faxback, email, telephone, and postal mail. The following is a brief list of some of these resources.

World Wide Web

Sun's Java Developers Connection, which has access to technical support, a Q&A database, online forums, technical articles, training courses, tips and techniques, and product discounts:

```
http://developer.javasoft.com
```

JavaSoft's home page:

```
http://java.sun.com
```

JavaSoft mirror site (SunSITE Singapore, National University of Singapore):

```
http://sunsite.nus.sg/hotjava/
```

JavaBeans component architecture:

```
http://splash.javasoft.com/beans/
```

HotJava Web page:

```
http://java.sun.com/products/hotjava/
```

SunTest home page, featuring cross-platform testing tools for Java:

```
http://www.sun.com/suntest/
```

List of places to email for technical help:

```
http://java.sun.com/mail/
```

Sun's Java Computing Web page:

```
http://www.sun.com/java/
```

Sun Microsystem's main Web site:

```
http://www.sun.com
```

Mail, Phone, Fax

Comments about the JDK can be emailed to

```
jdk-comments@java.sun.com
```

Sun's street address:

Sun Microsystems, Inc.

2550 Garcia Avenue

Mountain View, CA 94043-1100

USA

Other Java Resources

There are many other resources on the Web and elsewhere for Java- and JBuilder-related information. What follows is a brief description of the resources that have proved to be the most interesting.

World Wide Web

Finjan Inc., premier Java security solutions vendor and founder of the Java Security Alliance (JSA), whose members include Cisco, Raptor Systems, CheckPoint Software, Alta Vista, Milkyway Networks, and Secure Computing:

`http://www.finjan.com`

JARS provides ratings for Java applets that are available on the Web:

`http://www.jars.com`

Gamelan's collection of Java information, demos, and applets:

`http://www.developer.com/directories/pages/dir.java.html/`

Ask the Java Pro at `inquiry.com`:

`http://www.inquiry.com/techtips/java_pro/`

Laura Lemay's Web site (coauthor of *Teach Yourself Java in 21 Days*):

`http://www.lne.com/lemay/`

Charles L. Perkins's Web site (coauthor of *Teach Yourself Java in 21 Days*):

`http://rendezvous.com`

Moondog Software (Bill Giel) has some interesting applets and is where you can obtain jHelp 2.0 software:

`http://w3.nai.net/~rvdi/bgiel/bill.htm`

TeamJava, a no-cost registry for consultants and companies that provide Java-related services:

`http://teamjava.com`

Newsgroups

Newsgroups hosted by Usenet:

`alt.www.hotjava`

`comp.lang.java`

`comp.lang.java.*`

Newsgroups hosted by `msnews.microsoft.com`:

`microsoft.public.java.*`

`microsoft.public.internetexplorer.java`

`microsoft.public.inetexplorer.ie4.java_applets`

Macmillan Computer Publishing

Macmillan has an extensive Web site that has links to many other resources as well. Macmillan Computer Publishing is the parent company of Sams Publishing, Que, and New Riders.

World Wide Web

Macmillan's home page:

`http://www.mcp.com`

Mail, Phone, Fax

Comments or questions can be sent to

`support@mcp.com`

Sams Publishing's street address:

Sams Publishing
201 W. 103rd St.
Indianapolis, IN 46290-1093
USA

Sams Publishing's telephone numbers:

Orders: (800) 428-5331

Fax: (800) 835-3202

Customer service: (800) 858-7674

C

INDEX

Symbols

= (assignment operator), **40, 45**
  combining operators, 50
\ (backslash), **42**
&
  bitwise AND operator, 49
  logical AND operator, 48
- (bitwise NOT operator), **49**
^ (bitwise XOR operator),
  49-50
<< (bitwise left shift operator),
  49-50
| (bitwise OR operator), **49**
{} (braces), **35**
[] (brackets), **54**
: (colons), **81**
+
  concatenation operator, 46, 65
  unary plus operator, 46
&& (conditional AND operator), **48**
?: (conditional if-else operator,
  48, 73-74
|| (conditional OR operator), **48**
† (dagger symbol), **39**
-- (decrement operator), **45-46**
/ (division operator), **46**
/**, */ (documentation comment marks), **36-37**
> (greater than operator), **47**

>= (greater than or equal to
  operator), **47**
++ (increment operator), **45-46**
==
  is equal to operator, 47
  refers-to-same-object
    operator, 47
!=
  is not equal to operator, 47
  refers-to-different-object
    operator, 47
< (less than operator), **47**
<= (less than or equal to opera-
  tor), **47**
! (logical NOT operator), **48**
| (logical OR operator), **48**
^ (logical XOR operator), **48**
% (modulus operator), **46**
/*, */ (multi-line comment
  marks), **36**
* (multiplication operator), **46**
; (semicolons), **34**
>> (signed right shift operator),
  49-50
' (single-quotes), **42**
// (single-line comment marks),
  36
- (unary minus operator), **46**
>>> (zero-fill right shift opera-
  tor), **49-50**

A

About command (Help menu),
  220
abstract modifier, 159-160
Abstract Window Toolkit, *see*
  AWT
accelerators (menus), 244
accept( ) method, 692
access control, 149
  class methods, 156
  class variables, 155-156
  instance variables, 153-155
  modifiers
    abstract, 159-160
    final, 157-159
    package (default),
      149-151
    private, 152-153
    private protected, 151-152
    protected, 151
    public, 149
accessing array elements, 55-57
accessing string elements, 60-63
  AccessString.java listing, 61
AccessString class, 60
action events, 502
  ActionTest applet, 503-504
    listing, 505-507
ActionEvent class, 503
actionPerformed event handler,
  502

D

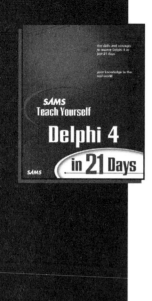

Sams Teach Yourself Delphi 4 in 21 Days

Reisdorph, Kent

Contains 750 pages of all-new content. The tutorial information for programmers and developers includes complete coverage of Delphi 4's enhanced features. Get up to speed with Delphi and learn advanced topics such as databases, Object-Oriented Programming, ActiveX, graphics, and Internet programming. Learn basic component creation, and focus on enabling applications for intranets, the Internet, and client/server environments. Explore ways to integrate Delphi into your enterprise. No other tutorial offers this level of coverage. A Sams Teach Yourself book is the perfect introduction to an upper-level development tool such as Delphi. This book is an all-new edition. It's the most complete beginning level tutorial for Delphi 4.

$39.99 US/$57.95 CDN　　　　　*Beginner - Intermediate*
0-672-31286-7　　　　　　　　*750 pp.*
Programming
Sams　　　　　　　　　　　　*Borland Press*

Delphi 4 Developer's Guide

Pacheco, Xavier; Teixeira, Steve

The Delphi 4 Developer's Guide is an advanced-level reference showing developers what they need to know most about Delphi 4. The authors deal with developers every day and offer sound skills, advice, and technical knowledge on the most advanced features of Delphi 4. This guide is the most advanced developers' book on Delphi 4. Written by members of Borland's Delphi development team, it shows you how to: build advanced-level components, create Visual Component Libraries, design and create enterprise-level applications, and more. On the CD-ROM are the book's complete source code, additional chapters from the book, examples, and sample components. This guide discusses issues about application design and frameworks concepts for client/server, enterprise, and desktop level database apps, along with Delphi's Multi-tier Distributed Applications Services Suite (MIDAS) and how it works with Delphi. Steve Teixeira and Xavier Pacheco are the award-winning authors of the *Delphi 2 Developer's Guide* and key members of Borland's Delphi development team. Learn the latest information on the best ways to build efficient, usable applications with Delphi 4, including Borland's new enterprise features, cross-component compatibility, and Internet-enabling capabilities.

$59.99 US/$85.95 CDN　　　　　*Advanced - Expert*
0-672-31284-0　　　　　　　　*1200 pp.*
Programming
Sams　　　　　　　　　　　　*Borland Press*

Charlie Calvert's Delphi Unleashed

Calvert, Charlie

Charlie Calvert's Delphi 4 Unleashed is an all-new edition, written by one of the best-known developers in the Delphi community. This advanced reference provides programmers with the information they need to build high-end Delphi applications and components. Calvert brings the newest technologies and features of Delphi into focus and shows programmers how to utilize them. Some features include: Building and integrating components with Java, Active X, and so forth; Internet-enabling applications and components; Internet and intranet applications and enabling; Delphi's Multi-tier Distributed Applications Services Suite (MIDAS) and how it works with Delphi; and client/server architecture and enterprise-wide development. The content for the book and CD is all new. This book tells programmers what the manuals don't—how to make Delphi 4 really work for them.

$49.99 US/$71.95 CDN   *Intermediate - Advanced*
0-672-31285-9   *1000 pp.*
Programming
Sams   *Borland Press*

Sams Teach Yourself Borland C++Builder 3 in 21 Days

Kent Reisdorph

The drag-and-drop power of Borland's C++Builder 3.0 is yours to command with Sams Teach Yourself Borland C++Builder 3.0 in 21 Days. In no time, you can rapidly build programs from reusable ActiveX controls, JavaBeans, and Delphi components. Using the methods taught in this book, you can increase your productivity and leverage your knowledge of C++ 3.0 and Delphi to develop mainstream applications. The proven, step-by-step techniques of the Sams Teach Yourself series show you how to accomplish specific tasks with this powerful new programming interface. Stop programming C++ the old-fashioned way, and start tapping into the visual programming power of Borland C++Builder 3.0! This is a key revision to an already-successful Borland Press book. It was released day-and-date with the release of Borland C++Builder 3, with 30 percent new and updated content by a well-known author in the Borland development community.

$39.99 US/$57.95 CDN   *Beginner – Intermediate*
0-672-31266-2   *832 pp.*
Programming
Sams   *Borland Press*
CD-ROM

Charlie Calvert's C++Builder 3 Unleashed

Charlie Calvert

Focused, in-depth explanations of the core features and complexities of C++Builder 3. Written by best-selling author and C++Builder expert Charlie Calvert and key members of the C++Builder team, this title provides you with what you need to know to take advantage of C++Builder 3's power. Develop Web applications by incorporating WebBroker, ActiveX, and Internet functions into your programs, write multimedia instructions for Windows with DirectX, and interoperate with OWL and Microsoft DLLs.

Connect to your corporate data with scaleable database tools, develop C++ programs visually with drag-and-drop methods, Internet-enable client/server applications for your entire network, and much more!

$59.99 US/$85.95 CDN　　　　*Advanced - Expert*
0-672-31265-4　　　　　　　　*1200 pp.*
Programming
Sams

Add to Your Sams Library Today with the Best Books for Programming, Operating Systems, and New Technologies

To order, visit our Web site at www.mcp.com or fax us at

1-800-835-3202

ISBN	Quantity	Description of Item	Unit Cost	Total Cost
0-672-31286-7		Sams Teach Yourself Delphi 4 in 21 Days	$39.99	
0-672-31284-0		Delphi 4 Developer's Guide	$59.99	
0-672-31285-9		Charlie Calvert's Delphi Unleashed	$49.99	
0-672-31266-2		Sams Teach Yourself Borland C++Builder 3 in 21 Days	$39.99	
0-672-31265-4		Charlie Calvert's C++Builder 3 Unleashed	$59.99	
		Shipping and Handling: See information below.		
		TOTAL		

Shipping and Handling

Standard	$5.00
2nd Day	$10.00
Next Day	$17.50
International	$40.00

201 W. 103rd Street, Indianapolis, Indiana 46290   1-800-835-3202 — FAX

Book ISBN 0-672-31318-9